W9-AWK-135

1999 MCSD CERTIFICATION REQUIREMENTS

CORE EXAMS (3 REQUIRED)

SOLUTION ARCHITECTURE (REQUIRED):

Exam 70-100: Analyzing Requirements and Defining Solution Architectures

DESKTOP APPLICATIONS DEVELOPMENT (1 REQUIRED):

Exam 70-016*: Designing and Implementing Desktop Applications with Microsoft® Visual C++® 6.0

Exam 70-176*: Designing and Implementing Desktop Applications with Microsoft® Visual Basic® 6.0

(Designing and Implementing Desktop Applications with Microsoft Visual FoxPro available later this year.)

(Designing and Implementing Desktop Applications with Microsoft Visual J++ available later this year.)

DISTRIBUTED APPLICATIONS DEVELOPMENT (1 REQUIRED):

Exam 70-015*: Designing and Implementing Distributed Applications with Microsoft® Visual C++® 6.0

Exam 70-175*: Designing and Implementing Distributed Applications with Microsoft® Visual Basic® 6.0

(Designing and Implementing Distributed Applications with Microsoft Visual FoxPro available later this year.)

(Designing and Implementing Distributed Applications with Microsoft Visual J++ available later this year.)

ELECTIVE EXAMS (1 REQUIRED)

Exam 70-015*: Designing and Implementing Distributed Applications with Microsoft® Visual C++® 6.0

Exam 70-016*: Designing and Implementing Desktop Applications with Microsoft® Visual C++® 6.0

Exam 70-024: Developing Applications with C++ Using the Microsoft® Foundation Class Library

Exam 70-025: Implementing OLE in Microsoft® Foundation Class Applications

Exam 70-029: Designing and Implementing Databases with Microsoft® SQL Server™ 7.0

Exam 70-055: Designing and Implementing Web Sites with Microsoft® FrontPage® 98

Exam 70-057: Designing and Implementing Commerce Solutions with Microsoft® Site Server 3.0, Commerce Edition

Exam 70-069: Application Development with Microsoft® Access for Windows® 95 and the Microsoft® Access Developer's Toolkit

Exam 70-091: Designing and Implementing Solutions with Microsoft® Office 2000 and Microsoft® Visual Basic® for Applications

Exam 70-152: Designing and Implementing Web Solutions with Microsoft® Visual InterDev™ 6.0

Exam 70-175*: Designing and Implementing Distributed Applications with Microsoft® Visual Basic® 6.0

Exam 70-176*: Designing and Implementing Desktop Applications with Microsoft® Visual Basic® 6.0

★ Core exams that can also be used as elective exams are counted only once toward a certification.

For complete information on MCSD Certification, visit **www.microsoft.com** and click on Training and Certification.

MICROSOFT CERTIFIED SOLUTION DEVELOPER

MCSD Analyzing Requirements Study Guide

(Exam 70-100)

Syngress Media, Inc.

Osborne McGraw-Hill

Berkeley   New York   St. Louis   San Francisco
Auckland   Bogotá   Hamburg   London   Madrid
Mexico City   Milan   Montreal   New Delhi   Panama City
Paris   São Paulo   Singapore   Sydney
Tokyo   Toronto

Osborne McGraw-Hill
2600 Tenth Street
Berkeley, California 94710
U.S.A.

For information on translations or book distributors outside the U.S.A., or to
arrange bulk purchase discounts for sales promotions, premiums, or
fund-raisers, please contact **Osborne McGraw-Hill** at the above address.

MCSD Analyzing Requirements Study Guide (Exam 70-100)

1234567890 DOC DOC 90198765432109

ISBN 0-07-211955-1

Publisher	**Technical Editor**	**Illustrators**
Brandon A. Nordin	Michael Lane Thomas	Robert Hansen
		Beth Young
Associate Publisher,	**Copy Editor**	
Editor-in-Chief	Eileen Kramer	**Series Design**
Scott Rogers		Roberta Steele
	Proofreader	
Acquisitions Editor	Joe Sadusky	**Cover Design**
Gareth Hancock		Regan Honda
	Indexer	
Project Editor	Valerie Perry	**Editorial Management**
Brian Miller		Syngress Media, Inc.
	Computer Designers	
Editorial Assistant	Roberta Steele	
Tara Davis	Jani Beckwith	

FOREWORD

From Global Knowledge

At Global Knowledge we strive to support the multiplicity of learning styles required by our students to achieve success as technical professionals. In this series of books, it is our intention to offer the reader a valuable tool for successful completion of the MCSD Certification Exams.

As the world's largest IT training company, Global Knowledge is uniquely positioned to offer these books. The expertise gained each year from providing instructor-led training to hundreds of thousands of students worldwide has been captured in book form to enhance your learning experience. We hope that the quality of these books demonstrates our commitment to your lifelong learning success. Whether you choose to learn through the written word, computer-based training, Web delivery, or instructor-led training, Global Knowledge is committed to providing you the very best in each of those categories. For those of you who know Global Knowledge, or those of you who have just found us for the first time, our goal is to be your lifelong competency partner.

Thank you for the opportunity to serve you. We look forward to serving your needs again in the future.

Warmest regards,

Duncan Anderson
President and Chief Executive Officer, Global Knowledge

January 12, 1998

Dear Osborne/McGraw-Hill Customer:

Microsoft is pleased to inform you that Osborne/McGraw-Hill is a participant in the Microsoft® Independent Courseware Vendor (ICV) program. Microsoft ICVs design, develop, and market self-paced courseware, books, and other products that support Microsoft software and the Microsoft Certified Professional (MCP) program.

To be accepted into the Microsoft ICV program, an ICV must meet set criteria. In addition, Microsoft reviews and approves each ICV training product before permission is granted to use the Microsoft Certified Professional Approved Study Guide logo on that product. This logo assures the consumer that the product has passed the following Microsoft standards:

- The course contains accurate product information.
- The course includes labs and activities during which the student can apply knowledge and skills learned from the course.
- The course teaches skills that help prepare the student to take corresponding MCP exams.

Microsoft ICVs continually develop and release new MCP Approved Study Guides. To prepare for a particular Microsoft certification exam, a student may choose one or more single, self-paced training courses or a series of training courses.

You will be pleased with the quality and effectiveness of the MCP Approved Study Guides available from Osborne/McGraw-Hill.

Sincerely,

Becky Kirsininkas

Becky Kirsininkas
ICV Program Manager
Microsoft Training & Certification

The Global Knowledge Advantage

Global Knowledge has a global delivery system for its products and services. The company has 28 subsidiaries, and offers its programs through a total of 60+ locations. No other vendor can provide consistent services across a geographic area this large. Global Knowledge is the largest independent information technology education provider, offering programs on a variety of platforms. This enables our multi-platform and multi-national customers to obtain all of their programs from a single vendor. The company has developed the unique CompetusTM Framework software tool and methodology which can quickly reconfigure courseware to the proficiency level of a student on an interactive basis. Combined with self-paced and on-line programs, this technology can reduce the time required for training by prescribing content in only the deficient skills areas. The company has fully automated every aspect of the education process, from registration and follow-up, to "just-in-time" production of courseware. Global Knowledge, through its Enterprise Services Consultancy, can customize programs and products to suit the needs of an individual customer.

Global Knowledge Classroom Education Programs

The backbone of our delivery options is classroom-based education. Our modern, well-equipped facilities staffed with the finest instructors offer programs in a wide variety of information technology topics, many of which lead to professional certifications.

Custom Learning Solutions

This delivery option has been created for companies and governments that value customized learning solutions. For them, our consultancy-based approach of developing targeted education solutions is most effective at helping them meet specific objectives.

Self-Paced and Multimedia Products

This delivery option offers self-paced program titles in interactive CD-ROM, videotape and audio tape programs. In addition, we offer custom development of interactive multimedia courseware to customers and partners. Call us at 1 (888) 427-4228.

Electronic Delivery of Training

Our network-based training service delivers efficient competency-based, interactive training via the World Wide Web and organizational intranets. This leading-edge delivery option provides a custom learning path and "just-in-time" training for maximum convenience to students.

ARG

American Research Group (ARG), a wholly-owned subsidiary of Global Knowledge, one of the largest worldwide training partners of Cisco Systems, offers a wide range of internetworking, LAN/WAN, Bay Networks, FORE Systems, IBM, and UNIX courses. ARG offers hands on network training in both instructor-led classes and self-paced PC-based training.

Global Knowledge Courses Available

Network Fundamentals
- Understanding Computer Networks
- Telecommunications Fundamentals I
- Telecommunications Fundamentals II
- Understanding Networking Fundamentals
- Implementing Computer Telephony Integration
- Introduction to Voice Over IP
- Introduction to Wide Area Networking
- Cabling Voice and Data Networks
- Introduction to LAN/WAN protocols
- Virtual Private Networks
- ATM Essentials

Network Security & Management
- Troubleshooting TCP/IP Networks
- Network Management
- Network Troubleshooting
- IP Address Management
- Network Security Administration
- Web Security
- Implementing UNIX Security
- Managing Cisco Network Security
- Windows NT 4.0 Security

IT Professional Skills
- Project Management for IT Professionals
- Advanced Project Management for IT Professionals
- Survival Skills for the New IT Manager
- Making IT Teams Work

LAN/WAN Internetworking
- Frame Relay Internetworking
- Implementing T1/T3 Services
- Understanding Digital Subscriber Line (xDSL)
- Internetworking with Routers and Switches
- Advanced Routing and Switching
- Multi-Layer Switching and Wire-Speed Routing
- Internetworking with TCP/IP
- ATM Internetworking
- OSPF Design and Configuration
- Border Gateway Protocol (BGP) Configuration

Authorized Vendor Training
Cisco Systems
- Introduction to Cisco Router Configuration
- Advanced Cisco Router Configuration
- Installation and Maintenance of Cisco Routers
- Cisco Internetwork Troubleshooting
- Cisco Internetwork Design
- Cisco Routers and LAN Switches
- Catalyst 5000 Series Configuration
- Cisco LAN Switch Configuration
- Managing Cisco Switched Internetworks
- Configuring, Monitoring, and Troubleshooting Dial-Up Services
- Cisco AS5200 Installation and Configuration
- Cisco Campus ATM Solutions

Bay Networks
- Bay Networks Accelerated Router Configuration
- Bay Networks Advanced IP Routing
- Bay Networks Hub Connectivity
- Bay Networks Accelar 1xxx Installation and Basic Configuration
- Bay Networks Centillion Switching

FORE Systems
- FORE ATM Enterprise Core Products
- FORE ATM Enterprise Edge Products
- FORE ATM Theory
- FORE LAN Certification

Operating Systems & Programming
Microsoft
- Introduction to Windows NT
- Microsoft Networking Essentials
- Windows NT 4.0 Workstation
- Windows NT 4.0 Server
- Advanced Windows NT 4.0 Server
- Windows NT Networking with TCP/IP
- Introduction to Microsoft Web Tools
- Windows NT Troubleshooting
- Windows Registry Configuration

UNIX
- UNIX Level I
- UNIX Level II
- Essentials of UNIX and NT Integration

Programming
- Introduction to JavaScript
- Java Programming
- PERL Programming
- Advanced PERL with CGI for the Web

Web Site Management & Development
- Building a Web Site
- Web Site Management and Performance
- Web Development Fundamentals

High Speed Networking
- Essentials of Wide Area Networking
- Integrating ISDN
- Fiber Optic Network Design
- Fiber Optic Network Installation
- Migrating to High Performance Ethernet

DIGITAL UNIX
- UNIX Utilities and Commands
- DIGITAL UNIX v4.0 System Administration
- DIGITAL UNIX v4.0 (TCP/IP) Network Management
- AdvFS, LSM, and RAID Configuration and Management
- DIGITAL UNIX TruCluster Software Configuration and Management
- UNIX Shell Programming Featuring Kornshell
- DIGITAL UNIX v4.0 Security Management
- DIGITAL UNIX v4.0 Performance Management
- DIGITAL UNIX v4.0 Intervals Overview

DIGITAL OpenVMS
- OpenVMS Skills for Users
- OpenVMS System and Network Node Management I
- OpenVMS System and Network Node Management II
- OpenVMS System and Network Node Management III
- OpenVMS System and Network Node Operations
- OpenVMS for Programmers
- OpenVMS System Troubleshooting for Systems Managers
- Configuring and Managing Complex VMScluster Systems
- Utilizing OpenVMS Features from C
- OpenVMS Performance Management
- Managing DEC TCP/IP Services for OpenVMS
- Programming in C

Hardware Courses
- AlphaServer 1000/1000A Installation, Configuration and Maintenance
- AlphaServer 2100 Server Maintenance
- AlphaServer 4100, Troubleshooting Techniques and Problem Solving

ABOUT THE CONTRIBUTORS

About Syngress Media

Syngress Media creates books and software for Information Technology professionals seeking skill enhancement and career advancement. Its products are designed to comply with vendor and industry standard course curricula, and are optimized for certification exam preparation. Visit the Syngress web site at **www.syngress.com**.

Contributors

Michael Cross (MCSE, MCPS, MCP+Internet) is a computer programmer and network support specialist. He works as an instructor at private colleges, teaching courses in hardware, software, programming, and networking. He is the owner of KnightWare, a company that provides consulting, programming, network support, web page design, computer training, and various other services. In his spare time, he has been a freelance writer for several years, in genres of fiction and non-fiction. He currently lives in London, Ontario.

Audrea Elliott (MCSD, MCP, MBA) has been an IT professional since 1978 and now works for Compuware in Madison, Wisconsin. She has in-depth experience in the design and implementation of client/server technologies and object-oriented technologies. She has worked in many IT roles, including programmer, network administrator, IT Manager, and Business Area Analyst. She is also certified in Function Point counting. A single parent, Audrea's hobby is dreaming of the day she has the time to have a hobby. She lives with her son surrounded by cornfields in a picturesque small town just south of Madison. Audrea may be reached at **aelliott@inwave.com**.

Terry Knaul (MCSE, MCSD) presently works for a national IT consulting firm. He has worked in the IT field for more than nine years with such companies as Procter & Gamble, Fidelity Investments, and Ernst & Young LLP. He is currently on assignment as regional IT manager with a global insurance company. He is a Microsoft Certified System Engineer (MCSE) as well as a Microsoft Certified Solution Developer (MCSD).

Terry also freelances as an application developer and web designer. In his free time he is an avid runner (having finished a marathon) and cycling wannabe who competes in triathlons.

Steven Jones (MCSD) has just finished a Masters of Divinity at the Cincinnati Bible Seminary; his first degree was a B.S. in Civil Engineering from the University of Pittsburgh. Currently, he's a Programmer/Analyst for Cincinnati State Technical & Community College, having also done programming work for the two institutions he's attended. Steve has an MCSD, and works primarily with MS SQL Server, as well as VB, InterDev, and Unidata.

Leigh Kendall (MCSD) is a Senior Technical Consultant for ASP Consulting Group, a California-based Siebel Systems consulting partner. Leigh has experience developing and implementing Client/Server solutions using such tools as Visual Basic, SQL Server, and Microsoft internet technologies including ASP and MTS. Leigh lives in Connecticut and can be reached at **www.aspinc.com**. When not glued to the PC, he's usually out walking his Siberian Husky, Tasha.

Thomas Huff (MCSD) has over a decade of experience in the field. Thomas hails from Silver Spring, Maryland where he works at PowerVision Corporation (**www.powervision.com**) as a Systems Engineer. He graduated magna cum laude from the University of Maryland, Baltimore County with a degree in Computer Science, and is currently pursuing a master's degree at Johns Hopkins University. In his spare time he enjoys science fiction, ice hockey, heavy metal, and skydiving.

Technical Review and From the Classroom Sidebars by:

Michael Lane Thomas (MCSE, MCSE+Internet, MCT, MCSD, MCP, MCP+Internet, MCP+SB, MSS, A+) is a computer industry consultant, anaylst, technical trainer, and president/CEO of theFastLane.com Inc. He has spoken publicly on some of the hottest technologies to hit the industry, such as XML, SQL, and Y2K issues, and has been heard at Microsoft-sponsored national technical conferences, special interest groups, and on Kansas City's airwaves on 980KMBZ radio.

Michael teaches Microsoft Official Curriculum (MOC) courses, ranging from BackOffice products such as Proxy, SQL Server, and IIS, to development technologies such as Visual InterDev, Visual Basic, COM, and Visual Studio. Michael is certified to teach over 40 Microsoft courses, with more on the horizon, but he prefers to focus on the most recent development courses because "that's where the fun stuff is!"

When not writing, Michael spends his time consulting and training, although he prefers the challenge of designing, building, and developing complex intranet, three-tier Web applications, and advanced Web-based solutions using the full range of available Microsoft technologies. Michael is currently waiting on beta scores for the SQL 7.0 Administration and Implementation exams to secure his MCDBA charter certification, to go with status as a charter MCSE+I and MCP+SB professional. Michael has successfully passed over 30 Micosoft exams.

After graduating from the University of Kansas with a B.A. and B.S. in Mathematics, Michael has continued his traditional academic pursuits with a slow but steady climb towards his M.S. in Engineering Management from the University of Kansas. Michael is a former contributor and technical editor for *Microsoft Certified Professional* magazine, and author, contributor, and/or technical editor for nine books to date. Michael can be reached at **michael@thefastlane.com**.

Acknowledgments

We would like to thank the following people:

- Richard Kristof of Global Knowledge for championing the series and providing access to some great people and information.

- All the incredibly hard-working folks at Osborne/McGraw-Hill: Brandon Nordin, Scott Rogers, and Gareth Hancock for their help in launching a great series and being solid team players. In addition, Tara Davis and Nancy McLaughlin for their help in fine-tuning the book—and a special thanks to Osborne's capable Production department for compiling all the pieces with speed and accuracy.

- Becky Kirsininkas and Karen Croner at Microsoft Corporation for being patient and diligent in answering all of our questions.

CONTENTS

xiii

PREFACE

This book's primary objective is to help you prepare for and pass the required MCSD exam so you can begin to reap the career benefits of certification. We believe that the only way to do this is to help you increase your knowledge and build your skills. After completing this book, you should feel confident that you have thoroughly reviewed all of the objectives that Microsoft has established for the exam.

In This Book

This book is organized around the actual structure of the Microsoft exam administered at Sylvan Testing Centers. Microsoft has let us know all the topics we need to cover for the exam. We've followed their list carefully, so you can be assured you're not missing anything.

In Every Chapter

We've created a set of chapter components that call your attention to important items, reinforce important points, and provide helpful exam-taking hints. Take a look at what you'll find in every chapter:

- Every chapter begins with the **Certification Objectives**—what you need to know in order to pass the section on the exam dealing with the chapter topic. The Certification Objectives headings identify the objectives within the chapter, so you'll always know an objective when you see it!

- **Exam Watch** notes call attention to information about, and potential pitfalls in, the exam. These helpful hints are written by MCSDs who have taken the exams and received their certification—who better to tell you what to worry about? They know what you're about to experience!

- **On the Job** notes point out procedures and techniques important for coding actual applications for employers or contract jobs.

- **Certification Exercises** are interspersed throughout the chapters. These are step-by-step exercises that mirror vendor-recommended labs. They help you master skills that are likely to be an area of focus on the exam. Don't just read through the exercises; they are hands-on practice that you should be comfortable completing. Learning by doing is an effective way to increase your competency with a product.

- **From the Classroom** sidebars describe the issues that come up most often in the training classroom setting. These sidebars give you a valuable perspective into certification- and product-related topics. They point out common mistakes and address questions from actual classroom discussions.

- **Q & A** sections lay out problems and solutions in a quick-read format. For example:

QUESTIONS AND ANSWERS

Why should I make my solution scalable?	Scalability takes into account growth within the organization. By making your solution scalable, it can handle increases in users, data, and other issues that will affect the performance and usability of the solution.

- The **Certification Summary** is a succinct review of the chapter and a restatement of salient points regarding the exam.

- The **Two-Minute Drill** at the end of every chapter is a checklist of the main points of the chapter. It can be used for last-minute review.

- The **Self Test** offers questions similar to those found on the certification exams, including multiple choice, true/false questions, and fill-in-the-blank. The answers to these questions, as well as explanations of the answers, can be found in Appendix A. By taking the Self Test after completing each chapter, you'll reinforce what you've learned from that chapter, while becoming familiar with the structure of the exam questions.

Some Pointers

Once you've finished reading this book, set aside some time to do a thorough review. You might want to return to the book several times and make use of all the methods it offers for reviewing the material:

- *Re-read all the Two-Minute Drills,* or have someone quiz you. You also can use the drills as a way to do a quick cram before the exam.

- *Re-read all the Exam Watch notes.* Remember that these are written by MCSDs who have taken the exam and passed. They know what you should expect—and what you should be careful about.

- *Review all the Q & A scenarios* for quick problem solving.

- *Re-take the Self Tests.* Taking the tests right after you've read the chapter is a good idea, because it helps reinforce what you've just learned. However, it's an even better idea to go back later and do all the questions in the book in one sitting. Pretend you're taking the exam. (For this reason, you should mark your answers on a separate piece of paper when you answer the questions the first time.)

- *Complete the exercises.* Did you do the exercises when you read through each chapter? If not, do them! These exercises are designed to cover exam topics, and there's no better way to get to know this material than by practicing.

- *Check out the web site.* Global Knowledge Network invites you to become an active member of the Access Global web site. This site is an online mall and information repository that you'll find invaluable. You can access many types of products to assist you in your preparation for the exams, and you'll be able to participate in forums, online discussions, and threaded discussions. No other book brings you unlimited access to such a resource. You'll find more information about this site in Appendix C.

A Brief History of MCSD Certification

Although the MCSD certification for software developers was introduced in the same year as the MCSE certification for system engineers, there are currently many more MCSEs than MCSDs. There are several reasons for this discrepancy:

- The MCSE was immediately understood as similar to Novell's CNE (Certified Network Engineer), but there was no popular credential competing with the MCSD.

- The learning curve has traditionally been steeper for system engineers than it has been for software developers, and the consequences of error are usually much more severe. (A software developer who has an off day might end up working late every day the next week, but a system engineer who has an off day might end up working at Burger King.) Consequently, there has been more demand from companies for a network certification, and more willingness to invest in employees receiving the appropriate training.

- The MCSD was considered by some to be more difficult than the MCSE. Although the MCSE required passing six tests (as opposed to the four required for the MCSD), there was significant overlap in the content covered on the MCSE tests. By contrast, the content learned for one MCSD test was of little value on other MCSD tests.

- While a network engineer would encounter most of the MCSE test concepts in their day-to-day work, even an experienced developer would have to deal with new material when preparing for an MCSD test. For example, on the original WOSSA 2 Exam, a level of understanding of ODBC was required that far exceeded the needs of almost all developers.

- Finally, while MCSE study resources were plentiful, there were few classes and fewer books covering the MCSD curriculum.

However, the popularity of the MCSD is starting to reach a critical mass. As the number of organizations dependent on custom-developed Microsoft applications increases, so does the desire of these organizations to objectively measure the skills of developers, and the willingness of these organizations to use these certifications as a factor in determining compensation. According to *Microsoft Certified Professional* magazine, developers with the MCSD certification reported a median salary of $71,500, while developers lacking any certifications reported a median salary of $56,500. (More

information is available by viewing the magazine's web site at
http://www.mcpmag.com/members/98feb/fea1pmain.asp.)

To Microsoft's credit, they have continually surveyed developers and employees and used this feedback to align their certification tracks with market needs. In June 1998, Microsoft revamped the MCSD program, providing new requirements and tests required to achieve this status. However, they did not discontinue the existing path, which leaves developers with the challenge of determining which to pursue.

Original and New MCSD Tracks

The primary difference between the original and the new MCSD tracks is the emphasis on architecture. The new track reduces the number of generalized architecture tests, but requires at least one test that covers distributed application development. A test-by-test comparison of the exams required is presented in Table P-1.

TABLE P-1 Test-by-Test Comparison of Original and New MCSD Tracks

Test	Original Track Requirements	New Track Requirements
1	Core: Microsoft Windows Architecture 1 (70-160)	Core: Analyzing Requirements and Defining Solutions Architectures (70-100)
2	Core: Microsoft Windows Architecture 2 (70-161)	Core: Desktop Application Development (in C++ 6, VB 6, FoxPro, or J++)[1]
3	Elective: One elective from Table P-2	Core: Distributed Application Development (in C++ 6, VB 6, FoxPro, or J++)[1,2]
4	Elective: One elective from Table P-2	Elective: One elective from Table P-2[2]

[1]Although the test choices for Test 2 and Test 3 are available as electives, the same test cannot be used to fill both a core and an elective test requirement.

[2]Tests 3 and 4 must cover different Microsoft products. For example, you cannot use Programming with Microsoft Visual Basic 4.0 for Test 3 and Developing Applications with Microsoft Visual Basic 5.0 for Test 4.

Note: Microsoft Windows Architecture exams were introduced to replace the original Windows Operating System and Services Architecture exams used for MCSD certification. Microsoft has already retired these, so they are excluded from Table P-1.

Tests Available for MCSD Certification

As of this writing, there are 27 exams that can be used to achieve the MCSD certification (although some of these will be retired soon). These tests are listed in Table P-2, sorted by the subject they cover.

| TABLE P-2 | | Tests Available for MCSD Certification |

Subject	Test Number	Full Test Name	Original Track	New Track
Architecture	70-160	Microsoft Windows Architecture 1[3]	C[4]	
Architecture	70-161	Microsoft Windows Architecture 2[3]	C	
Architecture	70-100	Analyzing Requirements and Defining Solution Architectures		C
Visual Basic	70-065	Programming with Microsoft Visual Basic 4.0[3]	E[5]	E
Visual Basic	70-165	Developing Applications with Microsoft Visual Basic 5.0	E	E

[3]These tests are scheduled to be retired by Microsoft. (Note that after Microsoft retires an exam, it usually remains valid for certification status, but only for a limited time.)

[4]"C" means that a test can be used as a core requirement. "Original" refers to the Original MCSD track; "New" refers to the New MCSD track.

[5]"E" means that a test can be used as an elective

| TABLE P-2 | | Tests Available for MCSD Certification *(continued)* | | |

Subject	Test Number	Full Test Name	Original Track	New Track
Visual Basic	70-176	Designing and Implementing Desktop Applications with Microsoft Visual Basic 6.0	E	C, E
Visual Basic	70-175	Designing and Implementing Distributed Applications with Microsoft Visual Basic 6.0	E	C, E
FoxPro	70-054	Programming in Microsoft Visual FoxPro 3.0 for Windows[3]	E	
FoxPro	(none)[6]	Designing and Implementing Desktop Applications with Microsoft Visual FoxPro	E	C
FoxPro	(none)	Designing and Implementing Distributed Applications with Microsoft Visual FoxPro	E	C
C++	70-024	Developing Applications with C++ Using the Microsoft Foundation Class Library	E	E

[6]Exams without a number are not scheduled to be available until later in 1999.

TABLE P-2		Tests Available for MCSD Certification *(continued)*		
Subject	**Test Number**	**Full Test Name**	**Original Track**	**New Track**
C++	70-025	Implementing OLE in Microsoft Foundation Class Applications	E	E
C++	70-016	Designing and Implementing Desktop Applications with Microsoft Visual C++ 6.0	E	C, E
C++	70-015	Designing and Implementing Distributed Applications with Microsoft Visual C++ 6.0	E	C, E
J++	(none)	Designing and Implementing Desktop Applications with Microsoft Visual J++	E	C
J++	(none)	Designing and Implementing Distributed Applications with Microsoft Visual J++	E	C
Access	70-051	Microsoft Access 2.0 for Windows-Application Development[3]	E	
Access	70-069	Microsoft Access for Windows 95 and the Microsoft Access Developer's Toolkit	E	E

TABLE P-2		Tests Available for MCSD Certification *(continued)*		
Subject	**Test Number**	**Full Test Name**	**Original Track**	**New Track**
Access	(none)	Designing and Implementing Database Design on Microsoft Access	E	E
Office	70-052	Developing Applications with Microsoft Excel 5.0 Using Visual Basic for Applications[3]	E	
Office	70-091	Designing and Implementing Solutions with Microsoft Office 2000 and Microsoft Visual Basic for Applications	E	E
SQL Server	70-021	Microsoft SQL Server 4.2 Database Implementation[3]	E	E
SQL Server	70-027	Implementing a Database Design on Microsoft SQL Server 6.5	E	E
SQL Server	70-029	Designing and Implementing Databases with Microsoft SQL Server 7.0	E	E
Internet	70-055	Designing and Implementing Web Sites with Microsoft FrontPage 98	E	E

TABLE P-2	Tests Available for MCSD Certification (continued)			
Subject	Test Number	Full Test Name	Original Track	New Track
Internet	70-152	Designing and Implementing Web Solutions with Microsoft Visual InterDev 6.0	E	E

Note that this test list is adapted from the content available at **http://www.microsoft.com/mcp/certstep/mcsd.htm**. This content frequently changes, so it would be wise to check this site before finalizing your study plans.

Choosing a Track

So which track should you choose? Good question! Although Microsoft is obviously providing more support for the New track, there are legitimate reasons for considering both options. Some of these reasons are described in the following section.

Advantages of the Original Track

- *You may already be part way there.* If you already have, or are close to obtaining, the Windows Architecture 1 or 2, you should pursue the Original track. These tests are of no value in the New track. Similarly, if you have already passed an exam such as Access 2 or FoxPro 3, that is a valid elective for the Original track but not for the New track (though of course, these exams will be retired soon).

- *You cover more architecture.* The system architecture exams are excellent overviews to client/server development. The Original track consists of two architecture tests, but the New track has only one.

- *You don't have to use the most recent versions of the tools.* If your current job responsibilities make it unlikely that you will be working with the newest versions of C++, Visual Basic, FoxPro, or J++, you should pursue the Original track. The New track requires that you pass two tests on one of these four environments, and it seems very unlikely that these tests will be adapted to support prior versions. In other words, if you are an expert in VB version 5 but won't have an opportunity to significantly use VB version 6 for at least a year, it will be very difficult for you to use the New track.

- *You can start now.* As of this writing, some of the tests used for the New track (for example, Desktop and Distribution for FoxPro and J++) are scheduled to be available soon, and haven't even been released in beta yet.

Advantages of the New Track

- *Your credentials will last longer.* The Architecture 1 and 2 exams required for the original track will be retired more quickly than any of the New track core exams. However, this may not be as much of a disadvantage as it may seem. Remember, all of the exams you take will be retired within a few years. The certification process is designed not just to determine which developers have achieved a base level of competency, but to identify which developers are doing the best job of keeping their skills current.

- *You can become more of a specialist in your chosen tool.* Arguably, because the New track offers more exams for each product, the Original track encourages product breadth while the New track encourages depth. Therefore, if you're selling yourself as a specialist, the New track may be an advantage. (Specialists often earn higher salaries, though sometimes generalists have steadier employment.)

■ *You'll be more closely aligned with Microsoft's strategies.* If you are just beginning to consider certification and haven't already invested time pursuing the Original track, you should probably pursue the New track. The changes made by Microsoft are a result of their research into the needs of the marketplace, and it couldn't hurt for you to leverage their investment. In addition, if Microsoft revises the MCSD requirements again, the transition would probably be easiest for those who used the New track.

■ *You'll be "New and Improved!"*

Of course, the best choice may be not to choose at all, at least not yet. As the tables in this chapter have shown, many of the exams are applicable to both tracks. For example, the Designing and Implementing Desktop Applications with Microsoft Visual Basic 6.0 Exam counts not only as a core requirement for the New track, but also as an elective for either track. You do not need to declare to Microsoft which track you are pursuing, so you can delay that decision until after you have passed your first test.

And with this book at your side, you're well on your way to doing just that.

The CD-ROM Resource

This book comes with a CD-ROM that contains test preparation software, and provides you with another method for studying for the exam. You will find more information on the testing software in Appendix C.

How to Take a Microsoft Certification Examination

Good News and Bad News

If you are new to Microsoft certification, we have some good news and some bad news. The good news, of course, is that Microsoft certification is one of the most valuable credentials you can earn. It sets you apart from the crowd and marks you as a valuable asset to your employer. You will gain the respect of your peers, and Microsoft certification can have a wonderful effect on your income.

The bad news is that Microsoft certification tests are not easy. You may think you will read through some study material, memorize a few facts, and pass the Microsoft examinations. After all, these certification exams are just computer-based, multiple-choice tests, so they must be easy. If you believe this, you are wrong. Unlike many "multiple guess" tests you have been exposed to in school, the questions on Microsoft certification exams go beyond simple factual knowledge.

The purpose of this introduction is to teach you how to take a Microsoft certification exam. To be successful, you need to know something about the purpose and structure of these tests. We will also look at the latest innovations in Microsoft testing. Using simulations and adaptive testing, Microsoft is enhancing both the validity and security of the certification process. These factors have some important effects on how you should prepare for an exam, as well as your approach to each question during the test.

We will begin by looking at the purpose, focus, and structure of Microsoft certification tests, and examine the effect these factors have on the kinds of questions you will face on your certification exams. We will define the structure of exam questions, and investigate some common formats.

Next, we will present a strategy for answering these questions. Finally, we will give some specific guidelines on what you should do on the day of your test.

Why Vendor Certification?

The Microsoft Certified Professional program, like the certification programs from Lotus, Novell, Oracle, and other software vendors, is maintained for the ultimate purpose of increasing the corporation's profits. A successful vendor certification program accomplishes this goal by helping to create a pool of experts in a company's software, and by "branding" these experts so that companies using the software can identify them.

We know that vendor certification has become increasingly popular in the last few years because it helps employers find qualified workers, and because it helps software vendors like Microsoft sell their products. But why should you be interested in vendor certification rather than a more traditional approach like a college or professional degree in computer science? A college education is a broadening and enriching experience, but a degree in computer science does not prepare students for most jobs in the IT industry.

A common truism in our business states, "If you are out of the IT industry for three years and want to return, you have to start over." The problem, of course, is *timeliness*; if a first-year student learns about a specific computer program, it probably will no longer be in wide use when he or she graduates. Although some colleges are trying to integrate Microsoft certification into their curriculum, the problem is not really a flaw in higher education, but a characteristic of the IT industry. Computer software is changing so rapidly that a four-year college just can't keep up.

A marked characteristic of the Microsoft certification program is an emphasis on performing specific job tasks rather than merely gathering knowledge. It may come as a shock, but most potential employers do not care how much you know about the theory of operating systems, testing, or software design. As one IT manager put it, "I don't really care what my employees know about the theory of our network. We don't need someone to sit at a desk and think about it. We need people who can actually do something to make it work better."

You should not think that this attitude is some kind of anti-intellectual revolt against book learning. Knowledge is a necessary prerequisite, but it is not enough. More than one company has hired a computer science graduate as a network administrator only to learn that the new employee has no idea how to add users, assign permissions, or perform the other everyday tasks necessary to maintain a network. This brings us to the second major characteristic of Microsoft certification that affects the questions you must be prepared to answer. In addition to timeliness, Microsoft certification is also job-oriented.

The timeliness of Microsoft's certification program is obvious, and is inherent in the fact that you will be tested on current versions of software in wide use today. The job-task orientation of Microsoft certification is almost as obvious, but testing real-world job skills using a computer-based test is not easy.

Computerized Testing

Considering the popularity of Microsoft certification, and the fact that certification candidates are spread around the world, the only practical way to administer tests for the certification program is through Sylvan Prometric testing centers. Sylvan Prometric provides proctored testing services for Microsoft, Oracle, Novell, Lotus, and the A+ computer technician certification. Although the IT industry accounts for much of Sylvan's revenue, the company provides services for a number of other businesses and organizations, such as FAA preflight pilot tests. In fact, most companies that need secure test delivery over a wide geographic area use the services of Sylvan Prometric. In addition to delivery, Sylvan Prometric also scores the tests and provides statistical feedback on the performance of each test question to the companies and organizations that use their services.

Typically, several hundred questions are developed for a new Microsoft certification examination. The questions are first reviewed by a number of subject-matter experts for technical accuracy, and then are presented in a beta test. The beta test may last for several hours, due to the large number of questions. After a few weeks, Microsoft Certification uses the statistical feedback from Sylvan to check the performance of the beta questions.

Questions are discarded if most test takers get them right (too easy) or wrong (too difficult), and a number of other statistical measures are taken of each question. Although the scope of our discussion precludes a rigorous treatment of question analysis, you should be aware that Microsoft and other vendors spend a great deal of time and effort making sure their exam questions are valid. In addition to the obvious desire for quality, the fairness of a vendor's certification program must be legally defensible.

The questions that survive statistical analysis form the pool of questions for the final certification exam.

Test Structure

The kind of test we are most familiar with is known as a *form* test. For Microsoft certification, a form usually consists of 50–70 questions and takes 60–90 minutes to complete. If there are 240 questions in the final pool for an examination, then four forms can be created. Thus, candidates who retake the test probably will not see the same questions.

Other variations are possible. From the same pool of 240 questions, five forms can be created, each containing 40 unique questions (200 questions) and 20 questions selected at random from the remaining 40.

The questions in a Microsoft form test are equally weighted. This means they all count the same when the test is scored. A useful characteristic of a form test is that you can mark a question you have doubts about as you take the test. Assuming you have time left when you finish all the questions, you can return and spend more time on the questions you have marked as doubtful.

Microsoft may soon implement *adaptive* testing. To use this interactive technique, a form test is first created and administered to several thousand certification candidates. The statistics generated are used to assign a weight, or difficulty level, for each question. For example, the questions in a form might be divided into levels one through five, with level-one questions being the easiest and level-five questions the hardest.

When an adaptive test begins, the candidate is first given a level-three question. If it is answered correctly, a question from the next higher level is presented, and an incorrect response results in a question from the next lower level. When 15–20 questions have been answered in this manner, the scoring algorithm is able to predict, with a high degree of statistical certainty, whether the candidate would pass or fail if all the questions in the form were answered. When the required degree of certainty is attained, the test ends and the candidate receives a pass/fail grade.

Adaptive testing has some definite advantages for everyone involved in the certification process. Adaptive tests allow Sylvan Prometric to deliver more tests with the same resources, as certification candidates often are in and out in 30 minutes or less. For Microsoft, adaptive testing means that fewer test questions are exposed to each candidate, and this can enhance the security, and therefore the validity, of certification tests.

One problem you may have with adaptive testing is that you are not allowed to mark and revisit questions. Since the adaptive algorithm is interactive, and all questions but the first are selected on the basis of your response to the previous question, it is not possible to skip a particular question or change an answer.

Question *seeding* is another technique where a select group of questions, called seed questions, are changed on a periodic basis. This decreases the chance that the individuals taking the exam will inadvertently share questions with others. It also allows updates to be made to the exam as technology changes.

Types of Test Questions

Computerized test questions can be presented in a number of ways. Some of the possible formats are used on Microsoft certification examinations, and some are not.

True/False

We are all familiar with true/false questions, but because of the inherent 50 percent chance of guessing the correct answer, you will not see questions of this type on Microsoft certification exams.

Multiple Choice

The majority of Microsoft certification questions are in the multiple-choice format, with either a single correct answer or multiple correct answers. One interesting variation on multiple-choice questions with multiple correct answers is whether the candidate is told how many answers are correct, as in

Which of the following controls can be used on a MDI form? (Choose all that apply.)

or

Which of the following two controls can be used on an MDI form? (Choose two.)

You may see both variations on Microsoft certification examinations, but the trend seems to be toward the second type, where candidates are told explicitly how many answers are correct. Questions of the "choose all that apply" variety are more difficult, and can be merely confusing.

Graphical Questions

One or more graphical elements are sometimes used as exhibits to help present or clarify an exam question. These elements may take the form of a database diagram, flow charts, or screenshots from the software on which you are being tested. It is often easier to present the concepts required for a complex performance-based scenario with a graphic than with words.

Test questions known as *hotspots* actually incorporate graphics as part of the answer. These questions ask the certification candidate to click on a location or graphical element to answer the question. For example, you might be shown the diagram of a three-tiered application and asked to click on a tier described by the question. The answer is correct if the candidate clicks within the hotspot that defines the correct location.

Free Response Questions

Another kind of question you sometimes see on Microsoft certification exams requires a *free response* or type-in answer. An example of this type of question might present a complex code sample including loops and error trapping and ask the candidate to calculate and enter the final value of a variable.

Knowledge-Based and Performance-Based Questions

Microsoft Certification develops a blueprint for each Microsoft certification exam with input from subject-matter experts. This blueprint defines the content areas and objectives for each test, and each test question is created to test a specific objective. The basic information from the exam blueprint can be found on Microsoft's Web site in the Exam Prep Guide for each test.

A practice case-based exam is available for download at **http://www.microsoft.com/mcp/exam/stat/sp70-100.htm**. This is the 70-100 Web site that lists all of the knowledge objectives covered in the exam. It is always a good idea to review this material before you take an exam.

Psychometricians (psychologists who specialize in designing and analyzing tests) categorize test questions as knowledge-based or performance-based. As the names imply, knowledge-based questions are designed to test knowledge, while performance-based questions are designed to test performance.

Some objectives demand a knowledge-based question. For example, objectives that use verbs like *list* and *identify* tend to test only what you know, not what you can do, as in this example:

Objective: Identify the ADO Cursor Types that support read and write operations.

Which two of the following ADO Cursor Types support write access? (Choose two.)

    A. adOpenStatic

    B. adOpenDynamic

    C. adOpenForwardOnly

    D. adOpenKeyset

Correct answers: B and D

Other objectives use action verbs like *connect, configure,* and *troubleshoot* to define job tasks. These objectives can often be tested with either a knowledge-based question or a performance-based question, as in the following examples:

Objective: Connect to a data source appropriately using ADO Cursor Type properties.

Knowledge-based question:

What is the correct Cursor Type to allow users to view new records created by other users?

A. adOpenStatic

B. adOpenDynamic

C. adOpenForwardOnly

D. adOpenKeyset

Correct answer: B

Performance-based question:

Your company supports several travel agents using a common data store, and each agent must be able to see the reservations taken by all other agents. What is the best application development strategy to allow users to see records modified and created by other users?

A. Use an adOpenKeyset Cursor Type to create the record set, and keep the same Recordset object open continuously.

B. Use an adOpenDynamic Cursor Type to create the record set, and keep the same Recordset object open continuously.

C. Use an adOpenStatic Cursor Type to create the record set, but destroy and create the Recordset object after every data update.

D. Use an adOpenForwardOnly Cursor Type to create the record set, but destroy and create the Recordset object after every data update.

Correct answer: B

Even in this simple example, the superiority of the performance-based question is obvious. Whereas the knowledge-based question asks for a single fact, the performance-based question presents a real-life situation and requires that you make a decision based on this scenario. Thus, performance-based questions give more bang (validity) for the test author's buck (individual question).

Test 70-100: Analyzing Requirements and Defining Solution Architectures

At the time of this writing, the Beta Exam was being evaluated. New test structures were introduced in this exam and conclusions based on the evaluation of the Beta Exam responses have not been formed. It is important that you watch the Microsoft Web site for late-breaking news on this exam. Again, the URL is **http://www.microsoft.com/mcp/exam/stat/sp70-100.htm.**

As with the other exams in this series, there may be 60 to 70 questions and approximately 90 minutes will be allowed to finish the exam. As you can see by the case-based practice exam, there will be a scenario followed by questions. For each type of question, there will be a button to click for instructions on completing the question. following a case study, expect to see not only multiple choice but all forms of questions. There may be a group of five different case studies followed by with anywhere from three to eight questions. The answers to these questions would be based on the information presented by that case study and would be unrelated to the other case studies. As you are answering the questions, if you are not clear on a point from the text, you may return to the case study to review it. If any multiple-choice questions were to follow the group of case-study questions, they would be unrelated to any of the previous case studies.

Testing Job Performance

We have said that Microsoft certification focuses on timeliness and the ability to perform job tasks. We have also introduced the concept of performance-based questions, but even performance-based, multiple-choice questions do not really measure performance. Another strategy is needed to test job skills.

Given unlimited resources, it is not difficult to test job skills. In an ideal world, Microsoft would fly MCP candidates to Redmond, place them in a controlled environment with a team of experts, and ask them to design, author, debug, and revise a Windows application. In a few days at most, the experts could reach a valid decision as to whether each candidate should be granted MCSD status. Needless to say, this is not likely to happen.

Closer to reality, another way to test performance is by using the actual software, and creating a testing program to present tasks and automatically grade a candidate's performance when the tasks are completed. This *cooperative* approach would be practical in some testing situations, but the same test that is presented to MCP candidates in Boston must also be available in Bahrain and Botswana. Many Sylvan Prometric testing locations around the world cannot run 32-bit applications, much less provide the complex networked solutions required by cooperative testing applications.

The most workable solution for measuring performance in today's testing environment is a *simulation* program. When the program is launched during a test, the candidate sees a simulation of the actual software that looks, and behaves, just like the real thing. When the testing software presents a task, the simulation program is launched and the candidate performs the required task. The testing software then grades the candidate's performance on the required task and moves to the next question. In this way, a 16-bit simulation program can mimic the look and feel of 32-bit operating systems, a complicated network, or even the entire Internet.

Microsoft has introduced simulation questions on the certification exam for Internet Information Server version 4. Simulation questions provide many advantages over other testing methodologies, and simulations are expected to become increasingly important in the Microsoft Certification Program. For example, studies have shown that there is a high correlation between the ability to perform simulated tasks on a computer-based test and the ability to perform the actual job tasks. Thus, simulations enhance the validity of the certification process.

Another benefit of simulations is in the area of test security. It is just not possible to cheat on a simulation question. In fact, you will be told exactly what tasks you are expected to perform on the test.

Study Strategies

There are appropriate ways to study for the different types of questions you will see on a Microsoft certification examination.

Knowledge-Based Questions

Knowledge-based questions require that you memorize facts. There are hundreds of facts inherent in each content area of every Microsoft certification exam. There are several keys to memorizing facts:

- ■ **Repetition**   The more times your brain is exposed to a fact, the more likely you are to remember it.

- ■ **Association**   Connecting facts within a logical framework makes them easier to remember.

- ■ **Motor Association**   It is often easier to remember something if you write it down or perform some other physical act, like clicking a practice test answer.

We have said that the emphasis of Microsoft certification is job performance, and that there are very few knowledge-based questions on Microsoft certification exams. Why should you waste a lot of time learning filenames, property values, and other minutiae? Read on.

Performance-Based Questions

Most of the questions you will face on a Microsoft certification exam are performance-based scenario questions. We have discussed the superiority of these questions over simple knowledge-based questions, but you should remember that the job task–orientation of Microsoft certification extends the knowledge you need to pass the exams; it does *not* replace this knowledge. Therefore, the first step in preparing for scenario questions is to absorb as many facts relating to the exam content areas as you can. In other words, go back to the previous section and follow the steps to prepare for an exam composed of knowledge-based questions.

The second step is to familiarize yourself with the format of the questions you are likely to see on the exam. You can do this by answering the questions in this study guide, by using Microsoft assessment tests, or by using practice tests. The day of your test is not the time to be surprised by the convoluted construction of Microsoft exam questions.

For example, one of Microsoft's favorite formats of late takes the following form:

Scenario: You have an application with . . .
Primary Objective: You want to . . .
Secondary Objective: You also want to . . .
Proposed Solution: Do this . . .

What does the proposed solution accomplish?

    A. Satisfies the primary and the secondary objective

    B. Satisfies the primary but not the secondary objective

    C. Satisfies the secondary but not the primary objective

    D. Satisfies neither the primary nor the secondary objective

This kind of question, with some variation, is seen on many Microsoft certification examinations.

At best, these performance-based scenario questions really do test certification candidates at a higher cognitive level than knowledge-based questions. At worst, these questions can test your reading comprehension and test-taking ability rather than your ability to use Microsoft products. Be sure to get in the habit of reading the question carefully to determine what is being asked.

The third step in preparing for Microsoft scenario questions is to adopt the following attitude: Multiple-choice questions aren't really performance-based. It is all a cruel lie. These scenario questions are just knowledge-based questions with a little story wrapped around them.

To answer a scenario question, you have to sift through the story to the underlying facts of the situation, and apply your knowledge to determine the correct answer. This may sound silly at first, but the process we go through in solving real-life problems is quite similar. The key concept is that every scenario question (and every real-life problem) has a fact at its center, and if we can identify that fact, we can answer the question.

Simulations

Simulation questions really do measure your ability to perform job tasks. You *must* be able to perform the specified tasks. There are two ways to prepare for simulation questions:

    ■ Get experience with the actual software. If you have the resources, this is a great way to prepare for simulation questions.

■ Use official Microsoft practice tests. Practice tests are available that provide practice with the same simulation engine used on Microsoft certification exams. This approach has the added advantage of grading your efforts.

Signing Up

Signing up to take a Microsoft certification examination is easy. Sylvan operators in each country can schedule tests at any testing center. You can reach Sylvan at (800) 755-EXAM. There are, however, a few things you should know:

■ If you call Sylvan during a busy time period, get a cup of coffee first, because you may be in for a long wait. Sylvan does an excellent job, but everyone in the world seems to want to sign up for a test on Monday morning.

■ An alternative to speaking with a human is to register using the Sylvan Prometric Web site at **http://www.2test.com**. You may also register online at **http://www.microsoft.com/Train_Cert/mcp/certstep/examreg.htm**.

■ You will need your Social Security number or some other unique identifier to sign up for a Sylvan test, so have it ready.

■ Pay for your test by credit card, if at all possible. This makes registration easier, and you can even schedule tests for the same day you call, if space is available at your local testing center.

■ Know the number and title of the test you want to take before you call. This is not essential, and the Sylvan operators will help you if they can. However, having this information in advance speeds up the registration process and reduces the risk that you will accidentally register for the wrong test.

■ If you need to reschedule your exam, you must call 24 hours ahead of the exam appointment and you may reschedule for the time and place of your choice.

Non-Disclosure Agreement

In exactly the same form as the Microsoft software installation process, you must agree to a nondisclosure statement. Clicking on the "I agree" option button signifies your signature and allows the test software to proceed. If you click on the other button indicating that you do not agree, the exam ends and you forfeit your exam fee. The new non-disclosure statement may be found at **http://www.microsoft.com/mcp/articles/nda.htm**.

Retake Policy

If the unthinkable were to happen—it happens to the best of us—and you do not pass the exam, the old policy was that you could retake the exam as many times it took to pass. That is all in the past. Now, if you do not pass after the second try, you must wait two weeks before trying again. Do you know how much information you can forget in two weeks?

Taking the Test

Teachers may have told you not to cram for exams, because it does no good. However, if you are faced with a knowledge-based test requiring only that you regurgitate facts, cramming can mean the difference between passing and failing. This is not the case with Microsoft certification exams. If you don't know it the night before, don't bother to stay up and cram.

Instead, create a schedule and stick to it. Follow these guidelines on the day of your exam:

- Get a good night's sleep the night before. The scenario questions you will face on a Microsoft certification examination require a clear head.

- Remember to take two forms of identification with you—at least one with a picture. A driver's license with your picture, and Social Security or credit cards are acceptable.

- Leave home in time to arrive at your testing center a few minutes early. It is not a good idea to feel rushed as you begin your exam.

- Do not spend too much time on any one question. If you are taking a form test, take your best guess and mark the question so you can come back to it if you have time. You cannot mark and revisit questions on an adaptive test, so you must do your best on each question as you go.

- If you do not know the answer to a question, try to eliminate the obviously wrong answers and guess from the rest. If you can eliminate two out of four options, you have a 50 percent chance of guessing the correct answer.

- For scenario questions, follow the steps outlined earlier. Read the question carefully and try to identify the facts at the center of the story.

Finally, I would advise anyone attempting to earn Microsoft MCSD certification to adopt a philosophical attitude. Even if you are the kind of person who never fails a test, you are likely to fail at least one Microsoft certification test somewhere along the way. Do not get discouraged. If Microsoft certification were easy to obtain, more people would have it, and it would not be so respected and valuable to your future in the IT industry.

1

Microsoft Solution Framework— An Overview

Welcome to your first steps to passing the Analyzing Requirements and Defining Solution Architectures exam. If you're experienced in analysis and design and have dealt with solution architectures, you may be wondering if you need to read this book. There are many methodologies out there that work well in theory, but are much less useful in the real (work) world. The Microsoft Solution Framework (MSF) consists of practices that have had proven success in the real world. Not only does reading this book bring you one step closer to becoming an MCSD, but it explains tried and true methods, from the real world.

In this chapter we'll introduce you to the principles and models that make up the Microsoft Solution Framework. We'll discuss what MSF is, what it's used for, and what it can do for you. While this chapter contains a substantial amount of information, it is merely a stepping stone for information that is covered throughout the book. By introducing you to the elements that make up MSF, you'll be able to build on this information as we go along.

CERTIFICATION OBJECTIVE 1.01

Identifying the Business Pressures on IT

The way business is conducted has changed more in the last 20 years than it has in the last two millennia. Technology has created the need for people to be educated throughout their entire lives. The Internet has even the smallest companies competing on a global scale. As companies merge, different technologies are combined, so that software needs to interact or run on different platforms, accessing different forms of information. Throughout this, there is new legislation that must be adhered to and buyouts to worry about, along with product cycles that are constantly growing shorter. Everyone, including Information Technology, feels the rapid changes washing over the business world.

New risks bring new challenges. No matter what problem you face, it's important that a company's technical and business goals parallel one another and work together toward common goals. While this may seem like common sense to you, people in Information Technology (IT) have traditionally been somewhat separated from the "suits" of the business world.

When computers first entered the corporate structure, the programmers and, to a lesser degree, network people, were early explorers who mapped the regions of the computer world. Often isolated from the business people in a quiet part of the building, these techies determined what could and couldn't be done with computers. While they followed the orders of upper management, communication of project goals was usually lax. Today, people have grown up with computers like settlers of cyberspace, and the importance of Information Technology is well recognized. The role of the explorers changed to those of cowboys and cowgirls, where programmers and network specialists work together with people in the business world. In many cases, the effectiveness of these hired hands determines the success of the company itself!

Now let's look at how Microsoft's Solution Framework deals with many of the problems facing business and Information Technology.

What Is the Microsoft Solution Framework?

The easiest way to achieve success is to follow in the successful footsteps of others. This doesn't mean you should wait to see what the competition is doing, and then put out a duplicate product, though that's been known to happen way too often in the real world. What it means is to learn to play like the big boys do, by following their game plans. That, in a nutshell, sums up what the Microsoft Solution Framework is about—it takes the best practices that are out there and integrates them into models, principles, and guides that the rest of us can use.

MSF is the most successful practices available for making software projects succeed. Unlike some models that are purely theoretical, MSF is taken from the experiences of IT professionals. Only the practices that have worked are incorporated into the framework. It is the amassed knowledge of Microsoft, its solution developers, partners, IT groups, customers, and product developers. It helps to integrate the business and IT environments, build teams that work, expose critical risks, identify and lower cost drivers, make improved development tradeoffs, create flexible designs, improve deployment, and anticipate the needs of customers and users. By using the resources, guides, and practices of the Microsoft Solution Framework, you not only create a better working environment, but also dramatically lower the odds that a project will fail.

Anyone who's worked on a software development project can tell you that the odds of a project succeeding or failing would make the most diehard gambler cringe. This is where risk management comes in. Under MSF, a risk is defined as the possibility of suffering some sort of loss, and is inherent to any project. This doesn't necessarily make risks a bad thing. Risk offers opportunity for a project. Earlier in this section, it was mentioned that it is not entirely uncommon for some enterprises to see what the competition does, and then follow their example. The competition absorbs all of the risks, as well as the benefits of taking a chance on a project. As we'll see in Chapter 3, risk management identifies, monitors, and deals with risks, so they don't become actual problems that can threaten a project's success.

In addition to the principles of risk management, the Microsoft Solution Framework provides models that can be used to enhance a project's success. MSF consists of seven models, which can be used individually or combined. As we'll discuss later in this section, you aren't limited to an "all or nothing" approach, and you can implement the models as your needs dictate. The MSF models are:

- Team model
- Process model
- Application model
- Solutions Design model
- Enterprise Architecture model
- Infrastructure model
- TCO model

Each of these models is used for very different purposes on a project to address different issues that determine a project's success. In the paragraphs that follow, we'll introduce you to each of these, then expand on them throughout this chapter and, of course, throughout the book.

The Team Model

The most fundamental resource of any project is the team that's working on it. Without an effective, expert team of individuals, nothing would get done. The *Team model* recognizes this importance, and provides team members with the power to use their expertise and creativity on a project, while holding them accountable for their actions.

MSF's Team model outlines well-defined roles for members of the team. Each role has its own mission, for which the members in that role are responsible. This allows members to not only have ownership over part of a project, it also allows them to focus on what they're working toward. The six roles and missions of the Team model are the following:

- **Product Management** Responsible for obtaining the customer's requirements of a product, and setting the vision for the product so everyone understands what it entails. This role also creates and manages a business case (explained in the next chapter), and manages the expectations of the customer so they understand what can and will be delivered.

- **Program Management** Responsible for making decisions that determine delivery of the right product at the right time. Ensures that the product meets the standards of the organization, as well as the interoperability goals.

- **Development** Responsible for building or implementing a product or service that meets the requirements and needs of the customer.

- **Testing** Responsible for making certain that a product works, and that issues such as bugs and errors are addressed before release.

- **User Education** Responsible for enhancing the user's experience and performance with a product, by making the product easy to understand and use.

- **Logistics** Responsible for a smooth rollout of the product. Ensures that the installation and migration of a product to support and operations groups goes smoothly.

Each of these roles works on their specific mission, and works toward achieving a specific goal that they are responsible for. Members know what they're hoping to achieve from their work, and what their purpose on the project is. Because people know what they're doing, and have ownership of their part in the project, the end result is a product of higher quality.

exam
ⓦatch

Expect to see numerous questions dealing directly or indirectly with the Team model and the roles that make up this model. This model is used in conjunction with other models, when applied to projects in the real world. As such, its importance will probably be reflected in questions dealing with it on the exam.

The Team model isn't an organizational chart to show who reports to whom, or which person on a team rules over another. Members of the team work together as peers. This isn't to say that leadership is dismissed. Team leaders are implemented to provide guidance and direction, so members can focus on the goals of their respective roles. Who the team reports to is left to the discretion of upper management.

The Process Model

The MSF *Process model* clarifies what people are working toward, and the progress achieved from that work. Process focuses the team on issues relevant to different phases of the project, and allows members to see that they're on the right track with a project. It does this by breaking the development cycle into four phases:

- Envisioning phase
- Planning phase
- Developing phase
- Stabilizing phase

By breaking the project into phases, large projects are less overwhelming and more organized. As we'll see later in this section, each phase is well defined. It outlines what needs to be done for that part of the project to culminate and the next phase to begin.

At the end of each phase, a major milestone is reached in the project. A *milestone* is a major turning point in the project that indicates progress. At each milestone, the team determines whether the customer's requirements are being met, and synchronizes their efforts so the project can succeed. Such milestones force the project to become results-oriented—one phase must be successful, and culminate in a milestone, before the next phase can begin.

The first phase in the Process model is the *Envisioning phase*. It is here that project requirements are defined. This phase keeps the team from spending effort on minor needs, or trying to make bad procedures or operations more efficient. For example, you don't want to spend great effort changing the color of the user interfaces in an enterprise application because someone wants it to have a marble appearance. Not only are the current needs of the customer evaluated, but future issues the business may face, similar issues faced in other departments, as well as what is causing the need in the first place are also addressed.

Once this is done, the Envisioning phase results in the *Vision/Scope Approved milestone*, where an agreement is made on the direction of the project and the nature of the solution. *Vision* sets the ultimate goals of the project, while *scope* recognizes the limitations. This takes into account that while it would be great to have 20 new features added to a product, the schedule may allow only 15, with the additional 5 appearing in the next version of the software. By reaching this milestone, a clear direction is established.

The *Planning phase* is where the customers and team members sit down to determine exactly what will be delivered and how it should be built. While the project's direction is specified in the previous step, this is where everyone agrees on a game plan: will we use Visual Basic, Visual C++, or some other program to build the software? Which features are most important, and where do we set our priorities? These are some of the issues discussed at this phase. It is also during the Planning phase that risks are reassessed, and estimates for schedules and resources are made. In the end, the *Project Plan Approved milestone* is reached, providing the functional specification and schedule. The functional specification created here is the combined plans of members in each role of the MSF Team model, and details the requirements and commitments of the project.

The functional specification and project plan are passed forward, and used in the *Developing phase* of the Process model. Using this information as a baseline, the product or service begins to be built at this stage. The development team sets a number of interim delivery milestones, where the product goes through several cycles of testing, debugging, and fixing. This happens until, finally, all development is complete, and the Scope Complete/First Use milestone is reached.

The *Scope Complete/First Use milestone* is where the product's functionality is assessed, and it is determined that rollout and support plans are in place before the product is delivered. Documentation is made about features dropped from the current version, and whether they will appear in future versions of the product. In addition, risks and new issues about the product are evaluated at this milestone.

The *Stabilization phase* has a primary focus on finding and fixing bugs that have appeared in the product. This phase occurs concurrently with code development, where the programming of the software product takes place. Once testing at this phase is completed, the product is delivered to operations and support groups, marking the *Release milestone*. At this milestone, the product is shipped and put into service.

One of the outstanding features of the MSF Process model is that risks are assessed early in a project. This proactive approach recognizes the risks involved in a particular project, so that they can be dealt with as the project progresses. At each milestone, the team members are able to synchronize their efforts, and address the issues and risks of the project, before critical problems arise that could jeopardize the project's success.

The Application Model

As its name suggests, the *Application model* addresses how applications are constructed to meet the needs of customers and users. This model promotes the use of COM (Component Object model) components. These components are reusable and can be shared by other applications your team creates. As such, rather than having to rewrite the same code in other applications, you can simply use previously created components.

The Application model breaks an application into a network of consumers and suppliers of services. A *consumer* is a program or component that uses the services of another component. The *supplier* provides the requested service to this consumer. A *service* is defined as a unit of application logic, which is used to perform an operation, function, or some sort of transformation on an object. For example, let's say you were creating an application that retrieves information from a database. To do this, you might decide to use COM components (such as ActiveX components) so you could reuse the code if your customer required the retrieval feature in other applications. The consumer component would then request the information, which could be located on the same machine or across a network, while the supplier would respond to the request for this data service and return the data.

This creates a multi-tier application (similar to a wedding cake, as shown in Figure 1-1). The user interacts with the application through a user interface and/or programmatic interface, which is the user services tier. The next tier controls sequencing, and enforces business rules and the transactional integrity of operations. The bottom tier is where data is stored, and where manipulations of data take place, like Create, Delete, Read, and Update services. When data is passed back up the tiers, Business Services transforms the data into information, so that user services can properly

---

FIGURE 1-1

Multi-tiered applications are built on User, Business, and Data Services.

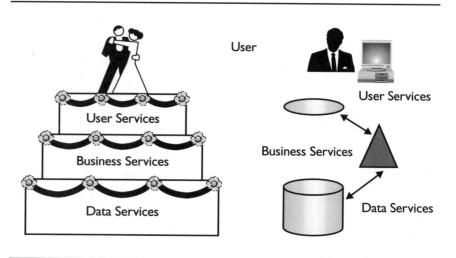

display or use it. Though the different tiers are separate from one another, they work together to provide services to the user.

In describing multi-tier application development, the Application model shows how programs are built on three services that can be consumed or supplied by COM components:

- User Services
- Business Services
- Data Services

User Services are associated with the user interface and/or programmatic interface, provided by units of application logic. The user of the application can be a person or another program. *Business Services* are used to enforce transactional integrity, business rules, and control sequencing. This service also transforms the data acquired from data services into meaningful information that the user can use. Finally, *Data Services* include Create, Read, Update, and Delete services, as well as such retrieval logic as order and joins. This allows Business Services, which is the consumer of data services, to be shielded from knowing where data is located, or how to access and implement it.

The Solutions Design Model

"Give the people what they want" should be the motto of this model. The *Solutions Design model* helps the project team anticipate the needs of the user, by bringing the user into the fold. While it is wonderful to discuss requirements with the customer, on many occasions you'll find that the customer isn't the person actually using the product. The customer buys the product, while the user is the person who uses it—they aren't necessarily the same people. It is important to get the users' input if a solution is to be properly aligned with the true needs of a business.

In the Solutions Design model, users become involved in the design process. By having them address key issues, such as usability and requirements, the team is able to determine whether an application will be used and will increase productivity. For example, if the application doesn't suit the end user's needs, and creates more problems than it solves, or the interface is difficult to use, the user may decide to keep the old system to get work done. Involving the user prevents problems later, including having the user rely on a help desk for assistance, or not using the product at all.

Beyond involving users, the Solutions Design model provides a strategy for designing business-oriented solutions that need to be created to suit a specific need. It brings together the Team model, Application model, and Process model so that resources can be focused on areas where they'll provide the most return.

The Solutions Design model is comprised of different perspectives. A *perspective* is an outlook or viewpoint on something, which in this case is the design process of an application. It is used to provide focus to the design process. These perspectives are:

- Conceptual
- Logical
- Physical

The perspectives are used to identify business and technical requirements of an application. The result of using this model is a better assignment of resources in your project, which can make things considerably easier for you.

Conceptual design is where the initial concept of the solution originates. It is here that the team develops an understanding of what the user needs from a solution. Scenarios and models are used to relay this understanding so that everyone involved in the project—team members, customers, and users—knows what is needed.

Logical design takes the information gathered from the conceptual design and applies it to technical know-how. While the requirements and needs of customers and users are outlined in the previous design perspective, it is here that the structure and communication of elements in the solution are established. The objects and services, the user interface, and logical databases are among the elements identified and designed in this perspective.

Physical design is where requirements from the conceptual and logical perspectives are put into a tangible form. It is here that the constraints of technology are applied to the logical design of the solution. Physical design defines how the components of your solution, such as the user interface and physical database, work together. Performance, implementation, bandwidth, scalability, reliability, and maintainability are all resolved and implemented through physical design. Because this perspective applies previous designs to a concrete form, you are able to estimate what resources, costs, or scheduling will be needed to complete the project.

In dealing with the three perspectives, it is important to realize that they are not a series of steps with clear cutoff points. You don't have to reach a specific point in one perspective before moving onto the next. In fact, one area of design may be used in conjunction with another, so that while one part of a solution is designed conceptually or logically, another is being coded or implemented into the final product. Since there are no stages with cutoff points or boundaries, you are able to return to the different design perspectives as many times as necessary. This allows you to refine your design by revisiting and redesigning your solution.

The Enterprise Architecture Model

Like the previous model, the *Enterprise Architecture model* is made up of four perspectives designed to help you focus on the key issues of a project:

- Business architecture
- Application architecture
- Information architecture
- Technology architecture

The Enterprise Architecture model provides guidelines for planning, building, and managing technology infrastructures. It helps to integrate the business, by making sure that changes throughout the enterprise are consistent and meet the needs of the business.

Business architecture is used to define how the business works. It determines what the business does, its strengths, and its future. By having a description of how the company works, and the functional and cross-functional activities it performs, you will have a better understanding of its requirements. You'll remember from the mention of milestones earlier that the first milestone in MSF's Process model results in the vision/scope of the project. The business architecture perspective aids in this, by establishing the perimeters or boundaries for requirements and development of vision/scope.

Application architecture is used to determine issues dealing with current applications and Application models, and what changes may be necessary to these areas. Here it is determined what Application models are currently used, integration issues unique to the current system, and where backlogs exist. It defines the interfaces, services, and Application models needed by a business, which are translated into development resources that are used by project teams. Application architecture provides the guidelines necessary for developing new applications and determining whether new Application models are required.

Information architecture describes how data and information are handled in a business so it can run effectively, and describes what the company needs to know to run the organization's business processes and operations. This includes such things as determining functional data requirements, information needs, and policies dealing with data management. This perspective also describes how information is bound to workflow. It is important to remember that data stores, such as databases, documents, and spreadsheets, exist not only on servers, but on the desktop computers prevalent in most enterprises. Because of this, information architecture deals with identifying where most of the critical information in an organization resides.

Technology architecture is a perspective that describes standards and guidelines for laying out the software and hardware supporting an organization. This perspective includes such things as operating systems, client/workstation tools, and hardware used by workstations and servers, printers, and modems. This perspective provides you with a vendor-independent, logical description of your organization's technology infrastructure.

The beauty and value of the Enterprise Architecture model is that it doesn't look at the enterprise from a single, stagnant viewpoint. Though comprised of four perspectives, there is only a single architecture that is being looked at in different ways. As we'll see later in this chapter, this model allows you to plan as you build an enterprise's architecture, resulting in a comprehensive view of the organization's technical infrastructure.

The Infrastructure Model

While the previous model deals with the software and hardware elements necessary in computing, the *Infrastructure model* defines all of the resources needed to support this environment. *Infrastructure*, under the MSF definition, is the total set of resources needed to support an enterprise computing environment. These resources consist of the following:

- Technologies and standards
- Operational processes
- People and organizational resources

Technologies and standards deals with the software, hardware, and standards that we introduced in the Enterprise Architecture model. *Operational processes* consist of the operating procedures, policies, and services that are used in the enterprise. These are the rules and regulations that are abided by in the organization. Finally, *people and organizational resources* deal with the skill sets and management available in the organization. These are human resources that are available as personnel, and can add their skills or management expertise to a project.

The Infrastructure model takes the knowledge of previously mentioned models, and applies it to rolling out a successful infrastructure. In doing this, you are reusing the expectations, functions, and roles of other models, rather than learning and applying new principles. The models used in the Infrastructure model are the Team and Process models.

In using these models as part of infrastructure, there are some differences from the original models. In the Process model, some names are altered to reflect their use in infrastructure. However, it is still milestone-based, and incorporates the principle of using tradeoffs. Priorities are made, as are decisions to sacrifice certain areas of a project so another may succeed. As is the case with process, the Infrastructure model makes such tradeoffs in the areas of schedule, scope, or resources. Tradeoffs are covered in greater detail later in this chapter.

In the Infrastructure model, team roles are expanded with wider responsibilities, and new roles are added to accommodate the task of such projects. The three roles added to the role of logistics are the following:

- Systems Management
- Help Desk
- Communications

Systems Management is responsible for maintaining accountability for the systems and technology. This accountability is inclusive to the continued operation of the technology. The *Help Desk* is responsible for providing assistance and ongoing support to the end user. Finally, *Communications* is responsible for maintaining video, voice, and data communications in the project.

FROM THE CLASSROOM

A Framework That Works

The Microsoft Solution Framework is a solid set of guidelines and processes that provides the patch to cover the gaping hole in application design and planning that many companies ignore these days. For this reason, numerous aspects of this framework will be covered directly on the exam, or a complete understanding of MSF will be expected. Be familiar with the basics of each and every model discussed. Pay careful attention to the Application model. Not only is this one of the most leveraged and clearly defined models, but it is the prime focus throughout Microsoft's Mastering Enterprise Application Design Using Visual Studio 6.0 (MOC1298) course, listed as one of the courses to which this exam maps. Keep in mind that application logic maps to the user services layer; business logic maps to the business services layer; and data retrieval logic maps to the data services layer.

Regarding the Team model, it is sometimes difficult to clearly determine the responsibility for each role. In some cases, roles are combined or performed by the same person. Some roles should never be performed by the same person because of conflicting goals of the roles. Be familiar with the associations of phases to milestones and interim milestones that comprise the core of the Process model. The Process model is fairly involved and complex and requires organization and communication skills. Keep in mind that reducing total cost of ownership is not the same thing as eliminating costs. Eliminating costs taken completely by itself is usually not a good thing. Eliminating costs without analyzing the value of the elements that are generating the costs is a recipe for reducing company competitiveness.

— *Michael Lane Thomas, MCSE+I, MCSD, MCT, MCP+SB, MSS, A+*

The TCO Model

The *TCO (Total Cost of Ownership) model* works on the basic premise that optimizing costs equals a better return on investment (ROI). In other words, by spending less, you have more money in your pocket. The TCO model approaches this objective by analyzing the cost areas in a business in a rational and proven method.

The first thing to realize with TCO is that cost isn't necessarily a bad thing. You could conceivably reduce the TCO of your company by selling every computer in the building ... The MSF TCO model addresses the value of elements that have costs attached to them. Rather than attempting to minimize the total cost of ownership, the TCO model seeks to optimize it. This allows the value of such elements to be retained, while lowering costs.

The key word in all this is *optimizing*. In the TCO model, there are a number of factors that can be optimized in an organization:

- **Cost model elements**   Used to show relative costs that are based on the averages in the industry.

- **Components**   The software and hardware used in an organization.

- **Operations**   The elements required by the computing environment to operate properly, such as maintenance, help desk, disaster recovery, and training.

- **Management**   The administration of such things as the network, data, systems, and repair.

- **Hidden costs**   Includes such things as vendor management, misdiagnosis, and end-user training.

- **Downtime and other costs**   Includes such things as development and testing.

When looking through these cost areas, you can see they encompass all areas of the computing environment. In addressing these areas, it is important to remember not only the cost of items, such as hardware or software, but also the labor required to develop, implement, and support them. As mentioned earlier, labor can cost considerably more than an actual hardware component, or the cost of a computer used to develop software. A majority of cost is associated with labor, and it is important to include that when estimating cost figures related to these areas.

In optimizing these cost areas, the TCO model uses an ongoing three-phase process. Although when one phase is completed you move to the next, the process continues and is constantly working to improve itself. The stages consist of the following:

- Benchmark and Baseline phase
- Improvement phase
- Management phase

In the *Benchmark and Baseline phase*, you use the TCO model to calculate cost baselines, benchmarks, return on investments (ROIs), and validations. The *benchmark* is the total cost that's based on averages in the industry, while your *baseline* is the actual cost of the acquisition, management, and retirement of technology. Information gathered at this phase is carried into the *Improvement phase*, where ROI is calculated. Based on a strategy you create, this is calculated by simulating the impact of your recommendations on improvement and estimated cost savings. Finally, the *Management phase* is where you measure what you actually achieved against what you hoped to achieve. The results of your work are compared to your objectives, which either validates or invalidates the strategy that was used.

on the
ⓘob

People with a background in networking are probably familiar with the importance of baselines and benchmarks. Without them you can't measure the normal or original condition. They give you something to compare changes to, and determine if things are better or worse after you implement new strategies.

Mixing and Matching Models So They Work for You

Using the MSF models isn't an all-or-nothing affair. You don't just pick one model for a project and run with it. The MSF models are mixed and matched together to best suit the project you're working on. For example, let's say you're working on a project designing an intranet. Though you may recognize immediately that you'll need to use the Infrastructure model, you'll also have to implement the Team and Process models in your project. Why? Well, for one thing, you won't get very far if you haven't put any members into a team to work on the project. The Process model is then used to focus the team.

Table 1-1 shows some combinations of MSF models that Microsoft suggests you use on certain projects. As you go through this table, you'll notice the importance of the Team and Process models, as they appear in each combination. These two models are fundamental to the common projects you'll encounter.

TABLE 1-1	**Project**	**Model**
Suggested Combinations for MSF Models	Deploying a standard desktop	Team Process Infrastructure TCO
	Planning a network architecture	Team Process Enterprise Architecture Infrastructure TCO
	Designing an intranet	Team Process Enterprise Architecture Infrastructure
	Building an intranet application	Team Process Solutions Design Application Infrastructure
	Building a messaging infrastructure	Team Process Enterprise Architecture Infrastructure
	Building an electronic commerce site	Team Process Solutions Design Enterprise Architecture Infrastructure

Without diminishing the importance of the other models in the framework, it is especially important that you understand the Team and Process models. These are the two most used models and you can expect to see a considerable number of questions regarding them on the exam.

In using these models it is important to realize that their success doesn't revolve around what technologies they're used with, but how well they're used. It is important to understand the nuances of each of these models as you use them. Rather than speeding through a project using MSF, with this book in hand like a recipe book, move slowly. It is more important to do things correctly than quickly with MSF models.

CERTIFICATION OBJECTIVE 1.02

Identifying Key Areas Where IT and Business Are Changing Together

The Information Age is significantly more complicated than previous ages. Global competition, the Internet, and government legislation and regulations have had an enormous impact on the business world, and subsequently, on Information Technology. We live in a world where people expect things immediately. This has led to one major fact in IT and business: those who get their product to market first and fastest, usually reap the greatest rewards.

As the face of business changes, Information Technology must keep up. This means that effective and proven measures must be taken to ensure a product meets all of the required standards, while still keeping within the constraints of schedules and budget. Throughout the Information Technology life cycle, MSF helps address these issues to ensure the success of a project.

In this section, we'll look at the key principles and methods of the IT life cycle, and see how the Microsoft Solution Framework applies to it. We'll also look at how business and IT have changed together, and inspired the need for flexible business solutions.

Key Principles and Methods for the IT Life Cycle

Information Technology has a life cycle, made up of three parts:

- Planning
- Building
- Managing

The first stage in the life cycle is to plan your project. *Planning* involves creating strategies and evolving an enterprise architecture that will drive, or is adaptable to, changes in the business. This moves into the *building* stage, where your product is moved from the paperwork of schematics to a physical form. Building takes information from the planning stage, and ensures that the business-driven application is created on budget and on schedule. From here, the product is *managed*, allowing it to be maintained and improved. In looking at Figure 1-2, you'll notice that the life cycle doesn't necessarily end with management, but flows back into the planning stage. This allows for new versions of the original product, causing this cycle to repeat itself indefinitely.

The first part of any mission is planning. If you haven't done this, but decided instead to take the "fly-by-the-seat-of-your-pants" approach, you're in for some serious problems. Any medium-to-large project you work on can seem very much like a grand-scale military attack. You need to decide what troops you'll need, figure a plan of attack, and plan a method of

The Information
Technology life cycle

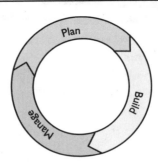

deployment. While this can seem relatively simple in a small organization, the complexities of projects tend to grow with the company.

In the planning stage, you determine current and future requirements of an organization. Where are you now, and where do you need to go to have future competitive advantages? Strategies are created at this point so you can reach the objectives you set for the teams you create. In doing so, you also use the Enterprise Architecture model, to drive and adapt to changes in your organization.

Once you've finished creating the necessary strategies and gathered the information you need, you move into the building stage of the IT life cycle. However, don't think that the bulk of your work now consists of coding. A weighty percentage of large IT projects fail at this point for a number of reasons. Information gathered to this point is insubstantial, such as poor or incomplete specifications, goals are unclear, the requirements are steadily changing, quality of coding is inferior, or there may be a lack of scope. It is here that you face some of the biggest risks your project will face.

Risk management is used at this point to identify and deal with areas of the project that can jeopardize success. In dealing with risks, you could simply put projects on hold until technologies, industry standards, and systems become commonplace. In doing so, you avoid many of the risks that present themselves in a project. However, you are also avoiding many of the opportunities that they present. Remember that the first ones to get their product to market usually reap the greatest rewards. When you avoid risks, you are avoiding opportunity as well.

This leads to two ways of dealing with risks in a project: proactive or reactive. *Reactive* means to wait until a risk turns into an actual problem and deal with it then. *Proactive* risk management means to monitor and deal with risks before they become a problem. As we'll see in Chapter 3, MSF's risk management process uses a proactive approach, so you get the most rewards, with the fewest problems.

During this stage in the IT life cycle, the Team model is used to implement small, focused teams on projects. In placing people in team roles, you should try to keep members in the same roles on different projects. This gives members a comprehensive understanding of their particular roles across an expanse of different projects.

At this time, the Process and Solutions Design models also come into play. During the building stage, you also need to consider and balance the budget, schedule, and resource constraints, which are the parameters of the Process model. Using this model, you can perform tradeoffs, so that one aspect of a project doesn't threaten the project as a whole. Later in this chapter, we will discuss tradeoffs in greater depth. The Solutions Design model is used during the building stage to acquire input from users, determine and fulfill their current and future needs, and provide focus in creating the product. Using these models you can build software products that meet and possibly exceed a user's expectations, while staying on schedule and budget.

Now that you've built and made changes to the enterprise by creating or updating new and/or improved software, or deploying a new infrastructure, it must be managed. Like risks, the MSF approach to managing change is proactive. Organizational change, or changes in the computing environment, must be dealt with accordingly, if people are to accept and use those changes.

In the management stage, the project is not looked at as completed, but viewed with an eye toward the future. Changes are evaluated, costs are analyzed, and areas of improvement are noted. Using the TCO model, the strategies used are evaluated for their effectiveness. Any areas of a solution that require intensive administration or maintenance or support are considered candidates for an integrated redesign using the Enterprise Architecture model. Information gathered at this stage can then be reapplied to future versions of a product.

Addressing the Growing Demand for Flexible Business Solutions

At the dawn of the 1990s, jobs began to be cut back. While downsizing was nothing new, corporations seemed to take this approach with an unparalleled voracity. According to U.S. government statistics, approximately 1.7 million manufacturing jobs disappeared between 1988 and 1993. While assembly line jobs are normally associated with manufacturing, it is important to note that a sizable portion of this number were back-office jobs. Despite the fact that they're a minority of the workforce, the human face of laid-off workers in the 90s belonged to that of white-collar professionals. Between 1988 and 1995, 18.6 percent of all middle-management jobs disappeared. Those still remaining in white-collar positions had to take up the slack. This meant taking on more duties than may have originally been in their job description.

These statistics illustrate the need for flexible business solutions in the enterprise. *Flexible business solutions* are applications that are adaptable, easily modified, and have the feature of a consistent interface. Such applications allow users to perform more activities and perform more complex duties, without having to learn new applications. Creating such applications requires the use of a good model, and that is where MSF's Application model comes into the picture.

The Application model allows you to design applications for flexibility, by outlining the development of multi-tier applications. These applications are built on User, Business, and Data Services. By separating the application into a network of services, this model allows the features in an application to be reused across physical and functional boundaries. This is done through the model's promotion of the Component Object model, which is also referred to as COM.

ActiveX Controls and OLE (Object Linking and Embedding) are built on the *Component Object model*. It is through this model that objects in an application are able to expose their functionality to other COM components or applications. COM isn't an actual programming language; it is a standard that defines how objects can expose themselves, the life cycle of an object, and how object exposure works across networks and processes. The beauty of COM components is that they are reusable, so rather than having to write the same code over and over, you can invoke components from existing applications. Since the interfaces for these components is the same regardless of the application using them, the user doesn't need additional training to perform a task.

Since COM is a platform-independent, distributed, object-oriented standard, it allows business applications and systems to be integrated with Internet technologies. This means you can use the Application model and COM to create applications that can access, or be accessed from, the Internet. Cross-platform support allows a user to access a COM component from Unix, Windows, or other operating systems, and still use its functionality.

The Application model sets out the rules, relationships, and definitions that form the application's structure. This allows consistency across all of the applications a user may use on the network or local computer. Users are able to easily move from one application to another on their desktop.

Identifying Problems That IT Must Overcome to Drive Business

There are two ways IT can drive business: forward or into the ground. Unfortunately, it's much easier to do the latter than the former. When you think of an enterprise like a human body, IT is the brain that runs the nervous system and which keeps an organization running. If you don't believe me, take a look at how many people suddenly stop working when a network or computer system goes down. When you see how important your role is, you see how vital it is to address problems properly, so the business can keep functioning.

There are two sources of problems you'll encounter in IT: technological and human. While each brings their own benefits to an organization and the design process, they also bring their own difficulties. There is no way of avoiding these two sources, so MSF provides ways to deal with them.

For technology, you must deal with the systems, utilities, and infrastructures that keep the organization up to speed. As the number of people in your organization grows, these areas must be improved to accommodate the population growths of users and enhancements in technology. For technology infrastructure, the Enterprise Architecture model provides guidelines to plan for future needs, while building to meet and manage current technological needs.

For the human source of problems, a big difficulty in IT is anticipating the needs of users. It is important to get users' input during the design process. While this brings forth difficulties of its own, as we'll see later, the benefits of user input far outweigh the problems.

Technology Infrastructure

Legacy systems and changing technologies can make you think you're fighting a losing battle. To support growth and drive business, the technology infrastructure of an enterprise needs to be constantly kept up to date. Operating systems, desktop and server hardware, network services, security, and APIs are all part of the technology infrastructure that needs to be planned, built, and managed.

Unfortunately, you can experience all sorts of problems when dealing with this issue. You may find it difficult to make any sort of change to the infrastructure, because you're having a hard enough time managing the current systems. If you're supporting legacy systems, you may find it difficult to define new technical guidelines. If you do manage to set such guidelines, you may find technologies have changed once standards are in place. If this isn't the case, you may find that departments in your organization prefer old systems and rebel against changes. The list of problems you may encounter with technology infrastructure can seem endless. Fortunately, MSF provides some hope.

The Enterprise Architecture model deals with technology infrastructure by providing a set of guidelines for planning, building, and management. With this model, planning takes place constantly as the business and its needs evolve and flourish. This "planning while building" doctrine helps keep you on top of the current system, while allowing you to plan ahead.

Without a proper means of dealing with technology infrastructure, there can be obstacles that go beyond the technology itself. Schedules may be set with an overly optimistic view of deployment, without taking into consideration that the application works as it should. You may find that projects are put on the back burner until certain technology issues are dealt with. If there is a need to decide on new technologies coming out, you may find your organization has no criteria for making such an evaluation. Such incidents not only deal with technology, but the practices and people in your organization.

While Enterprise Architecture focuses on technology infrastructure, the Infrastructure model aids you with the total resources necessary to support the computing environment of the enterprise. This not only deals with the technology infrastructure dealt with in Enterprise Architecture, but the technologies, standards, operational processes, people, and organizational resources needed in the computing environment. This model takes the roles and principles of the Team and Process models, and applies them to an infrastructure that works.

Anticipating User Needs

"Always leave the people wanting more" may be a great philosophy in entertainment, but it doesn't work in an application. It's vital that a program meet the needs of the user. Unfortunately, managing user involvement can be difficult at best. In fact, there are many development organizations that don't even bother involving users in project. The philosophy here is that "designing applications would be great, if it weren't for the users who use them."

When Windows 3.1 was the operating system of the day, users were screaming for a newer, better interface. When Windows 95 came out, many people disliked the new user interface, and decided they liked the old one better. People resist change in general, so it's not surprising that this resistance to changes in technology carries over to users. Users will have different preferences as to the layout, or the color or look of interfaces. Worst of all, when new features or functionality are delivered, users may want something different from what they originally asked for. The *Solutions Design model* is used to help anticipate user needs and overcome many of the obstacles in a project. This model has users brought into the project during the design process, so that they can address issues of usage before they become problems that support staff must deal with. By involving users early in the project, the benefits drastically outweigh any headaches such involvement might cause.

End users are the people who use the product on a day-to-day basis, and can tell you what specific needs the solution must address. These people work in the trenches with the product, and will work the software harder and considerably longer than team members in testing ever will. They will also be able to tell you what they require to properly use and keep using the product. By getting users involved, you not only find out the business and technical requirements of a user, but also get input on issues that will affect the product's success.

CERTIFICATION OBJECTIVE 1.04

Analyzing the Scope of a Project

When the vision for a project is being set, it's like writing a Christmas list. This isn't to say that nice customers get what they want, while the naughty ones get a product that has all the features of a lump of coal. The vision is the features and functionality you'd like to see in a product, and is much like a wish list. And like that wish list you make at Christmas, somewhere between the comic book and the pony, something's got to give! That's where scope comes into play. Scope is the opposite of vision, and reins in the features included in the vision, until it becomes something reasonable that the team can deliver.

There are many reasons for analyzing the scope of a project. One important reason is that projects can get so big that they may take too long to complete. Too many features can extend the development of a project to the point where it loses its value. If a project takes more than a year to complete, it may lose significant value to how fast technology evolves. If the project needs to be released by a certain point—such as income tax programs that need to be released before April—the product becomes completely worthless after a specific date. Besides time constraints, it is important to realize that the longer it takes to create a product, the more costs are involved. It's not difficult to suck the value out of a project by allowing the cost of labor and other resources to get out of hand.

Another reason for analyzing the scope of a project is morale. It is easy for team members and stakeholders to become disillusioned with a project. This can result when a project takes too long to complete, the amount of features and work involved being overwhelming, or because there appears to be no end in sight as the schedule keeps getting pushed up or new features keep being added. As team members become disillusioned, their productivity will drop. This can be avoided by determining and setting the scope of a project, and by using the models and principles of the Microsoft Solution Framework.

exam
ⓦatch

While morale is mentioned in several areas of this book, don't expect to see questions regarding this on the exam. It is an incredibly important issue in the real world and can greatly effect a project. However, while the models and principles of MSF can have the effect of improving morale, questions directly dealing with the emotional well-being of your team members and stakeholders aren't an objective of the exam.

Assessing Existing Applications

Before you create the specifications for a new application and set developers to work on coding a product, it's important to assess existing applications. There may be applications available that already suit the needs of the customer on the market. Buying software off the shelf may be cheaper than creating a new application that performs the same tasks. If you decide a new application does need to be created, applications that already exist on the system may provide services that your new program can use. Rather than rewriting the same code over and over, there may be existing components that can be incorporated into your software product. The reason to assess existing applications is simple: it can save you a considerable amount of needless work.

The Application model promotes the use of COM components, which are reusable and can be shared by other applications, by breaking the application into a network of consumers and suppliers of services. By using COM, components from one application are able to use the services of other applications. Because you are able to use components that were originally created in other applications, you don't have to rewrite the same code for a new application. A consumer component can be reused to access the services that were written in a previously created server component. While COM allows you to access the services of existing applications, you should determine whether a new application that uses COM should even be built. There are numerous off-the-shelf programs available, and you should determine whether to use them or spend time developing an application. In addition to buying or obtaining existing applications, you may need to work only with programs that already reside on user desktops. For example, let's say it is proposed that a database application should be created, because users are having problems understanding the complexities of Microsoft Access. You could spend considerable time creating such a program, or you could simply create forms in Microsoft Access that make the user's experience easier. By assessing existing applications, you can determine if it's cheaper to purchase or obtain programs that are already on the market rather than develop them. You can also determine if there is really a need for a new program, or if existing applications merely need to be reconfigured for users.

on the
Job

In dealing with customers, it is important to remember that the reason they're talking to you is because they aren't as knowledgeable as you. While you may know that they're asking you to build a product that already exists—and can be put on their company's desktops at a fraction of the price of what they're paying you—they may not know it exists. Once I had a company ask me to create a browser for their intranet. As I talked to them, they basically said they wanted the features of Microsoft Internet Explorer, but wanted their company logo, name, and a few other items. I suggested that rather than having me create a new program, I use the Internet Explorer Administration Kit to set up many of these features on their existing Internet Explorers. After this, I simply configured the Explorers the way they wanted them. Doing so saved them loads of money, and saved me a workload that wasn't even necessary.

Anticipating Changes in the Business Environment

It seems that a week doesn't go by without some company merging with another. If the organization you're working for experiences such a merger, you can expect changes to networks, standards, policies, and other areas that will influence Information Technology. If one company in a merger is dominant over another, then you can expect the dominant company's procedures and systems to become the norm. This is great if you're working for the dominant business in the merger, as you won't experience much in the way of change. If your luck is as good as mine, however, you'll be on the receiving end of having to learn new policies and procedures, implement new systems, and the list goes on.

It is important to keep abreast of changes in the business environment. If you're working in the IT department of a company, this means looking at the situations affecting your workplace. This means reading the information that comes across your desk (for example, memos), and having open discussions with customers and users.

The Microsoft Solution Framework recognizes the value of customer and user input. Customers are the people who purchase the product, and can provide higher-level information about changes expected in the business. They can provide information that the end user may not even be aware of. For example, they can tell you whether the organization will be connecting to the Internet, and whether users of the product will be getting access to the Net. Users are the people who actually use the product you're hired to create, and the Solutions Design model acknowledges the value of their opinions. Users work in the trenches with products, and may be aware of business changes that people higher in the company are not even be aware of! Remember that these users are hired for their special skills, and have knowledge that people commissioning the product's creation may not understand or know about. If you were creating an application for the accounting department, the accountants and bookkeepers would know about changes such as payroll policies and accounting procedures that people above them in the company don't know about or understand.

Another way to anticipate changes in the business is to stay current with changes in technology, industry standards, and other areas that revolve around the computing environment. It is important to know that things are changing, so you can anticipate changes that will be reflected in their products. For example, when Windows 95 first came out, it had a dramatic change in the features and functionality of applications. If you weren't aware that Windows 95 could use 32-bit applications, you would continue creating 16-bit applications as if they were for previous versions. Changes in operating systems and networks are inevitable at one point in the business. However, it is important to determine whether these changes will affect the business. Perhaps the company likes using Novell NetWare 3.12, and has no intention of changing anytime soon. It is essential to discuss changes with customers, users, network administrators, and people who will determine how and when such technological changes will affect the business.

Estimating the Expected Lifetime of the Solution

Everything in Information Technology has a lifetime associated with it. Nothing lasts forever, and there comes a time when your application will either need to be put out to pasture, or revised and recoded into a newer version. It is important that the expected lifetime of a solution be considered before you write your first line of code.

As you might expect, the difficulty of estimating a solution's expected lifetime ranges from child's play to what seems like brain surgery. For some applications, as mentioned in the cases of income tax programs, the lifetime is straightforward—after April a new version needs to be created, or the project is put to sleep. Most applications, however, aren't so simple, and you'll need to develop some researching skills to determine the lifetime. Having open discussions with customers and users can answer many questions for you. It's a simple principle: talk with the people who work with the application, and have the greatest knowledge of what the solution is for, to determine how long it will be used. Users of accounting programs can tell you when new legislation is released, while other users can tell you when new policies, procedures, or standards will make the current version of a product obsolete. Sources of technical information—such as TechNet and Microsoft's web sites—can help you determine when certain changes in computing will make a current version of a software product obsolete. Similar sources dealing with the business problems your solution addresses can also help you determine this.

Beyond going to the source, there is one rule of thumb to keep in mind when dealing with computing environments: technology changes quickly, and upgrades need to be performed at least once every three years. This means that hardware will need to be upgraded every two years to keep up-to-date with the latest standards. Since everyone else is releasing new solutions at least once every two or three years to meet with these standards and system requirements, you can estimate that your solution could have a maximum lifetime of three years. When creating mainstream solutions that are to be used by vast numbers of users in the general public, you can use this for estimating.

If you are creating solutions exclusively for the IT department, you can expect that the three-year maximum lifetime won't apply in many cases. For example, one large corporation I did some consulting for has only recently upgraded the computers to Pentiums. Before this, Information Technology was forced to create 16-bit and watered down 32-bit applications, as this was all that the older computers could handle. Solutions created far later than three years ago were still in operation. In such cases, its important to discuss with upper management when such changes will come into play. It is pointless to estimate an application's life at two years, if technological advances won't be implemented in the computer environment for another seven years.

In many cases, due to the swiftness of such changes in technology, you can also estimate that if your application takes longer than one year to create, most of its value has been lost. It is important that your applications make it to market as fast as possible so that you don't lose the value they offer on lost time. As mentioned earlier in this chapter—and expanded on throughout the book—the models and principles can help you get your product out, so that most of its lifetime isn't wasted on design and development.

By estimating the expected lifetime of a solution, you can determine when the next version of a product should start to be designed. It also helps you decide whether you should start on a current project or put it on hold until new policies, legislation, procedures, or technology come into effect. If your solution has an estimated lifetime of a year, but will take six months to release, it will have a lifetime of six months from release. You will also experience instances where the expected lifetime will be in the negative numbers. For example, if you have a product with a lifetime of six months, and it will take eight months to create, it will exceed its lifetime before it's even released! In such cases, it is far better to wait or start work on plans for the next version.

Assessing Time, Cost, Budget, and Benefit Tradeoffs

In any project, there are elements that can help move a project forward or act as obstacles to success. Three areas that regularly go either way in this regard are the following:

- Schedules
- Budget and cost
- Features

When it looks like there isn't enough time to complete the project, there are too many features to implement, or the costs of a project exceed the current budget, tradeoffs may become necessary. A *tradeoff* is where one element of a project is sacrificed so that another may fulfill the current needs. For example, costs may be cut or the schedule may be shortened so the project doesn't go over budget. The Process model helps you make better development tradeoffs, by defining variables and priorities that affect the issues of time, cost, budget, and benefits.

At one point or another, you've probably had someone tell you "we need it yesterday." Whether you've said it or thought it, the answer to this request may have been "fat chance!" There will be times when not enough time is given to complete a project. Perhaps your past performance was so impressive, that it was assumed you could do the same on a more complex or time-consuming project. Whatever the reason, time becomes an obstacle to the project's success.

The time allotted to projects is constantly shrinking. While pioneers in software development had considerable time to design, develop, and deploy applications, your teams will have time measured in weeks to complete a project. While you'll often find that the time scheduled for a project is enough to complete it, every once in a while you'll need to sacrifice time for another area. For instance, more people may need to be put on a project to meet the schedule.

Time can be a critical issue with software development. This is apparent when considering programs that deal with the Year 2000 (Y2K) problem, or income tax applications that are useless after April of each year. You'll remember that at the beginning of the Process model, the team schedules are submitted and put together into a large schedule. During the creation of such schedules, it is important that time-critical issues be scrutinized. Even if the project is on time and on budget, if it goes over a certain date, the program may no longer be needed.

On the flip side of this, projects can take too long to develop, and get too expensive. One fact that every book seems to skip over is that software development projects are supposed to make money! Revenue is an essential factor in any software being developed, and there isn't a product available that doesn't expect some productivity to increase, and money to be saved or made. Every project has a budget associated with it, and costs for producing the software incorporated into it. If the costs involved in a project cause it to go too far over budget, then a project may break even or run at a loss, thereby killing any reasons for starting the project in the first place.

Trading off the budget to keep schedules and features on track is often the easy way out when you're working in a large company, but it can come back to bite you. When you're working in the trenches, it's easy to forget that the company has only so much money to keep your mission going. The Process model helps to prioritize areas of a project, so that you don't kill your budget when making tradeoffs. The simple question, "What is most important?" is asked, allowing team members and stakeholders to determine what needs are most important to a project, and where cut-off points exist. By making certain features a priority, you are able to determine what can be dropped from the current project, and keep your budget from becoming victimized.

Versioned releases resolve many of the problems we've discussed. If there isn't enough time or money to include certain benefits in the current release, the features you planned to include can be passed forward. You've probably noticed versioned releases in using various operating systems like Windows, NT Server or Workstation or applications like those in Microsoft Office. Such programs have version numbers associated with them. For example, the last 16-bit full release of Windows was version 3.1. However, when they implemented the upgraded kernel for this operating system, it became Windows 3.11 (not to be confused with the Windows 3.11 associated with NT). This decimal number was used to indicate a minor update to the existing program. When Windows 95 was released, however, it contained major changes to the previous system. By using versioned releases of an application or system, you are able to improve or incorporate planned features in your application without destroying your budget or schedule.

Versioned releases also deal with another issue, common to project team members: ego. In a good team, members are proud of the features they've personally worked on or invented. Each member thereby feels that the feature they've worked on is essential to the product, and absolutely must be included. One problem with this is that there are so many features that they can't all be included by the release date. Another is that every time the product is almost ready to be released, someone decides to add more features. By versioning releases, such features can still be incorporated into the product, but will appear in the next version.

CERTIFICATION SUMMARY

The Microsoft Solution Framework consists of principles and methodologies that have been proven in the real world. MSF is comprised of the Team, Process, Application, Solutions Design, Enterprise Architecture, Infrastructure, and TCO models. Each of these models help to ensure the success of a project, and can be used together to enhance and improve a project.

In using MSF, its models and principles are applied to individual projects. In doing so, certain assessments and evaluations need to be made. The lifetime of the solution, changes in the business environment, tradeoffs that need to be made, and whether certain features should be included in current or future versions are addressed. MSF aids in these evaluations and assessments.

QUESTIONS AND ANSWERS

What's the difference between a benchmark and a baseline?	A benchmark is the total cost of the project based on industry averages. A baseline is the actual cost of the acquisition, management, and retirement of technology.
What are COM components and what are they used for?	The Application model promotes the use of COM components. These are reusable components in an application that can be shared by other applications. Because such client and server components are reusable, you can save on development time by using the features already available in existing components.
I'm not certain that all of the features a customer has requested can make it into the software by the release date.	Use versioned releases. Notify the customer that certain features will appear in the next version.

Understanding Model Names

The exercise will give you more in-depth experience with the concepts presented in this chapter. Match the model name in List A to the description in List B. Some names in List A may not be used. The answers to this exercise appear just before the Self Test at the end of this chapter.)

List A

a. Infrastructure

b. Enterprise Architecture

c. Solutions Design

d. Logical

e. COM

f. Process

g. Total Cost of Ownership

h. Product

i. Application

j. Strategic

k. Team

l. Business

List B

1. This model addresses how an application is constructed, breaking it into a network of consumer services and user services based on the Component Object model.

2. This model specifies roles for members of the project team, including the mission of the role and its responsibilities.

3. This model defines the total set of resources needed to support an enterprise computing environment.

4. This model partitions the project phases and focuses the team on relevant issues for each phase.

5. This model aids in optimizing the costs of a project.

6. This model helps provide focus to the business, application, information, and technology architectures of a project.

7. This model involves the users in addressing usability issues and other requirements of the application.

 # TWO-MINUTE DRILL

❑ MSF consists of seven models, which can be used individually or combined: the Team model, Process model, Application model, Solutions Design model, Enterprise Architecture model, Infrastructure model, and TCO model.

❑ MSF's *Team model* outlines well-defined roles for members of the team. Each role has its own mission, for which members in that role are responsible.

❑ The MSF *Process model* clarifies what people are working toward, and the progress achieved from that work.

❑ As its name suggests, the *Application model* addresses how applications are constructed to meet the needs of customers and users. This model promotes the use of COM (Component Object model) components.

❑ *User Services* are associated with the user interface and/or programmatic interface, provided by units of application logic.

❑ *Business Services* are used to enforce transactional integrity, business rules, and control sequencing.

❑ *Data Services* provide Create, Read, Update, and Delete services, as well as such retrieval logic as order and joins.

❑ The *Solutions Design model* helps the project team anticipate the needs of the user, by bringing the user into the fold.

❑ *Conceptual design* is where the initial concept of the solution originates. It is here that the team develops an understanding of what the user needs from a solution.

❑ *Logical design* takes the information gathered from the conceptual design and applies it to technical know-how.

❏ *Physical design* is where requirements from the conceptual and logical perspectives are put into a tangible form.

❏ The *Enterprise Architecture model* provides guidelines for planning, building, and managing technology infrastructures.

❏ The *Infrastructure model* defines the total set of resources needed to support an enterprise computing environment: technologies and standards, operational processes, and people and organizational resources.

❏ The *TCO (Total Cost of Ownership) model* works on the basic premise that optimizing costs equals a better return on investment (ROI).

❏ The *Solutions Design model* is used to help anticipate user needs and overcome many of the obstacles in a project.

Answers to Exercise 1-1

1. i.
2. k.
3. a.
4. f.

5. g
6. b
7. c.

SELF TEST

The Self Test questions will help you measure your understanding of the material presented in this chapter. Read all the choices carefully, as there may be more than one correct answer. Select all correct answers for each question.

1. Under MSF, how is infrastructure defined?

   A. The technology needed to support an enterprise computing environment

   B. The total set of resources needed to support an enterprise computing environment

   C. The standards needed to support an enterprise computing environment

   D. The public works that make up the city where resources are located

2. Which of the following is made up of the four perspectives of business architecture, application architecture, information architecture, and technology architecture?

   A. Infrastructure model

   B. Process model

   C. Enterprise Architecture model

   D. Architectural model

3. Which model breaks an application into User Services, Business Services, and Data Services?

   A. Process model

   B. Application model

   C. Tiered model

   D. Enterprise Architecture model

4. Which role in the Team model is responsible for the smooth rollout of the product?

   A. User Education

   B. Development

   C. Deployment

   D. Logistics

5. Which phase of the Process model results in the vision/scope approved milestone?

   A. Envisioning

   B. Stabilization

   C. Deployment

   D. Building

6. Which of the following represents the total cost based on industry averages?

   A. Baseline

   B. Benchmark

   C. Basemark

   D. Benchline

7. Which model has users brought in during the design process so their needs can be anticipated by the project?

   A. Enterprise Architecture

   B. Solutions Design

   C. TCO

   D. Application

8. The Application model promotes the use of COM. Which of the following are built on the Component Object model? (Choose all that apply.)

   A. ActiveX Controls

   B. OLE

   C. Solutions Design model

   D. System Management

9. The IT life cycle is comprised of three stages under MSF. What are these three stages? (Choose all that apply.)

   A. Plan

   B. Build

   C. Monitor

   D. Manage

   E. Stabilize

10. Which model expands the logistics role to include three new areas in a team?

    A. Team

    B. Logistics

    C. Infrastructure

    D. TCO

    E. Enterprise Architecture

11. The Process model breaks the development cycle into four phases. What are these phases?

    A. Envisioning, Planning, Developing, Stabilizing

    B. Envisioning, Planning, Building, Managing

    C. Vision/Scope, Planning, Developing, Stabilizing

    D. Envisioning, Planning, Deploying, Stabilizing

12. The Solutions Design model is comprised of different perspectives that provide focus in designing applications. What are these perspectives? (Choose all that apply.)

    A. Conceptual

    B. Logical

    C. Illogical

    D. Physical

    E. Planning

13. Which role in the Team model is responsible for making decisions that determine delivery of the right product at the right time?

    A. Product Management

    B. Program Management

    C. Logistics

    D. Development

14. What models make up the Microsoft Solution Framework?

    A. The Team, Planning, Application, System Management, Enterprise Architecture, Infrastructure, and TCO models

    B. The Product Management, Project Management, Development, Design, Testing, User Education, and Logistics models

    C. The Team, Process, Application, Solutions Design, Enterprise

Architecture, Infrastructure, and TCO models

D. The Team, Process, Product Management, Project Management, Development, Design, Testing, User Education, and Logistics models

15. Which phase of the Process model results in the Scope Complete/First Use milestone?

A. Envisioning

B. Planning

C. Developing

D. Stabilizing

16. Which phase of the Process model results in the Release milestone?

A. Envisioning

B. Planning

C. Developing

D. Stabilizing

17. Which service in the Application model is associated with the programmatic interface or user interface?

A. Data Services

B. Business Services

C. User Services

D. Application Services

18. Which of the following models promotes users becoming involved in the design process, so they can address key issues such as usability and user requirements?

A. Application

B. Team

C. Solutions Design

D. Process

19. In which perspective of the Solutions Design model are the structure and communication of elements in the solution laid out?

A. Logical

B. Conceptual

C. Physical

D. Planning

20. The Enterprise Architecture model consists of four perspectives. Which perspective deals with standards and guidelines for laying out the software and hardware supporting an organization?

A. Application

B. Business

C. Information

D. Technology

MICROSOFT CERTIFIED SOLUTION DEVELOPER

2

Using the Team, Process, and Application Models for Development Projects

CERTIFICATION OBJECTIVES

2.01   Understanding Microsoft's Team Model

2.02   Understanding Microsoft's Development Process

2.03   Identifying Common Service Needs Across Development Projects

2.04   Completing Different Phases of a Project in Parallel

O rganizing a project, and the people to complete it, can be a grueling task. The Microsoft Solution Framework (MSF) aids in this endeavor with models that outline the organization of a team, their goals, and the process of development. In using these models, a project team is able to see what they're responsible for, what progress they're making, and what they're working toward.

In this chapter, we will cover the Team, Process, and Application models introduced in Chapter 1. The Team model breaks a project team into different roles, with each responsible for meeting a particular goal. The Process model breaks the project itself into different phases, allowing team members to see where a project is going, and what progress has been made. Finally, we'll discuss the Application model, which breaks the actual application into different parts. By separating these large tasks into smaller parts, we will see that projects become more manageable and understandable.

CERTIFICATION OBJECTIVE 2.01

Understanding Microsoft's Team Model

When you think of a team, you might think of a group of people who work toward a common goal. In Microsoft's Team model, this isn't the case. Instead, a team is made up of six different roles, each with its own goal. As we'll see, by achieving these individual goals, the success of the project is ensured.

It is important to remember that the team model isn't an organizational chart. It doesn't define a hierarchical reporting structure. What it does do is identify the different roles, responsibilities, and goals that go into making a project work.

Creating Small Interdisciplinary Teams

You'll remember the old saying that "too many cooks spoil the soup." The same can be said for teams. When you have a large team, all sorts of problems arise. Confusion can result on the status of a project and the lines of responsibility, and elements of a project can be overlooked. It's also not uncommon for a couple of people to duplicate work, because one person doesn't know what the other is doing. This can easily be remedied by breaking a large team into small, interdisciplinary teams.

When a team exceeds ten or more members, it is recommended to break them into specialty teams. Each smaller team focuses on a specific goal, and is responsible for different tasks. Members are assigned to each team based on their expertise in specific areas, and are accountable for the quality of results in that area. Since these teams work parallel to one another, productivity increases because efforts are synchronized. It also results in a better product because teams are held accountable for results, and can clearly see the project goals.

Fundamental Roles in a Project Team

A project team is made up of six different roles. By placing people in roles that best match their skills, the quality and chances of success for a project dramatically increase. The fundamental roles in a project team are as follows:

- Product Management
- Program Management
- Development
- Testing
- User Education
- Logistics Management

Each role has different responsibilities, requires different expertise, and works toward a different goal. When team members succeed in these roles, the project itself succeeds. Team leaders can focus on managing, coordinating, and guiding the team, while team members can focus on achievement of their individual missions. In this section, we'll discuss each role, and see how the roles work on different areas to ensure the success of a project.

Product Management has a position of advocacy between customers who buy a product, and the team that creates it. To the customer, a product manager represents the team. To the team, a product manager acts as a customer representative. By representing one group to the other, Product Management clarifies what the customer wants and what the team can do. Thus, a shared vision of the project is created.

When Product Management represents the team, it has the primary responsibility of managing customer expectations. If the team feels that certain features won't be available until future versions, it falls on product management to let people know. This includes not only briefing customers, but also keeping senior management apprised of the team's assessment of product requirements in order to complete a project successfully. If the product falls short of what's expected, the project is considered a failure.

When Product Management represents the customer, this role has several responsibilities. First, it is responsible for obtaining the requirements of customers, and maintaining these requirements. This determines the needs of the customer, so that the product solves whatever business problems a customer is having. Once the customer requirements for a solution are understood, a business case is developed and managed.

A *business case* is a plan of action that's presented to senior management. Once a proposal has been made for a product or service, a business case is developed to back up that proposal with facts and evidence. It consists of the following:

- Analysis of the customer's business need
- A proposed solution to the business need
- Alternative solutions that were considered but rejected, and data exlaining why
- Quantitative and qualitative benefits of the proposed solution

The business case is maintained and modified as the project develops. Any changes are added to it, so the business case remains up-to-date and consistent with the project's progress.

Program Management takes the requirements outlined by product management, and turns this information into a functional specification and master project plan. The *functional specification* determines what is to be created, and the *master project plan* specifies how it will be done. In making the functional specification and master project plan, Program Management receives input from each of the other team roles. Though it promotes input from the other team roles, Program Management makes the final decision in cases where everyone can't come to an agreement.

Program Management holds responsibility for owning and driving the schedule and budget of a project. It also determines when to release the right product or service. By having ownership of the schedule and budget, Program Management makes sure that money is well spent and schedules are on track. Schedules are developed from estimates provided by each of the other roles. Since Program Management is responsible for the budget and schedules, it controls what features will appear in a particular version of a program. This keeps a function or group of functions from making a project going over budget or past its delivery date.

Development is in charge of building the product or implementing a particular service. This is done with adherence to the customer requirements and the specifications determined by Program Management. This role takes the functional specifications, and delivers a product or service that complies with them. Development offers input on designs, develops prototypes, and evaluates available technologies to be used. When and while this is done, development codes the different parts of a product, until it is finally built. Since it has first-hand knowledge of all this information, this role provides estimates of what's needed to deliver the product on a particular design.

Testing determines what problems exist in a product or service, so that these issues are addressed before it is delivered to a customer. This is by no means a random process. Schedules are created to specify when an area of the product will be tested. One day might consist of finding problems with documentation, while another is spent seeking out erroneous code. Strategies and plans are created to find defects, bugs, and errors in the product. This means that issues dealing with a particular product are known and addressed before it is released. In doing so, the problems can be fixed or workarounds can be developed.

User Education has the responsibility of representing the end user. This is different from Product Management's role of representing the customer— while the customer buys the product, it is the end user who actually uses it. It is User Education's role to ensure that an end user has a good experience with a product. In the grand scheme of things, user performance must be enhanced in some way by the product. To meet this goal, this role helps ensure that the product is easy to use and understand. For example, if a user interface is difficult to use, User Education steps in to help make it more manageable for the end user. This role is responsible for designing, creating, and testing materials that assist the user. Online assistance, manuals, wizards, and training materials fall into the realm of User Education.

Logistics Management is responsible for deployment and product support. This role ensures a smooth rollout, and makes sure that deployment is possible. Installation programs must work correctly, and installation sites are checked so they fit the necessary requirements for deployment. Logistics Management has to understand the infrastructure of a product, so they can provide training to operations and the help desk. By providing this information, support groups are able to assist the customer and end user.

Key Goals for a Project Team

Key goals help to focus and drive the team. They define what everyone is working toward, and as we'll see in the next section, help to define the team model itself. No matter what your team role, there are key goals that outline what everyone is working toward, and ensure the quality of a product. These goals consist of the following:

- Deliver within the constraints of the project.
- Deliver to specifications that are based on user requirements.
- Satisfy customers.
- Enhance user performance.
- Release only after knowing and addressing all issues.
- Ensure smooth deployment and ongoing management.

As we explore each of these goals, it quickly becomes apparent that if each one isn't met, the project will not be successful.

Delivering within constraints is a broad area that varies with each project. There are certain constraints that are constant in any project: time and money. Every project has a budget and schedule that must be kept. Imagine a software project for creating income tax returns. If it went past schedule, and was released at the end of May (a month after returns are due), the project automatically fails. A real-life example is Allstate, who in 1982 began a five-year, eight-million-dollar project to automate their office operations. A year after this deadline, the project's cost was $15 million, and it still wasn't finished. It was given a new time constraint, and the budget was readjusted to $100 million! Even though other goals may have been achieved, by not delivering within the constraints, the project itself failed.

"Always give the people what they want" is what delivering to specifications is all about. Product specifications provide detailed descriptions for project requirements. Let's say a company hired you to create a business application that accesses dBase files. As an extreme example, suppose you decide that Access databases are better, and create the program to access those instead of dBase files. The product specifications wouldn't be met, and you'd lose a customer and your reputation in one fell swoop. Product specifications are based on user requirements, and it is important for a team to meet those specifications as closely as possible. If a product isn't delivered to specifications based on user requirements, the success of the project is sacrificed.

Meeting the specifications falls hand in hand with another goal: customer satisfaction. Customer satisfaction means that the user gets what they expect from a product, and that it solves a targeted problem. If the customer is expecting a number of features in a product, and all features don't appear in the current version, it is important to inform the customer so they won't be unpleasantly surprised. This can be done through public relations, marketing, demonstrations, and promotions for launching the product. Always put the user first, and keep customer satisfaction a priority.

Enhancing user performance is the reason computers exist in business. Excluding entertainment, it's also the reason why people pay thousands of dollars for computers and software in their homes. If a project doesn't enhance the work or productivity of a user in some way, there was really no reason to start it in the first place. A project can be full of features and content, but if it doesn't do the job intended, it's a failure.

Nobody's perfect, so it follows suit that projects won't be either. All software contains defects, but it is important to release only after knowing or addressing all outstanding issues. This allows you to do one of two things: fix the problem, or have a workaround solution that can be added to documentation. Fixing the problem is preferred, but may not always be possible while keeping to the schedule. In such cases, you should offer a workaround, and add it to documentation. This keeps teams and customers from being blindsided by a defect. The worse thing to do is not to provide a fix or workaround, and leave the defect unidentified. By offering at least a workaround solution, the customer can use the software until a bug fix, patch, or new version is released.

Smooth deployment and ongoing management is an important part of the success of a project. All too often, applications are dumped on the end user with little or no support. Installation programs can fail, giving the user the impression that the application itself is defective. If they require assistance, they are faced with the dilemma that the only support available is in the form of ineffective help files, if even that. It is important that the deployment process is smooth, enabling the user to access and install the application with few if any problems. If they do experience difficulties, ongoing management is there to assist them. It is important that training, infrastructure, and support are already in place before the deployment of a project, so they can deal with project and user problems.

The Relationship Between Project Team Roles and Key Goals

There is a correlation between the various team roles and the key goals outlined in the previous section. Each goal maps to a different role, allowing team members to focus on the particular goal that relates to them. The six goals shape the team roles, and focus team members on what they are working toward.

Each team becomes responsible for the goal that relates to them, as outlined in Table 2-1. This allows every member of a team to have ownership of product quality, so that quality-related issues are addressed before projects reach the customer. Team members thereby become accountable for the success or failure of a goal that relates to them.

exam
Watch

The team roles and their related key goals have a symbiotic relationship. It is important to understand how one maps to the other, if you are to understand the purpose of each team role.

Team Role	Key Goal
Product Management	Satisfied customers
Program Management	Delivery within project constraints
Development	Delivery to product specifications
Testing	Release after addressing all issues
User Education	Enhanced user performance
Logistics Management	Smooth deployment and ongoing management

Scaling the Team Model

Now that we've established the roles and goals of a project team, the following question usually arises: what if you don't have enough people to fill each role? This is often an issue with smaller companies or smaller projects. Just because you don't have six people doesn't mean you can't use the model. It is important that each goal is represented, not that each role is filled by a different person.

Assigning more than one role to a person can scale the Team model. By having members share roles, each goal is pursued, and the project can achieve the same success. There are, however, two important things to remember while doing this:

- Development members should never be assigned extra roles.
- No member should ever be assigned conflicting roles.

It is wise to never give an extra role to Development for one reason: they are in charge of building the product, and you don't want to sidetrack them on other duties. It is also vital that you never give a member two roles that have a conflict of interest, or where the skills of one role are completely different from the other. For example, you wouldn't want to combine Logistics and Product Management, because the expertise for each is so different. Similarly, Program Management and Product Management would make a poor match due to conflict of interest. Product Management represents the customer, while Program Management is responsible for the schedule and budget. If a customer made a request for a feature, it might not be properly considered if it interfered with the budget or schedule. Conversely, the budget or schedule might be overrun to fulfill a customer request.

By reviewing the goals of each role, you can determine how a member can share roles. By determining the expertise of a member, and assigning two similar roles, the Team model is effectively scaled down.

Interteam Dependencies

As mentioned earlier, for a project to be successful, it is important that each goal be achieved. In this approach, there are teams of peers, who are dependent upon one another to complete the assigned project. This requires communication and cooperation between the different roles.

If one team role—or more specifically, a single goal—were not assigned to someone, the project itself would fail. Program Management relies on Product Management to supply the customer requirements and set the vision for a project. Development needs the functional specifications to build the project, and testing needs the built product to check for defects. Development relies on testing to enhance user performance, and logistics is required so that the product has a smooth rollout. In short, you need to achieve Point A to move to Point B before you can achieve Point C. Each team role relies on another, making the Team model symbiotic in nature.

In addition to the interdependency of the team roles and goals, there are dependencies to external groups. For example, Product Management relies on the customer to provide requirements for a project, while User Education has a dependent relationship with the end user. Remember that customers and end users aren't necessarily the same group. Customers buy a product, while end users are the people who actually work with the product. As seen in Table 2-2, most roles are interdependent with external groups.

Development and Testing are internally focused, so they have no external interdependency with other teams. This keeps them from being distracted from their roles of building and testing a product for defects. When these teams are insulated, they are able to focus on their work without having to worry about outside interference.

TABLE 2-2   Interdependency of Team Model with External Teams

Role	External Group Dependency	Reason
Product Management	Customer Senior management	Relies on customer to provide requirements, and manage customer expectations. Also works with senior management, technology, business architects, and steering committees to meet customer requirements.
Program Management	Customer	Creates functional specifications that meet the customer requirements.
Development	None	To avoid disruptions in work, which could compromise product quality.
Testing	None	To avoid disruptions in work, which could compromise product quality.
User Education	End user	Ensures user's experience is enhanced by the product.
Logistics Management	Operations and support groups	Trains support groups (such as help desk) and operations. Ensures smooth rollout and installation.

EXERCISE 2-1

The Team Model

Identify the Team model role described by each of the following team members. (The answers to this exercise appear just before the Self Test at the end of this chapter.)

I. Bob:

My concern is the resources available to the project. Resources in terms of available funds, available time, and available staff time.

2. Brenda

My concern is that the individuals who will use the application be able to understand the appropriate application of the programs to their daily work tasks.

3. Mark:

I focus on the rollout after the application is completed. A smooth transition from the old way of doing work assignments to using the new applications—including installation and any data migration—is what I'm after.

4. Jeffry:

I take the requirements and make sure the technical team understands them well enough to write functional specs from them. I also take the technical team functional specs and verify that the customer's requirements will be met.

5. Chris:

I have to make sure that all issues with the application have been addressed before the application is released. I also make sure it is functioning properly after each build in development.

6. Jan:

Our team builds the application according to the detailed design which is based on the functional specifications.

CERTIFICATION OBJECTIVE 2.02

Understanding Microsoft's Development Process

While the Team model shows who does what, the Process model deals with how things will get done. *Process* deals with the methodologies of technology and management. It shows the activities in an application's life cycle, from the time of conception to its initial release. By going step-by-step through the development cycle, process allows the project team to see their progress as tasks are completed.

If you're a developer who's experienced a Process model in the real world, you may be wincing as you read this section. While the purpose of process is to focus a team on relevant issues in the development cycle, bureaucracy often gets involved to the point where a team is bogged down by red tape. Rather than addressing priorities in a project, everything seems to have a policy attached to it, and developers are faced with having to address mundane issues. To keep this from happening, Microsoft's Process model balances creativity with distinct milestones to mark the completion of different phases of a project.

A milestone not only marks the point where one phase of a project ends and another begins; it also indicates the point in time that members of a team should synchronize their efforts. Each milestone is a point where team members can see if they are still meeting customer expectations. If the customer requirements change during a step in the development process, the team members can discuss and deal with the change. If a new risk to the project has arisen, that too can be dealt with when a milestone is reached. This keeps projects from getting too far into development before problems are addressed.

The MSF Process model is based on two proven models: the Waterfall model and the Spiral model. The *Spiral model* is also called the *Rapid Application Development (or RAD)* model. It breaks a project into sub-projects, each of which deals with different risks in a project. Since each risk is addressed in the sub-projects, all risks in a project can be identified individually. The *Waterfall model* views the life cycle as a flow of steps. When one step ends, a milestone is reached. The milestone indicates that the step is assessed, and the next step begins in the development process. By combining these two models, Microsoft's Process model allows a team to manage risks while focusing on results.

The MSF Process model breaks a project into four phases, each resulting in a definitive milestone:

1. *Envisioning*, which results in the Vision/Scope Approved milestone.

2. *Planning*, which results in the Project Plan Approved milestone.

3. *Developing*, which results in the Scope Complete/First Use milestone.

4. *Stabilization*, which results in the Release milestone.

Each of these phases, and their related milestones, are described in detail in the next section. They represent the state between milestones, which is also where the work is done to achieve a milestone.

The Four Externally Visible Development Milestones

There is a direct relationship between each of the four phases in the Process model and the four development milestones: you must complete a phase of the model before reaching a milestone. If you think of developing software like waging a war, each phase is a battle. When you win the battle, you have achieved a milestone—when you win all the battles, you've won the war. Rather than focusing on an overwhelming big picture, the four phases and their respective milestones allow you to keep your sights on the immediate battle for success.

The Envisioning phase comes first in the Process model, and results in the Vision/Scope Approved milestone. This phase answers the question: "What do you see us doing?" It involves understanding a customer's needs and the issues surrounding those needs. What issues are driving the need for the product or service, and what features should be incorporated to address future needs? By gathering information, and understanding the needs of a customer, the Vision/Scope Approved milestone can be achieved.

The Vision/Scope Approved milestone results when an agreement is made on the direction a project will take. To understand what this milestone represents, it is important to understand the meaning of vision and scope. *Vision* is an unbridled view of a project's goals, with no consideration given to the constraints of a project. *Scope* reins this in, by defining the limitations of a product or service, and determining what can be done within the project's constraints. By balancing these optimistic and realistic viewpoints, a shared vision of what the project entails is achieved. This shared vision is outlined in a *vision/scope document*, which specifies the direction and goals for a project.

The second phase of the Process model is *Planning*. There is usually some confusion between the Planning phase and the Envisioning phase, because it seems there is considerable amount of planning involved in envisioning a project. As far as Microsoft is concerned, planning is when the project team and customers come to an agreement on what will be delivered and how it will be built. It is here that the priorities and expectations for a project are set.

The functional specification is created during this phase. Each team submits its plans to create the functional specification and schedule for the project. It is during the planning phase that risks are reassessed, priorities are set, and estimates for schedules and resources are made. The functional specification, its associated project plan, and the schedules are used in the next phase of the Process model.

The result of the Planning phase is the Project Plan Approved milestone. This is basically a contract between the team and customer to go ahead with the project. Once all the details have been ironed out, the interested parties agree to continue with the project.

exam
ⓦatch

Remember that the Envisioning phase is where a common vision is set for a product, while the Planning phase is where an agreement is made on what will be built and how to build it. If you think of a marriage, a common vision is created before both parties say, "I do." While the Envisioning phase anticipates what will happen, the Planning phase is where the vows are made, and a go-ahead to continue is given.

Third in this lineup is the *Developing phase.* In the life cycle of an application, it is here that a product begins to reach maturity. The functional specification and project plan are used by the development team as a baseline to focus on developing the actual product. Rather than building the product in one shot, the development team uses the Developing phase to go through a number of cycles involving testing, debugging, and fixing the product. When it is determined that the product is ready for *Stabilization* (the fourth and final phase), the Scope Complete/First Use milestone is reached.

The team and customers get together at this milestone and review a number of key issues for the product:

1. First, the product functionality is evaluated to make sure it does what it is intended to do. If certain features aren't available in the current version, they are documented so they can be implemented in future versions.

2. Rollout and support plans are reviewed to make sure operations and support personnel will be ready for product release.

3. Finally, the team and customers address any additional issues before preparing to ship the product.

After the Scope Complete/First Use milestone, the product life cycle enters the Stabilization phase. It is here that more product testing is done, allowing bugs to be found and fixed before the release. When testing is complete, the project team hands over the product or service to Operations and Support. It is this handing over of the torch that marks the Release milestone. The product is shipped and put into service, and Operations and Support then have responsibility for managing and supporting the current version.

Making Project Tradeoffs: Setting Priorities with a Customer

Every project has to work within the constraints of time, resources, and the features requested by a customer. Early in a project, this is usually manageable. The customer outlines the features, schedules are created, and resources are organized. Unfortunately, there are always moments when a customer wants something added to a project, when you find that a critical feature was overlooked in the initial design, or some other problem crops up. When this occurs, tradeoffs need to be made if a project is to come in on time and within budget.

Tradeoffs are a matter of realizing that a project plan isn't concrete, and deciding what needs to give. There is no way you can keep the vision of a project so rigid that nothing can be traded off to meet new requirements or constraints. When tradeoffs are made, it is a matter of adjusting one element of a project to allow change in another element.

A project has three elements that are interrelated: schedule, features, and resources. The *schedule* is a timetable with dates that define when parts of a project are due, and when the finished product or service is due to be completed. *Features* are the requirements to be implemented into a product or service, and the quality and functionality of these items. *Resources* include such things as the people who work on the project, the technologies they work with, and the money available to use on a project. When working with these three elements of a project, changes in one element have a direct impact on at least one of the other two.

As shown in Figure 2-1, the three elements of a project have a triangulated relationship. Like three separate lines that make up a triangle, the three elements make up a project. Altering the size of any element will affect one, and usually two, of the other elements. For example, if a customer requires features to be added to a project, then the schedule must be adjusted so there is enough time to incorporate these features. Since time is money—and people like to get paid for their work—resources will need to be adjusted as well. If the due date cannot be altered, then more people and money will need to be infused into the project. As you can see, one element cannot be changed without directly affecting one or both of the other elements.

To establish priorities in a project when dealing with tradeoffs, a *tradeoff matrix* can be created to determine a strategy. This allows the team and customer to specify whether it is more important to stay on schedule, on budget, or to pass certain features off to future versions. A tradeoff matrix is simply a table that is used as a reference tool. By sitting down with the customer, the team management is able to agree on which elements take priority over others.

An example of a tradeoff matrix is illustrated in Table 2-3. A checkmark is placed in one of the blank cells to indicate that a particular element should be optimized, constrained, or accepted as a tradeoff. It is important that at least one of the three elements is accepted as a tradeoff, so the team has the power to control risks and changes in a product. As we'll see in the following paragraphs, where a checkmark appears in the matrix determines what strategies will be used to complete the project.

Triangulated relationship
of project elements

	Optimize	Constrain	Accept
Resources			
Schedule			
Features (Scope)			

TABLE 2-3

Tradeoff Matrix

The Resources row determines how money will be used in a project, which affects people and technologies. Remember that people on a project need to be paid, and computers and software will need to be purchased or allocated to these people. Whether resources are optimized, constrained, or accepted determines whether one of the following strategies will be used:

- Minimum Cost strategy
- Not-to-Exceed strategy
- Time and Materials strategy

A *Minimum Cost strategy* is used when the Optimize column of resources is checked. This means that the allocation of resources should be kept to a minimum, so that costs don't go too high. A *Not-to-Exceed strategy* occurs when the Constrain column is checked, meaning there is pressure to keep within the budget. A *Time and Materials strategy* occurs when the Accept column is checked, giving the team power to control risks and changes in a project by adjusting resources.

The Schedule row is used to control the ship date of a product or service. When the Optimize column of the matrix is checked for this element, an early-to-market strategy is used. This strategy sets declares that the ship date for the product or service is to be as soon as possible. When the Constrain column is checked, the schedule is kept to a specific time frame so that the ship date isn't altered. When the Accept column is checked, a tradeoff is made with the ship date, and it is accepted that the product will not meet its previous due date for release.

The Features (Scope) row is used to establish which features will be released for a current version. When the Optimize column is checked, a maximum benefit strategy is used, and it is accepted that as many features as possible will be shipped with the current version of the product. When

Constrain is checked, the scope is to ship the features that are essential for the product to function. When Accept is checked, it's acknowledged that a tradeoff needs to be made here, and features are dropped from the current version.

The Project Recap

A project manager wrote a brief project recap. Fill in the blanks. (The answers to this exercise appear just before the Self Test at the end of this chapter.)

"When we began talking to the customers about the project, we tried to list everything they would ever want in the application. Then we decided what was actually feasible to include. This resulted in completion of the _____ phase with the _____ milestone.

Once we had a fairly good idea of what the customer wanted, we could create our Gantt and PERT charts and consider the trade-offs between money, time, and risk. We were in the _____ phase which would end with the _____ milestone.

In the _____ phase we created our servers and consumers, explored what enterprise objects we could re-use and cycled through many iterations of design-build-test before we arrived at the _____ milestone.

At the point the technical team considered its work about finished we had to focus on open issues, develop deployment plans, and focus on verifying that the functionality satisfied the requirements. We were about to enter the _____ phase, which would result in the _____ milestone."

Multiple-Versioned Releases for Large Projects

Multiple-versioned releases boils down to this rule of thumb: you can't do everything at once, so don't even try. Is it a defeatist attitude? Not at all—it's just common sense. It's not unusual for projects to be held up for a great new idea that just has to be included. The problem is that there's always something more that could be added.

When the first version of Microsoft Windows appeared on the market, it was just a graphic interface that ran on top of DOS. If you didn't like typing commands, you could run Windows and just point and click to run a program. There were a number of other programs that did the same thing, but have since faded into obscurity. Bill Gates could have held back on releasing the first Windows—making an actual operating system, adding utilities and features to infinity—but chances are, Microsoft would then have become a footnote in computer history. There is high competition in software development, and it is important to get your product to the customer before someone else beats you to it. Versioned releases allow you to get a product to market, and have new features added in future releases.

The current version of a product should meet the current needs of the user. Users are then able to enjoy the functionality of a program, while new releases are being developed. In addition, users are able to grow as the application grows. Rather than being hit by a monolithic program, they are able to adapt as new features are added and old ones are retired. By incrementing a program in versions, you can address the most important requirements of the user, with additional features being added later, and still be first to market.

CERTIFICATION OBJECTIVE 2.03

Identifying Common Service Needs Across Development Projects

With the amount of downsizing occurring in the business world, employees are expected to take on a wider range of responsibilities in their jobs. No longer are people limited to specialized job descriptions that deal with a limited number of duties. There is an equally growing need for business applications to perform more tasks, and provide consistency in the way users view, locate, and modify information in applications.

To meet these needs, the *Application model* has been created. This model aids developers with the structure and standard design of applications. It aids developers in creating a service-based architecture for programs. This model breaks an application into a network of services. Through communication, each service in an application exposes its attributes to other services. This promotes the use of components in applications, and these components can be reused across development projects.

Defining the Application Model

The Application model provides rules and a representation for designing the architecture of an application, and breaks the application up into different layers of services. These services are used to enforce business rules, manipulate data, and expose features for using data. By using this model, you are able to form the structure of your application with flexibility in mind.

The model consists of three layers, which make up the application. These layers are explained in greater detail in the next section. In the order of top layer (where the user interacts with a program) to bottom layer (where data resides), they are as follows:

- User Services
- Business Services
- Data Services

Each layer provides services to higher layers and/or is a consumer of the services below it. Communications across these layers are called *service requests*. To communicate across these layers, the developer needs to know how to request a service and how to handle results. Requesting a service includes such things as making a function call, and knowing what arguments to pass. Handling the result of a service request means having code that properly deals with returned values. By allowing other programmers to know how to request services that you've developed, features of an application become reusable. In other words, other developers can now use something you've coded.

The Application model promotes the use of reusable components, which are commonly referred to as *COM components*. Services are meant for general use, and can be reused and shared by different applications. Rather than rewriting the same code over and over in a project, it is advisable to make use of existing components whenever possible. This means accessing features in the current application or accessing components in other applications.

FROM THE CLASSROOM

By Design

One of the most difficult tasks in making the transition to the use of proper design methodology involves the correct and proper separation of resources prior to implementing the designing or coding phases. One could safely venture to say that the area of design methodology that receives, unfortunately, the short end of the resource stick is that of design itself. Many developers have a tendency to try to rush into the implementation phase, expecting their vision of the final product to hold up; hence any additional headstart that can be achieved is bound to be beneficial. Oh, such wisdom!

Following this error in ways, the typical developer seeks to skip past, or handicap, the second process, planning, within the Microsoft Solutions Framework Process model. After gaining what is necessary from the envisioning process, the Planning process is often shorted, or concluded prematurely, so that the

Developing process can proceed. Take special care to avoid this, to the ultimate benefit of the project as a whole.

Besides the process model pitfalls, the Application model is also a common source of misunderstanding. The distinction between the layers is often fuzzy, leading to misguided design initiatives. Lacking a full understanding of the rationale behind the separating of the services can lead to coding tasks that yield inefficient functionality.

The Application model is the core design methodology behind a three-tier enterprise application. Proper separation of business logic, including COM component design and use, can yield vast increases in reusability, scalability, and application performance.

— *Michael Lane Thomas, MCSE+I, MCSD, MCT, MCP+SB, MSS, A+*

Services-Based Architecture

As mentioned in the previous section, the Application model is comprised of three layers of services: User Services, Business Services, and Data Services. Each of these layers has different characteristics, which address different aspects of a business application. These services are networked together, with one layer providing services to the layer above and/or consuming the services of the layer below.

The top layer of the Application model is *User Services*. This is what provides an application with an interface, which can be GUI (graphical user interface) or programmatic. A *programmatic interface* is used by other applications to obtain information, while a *GUI* is a visual display that's presented to a human user. The GUI provides navigation and consistent representations of data, and provides a way for the human user to interact with the application. Whether the user is another program or a human being, it is User Services that integrates a user with an application. It allows him, her, or it to perform various tasks and manipulate data.

Business Services resides on the middle tier of this three-layer model. Business Services responds to requests for information from User Services. It has the responsibility of communicating with the lower layer, where it does the following: takes the data, protects its integrity, transforms it into business information, and presents this information to the user interface. To illustrate this, let's say you had a sales program. If you used this application to retrieve the price of items including sales tax, you would start by entering the name of a product at the User Services layer. Business Services would request the data on this product from a database. Since you need the price including sales tax, it would add a percentage to the amount, and return this information to the User Services layer. To do such a business task, business rules are implemented at this level.

Business rules are policies used to determine how a business task is performed. A business task is determined by the requirements of an application. For example, if a customer required an application to print a list of orders from a database, this would be a business task. Business rules control the way business tasks are performed. For example, there is a common policy of adding sales tax to purchases, so business rules are added to applications that add a percentage to the value of items. Another example of a business rule would be adding a percentage to mark up a wholesale value to a retail value. In using such information, the correct information is presented to the user, rather than the raw data contained in a database.

As you can see by these examples, business rules would change more frequently than business tasks would in an application. While a business task to retrieve the marked-up value of an item would be a consistent business task, the business rule of what that markup was would change. If you were creating an application for a computer chain, one week the markup on RAM might be 50 percent, while the next week a sale might require a markup of 25 percent. Since business rules change faster than business tasks, it is advisable to encapsulate business tasks in components that are separate from the business rules and the actual application. This allows the components to be reused, and keep the business tasks and rules separate from one another.

Another name for the Business Services layer is *middle-tier services*. The reason for this is because there are some activities that take place at this layer that can't really be called a business service. There are a number of support services for an application that takes place at this layer. Such things as number crunching for math-intensive programs, security services (such as logon screens), and offloading graphics-intensive processing to a server's CPU are examples of such support. These activities are considered middle-tier services, as they don't apply to either of the other layers in the Application model.

exam
Watch

The middle layer of the Application model is a grey area that has a number of attributes. An easy way to remember the layers is to keep in mind that User Services integrates the user with the application, Data Services integrates data into an application, and everything else (i.e., Business Services and middle-tier services for application support) falls in the middle.

The bottom tier of the application model is *Data Services*. It is here that data is stored, defined, and retrieved. This layer provides Create, Read, Update, and Delete capabilities, and also protects the integrity of data. It services requests from Business Services for data, so the middle tier doesn't need to know where data is located, or how to implement or access it. For example, Data Services could consist of a database on a user's computer, a SQL server database on a network server, or a group of databases located on different platforms. When data is requested, this layer locates, stores, or modifies the data as per the request. The upper layers need not be concerned with this, since Data Services handles the entire request.

CERTIFICATION OBJECTIVE 2.04

Completing Different Phases of a Project in Parallel

By using modular design, you are able to complete different phases of a project in parallel and cut the overall development time. *Modular design* involves breaking a large project into smaller modules, or subprojects. This allows the developing phase to go through a number of cycles involving testing, debugging, and fixing the product. It also allows different areas of a project to be worked on in tandem.

By breaking these projects into smaller subprojects, a number of things occur. First, parts of a project are being developed parallel to one another. If a problem occurs in a module, the entire project isn't held up, because other modules are continuing to progress in development. For example, suppose ActiveX components are being developed for a project and the ActiveX server portion is experiencing problems. At the same time, developers of the ActiveX client portion (which is what users will primarily interact with in a client/server application) continue in their endeavors uninterrupted. Separating a project into smaller subprojects also separates problems in development.

The second benefit of breaking projects into subprojects is morale. While morale is often discussed in the military, the private sector often underrates it. *Morale* is having people feel good about what they're working on. The goals associated with the Team model address this issue. However, on big projects it often takes a considerable amount of time for one goal to be achieved. In the interim, people working on the project feel like they're trudging toward something that's way down the distant road. Subprojects allow developers to work toward smaller, more regular achievements.

To improve the morale of team members, subprojects can be implemented so that developers can see that something has been done, which helps drive them forward. When you're working on a subproject, you're able to stay fresh. Developers are excited that they've succeeded in completing one thing, and look forward to the next area of development. This speeds development time, since people on a team aren't dragging their heels feeling that nothing is getting accomplished.

Sharing Assets, Resources, and Skills

The Team model stresses that the people in different roles work as a team of peers. It should not be mistaken that these are people competing with one another on a project. While this sounds like a commonsense approach, all too often in the real world there is a hoarding of assets, resources, and skills between teams. For example, developers may need an extra computer to work on a project, and it is known that Testing has a spare. Rather than share this resource, it is kept from development with the excuse "we might need it!" While at face value this sounds childish, anyone who's had to go head-to-head with Accounting can testify that it may be difficult to have adequate resources assigned to a project. When one party is trying to keep the bottom line in the black, and another is trying to get the resources to complete a project, you have two parties with different goals that conflict with one another. As such, the importance of sharing becomes paramount.

on the ❗ ob

The foolishness of not sharing assets and resources can be seen in the experience of a colleague of mine. He was working for the government on a project. There was a rather archaic and overworked network server set up for developers, and no money was allotted for a new one. No one would part with spare computers, and this was slowing down the project as people were waiting incredible amounts of time to access information. Because my colleague managed the project, the powers that be felt he needed a good desk that would command some respect. He put in a request for a few thousand dollars, was given the money, and went out and purchased the parts to build a new server. The developers were happy, the project was completed, and he used this loophole every few years to request a new desk and keep projects running effectively. This illustrates two things: stupid things like this would never happen if sharing was the norm, and there is a reason that hammers and toilet seats cost thousands of dollars in military budgets!

In using the Process model, members of the project team get together and synchronize their efforts. This allows members of the team to determine if customer requirements are being met, and also gives them the opportunity to address internal issues. If members of Development feel that they are falling behind in their schedule, they are able to share this information with the other roles. The schedule can then be modified, or additional resources can be shared with members of the role who are facing problems. For example, if a member in another role is a speedy programmer and ahead in his or her work, this valuable resource can be shared with the other team to push Development up to speed.

Identifying Application Layers

Specify which application layer best models the following requirements: User Services, Business Services, or Data Services. (The answers to this exercise appear just before the Self Test at the end of this chapter.)

1. All dates must be displayed in *MM/DD/YYYY* format:
   _____

2. The user must select from a list of choices and is limited to only those choices: _____

3. Add a standard markup to the price of each inventory item:
   _____

4. Give all employees a 5% cost-of-living raise:
   _____

5. Given an inventory item number, find the current quantity in stock and its location: _____

6. After an inventory item has been shipped, reduce the current in-stock quantity: _____

7. ll fields that may be edited have a white background:
   _____

8. A long text comments field must wrap to the next line to fit on the user's screen: _____

Achieving Parallelism During the Development Process

The Application model can also be used as a model for separating members in the Development role of the team model into smaller subgroups. Rather than having a group work first on Data Services, then Business and middle-tier services, and finally on User Services, you can split Development into smaller groups that work parallel to one another. While one of these subgroups is working on one area of development, other groups are working on other areas at the same time. This creates faster development time, as the subgroups of the Development team are working in tandem to one another. Since they keep in close contact with one another through the Developing phase, they are able to address issues that arise as they are working on the different services of a project.

It is also important to remember that the roles of the Team model work parallel to one another. The model doesn't have five team roles sitting around, waiting for members in one role to finish. The model isn't linear, but has all of the roles working together in a parallel fashion. If a customer goes to the product manager and says, "Hey, I need this feature added," members in other roles don't stop working. As one feature is incorporated into the functional design, other services are being worked on. This is because when a modular design is used, the program isn't one monolithic program, but a group of modules that can be worked on in parallel. Each role can do their work on modules of the product, as new modules are incorporated into the design.

QUESTIONS AND ANSWERS

What is a milestone?	A milestone is the point at which one phase of a project ends and another begins. It is here that team members synchronize their efforts in a project, determine if they are meeting the customer's requirements, and discuss implementation problems.
What is a tradeoff?	Program managers work with resources, features, and schedules. At times, one of these areas may need to be modified to meet another area that has a higher priority. For example, a new feature required in a current version will either need the schedule changed, more resources to complete the project, or both.
Which change more frequently: business rules or business tasks?	Business rules generally will change more frequently than business tasks. While a task may be consistent, the rules associated with it may change a number of times.
I work for a small company and have only five people for my project team. How can I meet all my goals for the project if I don't have enough people to fill each project role?	Assign two roles, and thereby two goals, to one person. In doing this, make sure that the two roles assigned are similar in nature, and don't have conflicting goals.
It is taking awhile to complete a project, and it's affecting morale. How can I improve development time?	Break the large project into smaller projects. Different developers can work on the different parts in parallel and improve development time. It will also make them feel they're achieving something, allow them to look forward to the next sub-project, and improve morale.

CERTIFICATION SUMMARY

The Team model breaks a project team into six distinctive roles. Each role has an associated goal. When all of the goals in a project are achieved, the project is considered a success. If even one goal isn't met, the project is considered a failure.

The Process model is a milestone-based model that breaks a project up into four phases. At the completion of each phase, a milestone is reached. This model provides guidelines for planning and controlling a results-orientated project. This control is based on resources, schedule, and the scope of a project.

The Application model breaks an application down into different services, which are networked together. There are three layers to this model, with each layer consuming the services of the layer below and/or providing services to layers above. This model's structure allows for flexibility in designing solutions and promotes the use of components.

By completing different phases of a project parallel to one another, you are able to increase the speed at which a project reaches completion. Sharing resources, skills, and assets, and working on different parts of a project simultaneously, can help you meet the schedule and keep within budget.

 TWO-MINUTE DRILL

❏ Organizing a project, and the people to complete it, can be a grueling task. The Microsoft Solution Framework (MSF) aids in organizing a project with models that outline the organization of a team, their goals, and the process of development.

❏ The *Team model* breaks a project team into different roles, with each responsible for meeting a particular goal.

❏ The *Process model* breaks the project itself into different phases, allowing team members to see where a project is going, and what progress has been made.

❏ The *Application model* breaks the actual application into different parts.

❏ A *business case* is a plan of action that's presented to senior management.

❏ *Product Management* has a position of advocacy between customers who buy a product, and the team that creates it.

❏ The team roles and their related key goals have a symbiotic relationship. It is important to understand how one maps to the other, if you are to understand the purpose of each team role.

❏ A *milestone* not only marks the point where one phase of a project ends and another begins, it also indicates the point in time that members of a team should synchronize their efforts.

❏ The MSF Process model is based on two proven models: the Waterfall model and the Spiral model.

❏ The *Spiral model* is also called the *Rapid Application Development (or RAD) model*. It breaks a project into subprojects, each of which deals with different risks in a project. Since each risk is addressed in the sub-projects, all risks in a project can be identified individually.

❏ The *Waterfall model* views the life cycle as a flow of steps.

❏ The *Envisioning phase* is where a common vision is set for a product, while the *Planning phase* is where an agreement is made on what will be built and how to build it.

❏ The Application model consists of three layers, which make up the application. These layers are *User Services*, *Business Services*, and *Data Services*.

❏ *Modular design* involves breaking a large project into smaller modules, or subprojects.

❏ A *programmatic interface* is used by other applications to obtain information, while a *GUI* is a visual display that's presented to a human user.

Answers to Exercise 2-1

1. Bob: Program
2. Brenda: User Education
3. Mark: Logistics

4. Jeffry: Product
5. Chris: Test
6. Jan: Development

Answers to Exercise 2-2

Envisioning phase
Vision/Scope Approved milestone

Planning phase
Project Plan Approved milestone

Developing phase
Scope Complete/First Use milestone

Stabilization phase
Release milestone

Answers to Exercise 2-3

1. Data Services
2. User Services
3. Business Services
4. Business Services

5. Data Services
6. Data Services
7. User Services
8. User Services

SELF TEST

The Self Test questions will help you measure your understanding of the material presented in this chapter. Read all the choices carefully, as there may be more than one correct answer. Select all correct answers for each question.

1. What is the key goal of Product Management?

    A. Delivery within project constraints

    B. Delivery to product specifications

    C. Satisfied customers

    D. Smooth deployment and ongoing management

2. Which phase in the process model results in the Scope Complete/First Use milestone?

    A. Envisioning phase

    B. Planning

    C. Developing phase

    D. Stabilization phase

3. What milestone is associated with the creation of a vision/scope document?

    A. Vision/Scope Approved

    B. Project Plan Approved

    C. Scope Complete/First Use

    D. Release

4. Which of the following is associated with User Services? (Choose all that apply.)

    A. Creating a business plan

    B. Programmatic interface

    C. Graphical user interface

    D. Enforcement of business rules

5. Which of the following are elements of a business case?

    A. Analysis of the customer's business need

    B. Proposed and alternative solutions

    C. Quantitative and qualitative benefits

    D. All of the above

    E. None of the above

6. Which service in the Application model provides Create, Read, Update, and Delete capabilities to an application?

    A. User Services

    B. Business Services

    C. Middle-tier Services

    D. Data Services

7. Jennifer is a graphic artist who is working on a graphics-intensive application. To deal with this graphics-intensive process, the application she works with offloads some of the processing to a server's CPU. Which layer of the Application model has dealt with this situation?

    A. User Services

    B. Graphic Services

C. Middle-tier services

D. Data Services

8. How is testing performed by the members in the testing team role? (Choose all that apply.)

   A. Randomly check all areas of a solution.

   B. Schedules are used to determine when a product is tested.

   C. Business cases are used to put testers in the role of the potential user, so they can randomly check areas like a real user.

   D. Strategies and plans are used to find defects, bugs, and errors.

9. The WidgetSoft project has a budget of $25,000, and is to be completed by September 8. The project experiences a few problems. Though it is completed on time, it is over budget by $5000. Which goal has not been met?

   A. Delivery to product specifications

   B. Smooth deployment and ongoing management

   C. Delivery within project constraints

   D. None of the above. Since it was completed on time, all goals were met.

10. Which of the following is true of versioned releases?

    A. The current version of a program should meet the current requirements of the user.

    B. The current version of a program should meet future requirements of the user.

    C. The current version of a program should meet obsolete requirements.

    D. The current version of a program should meet all conceivable requirements of the user.

11. Which team role corresponds to the key goal of enhancing user performance?

    A. Development

    B. Testing

    C. Program Management

    D. User Education

12. Which team role corresponds to the key goal of a smooth deployment and ongoing management?

    A. Development

    B. Program Management

    C. Testing

    D. Logistics

13. Your project team has set up a meeting to establish priorities for a project to deal with tradeoffs. What tool will you use to determine a strategy for dealing with tradeoffs?

    A. Triangulated relationship

    B. Business case

    C. Shopping list

    D. Tradeoff matrix

14. Your project team has just completed the Scope Complete/First Use milestone. What phase will come next in the Development life cycle?

    A. Planning

    B. Envisioning

    C. Developing

    D. Stabilization

15. Project teams often depend on external groups. Which groups are members in the development role dependent on?

    A. Customers

    B. Senior management

    C. Operations and support teams

    D. None of the above

    E. All of the above

16. Project teams often depend on external groups. Which project roles have an external group dependency with customers? (Choose all that apply.)

    A. Product Management

    B. Program Management

    C. Testing

    D. Logistics

17. The project team has just handed responsibility for the product to Operations and Support teams, which is an indication of which milestone?

    A. Vision/Scope Approved

    B. Project Plan Approved

    C. Release

    D. Scope Complete/First Use

18. How do the different layers of the Application model communicate with one another? (Choose the best answer.)

    A. Service requests

    B. ActiveX components

    C. The Application model is a theoretical design. There is no need for actual communication.

    D. The layers perform different activities, and have no need to communicate.

19. Which of the following best defines a business rule?

    A. It is a policy that determines how team roles are assigned.

    B. It is a policy used to determine how a business task is performed.

    C. It is determined by the requirements of a customer, and used to specify the user interface.

    D. It is the criteria used in creating a business case.

20. How should you increment a large project into multiple-versioned releases?

    A. Ask what users want, then add all features requested at that time to the current release.

    B. Address the most important needs of the user, and add additional functionality to later releases.

    C. Add all possible features to a program, so that new ideas can be added later.

    D. See what the competition does first, then release a similar program.

21. Which of the following is not a phase in the process model?

    A. Envisioning

    B. Planning

    C. Developing

    D. Release

22. Which of the following best describes vision?

    A. It is an optimistic view of a project's goals, where no consideration is given to the goals of the project.

    B. It is an unbridled view of a project's goals, with no consideration given to the constraints of a project.

    C. It defines the limitations of a product or service, and determines what can be done within the project's constraints. It is synonymous with *scope*.

    D. It is a view of project priorities, which establish where tradeoffs in a project will take place.

23. The Team model is made up of six roles and six goals. In your zeal to get a project started, one of the roles isn't assigned to anyone, leaving one of the six goals not represented by anyone. How will this affect the project?

    A. The Team model is designed for redundancy. It won't affect the project.

    B. It will result in extra work for other members, but the Process model deals with this contingency.

    C. The project will fail.

    D. It depends on which role hasn't been assigned, and what goal isn't achieved, whether the project will succeed or fail.

24. Delivery within project constraints is a key goal addressed by the Team model. Which role is associated with this goal?

    A. Product Management

    B. Program Management

    C. Development

    D. Logistics

25. Which phase in the Process model ends in the Project Plan Approved milestone?

    A. Envisioning

    B. Planning

    C. Developing

    D. Stabilization

26. The Application model is a tiered model for solution development. From top to bottom layer, what are the tiers of this model?

    A. Data Services, Business Services, User Services

    B. User Services, middle-tier services, Data Services, Business Services

    C. User Services, Business Services, Data Services

    D. Business Services, middle-tier services, Data Services

27. Each role in the Team model has different responsibilities. Which of the following is a responsibility of User Education? (Choose all that apply.)

A. Acting as advocate for the customer

B. Designing, creating, and testing materials to assist the user

C. Smooth deployment and support management

D. Acting as advocate for the end user

28. You are working with a tradeoff matrix that has the Optimize column for Features (Scope) checked, indicating that a Maximum Benefit strategy will be used. What does this mean?

A. As many features as possible will be shipped with the current version.

B. Features essential to the main functionality of the product will be shipped.

C. Features will be dropped from the current version.

D. It means your job is in jeopardy.

29. What key goal in a project maps to the role of testing?

A. Delivery to product specifications

B. Release after addressing all issues

C. Smooth deployment

D. Delivery within project constraints

30. Which of the following is created in the Planning phase of the Process model? (Choose all that apply.)

A. Vision statement

B. Vision/scope document

C. Functional specification

D. Planning specification

31. Which of the following is a true statement?

A. Business rules change more frequently than business tasks.

B. Business tasks change at the same rate as business rules.

C. Business tasks change more frequently than business rules.

D. Business tasks change each time a business rule changes.

32. What are benefits of modular design in development? (Choose all that apply.)

A. It breaks a large project into subprojects.

B. It improves morale.

C. It allows different parts of a project to be developed parallel to one another.

D. It takes longer to complete a project.

33. You are using a tradeoff matrix, and notice that the Optimize column for the Schedule row is checked. What does this indicate?

A. The ship date for the product is to be as soon as possible.

B. The product will not meet its previous ship date.

C. The product is to be shipped at a later date.

D. The product must keep its current ship date.

34. Different roles of the Team model have dependencies on external groups. On which external group does User Education have a dependency?

A. Customer

B. Operations and Support teams

C. End user

D. Senior management

35. Which team role has the responsibility for creating the functional specification for a product?

A. Product Management

B. Program Management

C. Development

D. Logistics

36. You are using a tradeoff matrix and notice that the Accept column of the Schedule row is checked. What does this indicate?

A. The ship date for the product is to be as soon as possible.

B. The product will not meet its previous ship date.

C. The product is to be shipped at an earlier date.

D. The product must keep its current ship date.

37. You are working on a large project that's taking considerable time. This is affecting morale, and developers are getting depressed working on the project. What can you do to solve these problems?

A. Fire the developers and hire a subcontractor to finish the project.

B. Break the project into larger projects.

C. Break the project into smaller projects.

D. Scrap the project.

38. A milestone occurs at the end of a phase in the Process model. What does a milestone indicate? (Choose all that apply.)

A. The project is complete.

B. One phase of the project is complete, and another is ready to begin.

C. The point in time where members synchronize their efforts.

D. A phase needs to be repeated.

39. One of the roles in the Team model is Development. What is the key goal associated with this role?

A. Delivery within project constraints

B. Delivery to product specifications

C. Release after addressing all issues

D. Enhanced user performance

40. Which of the following is correct?

A. The Planning phase results in the Scope Complete/First Use milestone.

B. The Envisioning phase results in the Vision/Scope Approved milestone.

C. The Developing phase results in the Release milestone.

D. The Stabilization phase results in the Project Plan Approved milestone.

MICROSOFT CERTIFIED SOLUTION DEVELOPER

3

Risk
Management

T here are risks in every project, and the biggest mistake you can make is to ignore them and hope they'll go away by themselves. In this chapter we'll discuss proactive risk management, and find out how using this process helps you deal with risks before they become actual problems.

Proactive risk management is a five-step plan, in which risks follow each phase of the project until they are eliminated, become of minor consequence, or become a problem that is dealt with accordingly.

Using this approach involves a number of forms, charts, and tables that make managing risks relatively easy. Within a short time, you'll find that using this approach becomes second nature, and the possibility of loss is effectively kept at bay.

CERTIFICATION OBJECTIVE 3.01

Defining Risk Management

Risk is the possibility of suffering some sort of loss, and it is inherent to any project. The only way to avoid risk is to do nothing, and that means there is no chance of making any profit whatsoever from a project. Risks include anything from the project going over budget, to schedules not being met, to the project as a whole failing. There are all sorts of risks involved in any project, and that's why risk management is so important.

As we'll see later in this chapter, there are different ways of managing risks. In Microsoft's definition, though, *risk management* is a "discipline and environment of proactive decisions and actions to assess continuously what can go wrong, determine what risks are important to deal with, and implement strategies to deal with those risks." In other words, it's a way of dealing with problems before they happen. This involves implementing strategies that determine what risks are involved in a project and whether they're important enough to be a priority, and continually assessing problems that arise during the course of a project.

If you have already dealt with forms of risk management on a project, you know it can seem like a boring, tedious task that's bogged down in bureaucratic red tape. This need not be the case. The Microsoft Solution Framework (MSF) addresses the problems of risk management by creating a dynamic discipline that involves all members of a project. Microsoft's discipline of risk management is a five-step process, comprised of:

1. Risk identification
2. Risk analysis
3. Risk action planning
4. Risk tracking
5. Risk control

Rather than merely moving from one step to another in the process, risks are reassessed throughout the project. As new risks are identified, they are addressed with the five-step process. While we introduce these steps here, they are discussed in depth throughout the bulk of this chapter.

The issue of environment is crucial to good risk management. It is important that everyone involved in a project feels comfortable discussing potential problems with both superiors and subordinates. While people generally feel comfortable discussing risks with those who are below them in the chain of command, there is often a problem discussing potential problems with superiors. It can be a grueling experience telling your boss that a schedule can't be met or that features may not be included in the current version. In environments that don't promote good communication, this often results in risks becoming full-blown problems.

It is important to remember that identifying a risk and invoking a discussion about it, doesn't mean that you're saying a problem exists. A risk is a potential problem, which doesn't necessarily mean that it is inevitable and can't be avoided or remedied. It is the possibility of a loss, not a certainty. By having an environment where everyone involved in a project feels comfortable discussing risks, strategies can be employed to deal with these potential problems.

Risk Management Principles

The first, and most important thing, to remember about risk management is that risk is the possibility, and not the certainty, of loss. Though it's common for project teams to consider risks to be something negative, taking risks is important to progress. For example, let's look at something you can personally relate to right now, studying and taking the "Analyzing Requirements and Defining Solution Architectures" exam. You've probably identified certain risks in this: a schedule that needs to be met in taking the exam, possibly failing the exam the first time, and deciding whether to change jobs when you are certified. To deal with these risks, you've done some sort of risk management to lessen the odds of loss: you've adjusted your schedule to be prepared for the exam date, you've purchased this book and studied to avoid failing, and you've talked to management about a promotion. In taking these risks and managing them, you've pushed yourself forward and made progress toward becoming an MCSD. From this, you can see that just because a risk is identified in a project, it doesn't mean you're going to experience a loss.

The same goes for risk management in software development. Risk allows you to see where pitfalls may lie ahead, and manage them so they don't become a major issue and result in loss. Once you can see where the possibility of loss exists, you can take action so that losses don't occur, or deal with the problems once they've happened.

Good risk management requires having a project team assess risks throughout the course of a project. It is not uncommon for projects to make the mistake of identifying and assessing a risk at the beginning of a project, then failing to reassess the risk as the project progresses. For example, let's say you are working on a project for the Nutbar Company. At the beginning of the project, it looked as if time factors dictated that certain features wouldn't make it into the software you were creating. After some mitigation, you decide to subcontract some of the programming on this Nutbar project to a small software firm. End of risk, right? Not necessarily; if the subcontractor falls behind on coding and can't make your deadline, it could mean these features still won't be added. Without reassessing risks continuously, you run the risk that a potential problem will become a full-blown problem that results in loss.

The information gathered from the assessment of risks is used for making decisions on every phase of a project. Each team role (these are discussed in Chapter 2) must be aware of the risks involved in a project, and feel free to discuss those risks. If they aren't involved or made aware of the decisions made by others when assessing risks, it can snowball into further problems. To use the previous example, let's assume that the end result of the risk is that a feature isn't included. Development needs to know this, so they don't code the interface to access the feature. Testing needs to be aware of it, so they don't waste time trying to access and test the feature. As the project progresses from a concept to an actual physical product, the information gathered from the assessment of risks will influence what is done, how it is done, and whether actions are driving further loss.

There are risks inherent in any project. There isn't a project that's ever been undertaken that didn't involve some sort of risk. The major principle of risk management is dealing with the risk, and thereby lowering your odds that a loss will result. This means addressing the source of the risk, so that you don't have to deal with the consequences.

Sources of Risk

For every project there are a number of sources of risk. The source of a risk is an object, person, or structure that provides the possibility of loss in a project. For every source of a risk, there is a related consequence that can result from ineffective risk management. It's a simple matter of cause and effect. If you ignore the budget, you could wind up with cost overruns. If you ignore the schedule, it might slip. It is important to identify the sources of risk related to your particular project, so they can be properly addressed—and so you don't have to deal with the consequences.

A risk source is made up of three components: risk factor category, focus area, and risk factor. The *risk factor category* breaks the project into small groups, each of which contain individual risk factors. There can be many risk factor categories in a project, including the following:

- Mission and goals
- Customer and end user
- Organizational management
- Operational environment
- Development environment
- Development process

- Decision drivers

- Project characteristics

- Personnel

- Technology

- Schedule

- Budget and cost

The *focus area* is an area of the project that is being focused on for risk management. It can include such areas as component-based development, custom software development, packaged software deployment, infrastructure deployment, enterprise architecture planning, and management of enterprise programs. The *risk factor* is the final component of a risk source that is used to identify the risk. As we'll see, this can include such things as size of the project, availability of facilities, project fit, governmental regulations, and political influences.

Unfortunately, there is no simple list of risks and sources to memorize. While we discuss many of the common risks and risk sources in this chapter, it doesn't necessarily mean that you'll find them to be a possible threat to the success of a project. For example, when Microsoft introduced Windows 95, software development shifted to 32-bit programming for mainstream operating systems. While this technology shift was an issue for projects under development at the time (for Windows 3.1), the risk that this technology would change again wasn't an issue in the initial projects that followed. Just as organizations and projects are different, risks and risk sources can thereby be different. What may be significant to one project may not necessarily be the case on other projects.

One of the most common risk sources involved in any project is scheduling. Time is a limited commodity, and only so much of it will be given to a project team to complete a product. As such, a schedule has an extensive list of risks associated with it, including the following:

- **Schedules are overly optimistic.** Rather than including a bit of pessimism that some time might be lost, a best-case scenario is used. This often results in the project not being completed on time.

- **Target dates are moved up.**   When this happens, there is often a need for a tradeoff in other areas. Either the budget needs to be increased to pay for overtime and/or additional team members, or features need to be dropped. If there isn't a tradeoff, then this becomes a significant risk.

- **Delays in one area of the schedule have a cascading effect on other areas.**   When tasks can't be completed on time, it affects time allotted to other tasks.

- **The schedule is so intense that the pressure of meeting it reduces productivity, and causes the schedule to slip.**

- **Tasks that are necessary to the project's success aren't included in the schedule.**

In any project you're involved with, scheduling will have some risks associated with it. It is important to address these risks early in a project, as the project itself will follow this timeline. As the project progresses, the schedule should be reassessed. If it is found that it is unreliable, base any adjustments on how the project is going to date. The worst thing that can be done when an overly optimistic schedule is reassessed, is readjust it with great optimism. Remember to be realistic!

on the job

Schedules can be a major problem in risk management. People naturally want to impress their boss, and often create schedules that are based on best-case scenarios. It is important to be a little pessimistic in schedules, or the first time a flu bug hits your team, the schedule will slip. In addition, it is important that all of the tasks that are necessary to the project's success are included in the schedule. This may seem obvious, but after spending any length of time on a schedule, it's easy to miss something. A good rule of thumb for making sure everything's included is this: when you feel you've included everything in the schedule, don't submit it! Set it aside for at least 24 hours; then review it. This allows you to view it fresh, and certain things you've omitted from the schedule will often jump out at you.

Just as there is only so much time to complete a project, there is only so much money that will be allotted to it. If you've ever bashed heads with an accounting department, you know this to be true. Budgets are another common source of risk, and also have a number of risks associated with them:

- **The budget associated with the project is cut.** As a result, areas of the budget will need to be tightened, features may need to be dropped, and personnel may need to be dismissed. This can affect the morale of a team—and lower productivity.

- **Costs associated with the project change after the original budget is drafted.** Suddenly, more money is needed.

- **The budget doesn't take certain items into consideration.** It may not address the possibility of paying for overtime, adding additional staff, or hiring contractors.

These are but a few of the risks associated with the risk source of budget and cost. As with other risk sources, risks associated with budgets and costs should be reassessed throughout the life of a project. You need to be aware of how close you are keeping to the initial budget, and whether the budget meshes with reality. Since money is involved, depending on how much extra is needed, it is often the case that other areas of a project (such as features in the software) are traded off to keep within the original budget.

As we saw in Chapter 2, it is vital that everyone working on a project understands the mission and goals. The primary risk is that if project members don't understand what they are working toward and hoping to achieve, the project is destined for failure. The process of a project should be based on easily identifiable milestones. For this reason, we cover milestones in great detail in the next chapter. A common risk of missions and goals is that they are written in difficult to understand words, or cryptic language. You must be clear and straight to the point as to what each team role is working toward, and keep them up to speed on changes in the project.

Project characteristics are often a source of risk. Again, cryptic language and unclear wording in describing the specifics of a project can lead to confusion. If developers don't understand what features are being asked for, it can lead to immense problems. If an Exit function needs to be added under the File menu, say that! Don't ask for a "text-based feature to terminate said application and remove binary data from memory."

The most common risk for project characteristics is change. Customers or end users suddenly realize that certain features aren't needed, or decide that certain characteristics must be added. External environments, such as government regulations or technical standards, can also require changes in the project's characteristics. Laws, technical standards, and business rules can have the annoying habit of changing at the worst times in a project's life. When they do, you will be forced to change certain characteristics to meet these changes.

Anyone who has dealt with people realizes there are lots of risks involved. It is amazing the number of times that personnel aren't fully considered in risk management. Issues such as morale, relationships, and teamwork are often missed when identifying risks. These three areas relate to productivity. If personnel isn't properly motivated, or if morale is low, their productivity decreases. The same occurs if there is a poor relationship between team members, and a lack of teamwork. If developers and management don't get along, then the decision-making process slows down, and personnel will feel uncomfortable pointing out risks they've identified in a project. It is important to provide inspiring leadership, and to deal with any personnel issues immediately. Remember that without personnel, all areas of a project will stall and possibly fail.

on the
! job

Aside from the military, which takes morale very seriously, organizations and management sometimes seem to go out of their way to lower morale. One of the best superiors I've had did take this seriously, and promoted teamwork. The organization's upper management saw this, and chastised her for it. She was told "not to be friendly with them" and to basically earn respect and obedience through fear. This is something I've heard in several organizations. However, it is surprising the number of risks you can eliminate with personnel when they feel like a team, are motivated, have high morale, and look forward to doing their jobs each day.

In addition to more intrinsic risks involved with personnel, there are numerous other risks:

- **Hiring delays** When hiring personnel takes longer than originally expected, the project is at risk.

- **Failed prerequisites** These may include poor training, lack of critical skills, and delayed completion of projects that members are currently working on.

- **Poor work habits** Personnel are working slower than expected, or doing things that are affecting the productivity of other team members.

- **Unavailability** Certain personnel are available only on a part-time basis or tied up with other projects, or contract, permanent, or part-time personnel leave the project before it's completed.

When dealing with personnel, the risks involved are as numerous and different as people. Each project has its own risks involving personnel; these must be identified on a project-by-project basis.

Personnel risks must be evaluated continuously in a project. It is a bad idea to merely put together a team, and not assess the risks involved with personnel as the project progresses. It is possible for a team to initially work well together but fall apart over time. Some people don't work well together, and sometimes problem members need to be removed from a project. These are risks in themselves, and should never be dismissed or underestimated in their impact.

Other people-orientated risk sources are customers and end users. Customers and end users aren't necessarily the same. Customers pay for the product, while end users are the people who actually use a product. This in itself can make for interesting situations, since while the customer may approve a product, the end user may decide that it isn't satisfactory. Besides customers and/or end users disapproving of a product, other risks related to these sources include the following:

- Customer and/or end user insists on new requirements for the product.

- Customer and/or end user is dissatisfied.

- Input from the end user isn't acquired, so the product doesn't meet expectations.

- Expectations for completion of the project are beyond what development can provide.

- Customer is slow in making decisions or reviewing documentation regarding the project.

- Customer provides inadequate input regarding requirements.

Dissatisfaction from a customer or end user brings up another risk related to these sources: loss of the company's image. If your product doesn't meet expectations, or the project is looked poorly upon by a customer or end user, you can be sure that word-of-mouth about your company will be poor. This results in people thinking twice before buying your products, or hiring your software development firm.

Once you've worked on a computer for any length of time, you realize that technology has a plethora of risks. Networks go down and system requirements must be met before updated development suites (such as Visual Basic 6.0 and Visual Studio 6.0) can be installed. There is a rule of thumb that computer hardware components need to be upgraded every two years to keep up with the latest software technology. It used to be three years and still is in a best-case scenario, but changing market costs and depreciation of computers and other equipment have changed this rule. Beyond this, you will also experience that the customer's requirements for a project aren't possible, because technology hasn't improved enough to provide the features your customer wants. For example, web cams, which are used to transmit sound and images across the Internet, weren't available until relatively recently, but for decades a number of customers have been requesting the ability to chat face-to-face on the network.

Over the last few years, the development environment has been recognized as a risk source. Ergonomics has become a major theme in computing, with the theory being that if the environment is comfortable and conducive to good work, then productivity will improve. They're right! It is difficult to do good work if facilities are noisy, disruptive, uncomfortable, and/or crowded. While these are rather basic examples of ergonomic issues, it does give you an idea of how such things can affect the project.

Other risks of the development environment include facilities not being ready when the project begins. Imagine showing up for work, only to find there are no desks, chairs, working phones, or computers. One experience I faced was where they'd forgotten to deliver copies of Visual Basic to the office so we could develop software. In addition to things like this, where you get paid for fun-filled days of playing Euchre, the development environment also holds the risks of development tools not working as expected, or being chosen because they are cheap rather than functional. If you're ready to work with Microsoft Visual C++, and find you'll be using an unknown compiler called the Dead C Scroll, productivity is bound to suffer.

If you don't face problems with the development environment, you may find risks in the development process. If this is poorly managed, it can spawn numerous problems. If there is poor tracking of progress, you may not realize that a project is behind schedule until it's too late. In addition, if there is a bureaucratic adherence to policies and standards, you may find there is unnecessary work and additional overhead on a project. On the other end of the scale, if there is too much of a casual approach to software policies and standards, it can result in quality problems, miscommunication, or inevitably having to redo the same work on a product. The key to resolving this is finding a happy medium, where rules are adhered to, but not to an unreasonable level of following policies and standards.

Organizational management and the operational environment of a company must also be taken into account for a project to succeed. It is important to remember that the Information Technology department, and the project teams within them, are part of a larger organization. As such, the pressures of the organization's management and the company's operational environment have a major impact on a project's success. In fact, Microsoft states that many, if not most, projects fail because the pressures of the larger organization are ignored in risk management.

The company's operational environment and organizational management are two risk sources that hold an incredible amount of risks, and are often out of your control. While you have some control over the project's budget, (unless you're the owner) you don't have control over the entire company's financial health. Budget cuts, layoffs, and other cutbacks can upset the ability of a team to complete a project on time. In addition, there may be exhaustive pressure put on a project team by upper management. For example, it may be standard practice to burden a project team with incredible amounts of paperwork. Though meant to improve the performance of a team and project, too much can have people spending more time doing the paperwork than doing the actual work! If upper management is slow in making decisions, then this will also affect the project. Unfortunately, there is little you can do with these risk sources. If you were working on a project for Microsoft and had a problem with organizational management, they wouldn't let you fire Bill Gates. You can only add these risks into the project's overall plans and try to work around them.

The final risk source we'll discuss here is risk management. This seems like an oxymoron, but it's not. When risk management isn't taken seriously, or when the process of identifying and dealing with risks is skimmed over, you're tempting fate. Major risks associated with a project can be missed, and additional time must be spent backtracking over risk issues. If the risks are completely missed, then some sort of loss is involved. Schedules slip, and additional costs can cause projects to go over budget due to the initial half-hearted effort. It is important that risk management is taken seriously on projects, or these are but a few of the risks you will encounter.

EXERCISE 3-1

Risk Identification

Which items in the following list should be considered risks to the project? (The answers to this exercise appear just before the Self Test at the end of this chapter.)

1. Your project is scheduled for deployment in two months. Your Program Manager's Manager announced that she won a $15 million lottery.

2. Your project began in November and is expected to last six months. Your location is in the northeast United States. The weather service has predicted the coldest winter in history for the area.

3. Your customer is a government agency and new legislation has passed, moving your customer's responsibilities to another agency.

4. Your project was targeting both the 16- and 32-bit Windows platforms. The 16-bit platforms will all be replaced in two weeks. Your project's release date is next week.

5. The CEO of your organization just received his first notebook computer.

6. The database server for your targeted production platform was changed to RAID 5 technology.

7. A member of your development team who had a mental block understanding DCOM was laid off.

8. You were hired mid-project as an additional development resource because the project schedule was slipping. A week later you were told that one of your primary responsibilities will be skills transfer.

9. A team member's favorite hobby is competitive snow skiing. It is winter and it snows every third day.

10. Two members of the development team are husband and wife.

11. Your organization is merged with another and the resulting IT staff is now tripled.

12. Your organization is merged with another and the resulting IT staff count increased by 50 percent.

Risk Management Approaches

There are basically two approaches to risk management: proactive and reactive. *Proactive risk management* deals with risks before they become problems that result in loss. *Reactive risk management* deals with risks after they've occurred.

Proactive risk management requires implementing a plan to manage risks. The process used in this case must be measurable and repeatable. In other words, not only will you be able to document procedures and their results, but you will be able to use them in other projects. Earlier in this chapter, we mentioned how the MSF's proactive risk management model is basically a five-step process. This process is not only measurable in its success, but repeatable in that it has worked for numerous companies. Throughout the remaining sections of this chapter, we will discuss each of these steps in detail.

One approach to proactive risk management is elimination of risk sources and factors. This is basically a two-part process:

1. Identify the factors that cause the risk.

2. Eliminate these factors, so the risk is no longer present.

As we saw in the previous section, this isn't possible in a number of cases. For example, if you're having a problem with upper levels of organizational management, chances are you can't make personnel changes at that level. However, let's say you identify contractors as a risk source and you've found a particular contractor to have slow performance, or not deliver what's expected. Now that this has been identified, eliminate the risk source by not hiring that contractor. This could mean not hiring that particular problem contractor, or completely eliminating the risk source by developing the entire product internally.

Higher levels of risk management go beyond this, and actually involve a willingness to take risks. Since risk is only the possibility of loss, this doesn't mean that a loss will definitely result. Risk is therefore viewed as possible opportunity, where risks are identified, evaluated, and used to the team's advantage. With risk comes opportunity. The sources of risks are evaluated, and used as a means rather than an end. For example, if it is known that the development environment won't be ready immediately, there is an advantage in that your developers will have the opportunity to work on other projects until the environment is ready. If it is known that a subcontractor is usually two days late with delivering the work they've been assigned, then you can give a false due date that's four days before the actual time it's expected. By evaluating risk sources and risks effectively, you can embrace risks and use them to your advantage.

Preventing risk is the transition between the reactive and proactive approaches to risk management. During the planning stages of a project, a project team will consider the various risks in a project, and take actions to keep them from occurring. However, doing so doesn't really deal with the source of a risk, only the symptom of that particular cause. This is like handing a tissue to someone with a cold; you haven't found a cure to the common cold, you've only dealt with the symptom.

You've probably heard your father or grandfather use the phrase, "There's no point closing the barn door after the horses have run away!" This essentially captures the spirit of reactive risk management. Reactive risk management reacts to the consequences of risk rather than addressing the issues before an actual problem occurs. This may involve fixing problems after they've occurred, assigning resources at the beginning of a project to deal with problems after they've happened, or addressing the risk issues only after they become problems. In any case, the key to reactive risk management is that the risk has become a distinctive problem that has already occurred in the project.

FROM THE CLASSROOM

The Rewards of Risk Analysis

The potential for risks is far too often overlooked during the initial stages of a project. Often, only a cursory look is given to the issues that can drag a project from the lofty heights of the best-case scenario. Proper definition of project scope, adjustments for changing markets, and proper communication of required resources are paramount to reducing project risks.

One of the most common failures is accepting the inherent risk when the scope of a project is improperly defined. Clients, end users, and customers are often fickle in their expectations when a clearly defined project scope and analysis documentation are not produced. This failure opens the door to increased volatility in customer expectations, leading to greater risks taken with budgets, schedules, and customer satisfaction.

Failure to produce or communicate a proper list of project resource requirements, for example, can lead to some unexpected increases in risks. Beginning phase two of a proof-of-concept project, only to find that the client has migrated the entire development system to a virgin system without the necessary software, can certainly lead to increased risks of missing schedules or reducing functionality.

When analyzing risk, Microsoft emphasizes assigning a decimal, from 0 to 1, as a measure of risk probability. This can be used when assessing quantitatively the impact of a risk. Also, the Delphi method should be a familiar process, both for allowing collaborative input of risk analysis from team members, and as a good source of exam questions.

—Michael Lane Thomas, MCSE+I, MCSD, MCT, MCP+SB, MSS, A+

The Components of a Risk Statement

Earlier in this chapter, we saw that it is important for team members to be aware of the risks involved in a project. Relaying this information involves more than yelling across the office, "Hey Bob, the schedule is wacky! I don't think we'll make it on time!" This is where risk statements come into play. *Risk statements* are used to communicate the risks involved in a project, so that members can effectively manage them. This not only includes mentioning the symptoms of a risk, but what the result of a risk could be.

In creating a risk statement, you are delving into the first two steps of the proactive risk management process: identification and analysis. It is through these two steps that risks are assessed. *Risk identification* results in a list of risks that have the potential to cause problems in a project. *Risk analysis* evaluates the impact of the identified risks and considers alternatives to factors causing the risk. In the following section, we will go through each of these steps in detail.

Risk Identification and Analysis

The first step in the risk management process, and the process of creating a risk statement, is identification. Before anything else can be done, a risk must be identified. It is from the identification of risks that the project team can see what threats, opportunities, and possibilities face them in a project. By using this information, they can deal with risks before they become problems that might jeopardize a project.

Risk identification involves project members and stakeholders following a series of steps, which result in the identification and ranking of risk factors. This involves the following:

- Using risk factor charts
- Using risk assessment tables
- Discussing the risks openly and freely
- Ranking risks by importance

Risk factor charts are used to organize and categorize risks, so it can be determined how critical certain risks are to a project. In using the risk factor chart, members and stakeholders discuss and rank risks in order of importance. When this is done, a *risk statement* is developed, and the risk is entered on a master list.

A risk factor chart is used to determine whether a risk should be considered high, medium, or low. Though called a chart, it is actually a table used to document risk factors in a project. Risk factors are grouped by risk factor category and focus area, with one or more characteristics that describe the risk level. Risk factor categories are the categories of risk sources, which we previously discussed in the section on risk sources. The category determines what is being addressed in the risk factor chart. In the example shown in the following table, personnel is the risk category that is being addressed. The focus area narrows the view of this category, and focuses interest on a particular area of the category. This can include such things as enterprise architecture planning, software development, packaged software deployment, and component-based development. The risk factor characteristics are used within the risk factor chart to label the risk level as high, medium, or low.

Risk Factor	Low-Risk Cue	Medium-Risk Cue	High-Risk Cue
Hiring	Taking longer than expected.	Some unqualified people are being hired, and will require additional training.	Personnel department's union may strike, and no hiring will take place.
Key personnel	Three are tied up with another project, and will join a week into the project.	Two are available only part-time.	Two will not be available until late in the project.

What might be crucial to one project, may be of minor importance to another. As such, when ranking risks, you need to view the risk in the context of the current project. Just because you found a risk factor to be high ranking in a previous project, doesn't mean it rates as high on the current project.

Ranking the importance of a risk can be difficult. Project members and stakeholders come from different backgrounds and experience, so they will view the risks differently. In addition, their diversified roles on the project team will affect what they consider to be vital. For example, Development will consider coding issues more critical than testing issues. Because of this, you can't always expect agreement on how a risk ranks in the overall project. When this happens, it should be put to a vote. Majority rules is the easiest way to decide where the risk resides on a ranking of risks. If the vote is tied, then the worst case should be used for assessment.

Once risks have been identified in a project, the second step of the proactive risk management process comes into play. This is analysis. *Analysis* takes the raw data you've acquired, and converts it into information used in decision making. Analysis determines which risks pose the greatest threats and opportunities to a project, and thereby which risks the project members should work on. It is pointless to work on risks that are unlikely to occur, or have little or no impact on a project.

When analyzing risks, two important factors quickly become apparent: risk probability and risk impact. *Risk probability* is the likelihood of events occurring, while *risk impact* is the amount of loss that could result. These factors are what you evaluate when analyzing risks.

Risk probability is usually indicated by a numerical value expressed as a decimal number. Microsoft recommends using increments of 0.05, with a value between 0 and 1, as the standard way of expressing the probability of a risk. When calculating the probability of a risk in this manner, it must be more than 0 and less than 1. A risk probability of 0 means that there is no probability of loss, while a risk with a probability of 1 means that the risk has occurred.

While Microsoft recommends using decimal numbers, this may not be the only method you'll encounter in the real world. For example, it isn't uncommon to find the probability of risk indicated by a numerical value expressed as a percentage. The reason is because people will be able to recognize what this means without additional information. When calculating the probability of a risk, it must be more than 0 percent and less than 100 percent. A risk probability of 0 percent would mean that there is no possibility of loss, which means that the item shouldn't even be analyzed. If the probability is 100 percent, then it means that the risk has already become a problem.

Despite these other methods for showing risk probability, remember that these aren't the recommended methods endorsed by Microsoft. For the exam, you should remember that the decimal increments are the preferred method.

Risk probability is often more subjective than scientific. It is difficult, if not downright impossible, to give an accurate percentage of risk probability. For example, can you accurately predict that there is a 25-percent chance that the design of a software product needs to be reworked? There are several ways to provide estimation, but in many cases (such as this) it comes down to good old-fashioned guesswork! As we'll see, these "guestimates" are based on the experience of team members.

There are several methods that teams can use to estimate risk probability. One that is commonly used is having the person who is most familiar with the area of risk provide an estimate. Other members of the team then discuss this. Another common method is through group consensus, which is also called the *Delphi method.* Each member provides an estimate on their own, along with the logic and reasons behind the estimate. Once this estimate and justification have been submitted, the members receive the estimates, along with the ratings, and re-evaluate their own submissions. After re-evaluating their work, each member submits revised estimates, and then discusses these estimates until they come to a consensus.

While both of these methods are proven and commonly used, they rely on members to use personal experience to make educated guesses on what percentage of risk is involved.

A method of estimating probability that doesn't require percentage estimates is *adjective calibration.* This uses a scale of adverbs that describe the probability of a risk. For example, high probability, very likely, likely, unlikely, very unlikely, and improbable would describe the probability factor of a risk. On a sheet of paper, members would choose a word to describe the risk. Each of these words would have a percentage value, which the word is converted to. For example, likely might have a value of 50 percent. If most members said a risk was likely, then you would apply the value of 50 percent to this risk.

One of the funniest methods, which actually works, uses a *betting scheme*. This works as if you were betting money on particular risks; however, no money actually changes hands. To illustrate, let's use this example: "If the development tools are ready and in place on time, you win $60. If not, I win $50!" These bets are adjusted until you feel comfortable on either side of the bet. You then take the lower amount and divide it by the total amount of cash that's in the proverbial kitty. To use our development tools example, the lower amount is $50, while the total amount is $110 ($60 + $50). This means you would do the following to get the risk probability percentage:

$50 / ($60 + $50) = 45%

While this method seems strange at first, it does work and makes the process of estimating risk probabilities fun. People are naturally used to taking money seriously, and are used to dealing with cash in the real world. As such, it has a natural feel once it's been used a few times.

Risk impact is the second factor involved in risk analysis. It measures the size of loss, or severity of adverse effects, if a risk results in becoming an actual problem. It is measured in currency for risks with a financial impact, time increments (days and weeks) for risks with a time impact, or a subjective scale for other risks that don't fall into such obvious areas. By using a scale of 1 to 5, you can show the seriousness of the impact. High values are used to indicate high losses; medium values show a moderate loss to portions of a project; and low values show that there is a minimum impact on the project.

Estimating the size of loss is considerably easier than estimating risk probability. It is a matter of taking the data available, and calculating the size of loss from the numbers. If you are expecting facilities to be ready September 1, and you know that phones, desks, and other necessities may not be set up until September 8, then the size of loss is one week (seven days). In cases where there are numerous components to an area, such as several programming tools being estimated for the risk impact of development tools, you simply look at the size of loss for each of the components, then add them together afterward. For example, let's say you were looking at the size of loss from using the fictional Dead C Scroll compiler and Julie's Wacky Tracker. You would first estimate the loss of each tool individually. There was a two-week training time for Dead C Scroll users and one week for Julie's Wacky Tracker, and a day for each of three other tools. As such, you would add 2 weeks + 1 week + 3 days together, and find that the size of loss is three weeks and three days. By looking at the individual components of a focus area, you are able to see the overall size of loss when they are added together.

Risk exposure factors together risk potential and risk impact. Risk exposure is used to balance the likelihood of an actual loss with the magnitude of the potential loss. In other words, it is the overall threat of a risk to a project.

The way to determine the risk exposure is by using the following formula:

risk potential × *size of loss* = *risk exposure*

Risk exposure is equal to the size of loss multiplied by the risk potential estimate. To understand how this works, let's go through this example step by step. If you estimated that there is a 50-percent chance that facilities wouldn't be available on time, then your risk probability is 50 percent. If the amount of time it would take for the facilities to be ready is two weeks, then your size of loss is two weeks. By multiplying two weeks by 50 percent, you have a risk exposure of one week. Once you've gotten this estimate, you would incorporate an extra week into your schedule, so that the risk you're exposed to won't affect the overall schedule.

In finding the risk exposure of risks in a project, a *risk assessment table* is used. As shown in the following table, a risk assessment table documents the probability of loss and the size of loss associated with the risk. These two fields are multiplied to find the risk exposure.

Risk assessment chart

Risk	Probability of Loss	Size of Loss (Weeks)	Risk Exposure (Weeks)
Facilities won't be ready on time.	25 percent	4	1
Amount of paperwork is excessive, and may impact progress.	50 percent	1	0.43

The tables, charts, and forms generated during the risk management process are important tools. You can expect questions dealing with them on the exam. It is important to remember the purpose of these tools, what steps of the process they're associated with, and what items each contains.

Once these steps have been completed, you are ready to prepare the risk statement. The *risk statement* has a number of features in it, and includes information acquired in the identification and analysis stages. In creating the risk statement, there is a considerable amount of information that can be added to the form. However, the following must appear in the risk statement, or it will not be complete:

- Source of a risk
- Risk(s) associated with the source
- Expected result or consequence

You can see that a risk statement isn't a long document. Remember that you are completing a form, not writing a novel, when generating a risk statement. First, you mention the condition that is causing the risk. This is followed by the risk that is faced and consequences the project may encounter. For example,

> The job market is excellent for developers right now and the Company is having difficulty hiring enough people. Consequently, we are short two people on the project. Therefore, we don't have the personnel needed to meet the October deadline.

In addition to this basic information, there is additional information that is recommended on a risk statement, as shown in Table 3-1. When

TABLE 3-1

A Risk Statement Form

Risk Statement Item	Description
Related Risks	List of risk identifications that are related to this particular risk situation. Used for tracking risks that are interdependent.
Risk Condition	Description of the condition that might lead to a loss for the project.
Risk Consequence	Description of the consequences or loss that will occur if the risk becomes an actual problem.
Risk Context	A brief paragraph that provides background information. Used to clarify a risk situation.
Risk Exposure	This is the overall threat to a project. It is calculated by multiplying the size of loss by the probability of loss.
Risk Identifier	Used for reporting and tracking purposes, this identifies the risk statement. It can be a number, alphanumeric filing code, or a name.
Risk Impact	Represents the amount of loss that would occur if a risk became an actual problem.
Risk Impact Classification	Specifies where the risk is. For example, a risk could be legal, financial, strategic, or technical.
Risk Probability	Represents the likelihood that a loss will occur.
Risk Source	Specifies the focus area, risk factor category, and risk factor.

generating a risk statement form, it is advisable to go through this list, so you can be certain that you haven't forgotten necessary information. For your convenience, the risks in Table 3-1 are listed in alphabetical order.

exam
⚙atch

Review Table 3-1 before going into the exam. By and large, risk management is fairly straightforward compared to other models in the Microsoft Solution Framework. Where people often seem to have a problem is remembering the terms in risk management. Know what should go on a risk statement form, memorize what each term means, and you will be prepared for this part of the exam.

In stating a risk, you need to express it clearly and concisely. You don't need to dazzle other members with your command of the English language and mastery of technical jargon. It should be stated so that everyone who reads or hears it will be able to understand what you're saying. In addition, don't ramble on about the consequences of a risk. You should be straight to the point. If people are baffled and bored by what you're saying, it won't be given the proper level of consideration.

EXERCISE 3-2

Assessing a Project's Risk Exposure

The ABC project is an office automation project that will take all the organization's required paperwork and make an electronic version. (The answers to this exercise appear just before the Self Test at the end of this chapter.)

The project has gone through Vision and Scoping, and a project plan has been prepared. Your next task is to determine the project's risk exposure.

Create a risk assessment table for the ABC project. Keep in mind the following points:

- The purchasing department wants a Purchase Requisition form and a Purchase Order form. They would prefer them in Microsoft Excel because they know the application.

- The Accounts Receivable Department wants a Credit History form and a Debt Collection Request form. This department prefers to work in Microsoft Word.

- The Payroll Department wants an Hourly Time Sheet form, a Vacation Request form, an Employee Review form, and an Expense Reimbursement form. This department just received desktop computers a week ago and is still being trained in how to use a mouse. The risk they won't be able to learn before the forms are to be used is estimated at 25 percent. Some department members have been enrolled in another two weeks of intensive, off-site usage training.

- You and one other person comprise the development team and your due date is in three months. There is a 75-percent chance that you won't make that due date. If you don't, the forms supply will be depleted and must be re-ordered. This will cost $5000.

- You have to share a development computer for two weeks until your computer is delivered. There is a 30-percent chance that your computer will be delivered three weeks late.

- All but one form have been preprinted and are to be duplicated exactly. One form, the Expense Reimbursement Form has yet to be designed. There is a 50-percent chance it won't be completed until two weeks after the project due date.

- The development tools are the Microsoft Office Suite and Visual Basic. Although you and the other developer are fluent in VBA, you have never used Visual Basic and will receive no training. There is a 50-percent risk that this will delay the project completion by four weeks.

Setting Priorities

Priorities are often set by the risk exposure figure on a risk assessment table. This figure represents the overall threat to a project, and balances the probability of loss with the impact (or size) of loss that could occur. By ranking the risks by this figure, you are then able to create a Top 10 Risk List.

A *Top 10 Risk List* helps you to pick your battles, and show which risks are the highest priority in a project. Remember that risk analysis determines the threat of each risk, so you can determine which risks require attention. If you don't focus your efforts on a selection of risks, team members will spend more time performing risk management than they will performing their individual roles of development and testing. By using the risk exposure value, you can compare the different risks and find which pose the greatest threats and opportunities. The risks that rank as the highest ten are then placed on a separate list, which is identifies those risks that must be managed.

In ranking by risk exposure, it is important that all of the values representing risk impact are of the same units of measurement. This means that each of the size of loss values is, for example, either in weeks, dollars, or levels of impact. It is impossible to determine whether a week is of higher value than a dollar or the level of 3. As such, if you are using different units of measurement, you should convert them to levels of impact before attempting to prioritize them. By having a level of impact, such as a scale of 1 to 5, with 5 having the highest impact, you can then view the different risk exposures to determine which are top priority.

The Top 10 Risk List provides a way for team members and stakeholders to view the major risks that must be managed. It is used later to focus the team on developing a risk management strategy, which is implemented as part of the project. This document is included in the vision/scope document and the project plan, which are explained in Chapters 2 and 4 of this book

CERTIFICATION OBJECTIVE 3.03

The Risk Management Process

The steps of the risk management process we've covered so far—identification and analysis—lay the foundation for the remaining three steps. While the identification and analysis steps provide us with data, it is from this point on that data is transformed into information and then used to create an action plan to track and control the risks involved in a project.

In looking at this process, shown in the following illustration, it resembles a wheel moving over a road. This image does well in illustrating how the process as a whole works. The first steps of the process act as a foundation, or road, for the other steps. It is here that the risk statement is created, outlining the risks related to the project. The risks that are determined to pose the greatest threats are added to a Top 10 Risk List. Like a wheel going around and around, the risks are carried through the remaining steps, and dealt with until they are resolved or become actual problems.

We'll briefly discuss each of the five steps. While we've already examined the first two steps, as part of the process that leads to the creation of risk statements and Top 10 Risk Lists, we will explore the remaining three steps in detail.

In the *identification step*, we identified a list of risks that have the potential to cause problems in a project. In the *analysis step*, the impact of the identified risks was evaluated, as were alternatives to what is causing the risk. The risk statement and Top 10 Risk List created from these first two steps are then carried through the remaining steps of the risk management process.

The third step of the risk management process is *risk action planning*. In this step, the data that's been collected is transformed into meaningful information, which is used to generate strategies to deal with the risk.

The fourth step in this process is *tracking*. Just because strategies have been developed, doesn't necessarily mean that they will work. As such, it is important that the status of risks is monitored, as are the actions taken to prevent loss.

The final step is *control*. This step requires the team to control risk action plans, correct the plan if necessary, and make improvements to the risk management process. It involves reacting to indications that a plan is failing, setting a backup plan into action, or determining that the team must go back to previous steps in the process and implement new strategies.

In using proactive risk management, you don't go through the various steps and quit at step five. The process of proactive risk management requires risks to be assessed continuously, throughout the life of a project. These assessments are used for decision-making in every phase of a project. Risks are carried forward from one phase to the next, and dealt with until they are resolved or become actual problems. When they become a problem, they are then handled with reactive risk management.

Risk Action Planning

The third step of the risk management process is *risk action planning*. This takes the information gathered in the previous steps, and transforms it into decisions and actions. Up until now, risks have been identified and analyzed to determine which ones will be dealt with, and the level of threat they present. It is here that risks actually begin to be dealt with, and a plan is created to deal with them. Risks are addressed individually, and actions are developed to deal with them. Once developed, the risk actions are prioritized so that the most vital ones are addressed first. Finally, they are integrated into a risk management plan.

By addressing four key areas, the team can decide how the risk will be dealt with. These four areas are the core of risk action planning:

- Research
- Acceptance
- Management
- Avoidance

Each of these areas represents a method that determines what action will be taken on a particular risk.

Research is performed when there isn't enough information currently available. This route of action is taken when there is a need to further study a risk or acquire more information regarding its characteristics, or other areas are lacking in sufficient information. It is important to always consider whether additional analysis of a risk is required, so that the wrong action isn't taken.

With research there may be times when its advisable to hire someone to investigate the risk, determine its seriousness, and suggest further courses of action. While this isn't a regular occurrence in risk management, it does occasionally happen. Consultants are hired, or information dealing with the risk you're concerned about is available for purchase. This should be considered when the risk is highly serious. For example, if you were creating software for air traffic control, and had concerns about design problems or risks that could threaten life or property, it would be wise to research critical risks thoroughly.

Acceptance is when you're willing to live with what you've got. No further action is needed with a risk, and you are willing to accept the risk as it stands. This action should be taken only when you're comfortable with accepting the consequences of a risk should they occur, or if the risk no longer poses a significant threat.

Avoidance is the final area of risk action planning. By avoiding the risk without changing the scope, you are able to side-step the problem without affecting the overall project. For example, if you are unfamiliar or uncomfortable dealing with certain features of a software product, you could contract out that area to another reputable firm. If you were having a problem with facilities not being ready, you could arrange for other facilities that will be ready for when the project starts. By avoiding the problem, you are removing risks that threaten the project, without changing the project itself.

Management refers to determining if the team can do anything to lessen the risk's impact should it actually occur. There are three goals to risk management:

- Reduce the probability that the risk will actually occur.
- Reduce the extent or magnitude of loss that could result from the risk.
- Change the consequences associated with the risk.

Achieving the goals of managing risks involves creating and implementing strategies and contingency plans to deal with the problem. This often involves using some creativity in finding solutions to individual risks.

In managing specific risks, there are a number of strategies available. While entire books have been written on managing and resolving the risks of software projects, a few common ones are reviewed here.

When luck, the budget, and upper management are with you, you can reduce risks be putting more resources into the project. If there is a risk that the schedule won't be met, you can hire more people, and get more desks, chairs, and computers into the office space. Unfortunately, this may not be feasible in some projects if the budget is tight.

In cases where the risk is out of the team's control or can't be resolved, a workaround should be found to reduce risks. If the program has a bug that can't be resolved by a certain date, let upper management and marketing know about it. If the schedule isn't changed to allow the bug to be fixed, then information about the risk, its consequences, and a workaround can then be supplied to the customer and end user. This keeps everyone outside the project team from being surprised when the problem occurs. After release, a bug fix or patch for the problem can be released, and/or it can be resolved in the next version of the program.

Sometimes you can transfer the risk. In some cases, it is possible to move the risk from one area of a project to another, which thereby minimizes the risk. For example, if it is risky having a software feature in one part of the system, move it to another part that is better able to handle it. Moving the feature from the client executable to a separate component or the server part of the program can do this. If you are unfamiliar or uncomfortable with an activity in a project, you can transfer the risk by subcontracting part of the project to someone with more experience. For example, if there is a feature of a program that works with an Oracle database, and no one on your team knows anything about Oracle, this is a candidate for subcontracted work. While there are risks involved with contracting work out, the risks involved are less than those of allowing unqualified people to perform work they know little or nothing about.

When dealing with risks that are hardware-related, you may want to consider moving to different hardware. This strategy is often raised when dealing with system requirements, or graphic-intensive designs or images. For example, if your project requires that graphics or animations are created and added to the product, you may want to consider adding a few computers devoted to graphics production. The other time you'll generally want to change hardware is when software upgrades require it. This means upgrading or replacing the hardware to support updated software. For example, if you planned to program with Visual Basic 6.0, and most of the computers were 386s, you would need to upgrade to—or replace the hardware with—Pentium equipment.

Because nothing is perfect, you can't expect your plan of action to be foolproof, either. As such, it is important to have a contingency plan to fall back on. This alternative strategy goes into action when all efforts to manage the risk and avoid a problem fail. As an example of a contingency plan, let's say your team has office space reserved until January 2, when the project is complete. There is a risk that your team won't be finished by this date, and able to vacate the facilities on that date. To deal with this risk, you plan to negotiate with the team who will take over the offices, so they won't bump you out of there. As a contingency plan, you will arrange other office space to be used temporarily, until the project is complete. If all goes well, the contingency plan isn't used, but it exists should the original action plan fail.

When creating a contingency plan, it is important to agree on what will trigger the second plan, and deem the first a failure. In the case of our previous example, you don't want to wait until people get back to work the day after New Year's! It would be better to discuss the situation before people go on vacation, and the second plan still has time to be implemented. If time isn't an issue, then you would use values such as a dollar amount (for budget and cost risks) or a condition (such as strikes in a company you're expecting deliveries from). Whatever you choose, it is important to decide on it at the time the contingency plan is incorporated into the project. If you wait until you're suffering panic attacks, and the second plan should have already been activated, there was no point in even creating a contingency plan.

It is important to document all of this information so that you can refer to it throughout the project and use it in later steps in the risk management process. The following information that should appear on a risk action form:

- Risk identifier
- Risk statement
- Risk management strategy
- Risk management strategy metrics

■ Action items

■ Due dates

■ Personnel assignments

■ Risk contingency strategy

■ Risk contingency metrics and trigger values

A *risk identifier* is used for reporting and tracking purposes, and uniquely identifies the risk action form. It can be a number, alphanumeric filing code, or a name, but must be unique so that it can't be confused with other forms. If you have developed an automated risk action form, such as a database program with Access or Visual Basic, the risk identifier could be nothing more than a record number.

The *risk statement* is part of the analysis step in the risk management process. However, it is important that a risk statement appear on or with the risk action form. The risk statement describes the condition that could result in loss, and explains the consequences of what might occur if the risk became an actual problem. A risk statement on the risk action form could reiterate this information, state the risk identifier of the risk statement form, or have a copy of the risk statement form attached. To keep team members and stakeholders from having to flip through too many pages, though, it is often better to provide a paragraph or two on this information, and mention the risk identifier on the risk statement form. This provides a summary of what's involved, while allowing members and stakeholders the opportunity to refer to the original risk statement form.

Since this form details the strategy to be used in dealing with a particular risk, it would be remiss not to mention it! The *risk management strategy* provides a paragraph or more detailing the strategy to be used for managing the risk. This should also include any assumptions or observations that have been made about the strategy. The risk management strategy metrics provide the measurement to be used to ensure that the planned actions are working. To understand what metrics are, let's look at your strategy of studying to become an MCSD. You are probably using metrics of your own to gauge how things are going, such as how well you're doing on the questions at the end of each chapter. When dealing with risk management strategy metrics, you would use such things as a cutoff point for time or money spent dealing with a risk or a particular occurrence.

Action items detail the duties and actions to be performed in managing the risk. Basically, they outline what is to be done (as part of the strategy) to ensure the risk doesn't result in loss. Along with these action items are *due dates*, which show when certain actions are to be completed. *Personnel assignments* also appear on the risk action form, to show who is assigned to perform these action items. This allows team members to know, in writing, what their risk management duties are, when they are to be completed by, and who is responsible for doing what.

Finally, the *risk contingency plan* is included in the risk action form. This shows what the team strategy will be should the original plan fail. It consists of a paragraph or more describing what will be done if the risk contingency strategy trigger values are reached. These figures are also included on the form, and are used for determining when this fallback plan is put into action. Risk contingency strategy metrics also appear on the risk action form with these figures, to show whether the contingency plan is working. If it is not, the members will need to go back to the drawing board, and go through the previous steps to deal with the risk.

on the job

While each project has its own risks, you can use risk action plans and other documents from previous projects. It is advisable to keep these forms after a project concludes, by storing them in a binder or database. When storing them, note whether certain plans were successful or failed, and (if possible) why. When you go into other projects, you can then refer to these plans and forms. By remembering that you experienced a similar risk, and referring to these documents, you can learn from failed plans and use successful ones in your current project!

Risk Tracking and Control

Unfortunately, once an action plan has been implemented, you can't just sit back and let it take care of the risk unattended. Once the plan has been put into action, it needs to be monitored, and occasionally intervention is required. This is where the last two steps of proactive risk management come into play.

The fourth step in the risk management process is *risk tracking*. This takes place once an action plan has been put into play, and is where the team monitors the status of risks and the actions implemented to manage them. Risk tracking watches events unfolding as a result of the action plan, and monitors the risk metrics and triggers that determine whether the plan is successful or not.

Part of risk tracking involves updates and assessments of the Top 10 Risk List. This list provides a run-down of the most critical risks in a project, and ranks them from the highest possibility of loss (number 1 on the list) to the lowest (number 10). By reviewing this list on a weekly basis, you will be able to see if certain risks have gone down or up in rank. At the very least, this list should be evaluated monthly or when a milestone has been reached. An example of a Top 10 Risk List is shown in the following table. While an initial Top 10 Risk List will simply have ten items ranked from highest to lowest, tracking uses the list to show an item's previous ranking and its current ranking. This allows the team to see where risks are being dealt with successfully, and which risks are getting worse and may need serious re-evaluation.

Risk	Progress	This Week	Last Week	Weeks on List	Number of Times in Top 10 List
Development tools are delivered late.	Two of three updated tools have been delivered.	1	3	5	2
Redesign is required.	Redesign is proceeding at a good pace.	2	6	7	1

on the
()ob

One of the mistakes people make in risk management is monitoring the effects of risk action plans only after the project has been completed, and do little or no monitoring while the project is still running. This does allow you to see how a plan worked over the course of the entire project, but isn't really risk management. It keeps you from actually seeing how a plan is working at the time, when you can do something to keep a risk from resulting in loss. This postmortem approach is useful when evaluating an action plan as a whole, but don't do it instead of regular risk tracking.

The risks listed in the initial Top 10 Risk List may disappear completely from the listing. When an action plan works incredibly well, or the risk itself is eliminated, then other risks will be moved into the Top 10, as original ones are dropped from the list.

In creating a Top 10 Risk List, it is advisable to keep track of the number of times a risk has appeared in the Top 10. If its ranking has fluctuated repeatedly, and appeared in the listing numerous times, then it could be an indication that the action plan isn't working as well as it could. In such a case, you should look at why the risk is doing this. If progress isn't working as well as it should, or certain action items are bumping the risk up in the ranking, then personnel assignments or other areas of the action plan may need adjustment.

Another tool of risk tracking is *risk status reports*, which are used to identify four possible situations:

- A risk is resolved, and the risk action plan is completed.
- Risk actions are tracking the risk management plan.
- Risk actions are not tracking the risk management plan.
- Situation has changed.

When risk actions are tracking the risk management plan, it means that your risk action plan is following its proper course. If this is the situation, then you should let risk actions continue as planned, and leave well enough alone (unless something changes). If the risk actions aren't tracking the risk management plan, then changes need to be made to the risk actions or risk action plan. This means you must determine where things have gone awry in your plan, and how things can be corrected. When the situation dealing with one or more risks has changed, it means that the risks may need reassessment, or the activity needs to be re-planned.

The final step of the proactive risk management process is *risk control.* This involves responding to triggers that indicate a plan is failing or has failed, making corrections in the initial risk action plan, and making improvements to the process of risk management. The work done in this step can include informing someone that they are not following a plan, or performing action items, or revamping existing actions or plans so they work properly.

It is important to remember that no matter how good your plans are, or how well things *should* work, success in risk management always falls on how well people perform in risk management. If your team is halfhearted or doesn't care enough about performing their duties in managing risks, the risk action process will always fail. Some companies have actually found it beneficial to use a risk officer on projects. This is either a person in an existing team role (other than product manager, as it can be a conflict of duty) or a person hired in the job of finding and managing risks. This person points out the risks involved in a project, points out where things are going wrong and where the project may fail, and handles all the work of documentation. If problems with risk management traditionally pop up on projects in your organization, this may be an option to consider.

QUESTIONS AND ANSWERS

What is risk?	Risk is the possibility of suffering some sort of loss, and is inherent to any project.
I made a list of risk sources and risks during the last project I worked on. Can I just apply this list to the next project I'm working on?	No. Risk sources and risks need to be identified and dealt with on an independent basis. What may be a major risk source or risk on one project may not be of great issue on other projects. It is better to use the existing list as a reference, to see if risks experienced in other projects are appearing here. This helps you remember certain risks, but should not be used as a listing of risks that is passed from one project to another.
What is the difference between proactive risk management and reactive risk management?	Proactive risk management addresses risks before they result in loss. Reactive risk management is used when, or waits until, the risk becomes an actual problem. When this occurs, the consequences of the risk are dealt with.
How do I find what the risk exposure will be for a particular risk?	Multiply the risk impact (size of loss) by the risk potential (potential of loss). The answer will give you the risk exposure for that particular risk.

CERTIFICATION SUMMARY

Risk is the possibility of a loss. To increase your odds that risks don't result in a loss of some sort, risk management is used. Risk management involves identifying, addressing, and possibly eliminating the sources of risk. It is an environment and discipline of proactive decisions and actions.

Risks are inherent to any project, and it is important to identify risk sources and their associated risks so they can be dealt with accordingly. There is no standard set of risk sources on a project, so what may be a major risk source on one project may not be an issue on other projects. As such, you need to identify and analyze the risk sources for each individual project.

Proactive risk management involves five steps that work together in dealing with risks before they result in loss. These steps consist of identification, analysis, risk action planning, tracking, and control. Together they deal with risks before they become an actual problem.

✓ TWO-MINUTE DRILL

- ❑ *Risk* is the possibility of suffering some sort of loss, and it is inherent to any project.

- ❑ In Microsoft's definition, *risk management* is a "discipline and environment of proactive decisions and actions to assess continuously what can go wrong, determine what risks are important to deal with, and implement strategies to deal with those risks."

- ❑ A risk source is made up of three components: risk factor category, focus area, and risk factor.

- ❑ *Proactive risk management* deals with risks before they become problems that result in loss. *Reactive risk management* deals with risks after they've occurred.

- ❑ *Risk statements* are used to communicate the risks involved in a project, so that members can effectively manage them.

- ❑ *Risk identification* results in a list of risks that have the potential to cause problems in a project.

- ❑ *Risk analysis* evaluates the impact of the identified risks and considers alternatives to factors causing the risk.

- ❑ *Risk probability* is the likelihood of events occurring, while *risk impact* is the amount of loss that could result.

- ❑ There are three goals to risk management: reduce the probability that the risk will actually occur; reduce the extent or magnitude of loss that could result from the risk, and change the consequences associated with the risk.

- ❑ A *risk identifier* is used for reporting and tracking purposes, and uniquely identifies the risk action form.

- ❑ *Action items* detail the duties and actions to be performed in managing the risk.

Answers to Exercise 3-1

Items 1, 2, 3, 5, 8, 9, 10, 11, and 12 should be considered risks to the project. (Items 4, 6, and 7 pose no risk.)

Answers to Exercise 3-2

The risk assessment table that you create will reflect your analysis of the project details. Here is one possible interpretation:

Risk	Probability of Loss	Size of Loss	Risk Exposure
Team won't meet deadline.	75 percent	$5,000	$3,750
Expense Reimbursement Form design is late.	50 percent	2 weeks	0.43 week
Computer is delivered late.	30 percent	3 weeks	I week
Payroll Department staff are slow computer learners.	25 percent	2 weeks	.21 weeks
Developers may be slow learning Visual Basic.	50 percent	4 weeks	0.43 weeks

SELF TEST

The Self Test questions will help you measure your understanding of the material presented in this chapter. Read all the choices carefully, as there may be more than one correct answer. Select all correct answers for each question.

1. A risk has a risk probability of 100 percent. What does this mean?

   A. The success of the project is ensured.

   B. There is no risk, or chance of a problem occurring.

   C. The risk has already become an actual problem.

   D. The failure of the project is ensured.

2. Part of a project has been contracted out to a small software company. The developers at this firm were on strike for two weeks, causing work to fall behind by this amount of time. The owner of the firm tells you he's sorry, and that this strike has cost his software firm $5000 in business. What is the risk impact to your project?

   A. Two weeks

   B. $5000

   C. There is no risk impact. This impacts the contractor, not you.

   D. One week

3. What are the four key areas of risk action planning?

   A. Research, Acceptance, Management, Avoidance

   B. Research, Management, Transfer, Avoidance

   C. Identify, Assess, Action, Track, Control

   D. Assess, Research, Management, Avoidance

4. Which step in the risk management process results in the generation of a risk action form?

   A. Identification

   B. Risk analysis

   C. Risk control

   D. Risk tracking

   E. None of the above

5. Which step in the risk management process is the first time a Top 10 Risk List is generated?

   A. Identification

   B. Risk analysis

   C. Risk control

   D. Risk tracking

   E. None of the above

6. Which of the following represents the amount of loss that would occur if a risk became an actual problem?

   A. Risk category

   B. Risk impact

C. Risk exposure

D. Risk identifier

7. Which of the following deals with risks before they result in loss, or become actual problems?

   A. Reactive risk management

   B. Proactive risk management

   C. Preliminary risk management

   D. All forms of risk management

8. Which of the following is best defined as the overall threat to a project?

   A. Risk

   B. Risk context

   C. Risk exposure

   D. Risk probability

9. Which of the following must be included in a risk statement?

   A. The risk or risks that may be an issue to the project

   B. The source of a risk

   C. The expected consequence

   D. Risk control measures

   E. Crisis management issues

10. Which of the following best describes a risk?

   A. The certainty of loss

   B. The certainty that a problem will result

   C. The possibility of loss

D. An object, person, or structure that provides the certainty of loss

11. You are using a risk assessment table, shown next. What is the risk exposure of the project?

Risk	Probability of Loss	Size of Loss (Weeks)	Risk Exposure (Weeks)
Redesign required due to inadequate design.	20 percent	5	

   A. 20 percent

   B. 5

   C. .04

   D. 4 percent

   E. 1

12. Which of the following is not a goal of risk management?

   A. Reduce the probability that the risk will actually occur.

   B. Keep the consequences associated with a risk constant.

   C. Reduce the extent or magnitude of loss that could result from the risk.

   D. Change the consequences associated with the risk

13. Which of the following specifies the focus area, risk factor category, and risk factor?

   A. Risk probability

B. Risk source

C. Risk context

D. Risk consequence

14. Which of the following would contain a contingency plan to deal with a risk?

    A. Risk statement

    B. Risk action plan

    C. Top 10 Risk List

    D. Risk status report

15. Delays in one area have a cascading effect on other areas. It results in tasks not being completed on time. Which of the following risk categories is this most directly linked to?

    A. Budget and cost

    B. Schedule

    C. Action planning

    D. Risk management

16. Below is part of a table used in risk management. What is it an example of?

Risk	Probability of Loss	Size of Loss (Weeks)	Risk Exposure (Weeks)
Design is inadequate —needs reworking.	25 percent	8	2
Schedule is overly optimistic.	50 percent	2	1

    A. Risk assessment table

    B. Risk factor chart

    C. Top 10 Risk List

    D. Risk statement

17. Which of the following detail the duties and actions to be performed in managing the risk?

    A. Due dates

    B. Personnel assignments

    C. Action items

    D. Risk sources

18. You are filling out a risk statement form and reach an area that asks for the risk consequence. What information will you enter in this area?

    A. A description of the loss that will occur, or results of the risk if it becomes an actual problem

    B. A description of the consequences expected if the suggested action plan succeeds

    C. A description of how managing this risk will affect the schedule of the project

    D. A description of the alternative action plan

19. Which of the following best describes risk probability?

    A. It represents the likelihood that a loss will occur.

    B. It represents the certainty that a loss will occur.

    C. It represents that a loss has already occurred.

    D. It is calculated by multiplying risk exposure by risk impact.

20. When creating risk action plans, you have decided that no further action is necessary for a particular risk. What key area of risk action planning does this decision fall into?

    A. Research

    B. Acceptance

    C. Management

    D. Avoidance

4

Software Development Track Milestones

F or software development projects, the Process model is an invaluable tool for good project planning. This model is used to assist in planning and managing projects, and acting like a roadmap, it shows the activities that take place in a solution's life cycle. Starting with the conception of the solution, and going step-by-step through the development cycle to its release, the Process model allows members of the team to synchronize their efforts and see progress in a project by the activities that have been completed.

The Process Model

As we saw in Chapter 2, the Process model breaks a project up into four phases, with each *phase* culminating in a *milestone*. Milestones mark the point where one phase of the project ends and another begins, and indicate a point in the project where team members should synchronize their efforts. Milestones are customer oriented, and are used by team members to see if the project is still meeting customer expectations. This allows them to deal with changes required in a project, and assess the risks that will be associated with those changes.

In using the Process model, it's important to distinguish between project phases and project milestones. Each phase of the Process model is where the work is performed to achieve the milestone. People in the different team roles perform various tasks, working to reach the milestone at the end of each phase. These phases, and their associated milestones, are listed here:

- **Envisioning phase**   Results in the Vision/Scope Approved milestone.

- **Planning phase**   Results in the Project Plan Approved milestone.

- **Developing phase**   Results in the Scope Complete/First Use milestone.

- **Stabilizing phase**   Results in the Release milestone.

Through the work performed in these phases, you complete part of the overall project. The milestones at the end of these phases allow members of the project team to coordinate their efforts, and see what work has been done. It also allows them to see where they need to go forward to ensure the project's success.

The four phases of the Process model always follow the same order, starting with the Envisioning phase, and ending with the Release milestone of the Stabilizing phase. Each of the phases of the process model result in several deliverables. A *deliverable* is a tangible result of the work performed. It can be a document that outlines risks or one that lays out the features and functionality of the product, or it can be the completed product itself. This is something we'll see as this chapter progresses, and we discuss each of the four phases and their related milestones individually.

CERTIFICATION OBJECTIVE 4.01

The Vision/Scope Approved Milestone

The first part of any well-planned journey involves determining where you're going. That's what the Envisioning phase of the process model accomplishes. The design of any application is driven by the needs of the user, and this is what the envisioning stage works to understand. Tasks performed during this phase of the process model are geared toward determining what the project entails. The team looks at what issues are driving the need for the product or service, and what features should be incorporated to address future needs. This phase not only identifies the present needs of the organization, but attempts to predict future needs while allowing for growth. In doing so, an understanding of the customer's needs, and the issues surrounding those needs, is attained.

The Envisioning phase uses a proactive approach to determining what features should be included in a product. By spending some time to project where the organization may wish to expand their services, the team has a better understanding of whether to include certain capabilities in the project, thus likely saving money and time in the future. Through the use of versioned releases of the product, each of the current and future needs of the organization can be addressed. Though certain functionality may not appear in the current version of the product, it can be included in future versions.

Once both the customer and team achieve a shared understanding of what's expected from the application, the Envisioning phase reaches its major milestone: the Vision/Scope Approved milestone. It occurs when an agreement is made between the customer and team on the direction the project will take. As we'll see in the sections that follow, a considerable amount of work goes into reaching this milestone, which results in several deliverables. The information gathered during this phase, the work performed by the team, and the deliverables produced, are used by the team in other phases of the Process model.

Achieving Shared Vision for a Project Team

Calling this first phase of the Process model the Envisioning phase captures the goal of this first stage of software development. The Envisioning phase strives to achieve a shared vision for the project team. *Vision* is an unbridled view of a project's goals, with no consideration given to the constraints of a project. Vision looks at the project from the perspective of the business and user, and focuses on what elements these parties find desirable and what should be added to the project.

With vision, the constraints of a project aren't an issue. When you consider that any application is bound by technical constraints of operating systems, network configurations, and so forth, this may see strange. Any software development project is also restricted by the constraints of time, money, and available resources that affect how and when the project will be undertaken. However, these all hinder the imagination of team members and stakeholders. Vision doesn't acknowledge such constraints, because to do so would be a stumbling block to any of the exciting ideas that interested parties might have. You want people to have the utmost creative freedom at this point. Introducing constraints at this point only stifles people's creativity, and blurs the vision of what the project could be.

This isn't to say that the constraints mentioned aren't considered in the design of your product. That is where scope comes into play. *Scope* is a narrowing of vision that maps the vision of a product against technology and project constraints. Vision is a dream of what your application could become, and scope is a detailed analysis of that dream that defines whether certain aspects of the dream can become reality. Scope looks at whether features can be included in a current version—based on scheduling, cost, the availability of resources, and other issues—and determines if certain features must be put off for now, and included in future versions of the product. It defines the limitations of a product or service, and determines what can be done within the project's constraints. It balances optimism with realism, looking at what the customer needs and what can actually be done to fulfill those needs.

Through a balancing of vision and scope, a clear understanding of what the project entails is achieved. As we'll see later in this chapter, this shared vision is outlined in a vision/scope document. The *vision/scope document* is a documentation of this shared vision, and specifies the direction and goals for a project.

Team Focus

In Chapter 2 we discussed the different roles that make up the MSF Team model. In performing the various activities associated with the Envisioning phase, team members in these roles focus on different tasks to ensure the success of this phase of the project. This means that each team member brings a level of competence to a specific area of the project. The work done successfully in one area of the project complements the work done in other areas to ensure the success of the project as a whole.

In the Team model, the team leaders are entrusted with supervising, guiding, and coordinating the teams. Team members have clearly defined roles, which allow them to focus on specific areas of the project. At each phase of the process model, one of the team model's roles is accountable for planning, managing, and executing the tasks associated with a particular milestone. They "own" the responsibility of ensuring that the team achieves a milestone.

In the Envisioning phase, it is the responsibility of Product Management to see that the team achieves the Vision/Scope Approved milestone. This role is responsible for identifying user needs, the business problem, expected benefits of a solution, project vision, and the risks associated with the project. These are documented in the vision statement, which Product Management is responsible for creating and maintaining. In managing the expectations of a product, Product Management ensures that expectations are clearly communicated to both the project team and the customer. This allows both customer and project team to have a shared vision of what the project entails.

Program Management is responsible for setting project design goals. In doing so, this role establishes what factors will determine the project's success, and what metrics will be used to measure this success. Program Management is also responsible for documenting the solution, researching the existing infrastructure that will be used with the product, and chronicling the success factors and metrics. This allows the team to see how well they are doing on the project, and initial specifications that will be used in the product.

During this phase, Development assists Program Management with documenting the solution. This role also researches existing solutions. This allows the team to determine if there are applications already available that provide the features and functionality that the customer requires. In doing so, a decision can be made to use and/or purchase an off-the-shelf solution rather than developing a solution that does the exact same thing or to design the new application to work with existing applications.

User Education determines training requirements for users of the solution. In doing so, this role identifies and establishes communication channels that can practically be used to advise and inform users of the application. In addition to users, User Education also determines any necessary training requirements for project team members. If a new language must be learned by Development, or other team members require some other upgrading in education, it is up to User Education to ensure that training is available and provided.

Although there is no actual solution to test at this point, Testing must begin work on developing a testing process that will be implemented at a later stage. This role is responsible for developing the test criteria based on the design goals of the project. It determines the frequency and process of testing, logs risks, and risk rates, and establishes a mechanism for feedback on the solution.

Logistics has the task of identifying any possible constraints that may affect the project. Team members in this role must research and report on constraints, inclusive to materials that may or may not be available for the project. Logistics also identifies any shipping and delivery issues that may arise. Through the work performed by Logistics, a foundation is set for long-term management and support.

Defining the Vision/Scope Approved Milestone

The Vision/Scope Approved milestone occurs when the project team, customer, and stakeholders come to an agreement on key aspects of the project. This includes such elements as the vision and scope of the project, and the priority of which business requirements need to be addressed first. The team, customer, and stakeholders come to an understanding of how the solution will solve the organization's business requirements. Business constraints that could affect the project are identified, discussed, and agreed upon as potential risks. Other risks and assumptions associated with the project are also addressed, as is the time frame in which the functionality of the application needs to be available. The level of work needed in the next phase of the process model is determined, setting the initial foundation for the decisions on resources that will be made in the Planning phase. When an agreement is made on such elements of the project, the Vision/Scope Approved milestone is reached, and the team moves into the Planning phase of the project.

The way that team members, customers, and stakeholders come to this agreement is with the vision/scope document, which is also called a *vision statement*. This document outlines what each of these parties is agreeing to, by providing a conceptualization of how the project will look upon completion. Essentially acting as a contract, this document establishes the project's scope and vision, and provides direction to team members. It provides an explanation of how the solution will solve the organization's business requirements. It does this by utilizing scenarios the organization may experience, explaining specific features of the product, and defining the vision and scope of the project.

By agreeing to the contents of the vision/scope document, everyone demonstrates a clear understanding of what will be created. They agree and show understanding of the work that needs to be done, what the project entails, and what the finished product will be. This establishes clear design goals, and sets the foundation for work that will be done in ensuing phases of the Process model.

Interim Milestones

While each phase of the process model has an associated milestone, this may not be enough on larger projects. Larger projects can take so long to complete that the time between each of the four milestones lessens the benefits of a milestone-based process. Rather than being able to coordinate and synchronize their efforts, members of the team can lose effectiveness because it takes so long to move from one major milestone to the next. Instead of working as a team, and having one another's work complementing each other's, they become small groups of individuals that may lose focus on what the project is really about. This is where interim milestones become a vital part of the Process model.

Interim milestones are like mini-milestones. They occur between the major milestones of the process model, and provide additional coordination points for members of the team. This allows team members to get together and discuss areas of the project. Depending on the phase the team is currently in, the formal or informal meetings arranged for interim milestones may include addressing scheduling, specifications, or other elements of the project. Each phase of the Process model has interim milestones that can be used.

The Envisioning phase of the Process model has two interim milestones associated with it. These interim milestones are the *Vision Statement Draft* and *Design Goals Draft*. A draft is a rough or preliminary copy of a final document. The design goals draft provides the team with a chance to review the design goals of the project before they're included in the vision/scope document. This allows team members to discuss what they consider the design goals of the project to be, to add new goals, and remove ones that don't meet the actual vision of the project. Similarly, the vision statement draft allows the team to discuss and analyze the business problems, which are solved by the solution, and set the focus of the project. This allows the team to boil down the issues faced by the organization, and identify the problems and features that will solve these problems. Once the issues discussed in the vision statement draft are finalized, they are included in the vision/scope document (vision statement).

Identifying the Interdependent Roles and Shared Responsibilities of Project Team Members

Earlier in this chapter, we discussed how the different roles of the Team model work together on different tasks of the Envisioning phase. Product Management has ownership of the Envisioning phase, and is responsible for seeing that the tasks associated with this phase are carried out. Each of the roles of the team model works as a group of peers, depending on one another to carry out the activities they are responsible for.

If one of the team roles fails to complete their duties, then the Envisioning phase will fail to reach the Vision/Scope Approved milestone. Program Management relies on Product Management to supply the customer requirements and set the vision for a project. Program Management works with Development to document the solution, which provides information that Logistics and Testing require to fulfill their tasks. If the team requires training—such as Development needing education on new technologies—User Education must provide that training. Though existing in different roles, with different duties, each member must work together as a team if the project is to succeed.

Describing the Deliverables to Be Produced During the Envisioning Phase

A *deliverable* is a product of work that's generated from the activities of a given phase in the process model. Unlike interim milestones, which are points of time allotted for the team to synchronize their efforts, a deliverable is a physical component that results from the work that's been done. Each of the four phases results in deliverables that are used in other phases of the process model.

The Envisioning phase results in three deliverables: the vision/scope document, the risk assessment, and the project structure document. Each of these documents provides valuable information that is used to ensure the project's success.

The vision/scope document is used to explain the project. Basically, it describes what the project entails, and answers the questions of who, what, when, where, and how things will be done. It provides the team with direction, sets expectations for the team, and describes the criteria that the team will use for the design and deployment of the finished product. The vision/scope document consists of four distinctive components. These are the problem statement/business objectives, the vision statement, user profiles, and the solution concept. Each part of the document describes or explains a different aspect of the project, and serves to aid team members in completing their individual assignments.

The first part of the vision/scope document is the problem statement/business objectives, which outlines the rationale behind the project, and describes the needs and objectives of the organization. This is used to explain why the project is being undertaken. It answers the question of what needs and problems the solution is required to meet and solve.

The vision statement component addresses the issues raised in the problem statement/business objectives segment of the document. It outlines the long-term vision of the project. In essence, the vision statement is the meat of the document in that it's what people think of when considering vision/scope documents. Therefore, vision/scope documents and vision statements are often used synonymously. The statement provides information that guides the decision-making of the project team throughout the life of the project. It is also instrumental in providing the project team with a way of evaluating the project.

User profiles provide a way for the team to understand whom they're creating the software for. In short, it describes the end user of the application. The information contained in the user profile guides the team in communicating how much change the solution will cause for the user, by allowing them to assess the expectations, risks, goals, and constraints of the project. By understanding the end user, the team has a better success rate of meeting the end user's needs.

The final component is the solution concept. This part of the document provides the groundwork for creating specifications for the solution. It details how the team will initiate the planning process, and defines the work necessary to successfully complete the project. This allows the team to establish priorities for the project, and determine what features are necessary for the current version and which features should be passed forward to future versions. The major focus of the solution concept is defining the services that will comprise the application. These services fall into one of three categories: User Services, Data Services, and Business Services. From Chapter 2 you'll remember that these services make up the MSF Application model, which we'll discuss further in future chapters of this book.

Moving away from the vision/scope document, the second deliverable of the Envisioning phase is the risk assessment. As we saw in the previous chapter, a *risk* is the possibility of incurring some sort of loss. Left unchecked, a risk could jeopardize a project's success. A risk assessment is used to determine the likelihood of a condition or situation that could adversely affect the project. This assessment identifies risks that could emerge in the project, evaluates what impact they would have on the project, and provides general provisions for monitoring such risks.

In writing a risk assessment, you would identify each individual risk in the project. This could be as simple as a paragraph on each risk. It should mention what the risk is, how it could affect the project, how it should be monitored, and what could be done to deal with it. In short, you would address the who, what, when, where, and how of the risk. By identifying and determining the level of risk, you are better able to deal with it.

The final deliverable produced during the Envisioning phase is the project structure document. This document is used to outline how the project will be managed and supported. In addition, it details the administrative structure for the project team. While we'll discuss this document in a later section of this chapter, it's important to realize that the work done on this document doesn't end in the Envisioning phase. It is passed forward and updated at the Project Plan Approved milestone, when resources have been assigned to the project.

Defining the Tasks Leading to Vision/Scope Approval

Reaching the Vision/Scope Approved milestone requires an agreement between the customer, the project team, and any other stakeholders in the project. This agreement is on several key points dealing with the project:

- The overall vision for the project
- Which business requirements should be addressed first
- Setting a time frame for the project
- Risks that are associated with the project
- Business constraints that may affect the project
- The required effort expected to complete the project.

In going through each of these points, you can see that each is a major element of the project as a whole. Without agreement on these issues, the team, customer, and other stakeholders will fail to have a shared understanding of what the project entails.

It's important to remember that the Vision/Scope Approved milestone occurs when the vision and scope of the project have been agreed upon. The points listed above must be met to move on to the next phase of the Process model. If this hasn't occurred, the milestone can't be reached, and additional work is required.

on the job

The vision and scope of a document allow everyone involved in a project—team members, customers, users, and other parties alike—to have a clear understanding of the project. This is important because it is easy for different people to have different perceptions of a project. While one party may view the project as a spreadsheet program, others may see it as more of a database application. It's important to understand what the project is, as well as the features that will and will not be included in a version. Without a clear understanding, the project is destined for failure.

Setting the Vision and Scope for a Project

It's important for a project to have the vision and scope set if the project is to be successful. Vision is the perceptions of customers, users, team members, and other stakeholders of what the project will be. It allows for creativity, without being burdened by constraints or preconceived limitations. Scope narrows the focus of the project, by mapping the vision to realistic constraints and requirements. It is necessary to do this so you can achieve the vision of the project, without having to trash it as a pipe dream. By properly setting the vision and scope of the project, you can have a clear focus of what the project will be.

The Envisioning phase of the Process model not only allows the team to focus on the needs of the customer, but also has a focus on the team itself. There is a symbiotic relationship between the customer who buys the product, the user who uses it, and the team that develops it. Neither can do without the other, and none can ignore the others' importance to the project. A shared vision of what the project entails helps to enforce this relationship, as everyone is working toward a common and well-understood goal.

Once the team has a clear vision of what the organization and users prefer, desire, and need from a project, they are better able to commit to the project. The team members can feel that they're part of something, and see what they're working toward. This motivation translates into higher productivity on the part of each team member, and allows the team to feel they're working together toward a common goal.

The thoughts and ideas of each team member, the customer, business, and end user are given careful examination. This allows members to feel that their input is worthy, and not dismissed out of turn. Communication is a key factor. Allowing team members and stakeholders to openly discuss elements and ideas of the project means that the project has addressed the concerns of everyone concerned.

Communicating this vision of a project to other team members requires a combination of verbal and visual components. As we'll see later, a vision statement is used to outline the elements that make up the project in a clear and concise manner. Images, diagrams, and so forth can be created to illustrate how a feature or function should work in the product. You can also use existing applications that have similar features to elaborate how a certain feature or functionality in the application will work. Metaphors can be used to translate a feature or functionality in the project in a way that conveys a common image. You've probably used metaphors without even realizing it. A file or folder in Microsoft Windows is a metaphor for a binary unit or area or storage, but by using a commonly used metaphor to communicate its functionality, everyone can picture what the file or folder is and does. In Chapter 11, we'll discuss metaphors in greater detail. It's important to have clear communication among members of the team, so that they know what they're working toward, and can then determine how to get that work done.

Throughout the process of acquiring a shared vision of the product, it's important to keep one thing in mind: the business. Always remember that you're working to improve the productivity and answer some need that the organization has. While a feature or capability may be interesting to include in the software, it's useless if it doesn't actually serve the customer or end user. The components that make up your solution should always be practical for the organization and end users.

Writing the Vision/Scope Document

The vision/scope document is made up of several parts, which together map out what the project entails. These components of the document consist of the problem statement/business objectives, the vision statement, user profiles, and the solution concept. While we'll go through each of these parts of the document individually in this section, they shouldn't be thought of as individual deliverables of the Envisioning phase. Like chapters making up a book, these components make up the vision/scope document. Together, they provide the team with direction on what is necessary in the project. It explains who will use the solution, the expectations of the customer and end user, and the criteria that will be applied to designing, developing, and deploying the product.

The first part of the vision/scope document is the problem statement/ business objectives. In writing this component of the document, you're explaining the motivation and rationale behind the project. In short, you're explaining why the project is necessary. What business problem will the solution address? What does the organization hope to accomplish with this application? These are the fundamental questions answered by the problem statement/business objectives portion of the vision/scope document. By defining the problem and stating the objectives addressed with the solution, you can create a product that can directly address these issues.

Product Management acquires information that goes into the problem statement/business objectives through a variety of methods. Interviews can be conducted with customers and end users, as well as senior management— technology and business architects, steering committees, etc.—or IT professionals and sponsors in the organization. These are the people who will benefit from a good solution, and can provide valuable information on the needs and problems faced in the organization. In addition to these individuals, researching documents within the company can provide valuable information on the business's objectives and problems. Such documents include contracts and commitment documents, such as presentations, proposals, and cost justifications. The availability of such documents depends on the security of the organization. Certain military and corporate clients may be unwilling to divulge such information, for fear that it will leak out into the public. You need to be aware that the avenues available in researching for the problem statement/ business objectives portion will vary from organization to organization.

The vision statement portion of a vision/scope document defines the perception or understanding of the project. This is the long-term vision of the product, which will follow the software throughout its development cycle. It defines what the product consists of. This not only establishes what features are to be included in the product, but what features will be left out. It allows the team, customer, and end user to agree on whether certain aspects of the project should be passed forward to future versions.

Setting the features to be included in a product is an important point in design, as issues such as scheduling and budget can affect the vision of the product. This vision of what the project entails needs to be set early in the design of the application. It can be demoralizing for a team to expect to create an incredible product—based on what's included in the vision statement—only to have the vision change part way through the project. This can occur because the organization needs the product sooner than expected, or due to other issues not expected or considered during the Envisioning phase.

The contents of the vision statement aid the team in making decisions throughout the life of the product. The team can look at the vision statement of the product, and determine whether features or functionality meet the set vision of the product. It can help them evaluate their options, by allowing them to view what was originally envisioned as the finished product.

User profiles are a depiction of the user or group who will use the new solution. They identify who will be the users of the solution. As we'll see in greater detail in Chapter 9, user profiles allow the team to see from whom the requirements and information on the project is being obtained. Each department, unit, end user, and the business itself may have their own individual needs and goals on a project. User profiles outline the specifics of these users—such as the number of people in a department, geographical locations, and so forth—and allow the team to see if the needs and goals of certain users conflict or agree with one another. It also aids them in gauging the level of change the solution will have on these users. By knowing whom you're creating the solution for, you have a better chance of that solution being successful.

As we'll see in Chapter 9, the information gathered for the user profiles can come from a variety of sources. These include Joint Application Design (JAD) sessions, interviews with individual users, and surveys. When used with usage scenarios, which detail how a certain activity or task is performed, user profiles can be a valuable resource in understanding your solution's target audience.

The final portion of the vision/scope document is the solution concept. This part of the document details how the team will initiate the planning process and do the groundwork necessary for successful completion of the project. It includes elements such as the following:

- Project success factors
- A list of deliverables
- Operational concept
- Acceptance criteria for the project

Together, these elements provide the team with a means of establishing priorities, and setting the groundwork for tasks performed in the next phase of the Process model.

Project success factors are used to determine what will make the project successful. There are many different elements that can be used to determine this, inclusive of certain features or functionality in the program, time, monetary factors, comparisons, and so forth. What your team includes as factors will be used later to measure the success or failure of the project.

A list of deliverables is included in the solution concept portion to show what the project will produce. You'll remember that a deliverable is a tangible result of work performed. The listing of deliverables for the project shows what will make the product operational.

The *operational concept* is a conceptual documentation of how the solution will be implemented, and how users will use the new product. Basically, it is a rundown of what the solution will do, how it is used, and how it fits into the existing system. It also shows an understanding of the organization, department, or end user's workflow.

The *acceptance criteria* is used to show what is necessary in the project. If a project is to be considered acceptable, certain elements of the project must be satisfied before the product goes into production. A checklist of requirements is created. When a requirement is fulfilled, that particular element is checked off.

A major focus of the solution concept is on each of the types of services that comprise the application. These include User Services, Business Services, and Data Services. As mentioned earlier, these were discussed in Chapter 2, and make up MSF's Application model. It is important to determine where elements of your application will reside early in design, as this can affect the performance of an application. In future chapters of this book, we'll discuss each of the services in greater detail, and show how important it is to put the proper coding into the appropriate service.

Determining the Project Structure

As its name implies, the *project structure document* is used to outline the structure of the project. This includes information such as the following:

- How the project will be managed and supported
- The administrative structure of the project team
- Other information that may be helpful to the project team

The project structure document is a vital information tool that is passed forward to the Planning phase of the Process model. Upon reaching the milestone of this next phase of the Process model, the document is updated to reflect resource assignments to the project. Information included in the document at this point sets the foundation for future work.

The project structure document contains guidelines that can be used to manage and provide support for the project. This allows the team to understand how the project will be handled, and aids them when experiencing problems with the project. Through these guidelines, the project has a better chance of success, because management and support issues are handled early in the process.

Also included in the project structure document is an outline of the administrative structure of the team. This structure shows team leadership and whom the team reports to in the organization. This keeps team members from having to wonder and stumble around seeking approval on elements of the project, by allowing them to know the exact administrative structure of the project.

Additional information may also be included in the project structure document, which can assist team members throughout the project. This may include such things as e-mail addresses, telephone numbers, server and directory information, and any other information that may be helpful to the project team. This allows the team to quickly find other members of the team, and which members are in certain roles of the Team model. Through this information, the team can function much more effectively.

FROM THE CLASSROOM

The Software Development Process Model

The Process model is one of the most clearly defined models included in Microsoft's Solutions Development Discipline course.

It is used in both the Software Development and Enterprise Architecture Development processes. Since both activities use the Process model, complete with their own set of interim milestones and deliverables, it is very important to keep these independent sets of items distinct. Confusing them, for purposes of the exam, can result in extreme difficulties in sorting out the details of responsibility.

One of the more difficult aspects of understanding the Process model involves keeping track of the tasks performed by each role during each individual phase—specifically, those tasks performed by the Product and Program Management teams.

Be sure to memorize the interim milestones, the deliverables, and the relationship between the two. For each interim milestone, certain deliverables are considered necessary for completion of the interim milestone.

—*Michael Lane Thomas, MCSE+I, MCSD, MCT, MCP+SB, MSS, A+*

on the **Job**

It's not uncommon for much of the information in the project structure document to be posted to a Web page on the corporate intranet. A page with hyperlinks to e-mail addresses, locations of team members, and other information can prove beneficial to the team.

EXERCISE 4-1

Identifying Deliverables in the Envisioning Phase

For each description, identify the deliverable. (The answers to this exercise appear just before the Self Test at the end of the chapter.)

1. This component of a deliverable outlines the needs and objectives of the organization.

2. The issues raised in the problem statement are contained in this portion of the deliverable. This part also outlines the long-term vision of the project.

3. This portion of the same deliverable describes the end user of the application.

4. The final part of this deliverable provides the groundwork for creating specifications for the solution and defines the services that will comprise the application.

5. This deliverable defines the possibility of incurring loss by the organization as a result of the final application or the development process.

6. The final deliverable outlines how the project will be managed and supported.

CERTIFICATION OBJECTIVE 4.02

The Project Plan Approved Milestone

The Planning phase of the Process model culminates in the Project Plan Approved milestone. It is during this phase of the Process model that the team and the customer agree on what will result from the project, and how to proceed with development. Priorities and expectations for the project are set, and an agreement is made on what will be delivered, and how the product will be built.

This is similar to the Envisioning phase. The Planning phase takes the work done in the previous phase, and expands on it. During the Planning phase, risks involved in the project are reassessed, estimates for schedules and resources are made, and the expectations and requirements are applied to create a functional specification and project plan. As we'll see, the functional specification, project plan, and schedules are passed forward to the third phase of the Process model, which is the Developing phase.

Defining the Project Plan Approved Milestone

The Project Plan Approved milestone occurs when the work done in the Planning phase has been completed and approved by the customer. During this phase, resources are assigned to the project, and work from the previous phase is built upon. This work results in four deliverables:

- **Functional specification**   Describes the purpose of the product, and acts as a blueprint for the solution.

- **Risk assessment**   Updates the risk assessment document produced in the preceding phase.

- **Project schedule**   Provides an estimated timeline for each team; created by each of the six team roles making up the Team model.

- **Project plan**   Shows how each team will approach their part of the project; created by each of the six team roles making up the Team model.

The information provided in these documents determines the structure for the remainder of the project. When a consensus is reached, and the team members and customer(s) agree on the contents of the documents, the Project Plan Approved milestone is reached. Once this happens, the team can move on to the Developing phase of the project.

[Handwritten margin note: It appears as though separate plans are made by the 6 roles. How can this work. Shouldn't program mgmt be responsible for team focus / schedules]

Team Focus

As we saw in the previous phase of the Process model, each of the roles making up the Team model focuses on different tasks to reach the milestone. In the Planning phase, Program Management has ownership of the Project Plan Approved milestone. This means that Program Management is accountable for reaching this milestone. Program Management has the responsibility of planning, management, and seeing that the tasks associated with this milestone are successfully executed. If any of the roles in the Team model fail to complete their respective tasks, then the team's ability to reach the Project Plan Approved milestone is compromised.

In addition to having accountability and ownership of this milestone, Program Management has other duties on which to focus. Program Management creates the Program Management plan and schedule. This shows the estimated times and tasks that Program Management will require on the project. It is a plan and schedule that the Program Management team can commit to, so that no changes need be made to this in later phases of the project.

Product Management ensures that the expectations of the user are included in the design of the product. Members in this team role collect and analyze information that is germane to user expectations and is responsible for ensuring that these are met in the product design. This role is also responsible for creating the Product Management plan and determines a schedule for this plan.

Development also creates a project plan and schedule. This role focuses on creating their plan and schedule to revolve around development issues. Development identifies and evaluates options, and creates the physical design for the product.

User Education is responsible for determining the training needs of users. In deciding on what the users' needs are in this regard, a User Education plan and schedule are created. This not only includes plans on how to train and provide educational support for users, but also includes a means of measuring user performance. This allows the project team to see that the user's productivity and experience with the product is enhanced.

The Testing team is responsible for looking at the design created by Development, and evaluating it. This allows Testing to determine what should be tested after the product goes through development, and the Testing team is ready to begin checking the product for problems. This assessment of the design is applied to the Testing plan and schedule.

Finally, Logistics looks at what resources will be required to complete the project, and determines how they will be obtained. These materials are what will be used in creating the product, and without the necessary resources, the project will fail. This information is applied to the plan and schedule, which Logistics will create.

Interim Milestones

The Planning phase of the Process model incorporates three interim milestones to facilitate the process of achieving the Project Plan Approved milestone: Functional Specification Draft, Development Schedule Draft, and Ship Date Determination. These interim milestones involve developing two drafts, and setting a date for shipping the final released version of the product.

The *Functional Specification Draft* interim milestone is used to help produce the deliverable known as the functional specification. Since a detailed description and definition of the product must begin somewhere, it rests on the creation of the functional specification draft to start to come to life. This interim milestone maps to the functional specification deliverable, to some degree. It is considered met upon its ability to provide the Development, User Education, Testing, and Logistics roles with enough information to begin mapping out their contributions to the development project.

The *Development Schedule Draft* interim milestone is a rough draft of the overall development schedule to which Product Management, Program Management, Testing, User Education, and Logistics will attempt to synchronize their schedules. In essence, this interim milestone is used to set the tone or pace for the development team. Since the Development role is most closely linked to the critical path of development, it is beneficial to have this role responsible for helping to set the overall pace.

The *Ship Date Determination* interim milestone is the result of negotiating the functional specification draft and development schedule draft. The determination of a ship date helps to provide a goal which the entire team can strive to meet.

The Importance of a Functional Specification

Functional specifications have a special importance to any project, and it's important to create one before starting development on a project. To do so during or after development would be like an architect creating a blueprint as contractors are putting up the building, or a baker referring to a recipe once the ingredients have already been added. Because the functional specification describes the application, and its purpose, and serves as a blueprint for what will be developed, it's vital that one is created before development begins. This will allow the team members to refer to the document, and see what exactly needs to be done to create a successful application.

The functional specification is based on the needs and requirements of the business, customer, and/or end user. It provides a clear outline of what needs to be included, and what shouldn't be added to the finished product. Without a functional specification, the vision and scope of the project, which were set in the previous phase, may become lost. It is a representation of the needs and requirements to be included in the application, by showing the components that address each business requirement and need.

As a blueprint for the finished product, when customers and team members agree to its contents, the functional specification acts as a contract between the customer and the project team. It shows what has been agreed to be included in the product, what shouldn't be added or should be removed, and what features may be passed forward to future versions. If a dispute occurs during development, the customer and team can refer to this document to show exactly what the consensus was on certain components, features, or functionality. If the functional specification suits the needs and requirements of the user, the team is given the go-ahead to start development.

The Interdependent Roles and Shared Responsibilities of Project Team Members

As we saw earlier in this chapter, the Team model is based on the premise of a group of peers working together toward a common goal. That goal is the success of the project. Though each role has its own tasks, there are shared responsibilities and an interdependency that requires real teamwork.

Tasks Leading to Project Plan Approval

Within the team, there are specific tasks that cause various roles in the Team model to be interdependent on one another. The Program Management team must sign off that the functional specification/design specification will meet the desired requirements. The Program Management team agrees that there is sufficient accountability for each function and that the schedules are realistic. The Development team is charged with investigating possible risks and ensuring that these risks are manageable as well as being willing to commit to the schedules put forth in the Planning phase.

Outside of the team, members must work with the customer and end users of the product. The customer must sign off on the project before any development can begin. Customers must be at a point where they recognize the business benefits to be gained by the solution and the time frame in which the solution is to be delivered. If a customer either can't agree on the schedule or can't see the product as being beneficial, then the Project Plan Approved milestone can't be achieved. In such a case, the team will need to go back over the tasks they've performed, and try to reach a consensus with the customer on elements of the project and the time allotted to finish the product.

Each of the different team roles is responsible for creating its own plans and schedules. The plans outline what tasks each team will need to perform in the project, and how they will be handled. The schedules reflect a timeline for completing these tasks that the team feels they can commit to. As we'll see in the next phase of the Process model, these plans and schedules are respectively added to the master project plan and master project schedule. When added into master plans and schedules, they show the total amount of effort and time needed to complete the project.

Defining the Deliverables for the Planning Phase

During the Planning phase, four deliverables are produced: the functional specification, project schedule, project plan, and risk assessment. Together they define what the project is, how it will be undertaken, the risks involved in the project, and the time it will take to complete tasks associated with the project.

Deliverables

The risk assessment of the Planning phase is a reassessed version of the risk assessment document that's generated during the Envisioning phase. This document contains estimates and assessments of risks that could adversely affect the project if not addressed. By identifying the likelihood of risks, the team is better able to handle problems before they occur in a project.

A project schedule is generated by each of the six roles of the Team model. Team leaders work with members of their team to create a schedule that team members can commit to, and that reflects a realistic view of how much time is required to successfully complete their respective tasks.

A project plan is also created by each of the six roles of the Team model. As with project schedules, team leaders work with their teams to document how they will approach their part in the project. It shows how that particular team will tackle the project from this point forward. Team leaders look at the individual components contained in the functional specification, and map these functional components to tasks that team members perform. By putting these into a project plan, a strategy is produced on how the project will take shape.

The functional specification acts as a contract between the customer and the project team. It describes the application and its purpose, and acts as a blueprint for the solution. It also defines the visual design, functional interfaces, and data requirements. In short, it is a document that specifies the functionality of the solution. In doing so, it also acts as a contract between the customer and project team. By coming to a consensus, and agreeing to the contents of the functional specification, the team is able to then move forward into the Developing phase of the Process model.

Developing a Functional Specification

Once the vision and scope of the project have been set in the Envisioning phase, the work performed at this phase can be passed forward and applied to the functional specification. Information in this document is derived from the objectives and requirements of the business, user profiles, and usage scenarios. User profiles identify the user of the solution, while usage scenarios describe how user tasks are executed. This information is applied to the functional specification, and shows what is needed in the application.

Because Program Management has ownership of the Project Plan Approved milestone, this role is subsequently responsible for the functional specification. This doesn't mean that Program Management is alone in generating this document. Each role of the Team model is active in assisting Program Management. Team members contribute to the functional specification by adding components to the document that reflect their expertise. This includes reviewing contents and assessing risks of the parts they contribute.

Team members need to show that what's included in the functional specification can actually be built and delivered to the customer. If a customer requires a specific feature, and the team isn't sure that it can be provided, then the team must come to a concrete decision whether the feature should be dropped or passed forward to a future version. To show they can deliver what the customer requires, the team may develop prototypes. *Prototypes* are mockups of such things as visual interfaces, and provide the customer with something tangible to view. Developing a prototype allows the customer to see what they're getting, and can let the team determine whether certain items in the functional specification can actually be provided.

In developing the functional specification, the requirements of the business are broken up into different services. These services consist of User Services, Business Services, and Data Services. You'll notice that these are the three tiers of the Application model, which we discussed in Chapter 2. This aids the team in defining the visual design, functional interfaces, and data requirements of the solution. By separating the requirements into each of these three tiers, a distinct view of what the application will be, and how it will be created, is established. Team members can then use this information when building the application in the Developing phase of the Process model.

The functional specification should include interoperability issues that may affect the project. External interfaces, communication, components, and other issues that determine how the solution will interact with other applications and users should be included.

Developing a Project Plan

A *project plan* is a document containing the tasks, dependencies, assumptions, and approaches to handling specific aspects of the project. Each role of the Team model creates a project plan that shows how they intend to perform various tasks that are mapped from the functional specification. Because the functional specification shows each of the functional components that make up the project, these components can easily be applied to tasks that are necessary to complete the project.

A project plan is basically a plan of attack, showing strategies on how individual teams will undertake their particular responsibilities to the project. For example, User Education would create a plan that shows performance objectives, how user performance requirements can be fulfilled, and information that will reflect training plans that can be implemented later in the Process model. The project plan would also show budget and cost information, required resources, and other data necessary to successfully complete the project.

A project plan starts with a purpose statement. This is a brief report on what that particular team assumes should be achieved by their work. It shows that the team understands what goals need to be met. The plan then documents the strategy that will be used to meet this purpose.

Developing a Project Schedule

Schedules are an important part of any project. They show the amount of time required by team members to execute specific tasks, necessary in creating the product. For example, Development would create a schedule to show how long it would take to code different components making up an application. When each of these estimates are added together, the schedule would show the total time necessary to code the total solution. Schedules give team members reasonable deadlines to complete their work, and show the entire project team how long each team role requires to fulfill their tasks.

The tasks that require scheduling are taken from the functional specification. The team leaders map individual functional components, outlined in the functional specification, to tasks. The team leaders then assign these tasks to members of their team. Team leaders have the responsibility of creating schedules for this work that the team members can meet.

Bottom-up, task-level estimating should be used in creating project schedules. This means that the person who does the work determines how long that work will take. This provides a more realistic estimate of how long it will take to perform a task. These estimates are given back to the team leader, who applies them to the schedule.

There are two common problems that often occur in creating project schedules. Both of these deal with the people performing tasks associated with a project misdiagnosing the amount of time it takes to complete a task. Overly optimistic scheduling occurs when too little time is assigned to a job. Sometimes this isn't the fault of team members. There may be a deadline—such as the date of a trade show, or a seasonal requirement to the project (such as income tax time)—where a project must be completed or the benefits of the project are diminished. More commonly though, overly optimistic scheduling results from unreasonable expectations. They assume a task is less complicated than it really is, or have a greater faith in their abilities than is really there. On the flip side of this, some people may add time to their estimates, or estimate the task as taking longer than it really should. This can occur from team members having a lack of faith in their abilities, confusion over what the task involves, or any number of other reasons. In creating estimates, it's important that those estimates are an accurate reflection of the time it will take to complete a task.

EXERCISE 4-2

Identifying Deliverables in the Planning Phase

For each description, identify the deliverable. (The answers to this exercise appear just before the Self Test at the end of the chapter.)

1. This deliverable is a revision of one of the Envisioning phase deliverables. It contains estimates and assessments of issues that could adversely affect the project.

2. This deliverable is a group effort from each of the six roles of the Team model. It reflects a realistic estimate of task effort.

3. This deliverable documents how each team will complete their tasks in the project.

4. This deliverable describes the application and acts as a blueprint for the solution.

CERTIFICATION OBJECTIVE 4.03

The Scope Complete/First Use Milestone

The Developing phase is the third phase of the Process model, and culminates in the Scope Complete/First Use milestone. For those who love to code, this is the phase of the project that's highly anticipated. During this phase, the project moves away from design and the focus changes to developing the actual product.

The Developing phase is initiated when the customer has approved the design of the product, and ends with the creation of a software solution that's ready for testing and stabilization. When this end result is achieved, the Scope Complete/First Use milestone is reached. Work done in achieving this milestone revolves around building the product, and identifying any additional issues that need to be resolved before the product ships.

The functional specification, and other deliverables from previous phases—inclusive to the project plan—are used in this phase as a baseline, and provide focus in developing the actual product. As we'll see, these aren't the only deliverables that aid team members in creating the product. The project plans and project schedules of different roles in the Team model are combined into master documents, which are used to show team members the tasks to perform in the Developing phase, and allow the team to measure the work they do against what is actually required.

Defining the Scope Complete/First Use Milestone

The Developing phase signals that the design of the application is at the point where it can be developed and optimized. Each of the six team roles making up the Team model work to ensure the solution is developed to the best of their ability, resulting in a high-quality product. During this phase, coding begins on the solution, support and training facilities are identified, and an actual software product takes a tangible form. The development team builds the product, going through a number of cycles involving testing, debugging, and fixing the product. This occurs until it is ready to be passed forward to the Stabilizing phase of the Process model. The Scope Complete/First Use milestone is achieved when a consensus is reached that the solution, and its support and training mechanisms, are ready for testing and stabilization.

Team Focus

During the Developing phase, the team roles of Development and User Education have ownership. It is their responsibility that this phase of the project is properly planned and managed, and that the tasks associated with developing are correctly carried out. If they fail in doing this, the Scope Complete/First Use milestone won't be reached.

During the Developing phase, members in each of the Team model roles follow the individual plans that make up the master project plan. Later in this chapter, we'll discuss the master project plan and master schedule in greater depth. The main focus on this phase is developing the product, so that an efficient and high-quality solution is produced. Each of the team members work toward this, and communicate regularly with one another in achieving this goal.

Development also has responsibility for building the solution. They are required to code the solution, so that each of the components outlined in the functional specification are included and function properly. During the building of the product, the development team goes through a series of cycles, involving testing, debugging, and fixing the product. This in no way means that further testing isn't necessary. It ensures that basic functionality of the product performs as expected, inclusive of the solution starting and exiting properly. Basically, if the solution doesn't even work, then Testing will be unable to check specific features and functions in the program.

User Education also has the responsibility for identifying support and training facilities. By having support and training mechanisms established early in development, users will have a better opportunity to understand how to use the product.

Testing sets up usability testing procedures, which will be used in determining whether the application meets the user's need and expectations. In a later section of this chapter, we'll discuss the importance of this.

A major task addressed by all roles of the Team model, as well as customers, users, and other stakeholders, are issues that need to be addressed before the product is ready for shipping and deployment. These issues need to be addressed here because after this phase, it is generally too late to do anything.

Interim Milestones

The Developing phase of the Process model is provided with five interim milestones, presented here in loose chronological order. The interim milestones are not required to be obtained or reached in the order provided, but rather the order is allowed to vary from project to project. The order provided is merely considered optimal for reducing the impact of changes that may occur within the Developing phase. These interim milestones are *Visual Design Freeze, Database Freeze, Internal Release, Functional Specification Freeze,* and *Feature Complete.*

- **Visual Design Freeze**   This is the first interim milestone to be reached in the Developing phase. This milestone allows screenshots of the visual design to be acquired by Product Management and User Education to assist in documentation and packaging concerns. This interim milestone may be ascribed to the entire project, or just to internal releases as defined by the Internal Release interim milestone.

- **Database Freeze**   This interim milestone is reached once the database schema is solidified and decided upon. By freezing the database schema, the component interfaces may begin to be defined. This also allows the different Development teams for the separate application layers to begin parallel development tracks without fear of database changes forcing recoding of components.

- **Internal Release**   This interim milestone is usually reached several times, as several internal releases clustering different product features are tested and debugged. Depending on project size, many different Internal Release milestones may actually be reached prior to reaching the ultimate Scope Complete/First Use milestone. This interim milestone generally involves a release of code by the Development role once a level of reasonable stability has been obtained. This code has already undergone testing and verification of the daily builds from which the internal release is obtained. Part of this interim milestone is the production of a *testing release document (TRD)* to document the interim milestone and provide documentation for identifying untestable areas, known bugs, and general information about the internal release. In order to reach this interim milestone, the physical internal release must pass testing performed by the Testing role to ensure acceptable stability of the feature set.

- **Functional Specification Freeze**   This interim milestone is used to develop a final, formal functional specification for the product in order to fully define the product. Last minute tradeoffs in the product are solidified and the features are fully set into a completed specification. Although this is considered the final specification, keep in mind that minor changes are allowed after the product ships to account for last-minute visual changes.

- **Feature Complete**   This interim milestone represents the first internal release of the product that is fully functional—i.e., the first release against which full test scripts may be run. The final testing separates this interim milestone from the Scope Complete/First Use milestone and involves heavy systems testing to allow the product to move from alpha to beta status.

Tasks Leading to Scope Complete/First Use

The tasks performed by the project team revolve around creating a high-quality solution, which meets the needs and requirements of the customer. A great deal of work is performed during this phase of the project, inclusive of building the actual product. Each of the tasks performed works toward creating a product that is ready for testing and stabilization. Once the customer and project team agree that this has happened, the Scope Complete/First Use milestone is reached, and the next phase of the Process model is ready to begin.

During this phase, Development and User Education own responsibility for achieving the Scope Complete/First Use milestone. This is due to the fact that the Developing phase revolves around building the product, and setting support and training for the product. These two roles of the Team model plan, manage, and ensure that the tasks involved in this phase are properly executed by the other teams roles.

During the Developing phase, risk assessments are applied to create a risk management plan. The *risk management plan* outlines strategies that can be used to deal with problems before they occur. This is a proactive method of dealing with risks. If the risk has already produced a problem that will result in some sort of loss, the risk management plan should provide some method of how the team should react to the risk. You'll remember that these issues are discussed in greater detail in the previous chapter.

Development creates the source code and executables that make up the solution. This is where the design is applied to the building of an actual solution. As mentioned, this also includes a cycle of testing, debugging, and fixing the product. By writing and compiling the application, and then going through these cycles, many of the problems that can occur in the application are caught before testing and stabilization begins.

Performance support elements are set during this phase of the Process model. User Education creates a strategy by establishing how the solution will need to satisfy user performance requirements. This is used to determine areas where the application meets or fails such requirements.

Testing is responsible for creating test specifications and test cases, which can be used in the next phase of the Process model. These give team members in this role something to follow in testing the application. Through these documents, Testing will be able to find potential problems by taking the solution through a series of tests that match how the user will use the product.

Defining the Deliverables for Scope Complete/First Use

There are more deliverables produced during the Developing phase than in previous phases of the Process model. Many of these are built upon deliverables created in previous phases, but all provide the team with knowledge in creating a high-quality solution. One of the most distinctive deliverables at this phase is the solution itself. Source code, executables, and COM components are written and compiled, making up the application as a whole. As we'll see, though, this isn't the only important deliverable generated in this phase.

Deliverables

The Developing phase of the Process model produces a number of different deliverables:

- Frozen functional specification
- Source code and executables
- Performance support elements
- Test specification and test cases
- Master project plan
- Master project schedule
- Risk management plan

Each of these deliverables is used by the team to create a high-quality solution that meets the needs and requirements of the business.

Because development starts at this phase of the Process model, the functional specification is frozen at this point. The only changes applied to the design of the application are fixes. The *frozen functional specification* contains all of the features from the previous phase, but doesn't allow additional features or functionality to be added.

Source code is written, and executables and components of the application are compiled, during this phase of the Process model. This results from using a programming language (such as Visual Basic or C++) to write the programming code, and then compiling it into an actual program that can start, perform its functionality, and then exit. Considerable time and work is put into this by Development, who creates the physical solution that users will work with.

Performance support elements are identified and set. These elements dictate what user performance requirements are necessary, and are used to develop a strategy that can be used to analyze whether the application meets those requirements. By improving performance in areas that the user requires, the user's experience with the application will be enhanced.

Test specifications and test cases are created to show how testing will be performed in the next phase of the Process model. Test specifications show guidelines, rules, and approaches that will be taken to ensure that the product meets the standards, quality, and performance that are required from the application. Such specifications let the Testing team know what needs and requirements have to be met in the solution. Test cases provide scenarios that Testing can follow in order to find errors or malfunctions in the application. This allows Testing to test the product in ways that the user will use the product.

The master project schedule is the combined schedules of each of the six roles of the Team model. Team leaders provide schedules for each of their teams. These are schedules that team members can commit to, and reflect a realistic view of how much time is required to successfully complete their respective tasks. These are combined into a *master project schedule*, which shows the total scheduling of the entire project team.

The *master project plan* is similar to the master project schedule, in that each of the six roles provides individual components to create a master document. With the master project plan, team leaders submit plans of their teams. These include implementation, user education, logistics, testing, solution marketing, and budget plans. Together, they show how the team will tackle the project from this point forward.

Risk assessments from previous phases of the Process model are used at this phase to create a risk management plan. Risk management plans define how the team should manage risks. As we saw in the previous chapter, risk management can be proactive or reactive. Strategies contained within the plan show how the team can keep risks from resulting in loss, and how to deal with risks once they've become a problem.

EXERCISE 4-3

Identifying Deliverables in the Developing Phase

For each description, identify the deliverable. (The answers to this exercise appear just before the Self Test at the end of the chapter.)

1. This deliverable contains all of the features from the previous phase but allows fixes only to the design, no additional functionality.

2. The major part of this deliverable is the code that executes the functionality of the application.

3. This deliverable contains the support elements and performance requirements.

4. This deliverable includes the guidelines, rules, and approaches taken to ensure that the end product meets the standards, quality, and performance.

5. The combined schedules for the six project teams comprise this deliverable.

6. For this deliverable, team leaders submit analyses of their components that show how the team will continue the project.

7. This deliverable results from the risk analysis of the previous two phases.

CERTIFICATION OBJECTIVE 4.04

The Release Milestone

Once the Scope Complete/First Use milestone is achieved, team members are ready to move into the Stabilization phase of the project. The Stabilization phase is where product testing is performed, allowing bugs to be found and fixed before it is shipped or put into service. The goal of this phase is to make the solution a stable product that is ready for end users.

Once testing is completed during this phase, responsibility of the product is handed over to operations and support. When a consensus is made that the product is stable and testing is complete, the Release milestone is achieved. Operations and support staff will manage and support this current release of the software, and the project team can begin on the next version of the product or move on to a new project.

Defining the Release Milestone

The Release milestone is a mechanism for ensuring the quality of the product. It is during this phase of the Process model that testing and stabilization of the product take place. Once it's determined that testing is complete, and the software product is stable enough to be used, the Release milestone is achieved. This means that the product can be shipped or put into service, and users can now benefit from its capabilities.

In determining whether the product is ready for release, the customer and project team must come to a consensus. They must agree that the application has fulfilled expectations, and is ready for use. This can be determined when the following factors are met:

- The solution meets the requirements of the business, and all the users who were identified in the scope of the project.

- The new problems encountered have steadily declined, or now number at or near zero each day.

- A consensus is reached that the solution is supportable and possesses no quirks, and a support system for the solution has been implemented.

- The customer is satisfied that the product provides the solution as outlined in the scope.

The application is ready for release when these four steps have been accomplished. The quality of the product is the responsibility of each functional team, as well as the organization. By accomplishing these steps, the project team and organization can establish that this quality is met.

Team Focus

During the Stabilizing phase of the product, Testing and Logistics have ownership. It is their responsibility to plan, manage, and see that the necessary tasks involved in achieving the Release milestone are completed successfully. This results in the team releasing a high-quality, usable product.

As the primary goal of the Stabilizing phase is to create a stable product, it is here that Testing goes through the application to find errors and malfunctions in the product. If the application crashes due to certain actions, fails to perform certain functions, or has features that aren't included or don't work, the product must go back to Development to be fixed. In testing the application, the Testing team uses the specifications and test cases that were created in the previous phase.

Logistics ensures that the Operations, Help Desk, and other support staff are in place, and properly prepared for the release of the product. It is the responsibility of this role to ensure a smooth rollout of the product, and make certain that deployment of the solution is possible. Installation programs must work correctly, and installation sites are checked so they fit the necessary requirements for deployment.

Interim Milestones

The Stabilizing phase of the Process model is provided with six very closely related interim milestones: *Content Complete, Bug Convergence, Code Freeze, Zero-Bug Release, Release Candidate*, and *Golden Release*. Most of these interim milestones are grouped towards the end of the Stabilizing phase, and can be reached almost simultaneously on some projects. In order to reach these milestones, numerous beta releases may be required, effectively masking the true degree of effort required to obtain these milestones, from the standpoint of the Process model alone. In most cases, a great deal of effort precedes these interim milestones.

The *Content Complete* interim milestone involves the final editing and production of the support elements for the product by User Education. At this point, the content to be provided by User Education is finalized and full testing is performed for this material.

The *Bug Convergence* interim milestone is somewhat tricky to determine. This milestone occurs when the rate of bug resolution exceeds, for the last time, the rate of bug identification. In simpler terms, this interim milestone is considered to have been reached when the number of new bug fixes is greater than the number of new bugs. Although this may occur several times, the last such occurrence is considered the mark for the milestone.

The *Code Freeze* interim milestone and the *Zero-Bug Release* interim milestone go hand-in-hand in the development process. They are almost always reached simultaneously. The Code Freeze milestone occurs when the last known active bug has been resolved. Once Development has caught up with Testing in this manner, for the first time, then the Code Freeze milestone is reached. Immediately following this milestone, the product release built from this code is sent to Testing as a zero-bug release, and the Zero-Bug Release milestone has been reached.

The *Release Candidate* interim milestone is reached when a product version is returned from Testing and the following conditions are true:

- No Severity 1, 2, or 3 bugs are found.

- No Priority 1, 2, or 3 bugs are found.

- All files to be shipped with the final product are included with the release.

- No Severity 1 bugs are found for a preset length of time.

The generally accepted definitions for severity levels are as follows:

- **Severity 1**   Causes system crashes.
- **Severity 2**   Defined as a major problem.
- **Severity 3**   Defined as a minor problem.
- **Severity 4**   Defined as a trivial problem.

The generally accepted characteristics of Priority levels are as follows:

- **Priority 1**   Highest-priority bugs are completely reproducible, following a simple series of steps, and are given a severity of 1, 2, or 3. These bugs must be fixed.

- **Priority 2** High-priority bugs are very reproducible through somewhat complex or convoluted steps. These bugs should be fixed.

- **Priority 3** Medium-priority bugs are only intermittently reproducible, and only through a convoluted series of steps. The fix is not intuitive or obvious. These bugs are fixed last, and a product may ship with them.

- **Priority 4** Low-priority bugs are very difficult to reproduce. Fixes are not obvious. Only fix these bugs given a low-risk solution acquired without effort to ascertain.

The *Golden Release* interim milestone results in the final product release. This milestone coincides directly with the golden release deliverable. Upon full testing of the golden release, including archival of the release, this interim milestone will have been reached.

Effective Usability Testing

Usability testing is an important component in preparing for the employment of the solution. It gives you an idea of how well the solution meets the users' needs and expectations. Effective usability testing is accomplished by first defining the target audience to determine the test goals. When determining the goals, you should focus on tasks.

One method of usability testing is to provide an environment that's comparable to the target setting. Then, you need to allow the users a reasonable amount of time to try and work through any difficult situations that may arise with as little intervention as possible. Finally, you should record the results, preferably with a video camera, so the results can be reviewed later in fuller detail.

As we'll see in the sections that follow, there are other methods of determining the usability of a solution. The importance of establishing the usability of a solution is high indeed. If an application is unusable, the product will fail because no one will want to use it.

Beta Testing

Beta releases are test or trial copies of a product that are released to a limited number of users. These users are called *beta testers*, and they try out the product before the final version is released to the public. These beta testers use the product, and report bugs and problems with the solution to the team. Beta testing allows the project team to see how the solution works while being used by the target audience.

on the **job**

Beta releases of a product aren't uncommon, and are usually provided to users free of charge. There are exceptions to this, as was the case with the beta release of Windows 98. There are various reasons why users are willing to try out these beta releases before the finished product is ready. Some want to view the new version before it's on the market. Many teams will provide some sort of incentive for people to beta test the product, including a free copy of the finished product or a discount.

Release Candidates

On occasion beta releases will go through a number of different versions before the official, final version of the product is released. These are called *release candidates*. Each candidate contains fixes to bugs or problems reported by users.

Release candidates may also contain such things as different features, visual interface, and tools included in the product. This allows users to communicate what they like and dislike in the product, before the final version is released. For example, some users who are beta testing a product may find one version of the visual interface easier to use than another. While this isn't usually tested with release candidates, and more often determined with prototypes, it can be tested with release candidates of some products.

Defining the Deliverables for Release

The Release milestone is the final milestone of the Process model. The deliverables in this stage are the last ones of the project. After they have been produced and a consensus is reached to release the product, the project team is ready to move on to other projects or new versions of the current product.

Deliverables

The Stabilizing phase of a software development project results in the following seven deliverables:

- Golden release
- Source code and executables
- Release notes
- Project documents
- Performance support elements
- Test results and testing tools
- Milestone review

These deliverables are the result of work performed in the current and preceding phases of the project. As we'll see, many of these deliverables can be applied to future projects, or future versions of the current product.

The *golden release* is the finished product. It's also called a *golden master*, as this is the master copy of the solution. This is released to manufacturing, and is the copy from which all copies of the finished application will be made.

Source code, as well as executables and components that make up the application, are another deliverable of this phase. You'll remember that this was one of the deliverables from the Developing phase. The difference between the raw and compiled code of these two phases is that this deliverable has gone through testing, and is considered stable. The source code from the Stabilizing phase can be used for future versions of the product, and should be kept for this reason.

Release notes are documentation that describes updated features, and may contain information on the history of the solution. When such a history is included in the release notes, it describes what bugs or problems have been fixed in each version, or what features were added and removed from the product. Release notes allow users to view what has been done to the product in current and previous versions.

Product documents provide users and team members with information on the current version of the product. These documents describe features and functionality in the current version, and guidelines on how to use them. Such documents provide a clear view of the product's capabilities.

Performance support elements are updated during the Stabilization phase of the Process model. They are revised from the performance support elements established in the Developing phase.

Test results and testing tools are another deliverable produced during this phase. Testing tools are the utilities and tools used in automated and manual testing of the product. These include performance tools, as well as those that test features and functionality in the product. Test results are the documented results of the work performed by the Testing team during this phase. They show how the application merited during testing, and can be used when creating future versions of the product.

QUESTIONS AND ANSWERS

What are the phases and associated milestones of the Process model?	The Process model consists of four phases, with a milestone associated with each: Envisioning phase (Vision/Scope Approved milestone), Planning phase (Project Plan Approved milestone), Developing phase (Scope Complete/First Use milestone), and Stabilizing phase (Release milestone).
Who has ownership of the different milestones?	Product Management has ownership of the Vision/Scope Approved milestone, Program Management owns the Project Plan Approved milestone, Development and User Education own the Scope Complete/First Use milestone, and Testing and Logistics own the Release milestone.
Why are bottom-up, task-level estimates beneficial for scheduling?	Bottom-up, task-level scheduling has the person performing a task providing an estimate on how long the task will take to complete. Because the person doing the work has the best idea of how long it will take them to complete it, the estimates are more accurate.
Why should milestones be reviewed at the end of a project?	To determine issues that resulted from the current project. By knowing what problems occurred, and what was successful in the current project, you can apply that knowledge to future projects.

A *milestone review* is done to analyze how the project went in meeting each of the milestones in the Process model. Were there any problems that could have been avoided? How well did the team measure up in meeting these milestones? These are a few of the questions that are asked in a review of the milestones. By doing a milestone review, you can determine what issues, problems, and successes occurred. This allows the team to apply this knowledge to future projects.

EXERCISE 4-4

Identifying Deliverables in the Stabilizing Phase

For each description, identify the deliverable. (The answers to this exercise appear just before the Self Test at the end of the chapter.)

1. This deliverable is the finished product.

2. This deliverable provides the foundation for future enhancements and releases.

3. Any notes for the feature or history of the solution are contained in this deliverable.

4. This deliverable provides the users with instructions on how to use the features of the current release.

5. This deliverable is a revision of a deliverable in the previous phase and updates response times as well as other issues.

6. This deliverable is comprised of any automated or manual procedures used to verify functionality.

7. This deliverable documents the issues, problems, and successes that occurred during the project.

EXERCISE 4-5

Identifying Project Milestones

Identify the milestone associated with each attribute. (The answers to this exercise appear just before the Self Test at the end of the chapter.)

1. Agreement on product characteristics.

2. Bugs and problems encountered are near zero.

3. Identify the support and training requirements.

4. Estimate schedule and resource requirements.

5. Identify the time frame for the application to be functional.

6. Determine the level of work needed in the Planning phase.

7. Agreement on how to proceed with the development.

8. Set priorities and expectations.

9. Understand how the solution will solve the business requirements.

10. Re-assess risks.

11. The application has to be deployed to the appropriate users.

12. Agreement on vision and scope of the project.

13. Agreement on priority of business requirements.

14. Create functional specifications.

15. Identification of business constraints, risks, and assumptions.

16. Build, test, debug, and fix the product.

17. The customer concludes that the product is what they wanted.

18. The support system for the application is in place.

19. Write code that satisfies the solution.

CERTIFICATION SUMMARY

The Process model provides the roadmap needed for ensuring that product development does not fall off track. The Process model for software development is comprised of major milestones, interim milestones, deliverables, and phases.

The Process model is broken up into four major phases: Envisioning, Planning, Developing, and Stabilizing. Each of these phases has its own collection of interim milestones and deliverables. Each phase culminates in a final milestone that signifies the end of that phase.

The Envisioning phase culminates with the Vision/Scope Approved milestone. Leading up to this, the Envisioning phase includes Vision Statement Draft and Design Goals Draft interim milestones. The Envisioning phase physically results in an internal deliverable known as the risk management plan, and external deliverables known as a vision/scope document and a project structure.

The Planning phase concludes with the Project Plan Approved milestone. Prior to this milestone, this phase involves three interim milestones: Functional Specification Draft, Development Schedule Draft, and Ship Date Determination. During this phase, the physical deliverables include an internal risk management plan, and external deliverables are a functional specification, master project plan, and master project schedule.

The Developing phase finishes up with a Scope Complete/First Use milestone. During this phase, the interim milestones are Visual Design Freeze, Database Freeze, Internal Release, Functional Specification Freeze, and Feature Complete. These interim milestones contribute to the production of six deliverables: functional specification, risk management plan, source code executables, performance support elements, test specification plus test cases, and master project plan/schedule updates.

The final phase, Stabilizing, results in the Release milestone, with six interim milestones: Content Complete, Bug Convergence, Code Freeze, Zero-Bug Release, Release Candidate, and Golden Release. These result in seven deliverables. The external deliverables include performance support elements, release notes, and the long-anticipated golden release. The internal deliverables include testing document and tools, source code and executables, project documents, and the final milestone review.

TWO-MINUTE DRILL

❑ The Process model breaks a project up into four phases, with each phase culminating in a milestone. *Milestones* mark the point where one phase of the project ends and another begins, and indicate a point in the project where team members should synchronize their efforts.

❑ The four phases of the Process model always follow the same order, starting with the Envisioning phase, proceeding through the Planning phase and the Developing phase, and ending with the Release milestone of the Stabilizing phase.

❑ The design of any application is driven by the needs of the user, and this is what the envisioning stage works to understand.

❑ The Vision/Scope Approved milestone occurs when the project team, customer, and stakeholders come to an agreement on key aspects of the project. This includes such elements as the vision and scope of the project, and the priority of which business requirements need to be addressed first.

❏ A *deliverable* is a product of work that's generated from the activities of a given phase in the Process model. Unlike interim milestones, which are points of time allotted for the team to synchronize their efforts, a deliverable is a physical component that results from the work that's been done.

❏ It's important to remember that the Vision/Scope Approved milestone occurs when the vision and scope of the project have been agreed upon.

❏ The vision/scope document is made up of several parts, which together map out what the project entails. These components of the document consist of the problem statement/business objectives, the vision statement, user profiles, and the solution concept.

❏ The *project structure document* is a vital information tool that is passed forward to the Planning phase of the Process model. Upon reaching the milestone of this next phase of the Process model, the document is updated to reflect resource assignments to the project.

❏ Be sure to memorize the interim milestones, the deliverables, and the relationship between the two. For each interim milestone, certain deliverables are considered necessary for completion of the interim milestone.

❏ The Project Plan Approved milestone occurs when the work done in the Planning phase has been completed and approved by the customer. During this phase, resources are assigned to the project, and work from the previous phase is built upon.

❏ Functional specifications have a special importance to any project, and it's important to create one before starting development on a project. To do so during or after development would be like an architect creating a blueprint as contractors are putting up the building, or a baker referring to a recipe once the ingredients have already been added.

❏ The functional specification is based on the needs and requirements of the business, customer, and/or end user. It provides a clear outline of what needs to be included, and what shouldn't be added to the finished product.

❑ During the Planning phase, four deliverables are produced: the functional specification, project schedule, project plan, and risk assessment. Together they define what the project is, how it will be undertaken, the risks involved in the project, and the time it will take to complete tasks associated with the project.

❑ In developing the functional specification, the requirements of the business are broken up into different services. These services consist of User Services, Business Services, and Data Services.

❑ A *project plan* is a document containing the tasks, dependencies, assumptions, and approaches to handling specific aspects of the project.

❑ Schedules give team members reasonable deadlines to complete their work, and show the entire project team how long each team role requires to fulfill their tasks.

❑ The Developing phase is initiated when the customer has approved the design of the product, and ends with the creation of a software solution that's ready for testing and stabilization. When this end result is achieved, the Scope Complete/First Use milestone is reached.

❑ The Developing phase signals that the design of the application is at the point where it can be developed and optimized. Each of the six team roles making up the Team model work to ensure that the solution is developed to the best of their ability, resulting in a high-quality product.

❑ There are more deliverables produced during the Developing phase than in previous phases of the Process model.

❑ The Stabilization phase is where product testing is performed, allowing bugs to be found and fixed before it is shipped or put into service. The goal of this phase is to make the solution a stable product that is ready for end users.

❑ The Release milestone is a mechanism for ensuring the quality of the product. It is during this phase of the Process model that testing and stabilization of the product take place.

❑ Effective usability testing is accomplished by first defining the target audience to determine the test goals.

❏ The Release milestone is the final milestone of the Process model. The deliverables in this stage are the last ones of the project.

❏ A *milestone review* is done to analyze how the project went in meeting each of the milestones in the Process model.

Answers to Exercise 4-1

1. Problem statement/business objectives
2. Vision statement
3. User profiles
4. Solution concept
5. Risk assessment
6. Project structure document

Answers to Exercise 4-2

1. Risk assessment
2. Project schedule
3. Project plan
4. Functional specification

Answers to Exercise 4-3

1. Frozen functional specification
2. Source code and executables
3. Performance support elements
4. Test specification and test cases
5. Master project plan
6. Master project schedule
7. Risk management plan

Answers to Exercise 4-4

1. Golden release
2. Source code and executables
3. Release notes
4. Project documents
5. Performance support elements
6. Test results and testing tools
7. Milestone review

Answers to Exercise 4-5

1. Project Plan Approved milestone
2. Release milestone
3. Scope Complete/First Use milestone
4. Project Plan Approved milestone
5. Vision/Scope Approved milestone
6. Vision/Scope Approved milestone
7. Project Plan Approved milestone
8. Project Plan Approved milestone
9. Vision/Scope Approved milestone
10. Project Plan Approved milestone
11. Release milestone
12. Vision/Scope Approved milestone
13. Vision/Scope Approved milestone
14. Project Plan Approved milestone
15. Vision/Scope Approved milestone
16. Scope Complete/First Use milestone
17. Release milestone
18. Release milestone
19. Scope Complete/First Use milestone

SELF TEST

The Self Test questions will help you measure your understanding of the material presented in this chapter. Read all the choices carefully, as there may be more than one correct answer. Select all correct answers for each question.

1. You have decided to use the Process model on a software development project. Which phase will your team start with in using this model?

   A. Envisioning

   B. Planning

   C. Developing

   D. Stabilizing

2. Which of the following milestones are reached only after business constraints, which may adversely affect the project, are identified?

   A. Vision/Scope Approved milestone

   B. Project Plan Approved milestone

   C. Scope Complete/First Use milestone

   D. Release milestone

3. During the Planning phase, which team role is responsible for ensuring that expectations are met in the product design?

   A. Project Management

   B. Development

   C. User Education

   D. Product Management

4. Which of the following milestones demands the signoff that the functional specification/design specification will meet the desired requirements?

   A. Vision/Scope Approved milestone

   B. Project Plan Approved milestone

   C. Scope Complete/First Use milestone

   D. Release milestone

5. The project team has just achieved the Vision/Scope Approved milestone. What phase of the Process model will your team now use?

   A. Envisioning

   B. Planning

   C. Developing

   D. Stabilizing

6. You are creating a project structure document to outline the structure of the project you're currently working on. What information will be included in this document? (Choose all that apply.)

   A. Project plans

   B. How the project will be managed and supported

   C. Administrative structure of the project team

   D. Other information that the project team may find useful, such as e-mail addresses and phone numbers

7. You have reached the end of a project, and have decided to review the project to determine what went well, and which problems could have been avoided. Which deliverable is this?

    A. Master project plan

    B. Project plan

    C. Milestone review

    D. Golden master

8. You have reached a point in the project where no additional changes or additions will be made to the product. What deliverable does this represent?

    A. Master project plan

    B. Project plan

    C. Functional specification

    D. Frozen functional specification

9. You have reached a point in the project where no additional changes or additions will be made to the product. In what phase of the Process model does this occur?

    A. Envisioning

    B. Planning

    C. Developing

    D. Stabilizing

10. Which role of the Team model is responsible for the team achieving the Vision/Scope Approved milestone?

    A. Program Management

    B. Project Management

    C. Product Management

    D. Logistics

11. The project has reached the point where the application has been designed, and development has begun. Which milestone is the project team now working to achieve?

    A. Developing

    B. Stabilizing

    C. Scope Complete/First Use

    D. Release

12. You are looking through the deliverables produced during the current phase of the project, and notice that the source code includes fixes to bugs that were found during testing by the Testing team. Which phase of the project are you currently in?

    A. Scope Complete/First Use

    B. Developing

    C. Release

    D. Stabilizing

13. The project team is working to achieve the Scope Complete/First Use milestone. Which of the following team roles has ownership of achieving this milestone? (Choose all that apply.)

    A. Development

    B. Product Management

    C. Logistics

    D. User Education

14. The project team is working to achieve the Release milestone. Which of the following team roles has ownership of achieving this milestone? (Choose all that apply.)

   A. Development

   B. Logistics

   C. Testing

   D. User Education

15. Which of the following acts as a contract between the project team and customer? When approval is given on this deliverable, the project team is able to start development on the product.

   A. Golden release

   B. Frozen functional specification

   C. Functional specification

   D. Project plan

16. You have finished the product and are now ready to release the solution. What will you use to create copies of the application to release to users?

   A. Master release

   B. Golden release

   C. Zero-bug release

   D. Deployment release

17. You are creating a schedule for your team and decide to use bottom-up, task-level estimates. Who will provide the estimates required for performing individual tasks?

   A. Project Management

   B. Product Management

   C. The person performing the task

   D. The team leader of the person who performs the task

MICROSOFT CERTIFIED SOLUTION DEVELOPER

5

Infrastructure Deployment Track Milestones

CERTIFICATION OBJECTIVES

Y ou've learned about the MSF Team model and Process model. You've applied these models to software development. Now it's time to apply them to infrastructure projects. Why should a programmer, an MCSD, care about infrastructure projects? Because we do so much more than code. Much of what we do requires working with networks, hardware, and even phones. We increase our professional value by expanding our expertise out of the developer's cube into the real-world workings of the enterprise. In this chapter, we'll discuss the MSF guidelines for infrastructure deployment.

CERTIFICATION OBJECTIVE 5.01

Enterprise Architecture Overview

Enterprise architecture is built on the interdependencies of people, process, and technology. We have technology to aid productivity, and each team member brings unique skills and characteristics to the process. Figure 5-1 illustrates the MSF enterprise architecture.

Thinking about the architecture of our enterprise helps us to categorize the various components of an organization. It's a way of breaking down the whole into understandable pieces. Not only can you view the enterprise architecture of an entire business, but also the architecture of the IT organization, which is the focus of this chapter. The enterprise architecture consists of people, process, and technology.

FIGURE 5-1

Enterprise architecture consists of people, process, and technology.

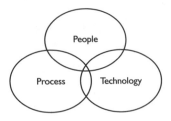

The Elements of the Enterprise Architecture

One crucial element of the enterprise architecture is *people*. People use technology, create processes, and provide the intellectual energy to keep our enterprise moving forward. In the end, the benefit comes back to people. Sometimes developers want people to adjust to the technology, and we may even want them to change processes because of how our technology works. A more balanced view of the enterprise architecture leads developers to value the people in the organization.

The second element of enterprise architecture is *process*. For example, computer departments commonly buy new desktop systems in batches after a bidding process. The bidding process is a well-established procedure for getting good prices. There are forms involved, relationships with vendors, and reasonable criteria for making a decision. Processes exist on every level of the organization, for everything from rudimentary daily tasks to the hiring of a new CIO. Every good programmer knows how to isolate the process from the people who use it, and from the technology it may run on.

The third element of enterprise architecture is *technology*. Technology doesn't mean just the network. It includes things like writable CDs, Visual Studio 6.0, and phones. Remember that the enterprise architecture is not limited to a location, nor is it identified by size. It's a model that we use to define organizational roles.

CERTIFICATION OBJECTIVE 5.02

Infrastructure: Overview and Drill Down

Let's understand the technology infrastructure of organizations by using an analogy. The infrastructure of a nation consists of things like roads, power facilities, waterways, airports, and phone lines. These are the systems that keep the country functioning. *Infrastructure* consists of both facilities and services. A school can be considered part of the infrastructure because of the service that goes on there, education, which produces people with the necessary skills to contribute to the larger enterprise.

Understand the relationship between enterprise architecture and technology infrastructure.

The technology infrastructure consists of the resources that support the organization's computing environment; that is, the systems that we need for the functioning of the computing environment. Figure 5-2 shows the relationship between the enterprise architecture and the technology infrastructure. Like the overall architecture, the technology infrastructure includes people and processes, as well as technology. The people in the infrastructure use, buy, and maintain the technology. Common processes in a technology infrastructure include network design, setup of personal systems, and training. The following are Microsoft's eight categories of the technology portion of the infrastructure:

- Data transmission links
- Local area network architecture
- Wide area network architecture
- Protocols and transports
- Network operating systems
- Computer hardware
- Computer software
- Domain/site models

FIGURE 5-2

People, process, and technology come together in the technology infrastructure.

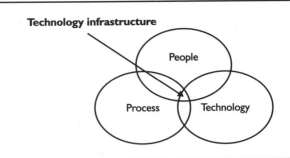

The technology infrastructure exists to meet the business needs of the organization. We are the roads and bridges, the power lines and coal mines of the organization; the job we do makes it possible for the rest of the organization to meet the business goals.

CERTIFICATION OBJECTIVE 5.03

Infrastructure: Deployment and the MSF Process Model

Deploying a new technology infrastructure element brings up issues such as the technical problems of getting operating systems to work together, dealing with aging hardware, getting enough server power for the job, and a number of resource allocations. Managers need to assign the appropriate resources to the task, establishing an appropriate budget. Managers also need to rally people around the business need that the new project is to address. Even with the best equipment in the world, you cannot neglect the workplace environment.

No one can fail to be impressed by the array of quality products Microsoft has produced in recent years. They have solved the problems involved in rolling out new technologies, and they share the answers with the rest of us.

At the core of the solution development discipline is the MSF Process model, the subject of the rest of this chapter. You've already seen this model applied to software development; now it's time to apply it to infrastructure deployment.

Develop a thorough understanding of the MSF Process model.

Figure 5-3 illustrates the MSF Process model. From the first spark of an idea, envisioning leads to the Vision/Scope Approved milestone. Planning will take you to the Project Plan Approved milestone. The Scope Complete/First Use milestone yields itself after a healthy dose of development. And finally, release signals the end of the Deployment phase. Working with the MSF model helps us to minimize problems, efficiently

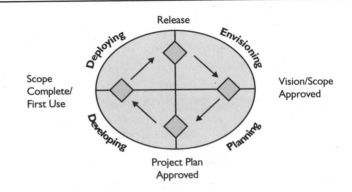

use resources, and achieve our business goals. The details of each milestone
and phase make up the rest of this chapter, the core of the infrastructure
deployment process.

FROM THE CLASSROOM

The Process Model

The Process model is an iterative process that allows for multiphase development projects to assume an organized, continuous, development process. It ensures the necessary emphasis on design and planning, which is often overlooked in many development projects. Special emphasis should be placed on the development of scope documents. Without a properly developed scope document, all aspects of a project are subject to increased risk and will not reach the desired milestones. Remember the SMART requirements of a vision/scope document: Specific, Measurable, Achievable, Results-based, and Time-oriented.

In preparation for the exam, or for leveraging the MSF Process model for the first time, become familiar with the interim milestones and deliverables that map to each of the four phases of the MSF Process model. It is also important to become familiar with the functionality and responsibilities of each of the six roles identified. Be able to match up a given project task with both the phase within which it should reside or be carried out, and the role responsible for carrying out the task.

—*Michael Lane Thomas, MCSE+I, MCSD,
MCT, MCP+SB, MSS, A+*

CERTIFICATION OBJECTIVE 5.04

The Vision/Scope Approved Milestone

When you achieve the first milestone of the infrastructure deployment process, you will have articulated a clear and inspiring vision and will have set an achievable scope for the project. A team effort must begin with a sense of vision. The larger the project, the more important a strong vision becomes. The vision motivates a team—it's the focal point around which they can concentrate their best efforts. A team with a strong vision has members who feel they are important to the overall goals, and are all committed to a common purpose.

Vision supplies the *why*, which inspires the *how*. Good team leaders communicate vision both verbally and visually. Developing vision is much more than coming up with a mission statement that you post on your wall. The overriding sense of purpose must be active in the minds of team members. Remind your people of the vision; get excited about it; show everyone how they can have a fulfilling part of the new mission. Once a team begins to congeal around the vision, it's ready to begin a phase of high-quality action.

Vision and scope work together. Vision points the direction; scope says how far. Scope helps team members see that real achievements can be met. Once the excitement of vision fades, the task can seem daunting, but scope reins in the vision and helps people see the end of the tunnel.

Achieving a Shared Vision for the Infrastructure Deployment Project Team

Vision grows from a business need. The sustaining force of vision is the value to the organization. Vision has to result in something good for the business. Everyone should be able to agree on the fact that your project will be beneficial to the college, bank, charity, investment firm, or manufacturer you work for.

Achieving vision and scope takes time, lots of communication, and some interim steps. Microsoft suggests some interim milestones to mark your progress along the way. Deliverables mark the conclusion of each step. The Envisioning phase culminates in the vision/scope document.

The Vision/Scope Approved Milestone Envisioning Phase

The process of envisioning brings the team to the Vision/Scope Approved milestone. At this milestone the members of the project team, the customer, and key project stakeholders reach a common agreement on the essential parts of vision and scope. These elements include the overall vision, the business requirements to be met first, time frame, risks, assumptions, business constraints, and the level of effort to give to the next phase, which is Planning. Envisioning is a very creative process, characterized by excitement and enthusiasm.

Vision

Vision addresses how the business will change with the new solution. It identifies the business problem and provides the context for the solution. The vision doesn't have limits. During envisioning, team members do not need to consider technical constraints. To reach the milestone, the differing ideas of vision must converge into a single agreed-upon statement.

Scope

During envisioning, people take the vision and compare it to the reality of the situation. This gives the vision appropriate scope. Scope includes the elements essential for success, as made clear by the customer. While deciding on scope, team members consider things like the urgency of various pieces of the solution, which things can wait until the next release, and the constraints and risks involved with the project.

Resources, schedules, and solution functionality each impact the shape of the project. More functionality demands more resources and time. Envisioning is the time to decide how much time and money the result is worth. The scope should let the project achieve solid results while keeping costs and risks down. With most projects, the law of diminishing returns will eventually kick in. Setting an appropriate scope will make sure that benefit is maximized.

Tasks That Occur During the Envisioning Phase

Before you reach the vision/scope document and the approval milestone, Microsoft suggests some helpful intermediate points to measure progress. A team should have a deadline for each of these points. These interim milestones are: Team Formation Complete, Draft Vision/Scope, and Final Vision/Scope. Table 5-1 describes the nature and effect of each milestone.

Team Formation Complete

Microsoft identifies six roles for members of a team: product management, program management, development, testing, logistics management, and user education. Team formation happens when particular team members take on each of these roles. During team formation, leaders match skill sets to roles, and each member commits the time necessary to complete the project.

Getting the right people for the job assures the quality of the product. Once the team has been formed, members take on a sense of ownership of the project. Reaching this milestone means that the project has gotten off the ground. Members have a sense that the project is underway. Once together, the core team can do the work of crafting a central vision.

TABLE 5-1   The Three Interim Milestones of the Envisioning Phase

Interim Milestone	Description	Effect
Team Formation Complete	Team roles have been scaled to the needs of the project. Skill sets are identified. Primary team members are assigned tasks.	Encourages ownership of tasks. Ensures the timelines and quality of deliverables.
Draft Vision/Scope	Has problem statement, solution concept, and procedure for training during the project. Identifies the customer.	Defines what the teams do and why. Ensures that participants are together on the nature of the problem and solution.
Final Vision/Scope	The deliverables have been produced. Success factors and business improvement metrics are documented.	Establishes viability. Team and customer understand their responsibilities.

Draft Vision/Scope

The two key elements of the vision/scope draft are the statement of the problem and the sketch of the solution. Make sure that your solution matches the problem! Establish the customer for the project. This is not always as simple as it might seem. For example, an IT department of a college may want to deploy an ATM network. Who is the customer here? All the potential users? The president of the college who got the grant for the network in the first place? Keep in mind that the customer will play a part in the rest of the process. You want to clearly identify the customer to allow them to participate in the following steps. The customer should see your draft statements at this stage, and give preliminary approval.

Final Vision/Scope

At this milestone the deliverables for the Envisioning phase are complete. When this milestone has been met, both customers and team members understand their responsibilities for the project. By this point, the viability of the project should be apparent to all.

Roles and Responsibilities of Infrastructure Deployment Team Members That Lead to Vision/Scope Approval

Each team member has a part to play in the Envisioning phase. Product management identifies the problem, and then documents the need. Product management also *articulates* the vision. Program management comes up with the design goals and documents the solution. Developers do the critical job of researching solutions and coming up with technical options. User education prepares by deciding on the requirements for training, as well as training scope. Testing creates criteria based on design goals. Logistics management reports on material constraints and considers long-term management and support.

Deliverables Produced During the Envisioning Phase

Table 5-2 describes the deliverables that the team produces in the Envisioning phase.

TABLE 5-2

Deliverables of the
Envisioning Phase

Deliverable	Content
Vision/Scope Document	Problem statement/business objectives Vision statement User profile Solution concept
Risk Management Plan	Identifies risks Identifies new technologies that should be monitored Identifies organizational issues that might impact the progress of the project
Project Structure	Defines how the project will be managed and supported Defines the administrative structure for the project team, such as reporting structure, meetings, and schedules

Writing the Vision/Scope Document

The vision/scope document, the deliverable that marks the Vision/Scope Approved milestone, has several necessary characteristics:

- It provides a clear direction for the team.
- It sets customer expectations.
- It approximates the risk involved in the project.

A baseline for planning, design, and deployment comes from the vision/scope document.

Vision/Scope Document:
Description of Deliverables and Content

The vision/scope document has four parts. The first is the problem statement and business objectives, which address what you want to do and why you want to do it. Next is the vision statement itself, the heart of the document. This statement articulates the direction of the business and shows how the project contributes to the mission. The user profile lists the people that the project impacts. Finally, the solution concept gives the timeline for the project and, of course, sketches how the team intends to solve the stated problem.

SMART Vision/Scope Document Content

A SMART vision/scope document is Specific, Measurable, Achievable, Results-based, and Time-oriented. If the vision for your project is vague and hard to measure, how will you know when you've reached your goal? A specific and measurable vision and scope can help the team recognize the progress they are making as well as giving the project a clear end point. The middle of a project is not the time to discover that you don't have the resources, expertise, and technology to get it done. You should be able to determine up front whether you can reach your objective. A good working timeline should be defined in the vision/scope document. In addition to the qualitative and quantitative measurement set out in the document, you should make sure that the document keeps the results in focus.

EXERCISE 5-1

The Envisioning Phase

Identify the role responsible for each of the following tasks. (The answers to this exercise appear just before the Self Test at the end of this chapter.)

1. Research potential technical solutions: _____

2. Determine the requirements for training: _____

3. Articulate the vision and identify the problem: _____

4. Determine the design goals: _____

5. Create criteria for test suites based on design goals: _____

6. Determine any material constraints: _____

CERTIFICATION OBJECTIVE 5.05

The Project Plan Approved Milestone

The main task of this phase is planning. Your vision is in place; you know what the problem/need is; and you have a good handle on a solution. Now you have to plan the many details of your project. Have you ever been in the middle of a seat-of-the-pants project and thought that some day we're going to do this the right way? Well, now is your chance. Just as a well-designed program tends to flow from your fingers and come together in good order, a well-planned infrastructure project puts peace in your soul.

Setting the Target for the Project Plan Approved Milestone

At the Project Plan Approved milestone, agreement has been reached on a number of important items:

- Project deliverables
- Functional priorities
- Risks
- Ship date
- Project plan
- Business requirements
- Conceptual design elements
- Design specifications
- Time and effort to complete project

Roles and Responsibilities That Lead to the Project Plan Approved Milestone

As with envisioning, three interim milestones occur during planning: Conceptual Design Complete, Design Specification Complete, and Master Project Plan Complete. Deliverables for this phase considerably outnumber those for envisioning. Table 5-3 lists each milestone with its measurement and effect on the project.

Deliverables to Be Produced at Project Plan Approved

The deliverables produced during this phase set the parameters and establish a guide for development. The Planning phase documents can and do still

TABLE 5-3	Milestones of the Planning Phase	
Interim Milestone	**Measurement**	**Effect**
Conceptual Design Complete	The vision, characteristics, distinctive benefits, and how the target audience will interact with the proposed solution are defined.	Structures the solution and ensures that activities adhere to the overall mission and objectives.
Design Specification Complete	Defines the technical components of the solution in detail and determines how they will be implemented.	Assigns technical detail to the structures defined in the functional specification.
Master Project Plan Complete	The master project plan includes the approach, dependencies, and assumptions of the project, as well as budget and cost information.	Ensures that all the participants have a common understanding relative to the functionality desired, resources required, and time constraints.

change with time; they are not set in stone. These documents belong to the Program Management role, who should alter them as the process helps to define itself. Figure 5-4 illustrates the deliverables for the Planning phase.

Conceptual Design Document

Conceptual design, a non-technical document, describes what the final product includes. This detailed document covers the functionality of the solution, how the product might impact the current infrastructure, and the relationship between user and product. The conceptual design document

FIGURE 5-4	The Planning phase has three deliverables.

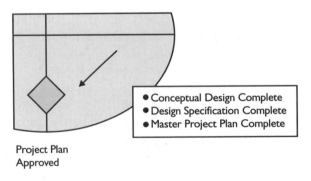

Project Plan
Approved

- Conceptual Design Complete
- Design Specification Complete
- Master Project Plan Complete

includes a vision/scope summary, which is a refined distillation of the results of the previous phase. Of course, the conceptual and logical design is fully detailed within the document. This deliverable also includes design goals, usability goals, constraints, and expectations. Besides acting as a guide to developers, the design goals give the testing team something to test. Detailed field surveys can be an important part of this deliverable. The project team must be able to gauge expectations for the solution. Documenting these expectations at this stage can be very helpful. Finally, the conceptual design document includes user profiles and usage scenarios. The scenarios focus on the environment as it will be, comparing it to the present environment.

Design Specification Drill Down and Detailed Descriptions of Deliverables and Content

While the conceptual design provided a non-technical view of the solution, the design spec itself fills in these technical details. Here's where you get into the fun stuff, thinking of hardware and all the nuts and bolts of your solution. Additionally, this deliverable lists standards and guidelines, change control methodology, the life cycle management plan, and the security plan. Table 5-4 presents these parts.

TABLE 5-4		
Design Specification Content	**Item**	**Description**
	Logical and physical design	The details of the team's solution.
	Standards and guidelines	Ensures that the proposed solution facilitates the communication, integration, and consistency of information between and within elements of the organization.
	Change control methodology	Framework for establishing why the change is needed, who is accountable for the change, what the impact of the change is, and how the change will be traced.
	Life cycle management plan	Considers the rapid evolution of individual and aggregate technologies, together with dynamic organizational factors.
	Security plan	Serves to ensure that data, resource, and service integrity are maintained during the project.

Master Project Schedule Drill Down and Detailed Descriptions of Deliverables and Content

The schedules contained in this deliverable are also not set in stone. Scheduling can be an iterative process, but the mechanism for dealing with project schedule changes must be established. The master project schedule evolves over time. This deliverable consists of a task list, implementation schedule, test schedule, preliminary training estimates, logistics schedule, and marketing schedule.

Master Project Plan Drill Down

The master project plan consists of the following plans: implementation, test, user education, logistics, solution marketing, and also a budget. The user education plan can be a key component of this deliverable. Your team should have an idea of what kinds of solutions it will take to help users work with the product. A needs assessment, purpose statement, and evaluation strategy are parts of the user education plan.

TABLE 5-5	Team	Role
Responsibilities of Each Team in the Planning Phase	Product Management	Project vision User needs analysis Schedule
	Program Management	Project design Project master plan/schedule
	Development	Technology evaluation Physical design Development plan/schedule
	User Education	User performance solution strategy Training needs
	Testing	Design evaluation Testing plan/schedule
	Logistics Management	Materials/facilities procurement Rollout plan/schedule

Defining the Focus and Deliverables of Each MSF Team and Their Role at Project Plan Approved

Table 5-5 gives a complete listing of each MSF team role during the Planning phase. As with all the other phases, each team has a very important role in planning. Ownership for the project really starts to take off in this phase, as each member gets a clear grasp on how they're going to contribute to the solution. The remaining deliverables are test lab setup, risk assessment, and business manager approval.

Test Lab Setup

Planning test lab setups includes deciding who will be responsible for the labs, what activities will be performed there, how the lab should be configured, and how to establish the guidelines and policies for the lab. Like the SMART vision/scope document of the previous phase, Microsoft suggests a BEST way to define the main focus of the test lab. BEST stands for:

- Baseline and backup, making sure that your system can return to the original state in the case of a problem

- Eliminate risk by working through the problems and coming up with acceptable solutions

- Stress testing the solution under full load

- Testing and tracking, testing transitional components and generating useful statistics

Risk Assessment

Risk assessment goes on through all phases, but planning is a good time to start eliminating risk. The team should prioritize and identify the most probable risks. Work on plans to mitigate these top risks and incorporate the plans into the project plan, providing necessary additional resources.

Business Manager Approval

The business manager approves the budget and resources required for the project. This deliverable represents the last element of the Planning phase. Once you've got your resources, you're ready to move to the next phase.

CERTIFICATION OBJECTIVE 5.06

The Scope Complete/First Use Milestone

This milestone comes as your hard work begins to pay off. The Scope Complete/First Use milestone occurs when your solution has been tried in a production environment and your team has consensus on the solution meeting the objectives of the vision/scope document. Figure 5-5 shows our progress through the Process model. The Developing phase has its own set of interim milestones and deliverables, which we will discuss in turn.

EXERCISE 5-2

The Planning Phase

Identify the role responsible for each of the following tasks. (The answers to this exercise appear just before the Self Test at the end of this chapter.)

1. Project vision, user needs analysis, and a schedule: _____
2. Project design and the project master plan/schedule: _____
3. Design evaluation and the testing plan/schedule: _____
4. Materials/facilities procurement and the rollout plan/schedule: _____
5. Technology evaluation, the physical design, and the development plan/schedule: _____
6. User performance solution strategy and training needs: _____

FIGURE 5-5

Developing leads to the Scope Complete/First Use milestone

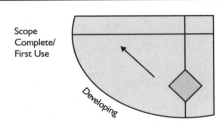

Scope Complete/ First Use

Tasks That Lead to the Scope Complete/First Use Milestone

As with other phases, interim milestones help developers track progress on the way to the completion of the phase, the Scope Complete/First Use milestone. In this section we'll look at each of the interim milestones and discuss how they fit into the Developing phase.

Identifying the Interim Milestones
Leading to Scope Complete/First Use

Three somewhat similar milestones happen along the way to Scope Complete/First Use. Each involves testing. The Lab Test Complete interim milestone makes use of a test lab, which the team planned in the previous phase. This lab does not mimic the production environment, but verifies the soundness of the solution's functionality. At Lab Test Complete, the pieces of the solution have been tested. Some problems will be discovered and alternatives tested.

The Proof-of-Concept Complete interim milestone takes place in the proof-of-concept lab. This lab, a successor of the test lab, does mimic the production environment. Here the whole model of the solution gets a test. The main goal of the Proof-of-Concept Complete milestone is to reduce as much of the risk as possible. Here's where you try the product without risking other enterprise resources.

The Pilot Complete interim milestone means that you're almost ready to begin deployment. During the pilot, your team deploys a portion of your system in the actual user environment. Hopefully the bugs have been worked out by this stage, but you'll likely find any that are left, without sharing them with the whole organization.

Listing the Interim Milestones
Leading to Scope Complete/First Use

Table 5-6 gives each milestone's description and effect.

| TABLE 5-6 | | Interim Milestones of the Developing Phase |

Interim Milestone	Description	Effect
Lab Testing Complete	Testing has been completed in an isolated technology infrastructure lab.	Validates the technology
Proof of Concept Complete	The solution has been installed in a controlled test environment that mimics the anticipated production.	Validates the solution
Pilot Complete	The solution has been tested in a limited, controlled production environment, and all known issues have been resolved or a contingency plan has been developed.	Real-world validation

Defining the Focus and Deliverables of Each MSF Team and Their Role at Scope Complete/First Use

Your team will produce five deliverables during the Development phase: pilot plan, training plan, capacity plan, business continuation plan, and rollout plan. Each MSF team has a role to play in developing these documents. Communication through this phase is essential. You want your teams not only to keep each other up-to-date on their progress, but also to let them share ideas and input. First, we'll discuss the deliverables, and then the roles of each team.

The pilot plan sets up the pilot test. It should contain all the necessary steps and procedures to run the test. Be sure that the plan accounts for each usage scenario. You'll want the pilot to give a realistic representation of the product. Keep in mind that the pilot happens once. The pilot plan sets the stage for escalation to deployment.

Scope/complete first use is the time for training. Your team should complete a training plan as a deliverable for this phase. Good training doesn't just teach users the mechanics of a solution; it also helps the organization get the greatest advantage possible for your project. With this in mind, your training plan should include a view of how job functions will change with the new solution, training logistics, and conclusions based on the user profiles.

The capacity plan functions as a kind of check to see if you've got enough of what you need. Is your infrastructure solution up to the job?

Your team must determine if the components of your system can handle their required functions. Additionally, the product should allow for growth, without going overboard. The capacity plan is also a good place to check if your solution fits the vision, at least in terms of being adequate for the job.

The business continuation plan reduces risk by establishing procedures to recover to an acceptable threshold of performance in the case of a disaster. The plan doesn't restore everything to its pre-failure state, but just gets things working enough so business can continue. To do this, your team must identify the critical systems that have to stay up, and what it would take to get them back up. Identify areas where load can be reduced; in other words, functions that are not essential and can be shut down to devote resources to the more critical operations. A recovery plan takes the enterprise back to normal from where the business continuation plan leaves off.

And finally, the rollout plan! This plan gets your team ready for the next phase. It contains step-by-step procedures for delivering the solution. The strategy includes who gets the product when, and who will give it to them. The plan addresses how to get this done with minimal disruption. A good key to success for the rollout plan is for your team to get consensus, participation, and ownership of the user community. Don't assume that everyone will think the product is as super as you do and worth the effort of change. Get the users involved and excited, and they'll make rollout a lot more fun.

Table 5-7 shows the role of each MSF team during the Development phase.

TABLE 5-7	Team	Role
	Product Management	Customer expectations Schedule
Team Roles During Development Phase	Program Management	Functional specification management Project tracking/communication Pilot plan
	Development	System compliance
	User Education	User/deployment team training
	Testing	Issue identification
	Logistics Management	Operations/support/systems administration Final release schedule

Describing the Process for Driving to the Release Milestone

As your team approaches scope complete/first use and starts to think about deploying, some tasks help to wrap up development. During this phase, your team has validated the project. You know now that it will work. Plans made earlier, such as conceptual design, design specification, and project plans should be in their final form and consistent with the solution you are about to deliver. As your team transitions to deployment, work on stabilization of the system, making sure everything is settled and functioning as load begins to increase. Also, take a look at the milestones reached so far, and review what when wrong, and what went right. Examine your successes and failures so the team can be ready for the Release milestone.

EXERCISE 5-3

The Developing Phase

Identify the role responsible for each of the following tasks. (The answers to this exercise appear just before the Self Test at the end of this chapter.)

1. Functional specification management, project tracking/communication, and the pilot plan: _____

2. User/deployment team training: _____

3. Issue identification: _____

4. System compliance: _____

5. Operations/support/systems administration, and the final release schedule: _____

6. Customer expectations and the schedule: _____

CERTIFICATION OBJECTIVE 5.07

The Release Milestone

Figure 5-6 shows how far the team has gotten in the process: we're almost there! The last phase, Deploying, leads to the Release milestone. Microsoft defines the point of release as when management of the system shift from the product team to the normal operations and support mechanisms. At this

FIGURE 5-6

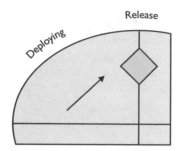

milestone the solution has been deployed and is considered stable. The customer has accepted the product and signs off in some way. Your team then moves on to the next project.

Defining the Release Milestone

Four milestones occur during the Deploying phase: Rollout Begins, Training Complete, Rollout Complete, and Stabilization Complete. Rollout Begins is pretty easy! Your team should pretty much be there having finished the pilot of the previous phase. Training has been ongoing for some time now, but as rollout continues, training concludes, as users jump on the system and take off. As your team reaches Rollout Complete, there may be some significant problems remaining that prevent you from handing over support to the operational staff. Your team must complete stabilization before your role can end.

Tasks That Lead to the Release Milestone

Table 5-8 describes each of the interim milestones in more detail. As your team reaches these milestones, a number of tasks are underway. Logistics management comes to the fore in this phase as they handle site preparation and rollout itself. In preparing the site, the team checks the site against operations requirements and sets up user administration.

During the previous phase, Development has adjusted the rollout plan to fit the solution. Now it's time for Logistics to execute the plan, providing

TABLE 5-8   Interim Milestones Leading to Release

Interim Milestone	Description	Effect
Rollout Begins	Deployment of the new technology solution is extended beyond the safety net of the pilot group.	Allows business to begin to realize incremental benefits from the solution.
Training Complete	Trainers, implementers, administrators, users, and operations personnel have all received the training they need.	Meets explicit training needs of all user segments.
Rollout Complete	Technology solution has been deployed to all of the targeted users.	Conveys the project business benefits to the customer.
Stabilization Complete	Rate of new problem reports has declined steadily and is at or near zero each day.	Facilitates the transfer of support for the new technology to the infrastructure management team.

the material and doing the legwork for getting the system in place. Logistics also sets up the appropriate help desk mechanisms for long-term support after your team withdraws.

The testing done up to now has been good and has eliminated a lot of problems, but you know that problems will pop up when the system hits the production environment. Now your labs switch over to solving real-world problems. Testing continues throughout deployment as you work to bring the solution to stabilization and optimize its performance.

Describing the Deliverables for the Release Milestone

The Deploying phase has two deliverables: post-rollout baselining of user profiles and usage scenarios, and project review. Do you remember the predictions of how the enterprise environment would change at the conclusion of the project? In the initial phase, your team developed a vision for a new system. In the Planning phase, your team took that vision and produced a document outlining the new environment. Now is the time to compare these predications to reality. How did your solution match what you envisioned? For the post-rollout baselining of user profiles and usage scenarios, you take the user profiles and usage scenarios of the previous phases and compare them to the result.

The project review examines the course you took in the deploying phase. Your team looks at what went wrong and what went right. The project review documents what you learned from your mistakes. Your team can then use these best practices for future infrastructure projects.

Describing the Focus for Each MSF Team Role at Release

Table 5-9 gives a complete listing of the role of each MSF team during the Deploying phase. As your team moves towards the goal, each segment still needs to focus on its role, keeping communication open throughout.

exam
ⓦatch

Remember how each MSF team role relates to each phase of the project.

TABLE 5-9	Team	Role
Team Roles During the Release Phase	Product Management	Promotion Feedback Assessment Signoff
	Program Management	Solution/scope comparison Project tracking/coordination
	Development	Problem resolution Release
	User Education	Need-specific training Training schedule
	Testing	Performance metrics Problem resolution
	Logistics Management	Site prep setup/support Rollout management Change approval

Identifying the Activities Leading to the Release Milestone and Laying the Foundation for Future Projects

Deploying culminates in the Release milestone. The solution achieves release when all the users identified in the scope have received the solution, the rate of new problems approaches zero, the solution can be supported by permanent staff, and the customer expresses satisfaction with the performance, quality, and functionality of the solution.

If you've achieved your vision, your team has indeed done something worth celebrating. During this happy time, you can receive feedback from users, review milestones, and prepare for future technology infrastructure projects.

EXERCISE 5.4

The Stabilizing Phase

Identify the role responsible for each of the following tasks. (The answers to this exercise appear just before the Self Test at the end of this chapter.)

1. Promotion, feedback, assessment, and signoff:_____

2. Solution/scope comparison and project tracking/coordination: _____

   _____

3. Need-specific training and training schedule: _____

4. Problem resolution and release:_____

5. Site prep setup/support, rollout management, and change approval:

   _____

6. Performance metrics and problem resolution: _____

EXERCISE 5.5

Phases of the MSF Process Model

Identify the phase for the following interim milestones and deliverables.

Interim Milestone	Deliverables	Phase
Conceptual Design Complete Design Specification Complete Master Project Plan Complete	Conceptual Design Document Design Specification Master Project Plan	
Team Formation Complete Draft Vision/Scope Final Vision/Scope	Vision/Scope Document Risk Management Plan Project Structure	

Interim Milestone	Deliverables	Phase
Rollout Begins Training Complete Rollout Complete Stabilization Complete	Post-Rollout Baselining of User Profiles and Usage Scenarios Project Review	
Lab Testing Complete Proof of Concept Complete Pilot Complete	Pilot Plan Training Plan Capacity Plan Business Continuation Plan Rollout Plan	

CERTIFICATION SUMMARY

The enterprise architecture consists of people, process, and technology. The technology infrastructure is an intersection of these three. The MSF Process model can guide infrastructure deployment projects. The model consists of four phases: Envisioning, Planning, Developing, and Deploying. Each phase concludes with a milestone: Vision/Scope Approved, Project Plan Approved, Scope Complete/First Use, and Release. Each of these phases includes interim milestones and deliverables. The MSF team model organizes the Deployment team into six roles: Product Management, Program Management, Development, User Education, Testing, and Logistics Management.

TWO-MINUTE DRILL

❑ The technology infrastructure exists to meet the business needs of the organization.

❑ Microsoft's eight categories of the technology portion of the infrastructure are: data transmission links, local area network architecture, wide area network architecture, protocols and transports, network operating systems, computer hardware, computer software, and domain/site models.

❑ The Process model is an iterative model that allows for multiphase development projects to assume an organized, continuous, development process.

❑ Remember the SMART requirements of a vision/scope document: **S**pecific, **M**easurable, **A**chievable, **R**esults-based, and **T**ime-oriented.

❑ The process of envisioning brings the team to the Vision/Scope Approved milestone. At this milestone the members of the project team, the customer, and key project stakeholders reach a common agreement on the essential parts of vision and scope.

❑ Microsoft suggests some helpful intermediate points to measure progress: Team Formation Complete, Draft Vision/Scope, and Final Vision/Scope.

❑ Microsoft identifies six roles for members of a team: Product Management, Program Management, Development, Testing, Logistics Management, and User Education.

❑ The vision/scope document has several necessary characteristics: it provides a clear direction for the team; it sets customer expectations; and it approximates the risk involved in the project.

❑ Conceptual design, a non-technical document, describes what the final product includes. This detailed document covers the functionality of the solution, how the product might impact the current infrastructure, and the relationship between user and product

❑ Planning test lab setups includes deciding who will be responsible for the labs, what activities will be performed there, how the lab should be configured, and how to establish the guidelines and policies for the lab.

❑ Your team will produce five deliverables during the Development phase: pilot plan, training plan, capacity plan, business continuation plan, and rollout plan.

❑ The rollout plan contains step-by-step procedures for delivering the solution.

❑ Four milestones occur during the Deploying phase: Rollout Begins, Training Complete, Rollout Complete, and Stabilization Complete.

❑ The Deploying phase has two deliverables: post-rollout baselining of user profiles and usage scenarios, and project review.

Answers to Exercise 5-1

1. Developer Team
2. Product Team
3. Testing Team

4. User Education Team
5. Program Team
6. Logistics Team

Answers to Exercise 5-2

1. Product Team
2. Testing Team
3. Developer Team

4. Program Team
5. Logistics Team
6. User Education Team

Answers to Exercise 5-3

1. Program Team
2. Testing Team
3. Logistics Team

4. User Education Team
5. Developer Team
6. Product Team

Answers to Exercise 5-4

1. Program Team
2. User Education Team
3. Logistics Team

4. Product Team
5. Developer Team
6. Testing Team

Answers to Exercise 5-5

Planning Phase
Envisioning Phase
Stabilizing Phase
Developing Phase

SELF TEST

The Self Test questions will help you measure your understanding of the material presented in this chapter. Read all the choices carefully, as there may be more than one correct answer. Select all correct answers for each question.

1. Complete this sentence: Enterprise architecture _____

    A. consists of people, process, and technology.

    B. is the intersection of people, process, and technology.

    C. consists of the Process model and Team model.

    D. means *technology infrastructure.*

2. Which is an example of an enterprise architecture process?

    A. Managers

    B. TCP/IP

    C. Billing

    D. Microsoft Project

3. Which is not a technology infrastructure category?

    A. Data transmission links

    B. Local area network architecture

    C. Protocols and transports

    D. TCP/IP

4. The MSF process model does not include

    A. Milestones

    B. Phases

    C. Teams

    D. Deliverables

5. Which milestone happens before the planning phase?

    A. Vision/Scope Approved

    B. Project Plan Approved

    C. Scope Complete/First Use

    D. Envisioning

6. Complete the following sentence: Vision addresses _____

    A. the nature of the solution.

    B. how the business will change with the new solution.

    C. team makeup.

    D. testing.

7. Which does not affect scope?

    A. Resources

    B. Schedules

    C. Solution functionality

    D. Planning

8. Which interim milestone occurs first?

    A. Draft Vision/Scope

    B. Final Vision/Scope

    C. Team Formation Complete

    D. Vision/Scope Approved

9. Which team has responsibility for articulating the vision?

    A. Development

B. Program Management

C. Logistics Management

D. Product Management

10. A SMART vision/scope document is

   A. Specific, Measurable, Achievable, Results-based, and Time-oriented

   B. Significant, Marketable, Achievable, Ready, and Testable

   C. Sloppy, Marked, Amiable, Red, and Typed

   D. Specific, Measurable, Action-oriented, low Risk, and Timely

11. The Conceptual Design Complete interim milestone is a part of which phase?

   A. Envisioning

   B. Planning

   C. Developing

   D. Deploying

12. Which is not an interim milestone of the planning phase?

   A. Conceptual Design Complete

   B. Design Specification Complete

   C. Master Project Plan Complete

   D. Lab Testing Complete

13. The security plan is a part of which deliverable of the planning phase?

   A. Conceptual design document

   B. Design specification

   C. Master project schedule

   D. Master project plan

14. Complete the following sentence: The master project schedule _____

   A. evolves over time.

   B. stays set.

   C. is good for the planning phase only.

   D. can by changed by development.

15. During planning, development is responsible for _____

   A. user needs analysis.

   B. project plan.

   C. technology evaluation.

   D. design evaluation.

16. Which test happens last in the developing phase?

   A. Pilot

   B. Test lab

   C. Proof-of-concept

   D. Design test

17. Which does the Lab Testing Complete milestone mark?

   A. Real-world validation

   B. Technology validation

   C. Solution validation

   D. Software validation

18. Which is not a deliverable of the developing phase?

   A. Pilot plan

   B. Training plan

   C. Rollout plan

   D. Project review

19. What does the business continuation plan do?

    A. Provides for transition to normal operations.

    B. Eliminates risk.

    C. Returns the company to an acceptable threshold of performance.

    D. Returns the company to pre-failure.

20. Which is not an interim milestone of the deploying phase?

    A. Rollout Begins

    B. Training Complete

    C. Rollout Complete

    D. Program Review

6

Designing Component Solutions—An Overview

I n this chapter, we'll discuss some of the problems commonly encountered in designing an application. This includes some of the challenges currently encountered in Information Technology, as well as a discussion on the ten common problems that lead to design failure and flaws.

Also in this chapter, we'll discuss the models and issues dealing with the design of component solutions. We'll see how MSF provides proven methods for designing applications and solutions that use components. In reading this chapter, it's important to realize that not everything is covered here. This information introduces you to some of the models, principles, and practices of designing these solutions, which we'll expand on in later chapters.

Success in Software Design

Designing software can be a bittersweet experience at best. While it's exhilarating to reach a major milestone in a project, and to see a product you toiled over being welcomed by users, the problems of reaching these points can feel overwhelming. Meetings, schedules, budgets, placing people in team roles, and so many other tasks need to be done before the first line of code is even written. If you're using outdated and obsolete models that worked well a decade ago but don't address issues faced today, you may be frustrated by the time that first line is written.

If you've used computers for awhile, you've probably come across a few different applications that failed to provide the benefits they promised, and perhaps a few that barely worked at all. It's important to remember that most problems with software development products aren't the result of bad coding, but bad design. Any programming code that a developer writes is based on information obtained during the design process. If the design is bad from the start, no amount of programming talent will be able to save the project.

Being successful in software design isn't as elusive as it may seem. One of the easiest ways to deal with design problems is to understand the obstacles others have encountered, and learn how to overcome or avoid them. As we'll see later in this chapter, there are a number of common problems that can lead to design flaws and failure. By discussing issues with people who have designed similar projects, you can often identify difficulties before they become major problems.

The importance of applying good models to a project can't be stressed enough. Software design and development is complex, and as we've seen in the previous chapters, models help to break down this complexity into manageable parts. While there are many models and methods available to you, it's important that the models you choose work well together. Otherwise, you could have one model that works well on its own, but jeopardizes the benefits of other models used in your project. By using models that work well together, and have proven their worth in real-world projects, you can minimize the possibility of failure in your project.

Identifying Business Environment and Information Technology Challenges

Anyone who's been in Information Technology for awhile can tell you that one of the biggest challenges are those faced by the business environment itself. Issues such as global competition and the need for new services and technologies to enhance the performance of workers have changed and continue to change the face of business. As the business environment changes, IT must try to keep up with the changing policies, security requirements, and other influences that influence the development of software products. To add to these challenges, it can be difficult trying to get the necessary information to develop a solution, because customers and users may not be able to communicate what they really want.

Unfortunately, as your team attempts to face these challenges, they may be hindered by a number of problems. Current methodologies used by the team may not allow additional user requirements to be added midstream. Members of the team may not fully understand what's required from a project, and even if they do, they may find their role in the project's success unclear. Schedules may be so demanding that they jeopardize the product's release date. Projects may be too big and complex, and there is a need to break these large projects into manageable parts. The design may be so flawed that it does little to enhance work performance, and actually slows it. Each of these is an important issue, and if the solution you're developing is hindered by these issues, it can affect how an organization is able to do business.

There is a symbiotic relationship between an organization and its IT department; neither can get along without the other. Because of this, it is important for Information Technology to use the proven methods to ensure their software development projects are successful. There is no time in IT to experiment with models, principles, and practices that may or may not work.

Exercise 6-1 tests your comfort level with designing solutions and the MSF model. (The answers to this exercise appear just before the Self Test at the end of the chapter.)

EXERCISE 6-1

Designing Solutions

Please indicate with a "T" or an "F" whether these statements are True or False.

1. You can use the same software models from 20 years ago for today's application designs. _____

2. Because the business environment continually changes, Information Technology must attempt to keep up with changing policies, security requirements, and other issues that change the way the organization does business. _____

3. Information Technology must use proven development and management methods to ensure projects are successful. _____

4. The MSF is a static methodology that clearly delineates what steps to take in the development process. _____

5. You may use mature analysis and design techniques with the MSF model. _____

6. Incremental internal release of a software product means a new version with added functionality is put into production. _____

7. Product management is responsible for estimating the development schedule and getting it approved. _____

8. Tradeoffs may be made between schedule features and resources. _____

9. Large projects should always be developed as a monolithic application to avoid losing functionality. _____

10. Daily builds may, in reality, be accomplished once a week. _____

Achieving Good Design with MSF

The models in the Microsoft Solution Framework provide you with the ability to address many of the challenges and difficulties faced by solution developers. It takes the best practices and principles used by companies like Microsoft, and puts them in a format that can be applied to any project you encounter. By being proven, you don't need to worry about having to test these models for effectiveness, and worry about the first projects you use them on failing.

Rather than being a static methodology, MSF is a framework of models that can be adapted and applied to an organization's specific needs. In fact, you can continue using the analysis methods, data modeling, and user interview techniques you're comfortable with, providing they can be adapted to evolving technologies. Each model in the framework is a flexible component, so you can adapt and combine the different MSF models with the methods and techniques your organization currently uses.

CERTIFICATION OBJECTIVE 6.02

Identifying Typical Problems That Lead to Design Flaws or Failure

Many of the problems and dissatisfaction customers have with software are the result of design problems. While the lines of code work, and the product functions as it should, mistakes in the design phase cause the project to be less than successful or to fail dismally. Like other areas of solution development, there are common problems that you can watch out for, and thereby avoid flaws and failure resulting from design. In this section, we'll cover ten of the common issues that lead to problems in design.

Of all the possible problems you can encounter in designing an application, the most common one you'll experience is the *design failing to deliver what the customer expected.* Often, this is a result of the customer not knowing what they really wanted. This may seem strange at face value, until you realize that people often find it easier to say what they don't want, rather than what they do want. Because of this, it is important for the designer and customer to sit down and come to a clear understanding of what needs to be included in the product. This is the purpose of a specification. You'll remember from Chapter 4 that the functional specification is the result of the Project Plan Approved milestone, and contains information on what needs to be done to create the product. Creating a specification requires a clear understanding of the project's end result, and the specific items to be included in the product. Once created, this information is used throughout the development process to create what customers and users expect.

The second most typical problem in design is *using inappropriate technologies to complete the project.* As you know from your own experience, developers and analysts learn and become experts in specific programming languages, DBMS (database management systems), and other technologies. Therefore, when they design an application, they use the tools they are most familiar with. Unfortunately, the technologies they incorporate in a product may not be the best ones to use. It's important to evaluate different technologies available, and determine which is best suited for your project and how it should be utilized.

The third most common problem in design is *scalability.* This deals with the number of people who will use your product. It's important to remember that just because your product works well with ten users, it may not work well with hundreds or thousands of users. Remember that each user added to a network's population eats up more resources. While your application may work well on a test network of a dozen or so people, its usability may crumble if it is not designed to deal with a significantly larger user base.

A *software product's ability or inability to deal with errors and other unexpected occurrences* is the fourth typical problem in design. Applications should have code added to deal with any errors that might occur, or messages sent to the application from the operating system or any servers the application accesses. When your software product needs to access resources, you should have *error-handling code* to deal with the possibility that the resource may not be there. Error handling involves having code (called *error handlers*) added to your program's code to deal with problems as they occur. For example, let's say your application needed to access a specific database, but the database had been moved to another location or accidentally deleted. Such error handlers would deal with this problem, and provide another course of action. Because of the importance of such code, you should add error- and message-handling code from beginning to end of your software product's development.

Fifth in our listing is the problems involved from *integrating business rules into a single application*. Business rules are rules on how data is utilized and manipulated, which adhere to the enterprise's way of doing business. Business rules reside in the business services tier, where the combination of such things as validation edits, logon verifications, database lookups, policies, and algorithmic transformations constitute the enterprise's way of doing business. Considering that over 80 percent of applications running on a Windows platform access data in some way, this is a significant issue for your software design. If business rules are integrated into applications and those rules change, you and your development team will need to change the code in every application. Because of this, you should put business rules in a central repository or server, so they can be accessed as needed. You can also avoid this problem by integrating business rules into COM components, which are then accessed by applications that utilize the rules. When a business rule changes, you modify the code in the COM component rather than in each application that uses the rule to access data.

Just as accessing data is vital, it's equally important that users are able to update records without a problem. Unfortunately, it's difficult to know how many of your product's users will be updating the same record at the same time. The sixth most common problem in design is *concurrency*, which is the designer's failure to account for numerous users updating the same records. When numerous users do heavy updates and inserts on frequently used pages of a database that contain the most current row, it can seriously bog down a system. In any database you design, you should take into account the maximum number of users who will concurrently use the database. If you are creating an updated version of an application that uses a database, analyze the current number of concurrent users. If it is a new design, try to determine the worst-case scenario of users who will concurrently use records in the database; then apply it to the design. Chances are, unless you're designing a desktop application used by a single user, more than one user will be accessing the same records simultaneously.

The seventh typical problem in design is *security*. This is a particularly important issue in software development, as the last thing you want is an unintentional intruder or malicious hacker getting into areas where they don't belong. Imagine a person who's getting fired reading about it through a supposedly secure database, or a hacker deleting and changing records. A number of problems could result from insecure access to data. When creating applications that access data, you should build stored procedures or server-side COM components that can control access to the data. As mentioned earlier, the use of COM components also allows you to integrate business rules on a server. By incorporating security into server-side components, you can change and enhance security procedures without having to recompile and reinstall applications on each of the workstations in your network.

Eighth in our listing of typical mistakes is *adding BLOBs to databases*. If you're a fan of B-movies from the 1950s, this comment has probably put some strange images in your head. A *BLOB* is an acronym for *binary large objects*, and includes such things as graphics, compiled code, tomes, and sound, which can cause serious performance issues. By including a data column containing such binary data, you can slow down the speed that data is accessed. Imagine a database of employees that includes an employee's photo with each record. Not only does the photo enlarge the size of your database, but it slows performance as users access each record. It is far better to leave the binary data in its original source file, and add a pointer from the database to that file. Views or SELECT statements can also be used to return only the data desired from a given table. You can also add a command button to your user interface that accesses the data on demand. This allows you to expand the amount of data shown, rather than displaying it automatically each time the record is accessed.

The ninth most typical problem deals with *buying third-party solutions*. The *Not Invented Here (NIH)* syndrome is based on ego, with a prevalent feeling that software products developed outside the organization should rarely be used. Considering that there are third-party solutions out there that are recommended by Microsoft, this is a narrow way of thinking. Never discount the value of other people's work. By designing your application to work with other applications already on the market, you can save time developing applications that already provide the functionality the organization requires. You may even find applications that already meet all of the requirements your organization needs. Not only can it save your organization or customer considerable amounts of money, it can save your team time to focus on other products that haven't been developed, or require a more customized approach.

Finally, the use of poor design models and the complete lack of design are the last problems we'll discuss here. New developers and those working on smaller projects can conclude that since it isn't a big project they're working on, design isn't needed. As such, they take a "code by the seat of your pants" attitude, and later find problems cropping up that could have been resolved through design. When models are used for designing an application, new or theoretical models that work well in a classroom are used. Unfortunately, you can experience problems because these models are purely academic and/or untested. It's for that reason that the models in the Microsoft Solution Framework should be adopted, as they've been used in the real world with success.

FROM THE CLASSROOM

Typical Failure by Design?

It is a common fact that a majority of application failures or flaws can be traced to deficiencies instituted during the design phase. Considering the importance the design phase places on the outcome of an application development project, traditionally low regard has been given to the ramifications of ignoring this phase of development.

Some of the most common pitfalls may have incredibly simple solutions. Yet it is the simplicity that often causes the development team or product manager to underestimate the negative consequences. The odds of failing to deliver the customer's expectations can quite often be significantly diminished simply by focusing on creating a clear and concise understanding of the project scope. For a product, clearly identifying the feature set to the mutual understanding of all parties involved can significantly reduce discrepancies in the future.

One potentially devastating issue involves focusing on using certain technologies simply to leverage existing skill sets, past the point of those skills producing a clear and distinct advantage. One common pitfall to avoid, therefore, is using a narrow focus when assessing the appropriate technologies to implement.

Given that proper design has produced a stable, workable, and efficient solution, failing to implement the necessary "open door" design policy can lead to significant scalability issues down the road. Failing to recognize design considerations that, given equal effectiveness, would produce a more scalable solution can severely crimp the ability to serve additional users when the application is a success.

Finally, keep in mind that the strict adherence to separation of functionality between the different services in a multi-tier application can yield the same potential application inefficiencies that failing to consider adequate database denormalization may produce. Developing a strict division between user, business, and data services can lead the developer to make decisions that ultimately may actually produce a less efficient and possibly less scalable design.

—*Michael Lane Thomas, MCSE+I, MCSD, MCT, MCP+SB, MSS, A+*

Microsoft's Process for Designing Solutions

As we saw in first few chapters of this book, the Process model describes the life cycle of a software development project. This life cycle lays out which tasks need to be completed, by breaking a project into four phases that culminate in milestones:

- *Envisioning phase,* which results in the Vision/Scope Approved milestone.

- *Planning phase,* which results in the Project Plan Approved milestone.

- *Developing phase,* which results in the Scope Complete/First Use milestone.

- *Stabilizing phase,* which results in the Release milestone.

Each of these milestones produces several deliverables, and is a point at which the development team synchronizes their efforts.

By outlining which tasks are performed at what time, and when efforts are to be coordinated and evaluated, these phases and milestones are a primary function of the Process model. However, this isn't all the Process model provides to your project. As we'll see in this section, the Process model has a number of principles and practices that help to ensure the success of your project, while providing flexibility to any project.

Interim Milestones

There are times when four milestones may not be enough. For delivery schedules that are over three months, you should consider establishing interim milestones. Interim milestones further break up a project, and provide additional points at which the team can synchronize their efforts. You can think of these as mini-milestones that occur between the major milestones of the Process model. By having interim milestones placed at regular increments in a project, your team can review issues concerning the project, coordinate efforts, and analyze whether each team member is performing according to schedule. After reviewing these individual schedules, Program Management can then assess what impact certain issues will have on the delivery schedule as a whole.

There are two kinds of interim milestones you can apply to any project you're working on. They are *externally visible interim milestones* and *internally visible interim milestones*. Which is used depends on a "need to know" basis. If the milestone applies only to members of your project's team and customers, users, or stakeholders don't need to be informed of the milestone, then it is considered internally visible. If you need to notify the organization itself about the milestone, then it is an externally visible milestone.

External interim milestones are known outside of the development team, and are announced to the organization. These include such things as meetings, where the team apprises customers and stakeholders of various aspects of the project:

- Management review meetings, which are regularly scheduled to inform those attending about the status of a project, and review requests for changes in the product.

- Post-functional specification baseline meetings, where those attending the meeting can approve freeze points in the functional specification of the product.

- Review and validation of a draft functional specification. Before the functional specification is created, a draft is created. This includes interim delivery of models, user task analysis, and other elements that will be incorporated into the final specification.

As you can see, external interim milestones are a way of synchronizing team members and the organization as a whole, so that everyone has a clear understanding of what is required and what is being created.

Internal interim milestones are not known outside the development team. The reason that no one outside of the team requires knowledge of these milestones is that they are only of use for the team itself. Internal interim milestones are used to coordinate the team, or get a clear perspective on how their work is progressing. They include such things as synchronization points, incremental internal releases, and short-term interval deliverables.

Synchronization points are determined by Program Management, and used to coordinate the efforts of your project team. At these points, the data model, business model, user interface, and system architecture are discussed. These points ensure that the functional specification is being followed and understood by team members.

Incremental internal releases are, as their name implies, releases of the product that are used internally by the project team. For every internal release, the development team delivers a number of features in the product for testing. The thought behind the release is to treat the product as if it were to be shipped with just these features. If testable, the release goes through a test/debug/retest cycle, which allows the team to determine problems and progress associated with the product. If the quality is as good or better than expected, then it achieves a *Zero-Defect milestone,* meaning that it passed testing without any defects and developers can work on the next set of features. If it fails, the developers hammer out the problems of the original code, and the process repeats itself.

on the
job

It is recommended that you use intervals of every three months for your internal releases. If you choose to use a different and wider time span, remember not to space the releases more than six months apart. If you do, you'll lose many of the benefits of incrementing internal releases.

Finally, short-term internal deliverables are used for assessing progress and risks of a project. As we saw in Chapter 4, each major milestone has a deliverable associated with it. By using internal deliverables that are made in increments of between five and ten days, the team can view how well they are proceeding before the major milestone is actually reached. This provides the team with realistic assessments of the project's progress, as well as risks associated with the product.

How Milestones in the Process Model Map to Team Roles

Due to the close relationship the Process model has to the Team model, the MSF Process model also shows who is responsible for reaching a milestone. For a particular milestone to be achieved, certain tasks must be planned, managed, and accomplished. Team members are accountable for seeing that these tasks are completed successfully. If a team member fails in this responsibility, then the milestone associated with that member's role isn't achieved either. This relationship allows us to directly map each team role to one of the four milestones in the Process model:

Milestone	Owner
Vision/Scope Approved	Product Management
Project Plan Approved	Program Management
Scope Complete/First Use	Development & User Education
Release	Testing & Logistics

The Process model provides ownership of responsibility to the different roles in the Team model. Each team member owns responsibility for planning, managing, and accomplishing tasks associated with particular milestones. For a milestone to be achieved, the team members associated with that milestone must fulfill their specific responsibilities.

Scheduling

One of the more interesting aspects of a project is determining how long it will take for your team to complete tasks, so the product can be shipped by a specific date. The reason this can be so difficult is that the future is uncertain, and a schedule is a prediction of how long the tasks comprising your project will take to be completed. Proper scheduling is vital to the success of a project.

The Process model incorporates a number of proven disciplines and methods for scheduling, which helps ensure that your product is completed on time, and with little difficulty. One of the most basic principles in the Process model is the use of *bottom-up estimating*. Bottom-up estimates work on a chain-of-command principle, with those who are lower in a hierarchy reporting work estimates to those above them. As illustrated in Figure 6-1, you can think of bottom-up estimating as being a ladder, in which estimates are passed from the bottom rung to the top. Each estimate is passed to whoever is at the next level until it is finally combined at the top level. In other words, the people who actually do the work submit estimates to team leaders and management, and the estimates are then put together into a master schedule of the project.

The benefits of bottom-up estimates reside in having the people who have experience with a task determining how long it will take to do it. For example, rather than having someone with managerial background decide how long it will take to create a feature component, the developer in charge of that feature decides how long it will take to program it. Because the person responsible for the task determines the work estimate, this also

FIGURE 6-1

Bottom-up estimating can be thought of as a ladder, with each estimate being passed to a higher rung.

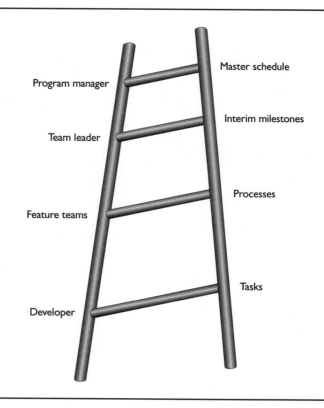

makes them accountable for success in meeting that estimate. This provides motivation to produce in a specific time what they said they could do, and encourages members to try for early milestones.

The thought of bottom-up estimates can seem contradictory to the Team model, because it uses an obvious hierarchy, while the Team model views the team as a group of peers. However, even though the Team model is based on the philosophy of a group of peers, there is a hierarchy of what work is performed first, and which members are in leadership roles. When going through the different team roles listed in Chapter 1 of this book, you'll see this hierarchy.

The first activity performed in a project is Product Management, which obtains the business requirements of a project, followed by Program Management, which has specific scheduling duties and determines when the product is delivered. The final activity in a project is Logistics, which ensures the smooth rollout of a product. In addition to this, Program Management has responsibilities over team leaders, who are responsible for feature teams, which developers are a part of. Though the hierarchy exists, the team is a group of peers, where the expertise of each member is put to the best use. The ladder analogy to bottom-up estimating in Figure 6-1 also helps in understanding the relationship the Team model has with bottom-up estimating. If you think of house builders working on the ladder, the carpenter is no less important than the painter. However, the estimates of when the carpenter finishes affect when the painter can start, and when the work as a whole will be finished. Though these workers are peers and equally important to the project, their estimates are passed up the ladder and combined into a master schedule of their project.

Because the master schedule is comprised of estimated schedules and variables, it is important that the people doing work in these areas of the project create their own estimates. Estimates on the time each activity will take are submitted, and these are put together into a master schedule. Unfortunately, after estimates have been made and submitted, problems may occur, which can cause these estimates to be wrong. The Process model offers two methods of scheduling for an uncertain future. One of these is prioritizing tasks by how risky they are. This is called *risk-driven scheduling*. Using this method, a task is prioritized by the customer. The customer determines how important tasks are by technical and business risks associated with them. Features and services that are vital to the project's success are given highest priority, and tasks that deliver less important benefits are given lower priority.

By prioritizing tasks involved in a schedule, the customer gains an understanding of what is risky about the project, while the team attains a clear vision about what features and services are important to the customer and end user. The team and customer gain a cohesiveness, and are able to decide which features will be shipped with the product, and when. In addition, since the team now knows which features are of high priority to a customer, they can give added effort to reaching early milestones for those tasks that are of greatest importance.

The other method is *adding buffer time to your schedule.* This is time that's added to a schedule to cover problems that may arise in individual tasks. Program Management adds this time to the end of the schedule, rather than to each task in the schedule. The reason for this is that some tasks may come in on time or early, so it would be impossible to add buffer time to each activity the team works on.

When you add buffer time to the end of a schedule, it's not an indicator that your team did a poor job of estimating the time it will take to complete different tasks. It is an acknowledgement that things happen that are out of your team's control. For example, people get sick and miss time from work, some tasks are more complex than they originally appeared to be, requirements change, and so on. Because of this, it is impossible to merely add up the estimates the team members submitted to get an accurate ship date. Adding up such estimates should only be used to create an internal ship date that the team strives to meet, while buffer time is added to this to create an external ship date, which is where the organization and/or customer sees the finished product.

Having said this, how much buffer time should be added to the schedule? There is no set number of days, weeks, or months to add to project schedules, because each project you deal with is different. While some products may take a couple of month to finish, others may take considerably longer. Each product needs to be addressed individually, but you should expect approximately one-third of your total development time to be buffer time. If unplanned events occur during development, this buffer time will keep your schedule from slipping. If, however, there are no unplanned contingencies to affect the schedule, the buffer time won't be used, so your product will be ready for early release.

Fixed Ship Dates

When we discussed the Process model in Chapter 2, we saw how tradeoffs can be made between schedules, features, and resources. This creates a triangulated relationship between these three elements:

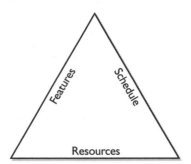

Just as if a change in any side of a triangle changes the other sides, any change in schedule, features, or resources will affect the other two elements. As an example, if layoffs caused you to lose several programmers from a large project, you would have a cutback in resources. This means you would either have to trade off features available for the release you're working on, or increase the time available to create the product. As you can see, trading off one element in the triangle affects the other two sides.

Despite the tradeoffs available through this triangulated relationship, fixed ship dates can aid in getting a project completed rapidly and on time. When a fixed ship date is used, the schedule side of the triangle becomes fixed, and can't be used as a tradeoff unless, of course, there is no other option except changing the schedule. Using a fixed ship date doesn't mean that you're carving a specific date in stone, and that missing this date will cause your project to fail. It means you're agreeing that the schedule isn't an element that can be traded off, and you're going to shoot for a specific date to have the product shipped by. In short, it is a way of thinking, and not a method of determining exactly when the product will be ready.

This mindset allows team members to focus on delivering the product, rather than delaying delivery dates. The fixed ship date is achieved by using the bottom-up estimates and buffer time to acquire a date that the team believes is realistic to deliver by. The team can then get creative to meet this date, and force the tasks to be prioritized. Because the schedule can't be pushed back, decisions must be made on how to produce the product by the set date. Any features that can't be added to the current version are looked at as a possible addition to the next versions, allowing the team to deliver only the most important features in the current version.

One of the other benefits of the fixed-date mindset is that it acts as a motivational goal. It's a way of setting a personal goal for members of the team; they are going to push themselves to get things done by a specific date. This enhances morale in the team, because they have a tangible due date that they're working toward. Since it's agreed that the date isn't going to be adjusted as a tradeoff, the team won't feel like they're going to have a career working on the same old project. They know when they'll need to have the tasks completed, so they can move on to something new and fresh.

Breaking Up Large Projects

Just as a slipping schedule can dishearten a team, so can projects that are large and complex. Listings of what is to be included, known as the *feature set*, may be lengthy and difficult to follow, due to the sheer number of features to be included in the product. It can easily feel overwhelming when viewing the project as a whole. When this is the case, you should consider breaking the large project into subprojects.

By breaking a large project into groups of related tasks, team members are better able to focus on specific aspects of a project. For example, let's say you were creating a calculator program for use by different types of users such as accountants, programmers, and networking people. You could split this project into subprojects of creating a financial calculator, programming a calculator, a component that calculates subnet masks, and so forth. This could further be split up into user interface, storage of user preferences, and so on. Rather than taking on the entire project in one fell swoop, developers can focus on the subproject of creating a group of features.

One of the benefits of breaking up projects is that developers are able to see small successes building toward a completed project. There is a certain amount of exhilaration in seeing that a subproject works, and knowing that you can now move on to the next stage of development. If there is a problem, it is easier to isolate it in these small feature groups than in large projects. These internal releases allow you to correct a problem before it affects the project as a whole.

Daily Builds and Smoke Tests

Imagine you're a teacher who doesn't believe in giving tests. When your students take their final exam, the class fails because they didn't understand the information you were attempting to put into their heads. If you had tested your class regularly, you could have caught and fixed this quickly. This little parable illustrates why daily builds and smoke tests are important in a software project. Daily builds and smoke tests are where you build your program daily by compiling it, and then run a series of tests on it to ensure that it functions as it should. Like the tests you took in school, the daily builds and smoke tests allow you to see problems quickly, and fix them before they get out of hand.

A *daily build* is where you build your executable program by compiling it. This allows you to see that the application compiles and links its files and components without errors. Once compiled, you can then determine if the program launches properly, without locking up the system or causing other unexpected events. Each day sections of code completed the previous day are added to the build. If the daily build works one day, and not the next, it can be determined that part or all of the code integrated into the current build is causing the problems.

Before performing a daily build, and making changes to erroneous code that causes problems, you should ensure that the project has been added to Visual SourceSafe (VSS). Visual SourceSafe comes with Visual Studio 6, and allows you to add files from your project to a database. If changes are made to your project files, and those changes cause problems, you can restore a previous version of the file. Since these previous versions were saved to the VSS database before the changes were made, you don't have to remove your changes before attempting to solve problems in your code in another way.

exam**✪**atch

Microsoft makes a valid point of stressing that a daily build is just that—it is built daily, and not weekly or monthly. Spreading out the builds over longer periods of time loses the benefits acquired from doing it in the first place.

In creating such daily builds, the code that's completed to date is added and compiled. This doesn't mean every line of code that was written the previous day, but all of the code that's considered complete and doesn't require any additional work. Once a developer is finished with a procedure, it is integrated with the daily build files and compiled. This keeps the development team from feeling that they need to complete everything they're working on in a day, or deciding not to start sections of code that won't be ready for the next day's build.

Once this is successful, you're ready to start the smoke test. A *smoke test* is used to detect major problems that go beyond seeing if the software launches properly. Because of this, a daily build isn't really valuable without a smoke test. While your application may compile without error, and create a nice little .exe file that launches correctly, the build doesn't tell you if the program performs the functions its designed to do, or if it "smokes" the computer system by causing major damage. The smoke test acts as the first real testing an application will experience, and keeps your program from deteriorating because of bad code being continually added.

A smoke test evolves with your software product. While an initial smoke test may be small, and determine if the words "Hello World" appear on the screen, it may take a considerable amount of time to do a smoke test later in the project. Therefore, you should consider creating an automated smoke test that checks major parts of your application without user intervention. That way you won't be required to spend a large amounts of time—30 minutes, an hour, or more—determining whether your program passes the smoke test.

In addition to testing the integrated code of your development team, you should have each developer smoke-test his or her own code. This ensures that the code is stable on its own, and won't be a problem in itself when integrated with the code of other developers. However, just as adding comments to code is heavily advised yet often overlooked, it is common for developers to bypass building and smoke-testing their code. After all, the real fun in programming is programming. However, if you have a developer who isn't performing daily builds and smoke tests of their own code, you should consider that person's work to be risky (at best).

on the **Job**

When possible, a separate computer should be used for code that's integrated for daily builds and smoke tests. This computer shouldn't have anything important on it, as you're not only testing to see that the major functionality of the program works, but also checking to see that the program doesn't harm the system. The last thing you want is to have a bad section of code reformat the hard drive of your network server, destroy critical information, or some other nasty event.

The daily build and smoke test should not be considered a replacement for the Testing role of the Team model. By performing daily builds and smoke tests, you're ensuring that the product is stable enough to reach an interim milestone. The daily build and smoke test are used to see that the software compiles and links files and components, launches correctly, and performs its activities without harming the system. After all, if the program won't start, harms the system, or doesn't have basic functionality, the people in Testing won't be able to do much. If Development can perform smoke tests without problems, then when completed, the application can be passed on to Testing to check for problems beyond this fundamental functionality. If it doesn't succeed in meeting the requirements of the daily build and/or smoke test, then the team must consider debugging or redesign.

CERTIFICATION OBJECTIVE 6.04

How Solution Design Relates to Enterprise Architecture

An enterprise is a business, such as a corporation, that uses computers in a network or an interconnected group of networks that can span different geographical areas. Usually the network will consist of a variety of platforms, operating systems, protocols, and/or network architectures. In creating enterprise applications, you'll need to design your software product for such things as networks, corporate intranets, or the Internet. Unlike desktop applications, enterprise applications can be split so part resides on a server, and another part resides on client computers. Hundreds or thousands of requirements may need to be addressed by the application, as users access the application and data on the server application.

This kind of development requires an understanding of the architecture of the enterprise's system of computers, and solid design models for creating these large applications. The Microsoft Solution Framework's Solution Design and Enterprise Architecture models provide the means of creating such applications. As we'll see, these models makes the design process easier by splitting large projects into smaller pieces, and promote the use of COM components. In using these models, any large project becomes much more manageable.

Modular Design and the Solutions Design Model

Modular design involves breaking a large project into manageable chunks called *modules*. These modules are designed to perform different and specific tasks and functions. They can be developed and tested individually, and then combined into the final project. Because you design modules as standalone components of a project, the code can be reused in different products that require the same functionality. In addition, by incorporating business rules into these components, you don't have to rewrite each application that uses the rules; you merely rewrite the code in the component that contains the business rule that needs changing. This saves you the trouble of having to rewrite the same code over and over in different projects, or different areas of the same program.

Using modular design requires implementing such things as stored procedures and components. Components are written with Class models, and use the Component Object model (COM). An example of a COM component is an ActiveX component. Such components allow you to split an application so that parts are spread across a network or a computer. These components are reusable and accessible to other programs. By using this method of design, you can split the design of your solution into two main tasks: creating reusable components (ActiveX, stored procedures, and so forth), and integrating those components into your application.

When you design an application with components, you need to determine and then organize or separate the customer's requirements. In doing so, you decide what each component will do, and what each component will require. This is where the Solutions Design model comes into play.

The Solutions Design model is highly focused on addressing the requirements and limitations of the customer, the user, and the enterprise itself. As we've mentioned in previous chapters, the user and customer aren't necessarily the same person or people. The customer is the person who's paying you to create the software, while the user is the person who actually uses your business solution. In designing a business solution, you need to address the issues regarding them, as they are the ones using and/or paying for the application. Because of this, the Solutions Design model has the customer and user involved in the design process. They are invited to address such key issues as usability and requirements, so you can determine how the application will be used and consequently how it will increase productivity. By involving the user, it keeps them from experiencing problems later, having to rely on a help desk for assistance, or not using the product at all.

In addition to the user and customer, the enterprise as an entity has its own requirements and limitations. In designing business solutions, you'll need to look at such things as what the organization does, what it produces, and what limitations will affect development. These limitations include such things as legal issues (e.g., including a certain percentage as tax to a price), business rules that determine how data is accessed, or technical issues like the network, operating systems, and hardware being used. Thus, you apply the needs of users and customers to the constraints of the organization.

on the job

While the Solutions Design model has you determine the requirements of the user, customer, and enterprise, there are often times when the three don't agree. Customers may want features that users don't, while users want features that your customer sees as unnecessary. To add to this, business rules, legislation and standards, or technical limitations may negate the wishes of the customer and user. In designing an application you act as an advocate for each group. Because the application is useless if it doesn't adhere to business practices, laws, or technical requirements, the enterprise should always be given priority. Since the software must be usable, the user should rank second in importance. You should always try to address these needs to the customer in an accessible manner. However, in the end, it's important to remember that the customer is the person signing your paycheck. In the end, regardless of the business's requirements and the needs of the user, it is the customer who has the final say.

The Solutions Design model brings together several other models in the Microsoft Solution Framework, to enable you and your staff to focus on where resources should be used to produce the most value and provide the most return. The models incorporated by Solutions Design are the Process, Team, and Application models. As we saw in the previous section, the Process model maps out the process of a successful software project, and the Application model helps you create flexible designs. The Team model is used to organize people who will be working on the project into a high performance group of peers. When used with the Solutions Design model, you have the foundation for a successful project that will anticipate user needs, and adhere to the requirements of the business and customer.

To identify the requirements of a project, three different perspectives are used in the Solutions Design model:

■ Conceptual design

- Logical design
- Physical design

These perspectives help focus the design process by identifying the business and technical requirements of a software development project. By understanding these requirements, you are then better able to assign the resources necessary for your project's success.

The *conceptual design perspective* is where the needs of the customer and user are determined, and the initial concept of the solution is conceived. Information gathered on what the user needs to do is applied to the requirements of the product. The conceptual design is non-technical. It details such things as the functionality of the application, how it will interact with the end user, and criteria for performance. Scenarios and models are used to relay the information so that team members, customers, and users can understand what's needed.

Once this information has been gathered, it can then be applied to the logical design perspective. Logical design is where user requirements are applied to the technical know-how of the team. In logical design, the structure and communication of elements making up your application are laid out. These elements include such things as objects, component and application structure, user interface, the logical database, and various services supplied and consumed by your application.

Once the requirements of the conceptual and logical design are established, the *physical design perspective* is used to put these needs into a tangible form. In physical design, the constraints of technology are applied to the logical design of the solution. It is used to define how the pieces that make up your business solution work together. This includes such elements as the physical database, user and programmatic interfaces, and other components. In determining this, issues like performance, implementation, bandwidth, scalability, reliability, and maintainability are resolved and implemented. Because this perspective applies previous designs to a concrete form, you are able to estimate what resources, costs, or scheduling will be needed to complete the project.

In working through the three perspectives that make up the Solutions Design model, you don't necessarily need to complete work in one perspective before moving on to the next. There isn't a specific cutoff point between one perspective and the next that allows you to have one part of a solution being coded while another is being designed conceptually or logically. As we'll see in the chapters that follow, the major separation between these perspectives is where specific tools are used in design. For example, in conceptual design, no development or development tools are used. Instead, wordprocessing, project management, financial modeling and planning, accounting, and other management information tools are used. While Visual Studio offers none of these tools, Microsoft Office, Microsoft Project, and other application packages are utilized. The benefit of being able to overlap these perspectives is that you can return to the different design perspectives as many times as necessary. In doing so, you can revisit, refine, or even redesign your solution without compromising the project as a whole.

Enterprise Architecture

When you think of architecture, you probably think of structures designed by architects, and you'd be right. Architecture is the art and science of building, and it is also the method whereby the components of a system are organized and integrated. *Enterprise architecture* deals with the planning and design of systems, utilities, infrastructure, and processes that support a business's needs and the business units of the organization. This involves planning the architecture before building it, as well as setting standards and guidelines to support the application and infrastructure systems.

The enterprise architecture model integrates the business by ensuring that changes made to the enterprise are consistent and meet the business's needs. This means elements of the architecture such as data management policies, APIs, and technical specifications are the same in each department of the organization. Rather than having one set of standards and guidelines for each area of the enterprise, it is consistent across the board. As we'll see, the model does this by not only looking at the current state of the organization, but where they are going or want to be in the future.

The Enterprise Architecture model also provides the guidelines you need to plan, build, and manage technology infrastructures. It is used when your team needs to do such things as design an intranet, plan a network architecture, or build a messaging infrastructure or electronic commerce site. This model aids you when you need to plan the technology that will be used to support and solve an application's requirements.

Like the Solutions Design model, the Enterprise Architecture model is comprised of different perspectives, which allow you to look at an enterprise from diversified viewpoints:

- *Business architecture* defines the business and its requirements
- *Application architecture* defines an organization's application portfolio
- *Information architecture* defines what an organization needs to know in running its processes and operations
- *Technology architecture* defines the hardware and software in an organization.

Though the Enterprise Architecture model is comprised of four distinct perspectives, it's important to remember that when using the Enterprise Architecture model, you're dealing with a single architecture that's being looked at in different ways.

exam ☖atch

To remember the different perspectives in the Enterprise Architecture model, remember the word "BAIT," with each letter representing the words Business, Application, Information, and Technology.

Business Architecture

In comparing the business architecture perspective to the conceptual design perspective of the Solutions Design model, it's easy to see a correlation. It is through these perspectives that the team acquires an understanding of project requirements. The needs of an enterprise application's users are obtained, and models that communicate the requirements addressed by the project are generated. Each perspective is the starting point to designing solutions that address specific business needs.

Business architecture defines the business and its requirements. It is here that you determine what problems an organization is experiencing, what they do, and what they require. This information is gathered by asking and answering such questions as:

- What does the enterprise do?
- What does the enterprise hope to achieve?
- What are the organizational structures of the enterprise?
- How do the elements in the three previous questions interact with one another?

Without knowing the information gathered from these questions, you will have an unclear view of what's required from your team. Information gathered through this perspective is what drives enterprise application development. After all, before you can solve business problems, you need to understand its requirements, and how the business works. Because business architecture is the foundation that an application or infrastructure is built on, any work you do after gathering information at this stage should trace back to the problems and requirements of the business.

Without knowing what an enterprise does, you won't be able to address the specific needs of the organization. It's important to understand what products and services are created, provided, and/or sold by an organization. This information has a direct impact on the requirements of the enterprise architecture, and the applications or infrastructure you'll create, manage, or upgrade.

If you don't understand the high-level goals and objectives of an organization, it doesn't matter what course of action you take. Therefore, you must discern what the organization hopes to achieve if you're going to move the enterprise from its current to future state.

It may seem strange that you need to inquire about the enterprise's major organizational structures. After all, what does that have to do with applications and infrastructure? The answer to is, a lot. This information can affect issues such as security, which affects who will require access to certain resources or features, or even if such issues are relevant to an application or infrastructure.

In addition to this, it will affect who your team deals with, the chain of command in dealing with problems, who will interact with the team on the project, and so on.

As the Enterprise Architecture uses the milestones of the Process model, this perspective corresponds to the envisioning phase. The information gathered on business requirements is used to create a vision statement, which outlines the assumptions and expectations of the project. Any information on the process is used for revising the vision statement. This is an informal document, and is reviewed and revised until a balance of what is desired and what can be delivered is achieved. As you'll remember from Chapter 2, by balancing these optimistic and realistic viewpoints, a shared vision of the project is achieved. By identifying and setting priorities for the project, the result is a vision/scope document that outlines the details of what a project entails.

In addition to these documents, the business architecture perspective includes a number of other tasks and deliverables. It is through this perspective that you determine the costs involved in the project, plan and maintain a budget, determine business projections, negotiate contracts, and manage personnel. In addition to these tasks, the business architecture perspective results in the creation of a business case, which is maintained and updated as the project progresses. A *business case* is a plan of action that's presented to senior management, and backs up a proposal for a project by providing facts and evidence about the project, and how it will be approached. For more information on business cases, review Chapter 2.

Application Architecture

Application architecture defines the application portfolio of the enterprise. In other words, it looks at what applications and application models are currently used in the enterprise, and then uses this information to determine what work needs to be performed by the team. When you consider that the purpose of a software development team is to develop software, it may seem strange that a perspective even exists that looks at other applications and models. However, in doing any work, you need to understand where you are before you know where you're going. Information gathered through this perspective allows you to see what work needs to be done, and determine the resources available to your team.

Application architecture defines the interfaces and services needed by a business, which are translated into development resources that are used by project teams. In other words, the user and programmatic interfaces determine the component and code libraries you'll use for your application, as well as standards documents, design guidelines, and models. It is important to determine the application models currently used by the enterprise, to see if they are compatible with the MSF models we're discussing here. There are older systems out there that use application models that trace back to the 1960s or earlier, and are in dire need of replacement. Ones that aren't quite so out of date may simply require revision. Application architecture provides the guidelines necessary for moving to new application models.

Through the information offered with this perspective, you can determine where application backlogs exist, and if new applications are required. This allows you to decide on whether an application needs to have its code revised, or if there is a need to create brand-new applications that adhere to new standards and have better performance. For example, if the network is slowed because of 16-bit applications designed for Windows for Workgroups, you would either revise the code or create new 32-bit applications for newly installed NT Workstations and Servers. Based on the priorities you set in the business architecture perspective, and the automated services that support business processes, you can determine how to approach a particular project.

In addition to aiding you in the applications your team creates, this perspective also has you look at whether your team should bother creating a product. Due to the number of software products on the market, you should investigate whether it would be better and cheaper to purchase software that's already developed from third parties. By simply examining what's already on the shelf, you may find that there are applications that provide the same (or better) functionality as what your organization wants you to create. In such cases, it may be more affordable to simply purchase the third-party product.

Never underestimate the value of steering your customer toward software that's already out there. Many developers forget that customers aren't as savvy with what's available, and assume that the reason they're being hired to create software is because software already on the market has been dismissed by the customer. For example, a customer may want you to create a spreadsheet program, and after discussing the requirements, you may realize they're talking about a product identical to Microsoft Excel. Rather than recreating the wheel, you could charge a consultation fee and go on your merry way. By suggesting software that's currently available to the customer, you may save them a considerable amount of money, and save yourself unnecessary work.

Because your application needs to become part of a system, and users have come to expect applications to integrate with their operating system and other applications, the application architecture perspective provides information on integration issues unique to the current system. Using this perspective, you can determine what issues will affect integration of a new application with a system.

This perspective corresponds to the logical design perspective of the MSF Solutions Design model, in which objects and services are determined and laid out. As we saw previously in this chapter, this includes defining the business objects, interfaces, services, and dependencies in the system. Information gathered through the application architecture perspective can be directly applied to logical design.

Information Architecture

Like application architecture, the information architecture perspective correlates to logical design. This perspective describes what the company needs to know to run the organization's business processes and operations, and how data and information is handled in an organization. Information gathered through this perspective is applied to laying out such things as logical databases, and determines such elements as functional data requirements, information needs, policies dealing with data management, and how information is bound to workflow.

Because the meat and potatoes of every business application is accessing and manipulating data, it is important to determine where data resides in an organization. It is important to remember that data stores—databases, documents, spreadsheets, and so forth—exist not only on servers, but on the desktop computers prevalent in most enterprises. If a software product needs to access such data, you must first determine where it resides. This will affect what features will be included in your application, whether components that implement COM and DCOM will be required to access data in various locations, and how your application will be designed. The information architecture perspective addresses these issues by identifying where most of the critical information in an organization resides.

Technology Architecture

Technology architecture falls hand in hand with the physical design perspective of the Solutions Design model, where logical design is applied to the real-world constraints of technology. Technology architecture is what provides standards and guidelines for laying out the software and hardware supporting an organization. This is important because it is the technology that determines whether elements of your application, or the software as a whole, will run. For any software product, there are requirements that must be met if the application is to function. These can include the following:

- Operating system
- Client/workstation tools
- Network connectivity components
- Hardware used by workstations and servers
- Modems
- Printers
- Other peripheral devices, software and hardware components

In looking these over, you may assume that all software must involve each of these elements. This isn't necessarily the case. For example, one software project may require the use of a modem, while another project you're working on does not. As you can see, different projects may use different technologies. With the technology perspective, you acquire a vendor-independent, logical description of your organization's technology infrastructure. This allows you to determine if the infrastructure will need to be updated to support new applications, or if the functionality of new applications created by your team will need to be limited.

Beyond the actual hardware and software requirements that support the application and information perspectives, the technology perspective defines the standards and services of the technology needed to support your organization. These include such things as APIs, network services, topologies, and technical specifications.

QUESTIONS AND ANSWERS

What is modular design?	Modular design breaks up large projects into smaller chunks called modules. They are designed to perform a different function or task, and can be developed and tested independently of one another, then combined into the final project. By designing these modules as standalone components of a project, they can be reused in other projects that require the same functionality.
How much buffer time should I add to my project's schedule?	About one-third of your total development time should be buffer time. This covers time spent dealing with unplanned events or occurrences.
What are the four perspectives of the Enterprise Architecture model?	The four perspectives of the Enterprise Architecture model are business, application, information, and technology (BAIT).
What perspectives make up the Solutions Design model?	The Solutions Design model is comprised of the conceptual, logical, and physical design perspectives.
When should I use interim milestones?	The buffer time involved with using interim milestones is a variable that generally needs to be determined from project to project. As a rule of thumb, though, if your project has a delivery schedule greater than three months, you should consider using interim milestones.

EXERCISE 6-2

Determining the Appropriate MSF Design Phase

In the second column, fill in the appropriate phase that corresponds to the architecture from the first column. (The answers to this exercise appear just before the Self Test at the end of the chapter.)

Architecture	MSF Solutions Design Phase
Application	
Business	
Technology	
Information	

CERTIFICATION SUMMARY

While there are numerous pitfalls you can encounter in a project, you can avoid many, if not most, of the problems by knowing what common problems to avoid, and using proven models that aid you in software design. The Microsoft Solution Framework provides models, practices, and principles that aid you in the design of applications and component solutions.

The Process model defines the life cycle of a project, by breaking your software project into four phases. These phases culminate in major milestones that allow a team to coordinate their efforts. In cases where you're working on complex projects with long delivery schedules, interim milestones should be placed at regular intervals in large projects. If your project has an overall delivery schedule of three months or more, you should give serious consideration to setting interim milestones in your project.

In addition to the use of milestones, the Process model aids in getting your application completed rapidly and on schedule. Risk-driven scheduling prioritizes the tasks associated with a project, while buffer time provides additional time to a project to deal with unforeseen events. Bottom-up estimates allow the people doing the work to create their own work estimates. Tradeoffs can be used to sacrifice one area of a project to keep other elements on track, while fixed-date mindsets keep your schedule from being sacrificed as a tradeoff. Finally, to ensure that your product is properly constructed during the course of the Process model, daily builds and smoke tests are used.

The Solutions Design model is comprised of the Conceptual, Logical, and physical design perspectives. Through this model, users become part of the design process by putting forth the requirements they feel are necessary in the product. The different perspectives of this model shouldn't be thought of as stages with clear cutoff points, as they allow the team to revisit, refine, and redesign perspectives at any point in development.

The Enterprise Architecture model integrates the business by ensuring that changes made to the enterprise are consistent and meet the business's needs, and provide the guidelines you need to plan, build, and manage technology infrastructures. This model consists of four perspectives: business, application, information, and technology (BAIT), which provide different ways of looking at the architecture.

TWO-MINUTE DRILL

- ❑ Rather than being a static methodology, MSF is a framework of models that can be adapted and applied to an organization's specific needs.

- ❑ Of all the possible problems you can encounter in designing an application, the most common one you'll experience is the *design failing to deliver what the customer expected*.

- ❑ The second most typical problem in design is *using inappropriate technologies to complete the project.*

- ❑ Interim milestones further break up a project, and provide additional points at which the team can synchronize their efforts.

- ❑ There are two kinds of interim milestones you can apply to any project you're working on: *externally visible interim milestones* and *internally visible interim milestones*.

- ❑ External interim milestones are known outside of the development team, and are announced to the organization.

❑ Internal interim milestones are not known outside the development team. The reason that no one outside of the team requires knowledge of these milestones is that they are only of use for the team itself.

❑ Synchronization points are determined by Program Management, and used to coordinate the efforts of your project team.

❑ Bottom-up estimates work on a chain-of-command principle, with those who are lower in a hierarchy reporting work estimates to those above them.

❑ A *daily build* is where you build your executable program by compiling it.

❑ A *smoke test* is used to detect major problems that go beyond seeing if the software launches properly.

❑ *Modular design* involves breaking a large project into manageable chunks called *modules*. These modules are designed to perform different and specific tasks and functions.

❑ The *conceptual design perspective* is where the needs of the customer and user are determined, and the initial concept of the solution is conceived.

❑ In *physical design,* the constraints of technology are applied to the logical design of the solution. It is used to define how the pieces that make up your business solution work together.

❑ *Enterprise Architecture* deals with the planning and design of systems, utilities, infrastructure, and processes that support a business's needs and the business units of the organization.

❑ The Enterprise Architecture model is comprised of different perspectives: business architecture, application architecture, information architecture, and technology architecture.

❑ To remember the different perspectives in the Enterprise Architecture model, remember the word "BAIT," with each letter representing the words *business, application, information,* and *technology.*

Answers to Exercise 6-1

1. False	6. False
2. True	7. False
3. True	8. True
4. False	9. False
5. True	10. False

Answers to Exercise 6-2

Architecture	MSF Solutions Design Phase
Application	Logical
Business	Conceptual
Technology	Physical
Information	Logical

SELF TEST

The Self Test questions will help you measure your understanding of the material presented in this chapter. Read all the choices carefully, as there may be more than one correct answer. Select all correct answers for each question.

1. Which milestone is owned by the User Education and Development roles in the Team Model?

    A. Vision/Scope Approved

    B. Project Plan Approved

    C. Scope Complete/First Use

    D. Release

2. Which of the following is an internal interim milestone?

    A. Synchronization points

    B. Management review meetings

    C. Post-functional specification baseline meetings

    D. Review and validation of a draft functional specification

3. Which role of the team model adds buffer time to the schedule, and where in the schedule is buffer time added?

    A. Program Management adds buffer time to the end of the schedule.

    B. Product Management adds buffer time to each task in the schedule.

    C. Program Management adds buffer time to each task in the schedule.

    D. Development adds buffer time to the end of the schedule.

4. What is the purpose of performing daily builds? (Choose all that apply.)

    A. Compiling files and components

    B. Linking files and components

    C. Exercising the system

    D. Ensuring that the application launches properly

5. What are the four perspectives of the Enterprise Architecture model?

    A. Conceptual, application, information, and technology

    B. Conceptual, logical, physical, and technology

    C. Business, application, information, and technology

    D. Business, logical, information, and technology

6. Which of the following best defines modular design?

    A. Modular design involves breaking a large project into modules that are designed to perform different and specific tasks and functions.

    B. Modular design is the design procedure for network applications that use modems.

    C. Modular design involves breaking large networking into modular networks that are designed to improve performance.

D. There is no such thing as modular design.

7. Which other models does the Solutions Design model tie together to focus resources so they produce the most value? (Choose all that apply.)

A. Process model

B. Modular model

C. Team model

D. Application model

8. What perspectives make up the Solutions Design model? (Choose all that apply.)

A. Conceptual design

B. Modular design

C. Logical design

D. Physical design

9. You are designing a business solution, and have decided that at this point in the project, you will adopt a fixed-date mindset. The customer now comes to you and decides that she wants several new features added to the product. If these features aren't added, in addition to the other features already incorporated into the solution's design, then the productivity of users will suffer. Which areas of the software development process can you trade off to implement these features?

A. Schedule

B. Resources

C. Features

D. Schedule and Resources

E. Resources and Features

10. You have a project with a delivery schedule of six months. What should you consider implementing?

A. ActiveX components

B. Interim milestones

C. Major milestones

D. Interim delivery schedules

11. For which of the following milestones does Product Management hold responsibility?

A. Vision/Scope Approved

B. Project Plan Approved

C. Scope Complete/First Use

D. Release

12. What kinds of interim milestones are there, and what is the difference between them?

A. There are no different kinds of interim milestones. They are only used for synchronization points for the team.

B. Internal interim milestones are announced to the organization, while external interim milestones have a beta release of the product available for public use.

C. Internal interim milestones are announced to the organization, while external interim milestones have a beta release of the product available for organizational use.

D. Internal interim milestones are known only to the project team, while external interim milestones are announced to the organization.

13. Which perspective defines the application portfolio of the enterprise?

   A. Business

   B. Application

   C. Information

   D. Technology

14. Which of the following Enterprise Architecture perspectives correspond to the physical design perspective of Solutions Design?

   A. Business

   B. Application

   C. Information

   D. Technology

15. Which perspective of the Enterprise Architecture model corresponds to the Envisioning phase of the Process model?

   A. Business

   B. Application

   C. Information

   D. Technology

16. In which of the following perspectives are the needs of the customer and user determined, and the idea of the solution is conceived?

   A. Technology

   B. Conceptual

   C. Logical

   D. Physical

17. In which of the following perspectives are the structure and communication of elements making up your application laid out?

   A. Technology

   B. Conceptual

   C. Logical

   D. Physical

18. Which perspective describes what the company needs to know to run the organization's business processes and operations, and how data and information are handled in an organization?

   A. Business

   B. Application

   C. Information

   D. Technology

19. Which perspective provides standards and guidelines for laying out the software and hardware supporting an organization?

   A. Business

   B. Application

   C. Information

   D. Technology

20. In which of the following perspectives are the constraints of technology applied to the logical design of the solution?

   A. Modular

   B. Conceptual

   C. Business

   D. Physical

7

Analyzing Business Requirements

C ontinual improvement of IT services and simultaneous reduction of IT costs are
conflicting goals. *Total Cost of Ownership (TCO)* is the process of creating a set of
repeatable tasks tailored for a specific organization. These tasks produce the analytical
results that suggest areas for improvement. It is then possible to track the resulting change.

Microsoft and Interpose, Inc., a Florida organization that is now part of
the Gartner Group, has developed a TCO methodology that maps to the
Microsoft Solutions Framework. This chapter explains the Microsoft-
Interpose TCO Model and discusses the practical application of TCO.

Business requirements are the foundation of analysis. The requirements are
the primary communication device between the business area experts and
the technical development team. Business requirements are transformed
into a set of technical specifications. These specifications are influenced by
the technical architecture of the target platform but must retain the intent
of the business requirements. This chapter describes the gathering of
business requirements.

CERTIFICATION OBJECTIVE 7.01

The Total Cost of Ownership (TCO) Model

Several TCO models exist, with varying degrees of success. The
Microsoft-Interpose model is simple, yet complex enough to support more
precise analytical conclusions. Although this model is flexible, a consistent
application of the principles must be followed with a high degree of
discipline. This strict discipline is necessary to get the most benefit from
the model.

Defining Total Cost of Ownership

The *Total Cost of Ownership (TCO)* is the dollar amount of expenses and
depreciated costs invested by an organization for each IT asset. Examples of

IT assets are a workstation on the network, an operating system, a printer, and a communication device such as a router or hub.

How TCO Works

The implementation of TCO involves creating a baseline set of data, recognizing the issues that the analyzed data represents, taking actions on those issues, and then measuring progress toward resolving the issues.

Creating a Baseline

An organization must first mark where they began. Some organizations may not know what IT assets they have, how the IT assets are distributed, or the true costs of each asset. There will be a set of tasks that an organization must accomplish, but the way the organization performs the tasks must be documented to create a repeatable process for the next iteration. The tradeoffs and decisions made must be documented at each step. Once the baseline is created, the results may be compared to industry averages.

Industry averages for the TCO model were collected from 120 different organizations. Although immature, these averages (called *metrics*) may be used to make rough comparisons between the industry TCO figures and a specific organization's figures.

Recognizing Problems

Once a set of TCO metrics has been collected, the data may be analyzed and compared to the industry averages and to previous TCO metrics of the organization. This analysis and comparison may indicate issues that need further investigation. If an issue is determined to be a problem, then a resolution may be proposed, but this resolution must consider the risks and the impact of the resolution on the IT organization.

Validation of Change

Once a resolution has been implemented, the metrics must be re-collected and compared to the previous set of metrics to determine the amount of change that the organization accomplished. Ideally, the resolutions implemented by the organization should result in positive changes.

People, Process, and Technology

People, process, and technology are interrelated parts of a comprehensive view of the TCO model. Balancing the proportions of water, lemon juice, and sugar makes good lemonade. Too much sugar and the drink is too sweet; too much lemon juice and the drink becomes too sour. A good IT department consists of a balanced mix of people, process, and technology. Some organizations attempt to buy their way into enhanced information technology maturity by purchasing the latest and greatest technology. The introduction of new technology by itself may have a detrimental impact. Microsoft endorses not only technology enhancements but also improvements in the information technology processes and upgrades in IT staff's technical skills.

Microsoft attempts to assist their customers' improvement efforts by offering enhanced technology and by attempting to support their customers in creating successes with that technology. Microsoft does this by making various forms of training available to the implementers of their technologies. The certification programs enable organizations to distinguish individuals who are successful with Microsoft technology. Microsoft also offers consulting services, an elevated support tier, and partnerships with other consulting organizations that have been effective in implementing Microsoft's technologies.

Costs

The Microsoft-Interpose TCO Model identifies seven categories of costs; five are considered direct IT costs and two are indirect IT costs.

Direct Costs

Direct costs are predictable costs such as scheduled replenishments of supplies such as printer paper or diskettes. Another direct cost is the scheduled upgrade of desktop computer hardware. These costs are reflected in a periodic IT budget and, because they are included in an IT spending plan, are identified as direct costs.

Some IT expenditures are not planned. One example is the replacement of a failed hard disk. Although the replacement was not planned and therefore the cost was not budgeted, this is still clearly an IT expense and would be categorized in one of the four direct categories.

The differentiation between direct and indirect categories highlights costs that have been buried in the costs of business departments that do not report any IT costs.

HARDWARE AND SOFTWARE COSTS   This category includes all capital expenditures such as costs to lease and depreciation on new computers or network equipment and upgrades to existing equipment. Also included are expensed software and software upgrades.

MANAGEMENT COSTS   This category includes all administration costs for the network, computers, shared disk drives and CD-ROM banks, and the labor costs for the staff to manage this equipment. Any travel expenses incurred by IT support personnel are also included in this category.

DEVELOPMENT COSTS   Systems application development, testing, documentation, and training are grouped in this category. Also included are the costs to tailor shrink-wrapped software for the organization and to update the documentation and training to reflect the tailoring.

SUPPORT COSTS   This category includes costs associated with the Help Desk, all support contracts, purchasing administration costs, and personnel management administration costs. IT supplies such as diskettes, CRT wipes, and ergonomic accommodations are also included here.

COMMUNICATION COSTS   Access charges and leased-line costs are included in this category. Just like individuals, businesses must pay telephone companies and long-distance carriers to install communication lines. After the necessary hardware is installed, monthly usage fees are normally billed to the organization. Although modems have become a standard part of a desktop computer, some organizations may categorize the cost of modems under communication costs.

Indirect Costs

This category includes costs not included in an IT budget. These costs are hidden in the expenses of the business departments of the organization. The business departments, also called *user communities*, are the parts of an organization that use IT services. Although these costs may add up to significant dollar amounts, sometimes detective work is needed to account for them because they may not be obvious. User interviews and review of Help Desk logs may reveal IT costs not previously detected. Examples of these hidden costs are discussed in the appropriate category descriptions.

END-USER COSTS   This category takes into account the time spent by end users helping their co-workers figure out how to do some task on the computer or solve a computer-related problem. For example, the time spent changing a screensaver or adding desktop options are included in this category. The cost of labor to recover a user's computer after they deleted the registry database or io.sys is also included, for example.

I have experienced variations on the theme of indirect end-user costs. In one organization, the user community did applications development in an effort to develop solutions in a timely manner. Unfortunately, the users discovered it was difficult to do the job they were hired to do in addition to the applications development role they had taken upon themselves. Although these individuals completed the application and the organization used it for five years, the application had numerous issues. It had not been tested thoroughly, the application was rarely enhanced, and the hardware/software platform had to be carefully preserved to allow the application to continue to execute. In this situation, there were many indirect IT costs that were never understood by the organization, and the individuals paid a steep personal price to implement the application.

Not included in this category are the costs of end users surfing the web or playing computer games.

DOWNTIME COSTS   The expense of lost productivity because the network went down is accounted for in this category. The costs of paying wages for time spent without adding value to the organization may be quantified. Perhaps the business community had to put in paid overtime to catch up after an unplanned network crash.

Also included in this category are the costs for unproductive time due to the network being down for planned maintenance. Most organizations attempt to schedule maintenance activities during weekend or off-hours to minimize this cost. Of course, if the organization works seven days a week, 24 hours a day, this cost may not be completely avoidable.

Scope of the Total Cost of Ownership

The Microsoft-Interpose TCO model applies only to the client/server world and client/server costs. The mainframe and all costs associated with it are excluded. This is no doubt because Microsoft is not in the business of writing software for the mainframe environment. Microsoft realizes that as components become increasingly more distributed, the difficulty in accurately measuring IT costs increases. Forecasting and change control then become almost impossible.

Also excluded are the costs or benefits resulting from a change in end-user productivity because of a change in the user's IT environment. Changes in the expense of conducting business are not included because of the difficulty of clearly relating the change to an IT action. The IT change may have served only as a catalyst for the impending business change, forcing the impact on the business to happen sooner rather than later.

The TCO model is based upon three assumptions:

- Three-year straight-line depreciation is used for hardware.
- Labor costs include overhead allocations.
- All costs are annualized.

TCO and IT Life Cycles

The TCO Model is a continuous improvement technique because it is designed to be like the Plan-Do-Check-Act cycle of the Quality Assurance realm. After a business has determined its current status by using a TCO assessment, the data is analyzed and issues are identified. These issues then become improvement projects. After improvement projects have been completed, another assessment must be made and compared to the previous one to see the impact on the organization. Here is how the phases of the TCO Model map to those of the MSF IT cycle:

IT Phase	TCO Phase
Manage	Analyze
Plan	Improve
Build	Manage

The Analyze Phase

In the Analyze phase, the IT costs are measured and documented. A critical factor is an accurate IT asset census. For many organizations this data may be obtained from current inventory management records or other financial data.

A repeatable process for this measurement must be established. This process must be kept simple and inexpensive to duplicate, yet it must be rigorously followed. The data must be collected consistently to yield any real value.

The industry-specific averages are also collected in this phase. These averages must come from the same type of industry as the organization. This is important because these industry averages are used to compare with the organization's data. The comparison creates a baseline report. The *baseline report* is the starting point to which, after changes have been made to the organization, the next set of data will be compared.

The Improve Phase

After a TCO assessment, issues are identified by comparing the TCO data to industry averages and to previous organization data. These issues may become improvement projects. What-If analysis may be valuable in this phase to simulate costs and benefits of an improvement project. Further modeling may simulate the impact of an improvement project on the enterprise.

These projects are then prioritized, and several may be selected. Then the tasks are completed to resolve IT issues. Resources are applied to the issues to ensure change.

Remember that the Improve phase is part of a cycle, and that the complete cycle is repeated. In the first cycle, the baseline data are established in IT assets, IT management, and IT costs. The improvement projects and the tasks to meet the improvement objective are the final deliverable from this phase.

The Management Phase

The activities in the Manage phase take the data collected from the two cycles of the Analyze phase and compare them to see if any progress has been made. The focus of this comparison is those projects identified in the Improve phase as the projects to be implemented in the current cycle. The industry averages are also used as benchmarks in this phase. There are four major activities for this phase:

1. Review and perhaps integrate new ideas. In the process of the Analyze-Improve-Manage cycle, practices will be identified as those that reduce IT costs. These practices may allow the organization to be more aggressive in its TCO improvement plans.

2. Institute the full revolution of the improvement cycle. An awareness of continual improvement begins to permeate the entire IT department once the full cycle has been completed and individuals can see the results of their efforts.

3. Monitor, track, and adjust the projects affected by the TCO results. The improvement projects must be managed like any project. They must have due dates and deliverables, and individuals must accept responsibility for accomplishments. These projects will usually compete with other IT projects for scarce organizational resources.

The costs and benefits must be reassessed at each cycle to determine whether stated goals have been met or have changed.

4. Adjust the baseline metrics. The baseline report is again generated in preparation for the next cycle.

TCO in the Enterprise

TCO specialists are available as consultants to perform the TCO assessment in approximately six weeks. The deliverables at the end of this period are as follows:

- **A completed TCO cost model spreadsheet**   A good example of a cost model spreadsheet is shown in Figure 7-1. This is generated from the Desktop TCO Calculator, which is available on the Microsoft web site (see the next section, "The Microsoft TCO Spreadsheet Tool").

- **A final presentation of findings and recommendations based on those findings**   This final presentation from the consultants may be given to the organization's top management.

- **Identification of the data sources and assumptions**   Assumptions should always be validated with the customer and re-validated at every opportunity. Conclusions from these findings must always take into account the source of the information and all assumptions.

- **A graphical analysis showing the comparisons to industry averages**   Once again, the Desktop TCO Calculator has graphical analysis of the data available in many different forms.

The Microsoft TCO Spreadsheet Tool

A spreadsheet tool is available from the Microsoft web site (**http://www. microsoft.com/office/tco/**) to assist in collecting data. The upside to this tool is that it is free for the download; the downside is that it contains no industry averages for comparisons. This tool is helpful for doing What-If analysis.

An excellent white paper for this topic may be found at **http://www. microsoft.com/solutionsframework/TCO/TCO.htm.**

The Spreadsheet Wizard consists of a series of screens that guide you through the data entry process and then format the information into an intelligible report at the end of the session, as well as performing all needed calculations. This whole Wizard is implemented in VBA in an Excel spreadsheet, so it is easily tailored. The first screen of the Wizard, shown in Figure 7-1, explains the algorithm for the ROI calculation.

Figures 7-2 and 7-3 show a report and a graph that the Wizard might generate based on sample data.

There are other reports and graphs available in the Wizard. The user may also return to the data collection screens and change the data. The complete studies can be found at **http://microsoft.com/office/tco.**

FIGURE 7-1

Screen 1 of the TCO/ROI Wizard

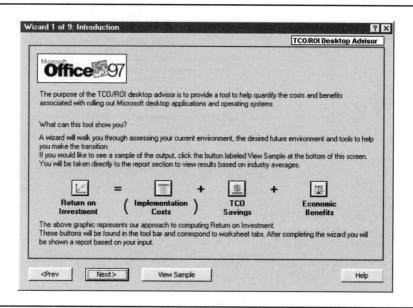

FIGURE 7-2

ROI report based on sample data

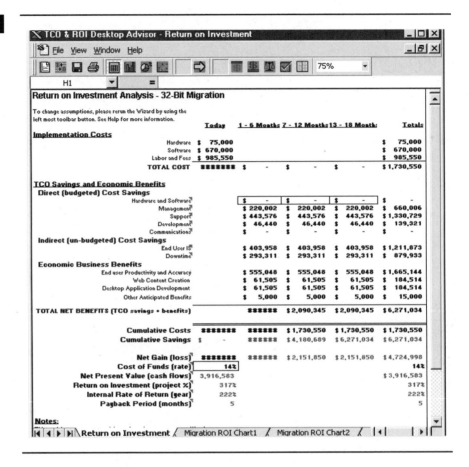

Exercise 7-1 will test your knowledge in identifying costs. (The answers to this exercise appear just before the Self Test at the end of the chapter.)

EXERCISE 7-1

Identifying Costs

Identify the cost categories for the following items:

1. Lease cost for the mainframe

2. Lease cost for the database server

3. Office Suite upgrade costs

4. Cost of networking closet racks

5. Salary and benefits of Networking Manager

6. Tuition for Networking Management School

7. Auto mileage for travel to Networking Management School

8. Consulting fees to tailor installed software

9. Development costs for credit card processing software

10. Salaries for the Help Desk Supervisors

11. Cost of diskettes, printer paper, and laser jet cartridges

12. Costs to inventory and monitor the supply of diskettes, printer paper, and laser jet cartridges

13. Purchase price of modem bank

14. Lease cost of T1 lines

15. Salaries of users unable to work because the network is down

16. Salaries of users fixing others' computer problems

FIGURE 7-3

Graphical analysis based on sample data

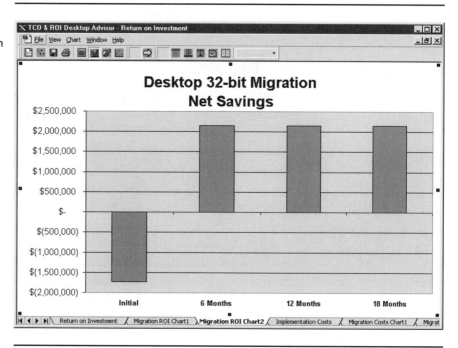

Analyzing the Extent of a Business Requirement

A previous chapter explained the first phase of the MSF cycle that resulted in the Vision/Scope milestone. We saw that the vision activity attempts to encompass all requests for functionality from the user community, while the scope activity attempts to set the boundaries of the project. Individual business requirements can be discussed only in context of the established vision and scope of the project.

exam
Watch

While taking the exam, carefully read each sentence in the scenario-based questions. Do not read anything into them. As in real life, opinions about the development issues are presented from different roles in the organization. The questions may be based on these opinions, and it is up to you to either remember them all or go back to the text of the scenario to review the opinions.

Establishing Business Requirements

Business requirements must be established by the business community, not by the IT group. Although the IT community may make suggestions to the business community, IT should not drive the definition of the business requirements. The users may not assume ownership of the final product claiming that IT forced requirements on them. IT should not assume they know the business plan. Application development history is full of examples of a brilliant solution developed for requirements that existed only in the minds of IT.

One of the best reasons for producing a printed requirements document is that it may serve as a contract between the business community and the technical team. Scope creep, the addition of newly discovered requirements by users, may be managed proactively with a Requirements document that is agreed on by both parties.

FROM THE CLASSROOM

Analysis of Business Requirements

The analysis of business requirements is not an exact science in all cases. Business needs change; therefore business requirements have a tendency to evolve, although this is not the biggest concern of the business community. Ensuring that the identified business requirements accurately match the true needs of the business is paramount to developing an application for which users will be willing to assume ownership. Such an application will contribute to the success of a business or department. On the other hand, an application developed using phantom business requirements, or born of the imagination of application developers or IT personnel, will most likely generate discord, inefficiencies, and occasional outright resentment towards the tool. Cooperation among the users, developers, and business community is paramount to the creation of a successful business tool.

Almost as important as the development of accurate and useful business requirements is the proper documentation of said business requirements. Production of a requirement's document provides a source of information that can be referred to by non-technical individuals to research and reference the base business requirements under use in the development of the business application. This document can provide a roadmap for current and future development efforts. Having the full range of identified business requirements identified in a single document can ensure less confusion, misunderstanding, and miscommunication during the development process.

—*Michael Lane Thomas, MCSE+I, MCSD, MCT, MCP+SB, MSS, A+*

Problems in the Requirements Analysis Phase

The Analysis phase is an excellent opportunity to begin identifying risks for the project. These risks may be closely related to the problems that appear in this phase. Problems may be organizational problems, people problems, business process problems, or regulatory or government problems.

The business community may legitimately not know their own business. One example of this situation is a government unit that must conduct business as instructed by legislation. The exact interpretation of legislative verbiage may need to be completed before business requirements can be defined.

Another variation is that the business community may not be able to imagine how their daily tasks may be interpreted into a computer application. Although the business requirements must be stated independently of any implementation decisions, it does help, for example, to work with users who have been exposed to several different alternatives of a list box. Sometimes it is necessary to discourage a user excited by the idea of getting a computer-based solution from designing the application as they are stating requirements.

The business community may believe that it is easy to develop applications, while the IT community may believe that it is easy to conduct the business. One by-product of requirements analysis may be an increased mutual respect between the business and IT communities in an organization.

Interviews

Before interviewing begins it is helpful to compile a list of individuals and an explanation of what perspective they can give to the analysis process. It is important to talk to people whose vision may differ from the overall, visionary perspective of the ideal world-as-it-should-be to the individuals responsible for working with the application daily and basing decisions on the information presented by the application.

There are several advantages to having this material before you begin. It aids in planning and helps to expedite the process. I attempt to prequalify the individuals I want to interview by sending a brief questionnaire that basically tries to answer the question of who has the power internally to get what they want. In the sales process a salesman attempts to prequalify a candidate mainly to find out if they have the real power to make purchase decisions.

If the application extends across departmental boundaries or even geographic boundaries, there may be conflicts of interest that appear during the interviews. I prefer to identify these areas and get all concerned parties into a war-room to make decisions about the tradeoff and hopefully reach a conclusion so that the project may go forward.

Documenting Requirements

The business requirements must be captured in terms understood by the business community. The requirements may be explained textually in a *business requirements document.* There are two major advantages to having a single document that defines the requirements for an application development project:

- It is a single-source repository for all requirements that may include supporting materials in the appendices.

- It is a document that the business community may review without IT expertise and then sign off on an agreement for the ensuing development effort.

Because of these two advantages, I prefer to treat all other tools for requirements gathering as an addendum to the requirements document. Use cases, storyboarding, and screen prototyping are extremely helpful in further defining areas of requirements that are difficult to make clear by the use of text alone. The products from these additional tools may be included in the Requirements document.

There are tools on the market to assist you in gathering requirements. Rational Software's product, RequisitePro, is one that not only performs as a repository for all textual requirements, it also integrates with Rational Software's SQA-Test and forms the foundation for test suits used in regression tests.

Requirements Analysis Conceptual Aids

There are a number of techniques available today to help you with the requirements gathering process. Use cases, storyboarding, and screen prototyping have already been mentioned.

One point at which to begin discussing requirements is with the definition of what kind of information needs to be kept by the business. The data is a very tangible need and one that provides an excellent springboard into discussions of functionality. Business users quickly understand the diagramming techniques involved in an Entity Relationship Diagram (ERD), and most users enjoy the data modeling process. The diagram is only a small portion of data analysis. The entities and all columns or fields must be defined. The relationships between entities must also be defined. Definitions should be captured as soon as an entity or field is mentioned. The risk of forgetting what was meant by a name increases with time. A sample ERD is shown in Figure 7-4.

Functional decomposition may be used to create a hierarchical tree-structure diagram, which, in the topmost layers, may suggest the structure of the workflow. See Figure 7-5 for an example. The diagrams are only part of the requirement. Each node must be backed up with a textual description, definitions of all tasks, and the identification of all data used in the process. The purpose of functional decomposition is to break down the tasks in a business process to a fine granularity. The lower functions may then be described precisely and in detail.

Screen prototyping, or storyboarding, aids the users in defining the workflow they want to use in the future. Some of this may be based on

---

FIGURE 7-4

An Entity Relationship Diagram

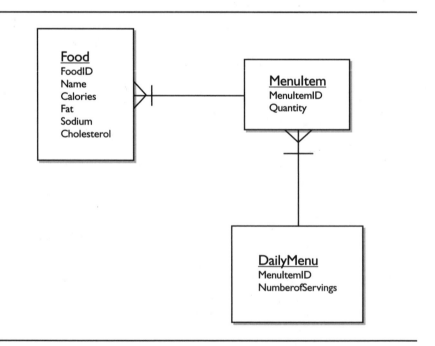

FIGURE 7-5   A Functional Hierarchy Diagram

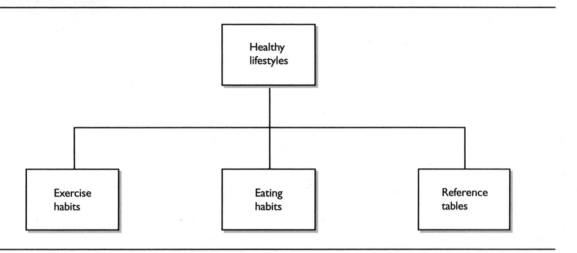

existing screens and production applications because that is what the user is familiar with. Although it may be difficult to get the user to think in revolutionary rather than evolutionary terms, the benefits will be that old mistakes or inconveniences are not duplicated in the new application. See Figure 7-6 for an example.

Data Flow Diagrams depict the information flow through the business functions. Here again a high-level business function may be further decomposed into a finer granularity. In these diagrams, each business process (the verb-noun pair in an oval) has information passed to it and in turn passes information to other processes. The name of the information is written above the arrow that points in the direction the information is going. See Figure 7-7 for an example of a DFD.

exam
Ⓦatch

Data modeling and the use of Entity Relationship Diagrams and business process modeling supported by both Functional Hierarchy Diagrams and Data Flow Diagrams are techniques that have been used successfully and are considered standard techniques that many business applications analysts will use. Please remember that the object of the exam is to test individuals on concepts that are proven in the field.

FIGURE 7-6

Screen prototyping, or
storyboarding

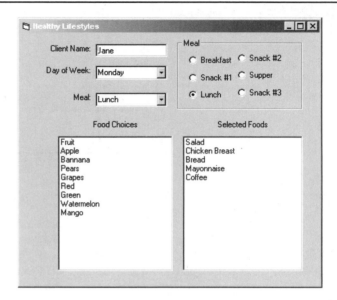

FIGURE 7-7   A Data Flow Diagram

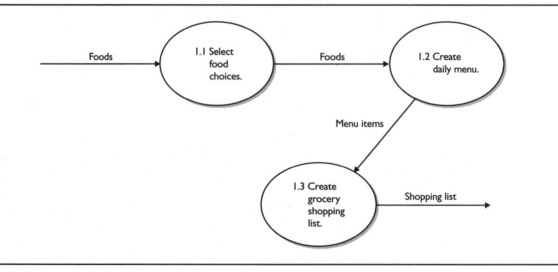

Identifying Risks

While proceeding through the Requirements Gathering phase, maintain a list of issues. As soon as they are identified, these issues should be assigned to an individual for further research, and that individual should then specify a due date that will fit their schedule. It may be that the individual cannot discover any more information about an issue. All unresolved issues become risks that must be taken into consideration. In this phase, the business risks are enumerated. Technical risks may then be added to the list as they are discovered, but these technical risks are not assigned to business users to investigate.

Ending the Requirements Analysis Phase

There are no obvious triggers that clue you in when one phase ends and another begins in the Applications Development process. To proceed from Vision/Scope to Analysis to Design is a progression along a continuum. Requirements should be complete but not too detailed. There are increasing risks in an application that remains in the Requirements Analysis phase too long. *Analysis paralysis* is the term used to identify development projects that stay in the requirements gathering phase too long. This is not, hopefully, the last chance to discuss requirements with the users and, as development progresses, issues can be clarified.

Establishing the Type of Problem to be Solved

Determination whether the type of application to be developed will drive the choice of technologies for the architectural design. This is discussed in more detail in Chapter 9. At this point in the Analysis phase, a high-level identification of the problem is sufficient. Will the application solve a messaging type of problem? Will it use communication technologies? Many applications require solutions arising from multiple problem types.

Establishing and Defining Customer Quality Requirements

The customer must dictate what level of quality they need to have built into the application. *Quality* in production applications means how often the application fails and what happens when it does fail. If a customer needs a program to be available 24 hours a day, seven days a week with no downtime, the design of the application and the technical architecture will need to accommodate these requirements. This is a much different application from one that needs to be available only during working hours to a localized group of business users.

Another consideration is the vitality of the Help Desk in the organization. If the Help Desk is already overworked and cannot tolerate an increased workload without additional resources, the application may need to have sophisticated help capabilities.

What happens to transactions when an application fails is a discussion with the customer that is often overlooked. Most transactional applications require the ability to roll back the data to a stable state if a transaction fails. How the rollback is controlled, i.e., whether by the database or by the application program, often dictates how much control the end user needs to determine how to recover.

Online documentation versus hardcopy documentation is a separate aspect of quality and is an integral aspect of the training decisions. If formal end-user training is planned, then the online help system may be a part of the training, and the hardcopy documentation may not be needed.

Minimizing the Total Cost of Ownership

Remember that the TCO is comprised of both direct IT costs and indirect costs. Difficulties in estimating TCO in the Requirements Analysis phase result from not knowing the amount of training needed, not knowing the level of Help Desk support that will be needed, and not having a good sense of the technical sophistication of the users. Specific aspects of TCO that can be defined in this phase are the number and location of users and their workstations, the targeted technical platform, the use of development consultants and their travel expenses, and the labor rates of the staff to manage the application and the technical platform.

Reliance on industry benchmarks at this date may be hazardous because of the immaturity of the cost data, but this should improve during the next decade.

Increasing the Return on Investment (ROI) of the Solution

A reasonable cost-benefit analysis may be difficult to create for one application, but this can form the basis of an estimated Return on Investment (ROI). Lower costs and increased benefits result in a better ROI. Although costs may be fairly simple to quantify, benefits may be difficult. If a new application saves an individual 50 percent of the time spent on a particular set of tasks, the fear-of-change factor may kick in and the extent of the savings may be hidden. Or the extent of the savings may be inflated due to overly optimistic estimates by the development team.

Analyzing the Current Platform and Infrastructure

Most business processes now have some form of automated support. I rarely find a project that starts without a production application. Unfortunately, the production application is often viewed as a time-saver and cost-cutter for the new development project. I have worked on many projects where the business community's idea of requirements analysis is the instruction to "Make the new application look exactly like the old application." The current production programs, hopefully, exist as source code. Other documentation may also exist for production programs. Some users assume that the requirements have been captured and are accurately reflected in the source code of the current production programs.

The assumption on the part of the users is that they do not need to be involved in the Requirements Analysis phase. This can be a serious mistake, because many users assume that the project will incorporate some amount of workflow analysis. I find myself repeating that if the only tool you have is a hammer, everything looks like a nail. The users must be convinced that the new application cannot be modeled on a workflow from even just five years ago. The danger is that the users may continue to do daily tasks because that is the way the tasks have always been done, and not because the task adds any value to the process.

Potential drawbacks to analyzing the existing application are that the software development platform may no longer exist, or may be an old, unsupported version, or may require that the IT requirements analyst learn a development tool that he or she has no desire to learn. Although a loop index in one language may appear the same as a loop index in other languages, the implementation of the construct may differ and may not be well documented in the older tools. If support cannot be found for the existing development tool, the only way to determine how the existing application works may be to play with the tool. This can be very time-consuming and resource-intensive.

One aspect of the production systems that is valuable is the definition of user's roles and responsibilities. The current roles may change drastically with new technology, and it is helpful to know what the roles were and how they will be redefined. It is natural for an end user to ask what happened to their daily report after the new application with advanced communication features does away with their perceived requirement. The analyst needs to see what the roles were and how they are changing to assist the end user to understand why the report is no longer being generated.

Incorporating the Planned Platform and Infrastructure into the Solution

A difficult aspect of Information Technology planning is enabling upgrades. Often, planned solutions in an application design must be reworked because the infrastructure of the hardware or foundational software is not ready. For example, if a network still has nodes running Windows 3.1 and these nodes, as well as Windows NT workstations, need to run an application, then either the application must be 16-bit or there must be two versions of the application, one compiled for 32-bit machines and another for 16-bit machines.

Multimedia or imaging applications often drive the need to upgrade the bandwidth of the network. Many of the older networks are 10 Mps and must be upgraded to 100+ Mps to provide adequate response time to handle graphics applications.

A common problem is upgrading hardware and not receiving it in time to roll out the application. These are all risks that must be identified and plans made to either circumvent the situation or to find a temporary fix.

Analyzing the Impact of Technology Migration

Changes in an organization must be handled with care. The best way to manage change is to plan before the change must be made. There are different aspects to changes caused by new computer systems. There are the technical and the social elements of a technology migration.

The technical aspects of changes in an organization's technical environment may include different computer hardware, different development tools, different shrink-wrapped applications, and perhaps even different storage or communication devices. Any and all of these may impact current applications upon which the organization is dependent. Any change in technology must be thoroughly tested before installation in a production environment. This may involve creating a complete test lab that simulates the current production environment, or installing an evaluation copy of software or a trial piece of hardware and ensuring that it works as expected.

One hardware/software issue that continues to plague development teams is the 16/32 bit architecture issue. If some of the target hardware platforms are running older operating systems, Windows 3.1 or DOS, 16-bit applications must be developed and maintained for these machines. If there is a mixture of architectures as in a network that has Windows 3.1, Windows 9*x*, and Windows NT, the choices must be considered. These choices are:

- The team writes code for the lowest common denominator, the 16-bit architecture, and loses out on the power of 32-bit systems.

- The team, using compiler directives, writes code for 16-bit and 32-bit architectures and then maintains two sets of compiled executables.

- The team only writes 32-bit code; individuals with 16-bit architectures won't be using the application.

The social aspects of change are sometimes even more important than the technical aspects. For example, in the process of rewriting an existing production application, the task of delivering reports to department managers was eliminated. Although the information contained in the reports was also online, and the managers had all been trained in accessing it, they complained that they weren't getting the same information. What they were not getting any more was the trigger of receiving reports that told them it was time to check the status of specific data. Once this was recognized, a small application was written to send them a reminder by e-mail.

Planning Physical Requirements for the Solution

Some physical requirements will be apparent in the Requirements Analysis phase, such as the need for bar-code readers in a retail application. But other technical architecture requirements may be dictated by the strategic IT plan. These may include a decision to keep all data on the mainframe rather than distribute it because of greater failure recovery or heightened security. Although the technical architecture may be sketched out in the Requirements phase, there is a danger in too much detail, because that may lock your solution into a dependency on specific technology.

Identifying Organizational Constraints

There are always some constraints on the product we are able to deliver. The less obvious ones may be issues that, if properly addressed in the upstream portion of the application development life cycle, may cease to be an area of contention even though they may still be an issue.

Financial Situation

Business users have fun in the visioning portion of requirements analysis because they can have anything they want, but as the requirements continue and resource needs become firmer, the cost of having everything may outweigh the benefits. Resources are ordinarily limited, and the development effort is normally limited by the availability of funds.

Company Politics

Politics within an organization may sway the acceptance of new applications. Although individuals high on the organizational chart may prove to be valuable allies for the acceptance of changes, individuals tasked with daily operations may hold more real political power. In the end, a wise applications development team takes into consideration the response of all concerned when it comes to changing the way an organization conducts business. This could also include communities outside of the organization such as the general public, suppliers, and distribution channels.

Technical Acceptance Level

Acceptance of new technology or a new software application relies heavily on the amount of understanding the users have of the new technology. If the users have a frame of reference, they find it easier to understand the new technology and they are always looking for the "What is in it for me" factor. If they understand the foundational concepts and see benefits to be gained, acceptance is greatly enhanced.

Training Needs

The need for end-user training should be stated in the Requirements phase as a targeted goal. If the end users will need only an hour of training, and that goal is much easier to react to than if they need a week of offsite training. Sometimes it is easy to forget that end users have assigned duties for which they are responsible. Extended training requires a shuffling of work assignments to get coverage for those duties.

Establishing the Schedule for Implementation of the Solution

Scheduling the installation of a new application must be accomplished with the involvement of a group of individuals. Of course, the end user for the application will be impacted. They may need to be trained, which means time away from their duties. The end user may also need additional help during the first attempts at using the application. The workload of these individuals must be lightened to give them enough time to get up to speed with the new application. Installation of new hardware may also require the end user to be away from their work area. If the workflow has changed drastically because of the new application, the workload of all affected end users may need to be adjusted to accommodate additional or lightened demands on their time.

Identifying the Audience for the Solution

The target audience for any technical solution falls into three main categories:

- The individuals who pay the bill.
- The end users of the application.
- The development team that is responsible for maintenance and enhancements.

The individuals who authorize payment often are influenced by the end users of the application and will pay based on the recommendation of the end user. If an application crosses departmental or geographic boundaries, this individual may be the only one in the organization who knows the overall success of the application.

The end users of the application may need to wait for a subsequent phase to get all the functionality they need to completely automate a process.

Exercise 7-2 will put into practice the business requirements analysis covered in this chapter.

EXERCISE 7-2

Identifying Requirements

The nutrition department of a large hospital wants an application to aid them in planning meals for special nutritional requirements such as low sodium diets, low cholesterol diets, low fat diets, or low calorie diets.

The lead nutritionist states, "We must be able to track for every food and quantity the sodium, calories, fat, and cholesterol that the food contains. We need the ability to combine these foods into recipes and then combine the foods and recipes into meals. What we need is a comprehensive catalog of foods. We don't care about instant response time so long as we don't have to wait too long."

The CIO states, "Because of our evolutionary upgrade plan for the client hardware, we cannot promise that when applications are first put into production they will all be running on 32-bit machines. We will have a mixed bag of NT, Windows 95, and Windows 3.1 for some time to come. Because the enterprise standard database is SQL Server, all applications needing database technology will use SQL Server and Access."

The CFO comments, "We also need to minimize overall the daily costs of meals."

Which of the following are valid business requirements? (The answers to this exercise appear just before the Self Test at the end of the chapter.)

1. There will be a foods database.

2. There will be a food table that contains the food name, sodium content, calorie content, fat content, cholesterol content, serving size, and cost per serving.

3. The application will run only on 32-bit client workstations.

4. There will be a recipe table that contains the foods that make up the recipe.

5. There must be two versions of the application, a 32-bit and a 16-bit version.

6. There will be a meals table that contains the foods and recipes that make up the meal.

CERTIFICATION SUMMARY

The TCO of a technical solution is calculated using both direct and indirect costs, and is an excellent approach to continuous improvement of the development process. The TCO lifecycle of Improve-Manage-Analyze roughly corresponds to the MSF life cycle.

Business requirements are derived from all levels of the business community. The requirements are then packaged in a form the business community can easily understand and will be able to sign off on. They then become the foundation of the Design phase, and can provide a base for testing during the development process.

✓ TWO-MINUTE DRILL

❑ Continually improveing IT services while simultaneously reducing IT costs are conflicting goals.

❑ *Total Cost of Ownership (TCO)* is the process of creating a set of repeatable tasks tailored for a specific organization.

❑ *Business requirements* are the foundation of analysis. The requirements are the primary communication device between the business area experts and the technical development team.

❑ Several TCO models exist with varying degrees of success. The Microsoft-Interpose model is simple, yet complex enough to support more precise analytical conclusions.

❑ *Total Cost of Ownership (TCO)* is the dollar amount of expenses and depreciated costs invested by an organization for each IT asset.

❑ The implementation of TCO involves creating a baseline set of data, recognizing the issues that the analyzed data represents, taking actions on those issues, and then measuring progress toward resolving the issues.

❑ *People, process,* and *technology* are interrelated parts of a comprehensive view of the TCO model.

❑ The Microsoft-Interpose TCO Model identifies seven categories of costs; five are considered direct IT costs, and two are indirect IT costs.

❑ The Microsoft-Interpose TCO model applies only to the client/server world and client/server costs. The mainframe and all costs associated with it are excluded.

❑ Also excluded are the costs or benefits resulting from a change in end-user productivity because of a change in the user's IT environment.

❑ The TCO model is a continuous improvement technique because it is designed to be like the Plan-Do-Check-Act cycle of the Quality Assurance realm.

❑ TCO specialists are available as consultants to perform the TCO assessment in approximately six weeks.

❑ While taking the exam, carefully read each sentence in the scenario-based questions. Do not read anything into them. As in real life, opinions about the development issues are presented from different roles in the organization. The questions may be based on these opinions, and it is up to you to either remember them all or go back to the text of the scenario to review the opinions.

❑ Business requirements must be established by the business community, not by the IT group. Although the IT community may make suggestions to the business community, IT should not drive the definition of the business requirements.

❑ One of the best reasons for producing a printed requirements document is that it may serve as a contract between the business community and the technical team.

❑ Data modeling and the use of Entity Relationship Diagrams and business process modeling, supported by both Functional Hierarchy Diagrams and Data Flow Diagrams, are techniques that have been used successfully and are considered standard techniques that many business applications analysts will use. Please remember that the object of the exam is to test individuals on concepts that are proven in the field.

❑ Determination of the type of application to be developed will drive the choice of technologies for the architectural design. At this point in the Analysis phase, a high-level identification of the problem is sufficient.

❑ The customer must dictate what level of quality they need to have built into the application. *Quality* in production applications means how often the application fails and what happens when it does fail.

❑ The TCO is comprised of both direct IT costs and indirect costs. Difficulties in estimating TCO in the Requirements Analysis phase result from not knowing the amount of training needed, not knowing the level of Help Desk support that will be needed, and not having a good sense of the technical sophistication of the users.

❑ A reasonable cost-benefit analysis may be difficult to create for one application, but this can form the basis of an estimated Return on Investment (ROI).

❑ Possible drawbacks to analyzing the existing application is that the software development platform may no longer exist, or may be an old, unsupported version, or may require that the IT analyst learn a development tool that he or she has no desire to learn.

❑ A difficult aspect of Information Technology planning is enabling upgrades. Often, planned solutions in an application design must be reworked because the infrastructure of the hardware or foundational software is not ready.

❑ Changes in an organization must be handled with care. The best way to manage change is to plan before the change must be made.

❑ Any change in technology must be thoroughly tested before installation in a production environment. This may involve creating a complete test lab that simulates the current production environment, or installing an evaluation copy of software or a trial piece of hardware, and ensuring that it works as expected.

❑ Although the technical architecture may be sketched out in the Requirements phase, there is a danger in too much detail because that may lock your solution into a dependency on specific technology.

❑ Scheduling the installation of a new application must be accomplished with the involvement of a group of individuals.

❑ If the workflow has changed drastically because of the new application, the workload of all affected end users may need to be adjusted to accommodate additional or lightened demands on their time.

❑ The target audience for any technical solution falls into three main categories: the individuals who pay the bill; the end users of the application; and the development team that is responsible for maintenance and enhancements.

Answers to Exercise 7-1

1. Mainframe costs are not included in TCO.

2. Hardware and software costs

3. Hardware and software costs

4. Hardware and software costs

5. Management costs

6. Management costs

7. Management costs

8. Development costs

9. Development costs

10. Support costs

11. Support costs

12. Support costs

13. Communication costs

14. Communication costs

15. Downtime costs

16. End-user costs

Answers to Exercise 7-2

The following are valid business concerns: 1, 2, 4, 5, and 6.

SELF TEST

The Self Test questions will help you measure your understanding of the material presented in this chapter. Read all the choices carefully, as there may be more than one correct answer. Select all correct answers for each question.

1. What costs are included in a TCO assessment?

   A. Fixed and variable Costs

   B. Direct and indirect Costs

   C. Budgeted and unbudgeted Costs

   D. Discretionary and involuntary Costs

2. What are the phase names of the TCO cycle?

   A. Plan, Do, Check

   B. Improve, Manage, Analyze

   C. Manage, Plan, Build

   D. Analyze, Develop, Test

3. Which is not a goal of the TCO Manage phase?

   A. Monitor, track, and adjust affected projects.

   B. Establish an improvement cycle.

   C. Re-establish the baseline.

   D. Create what-if scenarios to simulate the costs and benefits of improvement projects.

4. What is not within the scope of TCO?

   A. Mainframe costs

   B. Peer support of end users

   C. Downtime

   D. Travel costs for computer consultants

5. Which of the following is not a benefit of screen prototyping?

   A. The users aid in the placement of text and input boxes to create a sense of ownership of the screens.

   B. The flow of the screens from task to task is based on the recommendations from the business community.

   C. The user documentation can be developed earlier in the development life cycle.

   D. The prototype may then be used as the application.

6. What is not included in the end-user TCO costs?

   A. The labor costs to restore an end user's workstation after they deleted the registry database.

   B. The labor costs for the end user to install a favorite spreadsheet application.

   C. The cost to upgrade an end user's favorite spreadsheet application.

   D. The labor costs for the end users to play a networked game of hearts during office hours.

7. During the Requirements Analysis phase, the idea is expressed that for any one order there may be multiple lines of ordered items. Which technique is best used to model this detail?

A. Data Flow Diagramming

B. Entity Relationship Diagramming

C. Use Cases

D. Functional Decomposition

8. Which of the following organizational roles should be interviewed for the Requirements Analysis phase in a new payroll application?

A. The employees who get paid

B. The payroll clerk

C. The CFO

D. All of the above

9. Which of the following is not a technique used in gathering requirements from the business community?

A. Initial data modeling

B. Review of the inventory of hardware in use

C. Questionnaires

D. Interviews

10. Which of the following requirements might a warehouse manager state?

A. Need to know the cost of an item

B. Need to track the physical location of an item

C. Need to know the reorder quantity point of an item

D. Need to know the vendor of an item

11. Which of the following is not a step in the implementation of TCO?

A. Create a baseline set of data.

B. Recognize the issues that the analyzed data is highlighting.

C. Collect industry averages for analysis.

D. Measure progress toward resolving issues.

12. Identify the statement that is not a business requirement.

A. Create an application to manage health improvement.

B. Allow the user to choose each food from a list of items.

C. Create a report of all food ingredients for a daily menu sorted by food type.

D. Allow the user to enter favorite recipes and calculate the nutritional breakdown.

13. Select the business requirement from the following.

A. The application will run on NT 4 workstations.

B. The database for the application will be SQL Server.

C. Each food must have associated calories, fat, sodium, and cholesterol measures.

D. The application must have a web browser interface.

14. What role in the organization would state the following requirement: "Once a field has been entered and the return key pressed, the cursor must automatically position itself in the next field"?

A. The CFO

B. The CIO

C. The data entry clerks

D. The nutritional experts

15. Identify the tool not used in the Requirements phase of Applications Development.

    A. Data Definition Language

    B. Entity Relationship Diagram

    C. Data Flow Diagram

    D. Prototyping

16. Identify the best reason to generate a requirements analysis document.

    A. It can be used as an agreement contract between the technical team and the business community to manage scope creep.

    B. It can be used for training new additions to the programming team.

    C. A document can be mailed to geographically dispersed participants.

    D. Laser printer paper make the best airplanes because it creases nicely.

17. Select the reason why the technical team does not create the business requirements.

    A. The business users involved in the daily business activities know the business aspect better.

    B. The requirements document would be filled with acronyms and technical terms if the IT team stated the requirements.

    C. The document would be online rather than printed.

    D. The technical team is not involved until after the Analysis phase.

18. Select the analysis tool that aids in defining the workflow for the end user.

    A. Data Flow Diagrams

    B. Storyboarding

    C. Entity Relationship Diagrams

    D. Functional Hierarchies

19. The term *analysis paralysis* is best defined as:

    A. What happens when the lead analyst does not agree with the statement of requirements by the business users.

    B. A never-ending discussion of the minute details about how the application should function.

    C. An iterative process of Prototype-Review-Modify.

    D. The users cannot agree on the requirements.

20. Which choice does not have potential to constrain a development project?

    A. Financial situation

    B. Organization politics

    C. Training needs

    D. Vision statement for the business application

MICROSOFT CERTIFIED SOLUTION DEVELOPER

8

Narrowing Your Focus to Analyze Specific Business Requirements

CERTIFICATION OBJECTIVES

I n this chapter, we'll take a closer look at the requirements of the business, customer, and end user. Though it may seem from the previous chapter that determining such requirements should be completed, and you're ready to move on to designing your solution, there are specific needs that must be identified and analyzed more closely. In this chapter, we'll narrow our focus, and look at certain requirements that need to be looked at closely in a project.

For any project you work on, you need to look at issues that will affect the project, and determine how these issues should be addressed and/or implemented in the analysis of requirements. These issues include such things as security, performance, maintenance, extensibility, availability, scalability, and requirements that deal with human factors. In addition, you must look at any existing methodologies used by the business, and any business limitations that can affect the project. Finally, as we'll discuss in this chapter, you must identify any existing solutions that your solution must integrate with. When discussing such requirements for your solution with the customer, each of these elements must be addressed and analyzed. Even if the answer is "no, that isn't an issue for this product," it's important to know this before designing and coding the application. It's much easier to address such issues early, so you don't have to add and remove features later in the project.

CERTIFICATION OBJECTIVE 8.01

Analyzing Security Requirements

Security is always an important issue with any solution you design. It's important that only authorized users are allowed to use your solution and access data, and that any data your solution uses is kept safe and secure. This can be done through any combination of user accounts, audit trails, existing security mechanisms, fault tolerance, regiments of backing up data, and other methods. Even if very little security is required in an application, determining the sufficient amount is as important as if you'd implemented heavy security features.

Identifying User Roles

People who use applications fall into certain roles, which define the tasks users perform, the components they use, and the level of security needed. A *role* is a symbolic name used to group the users of a set of software components to determine who can access those components' interfaces. In analyzing the requirements of an application, it is important to identify the roles people play in an organization, and which roles will apply to the solution you'll create.

When identifying roles, you look at common groups that exist in an organization. For example, if you were creating a banking program, you would find that some of the common roles include managers and tellers. These would then be considered in designing the security of the application. Tellers might require access to features like depositing and withdrawing funds from accounts. However, the bank may not want tellers to have access to more advanced features in the solution, such as being able to freeze accounts and approve overdrafts. Such duties might fall on individuals fulfilling the role of manager. You would want to design the security of your application to take into account the roles of these people. People in the higher-level role of manager would be able to perform actions that aren't allowed by lower-level roles, such as teller.

While roles are generally associated with groups of individuals, you may also have certain roles that are geared toward a single user. For example, as we'll see next, you may have a person who's in charge of administering the application. This person would set up user accounts for the others who will use the solution. Another example would be a user who's assigned the role of doing regular backups on data, or who is responsible for maintaining user accounts. While these are still common tasks associated with the security of the application, and control what certain users can and can't do, these roles may be applied to only a single, solitary user.

The Administrator Role

Administrators typically are users who have the highest level of security access to features in an application, and to the data that the solution uses. Whether you decide to control access through the application itself, through a server application (like SQL Server) or the operating system (NT

Server), administrators are generally at the top of the authority chain. Common abilities associated with this role include the power to create and delete accounts, control the access of other users, and use any feature or functionality in the program.

The power of administrators is best illustrated by one of the most common passwords administrators use for their user accounts: "GOD." There is no role higher than that of administrator.

Administrators are in charge of the program and the security associated with it. Certain features of programs are often unavailable to users in lower-level roles, and some programs allow the administrator to determine how the solution functions. Such functionality includes determining where the data will be accessed from, and the availability of features.

Because administrators have such an incredible amount of power, you should severely limit the number of people who are put into this role. You wouldn't want to have every user of your application given administrator-level security, as it can cause serious problems, and considerable confusion. If you did, any user would be able to delete accounts, and control other users' access. The administrator is the person in charge of the program, and in control of the access given to others. Generally, the person who oversees others who use the application will be given this level of security. This might include the head of a department, a manager, an assistant manager, or other people in higher-level organizational positions.

It's vital that a person who's given administrator security is responsible, and realizes that they're in charge of the security. It's not unheard of for irresponsible administrators to increase the security access of their buddies, so they have complete freedom in the application. In addition, if too many people have administrator-level security, it will be impossible to track who is responsible for causing these and other security infractions.

The Group Role

Often, you'll find that there are a number of users who perform common activities, and need a shared level of access to application components and data. When this happens, these users can be put into a *group*, where they'll have the same level of permissions or rights. For example, if you had a group of people who needed access to a SQL Server, you could create a group called SQLUSER with the same levels of access. Each of these users will use the same data, access the same components, and share the same level of responsibility. Creating a special group in which to put them saves you the problem of having to assign the same permissions to their individual user accounts. Each user is simply added to the group.

The Guest Role

The *Guest* role is generally given the lowest level of security. As its name implies, people who are simply visiting the application, and don't require a high level of access, have the role of Guest. An example of this would be a banking solution, where people accessing the solution through a Guest account could see how many customers the bank has, the day's interest rate, exchange rates, and so forth. They aren't permitted to access sensitive information, or use many features or functionality associated with the program. Users who may not have a user account, and simply need to access low-level, unclassified material, use the Guest role.

The Client Role

Users in the *Client* role perform most of the activities in a solution. These are the common users of an application, who often add and modify much of the data your solution will access. In the bank application example, the tellers would be a client of the bank solution. Other types of clients might be data entry clerks or, if you were creating an accounting program, the accountants working in that department. The permissions associated with these users allow them to use the general features and functionality of the solution, and access data that's available to most of the people in that department or organization.

exam
ⓦatch

Many times, students who are taking the Microsoft exam confuse the Guest and Client roles, thinking of clients as customers, who often fall into a Guest role. It's important to distinguish between these two roles. Think of guests as visitors, and clients as workers on the client machines accessing a server. Think of the roles in this way to help keep the two separate.

Exercise 8-1 will give you some practice identifying user roles. (The answers to this exercise appear just before the Self Test at the end of the chapter.)

Identifying User Roles

Hammy Slam is a small company that makes imitation hamsters. They have over 50 models to choose from. They want you to design a solution that can be accessed over the company's intranet, which is also connected to the Internet. Darren takes care of this network, while Julie and Jennifer are responsible for backing up data and waiting on customers, respectively. Customers will use the application to enter the name of a product and see its availability and cost. Up to 20 employees of the company will use the application to access customer information, including customers' credit card information.

Administrators	Clients	Guests	

1. Based on the information given in the above scenario, determine who should be responsible for setting up accounts, applying security permissions to those accounts, creating new groups, and other administrative duties. Enter that name under the appropriate role in the table above.

2. Determine what special groups will be needed for the solution. Enter the name of the special group in the table above, and who will be in the role below that.

3. Determine who will access the lowest level of information, and will basically be visitors to the solutions capabilities. This role will have very few permissions attached to it. Enter them under the appropriate role in the table above.

4. Determine which user accounts will use general functions of the application, and enter them under the appropriate role in the table above.

5. Compare the table above to the completed one at the end of this chapter to see if your choices were correct.

Identifying the Impact of the Solution on the Existing Security Environment

In designing any solution that uses security features, you need to determine what impact your solution will have on the existing security environment. Basically, your solution will have one of three effects on existing security in the enterprise:

- Enhance it.
- Diminish or cripple existing security.
- Have no effect whatsoever on the existing security.

When identifying the impact of a solution on the existing security environment, you determine where the security features in your application will fall. In doing this, you look at each security feature in your solution individually, and then as a whole. While some features will have no effect, others may have a drastic impact on the overall security.

If your application sets permissions on specific user accounts, or sets rights on different folders on a hard disk, this may conflict with the security of the network operating system. For example, Windows NT Server controls the rights placed on folders on the server. If your application attempts to do the same, NT Server would stop the application from succeeding. On other operating systems, such as Windows 95, if your application attempted to set permissions on a folder where file sharing is disabled, an error would result. You need to determine how such actions will work with the existing security that's in place and controlled by the operating system.

If your application uses user accounts, it will act as another barrier against unauthorized users. Depending on how you set this up, and the type of application you're designing, a user account and password could be passed to the application. This occurs with Internet applications, when Internet Explorer 5 automatically provides the user account and password. This means any user using that particular browser can access the application and data. NT networks can also check the user's account to see if they have access to certain applications, files, and folders. Depending on the application, your security may diminish or have no effect on the current security environment.

Establishing Fault Tolerance

Fault tolerance is the ability of a solution to function regardless of whether a fault occurred. In short, it is non-stop availability of a solution. For example, let's say you created an application that accessed a database on a particular server. If that server went down, your solution would become useless, since the database is inaccessible. However, if the server portion of your solution made regular backups of the database to another server, the client portion of your server could simply switch to the secondary database, and users could continue to work. A fault-tolerant system keeps users working, despite any problems that occur.

One method of fault tolerance is the use of replicating databases. As we'll see in the next section, *replication* allows all or part of a database to be copied to other machines on your network. Because each database is a replication of the other, users see a consistent copy of available data. If a server goes down, users are able to still access data. They simply connect to another copy of the database, and continue to work.

A common method of fault tolerance is the use of *RAID (Redundant Array of Inexpensive Disks)*. There are several levels of RAID available with Windows NT, for example:

- RAID 0, Disk Striping without parity. This spreads data across several hard disks, but isn't fault-tolerant. If one hard disk fails, all of the data is lost. This means that RAID 0 actually makes your system less fault-tolerant. Rather than losing data on one hard disk when a fault occurs, you lose data on every disk in the striped set.

■ RAID 1, Mirroring. This creates an exact duplicate of data, by copying data from one partition to another (which should be on different hard disks). If you use a separate hard disk controller for each hard disk in a mirror set, it is called *disk duplexing.*

■ RAID 5, Disk Striping with parity. This spreads data across several hard disks and includes error-correction information. If any one disk fails, the operating system can use the error-correcting information from other disks in the set to restore the information. Once you replace the failed drive, RAID 5 allows the information to be restored to the new disk.

As you can see by this listing, only RAID 1 and RAID 5 are fault-tolerant. If you lose data due to a hard disk failure, each of these can keep you from losing the data. You should note that different operating systems support different levels of RAID. In addition, there are numerous hard disk manufacturers that make hard disks that support RAID.

As mentioned, RAID support is available through software such as Windows NT Server. There are also hardware-based RAID solutions. Hard drive controller cards are available that perform RAID functions. When hardware-based RAID is implemented, it reduces the workload on the processor, because the controller card deals with performing RAID functions. In addition, because RAID support is hardware-based, you can use RAID on operating systems that don't support RAID. Even though Windows NT has software-based RAID support built into it, Microsoft still recommends using hardware- over software-based RAID due to the benefits of hardware-based RAID.

exam
ⓦatch

Microsoft NT Server supports only Levels 0, 1, and 5 of RAID. While there are other levels of RAID—Levels 0 through 10, and Level 53— they won't appear on the exam. You should know the three levels mentioned here, especially 1 and 5, which are fault-tolerant.

FROM THE CLASSROOM

Solution Requirements Analysis

One of the most important aspects of solution development is the proper analysis of the requirements of the solution itself. Sometimes developers and programmers are overly eager to begin programming a solution without giving enough thought to concepts like security requirements, solution extensibility, and scalability concerns. Hopefully, developers will reach the point of giving real thought and analysis to performance considerations. Unfortunately, so many other areas of solution development and design offer numerous pitfalls for affecting the optimal functionality of a solution.

As the development of solutions shifts more into the web-enabling, globalization, and distribution of applications, a corresponding degree of concern should be placed on the security requirements of solutions. Failure to respect the interaction of security mechanisms provided by the different players in a distributed application can wreak havoc on the ultimate reliability of the solution. Since most developers are usually not of the SE-type, a full working knowledge of the idiosyncrasies of ACL, NTFS, IIS, and MTS role-based security is usually not present. This increases the odds of opening the door to security loopholes. For this reason, care should be taken to coordinate efforts with those having responsibility for maintaining security on your network to help determine the ultimate security level of the solution.

—Michael Lane Thomas, MCSE+I, MCSD, MCT, MCP+SB, MSS, A+

Planning for Effective Maintenance

No matter how well you design and develop an enterprise application, you can't expect it to run forever without some sort of maintenance. Areas in which you'll want to plan for maintaining the program include backing up data, and how user accounts will be maintained. If data is lost, and there isn't an archived copy of the database, it will mean that a new database will need to be created and all of the data will need to be reentered. In addition, new accounts will need to be added for users, while people who have left the company will need to have their accounts removed. Planning for effective maintenance means looking at what the application or service will require in terms of future use.

An important area in maintenance planning is a regular routine of backing up data. It's quite possible that at one point, the database could become corrupted, the hard disk storing the data could fail, or any number of other issues. If that data isn't backed up, it's quite possible, assuming there isn't any fault tolerance in place, that the data will be lost.

There are a number of different options when it comes to backing up data:

- Mirroring
- Replication
- Using backup software to store copies in a special format to other media. The terminology in SQL Server for this is *dumping*.

You can use one method, or several different methods, to ensure that there are several copies available for particularly sensitive data. Because of the importance of backups, we'll discuss each of these methods individually.

A convenient method of backing up data is *mirroring*. Mirroring is something we discussed when talking about fault tolerance, and involves data being copied to another storage device. Each time a transaction is made to the database, changes are also written to a second copy residing on another hard disk. This means you have two identical copies of the database at any given time. For added protection, you should have the mirror copy of the database on a second server. If one server goes down, work isn't disrupted, because the second server's database can be used. Many relational databases like SQL Server support mirroring, and once set up, your solution becomes virtually maintenance-free. Unfortunately, since every transaction requires writing once to each database, performance is diminished.

Replication is another method of backing up data that's virtually maintenance-free once it's set up. Replication has the entire database or portions of it copied to another server on the network. It is also an exceptional way of improving performance. Since the database is distributed across multiple servers, the workload can be balanced between the different servers. In other words, one user can make changes to a database on one server; another user can make changes on another server database; and a third can use another replicated database. The changes they make are replicated to each of the three databases. Each of these databases is an identical copy of the other, and because users are accessing the data through different servers, the workload of each server is less than if users were accessing data from a single server.

on the **job**

Replicating data is generally thought of as a method of balancing workloads across multiple servers, and keeping that data consistent between them. Though not generally considered a method of backing up data, it is still a valid method of keeping an additional copy of your data available in case of problems.

Dumping is when data is copied to an external device. While you could perform backups to the same hard disk containing the data, this wouldn't provide much safety if that hard disk crashed. Data is usually copied to external devices, which could be another hard disk, a tape drive, or other storage devices. When you dump a database, a snapshot of the entire database is made, and the data is copied in a special format to the external device. Any changes that have been made after the data is dumped to the external device are lost, unless the dump is supplemented with transaction logs. Dumping data is one of the most popular methods of creating backups.

Backups should be done regularly on data. How often depends on how often the data in the database changes. In companies where data changes as frequently as every hour, or even every few minutes, you may want to consider backing up the data hourly, or every few hours. If very few changes occur each hour, then daily backups should be performed. If a problem occurs, then the backed-up database can be restored, and only a minimal amount of data that was entered since the last backup is potentially lost.

In addition to backing up the database, you should also back up any configuration or user files. This will allow users to have their personal preferences restored in case of a failure. User accounts should also be backed up, so that you don't need to recreate an account for every group and user, and reenter information on every user of the system.

It's important to have some sort of strategy in place to maintain user accounts. A security role should be established to deal with account maintenance. When new employees are hired, the person in this role can create an account with the proper permissions for that person, and add them to any groups they will need to join. When employees are promoted, they may need new permissions, or have to be added to different groups. It's also important that when people are laid off or dismissed, their account is either disabled or deleted. This will keep them from reentering the system after they've left the company.

It's vital to remember to disable or remove a user's account after they've left the organization. Many companies have found out the hard way, that disgruntled users who have been fired, laid off, or put into retirement can wreak havoc on a system. The former employee logs on remotely to the network or application, and from there may modify or remove data. The employee may even add false data, by creating bogus users or creating false shipment orders.

Planning the Distribution of a Security Database

When security is required for a database solution, getting the database from a developer's computer to the computers where data will be accessed takes some planning. You need to do more than simply dumping the database on a server's hard drive. Without planning for distribution of a security database, you may find unauthorized users getting into data that they should not be allowed to access.

The level of security you can apply to your database is often reflected in the software being used on the network. For example, Windows NT Server allows you to control access at the file and folder level. When your database server is on an NT Server, you can control the access to your database file, or the folder containing your database.

User group accounts will also need to be set up for that database server. For more information on the different security roles, refer to the previous section on this topic. You can control access through accounts set up on the server's operating system (such as through User Manager in Windows NT Server), or you may be able to set up accounts through the DBMS. SQL Server enables you to create accounts and control access. However, this is dependent on the software, and the level of security available will be dependent on the type of software and database that are used and implemented for your solution.

When you think of a database application, you probably think of a single database residing on the hard disk of your computer, or some database or file server on the network. However, much of the data your solution accesses may be spread across multiple computers, and possibly on different networks. When the enterprise needs to have data on geographically dispersed computers, you may need to create multiple databases containing the same data on computers in different buildings, cities, or even countries. The databases will require data to be replicated between them, so that each database has the same data, or is able to find data residing in the other databases on the network. In addition to this, you will also need to set up security, to determine who may access each database.

When dealing with distributed or replicated databases, the database server on each network will need to have security permissions set up. Different accounts will need to be set up on each server, with the appropriate permissions applied to them. Generally, groups will be created as well, and individual accounts will be added to them. This controls who will be allowed to use the databases on each server. As mentioned, on Windows NT Servers, access can be set on a file and folder level. This means you can control access to the specific database file, or the folder containing the database. Replication must also be set up, so that changes to each database are replicated to the database on the other network.

Establishing the Security Context

The *security context* of a solution is made up of its security attributes or rules. This determines how a user is able to access, and what the user is able to do once access is achieved. It dictates how and when users are able to add, delete, and modify data, and use the features and functionality of an application. For example, when you log on to a computer, the password and your user account provide the security context for interaction with the operating system, and the applications and data on the computer or network. A personal identification number (PIN) would be entered by the user of a smart card, or a customer using an Automated Teller Machine. For a secure solution, you need to establish the attributes or rules that determine how and when users can access your solution and the data it uses.

Planning for Auditing

Auditing is where activities performed by certain or all users are documented to a file, allowing a user (such as the administrator) to see what these users have done. The record showing the operations a user performed is called an *audit trail.* The audit trail allows you to see what actions certain users perform, and determine where problems may exist with certain users.

Auditing can be effective in catching users who may pose a security risk. For example, let's say you had doubts as to whether a certain user was acting responsibly in your application. You could set up auditing on that particular user, and chronicle the user's actions. This would allow you to see when they logged on, what they did, and when they logged off. From this, you could determine whether the user was abusing their privileges, damaging the system, and basically doing things they weren't supposed to.

Identifying Levels of Security Needed

Different organizations, and different forms of data, have varying security requirements. If you're creating an application for a small business, to be used by a small group of users who are all highly trusted, the level of security required by the solution will be minimal. If you're creating a solution for the military, where different users will require different clearance levels to access data, the level of security will be drastically higher. When discussing the requirements of your application with customers, you should try to determine what level of security will be required of the solution. Is there a big concern over unauthorized users gaining access? If the organization's network is connected to the Internet, this may be of some concern. Will specific types of information need to have higher security? Which users will need to access certain data, and which ones shouldn't? These are all concerns that need to be addressed early in the project.

It's important to remember that security is a double-edged sword. Not enough security can leave your system open to all sorts of problems, while too much security will make your solution more of a pain to use than it may be worth. Every security feature you add to your solution is a blockade to keep unauthorized users out. However, as users move from having to enter passwords, wait for their access to be checked, and so on, your security features may be seen as overly restrictive and inhibiting to good and proper users. In determining the level of security required, it's important to strike a balance between accessibility and security.

Analyzing Existing Mechanisms for Security Policies

It's important to determine what existing mechanisms for security policies are already in place in an organization, before deciding on new ones that could conflict with or duplicate them. Imagine going through all the trouble of designing features for your solution that control access to folders or database files, only to discover that it will run on an NT server, which can already do this. Before determining what security mechanisms should be added to your application, you need to discuss with the customer what is currently in place.

Analyzing Performance Requirements

When a customer asks you to design a new solution, they want a quick and speedy program that obeys commands. When a command is given, there shouldn't be a long wait for a response. *Performance* determines how well an application works under daily conditions. This means that despite increases in the number of users accessing data, the volume of transactions over a given period, or other issues, the application performs as is required in a speedy and efficient manner. The solution performs calculations and operations quickly, and the user sees the solution responding fast to their actions and requests.

If all users had incredibly fast processors, networks that transferred information faster than the speed of light, and unlimited hard drive space, then performance wouldn't be a design issue. If every user used the same computer or network system, what you develop on your system would work on any system. Unfortunately, in the real world, companies have trouble keeping up with technology. Hard drive space is limited, networks are slow, and numerous users work on older, legacy equipment. Because of such considerations, it's important to determine how elements such as these will affect your design. You must analyze the requirements of the business, discover which elements exist in the organization, and determine how they may affect performance of the solution. Once this is done, you can then determine what needs to be added to the design to deal with the performance issues.

on the **!** Job

Many performance issues that arise once an application is built stem from the initial design of the solution. By not identifying and dealing with performance issues in the design of your solution, they often crop up later when the solution is developed. Dealing with performance issues once coding has begun is more costly and time consuming than in the Design phase of the project. Therefore, it's important that performance issues are addressed before the first line of code is even written.

There are basically two types of performance, and in determining the organization's performance requirements, you'll plan to deal with them through one of these ways:

- Real performance
- Perceived performance

Real performance is what most people think of, or assume is occurring, when they look at how well an application performs. It is the way that your solution carries out operations, does calculations, and runs. With real performance, the code is optimized, and actions are carried out swiftly.

Perceived performance gives the user the impression that the actions are occurring quickly, when in fact they are not. For example, when loading Visual Basic or Visual C++, you may notice that a splash screen appears. This shows the name of the application loading, and covers up the fact that it's taking some time for the program to load. Adding splash screens or other indicators to show that something is happening distracts the user from noticing that an activity is taking time to complete.

Transactions-per-Time Slice Considerations

One area that's important to identify is the number of transactions expected to occur over a given period of time. A *transaction* is one or more separate actions that are grouped together, and executed as a single action. One of the easiest ways of thinking of a transaction is withdrawing money from a banking machine. When you withdraw money, the program needs to check to see if there is enough money in the account. If there is, the amount of your withdrawal is deducted from your account balance, and this amount of cash is delivered. While the transaction is executed as a single action, there are actually multiple lines of code that need to be executed individually for the transaction to be completed.

In discussing the requirements of the business, you should find out how many transactions will occur over a given period of time. This will vary from one solution to another, but it is important to have this information so you can determine how many transactions your solution will deal with every second, hour, day, and so forth. For example, to use the bank machine example, bank machines in a small town may have only a few transactions every hour, while those in New York City could have thousands of transactions per hour. If you were creating the solution for New York City bank machines, you should consider designing it differently than the one in a small town to account for increased use.

Bandwidth Considerations

Bandwidth is the network's capacity to carry information, and is measured in data transferred per unit of time, usually seconds. For example, in using the Internet, you may have noticed that your digital data is transferred in bits per second (bps). When data is sent over the network cable, it uses a certain amount of bandwidth. In other words, it uses up so much of the capacity that the wire is able to carry from one computer to another.

For every network, there is a limited amount of bandwidth that can be used. If the amount of data being sent over the network gets too high, the network slows down. Therefore, you need to determine if the organization has sufficient bandwidth to support the data being sent over the wire (i.e., network cable). If it has more than enough bandwidth, then it will be able to support the current and future needs for data transfer. If it has just enough or not enough bandwidth, then the organization will need to consider whether to upgrade to a faster method of transmission, or add more network cables to give users multiple paths for transferring data.

exam
ⓦatch

To understand bandwidth, you may want to think of automobile traffic. When cars run on a city street with two lanes, there is only so much traffic that can be accommodated before you wind up with traffic jams. This gives you one of two options: make the cars go faster or add more lanes. This corresponds to networks, because when network traffic gets too high, the organization needs to consider whether a faster method of transmission is required (i.e., make the cars go faster), or more wires are needed to make up the network (i.e., add more lanes). Whichever method you choose will improve the performance.

The easiest way of determining the current bandwidth available on a network is to ask the network administrator. He or she should be able to tell you the current speed of the network, how it is laid out, and any other information that you require. In addition, you can find out about any changes that will be made before your solution is released.

There are two ways of estimating the amount of bandwidth needed. The first calculates bandwidth by the amount of bytes transferred by your server, while the second calculates by connections and file size. Which method you use depends on the data available to you. Performing these calculations will allow you to determine the bandwidth required, and what type of connection will be needed for the solution to perform well. For example, will an Internet connection require a 28,800 modem on the server, or will an ISDN or T3 connection be required? Before getting into these methods of estimating bandwidth, you need to know how bandwidth is measured.

Bandwidth is measured by the number of bits transferred per second (bps), but information you'll see on files transferred is usually in bytes. Statistics on the server(s) your application will reside on will show information in bytes transferred, while the file sizes of documents on a hard disk are displayed in kilobytes and megabytes. Estimating bandwidth requires converting bytes to bits. There are 8 bits in a byte, plus an additional 4 bits for overhead data. For either of the bandwidth estimation methods covered next, you'll need to use this information.

When you calculate bandwidth by the amount transferred by a server (e.g., NT Server, Internet Information Server, or Personal Web Server), you need to know how many bytes have been transferred over a certain number of hours. Once you do this, you use the following formula to convert this information into bits per second:

(Bytes × 12 bits) / hours × 3600 seconds

A byte is 8 bits of data plus 4 bits of overhead, which equals 12. When you estimate bandwidth by bytes transferred, you'll need to multiply the amount of bytes transferred by your Web server by 12. Because many servers record the amount of data transferred *per hour*, and bandwidth is *per second*, you'll also need to convert the number of hours to seconds. To do this, multiply the number of hours by 3600, which is 60 minutes in an hour multiplied by the 60 seconds in a minute (60 × 60). Having done this, you divide the number of bits by the number of seconds to get the bits per second.

The other method of estimating bandwidth is by using the number of connections and the average document size of what's been transferred. This translates into the following formula:

(Average number of connections per day / 86400) × (Average document size in kilobytes × 12)

While this seems pretty imposing, it's really not. The first part of the equation divides the average number of connections your site gets each day by the number of seconds per day (86,400). The second part of the equation multiplies the average file size by 12, which is the 8 bits of data and 4 bits of overhead. You multiply both parts of the equation to obtain your estimated bandwidth.

It just takes using these formulas a few times to master them. Once you've calculated the bandwidth used by your site, you can determine what kind of connection you'll need.

Capacity Considerations

Capacity is the volume or limit something can handle, and can have a direct effect on the performance of your solution. In the previous section, we discussed bandwidth considerations, which dealt with the capacity of data a type of network connection could handle. With bandwidth capacity, a method of transmission with high bandwidth has a high capacity for transmitting data, while low bandwidth would have a low capacity. The higher the bandwidth, the higher the capacity, meaning the greater amount of network traffic handled.

In addition to bandwidth capacity, it's also important to determine how many computers and users your solution will service. The more computers on a network accessing your application, and subsequently the more users, the more performance can degrade. It's important to know how many users and computers will be accessing your solution early, so your application can support the necessary number of users.

Besides your solution, you should try to determine if the server(s), on which any server-side components will reside, can handle the number of users you plan to support. Let's say an NT server is licensed to allow 50 simultaneous connections, and you know that 75 users will be accessing data or using the server portion of your solution that will reside on that server. This means that unless more licenses are purchased, 25 users won't be able to access your solution or its data.

Interoperability with Existing Standards

You should determine what standards currently exist in an organization when determining the performance requirements of your solution. Different organizations may utilize standards that must be adhered to if your application is to function properly and perform well. These are specifications for drivers, applications, networks, and so forth that dictate how certain elements of your application will interact with the existing system. If existing standards aren't conformed to, your solution may not function well (or at all), and may cause problems in other components of the system.

Peak versus Average Requirements

It is vital that you determine both peak and average requirements for your solution. *Peak values* show the highest amount of activity your solution experiences at a given time. For example, when users on a network log on to your solution in the morning, it will experience a higher amount of use than any other time of the day. *Average values* show the common amount of activity you can expect your solution to have. For example, even though 100 users log on to your application at the beginning of the business day, an average of 50 users may be using your solution at any other time during the day.

Peak and average requirements apply to almost any area of a project. In analyzing the business requirements of a project, you'll need to determine peak and average numbers of users, amounts of data storage and retrieval, and so forth. The peak and average values can then be applied to other areas of the project. For example, by determining when the peak and average times of activity are for your solution, you can determine when the best times are to perform maintenance. Rather than slowing down the network further by performing a backup, you can schedule maintenance for times when the average usage is low, and not at peak times.

Peak requirements can be determined by looking at the highest amount of activity that will occur at a given point. If an existing application is in use, you can look at the statistics of the server that your solution partially resides on, or by implementing auditing to see when people are using that server-side solution. For example, by looking at Performance Monitor in NT Server, you can see the top number of users accessing that server. The same can be done to determine the peak amounts of data transferred, or by looking at the statistics of the database, you can see the total amount of data transferred per day. By looking at this over a few days or a week, you can see the highest amounts of data or users. If this type of information isn't available to you, the organization will generally have an idea of who will use the solution. By taking the total number of users who will use the system over a specific time period, such as an 8-hour work shift, you can identify the peak value.

Average requirements are similarly determined. By calculating the total number of users, data transferred, or whatever element of the system you want to determine averages for, you can divide this by a specific period. For example, if 50 users access data one day, 10 another, and 60 on the third day, this would mean that 120 users used the solution over three days. By dividing this by 3 (the number of days), you can see that the average number of users per day is 40 users. By dividing this by 8, for the number of hours in a workday, you can see that 5 users per hour is the average requirement.

Determining Peak and Average Requirements

Universal Squeegee has offices in Detroit and Vancouver. These two offices are connected with a WAN line. They've asked you to design a solution that will be used at each location. There will be 300 users of the application, who will spend half their time using the solution. They will need to log on to the solution in the morning and at night, as well as log on and off at their lunch breaks, which is generally noon until 1 P.M. Modifications, additions, and deletions to the database will be replicated every 15 minutes over the WAN line, so that each office has relatively the same data at any given time. Each office is open from 9 to 5, Monday to Friday. (The answers to this exercise appear just before the Self Test at the end of the chapter.)

1. Based on the information given, determine the peak number of users who will access data.

2. Determine the average number of users who will access the system hourly.

3. Based on the peak and average use of the solution and network, determine when backups should be performed.

Response-Time Expectations

Response time is the difference in time from the end of a query or command to when the results of that query or command first begin to appear on the screen. For example, let's say a user made a query to a database server for all customers with the last name "Carruthers." The time from when this query is sent, to when the first names appear on the user's screen, is the response time. In other words, how long does it take for the computer to respond to the user's request?

Just as earlier we said that performance can be broken into real performance and perceived performance, there is real response time and perceived response time. *Real response time* is the actual time it takes for a server or solution to respond to a request. *Perceived response time* gives the impression that the response is actually faster than it really is. For example, let's say that when the user queried for all users with the last name of "Carruthers," there were a considerable number of records to look through, the network was busy, or other elements slowed the response time. If your solution put up a message box stating "Currently processing request," this response would make the user feel that the query was being processed quickly. It would also tell the user that the query is being processed, rather than leaving them wondering what was happening.

Existing Response-Time Characteristics

In determining response-time expectations, it's important to look at the existing characteristics affecting response times. In doing so, you can determine the characteristics of the system that are increasing response times beyond what is desired from the application. This is called *latency*.

Latency occurs when there is a longer wait than necessary or desired in response times. This can be an actual or perceived delay in response times. This can occur when data speeds are mismatched between the process and input/output devices, multithreading or prefetching is not being used, or there is inadequate data buffering. *Prefetching* is when your solution anticipates additional data or data requests, and *multithreading* is when multiple threads of execution are used to process a task. *Data buffering* is like a cache, where data is stored to improve the performance of various tasks being carried out. As we'll see next, there are a number of other barriers in a system that can affect the response time of an application, as well as the solution's overall performance.

Barriers to Performance

Despite how well your solution is designed, there are elements in any system that can keep your solution from performing as well as it should. Areas of a system that can serve as performance barriers include the following:

- CPU
- RAM

- Storage
- Operating systems and other programs your solution works with
- Network bandwidth capacity
- Network cards and modems
- Poor coding and/or design

Each of these, alone or in combination, can cause performance to degrade. It's important to identify what systems the solution will run on, so if necessary, the customer has the choice of upgrading systems, or accepting lower performance.

If a computer is slow and underpowered, then any application running on it will also be slow and inefficient. The server and workstations using your solution should have adequate processor, memory, and storage capabilities to support the application. If they don't, you'll find that performance suffers.

Any solution must work with other programs. After all, even a desktop application that doesn't interact with other applications must work with the operating system. When it comes to distributed applications, your solution will need to work with the user's operating system, network protocols, network operating systems like Windows NT or Novell NetWare, and other solutions with which the application may interact. If a system is using an older operating system, performance may be compromised. For example, if you were creating a solution for Windows 95, it could use 32-bit programming, while Windows 3.1 would have to use slower 16-bit programming.

Earlier in this chapter we discussed how network bandwidth can affect performance. It's important that the speed of the transmission devices and the media being used meet your solution requirements. If the bandwidth is too low, then network traffic problems can result. In addition to this, if the media is fast enough to carry the data but the network cards or modems being used are too slow, performance will suffer. In this case, a *bottleneck* will result. If you think of a bottle, the neck is narrow, so less can travel through than if the neck were wider like the base. In a network, if the modems or network cards are slow, the data has to wait for previous information to flow into the computer. Bottlenecks can be a big problem, and network cards and modems should be of sufficient speed to handle the amount of data a computer is expected to receive.

Poor design is the biggest problem in performance, with bad coding running a close second. By looking at areas that can improve the performance of your solution, and coding the solution accordingly, many performance issues can be resolved. However, it's important to remember that performance is often a matter of give and take. In a number of cases, increasing performance in one area will result in decreasing performance in another. For example, when dealing with Forms (containers used to hold other objects in your solution), this tradeoff becomes apparent. If all Forms are loaded at startup, the application will run faster as it switches from one Form to another. However, when an application uses a lot of Forms, loading them all into memory can gobble up memory. A rule of thumb is determining which Forms will commonly be used during the design stage, and then having these Forms loaded into memory when the application starts. Less commonly used Forms (such as one used for configuring preferences, or "About this Program" Forms) should not be loaded at startup. In designing and coding your solution, you'll need to know what areas need to be traded to improve performance in another.

CERTIFICATION OBJECTIVE 8.03

Analyzing Maintenance Requirements

As mentioned earlier in this chapter, maintenance is an important issue when it comes to designing good applications. This section deals with things such as regular backups and maintenance of accounts. It also deals with other issues that determine the upkeep of a solution, including how the solution is to be distributed, where it's to be distributed, staff considerations, and issues that deal with development.

While we'll discuss many of these in the sections that follow, it may seem that issues dealing with development should be handled much later in the project. How will source code versions be handled? What if another developer, other than the original author of the programming code, needs to make changes? How will that developer know what certain lines of code do? In designing an application, it is important to incorporate ways that allow the program to be maintained. Without an effective maintenance plan, problems can arise when changes need to be made to the application.

Throughout development, the source code will undergo numerous changes. Unfortunately, some changes may cause problems, and developers may need to revert to a previous version of the source code. Therefore, how versioning of source code will be handled should be discussed early, and a decision made on how it will be handled. Visual SourceSafe (VSS) is one answer to dealing with different versions of source code. Your code can be saved to a database, and if the development team wishes to use a previous version of that code, they can restore it from the VSS database.

As mentioned throughout this book, it's important to keep documentation on the different elements that make up your project. Source code is no different. An important aspect of making your source code maintainable regards documentation. This means writing down the objectives of your application, what aspects of your application do, creating flow charts, and so forth. Throughout the design process it is important to create such documentation, which can be utilized in later stages of design, and in the creation of Help documentation. Early in the project, it should be determined how documentation will be kept, and whether tools such as Visual Modeler or other tools in Visual Studio will be used.

To keep source code maintainable, developers should also be instructed to make comments in their code. *Comments* are a way of explaining what a procedure does, why a variable is included, or what particular sections or lines of code are there to do. Comments can be added to source code by using REM or by putting an apostrophe before a statement. Anything typed on a line that starts with REM, or anything on a line that is typed after an apostrophe, is ignored. When an apostrophe is used, anything after the apostrophe is ignored. The following shows two examples of comments:

```
' This is a comment

REM This is a comment as well
```

Adding comments allows you to remember why a line of code exists or the purpose of a procedure. This is important, because while a developer may know why code is being added at the time it's done, it is less evident months or years down the road. It's particularly useful to developers who are editing someone else's code. By looking at the comments of the original programmer, the new programmer can understand why a particular function or statement has been included.

on the job

The Y2K (Year 2000) issue shows the need for comments in source code. Many of the original programmers from that period are no longer in the business, or working for the company they worked for at the time the original source code was written. This means that the new programmers who are editing the code need to use the comments to determine the purpose of sections of code.

Finally, before moving to other issues, the final maintenance issue for development that we'll discuss here is the use of a consistent naming convention. Consistent naming conventions allow programmers to quickly determine the data type of a variable, what the variable is for, its scope, and much more information. An example of a commonly used naming convention is the *Hungarian Naming Convention*. This has prefixes added to the names of controls and objects, which allow developers to recognize the purpose of those objects and controls. For example, *cmd* is the prefix for a command button, *lbl* for a label, and *txt* for a textbox. By adding a prefix before the name of an object or control, such as lblAddress and txtAddress for the label and textbox of an address field, developers are better able to understand the type of object or control being used.

Breadth of Application Distribution

In determining maintenance requirements, you should identify the breadth, or scale, to which your application will be distributed. Will it be distributed to a single department in the organization, or marketed on the World Wide Web and on shelves to hundreds of thousands or perhaps millions of users? By discussing the scale of the application's distribution with the customer, you can determine the best method to distribute the solution.

Another important reason to identify the breadth of application distribution is to help set the vision for the application. If the customer wants a world-class solution, it will take longer to design and develop, and may need to compete with other solutions currently on the market. If the solution were a word processor, you would need to look at existing solutions with which yours will compete. On the other hand, if the solution was to be exclusively used by the business, it may not need to be of the caliber of large and expensive solutions already on the market. They may want something smaller, more geared to the organization's individual needs, which would take less time to develop and have no competition.

Method of Distribution

There are a number of methods of distribution that you can use to get your solution to the customer:

- Floppy disks
- CD-ROM
- Network or Internet distribution

Each of these has its own unique benefits and drawbacks. In many cases, you'll want to consider multiple distribution methods so that everyone who needs the product can actually obtain and install a copy of it.

Distributing solutions on floppy disk is the oldest method of getting applications to an end user. Although CD-ROMs have replaced the popularity of this method, it is still valuable, and should be considered as a secondary method of distribution. Most new computers come with CD-ROM drives already installed, and many older computers have been upgraded with CD-ROM drives. Despite this, there are still quite a few computers out there that have used up their connectors with hard disks, and don't have any more room for a CD-ROM drive. In addition, you may experience companies that can't afford to install one on every single computer in the organization. Because they have networks, the cost of doing so may be considered unjustified.

A drawback to using floppy disks is that the size of most applications today require a significant number of floppies to install a program. Users may spend considerable time swapping one disk for another in the process of installing the application. However, if a computer isn't connected to a network or the Internet and doesn't have a CD-ROM drive, installing from a floppy disk is the user's only option.

As mentioned, CD-ROMs are the most popular method today of application distribution. Although CD Burners, also known as Writeable CD-ROMs, have dropped in price, they're still around the price of a large hard disk. For smaller software development companies and independent developers, this can be hard on the pocketbook. However, the benefits drastically outweigh the initial cost of distributing solutions in this manner. Most users have come to expect programs to be available on CD, and enjoy the speed this method provides for installing solutions.

Distributing a solution through a company's LAN is an easy way of getting your solution to the user. A folder (i.e., directory, for DOS and UNIX users out there) is given the proper permissions to allow access to those installing the solution. They can then double-click on the setup program, and begin installing the solution over the network. The problem with this method is that if the solution is rather large, it can use up a significant amount of bandwidth and slow down the network. If this is the case, you may want to consider limiting the hours of availability to this folder. If not, you could also set up such distribution servers on different segments of the network. This would allow users to install the solution from a server that's in their department, or close to their location.

The popularity of the Internet has made it a good medium for distributing applications. Users with an Internet connection and the proper permissions, if required, can access the installation files for your solution. If only authorized users were to have access to these files, you could set up security on the web site to control access. This would be done through the web server and its operating system, such as Internet Information Server on Windows NT.

Maintenance Expectations

It's important to understand what the customer expects in terms of maintenance. This will aid in determining what will need to be put into place to support the solution, and any future versions that may be created. Because the business and customer should be included in the design process, it is important to understand their views on how ease of maintenance should be implemented through the project.

Maintenance Staff Considerations

The maintenance staff is the group of people who will support and maintain the solution once it's been implemented. This doesn't mean that they have anything to do with maintaining source code—that's in the realm of the Development team. Maintenance is responsible for maintaining regular backups of data, and may be responsible for such things as the maintenance of user accounts. However, user accounts are often controlled by network administrators, application administrators, or users who are given special permissions to help control accounts. In many cases, this is the same for backups, where a user is given special permissions so that they can back up data to an external device.

For particularly large organizations, where a considerable amount of data needs to be backed up and restored, a special staff of people may be responsible for these activities. In other organizations, maintenance may fall to a support staff that acts as help desk, computer repair, and other roles. Still other organizations contract outside workers, who come in when needed or only part-time to deal with maintenance tasks. Because of this diversity of who may maintain the product, it's important to determine where you'll need to pass on information about your product.

Location of Maintenance Staff

The location of the maintenance staff will have an effect on the design of the application. While location may not be an issue if they're located at the other end of a building or campus, it may be a serious issue if they're located at another office of the organization, perhaps even in another city or country. For example, if the maintenance staff were located in another country, and the offices were connected with a WAN line, you would want to consider replicating the data to the location of the maintenance staff. The staff could then perform backups on their end. If you didn't want to set up data replication, you would have this staff perform backups across the WAN line, during times when activity is low. This would keep the WAN from being bogged down during backups.

Knowledge Level of Maintenance Staff

It is important to determine the knowledge level of the maintenance staff so that they can properly maintain your solution. If they are unfamiliar with backup devices that will be used, or other elements applying to the maintenance of your solution, then training will need to be developed to upgrade their knowledge in these areas.

Impact of Third-Party Maintenance Agreements

Third-party maintenance agreements are contracts with companies outside the organization. This may be a person who comes in part-time to maintain the system, or a company that backs up data remotely. Regardless, it's important to determine if third parties are involved, so they can be informed about how to maintain the system.

CERTIFICATION OBJECTIVE 8.04

Analyzing Extensibility Requirements

Extensibility is the ability of an application to go beyond its original design. By incorporating extensibility into the design of your application, the solution is able to extend its capabilities, and provide additional functionality. A good example of extensibility is Visual Basic 6.0. Visual Basic 6.0 has an Add-in Manager, which allows you to add components called add-ins that extend the capability of the development environment.

In discussing the requirements of the application with the customer, you should try to determine whether extensibility is an issue, and if so, what areas of the application may need extended features. This allows your solution's functionality to grow with the needs of the customer, without necessarily needing to create a new version of the product.

Handling Functionality Growth Requirements

By incorporating extensibility into your design, you are able to benefit from other third-party programmers developing added features to your application. In addition, you are able to allow an added method of upgrading your application. Rather than having to create a complete upgrade with new features for a product, the features can be added through something like an Add-in Manager that's available as a menu item.

CERTIFICATION OBJECTIVE 8.05

Analyzing Availability Requirements

In determining the requirements of a business, it is important to determine the availability required from the solution. *Availability* is the ability of users to access and use the solution. The importance of this is simple: if the business can't use the functionality of the solution, then they can't benefit from it. For mission-critical solutions, where the business depends on the solution to be up and running for the company to do business, it is absolutely vital that your solution work. This means that despite any failures, the solution should be available.

Be sure to familiarize yourself with the following list of availability requirements, which are explained in the sections that follow.

Availability Requirements

- **Hours of operation**   When your solution will be used
- **Level of availability**   User access control
- **Geographic scope**   Location of servers and users
- **Impact of downtime**   Importance of data availability

Hours of Operation

Different companies have different hours of operation, which will determine when your solution will be used. If an organization isn't open after a certain time of day or during certain days of the week, the availability to data access during these times may be affected. The business may not want to have data available, to keep problems from occurring due to security breaches, or for other reasons. Sociological and religious beliefs may also come into play with this, if the customer has a conviction that employees aren't to work on specific days or holidays.

The hours of operation for external organizations will also have an effect on the availability of data. For example, if your solution accessed stock market data, the data available to be accessed would be dependent on when the stock exchanges were open. Due to different time zones, the Toronto Stock Exchange or New York Stock Exchange would close at different times than those in Tokyo, London, or other countries.

Determining the hours of operation can affect other areas of the project. This information can be applied to when the solution's data can or should be backed up. It also determines the times when your solution needs to function without problems, as well as the applications your solution interacts with.

Level of Availability

In addition to the when of availability, you should determine how your solution and its data should be available. At the beginning of this chapter, we discussed how different security roles can be applied to control access to data. This was used to control which users would be able to access the data and how. This applied to access at any given time. However, it's also important to determine if this access should be restricted or controlled differently during different times.

The level of availability may need to be different during specific hours or days of the week. For example, a real estate board may have you design an online solution where real estate agents can enter information on new listings they have for sale, or have sold. Because the board's offices are open only from 9-5, Monday to Friday, and the data must be approved before being posted, your solution may allow information on houses to be viewed at any time, but adding and modifying data would be restricted outside of those hours. This means that the level of availability would need to be controlled through your solution. Different features and functionality in your solution would be limited during certain periods. While some features work, others would not.

Like information on hours of operation, this information could be applied to other areas of your project. You could determine that when data is being backed up nightly, or other system events are run, users would have limited or no ability to access data. The level of availability could also affect how users would interact with other solutions. If a certain SQL Server is turned off at specific times, you could have your solution access data on a different database server. By determining the level of availability, you determine how your solution is used at specified times.

Geographic Scope

The geographic scope of the network will have an effect on how you design and develop your solution. Do users access servers in the same room that they're in, or are servers located on other floors of the building, or across a campus? If the network is larger than that, are servers on the other end of the city or country, or in different cities or countries? If it is a small network, geographic scope won't be as problematic, because users need to communicate only over a small distance. This means the computers will probably be able to use current protocols, and performance won't be affected (or affected much) by your solution being added to the current system. However, if computers are spread out over a large network, new protocols may need to be used to communicate with other systems, and traffic may increase due to users having to access data across large areas. The geographic scope can affect how your solution is designed, and the technologies that will be used in it.

Networks are not always limited to a number of computers in a single room or building. The Internet is a good example of that. As a global network, it also has the distinction of being the largest network on the planet. Even if your solution doesn't use the Internet, computers on your network may still be spread across multiple floors of a building, a campus, the city, or different countries. As such, the geographic scope could have an effect on how data is accessed, and from where.

If you are dealing with a large network, you should consider having data available on multiple servers. Changes to the database could then be replicated. With allowances for the time between data replication, this would allow each server to have the same data available. This decreases the workload of the one server. If users are given access to the server closest to them, it can decrease the amount of traffic on the network, because users won't have to go through a large section of the network to reach data. For example, let's say you had two offices in different cities connected by a WAN line. If your database resided on a single server, users would have to tie up the slow WAN line to access data. By having the same data available on a server at each office, and replication taking place over the WAN, users would need to connect only to the server at their location. Having users access data from the server that's closest to them results in substantially improved performance.

Impact of Downtime

Different organizations will experience downtime differently, depending on the importance of the solution that becomes unavailable. For example, a solution that's used for 911 calls would be extremely detrimental, while a personal information management solution—used to keep track of the boss's social calendar—may be seen as more of an inconvenience. Generally, when a solution doesn't function—for example, due to the system crashing or a lack of fault tolerance—it will affect the business in some way. If a video store's rental program goes down, they can't rent videos and they can't make money. The same goes for any other program used for sales or customer service. Therefore, it's important to determine what impact downtime will have on an organization.

Analyzing Human Requirements

With any solution you design, you should never forget the people who will actually use your application. You're not analyzing the requirements and designing a solution for the models, lines of code, bits, and bytes that make up the application. You're doing this for the human beings who will buy and use the solution. Because of this, any well-designed application begins with analyzing the factors that will affect these users.

Target Audience

Before you begin designing and developing your solution, it's important to understand for whom you're creating the solution. Who will be the users of your solution? This will be your *target audience*, and by understanding them, you'll be better able to create a good solution for them.

In defining your target audience, you should discuss with the customer which department, unit, or other entity the solution will serve. Will sales, accounting, marketing, or some other group of end users use the solution predominantly or exclusively? By determining who the end user will actually be, you can then obtain information from them, and discover what unique needs they expect to have addressed by your solution.

Localization

If your application will be used in different areas of the world or areas where different languages are used, your design will need to implement localization. *Localization* refers to adapting applications to international markets. This involves changing the user interface and other features so that people of other nationalities can use them. When localization is used, the design implements different character sets, language files, and so on. Features can be included in the application to allow users to change from one language or character set to another on the fly, allowing the same solution to be used, but different files to be accessed.

Accessibility

Accessibility refers to the ability for everyone, despite any disabilities they may have, to be able to use your solution. You should determine through the customer whether any users have disabilities that will require accessibility features. If not, you may decide not to implement accessibility features in your solution. If there are users with disabilities in the organization who will use the solution, or if you're creating a mass-market solution that will be sold off the shelf, you should consider incorporating such features into your design.

To provide accessibility for such users, you will need to implement features that allow users with certain disabilities to access your application. This may include using the following:

- Keyboard layouts for people with one hand or who use a wand
- Services for people who are deaf or hard of hearing
- Features that provide audio instructions or other features for the blind or visually impaired
- Services for people who have motion disabilities

The accessibility features that you implement will allow these users to effectively use the solution.

Roaming Users

Roaming users are users who access your solution from more than one workstation, and thereby require having their preferences available from more than one computer. Such users may need to move from one workstation to another in the organization, or may connect to your solution remotely through a computer they don't normally use. By discussing whether roaming users will be an issue for the program, you can implement profiles or features that address such user needs.

Help Considerations

Help should always be available to users, so they can find an answer to any problems or difficulties they experience with a solution. This includes online user assistance, such as help files, context-sensitive help, web pages with answers to frequently asked questions or problems, and other methods of assistance. Product documentation and user manuals should be available through the solution, or as printed material. In addition, you may also want to consider implementing a help desk or support staff, who can assist users in person, over the phone, or over the network or Internet.

Training Requirements

You should determine what training users would need to use the solution. Depending on the solution and the previous experience and education of the users, training needs may range from minor to intensive. You need to discover through the business or customer whether users have experience with previous versions of the product, similar solutions, or have little or no experience with solutions of this type (or perhaps with computers in general). Determining the level of training required will impact the training methods you implement in later stages of the project.

Training can be in a classroom setting. This may be in the form of a short seminar for upgraded solutions, or intensive training sessions that may take significantly longer. Online training can also be used, allowing users to access training through their computer. A web site can be set up with web pages that take the user through the features of the application, and how to use them. Streaming video or video files that users can download and play through a viewer can also be used. This allows users to see an instructor or some other presentation over the Internet or network, or by loading a video file that can be played on the computer.

Physical Environment Constraints

In discussing requirements for the solution, you should discern whether there are any physical environment issues that may affect the project. The physical environment is an actual facility or location, and can include where your solution will be used, the training area, and the facility where development will take place. As we'll see, when it comes to physical environments, there are a number of elements that may affect your project.

The physical environment will affect technologies used in your design, and how it will be implemented. For example, if you were designing a solution for an organization with buildings on either side of a major street, you wouldn't be able to rely on a network cable being run from one office to another. If underground cabling wasn't an option, you may have to add features to your solution that include such technologies as infrared devices, the Internet, or other technologies that would enable data to be transmitted from one area to another. If a larger expanse separated two areas, features that worked with microwave transmitters, the Internet, or other technologies might be used. As you can see, such networking issues would affect what you might include in the solution or service.

Another issue is whether the physical environment can support the people who will create, be trained on, and use your solution. It's important that your project team have facilities they can properly work in, with the room and resources they need to complete the project. Imagine a room that can't hold the number of people in your team, or Development finding there are no computers. Training facilities should also have enough computers to support users who will be in training sessions, and enough room so they can work. You should attempt to have wheelchair-accessible facilities, so that anyone who's physically disabled can reach the room where training is being held. While this is an issue of special-needs considerations, it crosses over into the realm of physical environment.

Special-Needs Considerations

As mentioned earlier, certain users with disabilities should be considered when addressing human factor requirements. This not only applies for accessibility in the solution, but to help and training considerations. In addition to providing printed material for user documentation, you may want to provide audio- or videotapes that detail the same information. This should also be discussed for any training sessions that will be used for teaching users how to use the solution. Audiotapes are useful for the blind and visually impaired, while sign language can be used in videotapes used for deaf and hearing-impaired individuals. In addition, you should also consider providing wheelchair-accessible facilities for people who are physically disabled. This will allow them to reach the training, and get the assistance they need to learn about your solution.

While these issues may seem like common sense, many training sessions have been in facilities that were inaccessible to people who are physically disabled. Visually intensive presentations have also backfired when dealing with an audience of blind and visually impaired people, while trainers have also experienced the foolish feeling of addressing a room filled with deaf people, without benefit of an interpreter to use sign language. Always discuss what considerations need to be made for such users, so they can have a good experience with your solution.

Analyzing Requirements for Integrating a Solution with Existing Applications

No application you create will be the only one existing on a system. At the very least, it will work with an operating system. It's not uncommon for your solution to work with other solutions on a user's computer or the network. Rather than reproducing the functionality of another solution that's already in use, it's much simpler and more efficient to simply have your solution work with the other programs already in place. To make your solution play well with others, though, you need to identify what programs your solution will interact with, and how those solutions will affect your design.

Be sure to go over each item in the following list when analyzing integration of your solution with existing applications. Each of the listed items is explained in the sections that follow.

Requirements for Integrating Existing Applications

- Legacy applications
- Format and location of existing data

■ Connectivity to existing applications

■ Data conversion

■ Data enhancement

Legacy Applications

Companies put a lot of money into application development, and purchasing off-the-shelf solutions. Therefore, they're often a little hesitant about putting these applications out to pasture. For example, after considerable cost in buying mainframe computers and creating programs for these beasts, they may not want to trash an entire system to be up to date. In addition, workstations may use older operating systems (such as Windows 3.1 or 3.11), because the company either can't afford to upgrade everyone at once, or decided that users of these systems don't need the upgrade just yet. Regardless of the reasoning, you need to determine which legacy applications and operating systems your solution will interact with, so that you can incorporate support for these legacy solutions and systems into your design.

Format and Location of Existing Data

Where data currently resides, and the format it resides in, should be identified so you can determine what technologies will be used in your design. If you're creating a new solution for new data, this doesn't become an issue. However, organizations that have been around awhile may require your solution to access data from older data stores or operating systems. Operating systems your solution may need to deal with include NT Server, AS/400, OS/390, Multiple Virtual Storage (MVS/ESA), Virtual Storage Extended (VSE), and Virtual Machine (VM). Data may be stored on mainframes, which use storage technologies like DB2, VSAM, or IMS. If SQL Server is used, then the data may be distributed. As you can see, there are many different storage systems your solution may need to work with. It's important to determine which of these may affect the design of your solution, so the design can incorporate technologies to access and work with these storage systems.

Connectivity to Existing Applications

It is important to determine early in the project if your solution will need to interact with existing applications, and how they'll need to connect to these applications. If this is the case, and methods of connectivity need to be determined, an analysis of how you connect to the application needs to be made. Certain drivers may need to be implemented or designed; where the other application resides should be established; protocols used by the other solution will need to be identified; and technologies used to connect to the application need to be determined. These things should be done early in the project, so that the necessary work can be incorporated into the design before coding begins.

Data Conversion

You should discuss with the business and customer whether data will need to be converted from the current format into a newer format. For example, if data is currently stored on the mainframe, they may want that data converted into another format for use on a different system, such as SQL Server. This should be determined early, so you can plan for the conversion in your project.

In addition, data may need to be converted into a different format for display. This is relevant for web-based applications, where the data may need to be converted into HTML for display on the Internet. In determining whether conversion of this type is necessary, you may also be discovering the type of application or output required from your solution.

Data Enhancement

It is important to determine whether there are any data-enhancement requirements that will need to be implemented as part of your design. This involves looking at the data being used, and the type of database that your solution will interact with, and determining if changes need to be made. For example, not all data types are supported by every development platform. If data being stored is of a type not supported by Visual Basic, Visual C++, or whatever programming language you're developing in, you will need to convert the data. If data is being stored in a database that doesn't support certain functionality, you will need to convert or migrate the data into one that will support it.

In addition, you should discuss any changes to the current database. This includes removing data that's no longer required, or adding new data tables, columns, and so forth to the database. The data format will influence the design of your visual interface, and determine what data will be accessed by the application.

An issue that's come out in recent years deals with the Y2K (Year 2000) problem. In previous years, programmers used two digits to represent the year. For example, 1998 would be 98 and 1999 would be 99; but the problem is that when the year 2000 hits, computers will read this data as 00—and the computer will consider this two-digit number as the year 1900. You will need to consider the Y2K problem in designing your solution.

CERTIFICATION OBJECTIVE 8.08

Analyzing Existing Business Methodologies and Limitations

An important part of creating a good solution, and having a project succeed, is taking into account the methodologies and limitations of the organization. This includes such things as how the organization conducts business, legal issues that will affect the solution, and the structure of the organization. These issues are addressed and applied to the design of the solution, and require analysis before the product can be developed and used.

Be sure to go over each item in the following list when analyzing methodologies and limitations of the organization. The listed items are explained in the sections that follow.

Methodologies and Limitations

■ Legal issues
■ Current business practices

- Organization structure
- Budget
- Implementation and training methodologies
- Quality control requirements
- Customers' needs

Legal Issues

Everybody hates the law, unless it works in their favor. Unfortunately, to get the law to work in your favor, you need to identify the legal issues that will apply to your situation. For solution design, this means looking at each of the legal issues that will affect the business and your solution. In doing so, you can create solutions that adhere to legal requirements, and thereby avoid problems that may occur from inadvertently breaking the law.

There are many legal issues that can affect a solution. For example, copyright and trademarks violations can result in a lawsuit, or cause significant problems for a business. Once a business has a copyright put on their logo, or has it become a trademark of the company, you shouldn't modify it in any way when applying a graphic of it to your solution. If you use a name or image that another company has a copyright or trademark on, the business probably will be sued.

Taxes are a common legal issue that need to be identified for sales software, and other solutions that require adding taxes to specific figures. Tax rates differ from province to province, state to state, or country to country. While one area may have a seven-percent sales tax, another may have a five-percent or eight-percent tax rate. In addition, there may be hidden taxes or special taxes that need to be applied to figures. An example of this is a food or bar tax applied to customer bills in a restaurant sales application. By failing to apply the correct tax, or not applying it at all, you can cause severe legal and financial problems for the business.

Regardless of the solution, it's vital to understand the legal issues that can affect your solution. There may be tax rates that need to be applied to the solution, or other legal issues that control what images, text, and so forth can be included in your solution.

Current Business Practices

Business practices and policies will determine the functionality of your solution. The policies and practices show how the organization conducts its business, and these policies and practices will be applied to the design of the solution. Remember that the design and development of a solution are driven by the needs of the business, and affected by the practices and policies within the business.

Organization Structure

Understanding the structure of the organization will help in the design of your project in a number of ways. First, it will help to understand how work flows through the organization, and how the work performed with your solution will be passed up the corporate ladder. For example, if you were creating a solution for processing payroll, the application may need to have data passed through several departments in the organization, before a paycheck can be cut. First, a manager may need to approve the number of hours worked by an employee. This may then be sent to an accounting officer at corporate headquarters, who approves the schedule and passes it to payroll. The check is cut and needs to be sent to the employee. This data on payouts will then be sent to accounts payable, who adjust the books to show this has been paid. As you can see, by understanding the corporate structure, you will understand how work flows through the organization.

Another important reason for understanding the structure of an organization is to know the hierarchy that your project team will deal with. Who do you go to for information on a particular department or division or the corporation? If the project team has a problem, what is the pecking order of who to go to for information and discussing problems on specific areas? Since you don't want to go over someone's head, and have that person as your enemy, it's wise to understand how the organization is set up, so you can deal with it effectively.

Budget

Budget determines the finances that can be allotted to your project, and is something that needs to be determined early. The budget will always be a limitation of your project, as no one is lucky enough to have an unlimited supply of wealth to pay for the resources necessary to create the product. This can determine the computers, tools, facilities, and other issues that will make up the project. It also affects the number of people you can have on your project team.

Since project members want to be paid for their labor, and there is a limited amount of money to pay these members, the budget will affect how many people will work on the project and for how long. Large projects with big budgets will have larger teams, which can consist of team leaders and multiple members in each role of the team model. Smaller projects with limited budgets may have a single person in each role of the team model, while even more limited budgets may require members to take on more responsibility and serve in more than one role. As you can see, by determining the budget of a project, you are subsequently determining how your team will be structured and the resources available.

With budgets, it's important to allot a percentage of funds for overtime, and to prepare for the possibility of the project going over schedule. If you planned that your project would take two months to complete, and it goes two weeks over schedule, this means that two weeks of paychecks and other bills will need to be paid. By not including a buffer for unanticipated events, you will go over budget, or possibly deplete the budget before the project is finished.

Implementation and Training Methodologies

Different organizations may have different methodologies that they use for training users and implementing new products. It's important to determine what requirements the customer may have in this regard, so that the affected roles of the team model can incorporate these into their respective plans. For example, User Education will want to acknowledge any special training methods that need to be used when creating their training plans. This is something we will discuss in greater detail in the chapters that follow. This information should be derived from the customer early in the project.

Quality Control Requirements

Quality control determines the number of defects your product will have and have removed by release, thereby affecting the quality of the product. In other words, the more errors and bugs your software has when it's released, the lower the quality of your product. There are two main ways of ensuring a high-quality product: good design and proper testing.

Many of the problems that occur in software could have been avoided in the Design phase of the project. By having open discussions on the requirements of the solution, you can avoid implementing features and functionality that aren't required in a solution, and put in what the customer feels is higher priority. Good design requires using good models, such as those we've discussed in the previous chapters, and following the methods we've discussed throughout this book. By using proven models and methodologies, you will improve the quality of your product.

Testing is responsible for finding defects in the product, which have occurred after Development has finished coding the software. When they find bugs and errors in the program, it needs to go back to the developers, who fix the problem. Testing then checks the newly coded software for any additional problems. This is because when code is modified, new bugs and errors may result. When Testing is complete, the level of quality control has been met, and the product can now be passed forward to the next stage of the project.

There is a direct correlation between quality control and the schedule of a project. It's been found that projects with the lowest number of defects have also had the shortest schedules. When a product is properly designed, the project will run smoother, and fewer defects will occur. When Testing finds defects, the code must go back to Development to be fixed. Additional testing time must be added to the schedule to ensure no further problems have resulted from the modified code. If a project has too tight a schedule, and needs to rush testing or allots too short a testing period, the number of defects in a product will be higher. This is because testing won't have enough time to properly test the product, and errors and bugs will slip through.

Customers' Needs

The needs of the customer are what drive the solution's design and development. Because of this, it's vital that you have a clear understanding of what those needs are, so you can design an application to address them. If you don't understand what the customer needs, the project will fail.

It's important to remember that the customer may not be the person who is actually using the program. That is the end user, and not necessarily the customer. The customer buys the product, and generally represents the interests of the organization. By understanding the customer's needs, you generally identify the needs of the business itself.

CERTIFICATION OBJECTIVE 8.09

Analyzing Scalability Requirements

Scalability accounts for the expansion of elements that affect your solution. It deals with such issues as the growth of user numbers, data, the organization, and cycle of use. As time passes, businesses may get bigger, more employees may be hired, and the amount of data stored and retrieved by your solution will proportionately increase. Because of this, it's important to identify and analyze scalability requirements so that your solution is able to handle such growth.

If a solution fails to account for scalability, it can quickly become ineffective and outdated. If a company planned to merge with another business, and the number of people using the application and its data doubled, you would need to know this before designing the solution. While the customer generally won't reveal information as sensitive as this, they will often tell you that there are plans for an additional number of users to be using the product after so many months or years. By taking such information into account, and scaling your solution to meet these requirements, your solution won't become useless once such growth occurs.

As the number of users, the amount of data being stored and retrieved, and the size of the organization increase, it can affect the usability and performance of the solution. If your solution can't effectively handle the growth, then a new version of the solution must be designed and developed. To keep a solution from requiring such upgrading before its time, scalability factors should be incorporated into the design.

Familiarize yourself with the items in the following list when analyzing scalability requirements. The listed items are explained in the sections that follow.

Scalability Requirements

- Growth of your audience
- Organization
- Data
- Cycle of use

Growth of Your Audience

Mergers, upsizing, expansion, and hiring less expensive employees after retiring high-paid ones are common topics in the news. From a solution design standpoint, this means an increase in the number of people who will use the solution. As the growth of audience increases, additional stress is placed on the system and network solutions used by this audience. By identifying such growth factors early, you can incorporate them into your design. Rather than designing a solution for the current number of users, you can plan to develop a solution that will support the number of users expected to use the application in the future.

Organization

Organizations grow just like people. While an organization may reside on a single campus today, it may have offices across the country or the world a year or more from now. Such growth can affect the performance and usability of a solution. Networks are spread out, WAN lines may be used, and technologies not currently in use today will be required later. It's important to identify the estimated expansion of the organization early in design, so these growth factors can be incorporated into the solution's design.

Data

As more users access a database, the amount of data being stored and retrieved increases proportionally. By determining the number of users expected in the future, and multiplying the current amount of data being accessed by that amount, you can determine the growth in data access.

However, new users aren't the only way that data storage may increase. For example, if the company experiences an increase in sales, more customers and orders will be added to a sales database. Here, the estimated growth of data is a reflection of increased sales. Similarly, if new types of data are stored to the database, this will also affect data growth. If pictures of employees were scanned and added to an employee database, this new infusion of data would mean that more data will be stored and accessed. Because of how data can grow over time—due to new types of data being used and increases in data access—you need to incorporate these growth factors into your design. By not doing so, performance and usability will suffer.

Cycle of Use

Early in a project, it is important to determine the cycle of use for your software. The *cycle of use* is the time that your solution will be in use, before new versions of the software will need to be released. This may be the result of the software being time-sensitive, so after a specific date, a new version is required. This is something that happens yearly with personal income tax software that's on the market. This not only affects when development of the new version must take place, but also when the current version must be released to the market. Another common occurrence is the need for new features to be implemented to support new needs. New releases may also be required due to more users having an effect on performance, resulting in a new version of the software required to support the new user population. As you can see, there are numerous elements governing the cycle of use. In many cases, these requirements affecting the cycle of use will vary from project to project. It is important to identify what will have an impact on the lifetime of your solution, and when use of the product dictates newer versions to be release.

QUESTIONS AND ANSWERS

Which levels of RAID support fault tolerance?	Fault tolerance is supported by RAID Levels 1 (mirroring) and 5 (disk striping with parity).
If only a small number of users are disabled, why do I need to bother with accessibility issues for them?	Many different types of users may use your solution. Some may have disabilities, while others may not. Despite this, each user is a vital player in an organization, and your product should be usable for all of them.
What is localization?	Localization deals with the locality in which a solution will be used. If different languages, character sets, and so forth are required, localization deals with these issues so the product can be used on an international market.
Why should I make my solution scalable?	Scalability takes into account growth within the organization. By making your solution scalable, it can handle increases in users, data, and other issues that will affect the performance and usability of the solution.

CERTIFICATION SUMMARY

Security is an important part of any solution. Security not only deals with keeping unauthorized users out, but keeping data used by your solution safe and secure. In analyzing the security requirements for your solution, you should determine the level of security required, and the mechanisms currently in place. You should determine whether authorization through user accounts, audit trails, existing security mechanisms, fault tolerance, regiments of backing up data, or other methods are required in your solution. By identifying the security requirements of a solution, and designing a level of security that matches the customer's and business's needs, you will be able to create a solution that is as secure as it is useful.

Performance determines how well an application will function under work conditions. If an application runs quickly and efficiently, it has high performance. If it works sluggishly, then it has low performance abilities. Areas to consider when analyzing performance requirements are the number of transactions that will occur over given periods of time, bandwidth, capacity, response time, and barriers that will affect performance. By properly analyzing performance issues and requirements, you can design robust solutions that run well in the workplace.

Your maintenance plan deals with the upkeep of the solution and its source files. This includes such things as a regular regiment of backups and user account maintenance, but also issues that deal with the source code of the application. To effectively maintain the source code of the solution, you should implement version control, such as through Visual SourceSafe, and implement the use of comments and consistent naming conventions. Effective maintenance also requires that you determine the breadth of the solution's distribution, and the methods of distribution to be used.

Extensibility is the ability of a solution to extend its features beyond its original design. Through extensibility, a solution can add components that are created by your development team or by third-party developers. This gives your solution the ability to grow with the needs of the customer, without requiring a new version of the product.

Availability is your solution's capability to function during the times of operation. With availability, your solution should run without problem, regardless of whether an error or failure occurs. This means implementing fault tolerance and error handling into your solution.

Human factor requirements deal with the factors that will affect the human beings who use the application. This includes such things as accessibility, localization, identification of the target audience, training and help, as well as other issues that govern the user's ability to effectively use the application.

Some projects may require that your solution work with other solutions that are currently in place in the organization. This means your solution may need to interact with legacy applications, operating systems, and data formats. You'll need to determine whether data needs to be converted into different formats, and how to connect with the data and existing solutions. By identifying this through discussion with the business, you can implement these requirements into your solution.

Scalability deals with growth factors that will affect the usability and performance of a solution. It deals with increases in the number of users, data storage and retrieval, cycle of use, and growth of the organization itself. By incorporating scalability into your design, the solution is better able to handle such factors.

✓ **TWO-MINUTE DRILL**

❑ For any project you work on, you need to look at issues that will affect the project, and determine how these issues should be addressed and/or implemented in the analysis of requirements.

❑ These issues include such things as security, performance, maintenance, extensibility, availability, scalability, and requirements that deal with human factors.

❑ It's important that only authorized users are allowed to use your solution and access data, and that any data your solution uses is kept safe and secure. This can be done through any combination of user accounts, audit trails, existing security mechanisms, fault tolerance, regiments of backing up data, and other methods.

❑ A *role* is a symbolic name used to group the users of a set of software components to determine who can access those components' interfaces. In analyzing the requirements of an application, it is important to identify the roles people play in an organization, and which roles will apply to the solution you'll create.

❑ Many times, students who are taking the Microsoft exam confuse the *Guest* and *Client* roles, thinking of clients as customers, who often fall into a Guest role. It's important to distinguish between these two roles. Think of guests as visitors, and clients as workers on the client machines accessing a server. Think of the roles in this way to help keep the two separate.

❑ In designing any solution that uses security features, you need to determine what impact your solution will have on the existing security environment.

❑ *Fault tolerance* is the ability of a solution to function regardless of whether a fault occurred. In short, it is non-stop availability of a solution.

❑ Microsoft NT Server supports only Levels 0, 1, and 5 of RAID. While there are other levels of RAID—Levels 0 through 10, and Level 53—they won't appear on the exam. You should know the three levels mentioned here, especially 1 and 5, which are fault-tolerant.

❑ Areas in which you'll want to plan for maintaining the program include backing up data, and how user accounts will be maintained.

❑ Planning for effective maintenance means looking at what the application or service will require in terms of future use.

❑ The *security context* of a solution is made up of its security attributes or rules. This determines how a user is able to access, and what the user is able to do once access is achieved.

❑ *Auditing* is where activities performed by certain or all users are documented to a file, allowing a user (such as the administrator) to see what these users have done.

❑ It's important to determine what existing mechanisms for security policies are already in place in an organization, before deciding on new ones that could conflict with or duplicate them.

❑ *Performance* determines how well an application works under daily conditions. This means that despite increases in the number of users accessing data, the volume of transactions over a given period, or other issues, the application performs as is required in a speedy and efficient manner.

❑ A *transaction* is one or more separate actions that are grouped together, and executed as a single action.

❑ *Bandwidth* is the network's capacity to carry information, and is measured in data transferred per unit of time, usually seconds.

❑ *Capacity* is the volume or limit something can handle, and can have a direct effect on the performance of your solution.

❑ You should determine what standards currently exist in an organization when determining the performance requirements of your solution.

❑ It is vital that you determine both peak and average requirements for your solution. *Peak values* show the highest amount of activity your solution experiences at a given time.

❑ *Response time* is the difference in time between the end of a query or command and when the results of that query or command first begin to appear on the screen.

❑ There are a number of methods of distribution that you can use to get your solution to the customer, including floppy disk, CD-ROM, and network or Internet distribution

❑ It's important to understand what the customer expects in terms of maintenance. This will aid in determining what will need to be put into place to support the solution, and any future versions that may be created.

❑ The *maintenance staff* is the group of people who will support and maintain the solution once it's been implemented. This doesn't mean that they have anything to do with maintaining source code—that's in the realm of the Development team.

❑ *Extensibility* is the ability of an application to go beyond its original design. By incorporating extensibility into the design of your application, the solution is able to extend its capabilities, and provide additional functionality.

❑ *Availability* is the ability of users to access and use the solution. The importance of this is simple: if the business can't use the functionality of the solution, then they can't benefit from it.

❑ You're not analyzing the requirements and designing a solution for the models, lines of code, bits, and bytes that make up the application. You're doing this for the human beings who will buy and use the solution.

❑ To make your solution play well with others, you need to identify what programs your solution will interact with, and how those solutions will affect your design

❑ An important part of creating a good solution, and having a project succeed, is taking into account the methodologies and limitations of the organization.

❑ *Scalability* accounts for the expansion of elements that affect your solution. It deals with such issues as the growth of user numbers, data, the organization, and cycle of use.

Answers to Exercise 8-1

Administrators	Clients	Guests	Backup
Darren	20 employees	Customer	Julie

Answers to Exercise 8-2

1. There will be a peak requirement of 300 users accessing the application.

2. Half of the total users will spend time using the solution. This means an average of 150 users per hour.

3. Since the solution will be accessed between 9 A.M. and 5 P.M., and replication will take place between the two offices every 15 minutes, backups should be done when the business is closed.

SELF TEST

The Self Test questions will help you measure your understanding of the material presented in this chapter. Read all the choices carefully, as there may be more than one correct answer. Select all correct answers for each question.

1. You are analyzing security requirements of the business, and want to establish the fault tolerance, based on what's available in the existing environment. You find that the organization's network uses NT servers. Which of the following levels of RAID will work with this type of network and provide fault tolerance? (Choose all that apply.)

   A. RAID 0

   B. RAID 1

   C. RAID 3

   D. RAID 5

2. Which of the following is the security context of an application?

   A. The security attributes or rules that determine access to the solution and data

   B. The effect that security features in an application have on the existing security environment

   C. The data and solution that are accessed

   D. The security attributes that determine the security environment, and keep the existing security environment from being modified in any way

3. You are planning for effective maintenance, and have decided to have data backed up at regular intervals to an external device. What method of data backup is this?

   A. Replication

   B. Mirroring

   C. Dumping

   D. Peeping

4. You want to combine your maintenance plan with fault tolerance. Which of the following methods will provide this? (Choose all that apply.)

   A. Replication

   B. Mirroring

   C. Dumping

   D. Striping with parity

5. After designing and developing an application that supports an average of 100 simultaneous users, the organization's users are now complaining that performance is bad at certain times of the day. When users log on to the solution in the morning and after lunch, or log off for lunch and at the day's end, the solution is incredibly slow. What is the most likely the reason for this?

   A. During design, the peak requirements for the solution weren't acquired and applied to the design.

B. During development, the peak requirements for the solution weren't acquired and applied to the code.

C. The design of the solution took peak requirements into account, but not average acquirements.

D. The bandwidth is too high to deal with this number of users.

6. There is a longer wait than desired in the time it takes for the database in your application to respond to requests. What is this called?

   A. Response time

   B. Legacy

   C. Lactation

   D. Latency

7. You have been hired to design a solution for a branch of the Canadian government, which is officially bilingual in English and French. All branches of this government require your application to support both languages. What must you implement into your design to accommodate this requirement?

   A. Latency

   B. Legacy

   C. Localization

   D. Parlezation

8. You are concerned about fault tolerance, and have decided to look into utilizing RAID. Which of the following can make your system less fault-tolerant?

A. Disk striping without parity

B. Disk striping with parity

C. Mirroring

D. Disk duplexing

9. You are determining where backups of data will be stored to for a computer with a single, large hard disk. Which of the following devices could store backups, so that in the event your hard disk crashed, the backup data would remain safe? (Choose all that apply.)

   A. Tape drive

   B. CD-ROM

   C. Local hard drive

   D. Network hard drive

10. You are analyzing security requirements of the business, and want to establish the fault tolerance, based on what's available in the existing environment. You find that the NT servers on the network are set up to use disk mirroring. What will this provide in terms of fault tolerance?

   A. Data will be spread across several disks, without error-correction information. If one disks fails, then data can be restored from the other disks in the set.

   B. Data will be spread across several disks, with error correction. If one disks fails, then data can be restored from the other disks in the set.

   C. Data will be copied to another partition on a separate hard disk.

D. Data will be copied to another partition on a separate hard disk, which also has a separate hard disk controller.

11. Which of the following have a direct effect on quality control requirements? (Choose all that apply.)

A. RAID

B. Testing

C. Design

D. Error correction control

12. Which of the following has a relation to quality control?

A. Schedule

B. Logistics

C. Process replacement

D. SQL Server testing

13. Which of the following refers to the ability of an application to go beyond its original design, so that it has additional capabilities and greater functionality?

A. Availability

B. Extensibility

C. Scope

D. Scalability

14. You need to determine the peak and average requirements of data being saved and retrieved from a database. On Tuesday, users of the previous database saved and retrieved a total of 20 GB of information. On Wednesday, they accessed 50 GB of data; on Thursday they accessed 60 GB; and on Friday they stored and retrieved 100 GB. What are the peak and average requirements for data access?

A. 57.5 GB average, and 100 GB peak

B. 50 GB average, and 100 GB peak

C. 100 GB average, and 57.5 GB peak

D. 60.5 GB average, and 100 GB peak

15. You are analyzing security requirements of the business, and want to establish the fault tolerance, based on what's available in the existing environment. You find that the NT servers on the network are set up to use disk duplexing. What will this provide in terms of fault tolerance?

A. Data will be spread across several disks, without error-correction information. If one disks fails, then data can be restored from the other disks in the set.

B. Data will be spread across several disks, with error correction. If one disks fails, then data can be restored from the other disks in the set.

C. Data will be copied to another partition on a separate hard disk.

D. Data will be copied to another partition on a separate hard disk, which also has a separate hard disk controller.

16. Acme Tire and Spatula have hired you to design a solution. The customer, Mr. Acme, has admitted that he won't use the solution, but has some suggestions nonetheless. He states that most of the users of this web solution you're designing

will be customers on the Internet. Sales will input information used in the solution, while accounting will make changes to any information that needs modification, such as tax rates. Which of the following will be your target audience?

A. The customer paying for the product (Acme)

B. The customer using the solution on the Internet

C. Accounting, who inputs tax and other data

D. Sales, who inputs data used in the solution

17. Backups are best associated with which of the following aspects of a solution?

A. Scalability

B. Availability

C. Maintenance

D. Extensibility

18. Testing has found bugs in the software they've tested. They send it back to the developers to fix the problem. After modifying the code, the developers are satisfied. Where will the software go next to ensure quality control?

A. Logistics

B. It will be shipped to the customer.

C. Testing

D. Program Management

19. You need to find a method of backing up data for a system that has no external storage devices, possesses a single hard disk, and has a network connection. Which of the following methods are available to you? (Choose all that apply.)

A. Dumping to network drive

B. Replication

C. Dumping to external device

D. Mirroring

20. You are analyzing security requirements of the business and want to establish the fault tolerance, based on what's available in the existing environment. You find that the NT servers on the network are set up to use RAID Level 5. What will this provide in terms of fault tolerance?

A. Data will be spread across several disks, without error-correction information. If one disks fails, then data can be restored from the other disks in the set.

B. Data will be spread across several disks, with error correction. If one disks fails, then data can be restored from the other disks in the set.

C. Data will be copied to another partition on a separate hard disk.

D. Data will be copied to another partition on a separate hard disk, which also has a separate hard disk controller.

9

Conceptual Design

CERTIFICATION OBJECTIVES

A s we saw in Chapter 1, conceptual design is the first perspective in the Solutions Design model. It is here that you look at activities performed by the users and tasks that must be performed to solve a business problem, and then lay the groundwork for your solution to deal with these issues.

As we'll see in this chapter, there is a considerable amount of work that goes into the conceptual design process. Information is gathered on users and their roles through a variety of methods; a perspective on the business is obtained; and usage scenarios are generated. These and other tasks set the foundation for your solution design, and are passed into the logical design of the solution.

CERTIFICATION OBJECTIVE 9.01

Understanding the Purpose and Value of Conceptual Design

When you were in school, you probably had to write essays on certain topics. The first step in creating the essay was coming up with a concept for the paper, and determining what issues it would address. This meant gathering information. It would be applied to subtopics included in the essay, which determined the overall structure of the paper. In the same way that your essays started with a basic concept and were based on the information gathered for the paper, conceptual design is where you determine what users actually need to do, and forge the basic concept of what your application will become.

Conceptual design looks at the activities performed by the business, and the tasks a user needs to perform to address a certain problem. Information is gathered through this design perspective, which is then applied to the logical and physical design perspectives. This information consists of input from users, who identify their needs and what is required from the application. In other words, they explain what they want to do and how they want to do it. In this process they tell you how they envision the application. By interviewing the people who will use the application, conceptual design allows you to obtain an understanding of the problems faced by a business, and identify the standards by which users will judge the completed product.

An application created for an enterprise is called a *business solution* because it's built to solve specific business problems. In other words, your application becomes the answer to the enterprise's question: "How are we going to deal with this problem?" Therefore, the development of an application is driven by the needs of the business. Regardless of where you are in the design process, you should be able to trace the current state of design to the business's needs. If you can't, it means that your team has lost focus on the application's purpose.

FROM THE CLASSROOM

Conceptually Speaking...

The most potentially damaging phase of designing a distributed application is the conceptual phase. Design flaws that are instituted in the conceptual phase can produce multiple logical or physical instances of application design or function that either do not address a business need or ignore user requirements. Design flaws can surface in many forms in the physical phase, including poorly scaling COM components, inefficient data service components, user interfaces that are difficult to navigate, poorly designed or bloated database structures, or resource-hungry tiers in general. While this is by no means an all-encompassing list, design flaws usually begin in the conceptual phase. Therefore, spending that extra effort to produce the best possible conceptual design can yield important benefits.

One of the key targets for ensuring that an application meets requirements is the proper identification of the end users. It is usually easy to identify the class of individuals who will navigate through the user interface as users, but many times, other classes of application users are completely ignored. If the information produced by the application is destined for vendors, partners, or remote offices, users may include many other groups of individuals. Also, end users may not be actual individuals. Departments, divisions, and the business or company itself should be considered users of the application. Failure to recognize non-physical entities properly as users of an application can detrimentally affect the conceptual design process.

—Michael Lane Thomas, MCSE+I, MCSD,
MCP+SB, MSS, MCT, A+

The conceptual design process is made up of several tasks, which are used to determine and substantiate the requirements of the application:

- Identifying users and their roles
- Gathering input from users
- Validation of the design

These procedures are important, because while you want to get user input, some users may request features that aren't necessary. For example, while a user may think it important to have a web browser included in a spreadsheet program, this wouldn't be essential if there were no connections to the Internet and no plans for a corporate intranet. By working through the tasks, you can determine which are valid and invalid requirements.

As with most things in life, it's important to know whom you're dealing with when designing an application. It's for that reason that the first step in conceptual design is identifying users and their roles. Because the purpose of conceptual design is to determine the business needs that drive application development, the term *user* can refer to a single end-user, the business as a whole, various units that make up the business, or other interested parties. As we'll see later in this chapter, the reason for this is to gain the fullest possible vision of what the application should be. If only individual end users were polled for input, the product would be usable, but wouldn't necessarily reflect the goals and needs of the enterprise itself.

In identifying the different users that provide requirements and perspectives used for the design of your business solution, user profiles are created. *User profiles* are documents that describe whom you're dealing with, and provide a depiction of the people and groups who use the system. This information is used to organize how data will be gathered, and identify from whom this input is gathered. These profiles can also be created at the time you generate usage scenarios, which we'll discuss later in this chapter.

There are many different techniques for gathering input, and each has its benefits and drawbacks. These include such methods as user interviews, focus groups, and surveys. These methods address the user's viewpoints and requirements, rather than technical elements that will go into the application. Later in this chapter, we'll discuss each of these and other methods for gathering input. It is through these techniques that you gain an understanding of what users need and expect from your application.

Once information has been gathered, it is applied to usage scenarios. *Usage scenarios* depict the system requirements in the context of the user, by showing how business processes are, or should be, executed. Usage scenarios take the raw data that's been gathered, and apply it to a step-by-step documentation of what occurs first, second, third, and so on in the execution of a specific task. This transforms the requirements you've gathered into the context of how features, processes, or functions are used.

The final step in the conceptual design process is validating your design. This presents your understanding of what's required from the product to the people who have a stake in the product's design. By taking the end user and other interested parties step-by-step through the usage scenarios you've created, you're able to determine if you've correctly understood what's required of the application. You can also create prototypes of the user interface, which allow the user to provide input on whether the interface suits their needs.

Conceptual design ends with several deliverables that are injected into the logical design of the application. Once completing the conceptual design process, you will have the following deliverables in your possession:

- User profiles, which identify users, their roles and responsibilities, and who played a part in providing information.

- Usage scenarios, which depict how the needs and perceptions of the system translate to actual tasks, by showing a step-by-step picture of how business processes are executed.

Once you've reached the end of the conceptual design process, you are generally ready to apply these deliverables to the logical design. If you need to, you can return to the conceptual design process to determine needs and perceptions of other features or functionality in your program. In addition, once one feature, function, or process has been conceptually designed, you can apply this to logical design, and then begin conceptually designing another element of your application. This provides great flexibility in designing your business solution.

Applying the Conceptual Design Process to a Business Solution

Conceptual design is the foundation of what your business solution will become. This design method is a perspective of the Solutions Design model, which ties the Application, Team, and Process models together. Conceptual design provides requirements that are passed forward to logical design, and used by the Application model to separate an application into distinct services. Conceptual design takes place immediately after the Envisioning phase of the Process model, and is the first description of what a system does to solve the problems outlined in the vision/scope document. Through conceptual design you get a specific description of what you've actually been hired to build.

The Team model is used to specify team members' responsibilities in the conceptual design of the product. While every member of the team is involved in the conceptual design, Product and Program Management have the greatest responsibility. Program Management has ownership of the conceptual design, and is responsible for driving the conceptual design process. Product Management is responsible for gathering user input and validating usage scenarios, which we'll discuss later in this chapter. Despite the fact that the major responsibilities lie with these two roles, each member of the team participates in the conceptual design.

Development is where coding of the program takes place, so this role aids in the conceptual design process by evaluating issues that would affect how the business solution is coded. Development evaluates the current and future states of the system, and helps to identify risks that may arise when the conceptual design is applied to the logical and physical design perspectives. Because the policies of a business can have an effect on the functions provided in a business solution, Development also has the responsibility of analyzing business policies. If the policies aren't complete or consistent, Development needs to catch this, so the product isn't built on false assumptions of what the rules of business entail. This ensures that the features going into the application don't conflict with the goals and interests of the business itself.

Since User Education has the responsibility for ensuring that users have a good experience with the product, this role has the duty of finding usability issues that appear in the conceptual design. User Education looks at the usage scenarios generated during conceptual design, and determines training and other forms of user education that will be required from changes to the current system. This allows the product to have support generated as early as possible in the project.

Testing acts as an advocate of the end user, and determines what issues may be problematic. This role looks at the conceptual design, validates usage scenarios, and identifies testability issues and conflicts between user requirements and changes to the system. This allows Testing to determine what issues will require testing later. By validating usage scenarios, Testing is able to determine whether changes made to the system are compliant with the requirements of the user.

Logistics has the responsibility for a smooth rollout of the product. By analyzing the conceptual design, they can identify rollout and infrastructure issues resulting from changes. This allows Logistics to be prepared for problems that could be faced by support and operations groups later. By identifying these issues early, during the conceptual design, the risks of problems occurring later are minimized.

CERTIFICATION OBJECTIVE 9.03

Gathering User Requirements and Gaining User Perspective

Requirements and perspectives are acquired from more than the end user who actually uses the product. As mentioned earlier in this chapter, the term *user* in conceptual design can refer to a number of different people, including the following:

- An individual end user who interacts with the system through a user interface.

- A department or unit in the business, comprised of many end users, with policies that dictate specific needs and requirements.

- The business itself, which has its own goals, interests, and needs.

- The customer, who pays for the business solution.

- Other interested parties, such as suppliers and support staff.

It is important to gather the viewpoints and needs of each of these groups, to gain a full vision of what the application entails. If you have input only from the end user, you miss information from key people who could guide your design.

In gathering user requirements, the business and the units within it become independent entities. The organization, and its departments and units, are seen as individual users with their own needs and perspectives. This is because the business will have interests that may be different from the person who actually uses your application. For example, a clerk acting as an end user of the application will be concerned with the interface, and the features that deal directly with his or her work. An accounting department interested in saving money may have interests directly opposed to that of a purchasing department. The business as a whole will have goals and interests of which each of these departments may not be fully aware.

In looking at these different groups and individuals, there is one common factor: each has a stake in solving the business problem. However, because each may have different interests, it is possible for their ideas to conflict or differ. To get the widest degree of input, it is important to identify each type of user if you're to properly gather requirements and gain user perspective.

When identifying users and their roles in the organization, it's important to document who they are, in addition to the information they provide. It's for this reason that user profiles are created in this first stage of conceptual design. User profiles are documents that describe the person or group with whom you're dealing. This includes their opinions toward the current system, and what they'd like to see in the new application you're developing.

Just as no two projects are exactly alike, you'll find that the information you gather will differ among types of users and projects. There are, however, common forms of information you'll gather no matter what type of projects or users you encounter:

- Requirements that are perceived to be important
- Staff perception of the current system
- Work responsibilities
- Experience
- Physical and psychological factors

This information is included in the user profiles you create. They address how the user views the current and future state of the system, their level of experience and responsibilities to the organization, and factors that will affect the development of the software product. By including this information, you get a complete picture of whom you're creating the product for, and what needs will drive application development.

Gaining Business Perspective

Because organizations and the units that make up the business are viewed as individual entities, it is important to create user profiles and gather information from them as well. Each department and unit, in addition to the business as a whole, while have its own goals, needs, and interests. This is always the case, regardless of whether you're dealing with a large corporation or a small video store.

While any user profile you create will include the information we discussed earlier, additional information needs to be added to the user profiles of a business, department, or unit. This is because you're dealing with groups of people, rather than individuals. The additional information helps to identify whom you're acquiring the requirements and perspectives from, and includes such things as the following:

- Name of the business, department, or unit (such as Accounting, Purchasing, etc.)
- Number of employees
- Their responsibilities, activities, or mission
- Perception of the current state of the system
- Perception of what's required in the business solution

The perceptions and needs gathered here are stated from an organizational standpoint. Any requirements or viewpoints from an individual person's standpoint are included in a user profile of that particular person (e.g., the customer or end user's profile).

In addition to the information listed above, you should also include a listing of terms, definitions, and jargon used in the organization. This not only allows you to understand what end users are talking about when you interview them individually, but gives you an understanding of language that may be included in the application itself. To give you an example of how important this is, let's say the organization that's contracted you to create an application is the military. The military is known for its use (or perhaps overuse) of abbreviations, specialized terms, and jargon. If you didn't know, for instance, that a unit you'd be tying into your enterprise application was referred to as *JAG,* and that the term was an abbreviation for the Judge Advocate General's office, your ignorance of the local jargon could lead to problems elsewhere. It's always important to know what people are talking about when you're trying to understand their needs and viewpoints.

Techniques for Gathering User Input

Once you've identified who you're going to acquire information from, you're ready to gather that information. There are many ways of gathering the input you need from users. These techniques include the following:

- User interviews
- JAD (Joint Application Design) sessions

- Focus groups
- User surveys
- Shadowing
- Consulting with the organization's Help Desk

While each technique has its own benefits and drawbacks, you can use one or several in conjunction to get the information you need on what's expected from your business solution.

User interviews are a common method of gathering input from users. In using this technique, you select a group of users from the organization to meet with your team. Each user meets with a team member individually, to discuss their views on what is needed in the application you're creating. In this informal meeting of two people, you're able to get detailed information on what the user feels are relevant issues to your project's design.

User interviews can be a time-consuming process, and you'll find that the value of the information you acquire depends on two things: the users you selected and the skills of the interviewer. If you choose a poor selection of users, they may not be able to tell you much about problems they've encountered or what they'd like to see in the new system. It's important to pick users who have been with the organization for awhile, and have enough experience to know what they're talking about. If you do have a good selection of users, you must have a team member with good interviewing skills. Often, it's useful to conduct mock interviews between team members. This will weed out the bad interviewers and determine who has the skills to conduct real interviews with users.

on the **job**

In conducting user interviews, it's vital that you make the user feel comfortable enough to discuss their views, needs, and any problems they have with the current system. Pick a comfortable setting for the meeting. Start the interview with a few minutes of idle chat, joke with them, and let them know that anything they say is in confidence. You'll be amazed at how often people hold back information, fearing that they'll be seen as troublemakers if they say bad things about the existing system.

JAD (joint application design) sessions can also be used to acquire valuable information from users. JAD brings team members, end users, and other interested parties together to design the concept of your product. In the session, you don't involve the user in the functional design of the application, but discuss the business concerns that will affect design. Remember, you're dealing with end users and executives who may know how to run a business, but not a computer. The session consists of everyone exploring what tasks need to be performed and why.

When creating complex applications, JAD sessions will often deal with specific features or functionality to be included in the design of the application. The people invited to these sessions have direct experience or knowledge pertaining to those aspects of the project. For example, if you were creating software that verified credit card applications, you might have one session with the users from the credit card company, and another that focused on the credit bureau that verifies an applicant's credit information. This allows you to get input on product components from people who will interact with them.

JAD sessions can last several days, and you will generally get huge amounts of information from the people attending them. Because of this, it is important to schedule time after these sessions, so your team can assimilate and organize the data. While it brings everyone together to discuss the issues, it's also important to realize that not everyone feels comfortable in group settings. Sometimes people feel intimidated by JAD sessions. This is especially true when a person is sitting across from their boss, or other senior management in the company. When conducting these sessions, it's important to keep it as informal as possible and make everyone feel they're part of a team. You can also use other methods of gathering input with JAD sessions, to ensure that everyone's point of view has been shared with the team.

Like JAD sessions, focus groups can be used to gather information from collections of people. *Focus groups* take a sampling of users, and bring them together to provide input on their needs and perceptions. Unlike other methods, a trained interviewer is used to solicit information from users, which makes focus groups more expensive to implement than other methods. This technique is commonly used when there are a considerable number of users involved. If you were creating an application that was to be used by hundreds or thousands of users, it would be impossible to conduct interviews with each user, or invite each of them to JAD sessions. Focus groups solve this problem by using a select group of individuals to represent the interests of people facing similar problems..

User surveys are a method that can get input from any number of users. They are cheap and fast to implement. In creating a user survey, you generate a document that addresses what you perceive to be important issues, based on information obtained from the vision/scope document. Users then answer questions in the survey to provide you with the input you need to design your application. Because each user answers the same standard questions, you can quickly tabulate the answers, and determine what are the most common requirements and issues faced by users.

The problem with this approach is that there is no real interaction with users. Dropping a survey form on their desk, or asking the user a series of standard questions, doesn't provide the user with opportunities to address issues not covered in the survey. While user surveys are a valuable tool, you should consider using them with other, more interactive forms of gathering input.

Another technique, *shadowing*, involves following the user as he or she performs the daily tasks your application will address. The user explains the tasks while performing them, and is encouraged to provide as much detail as possible. In following the user, you can observe and listen, or ask questions about the tasks being performed. This allows you to get the information you need first-hand, while seeing how the tasks you'll address in your application are currently performed.

For this technique to work, you need to have users available who will allow you to follow them around. Allowing someone to shadow your movements can be intimidating, and many people aren't willing to have someone watching them over their shoulder. An often-overlooked resource for acquiring user input is the Help Desk of an organization. Help Desks should keep records of the problems experienced by users, and the staff of a Help Desk can often provide you with information on common issues reported on an application. If you're improving an earlier or similar version of an application, you can use the Help Desk to determine issues faced by users.

Synthesizing Business and User Perspectives

Once you've determined the needs of end users, the business entity, and its departments, you need to combine the different perspectives into a single concept. This entails sifting through the information you've gathered to determine what will be included in the design. By going through the user profiles and gathered information, you see what common issues appeared, what end-user requirements conflict with the interests of the business or its departments, and what great ideas appeared that need to be incorporated into your application's design. In doing so, you acquire a common understanding of what's really needed for your product to succeed.

When synthesizing business and other user perspectives, it's important to ensure that no conflicts go into the final conceptual design. In weeding out these conflicts, it's important that the requirements of an end user don't go against the goals or interests of the department or the business as a whole. For example, let's say you were creating a software product for a lab that analyzed blood samples. In gathering input, several end users state that entering an input number for samples twice is redundant, and lowers their productivity. While it may seem like a good idea to remove this procedure from your design, the unit may have this in place as a quality assurance measure. This reflects the goals of the entire business and should not be removed. While a particular procedure in the system may appear to lower productivity for the end user, there may be a good reason it is in place.

Generally, a good rule of thumb is the bigger the user, the more important the requirement. Because of this, you can usually follow this order of importance, from lowest to highest: end user, units, departments, and finally business. At the same time, it's important to remember that changes in company procedures often occur from the input of people within the organization. If a suggestion from a user seems like a good idea, you should always check with senior management in the company to see how it will affect the goals and interests of the business and its units.

Constructing Conceptual Designs Based on Scenarios

A *scenario* is an outline or plot of a sequence of events. As an outline, it provides a point-by-point, step-by-step analysis that depicts the procedure that occurs when something is done. As a plot, it provides a paragraph or two that tells a brief description or story. To illustrate this, think of how you'd explain making a cup of coffee. You could give a description, and say, "When I make a cup of coffee, I first I set out my kettle, coffee, milk, and sugar. I then boil the water, and put a spoonful of instant coffee in a cup. I add the hot water to the cup, and add milk, sugar, or nothing to it." You could also write it down for someone like this:

PRECONDITIONS:

- Kettle, coffee, milk, and sugar are set out.
- Coffee drinker has access to these items.

STEPS:

1. Boil the water.
2. Add instant coffee to cup.
3. Add water to cup.
4. Add choice of milk and/or sugar or nothing.

POSTCONDITIONS:

Coffee drinker has a cup of coffee to drink or serve to others.

This would give you an outline of what occurs when a cup of coffee is made. In doing so, you've created a scenario of making a cup of coffee. Despite any technical knowledge of the process behind coffee manufacturing, anyone who reads the scenario can understand how to use it.

This same type of documentation is used in constructing the conceptual design of an application. Scenarios are used to provide a clear description of the requirements for an application, by outlining and plotting the sequence of events in performing some action. Scenarios address a business problem by depicting a process, function, or feature in your application in the context of how it will be used. It's for this reason that they're called "usage scenarios."

Because usage scenarios use normal, everyday language to describe how an activity is performed, everyone participating in the conceptual design of the application can understand it. Team members and users alike can review the usage scenario, and see the requirements of the application in the context of the business. This is of particular use later. When validating the design or making tradeoffs, users are able to view the requirements in a fashion that's easy to understand. The usage scenario provides straightforward documentation that can be used later to show how logical and physical designs map to the requirements of the user. As we'll see later, you can approach the usage scenario from different perspectives. These perspectives look at the usage of a feature, function, or process in different ways—the order in which work is process, the environment it's used in, the context in which it's used, or by the order in which tasks are performed. Regardless of how you approach the usage scenario, there are two basic ways of writing the documentation. As we saw with the coffee scenario at the beginning of this section, you can use narrative text or structured text.

Structured or numbered text provides a step-by-step procedure. In using structured text, you should start by mentioning what the usage scenario is for. Is it a business activity, a function? You would then identify what preconditions need to be in place before the first step can occur. If the preconditions aren't met, then the user can't proceed to the first step. Once these have been documented, you then write down the steps to take to achieve the desired outcome. If certain steps have steps of their own, you can document them, and provide details on that particular step. This creates a usage scenario for that step in the process. At the end of the usage scenario, you write down the postconditions of what occurs once the steps have been completed successfully.

Narrative or unstructured text tells a story from the perspective of the person you're interviewing, or the business itself. This gives it a bit of a personal feel, as it's basically the testimony of how things get done, what's required in performing an action, and individual observations. It begins by identifying what the usage scenario describes. Pre- and postconditions are stated in the narrative text, as are the steps taken to get to the end result.

Regardless of whether you use a narrative or structured text for your usage scenario, you can augment your scenario by using charts, workflow diagrams, prototypes, and other graphic representations. It's not uncommon to generate a table that outlines a usage scenario, by breaking a task into columns of who, what, when, where, and how. You can also mix the narrative and structured versions of usage scenarios, so that they are a combination of both.

exam
W a t c h

Usage scenarios are used to construct a conceptual design for your application, which is one of the exam objectives. There are different methods of constructing such scenarios in the context of the business and users. While these are included below to help you construct conceptual designs, the Task Sequence model, Workflow Process model, and Physical Environment models aren't directly addressed in the exam.

The Workflow Process Model

Many enterprises have a structured system about how work is routed through the organization. Policies exist in these organizations that dictate which department does what, and in what order. This controls the workflow, defining how work is processed. This ensures that jobs are properly authorized and can be audited.

The *Workflow Process model* is used to create usage scenarios that show how specific jobs are routed through an organization. For example, consider how a schedule turns into a weekly paycheck in an organization. The manager creates a work schedule, and documents whether employees showed up for work. At the end of the pay period, this may be sent to a district supervisor, who authorizes that the work schedule is valid. This is then forwarded to the payroll department, who authorizes and prints out a check. The schedule is then archived, a listing of payments is sent to accounting, and the check is sent to the mailroom to be sent to the employee. In creating an application that automates this system, you would need to understand this workflow. If it didn't adhere to the structure of these business activities, it could jeopardize the security of the process and render your application ineffective.

In using the Workflow Process model, you need to specify pre- and postconditions. These are the conditions that need to be met for work to be routed from one area to the next, and what is achieved by a particular step being completed. For example, if an expense claim hadn't been authorized, it wouldn't proceed to the next step in the workflow process.

In addition, you should define what forms are used in each step. This will aid in the logical and physical design of your application. By understanding the necessary forms and documents used by the organization, you'll be able to identify Business objects for your design. It will also give you a better understanding of how your user interface should be designed, so that it meets the basic structure of forms currently in use.

The Task Sequence Model

In designing an application that's geared to the needs of the user, you need to understand the tasks he or she does to complete an activity. It's for this reason that the *Task Sequence model* is used to create usage scenarios. This model looks at the series of actions, or sequence of tasks, that a user performs to complete an activity.

Earlier, we saw an example of the Task Sequence model. This showed the sequence of events that take place in making a cup of coffee. For creating such a usage scenario for your design, you discuss with the person you're interviewing (or through other techniques we discussed earlier) the steps they take to perform an activity. These are then written in the order each task is performed.

As with the other models, you can create a usage scenario with the Task Sequence model using either structured or unstructured text. Regardless of which you use, you need to identify the role of the user, and write the usage scenario from their perspective. The role of the user must be identified in the usage scenario so that anyone reading it can understand who is performing the activity.

Exercise 9-1 will give you practice creating a usage scenario. (One possible answer to this exercise appears just before the Self Test at the end of the chapter.)

Creating a Usage Scenario Using the Task Sequence Model

In this exercise we'll create a usage scenario for a video store, using the Task Sequence model. It will be written in structured format. In doing this exercise, read the interview below, then follow the instructions.

When a customer brings up a video to the counter, I take the customer's name so I can add the video rental to their membership account. I then take the SKU number of the video the customer is renting, and I add it to the customer's account. This shows that the customer is renting a particular video. I ask them if they would like video insurance. This is a $0.25 fee, and protects them from having to pay for the video if their machine ruins the tape. If they don't want the insurance, I have to record it, so the company knows that we asked and it was denied. I then see if they have any promotional coupons or discount cards, which give them free movies. After that, I calculate how much the customer owes, and print out a receipt for them to sign. I tell the customer how much they owe, and ask whether they want to pay by cash or credit card. The customer takes the video, and I go on to the next customer.

1. Get a piece of paper and pen, or a word processor, to document the usage scenario.

2. Identify the usage scenario. What type of function or business activity is being performed?

3. At the top of your document, identify the preconditions. These are conditions that must be met before the first step can be taken. If the preconditions aren't met, the activity as a whole can't take place. For example, one of the preconditions in this scenario would be that a database of customers and videos already exists.

4. Identify the user by his or her role. In the case of this scenario, it is the clerk. You will write from the clerk's perspective.

5. List the sequence of tasks involved in completing this activity. Start with the first step the clerk does; then ask yourself, "What needs to happen next?"

6. After the last step, identify the postconditions. What occurs when these steps have been completed? What is generated from the successful completion of these steps?

The Physical Environment Model

Usage scenarios are also valuable for understanding the physical environment that your application will be used in. This is because your design can be just as affected by where the application will be used, as how and why it's used. For example, a database application for a computer that isn't connected to a network will have everything located on a single computer. If all of the company's data is stored on a single server, then your application will need to access that data. If the company uses an intranet, it may access data in another building, city, or country. The differences in these environments will affect the design of your application, and the technologies that you incorporate into it.

The *Physical Environment model* looks at the environment in which an application will be used. In using this model, you document how an activity relates to the physical environment of the enterprise. This enables you to determine whether data moves to specific locations. With this model, you look at whether a process or business activity moves from one department to another, to other campuses, or across WAN or Internet links to other cities or countries. You also use this model to determine whether specific servers must be used. This allows you to see if your application needs to interact with an SQL server, a Microsoft Transaction server, an Internet server, or some other specialized or specific server in the organization. By looking at how information moves through an organization, you have a clearer understanding of how your application needs to be designed and built.

Designing the Future Work State: Identifying Appropriate Types of Solutions

From the usage scenarios, you gather the information that allows you to identify Business objects, as well as the appropriate solution type for your organization. Why is this important? Object-oriented programming uses code-based abstractions of real-world objects and relationships. That's what an object is. Business objects are abstractions of the people, places, things, concepts, relationships, and other objects that are represented in our application design. In the previous exercise, we can see that the customer account, payment, and video rental are objects that relate to our design. The Business objects would be translated into tables and columns that make up our database. They are also used in determining what variables and objects we use in our code and interface, so we can access that data. As we'll see, where this data resides and how it is accessed has a great effect on solution design.

Single-Tier Solutions

Single-tier solutions are common in desktop applications, where the user may not even have access to a network. With this type of solution, everything runs on the user's machine. If the application accesses a database, that database either resides on the machine itself, or is accessed through a mapped network drive. The mapped network drive is done through the operating system and, to the application, appears as if it's a local hard drive on that machine. Regardless of whether the database is accessed in this method, everything dealing with the application runs on the user's computer.

As we can see in Figure 9-1, the user interface, Business objects, and Data Service objects are all designed as part of the application. Data Service objects are used to consolidate data access. An example of this would be a custom COM component using ADO to connect to an OLE DB data source. Data Service objects are used to access and communicate with the data source. Business components encompass business rules and data components, and encapsulate access functions and data manipulation. The data components serve as a go-between or intermediary between the business components and data tier of the model.

Because the user interface and objects are built into the application, and the application and database run on a single computer, there is no interaction or need to design anything for other computers. You have no need to design components or code that works with servers. All business and data processing takes place on the user's computer.

exam
ⓦatch

Remember that with single-tier solutions, everything is located on one machine. While a hard drive may be mapped to a user's machine to access the database, it doesn't mean that another type of solution is being used. The user interface, the Business and Data Service objects, and the processing reside on the user's machine. The database is accessed through the user's machine. No additional components, software, or hardware are necessarily required with this type of solution.

Two-Tier Solutions

While single-tier solutions are designed for desktops, two-tier solutions are commonly designed for networks where users access a central data source. With *two-tier solutions*, the database doesn't reside on the user's computer. Instead, there is a database server that handles the management of data. A client application, which resides on the user's machine, is used to interact with the server. This client-server relationship allows processing to be shared by both machines.

In two-tier solutions, less work needs to be done by the application, because the database server handles data management. A database server, such as an SQL server, takes care of storing and retrieving data for multiple

FIGURE 9-1

A single-tier solution has the user interface, along with the Business and Data Service objects, built into the application.

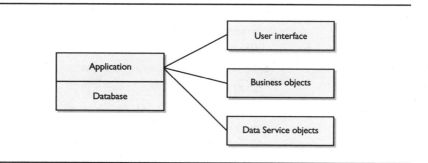

users. This relieves the application of a significant amount of data processing. The client portion of the distributed application contains the user interface, along with the Business and Data Service objects. As seen in Figure 9-2, this is unchanged from single-tier solutions. The only difference is that data resides on a different machine, which is accessed by the client through triggers, stored procedures, and/or SQL requests.

While two-tier solutions are a simple method of creating distributed applications, they can cause a considerable amount of network traffic. The network can become congested as numerous users attempt to access data from the single database. At face value, it may seem that the answer to this would be to replicate the database to different servers. This would allow traffic to be split among the different database servers. However, when doing this, users would have access to the same data. While one user

FIGURE 9-2

A two-tier solution distributes the application and the data source across a network.

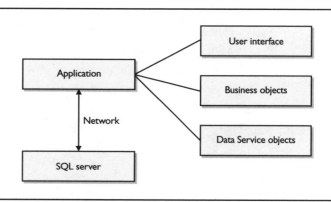

updates a record in one database, users of the other database won't see these changes. This means that, until the data is synchronized between the different servers, users will be using different data. These are some of the considerations to keep in mind when designing this type of application.

n-Tier Solutions

To create a distributed application that avoids the problem of network bottlenecks at the database server, you should consider using n-*tier solutions*. *n*-tier solutions are what developers commonly refer to when talking about three-tier solutions. As shown in Figure 9-3, this type of application splits the solution across several computers. The user interface still resides on the user's computer, and the database remains on the data server. However, the Business and/or Data Service objects are placed into a component or separate application that resides on a server, such as an application server, between the two computers. Rather than bogging down the database server with requests, the application on the user's machine makes requests to the component on the server between the two computers. If the server with this component gets bogged down, more application servers can be added to the network. Not only does this keep the database intact on one server, it also takes much of the processing requirements off the user's machine and onto a more powerful server. This makes for a much more efficient solution.

By splitting an application among multiple components, you have a great deal of flexibility as to where the Business objects and Data Service objects will be placed. While Figure 9-3 shows these as part of a component on an application server, you could also have either of them as part of the user's application. It is advisable to include Business objects, which include the business rules used by the organization, as part of a component. Should changes be made to a business rule, or Business objects need to be modified, you would merely create an updated component for the application server. Depending on the changes made to the Business objects, you wouldn't need to update the application on the machines of users.

While there is a close mapping between the physical placement of code and the number of tiers in your design, it should be stressed that your

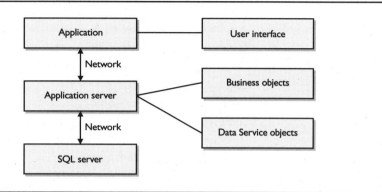

FIGURE 9-3

An *n*-tier solution distributes the activity among multiple computers.

application's tier design is a conceptual design issue, and not an issue of where on the system your code executes. The benefits of using tiers include faster development, the reuse of code, and easier debugging, which are not dependent on the physical location of your code. However, as we've seen, the physical or centralized location of code placement can be beneficial to your multi-tier application design.

CERTIFICATION OBJECTIVE 9.06

Defining the Technical Architecture of a Solution

If there were one type of computer system, one network, and one programming language that applied to everyone's needs, there wouldn't be a need for defining the technical architecture of your solution. Unfortunately, life is never that simple, and the technologies, standards, and platforms available are numerous, to say the least. Because of this, it is important to understand the current technology used by an organization, and what needs to be implemented in the future.

The relationship between technology and the design of your application is a double-edged sword. If your design requires certain technical resources to be used, then the organization will need to upgrade their computers, network, models, data architecture, and/or other systems. If the organization isn't willing to upgrade or can't because the older systems are still needed, then you need to adapt your design and use development platforms that adhere to these older technologies. Invariably, when either technology or applications require change, or can't change, the other is affected.

In defining the technology architecture for your solution design, you need to identify the necessary technical resources that need to be implemented or created to support the requirements of your application. This means determining what technologies are appropriate for your business solution, defining the data architecture for your solution, determining what are the best tools for developing the application, and deciding on what type of solution you'll be creating. In doing so, you'll need to look at the current state of technology used in an organization, and decide what the future state should be. In the sections that follow, we'll cover each of these issues individually.

exam
Watch

While the technologies covered here are those directly covered on the exam, you should try to have as much familiarity with as many as possible. The exam expects that you know at least one programming language before taking the exam, and have some experience with developing solutions.

Identifying Appropriate Technologies for Implementing Your Business Solution

There are many technologies that you can implement in your business solution: some new, and many that are older. By knowing what technologies are available, where they are used, and how they apply to your potential business solution, you can identify which will be the appropriate ones to use. Whether your application needs to access mainframes or the Internet, or utilize certain standards or technologies, it is important to know which ones will apply to your design.

EDI

EDI (Electronic Data Interchange) is a standard for transmitting business data from one computer to another. This business data can include such things as invoices and order forms. The data is sent in a format that both the sender and receiver (called *trading partners*) can understand. These trading partners make arrangements to exchange data through a point-to-point connection, which usually involves a dial-up connection. This allows the trading partner who was sending the data to transmit it to a BBS (Bulletin Board System) or directly to the receiving partner's computer.

Though it predates the Internet, EDI is still used as a method of electronic commerce. This is a method of making business transactions (buying and selling) over the Internet. You may have heard of electronic commerce by some of its other names: e-commerce, e-business, or e-tailing (for retail sales over the Internet). Because EDI was used to send documents through a point-to-point connection, with one computer dialing in to another, changes were necessary to the previous standard. The Internet removes the need for trading partners to directly connect with one another, so the previous standard needed to be revised so that EDI could be implemented into e-mail and fax messages.

EDI was developed by the Data Interchange Standards Association (DISA), and became the ANSI (American National Standards Institute) standard. This standard was ANSI X12. Due to its use by businesses, the International Telecommunications Union (ITU) incorporated EDI into the X.435 message handling standard. With this standard, data in various native formats can be added to messages, which allows transmission of EDI documents through e-mail and other messaging systems.

The way that EDI works is that business data is contained within a transaction set. A transaction set is a unit of transmission, made up of data that's framed by a header and trailer, which makes up the message being sent. The data itself is a string of delimited elements. A delimiter is a comma, tab, or some other indicator that separates one piece of data from another. This allows an application reading a segment of data to know where one element ends and another begins. Each element represents a single piece of data. For example, a data element could be an invoice number, name, or price. When put together and separated by delimiters, these elements make a data segment that represents the parts of the document or form. Upon receiving a transaction set, an application that uses EDI reads the data segment between the header and trailer, and uses it accordingly. This allows the application to save the data to a database, display it properly in the application's user interface, or perform whatever actions the application has been programmed to do.

While having had a considerably long run, EDI has begun to be replaced in recent years by XML-based languages, such as OFX. *XML (eXtensible Markup Language)* provides developers with a way to create information formats, and share the format and data over the Internet or corporate intranets. Although XML has been taking the place of EDI, EDI is still in use in many companies.

The Internet

The 1990s saw an incredible rise in the popularity of the Internet. It allows millions of people to access information on a business and its products. Using an Internet browser or other Internet applications, anyone with the proper permissions can transfer data to and from other computers connected to the Internet. It doesn't matter if they're using PCs, Macs, or UNIX.

The common denominator with the different kinds of computers connected to the Internet is the use of the TCP/IP (Transmission Control Protocol/Internet Protocol) suite of protocols. The TCP portion is responsible for assembling the packets of data that are transmitted over the Net into their original format. The IP portion is responsible for sending the packet to the correct IP address, ensuring that the packet reaches its proper destination. In addition to these, the TCP/IP protocol suite includes the following:

- **FTP (File Transfer Protocol)**   Allows users to transmit files efficiently over the Internet. Although other protocols have the ability for transmitting files, FTP is specifically designed for basic file transport.

- **HTTP (Hypertext Transfer Protocol)**   Allows for the transmission of web pages and other files.

- **SMTP (Simple Mail Transfer Protocol)**   Allows users to send and receive electronic mail (e-mail).

■ **UDP (User Datagram Protocol)** Allows users to to send and receive packets. Unlike TCP, however, UDP doesn't guarantee delivery of the packets.

■ **Telnet** Allows users with proper permissions to log on to remote computers over the Internet and execute commands as if logged on locally.

By adding controls and code to your application that utilize the TCP/IP protocol suite, you can create robust applications for the Internet.

In designing applications that use the Internet, there are a significant number of choices to make. First is determining what type of Internet application you need to design. There are applications that run on the server, the client machine, and applications that are initially stored on the server but downloaded from the Internet to run on the client. Standalone applications can be designed to access the Internet from your application, or browsers can be used to access data and applications from web servers. While we'll go through each of the technologies involved in these applications, the point is that a significant number of options are available to you when designing Internet applications.

If you need to design an application that accesses the Internet without a browser application, it can be done with ActiveX controls. These are controls that you can create, by writing code like you do when creating other objects. Depending on what you're using to develop the application, various ActiveX controls, which have the file extension of .OCX, are included with Visual Studio, Visual C++, Visual Basic, and so on. These controls are added like other controls (such as Textboxes and ListBoxes, for example) to a Form, which is a container object that appears as a window when your application runs. ActiveX controls that provide this functionality allow you to design standalone applications that run on a client machine, allowing users to exchange files and view documents on the Internet through your application.

In addition to standalone applications, you can write or add ActiveX controls to web pages, which are documents written in HTML (Hypertext Markup Language). By embedding such controls in your web pages, any user with a compatible web browser can utilize the control. Since ActiveX technologies are built on the Component Object model (COM), the user must be using a COM-compliant browser. If they are not, they won't be able to use the control. When a user's COM-enabled browser accesses the web page, the web server transmits the HTML document and your ActiveX controls to the user's machine. The user's web browser then displays the page and runs the control.

In addition to using ActiveX controls, there are Active documents. While developed in Visual Basic, Active documents cannot be used as standalone programs. Like HTML documents, Active documents must be viewed and used through a container application like Internet Explorer. These documents are downloaded from a server to the browser. Through the browser users are able to view data through a point-and-click interface. You can incorporate menus, toolbars, and other methods of navigation and functionality through the Active documents you create.

While the methods we've discussed have mainly dealt with the client end, *ISAPI (Internet Server Application Program Interface)* applications can be created for web servers in your organization. ISAPI is a set of calls that can be used in developing applications that run on ISAPI-compliant Internet servers. ISAPI applications are dynamic link library programs, with the file extension of .DLL, that load when your web server starts. Users can submit requests to these applications through their web browser, and view data that the application returns.

ISAPI applications are considerably faster than CGI (Common Gateway Interface) applications. While ISAPI applications are similar to those created with CGI, ISAPI applications load when the web server starts, and remain in memory as long as needed. When a CGI application is run, each instance of the application loads as a separate process and in its own separate address space. This means that if ten people use the CGI application, ten instances of it will be loaded. Not only does this take up more memory than ISAPI, it's also slower than ISAPI because of the numerous loading, unloading, and reading of extra instructions stored in separate address spaces.

Each of the technologies we've discussed here can also be used on a corporate intranet. An intranet is a network that uses the technologies of the Internet on a local area network (LAN), metropolitan area network (MAN), or wide area network (WAN). The difference between these types of networks is the area they cover. A LAN may service a building or campus, a MAN would have buildings throughout a city networked together, while a WAN would have computers networked across a state, province or country, or internationally. Utilizing TCP/IP and the technologies we've discussed, an organization can have its users accessing data as if they were on the Internet. They would use web browsers to receive HTML documents and Active documents, and use ActiveX controls.

Should corporations wish to allow people outside of the company to access the corporate intranet remotely, the accessible portion of the intranet is called an *extranet*. Using TCP/IP and a web browser, clients, partners, and other users with proper permissions can access data. This broadens the benefits of the intranet, and makes necessary data available to those outside the organization.

OSI

OSI (Open Standards Interconnect) is a reference model used to describe how computers communicate on a network. The OSI model was developed by the International Organization for Standardization (ISO) as a conceptual framework that allows developers, network personnel, and others to understand network communication. By using OSI, you can develop products that have the ability to properly transfer data between your product and those created by other developers.

OSI breaks up the tasks involved in network communication into different layers. Rather than having to look at how an application transmits data as one large task, it breaks it up into sub-tasks. You can then use or design protocols that fulfill each of these subtasks by mapping them to the different layers of the OSI model:

- **Application**   The layer that will be accessed by the network application you write. It isn't the application itself, but provides services that support e-mail, database access, file transfers, and so forth. At this layer, you identify whom you'll communicate with, define constraints on data syntax, and deal with issues of privacy and user authentication.

- **Presentation**   The translator of the OSI model, responsible for converting data from one presentation format to another. It translates data from a format that a network requires to one that your computer expects. The Presentation layer is responsible for converting character sets and protocols, and interpreting graphic commands. It is also responsible for the compression and encryption of data.

- **Session**   The layer responsible for setting up and tearing down *sessions,* which are connections between two computers. The session layer controls name lookups and security issues. These are used to find another computer on the network, and determine how the two computers can connect to one another. The Session layer also synchronizes the data that's sent, and provides checkpoints that are used to determine how much information has actually been sent. If the network fails, or the session is dropped for some reason, only data after the last checkpoint will be transmitted. This keeps an entire message from needing to be retransmitted.

- **Transport**   The layer responsible for complete data transfers from one computer to another. The Transport layer ensures that packets of data are delivered without errors, with no losses or duplication, and in the proper sequence. When messages are passed down to this layer from the Session layer, it breaks large messages into smaller packets. When the receiving computer receives these packets, it reconstructs them in the proper sequence, then passes the message up to its Session layer.

- **Network**   The layer responsible for routing and forwarding data to the correct destination. It ensures that when a packet is sent out on the network, it is sent in the correct direction to the correct machine on the network by determining the best route to take. It also breaks large packets into the smallest frames that the Data Link layer can accept. Frames are units of data that the Data Link layer passes onto the physical layer for transmission.

- **Data Link**   The layer responsible for error control and synchronization. It breaks up packets into frames that are passed to the Physical layer for transmission. In doing so, it adds a Cyclic Redundancy Check (CRC) to the data frame, which is used to determine if a frame has been damaged in transmission. This layer also adds information to frame that identifies segmentation, and what type of frame it is.

- **Physical**   The layer responsible for transmitting and receiving data in a bit format (a series of binary 1s and 0s). It is the physical connection to the network that deals with how data is sent and received along the carrier.

exam
Ⓦatch

Many people find it difficult trying to remember the different layers of the OSI model. A simple way to remember the layers is remembering the sentence "People Don't Need To See Purple Animals." The first letter of each word is the first letter of each layer in the model (from bottom to top): Physical, Data Link, Network, Transport, Session, Presentation, and Application.

In looking at the different layers of the OSI model, you can see that the layers can be broken into two distinct groups. The top four layers of OSI are used for passing messages from and to the user. The remaining layers, which are the bottom three layers of the model, are used for passing messages from the host computer to other computers on the network. If an application needs to pass a message, such as an error message, to the user, only the top layers are used. If a message is intended for any computer other than the host computer, the bottom three layers are used to pass the message onto the network.

The way the OSI layers work can be seen in the example of a message being sent from a user on one computer to a user on the network. The transmitting user's message starts at the Application layer, and passes down through the different layers of the OSI model. Each layer adds its own special, related functions and breaks the message up into packets, which can be transmitted across the network. Except for the Physical layer, each of the layers adds a header, which the receiving end uses to process the message.

Upon reaching the computer that belongs to the receiver of the message, the packets are passed back up through the layers of the OSI model. The headers that were added by the sending computer are stripped off, and the message is reconstructed into its original format.

exam

Watch

OSI is a model, but not an absolute and explicit standard. Although many models, protocols, and so forth are based on the OSI model, a number don't map to every layer. As a model, it provides a conceptual framework that can be used to understand network communication, but it isn't a standard that must be adhered to.

COMTI

Many organizations that have been around for awhile still use their old mainframe computers. These enormous, archaic machines are used because they contain data that the company still uses for its business. The problem is that users working on NT Workstations, Windows 9*x*, and other platforms that use NT servers on the network need a method of accessing this data. While you could program special interfaces to access this data, an easier solution would be to use COMTI.

COMTI is a component of Microsoft Transaction Server, and runs on Windows NT Server. When an object method call is made for a program on a mainframe, COMTI works as a proxy for the mainframe. It intercepts the method call, converts and formats the parameters in that method, and redirects it to the mainframe program that needs to be used. The parameters need to be converted and formatted because mainframe programs are older and wouldn't understand the formats used by newer operating systems like NT. When the mainframe program returns values and parameters to the NT Server, COMTI converts them to a format that NT can understand. These are then passed from the NT Server to whatever client machine made the initial request.

Because COMTI is a component of Microsoft Transaction Server, it follows that it would be used for transaction programs on mainframe computers. COMTI supports IBM's Information Management System (IMS) and Customer Information Control System (CICS)—mainframe transaction programs. When using COMTI with MTS, you can coordinate transactions with CICS and IMS systems through MTS. Since all processing is done on the NT Server, and standard communication protocols are supported by COMTI, no additional protocols are required, and no code needs to be written on the mainframe.

Any client application you design that implements COMTI needs to be used on a platform that supports DCOM (Distributed Component Object model). It doesn't matter whether the application is written in Visual Basic, Visual C++, Visual J++, or any number of other languages. DCOM is language-independent, but the operating system needs to be new enough to support DCOM in your client application. This means you can't use COMTI in applications that run on older systems, such as Windows 3.1 or older DOS versions. The client application needs to be running on NT Server, NT Workstation, Windows 9*x*, or other operating systems that support DCOM.

POSIX

POSIX (Portable Operating System Interface) is a set of open system environment standards based on the system services of UNIX. UNIX is an operating system that was developed by Bell Labs in 1969, and was written in the language "B" (for Bell). When the next version of this language was developed, it was called "C," and UNIX became the first operating system to be written in the new language. Since that time, it has evolved into the first open or standard operating system, and is used by many universities, colleges, Internet, and corporate servers. Because computer users wanted applications that were portable to other systems, without needing the code to be completely rewritten, POSIX was developed. Since it needed to be based on an open system that was manufacturer-neutral (meaning royalties didn't need to be paid), and that was already popular (as an obscure system would cause problems), UNIX was chosen as the basis for POSIX. It gave developers a standardized set of system interfaces, testing methods, and more (as we'll see next), which allowed applications to be used on multiple systems without being recoded.

While developed by the IEEE (Institute of Electrical and Electronic Engineers) as a way of making applications portable across UNIX environments, POSIX isn't limited to being used on UNIX computers. It can be used on computers that don't use the UNIX operating system, and has evolved into a set of 12 different POSIX standards. Each of these is defined by the word POSIX followed by a decimal point system:

- POSIX.0, which isn't a standard, but is an overview of the other standards.

- POSIX.1, the systems API (Application Program Interface). These are the basic operating system interfaces used in programming POSIX applications.

- POSIX.2, the IEEE approved standard for shells and tools.

- POSIX.3, the testing and verification standards.

- POSIX.4, the standard for real-time extensions and threads.

- POSIX.5, which defines the ADA language bindings to POSIX.1.

- POSIX.6, the standard for security extensions.

- POSIX.7, system administration standards.

- POSIX.8, the standards for application interfaces, networking, remote procedure calls, transparent file access, protocol-independent network interface, and open system interconnect protocol-dependent.

- POSIX.9, which defines the FORTRAN language bindings to POSIX.1.

- POSIX.10, the application environment profile for super-computing.

- POSIX.11, the application environment profile for transaction processing.

- POSIX.12, the standard for graphical user interfaces.

exam
ⓦatch

The two main interfaces for POSIX are POSIX.1, which defines the API for operating systems, and POSIX.2, which sets the standards for shells, tools, and utilities. These two standards were incorporated into the X/Open programming guide, and are primary standards of POSIX. Of all the standards comprising POSIX, these are the two you should remember.

Proprietary Technologies

A *proprietary technology* is one that's privately owned or controlled. When a company develops and/or owns a specific technology, it has control over how it is used. It can decide whether others can freely use the technology, which would make it an open technology. If it decides to make it proprietary, it can hold back specifications for that technology or charge a fee for its use. This keeps others from duplicating the product.

A major problem with proprietary technologies is that they prevent users from being able to mix and match that technology with other products on the market. If a customer purchases such a product from a developer or manufacturer, they are often stuck with having to work with or upgrade to other technologies from that company. While such products may solve a short-term problem, in the long term they are often a source of major difficulties.

The Technology Environment of the Company

It's impossible to escape the fact that the technology environment of an organization is what will support your application's requirements. If the current technology environment doesn't support the requirements of the application, you have one of two options: upgrade the technical resources so they do support the application, or change your design so that it works with what's already in place. To make this decision, you need to gather information on the current and future state of the environment.

Earlier in this chapter, we discussed a number of information-gathering techniques. These included interviews, JAD sessions, and so forth. By actively discussing the technology environment with people who have knowledge of hardware and software used in the company, you can quickly establish how your design will be affected. The people you would acquire this knowledge from include network administrators, management, team leaders from other projects, and so forth.

on the **job**

In discussing the technology environment with network administrators and other individuals who know about the systems in use, you may find that the information you need has already been documented and up to date. This would provide you with the facts you need, and preclude having to do unnecessary work, because all of the information is already available.

Identifying the current state and deciding on the planned future state of technology in an organization should be done as early as possible. It's important to determine the technical elements that will affect your design. This includes such things as the hardware platform to be used for the application, what database management system will be used, security technologies, and how data will be replicated. What operating system will be used, and can the features of that platform be used by your application? You'll need to identify the technologies used to access remote databases and mainframes, and how requests will be handled. If such issues aren't addressed early in the design, it can result in significant losses. Time, money, and effort will be wasted on developing an application for a technical architecture that isn't supported.

Another benefit of determining the current and future state of the organization's technology environment is that it helps to identify the skills that will be required to complete the project. If your application needs to implement EDI or Internet technologies, or access a mainframe, you can determine the skills required for your project, and decide on which people have those skills. This enables you to form a team with the necessary skills to make your project successful.

Current Technology Environment

The foundation of where you're going is where you are right now. You may decide that the application should obtain data from a database residing exclusively on an NT server, without realizing that all of the corporation's data is on a mainframe computer. Even worse, you could spend time, money, and effort planning to implement a technology in the future, only to find that the technology is already in place in the organization. It's important to understand the current state of the technical resources before planning changes. Not doing so can make or break the success of your project.

For the design of your application, you should document the current technology environment of the organization. This documentation should include as much detail, and show as much knowledge about the technology, as possible. Though most of the information will be written, you can include diagrams, charts, and physical environment usage scenarios to aid in understanding how the current technology environment is laid out.

In your documentation, you should outline the development tools currently in use, the technologies used in current network applications, and how the network itself is designed. Protocols should also be documented. You don't want to design an application that uses TCP/IP if the network uses IPX/SPX, and the network administrator refuses to implement that protocol. Much, if not all, of this information can be gathered through the information-gathering techniques we discussed earlier in this chapter.

Planned Technology Environment

From the information gathered on the current state of the technology environment, you're able to see changes that need to take place to support the application you're designing, as well as applications you plan to design later. It is through such planning that you take a hard look at where you are going with the technology environment, based on where you currently are. In doing so, you take the first steps toward developing a technical system architecture that can support the technical requirements of such business solutions.

It is important to document the future state of your technology environment. Such changes can be documented in a textual format, or listed in a chart form. In a chart, you could list the current state of the environment in one column, and the change that needs to occur in the next, and note what those changes entail in the third column. For example, let's say you wanted your current application to use 32-bit programming. If the current state of the environment is that workstations use Windows 3.11 (which uses 16-bit programs), then the planned state would be workstations using Windows 9x or NT Workstations. This would enable your team to use the latest development tools, create 32-bit programs, and use the latest APIs and technologies for that platform. This allows you to note where areas of the environment will remain the same, where changes need to be made, and what those changes to the environment will be.

In making such plans, you need to demonstrate that the future architecture will deliver at least one major business requirement to the environment of the organization. This may be meeting a business rule that determines how data is accessed, or such issues as performance aand ease of maintenance. No matter how nice you ask for the latest advances in technology, a company will only see the bottom line; that is, will the benefits of these changes outweigh the costs involved? Your plan should reflect the merits of such changes, describing how they will impact your application, the business requirements, and the productivity of the business as a whole.

In planning the future state of your technology environment, it's important to not only look at how you want things to change, but also how the changes will affect technologies that will continue to exist in the future state. Unless you're implementing a brand new system in your organization, a significant portion of the previous state will carry on. This could include such areas as security technologies, mainframes, and protocols. Ensure that you understand how your changes will affect these technologies, before they're put into effect.

Selecting Development Tools

Suppose you have to design a 32-bit program. After designing the business solution, you inform your development team to use Visual Basic 3 as the development tool. You know that all of the developers know that language and don't see a problem, until the application is completed. Unfortunately, the solution is a 16-bit application. Why? Because Visual Basic 4 was the first version of Visual Basic to offer 32-bit programming, and the last to offer 16-bit development. Oops. Not only would such a bad decision cause the solution to go back through development, but would also probably cost you your job.

Such a situation illustrates how important it is to select the right development tools to build your application. Your design may revolve around using Visual J++ when Visual Basic or Visual C++ is the better choice. Not only must you select the development tool that best suits your needs, but you also need to be aware of what that particular version of the tool offers. This means that upon choosing a tool, you must do some research on the different releases available to see if they're compatible with your needs and the environment those tools, and the programs developed with them, will be used in.

Unfortunately, in researching such development tools, you're bound to face biases. Visual Basic programmers will prefer that language and tool over Visual C++, C++ programmers will say the reverse, and Java programmers will say that Visual J++ is better than either of these. We will make no such recommendations. Each of the tools in Visual Studio 6 supports COM and enables you to create reusable components that can be used with each of the other tools in this suite. Generally, the best choice of a development platform revolves around the following:

- **Nature of the project**   Some tools are better suited to some projects than others, and should be decided on a project-to-project basis. This is due to the inherent strengths and weaknesses in the languages themselves. This, combined with the type or nature of the project, will make some tools more suitable for certain projects.

- **Skills of the development team**   Developers will develop quicker if they use a language and tools they're familiar with. This means the application can be built faster.

- **Cost and schedule**   If there isn't time to retrain developers on new tools, or the budget doesn't allow it, you can't send developers for retraining.

In short, you need to select development tools based on the project, the skills of the people involved in the project, and other resources available. By knowing the features and functionality of the various tools available, you can make such a determination.

on the **job**

Selecting the proper tools must be done early in the design to allow time for retraining and/or familiarization with those tools. It's not uncommon for developers to be sent out on a weekend or week-long class, and then be expected to master how to develop an application with their new knowledge, in a new language, with new tools. No matter how good the training session, it takes time for developers to hone their new skills. By selecting the development tools early in the design phase, you provide your team with the time it takes to do this. By the time your solution is designed and ready for development, your development team will be ready to do what you need.

Visual Basic 6

Microsoft Visual Basic 6 is based on the most commonly used programming language in computing: BASIC (Beginners All-Purpose Symbolic Instruction Code). Though based on the original language, it isn't the BASIC you may have learned in high school programming. There are hundreds of keywords, functions, and statements for the Windows graphical user interface (GUI). In addition, you don't write code through a console or text-based interface. Visual Basic allows you to add pre-built and custom controls to Forms, which become Windows when the application is run. This WYSIWYG (What You See Is What You Get) method of designing an application's interface makes programming significantly easier.

In addition to the comparative ease of learning this programming language, Visual Basic 6 comes with a number of features that allow applications to be developed rapidly. One such feature is the ability to create databases, front-end applications, and server-side components in various database formats. Such databases include Microsoft Access and SQL Server. Another feature of Visual Basic 6 (VB6) is the ability to create applications that access documents and applications across intranets or the Internet, and the ability to create Internet server applications, such as those used by Internet Information Server. Visual Basic 6 also includes ActiveX controls that you can add to forms to create applications quickly.

Perhaps the greatest strength of using Visual Basic is that it uses a simplistic syntax, and that people who know VBA (Visual Basic for Applications) can quickly be moved into the role of Visual Basic developers. VBA is used in all of the applications included in the latest versions of Microsoft Office, as well as other solutions put out by Microsoft. Because of this, you may already have an installed base of developers who can migrate from VBA to VB. Due to the simple syntax, Visual Basic also serves as an excellent language for new developers. It is easier to learn than many other languages out there, such as Java or C++, and can be used for the rapid development of solutions.

In addition, VB6 provides a number of Wizards, which can be used in creating or migrating an element that can be used in the applications you create. Wizard programs take you step-by-step through the process of a particular task—such as creating toolbars, property pages, or even applications—and result in a completed object or product when finished. These can then be built upon by adding additional code. The Wizards provided in Visual Basic 6 include those shown in Table 9-1.

TABLE 9-1	Wizard	Purpose
Wizards Included in Visual Basic 6	Application Wizard	Used to create functional applications that you can build upon later.
	Data Form Wizard	Used for generating VB forms from information obtained from the tables and queries of your database. The generated forms include controls and procedures, which you can build upon by adding additional code.
	Data Object Wizard	Used for creating the code used by COM data objects and controls that display and manipulate data.
	ActiveX Control Interface Wizard	Used to create public interfaces for the user interfaces you've created for ActiveX controls
	ActiveX Document Migration Wizard	Used for converting existing forms into ActiveX documents.
	ToolBar Wizard	Used for creating custom toolbars. This is new to VB6.
	Property Page Wizard	Used for creating property pages for user controls.
	Add-in Designer	Used for specifying properties of add-ins. This is a new addition to VB6.
	Class-builder utility	Used for building the hierarchy of classes and collections in your project.
	Package and Deployment Wizard	Used for creating setup programs for your applications, and distributing them. This is new to VB6, though it is based on the previous Setup Wizard included with previous versions.

Visual C++ 6

Though a more difficult language to learn for beginners, Visual C++ is incredibly powerful for creating all sorts of applications. Visual C++ is based on the C++ language (which has its origins in the languages of "B" and "C"), and is used to create many of the applications you've used in Windows. Like Visual Basic, Visual C++ provides a visual GUI that allows you to add pre-built and custom ActiveX controls in a WYSIWYG manner. Code is then added to these controls, enabling users to view and manipulate data, or access whatever functionality you decide to include in your programs.

The difficulty involved in learning this language and the power of developing with Visual C++ can serve as serious drawbacks to developing with C++. It uses complex syntax, which can make Visual C++ difficult to learn and use. Even when developers have backgrounds in other languages like Visual Basic, learning this language can be problematic. This, and the very power it provides, can and generally does lead to slower development times. You should attempt to determine whether your solution will actually need the power that C++ provides, as it may be overkill for some projects.

Also like Visual Basic, Visual C++ provides a number of Wizards that can easily be used to accelerate the speed of development. These Wizards are straightforward to use, and take you through each step in the process of a particular task. The Wizards provided in Visual C++ are listed in Table 9-2.

Visual J++ 6

If your development team consists of a group of Java programmers, you'll probably want to go with Visual J++. In terms of complexity and power, J++ generally falls between Visual Basic and C++. Using this development environment, you can create, modify, build, run, debug, and package Java applications for use on the Internet, your corporate intranet, or as Windows applications. While the Java language is most closely associated with the Internet, this doesn't mean you can't create applications used on a Windows platform that doesn't have access to the Internet. Visual J++ 6 uses the Windows Foundation Classes for Java (WFC), which enables programmers to access the Microsoft Windows API. Through WFC you can create full Windows applications in the Java language.

TABLE 9-2	Wizard	Purpose
Wizards Included in Visual C++ 6	ATL COM AppWizard	Used to create Active Template Library (ATL) applications.
	Custom AppWizard	Used for creating custom project types, which can be added to the list of available types.
	MFC AppWizard	Used to create a suite of source files and resource files. These files are based on classes in the Microsoft Foundation Class (MFC) library. C++ includes two versions of this Wizard: one is used to create MFC executable programs, while the other creates MFC dynamic link libraries (DLL).
	Win32 Application	Used to create Win32 applications, which use calls to the Win32 API instead of MFC classes.
	Win32 Dynamic Link Library	Used to create Win32 DLLs, which use calls to the Win32 API instead of MFC classes.
	Win32 Console Application	Used to create console applications. These programs use the Console API so that character-mode support is provided in console windows.
	Win32 Static Library	Used to create static libraries for your application.
	MFC ActiveX ControlWizard	Used to create ActiveX controls.
	DevStudio Add-in Wizard	Used for creating add-ins (in-process COM components) to automate development tasks. The add-ins are dynamic link library (.dll) files, which are written in Visual C++ or Visual Basic.
	ISAPI Extension (Internet Server API) Wizard	Used to create ISAPI (Internet Server Application Programming Interface) extensions or filters.
	Makefile	Used to create MAKEFILE projects.
	Utility Project	Used to create utility projects.

Like the other development tools we've discussed, you can create applications with Visual J++ through a GUI interface. By adding various controls to a form and then assigning code to those controls, you can rapidly develop applications. In addition, you can use the various Wizards included with Visual J++ (like those shown in Table 9-3) to quickly develop the applications you design.

Visual InterDev 6

Web designers and web application developers will get the most benefit from Visual InterDev. This development tool provides a number of features including design-time controls, and (as seen in Table 9-4) wizards to aid in creating such applications. As the second version produced of Visual InterDev, Version 6 is the first version to have a WYSIWYG page editor, which allows you to add controls to your applications just like the other development tools we've discussed. Rather than having to know how to raw code cascading style sheets (CSS), or possess a knowledge of HTML, Visual InterDev includes an editor that allows you to create and edit cascading style sheets (CSS). It also offers tools that allow you to integrate databases with the web applications you create.

TABLE 9-3	Wizard	Purpose
Wizards Included in Visual J++ 6	Application Wizard	Used to create functional applications that you can build upon later.
	Data Form Wizard	Used for generating forms from information obtained from a specified database. The controls on the form are automatically bound to the fields of that database. This includes Microsoft Access databases, and those accessible through Open Database Connectivity (ODBC).
	WFC Component Builder	Used to add properties and events to WFC components.
	J/ Direct Call Builder	Used to insert Java definitions for Win32 API functions into your code. In doing so, the appropriate @dll.import tags are also added to your code.

Wizard	Description
Sample Application Wizard	Used to install sample application from the Visual InterDev Gallery and third-party web applications.
Web Application Wizard	Used to create new web projects and applications, and to connect to existing web applications.

Visual InterDev 6 provides a number of powerful features that can be used when creating web applications and other distributed applications. First and foremost, the Data View window in Visual InterDev 6 enables you to launch tools to manage your database, and enables you with a live view of data. In addition, the Quick View tab in Visual InterDev provides instant page rendering without the need to save, while color coding of script allows a clearer way of viewing the script developers are writing or have previously written. Visual InterDev 6 also has debugging support, enabling developers to find problems in their code before it's passed forward into testing or use.

Visual FoxPro 6

Visual FoxPro is a development tool that enables you to create robust database applications. Using Visual FoxPro, you can create databases, queries, tables, set relationships, and interfaces that your users can use to view and modify data. It includes a Component Gallery, which is used as a central location for grouping and organizing objects like forms, class libraries, and so forth. Included in the Component Gallery is the Visual FoxPro Foundation Classes, which are database development tools and structures, components, wrappers, and so forth, which allow you to quickly develop applications without having to rewrite incredible amounts of code. Visual FoxPro also includes the Application Builder, which enables developers to add, modify, and remove tables, forms, and reports quickly. Finally, the Application Framework feature of Visual FoxPro provides common objects used in applications. Together, they are the means to creating database applications rapidly. Visual FoxPro Wizards are described in Table 9-5.

Wizard	Description
Application Wizard	Used to create projects and a Visual FoxPro Application Framework. When this is used, it will automatically open the Application Builder, which allows you to add a database, tables, reports, and forms. This is a new Wizard to Visual FoxPro.
Connection Wizard	Used for managing transfers between the Visual FoxPro class libraries and models created in Microsoft Visual Modeler. It includes a Code Generation Wizard and a Reverse Engineering Wizard as part of it. This is a new Wizard to Visual FoxPro.
Database Wizard	Used to create databases. This is a new Wizard to Visual FoxPro.
Table Wizard	Used to create tables.
Pivot Table Wizard	Used to create pivot tables.
Form Wizard	Used to create data entry forms from a specified table.
One-to-Many Form Wizard	Used to create data entry forms from two related tables.
Report Wizard	Used to create reports.
One-to-Many Report Wizard	Used to create reports. The records in these reports are grouped from a parent table with records in a child table.
Query Wizard	Used to create queries.
Cross-tab Wizard	Used to create cross-tab queries, and display results of such queries in a spreadsheet.
Import Wizard	Used to import data from other files into Visual FoxPro.
Setup Wizard	Used to create a setup program for your application.
Web Publishing Wizard	Used to display data in an HTML document. This is a new Wizard to Visual FoxPro.

	Wizard	Description
TABLE 9-5 Wizards Included in Visual FoxPro 6 (continued)	Graph Wizard	Used to create graphs from tables in Visual FoxPro. It does this by using Microsoft Graph.
	Label Wizard	Used to create labels from tables.
	Mail Merge Wizard	Used to merge data into a Microsoft Word document or a text file.
	Views Wizard	Used to create views.
	Remote View Wizard	Used to create views using ODBC remote data.
	SQL Server Upsizing Wizard	Used to create SQL Server databases that have similar functionality to Visual FoxPro databases.
	Oracle Upsizing Wizard	Used to create Oracle databases that have similar functionality to Visual FoxPro databases.
	Documenting Wizard	Used to create formatted text files from your project's code.
	Sample Wizard	Demonstration of a Wizard. This is new to Visual FoxPro.

Determining the Type of Solution

There are many types of solutions you can create for a network, that go beyond the capabilities and limitations of standalone applications. Standalone applications run completely on a single computer, and don't require a connection to a network. When your application does need to access objects, components, and/or data on other computers, then the design of your solution must be expanded to become one of the following:

- Enterprise solution
- Distributed solution
- Centralized solution
- Collaborative solution

In the sections that follow, we'll discuss each of these solution types. The type of solution you choose for your design will be determined by the number of users accessing data and using your application, where the data source and application will be located on your network, and how it is accessed.

Enterprise Solution

Once organizations began to interconnect their LANs together, the need for solutions that could effectively run on these larger systems was needed. That's where enterprise solutions came into play. They're called *enterprise solutions* to cover the numerous types of organizations, large and small businesses, charities, and so forth, that use computers, and have a need for solutions that can handle the possible hundreds or thousands or users that will use these applications. In addition, hundreds or thousands of requirements may need to be addressed by the application, as users use the application and access data on the server application. Because of these and other factors, designing and developing enterprise solutions can be incredibly complex.

While there are many enterprise solutions in the real world, they all generally have the following in common:

- They are about the same size.
- They are business-oriented.
- They are mission-critical.

To help you understand these attributes, and how they affect an enterprise application, we'll discuss each of them individually.

Enterprise solutions are generally large in size. They're spread across multiple computers, and can be used by numerous users simultaneously. Designing solutions for the enterprise requires an expanded scope of knowledge to deal with a larger environment. While the different models of MSF are used in a similar manner, enterprise solutions mean that these models need to be used on a grander scale. This means there is an overwhelming need to use a good framework, such as MSF. It would be impossible to tackle such a project on your own, without recruiting people into the various roles of the Team model. Teams are organized to take on the various tasks involved in developing, testing, and so forth using the Team model.

Teams of developers will generally create such an application, keeping in mind that each part of the application they code will be used by multiple users on multiple machines. Parts of the enterprise application will reside on different computers, distributed across the network. ActiveX components can be used with this, allowing the software to communicate and interact across the network.

To say that an enterprise solution is *business-oriented* means that it's required to meet the business requirements of the organization for which it's created. Enterprise solutions are encoded with the policies, rules, entities, and processes of the business, and they're deployed to meet that business's needs. Any enterprise solution you design must function in accordance with the practices and procedures of the enterprise.

When your enterprise solution is said to be *mission-critical*, it means that the application you're creating is vital to the operation of that organization. For example, insurance companies use applications that store policy information in a database. If this application stopped working, none of the insurance agents could input new policy information or process existing policies. This affects the operation of the enterprise. As such, enterprise applications need to be robust, so they are able to function in unexpected situations, and thereby sustain continuous operation. They must also allow for scalability, which means they can be expanded to meet future needs, and have the capability to be maintained and administered.

Distributed Solution

Distributed solutions are applications where the objects, components, and/or data comprising the solution are located on different computers. These computers are connected through the network, which thereby connects the elements of the application to one another. For example, a user's computer would have the user interface portion of the solution, with the functionality to access a component containing business rules on an application server. This application server's component might contain security features, and determine how the user accesses data. By looking at the user's account, it would determine if the user could access data residing on a third computer, the database server. Because each computer has a different portion of the application, each computer also shares in processing. One CPU handles the user interface, the CPU on the second computer handles processing business rules, while the third processes data. This increases performance, and reduces the amount of resources required by each individual computer.

Data can be spread across a distributed application in different ways. If your solution is to be used by numerous users, you can create an application with the user interface on the user's computer and the database program on a server. This is called a client-server database. The computer running the user interface is called the *front-end* or *client portion* of a distributed solution. The client (front-end) makes requests from the server, which is called the *back-end* of the distributed solution. Typically the front-end or client will run on a personal computer (PC) or workstation, although if the user is working on a server as if it were a workstation, it can run on a server computer. In either case, the client makes a request to view or manipulate data from the server, which processes the request on behalf of the client. This back-end portion of your distributed solution can service such requests from many users at the same time, manipulate the data, and return the results to the client portion on the requesting user's machine. Because numerous users are taken care of, the server requires a significant amount of storage space for the data files, as well as enough processing power to keep performance from suffering.

If such a distributed solution does degrade in performance from too many users, you can consider creating a distributed database. In such a solution, you create two databases that use the same data on two different servers. You then set up these databases to synchronize their data, having one database replicate its changes in the other at specific times. This is often useful when geographical reasons dictate the need to distribute a database, as might be the case if two branch offices opened in different countries, and needed to use the same data. Since it would be expensive and slow to have users connect to a single database using a WAN, you would set up a distributed solution with distributed databases. Users in each location would use the database closest to them, and these two databases would then synchronize with one another.

If a database isn't heavily accessed, or is used by a small number of users, you can create a distributed application where the data files are located on a server and the database application is located on the client. This is the kind of application you could create with Microsoft Access. The database program manipulates files directly, and must contend and cooperate with the other users who are accessing that particular data file. Because of this, if numerous users are accessing the same data file or files located on the same server simultaneously, the network can become bogged down with traffic, and the database's performance can suffer. In addition, the server will require significant storage space to contain the databases users will access.

Centralized Solution

A *centralized solution* is an application in which everything resides on a single computer, and is accessed by users on smaller, less powerful systems. Centralized solutions are associated with mainframes, which are accessed by terminals or terminal emulation programs. Such terminals can be smart or dumb terminals. *Dumb terminals* have no processing power, and are an output device that accepts input and data and displays it. *Smart terminals* do have processors, and are considerably faster than their dumb counterparts. The terminal emulation programs allow more powerful computers, such as PCs, to fool the mainframe into thinking that it's a terminal, allowing the computer to access data from the mainframe remotely. When such requests for information are made, they are sent over the network or communication lines to the mainframe. The centralized solution then retrieves the data, with all processing taking place on the mainframe. It then transmits the data back to the requesting computer, and displays it on the terminal.

Collaborative Solution

Over the last number of years, a growing need in business has been the ability for people to work together with computers. When one person has completed (or is nearing completion) of his or her work, it must be passed onto another worker in the company. This collaboration between the two employees requires that the work each does must be consistent and able to mesh with the other's. In the case of several designers working on different components of an application, the different designs would need to work together. This means that as each portion of work is added together to form the complete design of the solution, each person's design would have to mesh together, or errors would result. In addition, information may need to be transferred from one individual to another in a particular order, following a specific workflow. The first person may need to send his or her work to another designer, who in turn puts the different designs together into a complete design, and then sends it off to the team leader for analysis and approval.

This is where collaborative solutions are necessary in an organization. *Collaborative solutions* are also known as *groupware*, and allow groups of people to share data, and interact with one another. Collaborative solutions fall into one of two categories, with the first category being a requirement of the second:

- Collaborative solutions that allow users to share data with one another, or enhance data sharing.
- Collaborative solutions that allow users to interact with one another from different computers.

The first of these types of collaborative solutions allows two or more users to share data, and can include such things as linked worksheets or documents, Internet, or Internet applications that display dynamic web pages. The second type of solution enables users to interact with one another, and could include such features as providing e-mail, Internet Relay Chat (IRC), or other methods of communication in an application. No matter which type of collaborative solution you design, it's important to remember that groups of people will be sharing data and interacting with one another. At no time should the user feel isolated from other members of their team, and they should always be able to benefit from collaborating with others in their work.

In designing collaborative solutions, you need to determine how the flow of information needs to move through the company. This can be determined by creating workflow diagrams and usage scenarios. In addition, you need to establish whether work needs to be sent only through a specified workflow, or if users will need to interact with one another as well. This will enable you to determine what features to include in your collaborative solution.

Choosing a Data Storage Architecture

Since no one wants a database application that doesn't store data, choosing a data storage architecture is an important issue. Data Architecture addresses the flow of data through every stage of the data cycle: acquisition and verification, storage and maintenance, and retrieval. Not only does the data storage architecture address what database management system (DBMS) will be used, it also addresses issues dealing with the effective storage of data. This includes such things as volume considerations, the number of transactions that take place over a certain time period, how many simultaneous connections to the database will occur, and so forth. These and other elements of the data storage architecture will affect the overall performance and effectiveness of your database application.

Volume

An importation consideration in determining data storage architecture is the amount of information to be saved, and how large your database will become. Different databases have different capacities, and can accept greater and smaller amounts of data. For example, SQL Server has a capacity of over 1 Terabyte per database. In contrast, Access or Jet databases (.mdb) have a capacity of 1 Gigabyte per database, but because you can link tables in your database to other files, the total size is limited only by the available storage capacity. The volume of information to be saved to your database should be estimated before deciding on the type of database you'll use. If you fail to look at how much data may fill the database, you may find that the storage capacity of a particular database is insufficient for your needs.

If you're creating a database application to replace an existing one, you should look at how much information is being stored in the database by each user. This will give you an effective measure of the volume of data to be stored in the new database. You should also take into account growth factors in the number of users who will be saving data. For example, if 100 users were each saving 1MB of data a month, and there are plans to hire 20 more people for data entry over the next three years, you should figure that 120 MB of data will be saved monthly (120 users × 1 MB / month). By looking at the current trends of data storage, you're able to determine the volume of data to be stored in your future database.

If you're creating a new database application, and information on the volume of data being stored isn't available, it can be considerably more difficult to determine the storage needs of your customer. This is where it becomes important to look at the usage scenarios, and look at the kinds of data to be stored, as well as find out how many users will be accessing the database. By seeing what the database will be used for, the type of information to be stored, and the number of users, you can then determine the volume of information to be stored.

Number of Transactions per Time Increment

A *transaction* is a group of programming statements that is processed as a single action. To illustrate this, let's say you were creating an application for an Automated Teller Machine (ATM). If a user were to make a withdrawal from his or her account, the transaction would probably start with checking to see if there was enough money to withdraw from the account. If there was enough money, then the transaction would continue to adjust the user's account, and give the user the proper amount of cash. Each of these would be carried out as a single action, a transaction.

Different organizations will have a different number of transactions carried out over certain time periods. While the ATM of a small bank in the middle of nowhere may have a few dozen transactions carried out in a day, a single machine in the middle of New York City could easily carry out thousands of transactions in the same time period. While the first of these could use a Visual FoxPro or an Access/Jet database to handle such activity, the second would be overwhelmed if such a database were used. However, SQL Server databases, or an application working with Microsoft Transaction Server, would be able to handle such heavy activity.

SQL Server databases can handle a high volume of transactions, and should always be considered when creating applications that use mission-critical transactions. An example of this is our ATM application. If the network were to go down in the middle of a transaction, you wouldn't want the amount of a withdrawal deducted before the user got his or her money. This would cause problems for not only the user of this application, but also for the bank. SQL Server logs every transaction, such that if the system fails, it automatically completes all committed changes while rolling back changes that are uncommitted. Visual FoxPro and Microsoft Access/Jet databases don't have the ability to automatically recover after a system failure like this, meaning that data is lost if the system goes down.

It is important to determine the average number of transactions that will occur over a specific time increment for each project on which you work. This number will generally be different for each project you work on, and where it is used. It's important not to use figures gathered from other projects, as these may be incorrect for what you can expect from the current project. Also, if there are several locations using a previous version of the database application, you should gather information on the number of transactions that occur over a specific time increment, and then average them. This will give you an accurate picture of what to expect.

Number of Connections per Session

For your database application to work, it needs to connect to a specific database for a period of time. The period between the time that a user connects with a database and the time that the connection is released is called a *session*. In other words, when the user logs on to the database, or the application connects to the database on the user's behalf, the session starts. When the user logs off, the session has ended, and the connection is released.

With desktop applications, you can assume that only one session will be used with a database, unless more than one instance of the application is open at that time. With network applications, it isn't that simple. You may have dozens, hundreds, or even thousands of simultaneous connections to a single database at any given time. Therefore, you need to consider how many sessions will be required when designing your application.

Different databases provide a different number of sessions or user connections to occur at the same time. For example, Access databases and those that use the Jet database engine (.mdb) allow 255 concurrent users to be connected to a single database. SQL Server 6.5, however, allows a maximum of 32,767 simultaneous connections. This is a theoretical limit, and the actual number of connections is dependent on the resources (such as RAM) on the server running SQL Server. As you can see, more powerful databases provide a greater number of sessions.

In determining the number of sessions available, you should also consider the effect it will have on resources and performance. Each session open on a database server takes up memory. For example, while SQL Server's maximum simultaneous connections is 32,767, this value may be less. This is because the number of connections available is based on available memory and application requirements. The reason this is so is because each user connection takes up memory. For example, in SQL Server 6.5, each user connection takes up 37 KB, while SQL Server 7 incurs an overhead of about 40 KB. This increases the amount of overhead, and decreases the amount of memory that can be used for buffering data and caching procedures. Whatever computer you designate as the database server should have a considerable amount of memory to ensure that enough connections can be made.

Scope of Business Requirements

In choosing a data storage architecture for your solution, it is fundamental that the scope of business requirements is given paramount consideration. The requirements of the business should always determine the data storage architecture. Because the application is driven by the business requirements as well, it follows suit that this will help in making the data storage architecture also meet the requirements of the application.

Extensibility Requirements

Extensibility is the ability to extend the capabilities that were originally implemented. This includes such things as extended feature sets, or support for ActiveX controls or Automation. The extensibility of the data architecture you use should always be considered, so that the database won't need to be completely scrapped when new features are required in the future.

Microsoft Access has support for ActiveX controls. This includes ActiveX controls that bind to a row of data. If the control binds to more than one row of data, Access will not support it. It also won't support ActiveX controls that act as containers for other objects.

Microsoft Access also has the ability to control Automation servers (formerly known as OLE Automation Servers or OLE Servers). An *Automation server* is an application that exposes its functionality, allowing it to be used and reused by other applications through Automation. Access has the ability to control such servers because it's an Automation server itself. This means that if your application, even an Internet application, needed to use the functionality of Access, you could control access through your program with Automation. This extends the capabilities of Access to other programs.

Unlike Microsoft Access, Visual Basic (VB) and Visual FoxPro (VF) allow you to create custom Automation servers. This is because both VB and VF allow a greater degree of programming ability, allowing you to create your own applications that can use or be used by other applications.

Visual Basic ships with the Jet database engine, which is what Microsoft Access and Microsoft Office use. This isn't to say that VB comes with a free copy of Access, just that it uses the same database engine, and that Visual Basic provides the ability to create databases. Admittedly, these databases are less sophisticated than those created with Access or FoxPro. In addition, there are major differences in the extensibility of database applications created with Access and VB. Like Access, Visual Basic 6 and Visual FoxPro 6 support ActiveX controls. However, each of these supports controls that act as containers and those that bind to one or more rows of data.

Reporting Requirements

Reports are a common need of users, requiring data to be printed or displayed in a specific format. Microsoft Access and Visual FoxPro have offered Wizards in current and previous versions to make the creation of reports easy. The Professional and Enterprise versions of Visual Basic 6 now includes a report writer, which has a number of features, including the drag-and-drop functionality of creating reports from fields in the Data Environment designer. Each of these products also has the ability to create reports in an HTML format, allowing you to post your reports to the web.

SQL Server 7 has full integration with Microsoft Office 2000, and as such, enables users of SQL to use the reporting tools in this version of Microsoft Access. In addition, you can use office web components to distribute any reports you create. Because SQL Server 7 is the first database with integrated Online Analytical Processing (OLAP), it is the best database to select if your customer requires this type of corporate reporting.

Number of Users

The number of users who will use the database storage architecture will have a dramatic effect on the type of database storage you use. As mentioned earlier, Microsoft Access and Jet databases can handle up to 255 concurrent users. SQL Server can handle up to 32,767 simultaneous user connections, but (as previously stated) resources available on the system running SQL Server determine this maximum. Visual FoxPro doesn't have a specific limit, but is determined by the system's resources. Despite this, it shouldn't be used for a large number of users, as would be the case for SQL Server.

If a large number of users are expected to be using the database, you should always consider using SQL Server. On a system with good hardware, supporting a small number of concurrent users, it is doubtful that anyone would notice any performance issues. In such a case, unless the developer wanted to take advantage of SQL Server's extended functionality, you could use Access, a Jet database created with Visual Basic, or a Visual FoxPro database. However, as the number of users grows, and performance decreases, it is wise to migrate to SQL Server. If you expect a large number of users to begin with, then SQL Server is the data storage architecture of choice.

Type of Database

As we've seen, different database management programs have different capabilities and limitations that must be considered. Even though your design and application code may be flawless, if the wrong database is used, everything can fall apart. Because of this, it's important to know the functionality offered by the database types available.

In determining the type of database to use, cost should be a consideration. Microsoft Access and Visual FoxPro are relatively inexpensive. The same can be said for Visual Basic, which allows you to create Jet databases for use with your applications. However, SQL Server is considerably more expensive, and may not be affordable to use as part of a database application for a small business. For such smaller businesses, Small Business Server would be a wiser choice. In addition, while SQL outperforms each of these other databases, little performance value will be noticed if only a small number of users will be accessing the database. In such cases, SQL would be overkill.

Though we've discussed how different types of databases should be used in different situations, Table 9-6 shows some of the important differences in the database products on the market. While these are just a few of the attributes of each database type, this table will enable you to view the differences quickly before going into the exam.

Exercise 9-2 tests your knowledge in identifying different types of solutions. (The answers to this exercise appear just before the Self Test at the end of the chapter.)

TABLE 9-6 Information on Different Databases	**Attribute**	**Access/Jet (.mdb)**	**Visual FoxPro 6**	**SQL Server 7**
	Capacity	I GB. However, because you can link tables in your database to other files, this means the total size is only limited by the available storage capacity.	2 GB per table	1,048,516 TB per database
	Number of concurrent users	255	Unlimited	32,767 user connections

Identifying Different Types of Solutions

Supply the name of the type of environment in each of the descriptive passages below:

1. A publishing company hired a group of writers to write various sections of a book. This book reflects a wide range of technical expertise. Each writer is considered an expert in their professional area. They are physically located all over the world. Because the publishing company wants to ensure the text flows well from one topic to the next, it provides the applications that allow video conferencing, meeting tools such as electronic whiteboards, and a text delivery mechanism.

2. ABC, Inc., a publisher of children's education books, has two Novell Netware LANs and four NT domains. One of the Netware LANs is in the sales department that takes phone orders for books. They also have an Internet presence with an online store. Their sales application consists of multiple user interfaces and three major components: customer, order, and product. SQL Server is the database server. The sales application is considered a mission-critical application.

3. A small government agency has a bridge to a mainframe computer that hosts its data and all of its applications. The applications are all written as a text-based or console application. Each worker has a personal computer on their desk. These computers are licensed to run an office application suite and a terminal emulation application. Most of the workers invoke the terminal emulation program to connect to the mainframe and run the mainframe applications.

4. Fun 'n' Games, Inc. manufactures toys for the preschool market. This organization has a multi-domain NT network with a major accounting and manufacturing application. It also has a mainframe that hosts its data. The purchasing department has an application that consists of a vendor object and a product object. Because it has multiple factory locations across the continental United States, the purchasing department wants to centralize the purchasing duties. The corporate offices have a user interface written in Visual Basic that captures data on the mainframe. The business rules for the vendor object run on a dedicated application server, while the product object runs on the server that also hosts the vendor's electronic catalogues.

Testing the Feasibility of a Proposed Technical Architecture

Once you've determined what your technical architecture should be, it is time to test whether that architecture is feasible. This is important because while a proposed technical architecture may seem well-planned at face value, deeper analysis may show that it has the potential to cause your project to fail. In testing your architecture, you need to show that business requirements, usage scenarios (use case scenarios), and existing technology constraints are all met. If testing shows that these areas aren't met, or fall short in some areas, then you must assess the potential damage of these shortfalls. In other words, will it make a difference or cause the project to fail?

Because the design of your project is conceptual at this point, there are no actual applications or databases that you use in your testing. Prototypes or test applications can be developed, allowing Testing to have something concrete to work with. While prototypes don't provide the functionality of the actual application, or give a visual demonstration of what the GUI will look like, they may be beneficial in seeing whether certain requirements have been met. In Chapter 11, we'll go into prototypes in greater detail.

The primary method of testing whether requirements have been met is to go through the various documentation that has been generated to this point. This includes the business and user requirements that have been outlined in the vision/scope document, usage scenarios, and documentation on current technology. By comparing these to your technical architecture, you can determine whether the requirements have been met.

exam ⓦatch

On the exam you'll be given a case study with proposed solutions, and a series of choices. This is not a memory test. You can refer to the case study as many times as you wish.

Demonstrating That Business Requirements Are Met

The requirements of the business are what drive application design and development, and it's extremely important that these requirements are met in your design. The business requirements are the reason that you've been hired to design the solution in the first place. As such, you want to be able to demonstrate that these requirements have been given the attention they deserve, and that they are addressed in the design.

By going through each of the requirements outlined by the business, and documenting where they are addressed in your design, you are able to show that the various requirements have either been met, fall short, or haven't been addressed at all. Basically, this is simply a matter of going through the requirements, and checking each one off that has been addressed in the design. Documentation should be made as to where or how the requirement has been met, so team members can easily refer to where the requirement is met. As we'll see later in this chapter, if these requirements haven't been addressed, it's important to either revise the design so they are addressed, or have a good reason why they can't be included.

Demonstrating That User Case Scenarios Are Met

User case scenarios or usage scenarios are a vital tool in the design of your application, and show how the application will be used. By comparing the design of your technical architecture to these scenarios, you can determine if the solution actually follows the way certain activities must be carried out. For example, if you've created a collaborative application, you can view whether the design follows the way in which work is actually performed in the office. You can see whether the solution you've planned to create will actually serve the way users do their work in the organization.

Demonstrating That Existing Technology Constraints Are Met

It's important to determine whether existing technology constraints are met early in the design process, so that technologies aren't incorporated into the design that won't work in the current environment. For example, if an organization had a network that didn't use TCP/IP, had no connection to the Internet, and had no intention of implementing an intranet, then using Internet technologies as part of your design would be pointless. If every user in the organization ran Windows 3.1, then you'd be limited to 16-bit applications, as 32-bit applications wouldn't run on this platform. As you can see, the existing technologies used in an organization have a great impact on how the application can be designed.

It's important to know as much as possible about the current technology constraints, so that you can show that they have been addressed in your design. This allows you to go through the design of your application, and identify areas of the design that will fail to work or have poor performance with these constraints.

Assessing the Impact of Failure to Meet Requirements

If certain requirements aren't met, or fall short of what was previously expected, it is important to assess the impact this will have on the project's success. The requirements for your solution will have varying degrees of importance. While some may be a minor inconvenience, or may be added to the solution in future versions, others may cripple your design and cause it to automatically fail.

While business requirements drive the design and development of a solution, some requirements may be more important than others to the customer. If a business requirement is mission-critical, then the organization can't function without that particular requirement being met. This means that mission-critical requirements that aren't met will cause your project to fail. Other requirements may be more flexible, and can be dropped from a feature set until a later time. For example, if the customer wanted the ability to connect to a corporate intranet through your solution, but no intranet currently existed, this could be included in a future version. Because of the varying impact of shortfalls in meeting business requirements, it's important to assess the potential damage to your project early. By holding meetings with customers and users of your solution, you can often determine this quickly.

Because usage scenarios show the way that certain activities get done, failing to meet a usage scenario may keep users from performing their duties. Imagine designing a solution for a video store, and failing to meet the usage scenario that details the rental of movies. Needless to say, such a shortfall would be devastating. While this is an extreme example, such things as technology constraints may keep your design from fulfilling a usage scenario. There may be a need to provide a workaround, another method of performing the task, until it becomes technically possible to fulfill the scenario.

If a solution fails to meet the technology constraints of an application, you need to determine whether the technology needs to be updated, or your design needs to be revised. If a business requirement is mission-critical, and can't be implemented without upgrading the current environment, then the organization will need to know that the solution will fail without these changes. If a business requirement isn't mission-critical, then the customer will need to choose between dropping that particular feature, or upgrading a current technology.

Developing an Appropriate Deployment Strategy

The sooner you develop an appropriate deployment strategy, the better prepared you'll be when the time comes to actually deploy your application. There are numerous ways available today to deploy an application. These include floppy disk, CD-ROM, over the local network from a server containing the necessary setup files, or over the Internet or a corporate intranet. How you choose to deploy your solution will depend on who is installing the solution, what methods are available for use by your users, and which are feasible for the organization.

In most cases, it is the end user who will obtain and install a copy of your application on his or her computer. While end users have a great deal of knowledge on the day-to-day functionality of applications, their experience with computers, networks, and installing applications can vary greatly. Therefore, it is important to offer instructions in simple, plain language, so no technical jargon will confuse them.

In many organizations, a network administrator or support staff will aid the user with installing the solution. Either they will completely install the application on their computers for them, or they'll provide assistance when called upon. In these cases, you should provide a knowledge base or additional information on how they can support users through the installation. In addition, these people are the ones who are usually responsible for installing server-side components or back-end applications that work with the end-users' front-end applications. It is important to provide them with detailed instructions on how to perform these tasks.

Floppy-disk deployment is the oldest method of deploying a solution, but has been overshadowed in popularity in the last few years by CD-ROMs. Often, new developers will consider floppy-disk deployment to be a waste of time. Large installations may take numerous disks, and significantly more time to install, as the user must labor through the process of switching one disk for another through the installation process. However, this method of deployment shouldn't be completely discounted. There are users out there who don't have CD-ROM drives on their computers, and no network connections, and can use only this method of deployment. Organizations with older computers still in use, that don't have CD-ROM drives installed, rely on floppy deployment. In such cases, they can't afford to upgrade all of the computers in the organization with CD-ROM drives, or are slowly upgrading each of the systems over a period of time. In planning a deployment strategy, it's important to consider these issues, and offer floppy disks as an alternative method of installation.

As mentioned, CD-ROMs have become the most popular non-network method of deploying a solution. Most off-the-shelf applications you buy today are on CD, and most computers sold today come with CD-ROMs as part of the package. Despite this, CD-ROM deployment is a more expensive method of deployment. This is because you need to purchase a special device to create writeable CDs. While CD-ROM burners have drastically dropped in price over the last few years, they are still somewhat pricey, about the price of a large hard drive. In addition, writeable compact disks must be specially purchased, so that you can write your installation files to this media. Despite these issues, which will be of greater concern to smaller developers than larger ones, or organizations with their own development staff, the benefits of CD-ROM deployment are great.

You need to consider what percentage of your intended users has CD-ROM drives on their systems before using this method of deployment. In some cases, CD-ROM deployment may be your only method of deployment. There are a number of organizations that don't allow users to have floppy disks on their machines, for fear the user may save critical information to the floppy and walk out with it. If users don't have a network connection, then CD-ROM deployment will be your only available method.

If your network has a server that users of your application have access to, then you should consider network-based deployment. In this method of deployment, the installation files are saved in a network directory on a server. Users can then access the directory and begin installing from the files on this server. The drawback to this is that if numerous users are installing simultaneously, then the network can become bogged down from the increased traffic. It is, however, an extremely useful method of deployment, especially in cases where a specific person is given the duty of installing applications for the user. When the network traffic is low, such as after business hours, the installation can take place on the network with no disruptions.

Intranets and the Internet are also common methods of deployment, and similar to network-based deployment. In this method of deployment, the installation files are put on a web server that users can access. They then download and/or install the files from the directory on that web server. As is the case with network-based deployment, this can slow down an intranet. While this isn't an issue with Internet deployment, it is an issue for corporate intranets. Therefore, you may wish to limit the times or number of connections to access these files.

It's often wise to plan on setting up a test network of ten or so computers to test your deployment strategy before actually implementing it. This will allow you to determine problems that users may incur when trying to obtain and set up your solution on their computers. While this doesn't become relevant until after the application is completed and ready for deployment, it is something that's worth planning for. It may help you to identify and solve problems before your users actually experience them.

Validating and Refining the Strategy: The Value of User Feedback

Once usage scenarios have been created, or when you're ready for feedback on your design of a user interface, it's important to validate your design with the user. This means getting user feedback on your design, and ensuring that it suits their needs and expectations. In validating your conceptual design, you gather together the users you've obtained information from and solicit their opinions and input.

A common method of doing this is walking the user through the usage scenarios you've created. At points along the way, you can ask for their input directly, or invite them to jump in and comment at any point. Generally, you'll get considerable feedback from the user, which allows you to determine whether you're on the right track.

As we'll see in great detail in Chapter 11, prototypes of the user interface are another method of validating your design. This entails creating a mock-up of the user interface, and inviting feedback from users. Using this method allows you to catch problems in your interface design early in the development process.

Once you've gotten the input you need from users, you then go back and refine or redesign the work you've done so far. While this seems like a lot of work, it is considerably easier to correct problems early in the design process, than to wait and have to refine or redesign your application once program code has been added. The rule here is to try and get it as close to perfect early in the game.

QUESTIONS AND ANSWERS

Which is the best language to use in creating an application?	The choice of language for development depends on the inherent strengths and weaknesses of the language, and the specifics of the project you're working on. There is no overall "best" language. The programming language should be chosen on a project-to-project basis.
Based on the number of users, which type of database should I use for my application?	Visual FoxPro, Access, and Jet databases are useful for smaller amounts of users. If you expect a large number of users, in the high hundreds or even thousands, SQL Server should be considered.
Why is it important to validate the conceptual design?	It ensures that your vision of the product matches the customer's and end-users' vision. This guarantees you're on the right track with your design, and helps to keep design problems from cropping up in later design stages.

CERTIFICATION SUMMARY

Conceptual design is the first step in designing your solution. Here, the activities performed by the users are identified and analyzed, as are tasks that must be performed to solve a business problem. Through the conceptual design process, you lay the groundwork for your solution to deal with these issues. This process is made up of several tasks, which include identifying users and their roles, gathering input from users, and validating the design.

Because the design of the solution is driven by the requirements of the business, it's important to gain a business perspective for your solution. It's also important to gain a user perspective, and understand the requirements of the person who will actually work with the solution.

Through information gathered on the requirements of the business, customers, and end users, you are able to design a solution that meets these needs. Usage scenarios can be helpful for this purpose, showing how tasks will be performed by the end user. From these scenarios, you can build a conceptual design based on the scenarios, and have a design that maps to the needs of the organization and end user.

In defining the technical architecture of a solution, you determine models and technologies that can be used for your solution's design. Models, such as the OSI model, can be used to aid in understanding how your solution will communicate with applications on other computers. In addition, you will need to identify whether Internet technologies are required, and determine the language used to develop the solution. Each programming language and platform has inherent strengths and weaknesses. It's important to look at how these will specifically relate to the project, and determine which is the best to use.

 TWO-MINUTE DRILL

- ❑ Conceptual Design is the first perspective in the Solutions Design model. It is here that you look at activities performed by the users and tasks that must be performed to solve a business problem, and then lay the groundwork for your solution to deal with these issues.

- ❑ Conceptual design is where you determine what users actually need to do, and forge the basic concept of what your application will become.

- ❑ An application created for an enterprise is called a "business solution," because it's built to solve specific business problems.

- ❑ Design flaws that are instituted in the conceptual phase can produce multiple logical or physical instances of application design or functionality that either do not address a business need or ignore user requirements.

- ❑ In gathering user requirements, the business and the units within it become independent entities. The organization, and its departments and units, are seen as individual users with their own needs and perspectives.

❑ Because organizations and the units that make up the business are viewed as individual entities, it is important to create user profiles and gather information from them as well. Each department and unit, in addition to the business as a whole, will have its own goals, needs, and interests.

❑ Once you've identified whom you're going to acquire information from, you're ready to gather that information.

❑ Once you've determined the needs of end users, the business entity, and its departments, you need to combine the different perspectives into a single concept. This entails sifting through the information you've gathered to determine what will be included in the design.

❑ By going through the user profiles and gathered information, you see what common issues appeared, what end-user requirements conflict with the interests of the business or its departments, and what great ideas appeared that need to be incorporated into your application's design.

❑ A *scenario* is an outline or plot of a sequence of events. As an outline, it provides a point-by-point, step-by-step analysis that depicts the procedure that occurs when something is done.

❑ Usage scenarios are used to construct a conceptual design for your application, which is one of the exam objectives. There are different methods of constructing such scenarios in the context of the business and users. While these are included below to help you construct conceptual designs, the Task Sequence model, Workflow Process model, and Physical Environment model aren't directly addressed in the exam.

❑ The *Workflow Process model* is used to create usage scenarios that show how specific jobs are routed through an organization.

❑ In designing an application that's geared to the needs of the user, you need to understand the tasks he or she does to complete an activity. It's for this reason that the *Task Sequence model* is used to create usage scenarios.

❑ Usage scenarios are also valuable for understanding the physical environment that your application will be used in.

❑ The *Physical Environment model* looks at the environment in which an application will be used.

❑ From the usage scenarios, you gather the information that allows you to identify Business objects, as well as the appropriate solution type for your organization.

❑ *Single-tier solutions* are common in desktop applications, where the user may not even have access to a network.

❑ Remember that with single-tier solutions everything is located on one machine.

❑ With *two-tier solutions*, the database doesn't reside on the user's computer. Instead, there is a database server that handles the management of data.

❑ *n*-tier solutions are what developers commonly refer to when talking about three-tier solutions.

❑ While the technologies covered here are those directly covered on the exam, you should try to have as much familiarity with as many as possible. The exam expects that you know at least one programming language before taking the exam, and have some experience with developing solutions.

❑ If the current technology environment doesn't support the requirements of the application, you have one of two options: upgrade the technical resources so they do support the application, or change your design so that it works with what's already in place.

❑ Since no one wants a database application that doesn't store data, choosing a data storage architecture is an important issue.

❑ Once you've determined what your technical architecture should be, it is time to test whether that architecture is feasible.

❑ On the exam you'll be given a case study with proposed solutions, and a series of choices. This is not a memory test. You can refer to the case study as many times as you wish.

❑ The sooner you develop an appropriate deployment strategy, the better prepared you'll be when the time comes to actually deploy your application.

❑ Once usage scenarios have been created, or when you're ready for feedback on your design of a user interface, it's important to validate your design with the user.

Answer to Exercise 9-1

The usage scenario that you create will reflect your analysis of the project details. Here is one possible interpretation:

PRECONDITIONS:

- Database of customers and videos exist.
- Clerk has access to database.
- Customer has selected a video to rent.
  1. Clerk finds customer's membership account.
  2. Clerk documents the SKU number of the video in the customer account.
  3. Clerk obtains whether customer wants video insurance.

     If customer wants video insurance, clerk adds $0.25 fee to account.

     If customer doesn't want video insurance, it's recorded and no fee is added.
  4. Clerk specifies whether promotions or discounts apply.
  5. Clerk adds total cost of rental.
  6. Clerk prints out a receipt for the customer to sign.
  7. Clerk determines method of payment, and takes payment.

     Cash

     Credit

POSTCONDITIONS:

Receipt exists showing proof of rental.

Answers to Exercise 9-2

1. Collaborative solution type
2. Enterprise solution type
3. Centralized solution type
4. Distributed solution type

SELF TEST

The Self Test questions will help you measure your understanding of the material presented in this chapter. Read all the choices carefully, as there may be more than one correct answer. Select all correct answers for each question.

1. You are gathering information for the conceptual design of your application. In doing so, you identify the users who provided information, as well as their responsibilities and roles. What documentation will put this into?

   A. User profile
   B. User scenario
   C. Usage scenario
   D. Vision statement

2. You are gathering information for the conceptual design of your application. In doing so, you document how the needs and perceptions of the system translate to actual tasks. You do this by writing down a step-by-step procedure of how business processes are executed. What kind of documentation is this?

   A. User profile
   B. User scenario
   C. Usage scenario
   D. Vision statement

3. Which role of the Team model has ownership of the conceptual design, and is responsible for driving the conceptual design process?

   A. Product Management
   B. Program Management
   C. Development
   D. User Education

4. Which role of the Team model is responsible for gathering user input and validating usage scenarios?

   A. Product Management
   B. Program Management
   C. Development
   D. User Education

5. You are gathering information for the conceptual design of your application. You bring together team members, end users, and other interested parties to design the concept of your product. In the days that follow, you discuss business concerns that will affect the project. What information-gathering technique are you using?

   A. User interviews
   B. JAD sessions
   C. JAG sessions
   D. Shadowing

6. You are designing a database application for a user. The application will reside on the user's machine, but the user will connect to the database through a mapped network drive. What kind of solution is this?

A. Single-tier

B. Two-tier

C. Three-tier

D. *n*-tier

7. A company has asked you to design a new database application, which will get data from a SQL server. The company currently has a solution in place. Applications on users' machines make requests directly to the SQL server, with no other servers being used in this process. The problem is that the network is slow because there are so many requests being made to the database server. The company insists that the database isn't to be broken into multiple databases in your design. What type of solution will you design?

A. Single-tier

B. Two-tier

C. *n*-tier

D. None. It is impossible to redesign the solution based on this criteria.

8. The company for which you are designing an application asks if you can add browser functionality to the application. When a user clicks on a toolbar button, or a menu item, this will bring up a Window that allows the user to browse the Internet. What technology will you incorporate into the application's design so user's can have this functionality?

A. Active pages

B. EDI

C. ActiveX controls

D. POSIX

9. You are designing a business solution using the OSI model. This solution will access a database, and have built-in e-mail capabilities. Which layer of the OSI model will the written solution directly access?

A. Physical

B. Application

C. Internet

D. Transit

10. Your design includes COM components that can be reusable with other business solutions you create with development tools in Visual Studio 6. You need to select a development tool that supports COM. Which will you choose?

A. Visual Basic 6

B. Visual C++ 6

C. Visual J++ 6

D. All of the above

11. You have designed an application for your organization, but realize that with recent upgrades to the computers, the development team will need retraining. Your development team knows the Beginners All-Purpose Symbolic Instruction Code, and has experience creating text-based, console applications. For your application, they will need to create Windows applications and ActiveX documents. What will you have them retrained in?

A. Visual C++, and then have them create ActiveX documents with the ActiveX Document Migration Wizard

B. Visual Basic, and then have them create new ActiveX documents with the ActiveX Document Migration Wizard

C. Visual Basic, and then have them convert forms they create to ActiveX documents with the ActiveX Document Migration Wizard

D. Visual J++, and then have them convert forms they create to ActiveX documents with the ActiveX Document Migration Wizard

12. You have designed an application that will run on Windows. The computers that will use the application will have no network connection. Your development team consists of developers who specialize in Java programming. Which development tool should you use to develop the application you design?

A. Visual C++

B. Visual Java

C. Visual J++

D. None. Java is used only for Internet applications, and can't be used for Windows applications.

13. You have designed a solution that will access data stored exclusively on a mainframe computer. When a request is sent to the mainframe, it will do all of the processing: retrieving the data, transmitting it back to the requesting computer, and displaying it on the terminal. What kind of solution is this?

A. Standalone

B. Centralized

C. Distributed

D. Client-server

14. Splinky Sprockets has offices based in New York and London. New York is the main office, and 60% of the work is done there. Users at each of these locations need access to the same data, and both offices are connected with a WAN. What kind of solution will you design for this company, so that users have access to the same data, without having to wait long periods to connect to the database over the WAN?

A. Create a distributed solution with a database located on a server in New York. Have front-end applications on each of the users' computers to access this database.

B. Create a centralized solution. Have users connect to the database over the WAN line.

C. Create a distributed solution with a distributed database. Front-end applications will access the database residing on the server at their location, and the databases will be synchronized to replicate the data at certain intervals.

D. Create a collaborative solution, allowing data to be shared between each of the users. Users can interact with one another, and have their work follow a specified flow of information.

15. SuperDupe Comic Books has asked you to design an application for them. Their problem is that art drawn on computer for

their comic books needs to go from the computer artist to the writer. Once the text has been added to the artwork, it then goes to the editor for approval, who sends it to copy editors and finally publishing. Any work generated by one user must be compatible with the work done by others. What kind of solution will you design? Choose the best answer.

A. Centralized solution, allowing all users to access the same data from a central location

B. Standalone, allowing work to be printed or passed to other users on floppy disk

C. Distributed solution, allowing all users to access the same data from a single server

D. Collaborative solution, allowing data to be shared by users, and sent in a specified order from one user to another over the network

16. Your local community has decided that the 911 emergency system currently in use is terribly out of date, and has hired you to design a new solution to store information taken by the operators of 911 calls. This information is critical, and needs to be able to complete committed transactions even in the event of a system failure. You need to determine what will be used to store this data. Which of the following will you choose?

A. Jet database created in Visual Basic 6

B. Visual FoxPro 6 database

C. Access 97 database

D. SQL Server database

17. You are designing a database for a large insurance corporation. At any given time, up to 20,000 users will be accessing the database to store or retrieve information on policy holders. You need to determine what will be used to store this data. Which of the following will you choose?

A. Jet database created in Visual Basic 6

B. Visual FoxPro 6 database

C. Access 97 database

D. SQL Server database

18. The network you're designing an application for consists of 100 users. The network has no connection to the Internet, and no corporate intranet currently in operation. Fifty of these users are low-level employees who don't have floppy drives. Twenty-five of these users are high-level employees who have both floppy drives and CD-ROM drives. You want to choose a method of deployment that will allow all of these users access to installation files. What method will you choose?

A. Floppy-disk deployment

B. CD-ROM deployment

C. Put installation files on a web server, allowing users to access the installation files

D. Put installation files on a network server, allowing users to access the installation files

19. You have designed a database solution where users will access data from a server. A front-end application is designed as the GUI, allowing users to view and manipulate data. This front-end sends requests to a back-end application residing on the server, which can handle requests from multiple users simultaneously. Processing is shared between the front- and back-end applications. What kind of solution have you designed?

    A. Standalone
    B. Centralized
    C. Distributed
    D. Static

20. You are designing a distributed application for a company. Users will access data from a database server on the network. You need to design an application that will reside on each user's machine that will access data from the database server. No other servers will be used in your design. What type of solution will you design?

    A. Single-tier
    B. Two-tier
    C. Three-tier
    D. *n*-tier

MICROSOFT CERTIFIED SOLUTION DEVELOPER

10

Logical Design

CERTIFICATION OBJECTIVES

L ogical design encompasses all parts of your application, including the User Services or Presentation layer, Business Services, and Data Services. The user requirements and business rules gathered and established in the conceptual phase of development are now ready to be mapped to a logical model. However, progressing to the logical phase of development does not mean you're done with the conceptual phase. As you progress through the logical phase you will often find yourself circling back to the conceptual phase to gather more facts and clarify requirements. As we will see, this is just one of the benefits of logical design.

In this chapter, we will examine the process of deriving our logical model from the conceptual model. We will look at the basics of logical design and see the important role a thorough design plays in the success of distributed applications. We will examine the steps required to transform our conceptual design model into a logical design model, while incorporating the business rules and user requirements gathered in the previous phase. In the next section, we gain an understanding of component interfaces; what they are and why we need them, and the contractual relationships they require. We then take a look at the structure of the three-tier services model, what it is, and why you would want to use such an architecture. Next, we will explore the Presentation layer, or user interface, and the benefits of prototyping. In the final sections, we examine object dependencies and then assess the potential impact of our logical design.

CERTIFICATION OBJECTIVE 10.01

Logical Design Basics

Logical design is the process of taking the user requirements that we gathered in the conceptual design phase and mapping them to their respective business objects and services. In this stage of development we are not concerned with the physical aspects of our design, such as where certain components will reside or how many servers are involved. Our only concern here is to create a high-level abstract model, independent of any physical model. Mapping our logical model to a physical model is the next step in development. We have seen that the progression from the conceptual phase to the logical phase is not the final progression. Similarly, the progression from the logical phase to the physical design phase is an iterative process. However, the physical design should not be started until we have a thorough understanding of the objects and services that comprise our application. A premature migration to the physical design phase without a solid logical design will only hinder the flexibility of our application later on.

This high-level abstract model allows us to distance ourselves from the many details we gathered in the conceptual phase and organize them without getting bogged down in the intricacies of each particular requirement. It allows us to focus on one requirement at a time while maintaining the vision of the application as a whole. This high-level approach provides us the opportunity to gain a deeper understanding of the relationships that exist between the requirements and objects.

The Value of Logical Design

A good logical design is a critical step in correctly identifying the components and objects, and their services, that were established in the conceptual model. With proper analysis, a logical model will also facilitate the development of later phases, and improve the flexibility of the application model. Thoroughly breaking out the requirements into their respective objects will allow you to design the objects in such a way that they provide only the services they need to.

EXERCISE 10-1

The Value of Logical Design

1. Think of an idea for an application at work or for a client. Imagine what it would be like to simply sit down at your workstation, with nothing more than a list of what you think the application should be able to do, and start developing it. Where would you start?

2. Using this same idea, now imagine what it would be like to be handed a logical design or class diagram with all the objects for the application outlined with the methods and functionality they will contain and the relationships between them. Now where would you start in your development process?

3. Compare these two scenarios and think about which one would allow you to be more productive with a higher probability of satisfying the end user, and why.

Organizing Logical Structures

Once your objects have been identified, you need to organize them in terms of the services they provide, and the relationships they have with the other objects. There are many questions that need to be asked of the objects based on their functionality and how they interact with the other objects. We will be exploring these issues later in the chapter. For now, just remember that even though some objects may not have direct relationships with each other, they all interact with one another in some capacity and are composed of certain functionality.

Organizing Logical Structures

1. Think of an application you've written where all of your code was contained in modules (referred to as a *monolithic application*) rather than broken out into classes or objects. How would you apply some of the principles of logical design to modify that application so that the code could be based in classes instead?

2. Which application do you think would be easier to modify as requirements change or are added? Which would be easier to subsequently debug and maintain?

on the job

One tool that is extremely helpful in modeling an application is Microsoft Visual Modeler. Figure 10-1 illustrates the class diagram window of Visual Modeler, showing a logical design view of a sample file that ships with it. Visual Modeler is a graphical object modeling tool included with the Enterprise Editions of Visual Studio 6 and Visual Basic 5. Visual Modeler facilitates the entire process of creating your application model, from designing and organizing objects and their relationships to creating classes and generating code. Note, however, that in Visual Modeler the definition of Data Services is not quite the same as in a distributed application. In a distributed definition, Data Services usually refers to the database, whereas in Visual Modeler, Data Services refers to the data components that will reside in the middle tier, or the Business Services layer.

The class diagram window of Visual Modeler

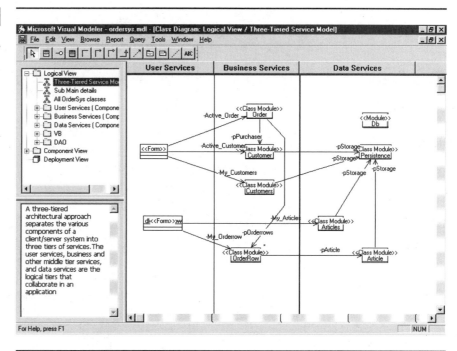

Importance of Core Principles

As you begin the preparation for logical design, there are several key considerations that also happen to be benefits of a three-tiered application design model. They are scalability, reliability, and efficiency. As you design your objects, let these factors be a driving force in the way you organize your logical structures. Although these concepts apply also to the physical design, they are equally important here, in the logical phase. How granular do you want to make your components? Will they maintain state, or will they be completely stateless to maximize scalability? What threading model will you use? How will you break your requirements into objects to maximize your object's performance? Questions like this need to be considered here, but you must be careful not to overlap your thinking too much at this time into the physical design perspective.

Deriving a Logical Design from a Conceptual Design

Creating a logical design consists of mapping the business rules and user requirements identified in the conceptual phase to objects. These *objects*, which can most readily be identified from the user requirements as nouns, also provide services. These s*ervices* in turn represent the rules and requirements of the business domain that you are modeling. It's important to note that in the logical design phase, we are not defining technical requirements. The sole purpose of the logical model is to translate user requirements and business rules into objects and determine the type of relationships the objects have with each other.

As discussed in Chapter 9, *conceptual design* is the process of determining the functional requirements and usage scenarios for the application. The outcome is a set of documents outlining the applications background, requirements, and implementation plan. It provides the basis for the logical design phase. The logical design, on the other hand, will result in diagrams such as the Visual Modeler diagram in Figure 10-1. It will also include the definitions of the interfaces, or the interface contract that we shall discuss later in the chapter.

exam
ⓦatch

Watch out for questions that try to confuse you on the differences between logical models and physical models. Keep in mind that the layout of your logical model does not correlate to a physical implementation of your application. It defines the relationships and interface contracts that exist between your objects and any external objects involved, such as other systems. It does not imply any type of physical or technical implementation.

Deriving the Components and Services of the Logical Design for a Business Solution

When determining the objects necessary to support the user requirements, it's important that you keep your objects as focused as possible. In other words, your objects should only provide services related to their intended purpose. For example, if you have a Customer object, it will be responsible for such services as adding new customers, updating customer information, deleting customers, and any other activities necessary to support the requirements specific to a customer as established in the conceptual phase. Therefore, the Customer object should not be doing other things such as updating inventory for a customer. Although the activity is customer-related, it should be the responsibility of, say, an Inventory object. The Inventory object, given a customer ID, would in turn modify inventory data on behalf of the customer. It is vital to the flexibility of your application to keep your components as self-contained as possible. This has other benefits in that such a design will also facilitate code reuse. The Customer object, if kept modularized to performing only customer-related activities, could then be reused in an entirely different application without modification. Another added benefit is that code can be developed by multiple developers in parallel, each working on separate self-contained units of logic. This modular or component-based design is easier to debug and develop, since each unit can be tested for its own functionality independent of other code.

The functionality that you design into your objects is referred to as *component granularity*. The more activities or services that your objects support, the coarser their granularity. The fewer services your object provides, the finer its granularity.

exam
Watch

Be aware of questions concerning component granularity. Remember that component granularity refers to the number of services or methods a component has. It does not refer to a component's properties. A component is referred to as being either coarse or fine. The fewer methods a component offers, the finer its granularity. The more methods it contains, the coarser it is. In addition, stateless components (that is, components that have methods, not properties) in a distributed application are preferred. If you need to maintain component state, then you may want to investigate using the MTS Shared Property Manager as opposed to designing your components with properties to maintain the state.

CERTIFICATION OBJECTIVE 10.04

Distinguishing Between Objects, Services, and Components in a Logical Design

In this section, we will begin our review of the process of transforming our user requirements into their respective objects. These objects will contain services and properties, or attributes, which will represent the behaviors and characteristics of our objects.

Let's review the basics of what we will be discussing. *Objects* are the things from our requirements that we are modeling. They are often identified in the requirements as nouns. For example, if you scan through the requirements from the conceptual design phase, you may notice items being discussed such as a customer, an order, or an invoice. These things (nouns) are objects. These objects will have services. *Services* are the objects' behaviors, or more technically, the methods of the object. They perform actions such as adding a customer, deleting an inventory item, or creating an invoice. The term *component* is not to be confused with object. An object and component are not the same, although you may see them referred to as such. However, an object is instantiated from a class, whereas a component consists of precompiled binary code.

Identifying Objects

Before we continue, let's review a few more terms. *User requirements* is the list of items that the application needs to be able to accomplish. These were established in the conceptual design phase and are commonly identified by interviewing users to determine what they demand from the system. Another term is *usage scenarios* (also called case scenarios), which were established in the conceptual phase. *Case analysis* is the process of modeling how the user or users interact with the system. This can often be captured through careful observation of end users interacting with their existing systems, whether automated or manual processes.

The most common technique for identifying objects is to pick them out from the usage scenarios. Although this may seem like a rather straightforward approach, it is quite likely that different people will come up with different, albeit similar, sets of objects or representations. It's important to remember that there is no one correct set of objects. What is important, however, is to come up with a set of objects that accurately reflects the business problem at hand.

Clearly, one could get carried away and start identifying every noun as a potential object. This is not the point. In order to qualify as an object, it must posses two characteristics: It must have behaviors and attributes (that is, methods and properties). The object must also either generate information or receive information.

EXERCISE 10-3

What's in a Name?

1. Think of an application that you've been involved with in the past. How did you pick names for code modules or classes?

2. In hindsight, if you could rename these modules or classes, would you name them differently? Why?

EXERCISE 10-4

Identifying Objects

1. Think of something that you use and depend on every day. What are the objects associated to using this object? What are the methods

and properties? For example, think of your car. It has an Engine object with methods such as accelerate and decelerate. It also has properties such as temperature and fuel level.

2. Think of some other ordinary objects you interact with every day, and try to break them down into objects.

Identifying Services

Services are an object's behaviors. These behaviors are the actions that they perform and are executed through the use of methods. The process of identifying services is very similar to the method we used to identify the objects in the previous section. Here again, we'll look through our usage scenarios. However, now we'll be looking for verbs instead of nouns. Verbs will help identify the actions that our objects need to perform. These in turn will be translated into methods or services. Again, as in identifying objects, one could get carried away with picking out all the verbs. What is important is to focus on the business-related actions. In addition, not all objects will have services or perform any actions. Some will simply be providing data. We'll discuss this in the next section when we look at identifying attributes.

When identifying services, keep these points in mind: Is the action initiated from within the application, or is it the responsibility of another system? Make sure that the action can be associated to an object. In other words, will this action be performed by an object you identified, or will it be the recipient of data from this service? And lastly, use only active verbs.

EXERCISE 10-5

Identifying Services

Using the object or objects from Exercise 10-4, list the services that they provide. For example, using our Car object, we said that the Engine object had accelerate and decelerate methods. What else do these objects do? What other actions do they perform?

Identifying Attributes

Attributes, also know as *properties*, are things your object knows. It's the data that's associated to the object. Attributes, which I'll refer as properties, are also things that other objects need to know about and that help establish the relationship between objects.

For example, a Customer object will have properties such as name, address, and customer ID. These are things it knows about itself. It may also have a property that allows another object to know about it. For example, this customer may have multiple addresses. The Address object that stores addresses for all customers will need to associate its address data with a customer and will therefore need to know the customer ID of the data it's storing.

To assist in identifying these properties, we return to our usage scenarios and list of requirements. What items need to be tracked? These will be the things that our objects need to know about and remember. Each item that needs to remembered will become associated to an object as a property or attribute.

<table>
<tr><td>**EXERCISE 10-6**</td></tr>
</table>

Identifying Attributes

1. Continuing with our car example, identify some of the properties it has. For example, our Engine object has properties such as fuel level, engine speed, and temperature. What other properties might it have?

2. In preparation for the next section on object relationships, think about what properties our Car object might have that other objects may need to know about.

exam
ⓦatch

Remember, we're designing distributed components, and these components should be stateless. In the context of a distributed environment, attributes, which are nothing more than properties of an object, become arguments to a method call. You no longer set an object's properties by making property calls. Instead, you pass them as arguments to a method, which in turn updates the object's properties all at once.

Identifying Relationships

The objects you have identified thus far in the logical design phase have certain types of relationships with the other objects in the logical model. Identifying relationships among your objects involves once again reviewing your usage scenarios and user requirements. Pick out the nouns and/or objects you identified and note the verbs and other connecting phrases between them. Table 10-1 lists the three major types of relationships objects can have and provides a question to ask to assist in identifying the

TABLE 10-1	The Three Major Types of Relationships Objects Can Have	
Relationship	**Description**	**Question**
Ownership/ Container	Commonly referred to as a *parent-child* or *one-to-many* relationship. This is where one object *owns* or *contains* another type of object. This is perhaps the most important and common type of relationship. They are used to implement object collections. For example, an Invoice object will contain or own InvoiceItem objects. Therefore, the Invoice object has an InvoiceItem object, and the InvoiceItem object is owned by the Invoice object.	Does this object belong to another object, or is it owned by another? Does this object own or contain any other objects?
Generalization/ Subclass	In this type of relationship, an object *is* a specific type of another object. These are often identified when different objects have similar properties. Often they can be combined, and one general object can be developed. For example, you may have a Server object, a Workstation object, and a Laptop object. They all share similar properties and can therefore be combined into one Machine object. Then, you can implement a Workstation object that uses only the properties specific to a workstation.	Is this object a type of another object?
User/ Collaboration	This is where objects employ the services of other objects. They aren't a specific type of another object, nor are they owned by another object. They simply rely on some other object's specific functionality or service. For example, a Car object might *use* a Fuel object to refuel. This Fuel object could also be used by a Truck object. Using our previous example, the Car and Truck objects could themselves be a type of MotorVehicle object.	Does this object use another object? Is this object used by another object?

relationships. The relationship types may have more than one name, as noted in ther first column of the table.

EXERCISE 10-7

Identifying Relationships

1. Using the Car object example, recall the objects you identified in Exercise 10-4. What objects have relationships? Do they all have relationships?

2. List the object relationships and identify the type of relationships they have. Don't forget to combine similar objects when possible into one general object. Refer to Table 10-1 if necessary.

CERTIFICATION OBJECTIVE 10.05

Incorporating Business Rules into Object Design

Business rules define the logic of how data is manipulated by your components. These rules mirror the way the business domain you are modeling operates or does business. Implementing the business rules and processing in business objects has three major benefits. Objects designed this way have the following characteristics:

- Easier to maintain
- Easier to enhance
- Easier to reuse

The majority of this business logic should be implemented in the middle tier or Business layer more specifically, as we will explore later in the chapter. The reasons for this are simple. Implementing the business logic in the middle tier allows developers to easily change and update the components as the needs of the business change without impacting the database or client application. Things such as validation edits can be placed in the Presentation layer to make the client application more dynamic. In addition, some rapidly changing rules, say a web-based application, may be more appropriately implemented in the interface itself to facilitate updates to changes.

Which objects you place the business logic in depend on the purpose of each object. For the most part, objects should be as self-contained as possible. By keeping an object's functionality limited to specific services, it allows the component to specialize and therefore be more reusable, on both a code level and a component level.

CERTIFICATION OBJECTIVE 10.06

Articulating the Purpose of an Interface Contract

The *COM (Component Object model)* establishes a standard by which objects communicate with one another. It describes a format in which COM servers expose their interfaces and how clients locate and use them. *Interfaces* are the methods that the object exposes and are the gateways of communication between objects. They are what allow objects to communicate with one another and exchange data. Without these interfaces, objects would not know how to request or provide services to one another. An interface therefore represents a contract between a client component and a server component.

Once the interface for an object has been established, and other objects rely on the known interface, it must be immutable. Changes to an object's internal implementation can occur as long as the interface to access this functionality remains unchanged. If the interface is changed, then client components that use the existing interface will break. If new functionality is needed in the component, it is usually best to implement it by adding an additional interface to the component.

Constructing an Interface Contract

An *interface contract* is a declaration of any preconditions for using the service, and the calling conventions. *Preconditions* are conditions that must exist prior to using the service. For example, a database with certain tables may need to exist in order for the service to return the requested data. *Calling conventions* consist of the syntax to employ the service, the input parameters it accepts, and the output parameters the service will generate.

The definition of the interface should be published before implementation of it has started. This allows development against this interface to proceed as a black box, without having to know anything about the internal implementation of the services. This provides a consistent standard to develop against. Once this interface is published, it becomes a contract between the client and the service and cannot change, even though the internal implementation of the service may change.

The Three Service Layers of the Application Model

In this section, we examine the three service layers. These layers are based on the services model, which is a way of designing an application as a set of specific functionality that is used to fulfill client or consumer requests. By modeling the application this way, a higher level of reuse can be achieved through better code and component reuse. The service's definition is the contract between the service and the client. It is this contract that allows for increased reuse and a more consistent development environment.

The three categories of services in the typical three-tier application are shown in the following table. We will explore them in further detail in the remaining sections.

Service Layer	Description
User Services	Also called the Presentation layer. It is where the user interface is implemented.
Business Services	Where the business rules and logic are implemented.
Data Services	Where data is stored. Defines the storage and retrieval of persisted data.

Figure 10-2 illustrates the relationship of the three service layers.

FIGURE 10-2

The three service layers

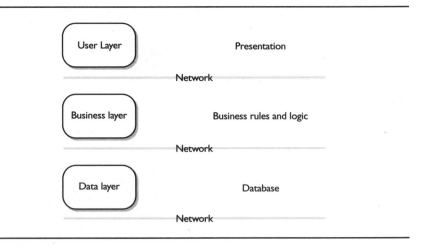

The User Layer

The *User layer* is the interface of the application. It provides the visual representation of data collection and display. In this layer, the interface is divorced from any implementation of the business logic, with the exception of perhaps some validation edits. Although these edits could be implemented solely in the Business layer, duplicating this logic in the User layer can make for a richer and more interactive interface. The User layer will provide for immediate feedback of the validation. If this logic is implemented only in the Business layer, the user will not receive any feedback until the data is saved via the appropriate service.

By excluding business logic in the User layer, we allow our Business layer components to be more self-contained and therefore more reusable and maintainable.

The Business Layer

The *Business layer* is where all of our business logic and rules are contained. They are encapsulated in the business components and are responsible for servicing the requests from the User layer. They act as the liaison between the Data layer and the User layer. When the User layer executes a business task, the Business layer is responsible for accessing the Data layer and retrieving or saving the data with the appropriate business rules being applied or enforced.

Because business rules can change, encapsulating them in components that reside in this layer allows for changes to occur without affecting the User layer or Data layer. In addition, business rules that are subject to frequent changes could also be placed in scripts, for example, in the case of a web-based application. However, this implementation does not provide the protection that compiled components do from prying eyes, since you could view the script's source code in the browser window. For example, say you have a service called "Calculate discount" which determines the discount provided to a customer depending on various factors such as buying patterns and the amount of revenue this customer has generated. If the decision is made to change the rules or logic that determine the amount of the discount, only the component needs to be updated. The User layer remains unaffected, since this logic is encapsulated in only this one component. Now, the next time the "Calculate discount" method or service is called by the client application (User layer), it will receive the newly modified service. This is also an example of where the interface or interface contract remains static, but the service's internal implementation changes to either improve performance or adapt to changing business rules.

The Data Layer

The *Data layer* is responsible for maintaining, accessing, and updating data, based on requests from the Business layer. These services may consist of one single data store, such as SQL Server or some other database, or they may be comprised of a variety of sources. For example, to fulfill a client (User layer) request, the Business layer may be requesting data from the Data layer that actually resides in a database, a mainframe computer, and a collection of other non-heterogeneous databases. However, none of this is important to the User layer; all it's concerned with is using the Business layer to request services.

Separating the Data layer from the rest of the application allows changes to be made to the Data layer without affecting the User layer or the Business layer.

exam
ⓦatch

Remember, the Data layer is not where your components will reside. Your components will be in the middle tier, or the Business layer. The Data layer is concerned with the storage and retrieval of your data into some sort of storage device, such as an RDBMS like SQL Server. Also, recall from earlier in the chapter that Microsoft Visual Modeler will display your components in a Data Services section, but this is not the same as the Data Services layer in a Distributed Application model.

CERTIFICATION OBJECTIVE 10.09

The Benefits of the Three-Tier/Three Service Layer Approach

Encapsulating and separating the functionality of the user interface, business logic, and data services into their own layers provides several benefits. As we have seen so far, this separation allows changes to be made to the individual layers without affecting the other layers. There are other benefits. Due to COM standards, application components are language-independent. In other words, they can be developed using any language as long as the language generates interfaces that adhere to COM standards. Components can be run on a central application server to ease development, deployment, and maintenance. Or, the components can be run on several application servers to spread the processing load to achieve better scalability. This is referred to as *load balancing*.

Database connections and resources are utilized more efficiently, since the database is interacting with only the application components and not all of the clients. Typically in a two-tier application, when a client connects to the database it connects early, when the user first logs on to the system, and the connection is held until the client logs off. Conversely, in a three-tier application, the component is responsible for the connection management and typically connects late or only when needed, and then releases the connection. On this note, database drivers such as ODBC drivers are no longer required on the client workstation, reducing client setup and maintenance issues.

Security is enhanced and simplified since access is done on a component basis and not by all the client applications. The middle-tier components are accessing the resources and therefore can be controlled more easily.

Accessing resources external to the application also becomes simplified, as this can be encapsulated within an application component. Now, external resources become application components in the eyes of the client application. Such details are now transparent and can be modified with no impact on the other layers.

As we can see, there are many benefits to designing an application in accordance with the three-tier/three service layer approach. Although it may involve more up-front design and planning time, the long-term benefits of easier maintainability, reuse, and scalability far outweigh those costs.

FROM THE CLASSROOM

Logically Speaking

The transition from the conceptual phase of application design to the logical phase provides the basis for all development efforts that will transpire from that point on in an application development project. Developing a strong logical design will not only reveal potentially large development pitfalls which can then be successfully navigated past, but will also provide a roadmap for developers joining a project later on and needing to come up to speed quickly.

Designing components as both stateless and of a sufficiently fine granularity are highly recommended factors that should be design considerations established or initially supported during the logical design phase. Knowing that any components designed to run within MTS should be stateless, for example, should initially be enforced within the logical design phase. Establishing a sufficiently fine granularity in provided services on a per component basis starts with the logical design phase. Simplicity in

component design can yield increased reusability, scalability, and extensibility.

During logical design, a strong correlation can be made between the proccess of denormalizing a database schema and the identification and design of components. For example, a customer's address can be simultaneously modeled logically as Customer and Address objects and in a database as Customer and Address tables, which are connected through a foreign key.

Following a proper three-tier distributed application development methodology can provide large increases in overall scalability and reusability of code components. It is important to understand the separation of User Services, Business Services, and Data Services when designing an application. Spending the necessary time on the logical three-tier design aspects will be well worth the effort.

—Michael Lane Thomas, MCSE+I, MCSD,
MCT, MCP+SB, MSS, A+

Using Paper Prototypes and Metaphors to Design User Services

The user interface is one of the most visibly important aspects of the application. This is the part that users can actually see and touch. They interact with it on a daily basis to perform their tasks. It doesn't matter how technically advanced or sophisticated your application is or even how fast it is. If your users don't like the interface and find it difficult to work with because it's not what they wanted or expected, then your application is a failure. Fortunately, using a three-tier approach affords you much flexibility when it comes to designing the interface. By using a component-based architecture, you can potentially have multiple user interfaces developed using a variety of technologies. For example, you might have a Visual Basic- or Visual C++-based interface, a web-based interface using Active Server Pages (ASP) and HTML, or even a Microsoft Office-based interface using components like Word and Excel.

However, understanding what the users want and how they will interact with the interface is often difficult to ascertain. This is where using common metaphors that are readily understood, as well as prototypes, comes in. It's possible to use the RAD features of development tools such as Visual Basic to design a quick and dirty prototype, but most often, using a simple paper-based prototype and examples of screenshots is easier—at least for the initial stages. It's easier to develop, and it's easier for the end users to understand and work with.

Designing paper prototypes does not have to get overly fancy. As long as they convey the goals of the user identified in the usage scenarios, and the users are satisfied and everyone agrees on things such as screen layouts and application flow, then these paper prototypes can be converted into an interface design document and used as the basis for the real thing. Use common metaphors when working with paper prototypes. Don't use computer jargon to explain application functionality to users. Use phrases such as "add an inventory item to the stock" and "add a customer to the customer list" instead of "create inventory item" and "add customer." Users will have an easier time understanding and relating to tasks when explained in everyday terms.

on the !job *Depending on your tool set and the environment you are developing for, whether it's a traditional Windows application or a web-based application, you may find that it is often easier and more productive to do your prototyping with something other than the tool you are developing in. For example, Microsoft Excel makes screen mock-ups a snap. Also, they're easy to distribute to end users involved in the design process, and most people are familiar with Excel. This facilitates the design process and can alleviate some of the burden from you as the developer, because your end users will be able to modify the mock-ups directly. This can often be an easier way for them to communicate their UI preferences as opposed to a verbal or textual description. As an added bonus, I find that one of the thorniest aspects to prototypes is reports. Users can't always tell you what they want, but they can usually show you!*

Object Refinement

As developers and end users work with the initial prototypes, it provides the opportunity to work through the usage scenarios developed in the conceptual phase. It allows the usage scenarios to be mapped to the actual tasks via the interface that users will be interacting with. This process will undoubtedly reveal changes that need to be made in the logical design of the business objects. This is not a sign of incomplete analysis, but rather a normal process, because the whole Application Design phase is an iterative process.

This *prototype phase* allows us to validate and refine the initial set of business objects we developed from the usage scenarios and requirements list. In terms of validating our logical design, it's important that for each usage scenario identified there is a corresponding object service that will perform the activity. Equally important is to make sure that every object and service listed in our logical design can be mapped back to a usage scenario. If they can't, then they may be unnecessary.

As we mentioned, the first set of objects identified is usually incomplete and sometimes incorrect. There are some things to look for when refining your object design. Objects should be specific and unambiguous. If the object is irrelevant to our application or beyond its scope, it can be omitted. Look for redundancy. Sometimes objects will share similar properties and can be combined into one object. Some properties may actually need to be broken out into their own business object.

EXERCISE 10-8

Object Refinement

1. Let's assume you've identified the following objects from a list of requirements: a Customer object, a Prospect object, and an Employee object. Which objects can be combined, and why?

2. While working with your end users on an initial prototype, you realize that there are several tasks they would like the system to be able to perform that were not identified in the usage scenarios you used to develop your initial set of objects. How do you proceed?

Risk Mitigation

Following a methodical and structured, yet iterative, approach to logical design is the best way to assure a successful logical design that correctly reflects the application's requirements, and will allow a successful physical implementation.

Perhaps the major source of risk in logical design is usage scenarios that aren't represented by an object and service, and conversely, objects and services that can't be traced back to a usage scenario. When this occurs, the conceptual view and logical view are no longer synchronized. Other risk factors to avoid are a lack of coordination with corporate development standards and architecture. If your logical design does not adhere to or correspond to the corporate development standard, it may make it more difficult to integrate your application. If your logical design is dependent on external systems, it is likely to be impacted when and if those external systems are modified.

EXERCISE 10-9

Risk Mitigation

1. You have integrated a feature into your logical design because it's new technology and you think it's cool. Do you think this poses any risk? If so, to whom?

2. Your logical design relies on an external system for some relatively static data that will be used for monthly reporting. How might you design your application to eliminate the risk to your application if this external system is modified?

Identifying Dependencies

Dependencies can arise between your business objects as you progress through the logical design process. Although it's desirable to design your business objects so that they are as self-contained as possible, this is not always possible. Therefore, you must take into account these dependencies. Some dependencies are based on the nature of the relationship. For example, an Orders object would assume the existence of a Customer object, which would use the Orders object's services. In this example we could say that the Customer object "has" an order or, conversely, the Orders object is "owned" by a Customer object. We looked at these types of relationships earlier in the chapter. It's important to identify these dependencies and redesign the object so that these dependencies are minimized by abstracting services that are likely to change often into their own object. Minimizing dependencies, to the extent possible, will ease component maintenance when business rules change.

In this section, we examine various aspects of these dependencies. First we'll take a look at how objects can trigger events in response to activities. Next, we examine the steps required to coordinate object dependencies and how timing can affect them. And finally, we review common business rules and explore how best to accommodate them in your design.

Triggering Events

Business objects have services and attributes (methods and properties). In addition, objects can also trigger events in response to certain conditions.

These conditions may exist as a result of a particular method call or service being invoked, or they may be the result of a particular property being set.

Events provide a form of notification that lets the client application or calling object know that something has occurred or informs them that a service they invoked is now complete. For example, as a result of calling a Delete Inventory method on an object, the inventory level may fall below the minimum stock level. This may fire a Trappable Warning event notifying the calling object or the client application. It may even be an external system that could receive this event.

Coordination Requirements

Because objects can have dependencies upon one another, either through the types of relationships they have or, less directly, through events, it's important to anticipate and account for these dependencies in your logical design.

These dependencies may be presuppositions of certain conditions. We saw this in our example in the previous section, with the Orders object relying on a Customer object to consume its services. Taking this one step further, the Orders object and Customer object may both depend on the existence of a database table to persist their information. All of these dependencies, albeit somewhat implicit, must be accounted for and clearly documented in the logical design.

Timing

The subject of timing relates to the order in which dependencies are invoked. Each dependency between objects that you have identified in your logical design will have an order of invocation. In other words, there is a logical path of dependency that must be adhered to in order for the objects to function as expected. Using our Order and Customer objects again, there is an issue of timing here as well. An order cannot be placed for a new customer until there is a valid customer. Likewise, a Customer object cannot be deleted if that customer has outstanding orders.

Common Business Rules

There may be objects in your logical design that use the same business rules in their services. These business rules are prime candidates to be abstracted into their own encapsulated object or objects. By abstracting these common business rules into a common business object, you minimize the impact on your application when these rules change. As with the design of your other objects, try to keep these new objects as self-contained as possible and anticipate which rules will be the most dynamic or subject to change in the future, and put them in their own object.

By abstracting common business rules into self-contained objects, you can avoid having to make changes to multiple components when the business logic for a service changes.

CERTIFICATION OBJECTIVE 10.12

Assessing the Potential Impact of the Logical Design

In this section, we explore the potential impact of the logical design on various aspects of a distributed application and the characteristics that define a distributed enterprise application. These same attributes also determine the level of success achieved once the logical model has been implemented physically and the application is in use. In today's business environment, it's critical that a high level of success is achieved in each of these aspects.

We'll begin by looking at the issues surrounding performance. Next we examine the areas of application maintainability, extensibility, scalability, and availability. Finally, we look at the issues of security and how they relate to a distributed component environment.

Performance

Forecasting the performance of a distributed application can be difficult. Therefore, it's necessary during the logical design phase to design your application with this in mind. It's important to look at all layers of the three-tier model to ascertain the impact on performance. Some items to review would be the following:

- What type of interface is being used? And are the target workstations capable of running this efficiently?

- What language will be used to develop the components?

- What type of data store is being used? Will it provide adequate performance?

- How many users are anticipated? Can the network handle the throughput?

- Where will the application components reside? On the workstations, or on an application server in the middle tier?

- Have all the objects been consolidated to remove any redundant objects and business rule processing?

Maintainability

Application maintenance is as important as any other part of the development cycle. A lack of planning can have serious negative implications later in the cycle when it comes time to modify the application. Designing objects that are well-thought-out and as self-contained as possible will provide for easier modification when it comes time to change the implementation of a service or the logic in a business rule. This also applies to the user interface. Building a solid foundation of self-contained and well-organized objects will allow for the development of multiple interfaces if necessary.

Extensibility

Does the logical design you've developed lend itself to being *extensible*? In other words, in addition to being maintainable, is it possible to add additional features to the application and its components without impacting other parts of the application? Remember from our discussion on interface contracts that your components will rely on other components and consume their services through their interface. Part of being extensible is being able to add functionality without breaking existing functionality. Depending on whether you are making changes to the internal implementation of an existing service, or adding additional services, will play a key role in how this functionality is added. If you are adding new services, it is best to add an additional interface to the component as opposed to changing an existing one and breaking any component that currently relies on it. If you're simply modifying the internal implementation of an existing service, then all you need to do is update the component with the new one. That's the benefit of a distributed component design.

To the extent possible, try to anticipate future needs and design them into your initial logical design.

Scalability

Scalability is how well an application performs as the number of users increases. Scalability is critical to handling the large volumes of requests made on a system in an enterprise environment. You can increase scalability to a limited extent by throwing more powerful hardware at a poorly designed application. This is limited however, and is by no means a substitute for proper application design. When an application is properly designed and the only change necessary to handle more users is to increase the capability of the hardware, the application is considered scalable.

There are several factors to keep in mind during logical design that will contribute to a more scalable application. Since this is a distributed application, your components will probably be running within some sort of object broker such as MTS (Microsoft Transaction Server). MTS provides several features that increase the scalability of your components. By using

MTS you can take advantage of such features as *connection pooling*. This allows your components to connect to data sources using a previously established connection. This dramatically reduces the overhead and wait time associated with connecting to a database. This can also be taken advantage of further by making sure your components request a connection on an as-needed basis, only when necessary, and then release it as soon as they are done with it.

Object pooling (not supported in this version of MTS 2.0) will allow your components to be recycled. In other words, MTS will take the component from a pool of available objects, if any exist, saving the overhead of COM instantiation; otherwise it will create a new instance of one. Currently, MTS creates objects on a just-in-time basis when the component is requested by a client. When the client is finished accessing the components method(s), it calls the MTS interface IObjectContext method SetComplete or SetAbort to instruct MTS to deactivate the component. This resets the component's internal variables to nothing and removes it from the server's memory while the client still holds a pointer or reference to it. The client can then call another method on the object, in which case MTS reactivates the object. As far as the client is concerned, this is the same object it used before.

Your objects can further take advantage of MTS by developing stateless components. *Stateless components* do not maintain state between method calls and call either SetComplete or SetAbort after each method call. This will allow MTS to activate and then deactivate the component more quickly. This allows for fewer server resources to be consumed and for a shorter amount of time, contributing to overall scalability.

Availability

How well your components perform and handle unusual exceptions will contribute in some part to the availability of the system. In component terms, this would be referred to as its *robustness*. Your components should anticipate errors and other unexpected scenarios and handle them gracefully through error handling, ideally without affecting the state of the application or other components, and without corrupting data. As we mentioned in the previous section when we discussed scalability, MTS also provides protection against data corruption through the use of transactions. MTS provides full two-phase commit transaction services and handles the complexities for you. By enrolling your components that comprise a transactional unit into an MTS transaction, you are guaranteed that your components will either succeed as a unit in modifying the target data, or fail as a unit. MTS provides the transaction management infrastructure allowing you to focus on the business services and robustness of your component.

Security

There are many options when it comes to implementing security. The exact configuration you choose depends largely on the application and the environment in which the application will run. Your application must provide protection for the application components and the data store, and it must ensure privacy of data for your users.

In terms of securing your middle-tier components, you can use DCOM (Distributed Component Object Model) for authentication. If you decide to use MTS for any of the reasons we've discussed, then you can also use MTS to handle authentication of the middle-tier components. Connections made to a data store such as SQL Server will be made through your middle-tier components. Depending on the identity that these components are running under, you have several options for authentication with SQL Server.

You can use SQL Server's standard security, which will log the component in with a standard SQL login, or you can use integrated security and map NT logins to SQL logins, taking advantage of the NT security model. In addition, MTS provides role-based security for the secure activation of packages. MTS packages are a group of related components. With role-based security or, as the documentation refers to it, declarative security, roles are defined for the package through the MTS Explorer and allow you to assign various levels of access to components and methods within the package based on these roles. Roles are then assigned NT users and/or groups of users. When components within the packages are requested by a client during runtime, they are subject to the security granted to the role of the package.

CERTIFICATION SUMMARY

The process of logical design involves mapping the user requirements gathered in the conceptual design phase to business objects and services. This high-level abstract model allows us to focus on the overall vision of the application and see the many aspects of the application in a more organized fashion. A solid logical design is critical in correctly identifying the required objects and facilitates development of later phases.

The objects and services required in the logical phase can most easily be identified from the user requirements and usage scenarios by identifying the objects and verbs, respectively. When identifying the necessary objects, keep them as self-contained as possible. A component's functionality is referred to as its granularity. It can be coarse or fine. If it's coarse, it contains many methods. If it's fine, it contains few methods.

The most common technique for identifying objects is to pick out the objects from the usage scenarios. There is no one right set of objects. What's important is that they reflect the business domain you're modeling. To identify the services of the objects, pick out the verbs in the usage scenarios. The properties or attributes of the object are what it needs to know and what information needs to be tracked. Objects have the following three types of relationships: ownership (owns or has), generalization (is), and user (uses).

Business rules define the logic of how data is to be manipulated by the objects in your logical design. Placing business logic in components allows the rules to be easily modified without impacting the rest of the application.

Interfaces are an agreement between objects or client and server as to how a service is to be consumed. Once defined and published, they become an immutable part of the service. An interface contract is a statement of any preconditions for using the service and the calling conventions of the service. The calling conventions detail the syntax, input parameters, and output parameters.

The three service layers consist of the User layer, Business layer, and Data layer. The User layer is responsible for the presentation of the application or user interface. The Business layer is where the components that contain the business services reside, and the Data layer defines the storage of persisted data.

Benefits of a three-tier/three service layer approach include component encapsulation. Business logic or services can be altered within one component without affecting other components. Middle-tier components can take advantage of pooling of database connections, can be run on a centralized application server to achieve load balancing, and can ease maintenance and deployment. Security is enhanced and simplified, along with access to external systems.

Building paper prototypes allows developers to work through the usage scenarios developed in the conceptual phase and begin to validate the logical design. At this point, object refinements will be discovered. Logical design risks are reduced since there is a validation process of mapping the logical design to the conceptual design and vice versa. The major source of risk is when the logical design and conceptual design do not agree.

Some object dependencies are based on implicit relationships such as an ownership relationship. However, minimizing object dependencies to the extent possible will help ease component maintenance when business rules change, particularly in relationships with external systems. Consolidating common business rules into self-contained objects will help avoid makng changes to multiple components when the business logic for a service changes.

There are many factors to weigh when assessing the impact of your logical design. To achieve success, your application must be efficient, maintainable, extensible, scalable, reliable, and secure. Taking these factors into consideration early in the development of the logical design phase will help you ensure that the application successfully meets these criteria.

TWO-MINUTE DRILL

- ❑ *Logical design* is the process of taking the user requirements that we gathered in the conceptual design phase and mapping them to their respective business objects and services.

- ❑ Once your objects have been identified, you need to organize them in terms of the services they provide, and the relationships they have with the other objects.

- ❑ Visual Modeler is a graphical object modeling tool included with the Enterprise Editions of Visual Studio 6 and Visual Basic 5. Visual

Modeler facilitates the entire process of creating your application model, from designing and organizing objects and their relationships to creating classes and generating code.

❑ As you begin the preparation for logical design, there are several key considerations that also happen to be benefits of a three-tiered application design model: scalability, reliability, and efficiency.

❑ The functionality that you design into your objects is referred to as *component granularity*. The more activities or services that your objects support, the coarser their granularity.

❑ *Objects* are the things from our requirements that we are modeling.

❑ *Services* are the objects' behaviors, or more technically, methods of the object.

❑ The term *component* is not to be confused with *object*. An object and component are not the same thing, although you may see them referred to as such. However, an object is instantiated from a class, whereas a component is precompiled binary code.

❑ *User requirements* is the list of items that the application needs to be able to accomplish.

❑ *Case analysis* is the process of modeling how the user or users interact with the system.

❑ *Services* are an object's behaviors. These behaviors are the actions that they perform and are executed through the use of methods.

❑ *Interfaces* are the methods that the object exposes and are the gateways of communication between objects.

❑ An *interface contract* is a declaration of any preconditions for using the service, and the calling conventions.

❑ *Preconditions* are conditions that must exist before the service can be used. For example, a database with certain tables may need to exist in order for the service to return the requested data.

❑ *Calling conventions* consist of the syntax to employ the service, the input parameters it accepts, and the output parameters the service will generate.

❑ The *User layer* is the interface of the application. It provides the visual representation of data collection and display.

❑ The *Business layer* is where all of the business logic and rules are contained. They are encapsulated in the business components and are responsible for servicing the requests from the user layer.

❑ The *Data layer* is responsible for maintaining, accessing, and updating data based on requests from the business layer.

❑ *Scalability* is how well an application performs as the number of users increases. Scalability is critical to handling the large volumes of requests made on a system in an enterprise environment.

❑ *Object pooling* (not supported in this version of MTS 2.0) will allow your components to be recycled.

❑ The ability of your components perform and handle unusual exceptions will contribute to the availability of the system. In component terms, this would be referred to as its *robustness*.

SELF TEST

The following Self Test questions will help you measure your understanding of the material presented in this chapter. Read all the choices carefully, as there may be more than one correct answer. Choose all correct answers for each question.

1. Which statement best describes logical design?

   A. Logical design involves determining what attributes objects will have.

   B. Logical design is the process of identifying object behaviors.

   C. Logical design involves identifying objects and services from the conceptual design.

   D. Logical design is the physical implementation of conceptual design.

2. How is the logical design influenced by physical limitations?

   A. The logical model must be in accordance with available hardware.

   B. You must know what kind of hardware the components will run on before designing them.

   C. Available hardware capacity will determine the components' degree of granularity.

   D. Logical design is independent of physical limitations.

3. What is a benefit of logical design?

   A. It can facilitate later phases of design.

   B. It helps in planning hardware requirements.

   C. It provides for good documentation.

   D. It helps establish the database design.

4. Which attributes are present in a distributed application?

   A. Scalability, reliability, transaction management

   B. Scalability, reliability, efficiency

   C. Performance, scalability, transactions

   D. Efficiency, transactions, scalability

5. Why should objects provide as many services as possible?

   A. It simplifies development.

   B. Performance will be increased because there will be fewer components.

   C. They should contain attributes instead of services whenever possible.

   D. They shouldn't. They should be as self-contained as possible.

6. *Component granularity* refers to which of the following statements?

   A. The number of properties a component has

   B. The number of services a component provides

   C. The physical size of the component

   D. The number of input parameters a method call takes

7. What is the easiest way to identify objects from the usage scenarios in conceptual design?

   A. Nouns are usually the best way to identify objects.

   B. Names are usually the best way to identify objects.

   C. Any phrase that contains a verb.

   D. This is what the prototype is for.

8. What is the difference between an object and a component?

   A. There is none.

   B. An object has services; a component has methods.

   C. An object is instantiated from a class; a component is precompiled binary code.

   D. An object has properties; a component doesn't.

9. What is a usage scenario?

   A. It's the same thing as user requirements.

   B. The way in which the application uses the hardware.

   C. It's the way in which users will interact with the system.

   D. It describes the needs of the users.

10. What characteristics must an object posses?

    A. It must be something the system needs to know about. In addition, it must have behaviors and/or attributes.

    B. It must have behaviors and/or attributes.

    C. It must be able to store and retrieve data.

    D. It must rely on other objects.

11. What are services?

    A. They are the things the object knows.

    B. It's how an object performs an activity.

    C. Services determine how the data will be saved.

    D. They are the actions an object performs.

12. What are properties?

    A. They are the things the object knows.

    B. The rules that determine how a service is carried out.

    C. Properties represent attributes.

    D. They identify relationships between objects.

13. What are the three types of relationships objects can have?

    A. Ownership, Generalization, User

    B. Ownership, Container, User

    C. Ownership, Generalization, Subclass

    D. Ownership, Subclass, Container

14. What is business logic?

    A. It determines where the components will reside.

    B. It determines how many services an object will have.

    C. It defines how an object will manipulate data.

    D. It defines how an object will retrieve data.

15. Where should business rules be implemented?

A. In the User Services

B. In the database, using stored procedures and triggers

C. In the Presentation layer

D. In the middle tier

16. Which statement is true? (Choose all that apply.)

A. An interface is a way of defining object properties.

B. An interface should be immutable.

C. An interface is just another term for service.

D. An interface defines an object's services.

17. What are the three service layers?

A. User layer, Business layer, and Data layer

B. User layer, Presentation layer, and Data layer

C. Presentation layer, Data layer, and Data Services

D. User layer, business services, data layer

18. Which phrase correctly identifies the user layer?

A. The User layer contains user-related business logic.

B. The User layer defines the data access strategy.

C. The User layer defines the user interface.

D. The User layer is the logical representation of the Presentation layer.

19. Which best describes the Business layer?

A. It acts as the liaison between the Data layer and the User layer.

B. It acts as the liaison between the User layer and the Presentation layer.

C. It acts as the liaison between the User layer and the business logic.

D. The Business layer is only in the Logical Design model. It is not physically implemented.

20. The Data layer consists of which of the following?

A. One database only

B. A variety of data sources

C. Any number of data sources, as long as they are all the same type

D. Any data source as defined by the application requirements

21. What is the main benefit of the three-tier approach?

A. It uses more hardware.

B. It's easier to implement and deploy.

C. It's easier to maintain and adapts better to changing business needs.

D. There is none.

22. What is a benefit of prototyping?

A. It allows developers a chance to test the usage scenarios.

B. It gives developers a chance to learn new development tools.

C. It lets users see an early cut of the application.

D. It allows users to express what they need the system to do.

23. What is the major source of risk in logical design?

  A. Not finding enough objects for the nouns.

  B. Finding more services than are needed.

  C. The conceptual design and logical design don't reflect each other.

  D. The conceptual design and logical design are too complex to model.

24. How can you avoid having to modify multiple components when a business rule changes?

  A. Implement all the rules in the User layer.

  B. Store them in the database as triggers.

  C. Use a two-tier approach instead.

  D. Encapsulate them into their separate objects by commonality.

25. Which phrase indicates that the application is scalable?

  A. Adding more users causes a major performance hit.

  B. Adding more hardware seems to help slow performance.

  C. When only hardware capacity is increased, more users are able to use the application.

  D. More connections must be made available to handle more users.

MICROSOFT CERTIFIED SOLUTION DEVELOPER

11

Integrated Design

CERTIFICATION OBJECTIVES

T his chapter takes you through the Solutions Design model, and shows how it works with the Application, Team, and other models in the Microsoft Solutions Framework. We'll discuss issues dealing with the conceptual, logical, and physical design of an application. We'll also discuss user and programmatic interfaces, which are used by the applications and components you create.

Focusing on the design perspectives of the Solutions Design model, we'll discuss data model development, and discuss issues dealing with database design. Because most applications running on Windows access data in some way, this is a particularly important topic.

CERTIFICATION OBJECTIVE 11.01

The Three Tracks of Solutions Design

Business solutions are based on the needs of customers and users. *Solutions Design* is a valuable model that provides different perspectives on how to design a business solution, and is essential in designing component-based solutions. As we've seen in previous chapters, the Solutions Design model is made up of three separate processes:

- *Conceptual design,* which identifies an application's requirements through specifications and usage scenarios.

- *Logical design,* which maps these requirements to abstract business objects and the services these objects need to provide.

- *Physical design,* which maps the business objects and services to physical components.

Although information from one perspective is applied to other views, it's important to remember that these aren't stages with clear cutoff points. Remember though, that you should always start with conceptual design and then proceed through the other design views; these perspectives will often overlap, and you may find the need to return to a previous perspective. As you're coding on one component of your application, you may still be identifying requirements for another component in an application. This is a benefit of the model: it is flexible and doesn't force you to complete one step before proceeding to another step.

The conceptual design process is made up of several tasks, which are used to determine and validate user needs and perceptions of what the application should be. These tasks consist of identifying users and their roles, gathering input from users, and validating the design. As we saw in Chapter 9, this includes creating user profiles, data gathering techniques, and documenting usage scenarios. Through these various tasks, you're able to acquire, document, evaluate, and validate the user's vision of the completed application.

The information obtained through conceptual design, that is used to create usage scenarios, is passed forward into the logical design of the application. Through this perspective, the structure and communication of elements in the solution are laid out. Elements like the user interface, logical databases, objects, and services are also identified and designed. The tasks that make this possible consist of identifying business objects and services, defining the interfaces, identifying business object dependencies, validating the logical view, and revising and refining the design. Each of these tasks is essential for the logical design to be completed, so that information from the design can be passed to the physical design.

The first of the five tasks in logical design is identifying business objects and services. *Business objects* are abstract representations of real-world things or concepts (such as orders and customers). You can consider something to be a business object if one or both of the following are true:

- It is something (or someone) the system is required to know about.

- It is something (or someone) the system gets information from, or provides information to.

Business objects are essential because they define what data will appear in the finished application.

The second task of logical design is defining the interfaces to be used in the product. When defining interfaces in the logical design, you aren't designing a user interface that the end user interacts with, filled with buttons and textboxes and so forth. Instead, you're outlining what's required to call on a particular service. Defining an interface requires listing a statement of preconditions and conventions (syntax, and input and output parameters) needed to call the service. In doing this, you define what one component needs to do to call on the services of another particular component.

The third task is identifying business object dependencies. When one business object calls on services in another business object, this is called a *business object dependency.* In other words, one business object depends on the services and existence of another business object. For example, let's say you were designing a database application for a credit card company. When a customer buys a product, the amount of the sale needs to be deducted from their credit limit. This means the sale depends on the existence of the customer account in the database. If the customer didn't exist, then the sale couldn't be deducted from the credit limit.

The next task is validation, where the work done to this point is compared to the conceptual design. This ensures that the logical design still matches the requirements in the usage scenarios. If these requirements aren't met, then the logical design is considered invalid.

Finally, revision and refining of the logical design deals with any problems, and improves the design. This can occur several times before the work performed in the logical design perspective is applied to the physical design of the application. Through these multiple iterations, any problems with the design can be hammered out. This keeps errors in the logical design from being passed on to the physical design, where they could adversely affect the finished product.

Physical design is where the business objects and services defined in the logical design are mapped to actual components that make up the software product. These abstractions of business behavior are transformed into a design of how the system will actually be implemented. While the conceptual and logical design perspectives are technology- and vendor-independent, physical design applies the abstractions in logical design to the physical constraints of technology. How the system is implemented and how it will perform are both issues of this perspective.

In physical design, business objects and their related services are mapped to physical components. Components are created using development languages like Visual Basic, Visual C++, Visual FoxPro, and Visual J++. In creating components, you encapsulate one or more services into

- An executable, which has the file extension of .EXE
- A dynamic link library, which has the file extension of .DLL

Because these services are encapsulated into the component, you need a way of accessing them. Services available from components are accessed through programmatic interfaces. Using standards like COM, DCOM, or ActiveX, you create one component that calls upon the services of another component. The calling component is called a *consumer*, because it consumes the services supplied by the other component, which is called a *supplier*.

Components can be reused in other projects that require the same functionality. For example, if you had a component that calculated sales tax in one program, you could use the same component in other programs that required the same function. This saves you the trouble of having to rewrite the same code over and over in different projects, or different areas of the same program.

In creating this network of consumers and suppliers of services, the Solutions Design model incorporates the use of the Application model. As mentioned in Chapter 6, Solutions Design ties together the Process, Team, and Application models. We'll discuss Team roles in Solution Design later in this chapter, and we've discussed the Process model in previous chapters. When it comes to the creation of components, the Application model is valuable.

The Application model, which is also known as the Services model, organizes an application's requirements into specific services. Generally, the requirements of an application fall into one of three tiers:

- *User Services,* which is associated with the user and/or programmatic interface.
- *Business Services* (and other middle-tier services, which can include such things as graphic services), which is associated with business rules and logic.
- *Data Services,* which is associated with the data accessed by your application.

It is through the User Services tier that the end user interacts with your application, through a user interface and/or programmatic interface. Through this tier, the functionality of application sequencing and display is handled. Business Services, and other middle-tier services, control sequencing and enforce business rules and processes.

Data Services stores and manipulate the data, and handles data operation transactional integrity. It's through the Database Management System (DBMS) in the Data Services tier that Create, Delete, Read, and Update services take place. When data is passed back up the tiers, Business Services transforms the data into information so that user services can properly display or use it.

User Interface

The user interface provides the end user with the ability to view and manipulate data, through units of application logic. It is associated with the User Services tier, which is also known as the Presentation layer. The user interface can be an executable program that a user starts on a workstation, or a separate component that's placed on a container object like a Form. A Form is a container for other controls, which appears as a window to the end user when your program is compiled. For example, you could place an ActiveX control on a Form, which might allow the end user to view or manipulate data in a database. As we'll see later in this chapter, there are many different controls you can use in a user interface for navigation or interacting with data.

Business Process

The middle tier of the Application model is comprised of a number of services, but is primarily associated with Business Services. The services on this tier apply business rules to tasks that an application performs, and are used to enforce transactional integrity, business rules, and control sequencing. For example, let's say that you're designing a banking program that allows people to withdraw money from an account. Before the money can be withdrawn, the application checks to see if there is enough money in the account to make the withdrawal. If there is, the transaction continues; if not, it is cancelled. In such an application, there is a business rule of needing to have more than the amount withdrawn. When business rules are added to a program, they are added at this layer.

The middle tier is also known as the *Application Server tier*. It is the layer between the user interface and a database. Generally, this is where a web server will reside in Internet applications, and where business objects (COM components that retrieve and process data) are instantiated. Because business rules change more often than the actual tasks a program needs to perform, they are prime candidates for being a component of a program. By having such rules incorporated into components, the entire program doesn't need to be changed, just a component of that application.

Database

Most applications on the market today need to access some form of data, whether it's in a database or some other data source. This makes the Data Services tier of the Application model important to most of the products you design. The Data Services tier is also called the *Data Source tier*, and is responsible for defining, maintaining, and updating data. It provides Create, Read, Update, and Delete services, as well as such retrieval logic as order and joins. This allows Business Services, which is the consumer of Data Services, to be shielded from having to know where data is located, or how to access and implement it.

When a request is made for data, Data Services is responsible for managing and satisfying the request. This ability to manage and satisfy requests can be implemented as part of the database management system (DBMS), or as components. The data is then passed back up to the middle tier, which transforms the data acquired from Data Services into meaningful information for the user. The data is then presented to the user through the user interface.

Designing a User Interface and User Services

Imagine going to a library, and finding that the building has no windows or doors. While the books you need are contained inside, along with librarians and services for information, someone forgot to design a practical way of getting to these resources. Sound silly? Perhaps, but this scenario isn't unheard of in application design. Teams can spend considerable time creating a functional database, and applying business processes to various components, but if the product has a poorly designed user interface, it isn't functional. The user interface is the way end users access information through your program. Having a poorly designed user interface is like building that inaccessible library; the system may technically work, but no one can access it.

In designing the user interface services for your application, it's important to keep the end user in mind. The user should always feel in control of the application, rather than feel that the application is controlling him or her. The interface should follow the design methodology that's common to Windows applications, so that if the user has experience with one application, they can quickly navigate and use the software you've designed. This means setting up menus, controls, and other forms of navigation in a fashion that's similar to other Windows programs on the market.

If the user has difficulty with a control or feature, you should provide online user assistance. This includes implementing such things as ToolTips, help files, and status bars in your application. This enables users to solve problems with the help features in your program, rather than bothering a Help Desk every time they experience difficulties.

It's important to remember that the user interface is the "face" of your application. This is what the user sees, and is really an interface between the human and the computer. As such, you want to put your best face forward. It's important to create an esthetically pleasing interface for the user, one which is both functional and friendly. For example, color schemes should not be hard on the eyes, navigation schemes should be consistent, and the controls and menu design should be intuitive. In addition, the controls you choose should be appropriate to the functions they provide. The design of your user interface and services is the most visible display that you've designed a quality product, and helps to ensure the overall success of your project.

on the
Job *It's important to have a good design for your user interface the first time you release your product. Make sure the user interface is set up the way you want it, so you don't need to drastically change it in future releases. If you have a peculiar way of navigating or the menus are designed differently from other Windows products, users may grow used to these peculiarities. When you try to correct the design in later releases, they may find it difficult to adjust to the new interface.*

Specifying Navigation Tools for the User Interface

To work with a user interface, you need a way of accessing and navigating between different objects, like Forms and controls. Without a consistent and effective way of getting from Point A to Point B in a program, users are stuck looking at a single screen. Implementing navigation into your application is done with controls and menus. After adding these to a Form, code is then added to the control or menu item. Then a user is able to navigate through an application, and get to other Forms, dialog boxes, or applications.

Menus are common to user interfaces, with a menu bar displaying across the top of an application window, below the title bar. Menu bars contain *menu titles*, which identify groups of commands, called *menu items*, that have similar purposes. For example, under a Help menu there would be help items, and items under a File menu would do things like open and close files. When you click on a menu with your mouse pointer, a drop-down menu appears containing these menu items. Upon clicking on a menu item, program code associated with that item is executed.

What your menu bar and drop-down menus contain is highly dependent on the functionality of your application, and how the user will interact with your application. For example, if your interface doesn't use multiple windows, you wouldn't have a Window menu title. Similarly, if your application doesn't require users to insert graphics, text, or objects into the interface, you don't need an Insert menu title in your title bar. In determining the menu items that will appear in the drop-down menus, determine what commands will be provided to the user, and then organize them accordingly.

While the content of the menu bar and drop-down menus varies from product to product, there are certain conventions that you should adhere to. File should always be the left-most menu title on your menu bar, and contain the commands that allow the user to exit the program, close windows, and open or create new files. If the application requires editing features (such as cutting, copying, or pasting items from the clipboard), you should place the Edit menu title directly to the right of the File menu title. The right-most menu title on your menu bar should be Help, which contains online user help. Other menu titles appearing on the menu bar would be placed between these.

Command buttons are another common element of a user interface. They have the appearance of push buttons, and are used to begin, end, or interrupt a process through programming code that is added to the button. In other words, when the button is clicked, the code associated with that event is executed. In terms of navigation, you could associate code with the button to open a Form, so that users can move from one part of the application to another.

While it is important to provide users with the ability to invoke the commands associated with menu items and command buttons, it is equally important to know when to prevent a user from invoking a command. For example, let's say you created a user interface that took a user step-by-step through the process of entering customer information. On the user interface, you placed command buttons with the captions Back and Next on them, which respectively moved the user back to a previous step or on to the next step. If the user were on the first step in the process, he or she wouldn't be able to move back. At that point, your Back button should be disabled or invisible. When a button or menu item is disabled, it appears greyed-out and nothing will happen when the user clicks on it. When it is invisible, the button or menu item doesn't even appear on the screen. This keeps a user from trying to execute code associated with a menu or control, when you don't want them to. By not implementing this into your design, users may think something is wrong with the control, or it may cause an error when improper code is executed.

When navigating to the objects on your interface, different users will use different methods. One user may use a keyboard, while another uses a mouse, while still another uses a pen. With these devices, the user is able to do the following:

- Identify an object, through such things as ToolTips, which are discussed later in this chapter

- Begin, end, or interrupt processes associated with objects through programming code.

- Access an object, to do things such as entering text into a TextBox object.

Because different devices will probably be used to navigate your interface, it follows that this can affect how you will design it. You need to know what these devices are, and how they'll be used to interact with your application.

Microsoft considers the mouse the primary input device for applications running under Windows. When a user moves the mouse, a pointer moves in the same direction on the screen. This allows the user to move the mouse up, down, and sideways to navigate to your menu and other objects on your interface. When the user reaches an object they want to access, the buttons on the mouse device are clicked or double-clicked. This invokes the click event of the object, so that code associated with that event is executed.

Using a mouse takes some coordination. New users often have trouble moving the mouse on their desk to get the pointer on the screen to go where they want. Because of this, new users will often use a mixture of mouse and keyboard input to get your application to do what they want.

Trackballs are another common input device, but are considered a mouse. While a ball located under the mouse device rolls over a pad, moving the pointer on the screen, a trackball looks something like a mouse turned upside down. The trackball device remains stationary on the user's desk, and the user rolls their hand across a ball on top of the device. This results in the same behavior as when a mouse is moved. Buttons located on the trackball device allow clicking and double-clicking.

Pens are devices that allow the user to navigate as they would with a mouse, but also allow them to draw and write on the screen. When navigating, the user moves the pen without touching an input surface, and a pointer moves across the display screen. When used as a writing or drawing tool, the pen touches the input surface and this causes an action called *inking*. Inking is where the pen's input causes lines to be drawn on the screen. While the pen allows the user to navigate as they would with a mouse, Table 11-1 illustrates how the behavior of the pen is different from that of a mouse. No clicking or double-clicking is used, because pens don't come with buttons that provide the same functionality as a mouse.

Pen devices are often used in settings that need the functionality of a drawing utensil and the navigation abilities of a mouse, such as in Graphic Art or Advertising departments. Because the pen is used as both a pointing device and a drawing or writing tool, there may be times when the user will need to switch between these operations. In other words, while they are drawing something in a window of your application, they may need to point to a menu

TABLE 11-1	Action	Description
Behavior of a Pen, and How It Is Similar to a Mouse Device	Pressing	Pressing the tip of the pen to the input surface identifies an action, which is similar to that of a mouse press.
	Tapping	Pressing the tip of the pen on the input surface and then lifting it without moving the pen, results in an action identical to clicking button 1 (e.g., left mouse button) on a mouse. This is usually used to select an object, activate a button, or set a text insertion point.
	Double-tapping	Tapping the pen-tip twice in rapid succession results in an action identical to that of double-clicking button 1 on a mouse.
	Dragging	Pressing the tip of the pen on the input surface and moving the pen, you are able to perform one of two actions: dragging or drawing. During inking sessions, you can move the pen to draw or write on the screen. During non-inking sessions, you can use the pen to drag objects in a fashion equivalent to dragging an object with a mouse.
	Barrel tapping	Holding down the barrel button of the pen while tapping has the same effect as if you were using a mouse and clicking mouse button 2.
	Barrel dragging	Holding down the barrel button of the pen while dragging has the same effect as if you were using a mouse and dragging with mouse button 2.

or object on the screen. Because of this dual functionality, you should incorporate some way of switching modes of operation for the pen in your software. To do this, you could use timing, so that if the user holds the pen in the same spot for a predetermined time, it will switch modes. You could also place a button on the toolbar or a shortcut key that allows the user to change whether the pen is used as a drawing tool or pointing device.

Each of the devices we've discussed requires some sort of visual interaction. If the users of your application include visually impaired or blind users, they won't be able to see (or may have trouble seeing) pointers appearing on the screen. In such cases, a keyboard will be the primary method of navigation.

This isn't to say that keyboard navigation is used only by the visually impaired or blind. After the mouse, a keyboard is the second most common device used for navigation in Windows applications. The keyboard allows a user to move from object to object and across fields of text in an application.

By pressing the appropriate keys on a keyboard, users are able to move about the window, and/or jump from one object to another. On a keyboard, there are four ARROW keys and the TAB, HOME, END, PAGE UP, and PAGE DOWN keys. These are called the *navigation keys*. By tapping one of these keys, you move an increment. For example, by pressing the RIGHT ARROW key, the insertion point moves one character to the right. If you press a navigation key and the CTRL key simultaneously, this increases the increment. Pressing the RIGHT ARROW and CTRL key at the same time moves the insertion point one word to the right.

In applications that use TextBoxes, control buttons, and other objects, users can navigate from one object to the next by pressing the TAB key. The order that determines which object you move to when pressing the TAB key is determined by the Tab Index property of that object. When you put a control on a Form, the Tab Index is set in an order corresponding to that in which the controls are arranged. For example, let's say you put a command button, a TextBox, and another command button on a Form. By default, when the user presses the TAB key, he or she will move from the first button to the TextBox, and then to the final command button (i.e., the order in which these objects are placed on the Form). To change the Tab order, you would change the value of the Tab Index. The value of the Tab Index starts at zero, so the first object you want the user to start from would have a Tab

Index of 0. The next object they move to when pressing TAB should have a Tab Index of 1, and so on.

When setting the Tab order of objects in an application, you should set the Tab index of objects to correspond to the way a person reads. Since people who read English read from top to bottom, and left to right, the object at the top left of your application interface should start the Tab order. The last object you want the user to Tab to should have the highest Tab Index value.

You can also aid keyboard users by implementing access and shortcut keys in your application. Access keys allow a user to move to a particular menu item or object by holding down the ALT key simultaneously with another key. You can tell if a menu item or title has an access key used, because the letter for that access key (the one you press at the same time as the ALT key) appears underlined. For example, to access the File menu, you would know to press the ALT-F key combination. This opens the File menu, allowing you to move to a menu item by using navigation keys or another access key. Shortcut keys are different from access keys, as you don't need to navigate to a menu item to execute it. By holding down the CTRL key and another specific key, you can invoke a command and execute code automatically. As we'll see later in this chapter, access keys and shortcut keys are commonly used by experienced users of an application.

EXERCISE 11-1
Specifying Navigation Tools for a User Interface

Baltimore Access Technologies is a company that provides applications for the blind and visually impaired. They have asked you to design the navigation for the user interface of a database application that will be used by their clients. The application will be a Wizard, moving from one screen to the next. Audio instructions will be provided on each screen. Based on the user needs of this application, you will need to decide which types of user navigation will be appropriate.

1. Determine what tools for navigation will be used. Because the users will be blind or visually impaired, you could dismiss any tools that require visual interaction. For example, the mouse and barrel pens would be dismissed for navigation. Write each of the appropriate tools on a piece of paper.

2. Because you will be using a keyboard as the navigation tool, determine what forms of navigation will be appropriate. List each of the navigation methods that would be appropriate.

3. Determine which navigation methods will be appropriate, based on the type of application used. While a keyboard can access menus and menu items, such navigation methods may not be appropriate for the Wizard application that is being developed.

4. Review the navigation methods you've listed, and compare them again to the user and application requirements of the case above. If they meet the requirements, you've identified which navigation methods can be used.

Determining the Input Validation Procedures to Integrate into the User Interface

No matter how intuitive you make your interface, one fact remains: people are unpredictable and imperfect. Users may make all sorts of mistakes. They can easily put the wrong information into a field. It's easy to input a customer's last name in a TextBox designated for customer first names, or leave an address field blank, making it impossible to ship orders or contact them. Worse yet, entering data into the wrong field could lock up your program, which could happen if a user entered a customer's surname into a field that expected numerical input. Just imagine your application trying to add sales tax to the data input of "John Doe."

Input validation procedures ensure that the correct information is put into fields, and fields that require information aren't left empty. Such procedures check the input entered into TextBoxes and other fields before they're processed. These procedures can be added to the object itself, and check input as it's typed, or added to an OK button (or similar command button) that the user has to click on before the data is processed. If the information is not what's expected, then a warning—such as a message box—should appear informing the user of the error. This provides as a failsafe, keeping incorrect or insufficient data from being saved to a database, or erroneously processed.

Determining Where Input Validation Procedures Should Be Used

Hard Exam Systems takes calls from people who want to become Hardly Certified Professionals. The exams they book usually cost $100. As a promotion, they offer coupons worth $100. Some exams cost more than others, so two coupons occasionally cover the cost of a single exam. At no time are more than two coupons allowed to be used. The order form interface is shown here:

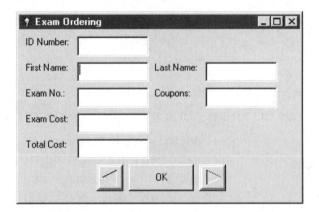

Users of this interface either type in an ID number or the customer's first and last name to bring up an existing account when the OK button is clicked. ID numbers start with the first three letters of the customer's last name, followed by a six-digit number. They then type in the exam number the customer wishes to take, which automatically generates the exam cost. The cost, minus the value of the coupon, is shown automatically in the total cost field. What input validation would you add to this screen? (The answers to this exercise appear just before the Self Test at the end of the chapter.)

Looking at each individual field, and the criteria given in the explanation above, try to determine what type of input validation is required. On a piece of paper, write the field and the input validation it will have. Follow these steps to determine what input validation is required for necessary fields:

1. Determine what conditions must be met for certain fields. For example, the first three fields (TextBoxes) have a common use.

2. Determine whether certain fields should reject certain types of input such as strings, integers, and currency.

3. Determine if any fields shouldn't accept any type of input. Some fields only return information, and shouldn't accept any input.

4. Determine which fields (if any) require input in a specific format. For example, in some applications, certain fields, such as zip code or postal codes, require a specific amount of information, such as five numbers for a zip code.

5. Determine what ranges of numbers are acceptable for certain fields; over a specific value or under a specific value could cause errors.

Evaluating Methods of Providing Online User Assistance

Online user assistance is the answer to a user's frustrated cry of "Help!" and an important part of software product design. There is nothing more frustrating and overwhelming to the user of a new application than trying to understand how to get your program to perform necessary actions, what certain buttons are for, and why a feature is even included in the software. Online user assistance allows the user to get the answers they need, without having to pick up a book or the phone.

You can provide many types of online user assistance. Some online help displays information automatically (based on the context of commands), while other help requires the user to make an explicit selection before the information is presented to them. Regardless of the type of user assistance you provide, the information should be presented in a simple, efficient, and relevant fashion, so that users won't get lost in the instructions. Once you've dealt with computers for any length of time, it's easy to forget that not everyone knows as much as you do. Because of this, it's vital that you relay the information in a clear and concise manner.

In evaluating the methods of online user assistance, it is important to know what information to include and what questions need to be answered. For example, if a user were to move the mouse over a particular object, you wouldn't want detailed instructions for that object to appear. In such a case, a brief explanation of what that object is, or what it is used for, would be all that's necessary.

In this section we'll discuss three common types of user assistance: status bars, ToolTips, and Help files. These are basic methods of online help that you've probably seen in a number of applications. In covering them, we'll discover how, where, and why they're used, as well as discuss some common guidelines for what information should be contained in them.

Status Bars

You've probably seen status bars when using Microsoft applications, such as Word, Internet Explorer, or Windows Explorer. These are bars that reside at the bottom of the user interface, and contain information about selected objects, their context, or the status of an operation. Being a contextual form of user assistance, status bars answer such questions as what an object is, why that object might be used, or how your application is proceeding with a current operation.

Status bars can be used to display descriptions of a command or object. As illustrated in Figure 11-1, if you used your mouse to point to the Select

FIGURE 11-1

Status bars provide contextual user assistance.

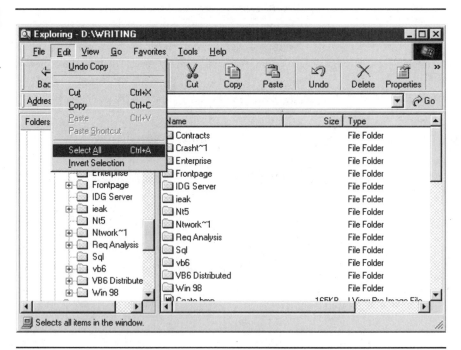

All command in the File menu of Windows Explorer, the status bar would say, "Selects all items in the window." If the object or menu item contained additional commands, you should use the status bar to explain the type of commands contained in that menu or object. For example, in a word processing application, if you moved your pointer over a Format menu, your status bar should display something like "Contains commands for formatting text."

As its name indicates, status bars are also meant to show the status of a current operation. For example, if you had a program that downloaded files from an Internet server to your workstation's hard drive, the status bar could display the status of your download. In this case, when your application is downloading the third in a series of ten files, it might state "Downloading 3 of 10 files." In showing the status of an ongoing process, you can also design the status bar to include a progress indicator control, or similar methods of providing feedback. This gives the user a graphical display of how much of a file has been saved, printed, or whatever the current operation is. While such information can be provided through dialog or message boxes, status bars allow the user to see how the operation is progressing, without having the current window obscured.

It's important to provide constructive information in your status bars. This means not only providing descriptive information, but also explaining why a particular command is unavailable or disabled. If a user is attempting to use the Paste command in the Edit menu of your application, they may wonder why it appears greyed-out. In such a case, you could provide status bar information saying "This command is not available because no items have been Cut or Copied." By providing such messages, you will enhance the user's experience with your application, and save them from their own mistakes of overlooking steps when performing a task.

When writing status bar messages, you should avoid any jargon. There is nothing worse than help text that contains words a user may find difficult to understand. Remember what it was like when you first started with computers. Don't use words that only a programmer or sophisticated user would understand.

A good approach to writing online help is to write it as if it's for a specific person. Think of a person you know who has little knowledge of computers or applications, and then write your text as if you were talking or writing to that particular person. Once you've approached it in this manner, then start your text with a verb and describe the action your command performs. For example, "Deletes the selected text."

Because the status bar is located at the bottom of your user interface, and most (if not all) of your toolbars, menus, and other commands will be at the top of the interface, you should consider using a status bar as a secondary means of help. You should never use status bars as the sole or primary means of user assistance. Since the status bar is so far away from such commands, users will often not notice information displayed in the status bar. As such, you should implement other forms of online help, such as ToolTips.

ToolTips

ToolTips are small, colored boxes containing information about your application. They appear when the user's mouse pointer rests on an object. You've probably seen a ToolTip when you rested your pointer on a button in a toolbar, and the name of that control appeared in a small colored box. This is the most common use for ToolTips, although they can be used for any control. For example, you can use ToolTips to display navigational information, or indicate what action a particular control would take if it were clicked. As shown in Figure 11-2, you can use ToolTips to inform the user that clicking a Back button will take them to a directory they were previously in.

You can add ToolTips to your user interface by using the standard toolbar control in Visual Basic or Visual C++. In using the toolbar control, support for ToolTips is automatically provided. You can also use a ToolTip control for use with other controls added to your user interface.

If you want to make your own ToolTip control, you should adhere to the way ToolTips are displayed with the standard control. ToolTips should display when the mouse pointer rests for a short period of time on a control, and should display after the pointer. When the user moves the pointer off the control, or after a specified timeout, the ToolTip should disappear. If the user moves the pointer onto another control, the first ToolTip should disappear and be replaced by the ToolTip of the new control. Be sure to

FIGURE 11-2

ToolTips are boxes containing useful descriptive information. They appear when a mouse pointer rests on a particular object.

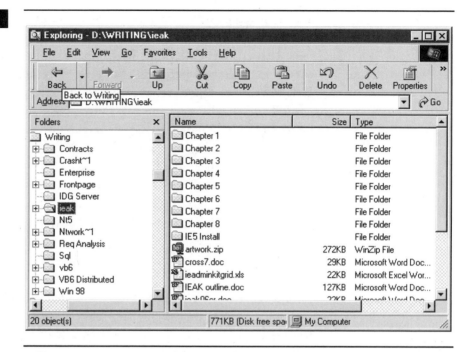

follow the standards used by other applications so users will have better access to your ToolTips.

Help Files

When people hear the words "user assistance," they often think of Help files. Help files contain organized information that is displayed when the user presses F1, selects a Help feature from the Help menu, or performs another action that invokes a Help display. When incorporating Help files into an application, you provide the user with a source of reference or online documentation. This can serve as a user's guide or documentation of the software's features, containing text and graphics to enhance the user's experience with your product, and lower the need for users to call help desks for assistance.

There are two kinds of Help files you can use for your software product: standard (which has the extension .hlp) and HTML (which has the extension .chm). Standard Help files are stored in a binary format, and are compiled with a special compiler. HTML Help files are created using the Hypertext Markup

Language, using a text editor (like Notepad) or a graphical editor (such as FrontPage 98). Once the HTML document is created, a special compiler is used, such as the HTML Help Workshop that comes with Visual Studio 6, to convert the document into an HTML Help file. Once you've created your Help file, the file must then be associated with your application through whatever development program (e.g., Visual Basic or Visual C++). This is done by setting the Help properties of your application, and can be done at design time (when you're creating your application) or programmatically.

When designing Help files, and/or the interface they are to be displayed in, you should follow certain conventions and standards. These not only explain how to design the interface used to display your Help files, but how the information should be presented. By providing the user with Help files in a manner consistent with other Windows applications, you keep them from requiring assistance on how to use the Help features in your product.

If you wish to design an interface for your online Help, you should include features similar to those in Figure 11-3. While this figure shows two different interface designs, upon closer inspection you'll notice similar features in each. The Help file is displayed in a main help window, and not in a pop-up window. The top of the interface has a menu bar with File, Edit, and Help entries, as well as toolbars and commands for navigation and printing topics. "Bookmark" or "Favorites" features are also provided, allowing a user to mark particular topics that he or she uses frequently. Each interface also provides a method of accessing the Contents of the Help file, which list topics as a Table of Contents would in a book. In addition to these standard features, other functions may be added to the interface to assist the user in navigating to different topics.

When writing Help files, it is important to include a title for the topic. A title is used to identify the topic, and provides a landmark in Help for locating particular topics. Any title you choose should match titles used in the Topics section of your browser.

Hyperlinks can also be used in your Help file, to allow users to jump to other Help topics or provide additional information. When the user clicks on a hyperlink, information in the window changes to another topic, a topic in another Help file, or another area in the same topic. Hyperlinks appear as underlined text when the Help file is displayed, but you can also use graphics or buttons to provide the same functionality.

FIGURE 11-3

Two examples of common
interfaces that display
Help files

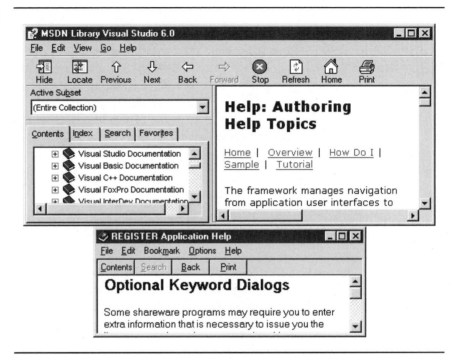

EXERCISE 11-3

Evaluating Methods of Providing Online User Assistance

Hard Exam Systems uses the GUI shown here for booking exams:

New employees are having trouble understanding what to do on the
screen. For example, they don't realize they should enter either the ID

number *or* the first and last name (not both) to specify a customer account. They also don't realize what the OK button is for (to bring up the user account after entering either the ID number or customer's name). The two arrow buttons (for navigation) are another source of confusion. Truly baffled users would appreciate lengthy instructions on how to use the GUI. The company would like you to determine what forms of online user assistance to provide. (The answers to this exercise appear just before the Self Test at the end of the chapter.)

1. Determine which type of online user assistance can best provide a brief description. This can be used to explain how the navigation buttons function.

2. Determine which type of online user assistance can provide brief instructions on how to use fields. These can be used to briefly explain what users should do. What is a drawback of this type of assistance?

3. Determine which type of online user assistance will provide longer instructions, and detailed help. Where should the menu to access this Help reside on a menu bar? What function key could be used to access it?

Establishing Appropriate Types of Output

When computers were first becoming commonplace, they were predicted to save trees by the forest-load. After all, with data being stored electronically, there would be no need for things to be filed away on paper. As the sales of printers and plotters will testify, paper is still one of the most common forms of output in desktop and distributed applications.

When creating applications with Visual C++ or Visual Basic, you can implement a standard Print dialog box into your application. From information obtained from the operating system your application runs on, it can determine what printer to print a file to. It also allows the user to choose how many copies to print and format, and which pages. Code is added to the dialog box to print in the format selected.

Output isn't limited to printers. In designing your application, you need to determine whether output needs to be sent to printers, routed to e-mail, or faxed. You also need to investigate whether output from your application should be saved as a particular file type. For example, if output from the application would then be used by an off-the-shelf program, such as Microsoft Excel, you would need to save the output as an Excel spreadsheet. If output were to be displayed on the Internet, you would save it in an HTML file format. In designing your application, it is important to discuss how output from your program will be used, and what formats will be required.

Establishing Appropriate Types of Output

Baltimore Access Technologies has a staff of 100. Fifty of these people are either blind or visually impaired, and "read" information through a web browser on computers with voice synthesizers. Thirty of the employees are often on the road, and connect remotely to the network through the Internet. The remaining 20 staff members prefer to read information on paper printout, and require copies of documents to be filed on cabinets. A copy of the information needs to be archived on the intranet server. What types of output are appropriate for the application you're designing? (The answers to this exercise appear just before the Self Test at the end of the chapter.)

1. The needs of the user, and those of the application, determine appropriate types of output. Determine what special needs must be met by your application.

2. Determine what types of output will address the needs of users.

3. Determine what special features can go into your application to address these needs.

CERTIFICATION OBJECTIVE 11.03

The Value of Prototypes

A picture paints a thousand words, and therein lies the value of prototypes. Prototypes are used as mock-ups of what you propose the final product will look like. A prototype is a user interface with little or no code associated with the objects and commands of your interface. This allows end users, customers, and interested parties to have a visual representation of what you understand their needs to be and plan to incorporate into the user interface. Users and team members discuss elements of the user interface before the application is actually built. If any of these parties have a problem with elements of the user interface, they can bring them up during the discussion, allowing issues in the design to be addressed early in development.

As mentioned in Chapter 9, prototypes are used to validate application design. This enforces that the designer has actually understood what the business needs, as well as the needs of the end user. Because the user interface is how the end user interacts with the program, it is vital that any application you create has a good user interface. By demonstrating a prototype, you can say, "This is what it'll be like," and allow beta users to address what they love and hate about the interface.

In creating a prototype, you are basically building a smoke-and-mirrors version of your program. While it looks like an application, you don't want to put very much code into it. After all, if the entire interface or parts of it are disapproved, you have to throw that out and start fresh. As such, you should only put the most basic code into it. Allowing the command buttons to navigate to other screens, or loading a canned graphic to show the results of a graph, will adequately demonstrate the functionality of the application without writing very much code. When creating a prototype, it's important to remember that you're building a mock-up of the application, and not the application itself.

If you don't want to create a working prototype that has code written into it, you can still benefit from the simple display of what the interface will look like. You can create screenshots, print them out, or display them through a program like Microsoft PowerPoint, and allow users to view the proposed interface. By printing out the prototype, users can jot down their comments directly on the printout. However, no matter which method of demonstrating a prototype you use, you will almost always get valuable feedback from your intended audience.

on the **job**

There have been more than a few occasions where a demonstration of a prototype meant the difference between landing or losing a software contract. When trying to pitch a business solution to a company, prototypes are great for demonstration purposes. Rather than proposing an application with a feature list, you can actually show them what they're getting. By bringing printouts of the user interface, or a working prototype, you can quickly impress a client.

Constructing a Prototype Interface Based on Business Requirements, Interface Guidelines, and Organization Standards

In constructing a prototype user interface, your first consideration is determining what kind of prototype you want to create. Prototypes fall into two categories:

- Throwaway
- Evolutionary

A *throwaway prototype* is created for the sole purpose of getting feedback from users, and validating the design of the user interface. In other words, when you're done with it, you throw it away. An *evolutionary prototype* is incorporated into the building of the actual product. This means you use the approved parts of the prototype as the user interface for the actual business solution.

Throwaway prototypes have virtually no code attached to objects and commands in the user interface. When a user clicks on a menu item, either nothing will happen, or a Form or pre-made graphic will appear. For example, let's say you created a spreadsheet program. When you clicked a command button to transform figures into a graph, a simple graphic would appear. The prototype wouldn't actually do any computations. Throwaway prototypes allow the user to see what the program is meant to do, but don't actually do anything. After validating the design and getting the user feedback, the prototype is discarded.

Evolutionary prototypes usually contain more code than the throwaway type. This is because the team realizes they will build the actual program on top of the prototype. This isn't to say they do loads of work writing code into the prototype, because any code written may be discarded if the prototype is disapproved. However, the evolutionary prototype often includes the basic code that's easy to write and has little chance of being tossed away. Developers will often include features like Open, Close, and Exit that are basic to the operation of the application. There is little chance of such features being disapproved, and they will almost definitely be passed forward into the final product.

No matter which type you construct, it's important to remember that you're making a representation of the final product. As such, you apply the business requirements, user interface guidelines, and organizational standards that dictate the development of the final product. In other words, you follow the design as if you were creating the real thing. If security specifies that users shouldn't be able to save data to their floppy, don't display a Save to A: feature in the prototype. If organizational standards require a customer ID number for orders, show a field for this information on the user interface. If your prototypes are convincing, users can (and often do) think you're showing the actual final product. They may get annoyed if their requirements seem to be disregarded in the prototype. It is vital to show an accurate representation of the final product through the prototype.

Establishing Appropriate and Consistent Use of Menu-Based Controls

In the section on navigation, we discussed some of the ways in which you can establish appropriate and consistent use of menu-based controls. Menu titles and items should follow the layout used by other Windows applications, so the user isn't confused by your menu layout. In addition, items should be placed under the appropriate menu title, so users aren't constantly searching for an item.

Because a prototype is "smoke and mirrors," you usually don't need to apply programming code to the items appearing under menu titles. If a particular tool appears under the Tools menu title, you can have no code associated with that item, or have it open another Form that shows what the interface for that tool will look like. If you do attach code to a menu item, try to keep it as simple as possible. Remember, you may have to change that item, or throw out the interface once users have finished reviewing the prototype. The main point of using menus in your prototype is to show what the menus in the interface will look like, not to create the menu system for the finished product.

When users navigate from one Form to another, the setup of your menu should always be consistent. While some menu items or menu titles may not need to appear on certain Forms, those that do appear should be in the same place as other Forms the user has seen. For example, let's say the first menu bar of your user interface has the following menu titles: File, Edit, View, Insert, Help. When a user moves to another window of your interface, the titles should appear in the same order, and not like this: File, View, Insert, Edit, Help. Mixing menu titles and items around is very confusing to a user.

Establishing Appropriate Shortcut Keys (Accelerated Keys)

Shortcut keys, which are also called *accelerated keys*, allow users to quickly access features of your product. Rather than having to navigate to a menu title, access the menu, and then select a menu item, users can press a combination of keys on their keyboard to access the same command. For example, let's say you had an Undo feature under the Edit menu of your application. Rather than accessing this item from the menu, it's common for applications to allow users to press the CTRL key and Z key simultaneously. CTRL-Z allows the user to undo their last action. This allows users who are more comfortable with their keyboards, such as power users, visually impaired or blind users, or users who grew up on DOS, to invoke commands without using the menu system, toolbars, or controls of your application.

Commonly used commands are prime candidates for shortcut keys, and they are easy to implement by using the properties of your control of menu system. Because it is easy to apply shortcut keys to commands in the user interface, you should consider implementing them in prototypes that evolve into the actual product. This keeps you from overlooking adding the shortcut key later, when code is being added to the user interface. When a shortcut key is applied to a menu item, the keys to use automatically appear to the right of the menu item. For example, a shortcut key to print would appear beside the menu item as Print CTRL-P. This is useful in both throwaway and evolutionary prototypes, as it shows the user that shortcut keys will be implemented in the final product.

To keep from confusing your users, you should use common shortcut keys in your application, and not use those keys for invoking other commands in your application. For example, CTRL-Z is a common shortcut key to undo a previous action in Windows applications. As such, you shouldn't use this combination of keys for other functionality in your application. Table 11-2 shows a listing of such common shortcut keys.

Access keys are often confused with shortcut keys, but they are quite different. Access keys allow the user to access a menu title, item, or object by pressing the ALT key with another key. When an access key is applied to menu titles, items, and objects, the letter to press with the ALT key is underlined, such as File. In this case, you would press ALT-F to open the File menu. Access keys allow keyboard users to navigate your application quickly without using the mouse. In general, applications should be

Shortcut Key	Action
CTRL-C	Copies the highlighted text
CTRL-O	Opens a file
CTRL-P	Prints
CTRL-S	Saves the file
CTRL-V	Pastes the highlighted text
CTRL-X	Cuts the highlighted text
CTRL-Z	Undoes the last edit or action
CTRL-ESC	Accesses the Windows Start menu
CTRL-F6	Displays the next child window in an MDI application
CTRL-ALT-DEL	Reserved for system use. Examples of its use include bringing up the Close Program dialog in Windows 9x, and restarting the machine in DOS/Windows 3.x.
SPACEBAR	Equivalent to clicking mouse button 1
ESC	Cancels the most recent action
F1	Displays contextual help
SHIFT-F1	Displays context-sensitive help (i.e., "What's This?" help)
SHIFT-F10	Displays the currently relevant pop-up menu.
ALT	Activates or deactivates the menu bar
ALT-TAB	Switches to the next primary window or application, or bring up the window to switch tasks
ALT-ESC	Switches to the next window
ALT-SPACEBAR	Displays a pop-up menu for the window
ALT-HYPHEN	Displays a pop-up menu for the active child window in an MDI application
ALT-ENTER	Displays the property sheet for the current selection
ALT-F4	Closes the active window
ALT-F6	Switches to the next window in an application (between modeless secondary windows and the primary window)

Shortcut Key	Action
ALT-PRTSCN	Captures a screenshot of the active image to the clipboard
PRTSCN	Captures a screenshot of the entire desktop to the clipboard

TABLE 11-2

Common Windows
Shortcut Keys *(continued)*

designed so that shortcut keys can be replaced by a sequential series of access keys.

In creating menu systems, it is easy to implement access keys by putting an ampersand (&) before the letter to be used as an access key. Due to this ease of implementation, you should incorporate access keys into the prototype. If they aren't used, end users will usually jump at the fact that the interface doesn't have certain letters underlined in the menu system. This gives an incomplete look and feel to the prototype, which is something you want to avoid.

EXERCISE 11-5

Constructing a Prototype User Interface

Jim Hardley and Bob Goode have hired your team to design and develop an application. A member of your team has created the prototype of a screen (shown here) to be included. (The answers to this exercise appear just before the Self Test at the end of the chapter.)

1. Determine if the prototype uses menus appropriately.

2. Determine if the prototype uses shortcut keys appropriately.

3. What other changes would you make to improve the design of this interface?

4. Using the development tools you're familiar with (i.e., Visual Basic and Visual C++), create a corrected version of the prototype with appropriate and consistent use of menus, access keys, and other elements of the user interface.

CERTIFICATION OBJECTIVE 11.04

The Significance of Metaphors

A *metaphor* is a term or phrase that suggests a resemblance to something else. Metaphors convey an image. For example, "The Internet is a vast spider web with threads connecting people all over the world." Metaphors can be used for objects in your application. You've probably noticed some metaphors in using Windows and Windows applications: for example, files holding data are stored in folders, which can be stored in cabinet files (like filing cabinets). This allows the user to associate such elements with non-computer items they've had experience with. Users are able to work with the object as a metaphor, relying on the representation and not knowledge of the underlying technology.

When designing your application, you should try to apply metaphors to the objects that are used. Icons used for toolbars should properly represent what they're used for. For example, an icon of a trashcan represents deleting an item, a floppy disk represents saving a file, scissors for cutting, and a clipboard or paste can for pasting from the clipboard. This allows the user to automatically associate the metaphor with a distinct action. Any original features appearing in your application should also follow suit. In doing so, the user has a better understanding of how to use your software, without needing to constantly refer to user assistance.

Developing Data Models: Database Design Activities

A business solution that accesses data won't be of much use if the database has a poor design. To design a database that works effectively with your program, you need to determine and define the input data. This is what data modeling is all about. Data modeling is where you define the structure of your database, through a process of:

1. Identifying the data and data requirements of the business.
2. Documenting this information.
3. Implementing the requirements into your application's design.

Through this process, you're able to gather and incorporate into your design valuable information that will enhance your application. This includes such things as data types to use in the database, data integrity, and, as we'll see, other integral pieces of information necessary to the successful design of a database.

The first step in creating a data model is reviewing the existing data structures used by an organization. This allows you to see how data is currently stored and used. By reviewing this, you can determine if the current data models and processes meet the requirements of your application, or if a completely new data model needs to be created.

Identifying data and data requirements is an important first step in the design of your database. This looks at what data needs to be accessed and stored, and the associated processes going along with it. Identifying data and its associated processes can also affect such things as output requirements, and the design of certain aspects of your application. For example, if customers need to access the ordering system over the Internet, it will not only affect how security will be set up in the database, but also determine that the information will be accessed online. In this example, data accessed by these clients would include the product, price, and description data stored in the database. In addition, they'd need to input some sort of customer information. By evaluating the processes used to access data, and whether data needs are required but not being met, you can determine how your database should be designed.

When interviewing users and analyzing the structure of the current database, document what kind of data will be used in the new database design. Data describes the people, places, and things that will be stored in the database. These items can be customers, employees, cities, products, and so on. When documenting these items, you should include the following information, which will be used later in your design:

- The name of the data item—for example, company, city, and state
- Description of the item
- Data ownership, which explains who will be responsible for the data
- Characteristics, which explain attributes of the data
- Processes, relationships, and events, which explain how the data is created, modified, and used

Through this information, you are able to combine these items into groups of data, identify how they relate to one another, and plan how they will be used.

Grouping Data into Entities by Applying Normalization Rules

Once you've identified the data that will be used, you need to organize it into an efficient database. After all, databases aren't mishmashes of information. They consist of tables, keys, columns, rows, and relationships. A process called *normalization* is used to organize and refine the data.

Normalization is a set of rules that the logical database design should satisfy. These rules are called *Forms*, and they ensure the proper design of your database. These Forms include the following:

- First Normal Form, where you determine that there are no duplicated groups or multi-value columns in the database.

- Second Normal Form, where you ensure that the non-key fields in your database depend on the entire primary key, and not just part of it.

- Third Normal Form, where you determine that non-key fields don't depend on other non-key fields.

- Fourth Normal Form, which requires that independent data entities are not stored in the same table when those entities have a many-to-many relationship with one another.

- Fifth Normal Form, which dictates that you should be able to reconstruct an original table from the tables created from breaking up the original table.

In the sections that follow, we'll show how to design the logical database so that it adheres to the rules that make up normalization. We will discuss only the first three Forms, as the last two are often disregarded in database development.

Normalization starts with the data you identify, and groups it into elements that make up the database's structure:

- **Entities** Representations of concepts or ideas, created from the values of its attributes. Of the specific types of entities, there are Associative, Kernel, and Characteristic. *Kernel entities* are entities representing core concepts. They are strong entities, and can exist in the database without the existence of other entities. *Characteristic entities* are entities that provide characteristics of another entity. They are weak entities, and thereby can't exist in the database without the existence of a kernel entity. *Associative entities* (also called *intersection entities*) are entities that associate two or more entities. As we'll see later, they are used to reconcile many-to-many relationships into two one-to-many relationships.

- **Attributes** Properties of an entity. These are the data elements that define the characteristics of the entity.

For example, an entity could be you, and the properties that make up you as a person would include height, weight, age, and sex. When applied to your database structure, the entity would be a table. The attributes would be the cells, fields, or object properties that make up the data entity.

In your database, you'll need to choose a specific attribute, or a combination of attributes, that uniquely identifies that particular entity, and no others. This is called an *identifier*, but is also known as a *primary key, key,* or *property value,* depending on the database management system that you're using to create the database. Identifiers are used to allow entities to be unique from one another, as they can often have identical attributes. For example, let's say you were creating a database of employees. Unless the company consists of two people with unique data, many of the entities making up the database will have identical attributes. Two or more people may have the same name, many will be of the same sex, others will work in the same department, and so on. To keep two or more entities from being confused with one another, an identifier is used. In this case, the identifier could be a social security number (or, for Canadians, Social Insurance Number), an employee number, or any other attribute that will be unique to any specific entity.

Database tables are then grouped into databases that are used by your application. To keep information from being repeated in your tables, you determine what information is repeated. For example, if you were creating a database of customers and orders, you would find that many customers are ordering the same products. These products could have attributes of a name, size, order ID, and so forth. To keep this same information from appearing over and over again in a table, you would separate the information into two tables: one for customer information, and the other for product information. Normalizing the one table, to create two related tables, keeps data from being duplicated.

While we'll see how normalization is used to set up relationships between tables in the next section, it's important to recognize the main purposes of normalization:

- Eliminating duplicated and redundant information from tables.

- Accommodating future changes to the data structure.

- Minimizing the impact of these future changes on applications that access the database.

Because normalization eliminates duplicate information from tables, it creates an efficiently designed database for your application. However, normalization alone generally creates databases that are inefficient performance-wise. As we'll see later in this chapter, *denormalization* is used to increase performance.

exam
ⓦatch

Normalization is a relational database design theory that is fairly complex. It's based on a branch of mathematics called set theory, on which entire chapters and books have been written. Fortunately, for the exam, you don't need that level of in-depth knowledge of normalization. You do need to know how to use normalization to group data, understand the rules of normalization, and other concepts covered in this and other sections of this chapter. In addition, while being originally created as a theory applied to relational databases, it's also common practice for indexed files.

EXERCISE 11-6

Using Normalization to Group Data into Entities

Using normalization in this exercise, we'll break a database into different entities, attributes, and tables. Because not everyone reading this book will have a DBMS, such as Access or Paradox, you can use the tables just ahead.

When interviewing the owner and staff of a local video store, you're told that it is common for customers to special-order videos. In taking orders, customers are set up with their own customer ID number, and information on their name, address, and phone number is taken. The customer requests a particular movie, which is currently organized in a purchasing book by an order number, and has information on the movie's name and price. As a service to our customers, we also want to be able to search the database for movies currently and previously ordered by the customer.

1. In the following table, write one attribute in each column. This will identify the attributes you can group into entities.

Attributes						

By looking over the interview information, we can see that the different attributes consist of the customer ID, customer name, address, phone, movie ID, movie name, and price.

2. By identifying redundant information, determine which attributes can be grouped into entities. In looking at the information from our interview, we can see that customers will probably order more than one movie. This means if we were to use a single table, customer information would be repeated many times for the same table. As such, we need to break the single table into two tables: one titled Customers, and the other titled Movies. Do this in the tables provided here.

By looking over the data from our interview, we can see that customers are one entity and movies are another. The customer ID number, name, address, and phone number would apply to the customer entity, while the order number, movie name, and price would apply to the movie entity.

3. Determine which attribute of the entity will be used as the identifier. In looking at the different attributes, we can see that the customer ID number can be used as the identifier for the Customer table, while the order number would be the identifier for the Movie table.

Choosing a Foreign Key to Enforce a Relationship Between Entities to Ensure Referential Integrity

In the previous section, we showed how tables use identifiers to uniquely identify data entities. When one column in the table is used as an identifier, it's called a *primary key*. If more than one column is used as an identifier, it's called a *composite* or *compound primary key*. Whether one or more attributes is used, the primary key is used to identify the rows that make up a table.

In addition to primary keys, there are also *foreign keys*, which are columns or combinations of columns with values that match the primary key of another table. The values of a foreign key are often unique and copy those of the primary key in the other table. However, as we'll see in the next section, this isn't always the case.

exam
ⓦatch

Don't confuse foreign keys with primary keys. Primary keys identify rows that make up the table, while foreign keys are used in relationships to reference other tables.

Using the primary key of one table, and the foreign key of another table, you can link two tables together in a *relationship*. Relationships link two tables together, by having the primary key of one table referenced by the foreign key of another table. For example, let's expand on the earlier exercise of the video ordering system. As you recall, we identified attributes, grouped them into entities, and split the data into two tables. We did this so that we wouldn't have to constantly re-enter the customer information (name, address, and phone number) for every video that was ordered. In the customer table, we used the customer ID as the primary key. By setting up a new column in the Movies table called customer ID, we can use this new column as a foreign key. All customer IDs entered into the foreign key would match those of the primary key in the Customers table, through *referential integrity*. We'll discuss referential integrity in greater detail later, but it should be mentioned here that when referential integrity is set on a relationship, you ensure that for every row existing in a foreign key, there is a corresponding row in the primary key. Depending on the DBMS used, a relationship is either set up automatically (as is the case in SQL Server), or you would need to manually set up a relationship between the two tables, by having the customer ID entered into the foreign key (the column in Movies) point to the primary key of the Customers table. When a staff member enters the customer ID into the foreign key, it references the information for a particular customer. In other words, if the customer ID entered into the foreign key is 21, it would reference the row of the other table that matches the primary key of 21. By having the relationship between the primary key of one table and the foreign key of another, we are able to reference information between them.

We'll elaborate on the different relationships possible for tables in the next section, but this illustrates the importance of primary keys and foreign keys. The foreign key you create creates a link between the two tables. Whatever column or columns you choose to use as the foreign key need to have values that match the values entered into the primary key. Then, when you enter a value into one column, it can match it up with the column in the other table.

In setting up relationships between two tables, a possible problem arises. Since one table points to another, what happens when you delete information from one table that points to information in another table? For example, if you deleted a customer from the video ordering system we've been discussing, there would still be information on all those video orders in the other table. In other words, if John Smith special-ordered a video, and his customer account was deleted, the order would still be lurking in the other table. When the video came in, there would be no way to contact the customer, since his account was deleted. Another problem that could occur is someone entering a value into the foreign key that doesn't correspond to a row in the primary key table. For example, the customer ID of 33 is entered into the foreign key of the Movie table, but there is no customer 33 in the primary key of the Customer table. To keep these problems from occurring, referential integrity is used.

Referential integrity is a system of rules that can be applied to relationships through your DBMS. When you set referential integrity on a relationship, you are ensuring that for every row existing in a foreign key, there is a corresponding row in the primary key. It also keeps related data from being changed or deleted, because you need to delete the relationship between tables before you're able to delete the primary key.

Before referential integrity can be enforced, several conditions must be met:

- The related tables must belong to the same database.
- The primary key and foreign key must have the same data type and size.
- When you set a relationship to a foreign key, the column must be a primary key or have a unique constraint. A *unique constraint* is a non-primary key with a constraint that ensures that no duplicate values can be entered in that column.

If any of these conditions is not met, you won't be able to set referential integrity through your DBMS.

Specifying Relationships Between Entities

As mentioned earlier, a relationship is a link between entities. This link is established through the primary key of one table and the foreign key of another table. By setting up a relationship between tables, you allow one table to reference information contained in another.

One issue dealing with relationships is what kind you will choose. While one table can reference another, you will need them to be referenced in different ways. For example, in a video database, one customer may rent many different movies. However, each movie will have only one director. This means that while the Customer and Movie tables will have one kind of relationship, the Movie and Director tables will need another kind of relationship. Because different tables are referenced in different ways, there are three kinds of relationships you can apply to tables:

- One-to-many
- Many-to-many
- One-to-one

As we'll see, the type of relationship you choose depends on how you want one table to reference another.

One-to-many relationships are the most common type of relationship used in databases. In a one-to-many relationship, a row in one table can have many matching rows in a second table, but the second table can match only one row in the first table. For example, let's say you have two tables for a paternity database. One table has information on fathers, while the other table has information on children. While each father can have many children, each child can have only one biological father. As such, the table on fathers could have many matching rows in the table of children, but the rows of related children would match a single row in the table of fathers. In creating such a relationship, you would need to have a column in the fathers table (the "one" side of the relationship) being a primary key (or have a unique constant), while the other table would be defined as a foreign key.

Many-to-many relationships can have each table matching multiple rows in one another. To use the example of a video database, let's say you had one table of actors and another table of movies. Many actors will act in a single movie, and each movie stars different actors. As such, each table will have many matching entries in the other.

To create a many-to-many relationship, you need to create an additional table, which is an Associative Entity. You may have heard this referred to as a *junction table* or *link table*. The Associative Entity is used to associate the two tables, and has a primary key that consists of foreign keys from each of the other two tables. To continue with our example of a video database, you would create two tables, Actors and Movies, which would have primary keys of their own. Let's say the primary key of the Actors table is called ac_id, while the primary key of Movies is mov_id. You would then create an Associative Entity, whose primary key would be a combination of the ac_id column in Actors and the mov_id column in Movies. After creating these tables, you then create a one-to-many relationship from the Movies table to the Associative Entity, and another one-to-many relationship from the Actors table to the Associative Entity. In creating two one-to-many relationships from each of the two tables to the Associative Entity, you create a many-to-many relationship.

One-to-one relationships are the least-used type of relationship. This is because one row in a table can match only one row in another table. For example, if a single ID card is assigned to a single person, you could create one table of people's personal information, and a second table of ID numbers. Each person would be associated with only a single ID number, so a one-to-one relationship could be created. You could create the one-to-one relationship if both related columns are primary keys or have unique constraints.

While such relationships are pretty uncommon, they do have their uses. As we saw with the example of ID cards and numbers, you could use the one-to-one relationship to isolate sensitive information for security reasons. It's also useful for temporary data that you plan to delete within a short period of time. If you have a temporary table that needs to be created, and is defined as temporary by the DBMS, the information you plan to delete can be removed quickly by deleting a table. If you are dealing with a table that has an incredible number of columns, and have trouble sifting through them, you could break up the table into two tables, and then create one-to-one relationships. This would allow you to keep all the data, but organize it more effectively. Such organizational reasons also apply when you're storing information that applies to only a subset of your main table. In such cases, it's often more effective to break up the table, and create one-to-one relationships.

Identifying Business Rules That Relate to Data Integrity

When you have integrity, you control your actions in a correct and consistent manner. While this is something you should expect of yourself and the people you deal with, it's also something that's expected from a good database. While the work we've covered so far is vital to good database design, it's useless if the values stored and retrieved by your application are invalid. After all, a database application is of little use if it can't control data access in a correct and consistent manner. This is what *data integrity* is all about.

In designing your database, it's important to identify business rules that can be used to ensure the integrity of your application's data. In doing so, you'll be able to determine how and under what conditions the application will store and retrieve data. The business rules are identified through interviews and other techniques mentioned in Chapter 9, and the usage scenarios that are generated from these methods of information gathering. Through these sources of information, you can determine how, why, and when data should be accessed. You then apply the data access business rules to any of the following situations:

■ When your application needs to insert, update, delete, or view data

■ Application-based referential integrity

■ Data security

■ Data validation

■ Multi-file data access

As we discuss each of these situations individually, you should remember that you're not limited to applying business rules to one or the other. In fact, many or all of these situations would arise on almost any project, and indicate that consideration needs to be given to applying business rules to data access.

The heart of a business solution is its ability to manipulate data. How this manipulation is performed is determined by the business rules that are applied to data access. When this is done, the data access business rules control how the business solution views, inserts, updates, and deletes data. For example, if you were creating a banking program that processed customer transactions, you would want to ensure that customers had money in their accounts before they were allowed to withdraw funds. In such a program, a business rule would automatically check the customer's account balance before inserting the amount of the withdrawal into a debit column of the bank account, and updating the account balance.

Another common use for business rules is application-based referential integrity. Relational databases like Microsoft Access allow you to set referential integrity through the DBMS. The information that handles referential integrity is itself stored within the database file. However, indexed files like VSAM don't have this capability; they're generally just storage engines for raw data. As such, referential integrity is handled through business rules that are incorporated into your application's code. In your application you create custom code procedures that determine how primary keys, foreign keys, constraints, and other issues will be dealt with.

This isn't to say you can use application-based referential integrity only in indexed databases. There may be times you want to enforce the referential integrity of relational databases through your application. This commonly occurs when the limitations of the database create a situation where triggers, constraints, and stored procedures are insufficient. When this happens, you need to enhance referential integrity through the code of your application. Another common occurrence is when the DBMS makes it too complex to effectively implement referential integrity, and it's easier to enforce through code in your application. Because of this, it is important to determine the limitations and complexities of the relational database you're using, and see if it is expedient to enforce referential integrity through your application's code.

As we saw in Chapter 8, security is an important issue in many of the applications you design. Business rules can be used to determine who gets access to your data, and how they can use it. By implementing business rules into your application's code, or by having your application work with other programs (such as SQL server), you can protect data by limiting who has access to the data, how they can manipulate the data, and what features of data manipulation they can use.

Data validation ensures that the values users type in are correct and accurate, by validating the data in one of several ways:

- Data type validation
- Range checking
- Code checking
- Complex validation

Each of these types of data validation is important to an application. If a user inputs incorrect information, errors can result, which could possibly lock up the application, or return incorrect information.

Data type validation looks at the type of data a user inputs, and determines if it is the correct type. For example, if the user tried to type his or her name into a numeric field in a calculator program, it would result in an error. To avoid this, data validation looks to see whether the field accepts numeric, alphabetic, or some other type of data.

Range checking is a type of validation that looks at the range of a particular data type. As we'll see later in this chapter, each data type has a minimum or maximum value. For example, if a field holds integers, it can hold any value between −32,768 to 32,767. If a user tried to type a number below or above this range, an error would result. Range checking is used in applications to check whether a value falls within the range of the data type.

In a number of the applications your create, *code checking* may be used to determine whether certain actions are taken. For example, in creating a retail sales application, different products may be taxable and nontaxable items. Depending where the application is used, different taxes may be applied. To resolve how products are taxed, retailers generally use tax codes. The code is typed in, and depending on this value, taxes are automatically applied to the sale price. Applications commonly use lookup tables or validation tables for this code checking. Input is looked up on the table, so the appropriate action can be performed.

In addition to the previously mentioned forms of data validation, which check the basic input of the user or lookup values, there may be times when more *complex validation* procedures are required. A good example of this would be an application used by an insurance company. With health insurance, you're allowed to claim a certain number of dollars for medical care each year, and a certain number over the lifetime of the policy. Because of this, the application would have to compare the amount currently being claimed to see if it's over the yearly limit, and then determine if the policy holder has gone over the policy's total limit. If it were over, the claim would be denied. If it were not over the limit, this complex data validation routine would commit some other action.

Moving away from data validation, another important use of business rules is multi-file data access. This occurs when your application needs to process a series of records as part of a decision process. To use the previous example of a medical insurance program, your application would need to review the policy holder's previous claims, to ensure that a fraudulent claim isn't being submitted. After all, there are only so many heart transplants a policyholder will undergo. The business rule goes through the chain of records, and repackages them so that the agent can use the information provided.

Incorporating Business Rules and Constraints into the Data Model

When incorporating business rules into your data model, it's important to remember that the business rules for your application aren't the only game in town. Consideration should be given not only to how your application works with the data, but also how business rules belonging to other applications will affect the data, and how often the business rules change. Business rules should keep your data accessible, correct, and secure. They shouldn't become problems for other applications and a hindrance for change.

When incorporating business rules, you need to look at the business rules of other applications. If other applications are using an older business rule, or one that contradicts the business rules in your application, it can affect the data. While your application performs its actions correctly, it may seem to be causing errors because of the business rules in the other application. In addition, you should determine whether other applications would benefit from using the business rules you're incorporating. Business rules change, and you should consider how your implementation of them would affect the ease or difficulty of modifying them later. When business rules are made part of an application's code, it can be difficult changing the business rules later. You'll need to change the code, recompile, and then reinstall on every workstation that uses the application. If the business rules are the only change to the application, this is unproductive. If business rules change frequently in an organization, it can also be frustrating.

Because of changes in business rules, and the need for other applications to access them, you should consider implementing business rules into COM components, such as ActiveX components. By incorporating them in this fashion, they are separate from the code of your application, and can easily be changed without having to change the code and recompile the application. By exposing properties and methods of the COM component, other applications can benefit from the business rules.

In addition to business rules, you can also incorporate constraints into your database. *Business rules*, also known as *business logic*, are the policies and procedures that dictate corporate behavior. *Constraints*, on the other hand, are business requirements that enforce what a user can input into specific columns of your database. Because constraints limit the values entered into a field, they keep users from entering data in a format incompatible with other values held in that column. They are also another way of enforcing referential integrity of data.

Despite the ability to put business rules and constraints into the data tier, it's important to remember that business rules/logic and requirements predominantly belong within the middle tier of your application. Whenever possible, the business rules and requirements for your application should be put into the middle tier, and avoid placement in the data tier.

Check constraints can be incorporated into a data model to specify what data formats and values are acceptable. For example, let's say you had a field for Canadian postal codes, which are a combination of letters and numbers, such as N5X 2L8. With a check constraint, you can keep users from entering only letters or only numbers into that field. With American zip codes, you could apply a constraint that accepted only a specific number of digits. If a user typed in 90210, the constraint would keep users from entering more than five numbers in a field for the zip code. You can apply check constraints to different columns of your database, or you can apply one or more constraint per column.

Default constraints are used to enter a specific value when a user doesn't enter anything into a field. If a user skips over a field, a default value is automatically entered for them. This can be a comment, such as "To be filled in later," or another value that reflects a common or expected answer. For example, if you were creating an application for subscriptions to a men's magazine, you could expect that most of the people ordering subscriptions would be male. As such, you could have a default constraint used to enter "Mr." unless another explicit value (i.e., Miss, Ms., or Mrs.) was entered.

Unique constraints ensure that only unique values are entered into columns that aren't primary keys. Just because a column isn't a primary key, it doesn't mean that duplicate entries can be allowed. Imagine if your application issued two people the same security ID, Social Insurance number, or Social Security number. Allowing duplicate entries could cause problems later. If you have a specific column that requires a unique value, this constraint will ensure that no duplicate value is entered.

Primary key and foreign key constraints can also be applied to a database. Primary key constraints ensure that duplicate values aren't entered into primary key columns. Foreign key constraints ensure that the value entered into a foreign key column match a value in another table's primary key column. Such constraints also restrict NULL values, thereby forcing the user to enter some value into the field.

Identifying the Appropriate Level of Denormalization

While rules of normalization are vital to good database design, it's important to know when to break the rules. There are times when a severely normalized database will decrease performance. By rearranging your database, and pulling away from the rules of normalization, you may be able to make your database work faster. By identifying an appropriate level of denormalization, you're able to address such performance considerations.

Denormalization allows you to selectively identify which tables and columns can break away from the normalization techniques you've used in your database. In other words, you intentionally violate the rules of normalization as a tradeoff for performance. This means that you must first start with a normalized database, and then select areas that will benefit from denormalization. At no time should you ever denormalize the entire database, or not bother to use normalization at all. Denormalization enhances performance, but shouldn't lower the security or functionality of the database in any way.

Defining the Attributes of a Data Entity

Earlier in this section, we mentioned how important it is to identify and define the characteristics or attributes of the data to be used in your design. Data reflects the people, places, and things a business needs to record facts on, which are used to run the business. Because the data entities in your application will reflect different items, it follows suit that these items will have different characteristics. One may reflect a location, such as an address or country; while another may reflect measurements, such as height, weight, and so forth. Other characteristics may be of value, such as currency or productivity; while still others may be conceptual (names or identification numbers) or relational (such as units within departments, which reside in organizations). No matter what data entity you encounter, each will always have attributes that define them.

The attributes of the data entity identify its data type. As shown in Table 11-3, different data types are used to store different kinds of data, and each kind uses varying amounts of storage space. This shows us that when creating your data model, it's vital to determine the kinds of information that will be stored in the recordsets of your database. If your database has the wrong data type, it can affect performance and limit user input. Imagine a customer service rep attempting to enter a customer name into a field that only accepts numbers, or needing to enter a number that's too large to input into a field, and you'll see the dilemma. In developing a data model it's important to define the data that's used, and determine the type, size, and default data that will be entered.

TABLE 11-3

Data Types

Data Type	Description
Boolean	Can accept values of True or False. Storage space: 2 bytes.
Byte	Numbers ranging in value from 0 to 255. Storage space: 1 byte.
Currency	−922,337,203,685,477.5808 to 922,337,203,685,477.5807. Storage space: 8 bytes.
Date	Dates ranging from 1 January 100 to 31 December 9999. Storage space: 8 bytes.
Double	−1.79769313486232E308 to −4.94065645841247E−324 for negative values and from 4.94065645841247E−324 to 1.79769313486232E308 for positive values. Storage space: 8 bytes.
Integer	−32,768 to 32,767. Storage space: 2 bytes.
Long	−2,147,483,648 to 2,147,483,647. Storage space: 4 bytes.
Object	Used to refer to objects. By using the Set statement, a variable declared as an Object can then have any object reference assigned to it. Storage space: 4 bytes.
Single	−3.402823E38 to −1.401298E−45 for negative values and from 1.401298E−45 to 3.402823E38 for positive values. Storage space: 4 bytes.
String	Codes in the ASCII character set (the first 128 characters on a keyboard), and special characters (such as accents and international symbols) making up the remaining 128.
Variant	Default data type. Used when no data type has been specified. It represents numeric values ranging from −1.79769313486231SE308 to −4.94066E−324 for negative values and from 4.94066E−324 to 1.79769313486231SE308 for positive values. Storage space: 16 bytes.

Developing a Database That Uses
General Database Development Standards and Guidelines

When you're developing a database, you should use general database development standards and guidelines. This means designing the database using the concepts we've covered so far, and first determining whether data for your database already exists in a different format. In the logical database design, this introduces the need to decide whether to use existing data, attach or import it into another database, or not use it at all. It also introduces whether certain guidelines and standards must be used. Depending on the database product you use to create your database, different guidelines may be suggested and offered.

Regardless of the type of database you create (e.g., Access or Oracle), there are certain guidelines and standards you should follow. Naming schemes are important to use in developing database applications. You should always keep the names of data objects short and descriptive. This will make it easier to remember the name of a data object during the design and development of the database. If columns have long names that are difficult to remember and that don't reflect their purpose, you'll find that you're spending considerable time looking up those names.

You also shouldn't use the same name for multiple objects or fields in your database. This can lead to confusion for developers, as they may refer to the wrong object if both have the same name. Similarly, if you have more than one field with the same name, it's very easy for developers to use the wrong field for data access. For example, if you have a column called Name in a table of publishers, and another column called Name in a table of authors, it is possible that the wrong attribute will be used in your application. The developer will see that the Name field needs to be used on a Form, but could use the wrong one.

Standard naming conventions should be used for your database application. In Appendix D of this book, the Hungarian naming convention is discussed, and it is suggested that you use it. If you choose not to use this naming convention, you should create your own naming convention or use the one currently in use by your organization. Also, it's important to note that some database products have well-defined naming guidelines, and you should follow those. The naming scheme should be decided on during the design of the database, and then used during development.

Synchronizing and Coordinating the Three Tracks of Solutions Design

As we saw earlier in this chapter, the Solutions Design model is made up of three processes: conceptual, logical, and physical design. Although you start with the conceptual design, and work your way to the physical design of the application, there is often overlap between each design phase. There's no clear cutoff point in moving from one process to the next, and you may often find that you'll revisit or redesign certain parts of your project while others are being finished. There is a considerable amount of work in designing a solution, and no one person in your team can do it all. Therefore, synchronizing and coordinating the different tasks that make up the Solutions Design model requires putting the right person on the right job.

At each point in the design process, each participant in the Team model has specific duties that are crucial to the success of the project. These duties vary as the design of the business solution moves through the conceptual, logical, and physical design phases. A team member may be responsible for performing one activity in the conceptual design, but that responsibility may change as the business solution progresses through the logical and physical perspectives.

Throughout the different processes of conceptual, logical, and physical design, one thing remains constant: Program Management has ownership. The Program Manager is responsible for driving the overall design process, and has the responsibility of coordinating and synchronizing the other members of the team. In performing activities that vary from one design phase to another, Program Management is always in the position of being accountable for the overall success of the business solution's design.

During the conceptual design of the product, Program Management and Product Management have the greatest responsibilities. Program Management owns responsibility for the conceptual design's success, and drives the actual conceptual design process. Product Management is responsible for gathering the information used in conceptual design, and has responsibility for driving the validation of usage scenarios created at this phase in the Solutions Design process. As seen in Table 11-4, members of each of the other teams have their own responsibilities. Each team member addresses issues that align to his or her particular role in the Team model, but the major duty of each role is to identify risks in their area of expertise, which may have an impact later.

Activities and information gathered in the conceptual design process are applied to the logical design of the application. The usage scenarios that are created in conceptual design are used to derive the business objects and related services used in the solution, and specify interfaces between the system and other elements (such as other users, systems, and components). It is here that the structure of the system is laid out, and it is determined how components will communicate with one another. Once the tasks involved in logical design are completed, the results are applied to the physical design.

TABLE 11-4	Role	Conceptual Design Responsibilities
Team Roles and Responsibilities in the Conceptual Design Process	Product Management	Gathers user input, and has responsibility for driving the validation of usage scenarios.
	Program Management	Has ownership and responsibility for driving the conceptual design process.
	Development	Aids in the evaluation of current and future states of the system. Analyzes business policies, and helps identify risks that may arise from the conceptual design in the logical and physical design stages.
	User Education	Looks at usability issues that appear in the conceptual design. Analyzes usage scenarios to determine training and other user education required from changes to the current system.
	Testing	Validates usage scenarios and determines changes required for the system to be compliant with user requirements.
	Logistics Management	Responsible for rollout and infrastructure issues resulting from changes.

FROM THE CLASSROOM

Whose Role Was That?

Microsoft's Solution Framework provides numerous models that apply to almost any type of application development project in existence. Not all models, or roles defined within the Team model for that matter, need to be leveraged or implemented. In the case of the roles listed as a part of the Team model, oftentimes, numerous roles will be assumed by the same person. Be careful to avoid grouping roles that have inherently different goals in mind during certain aspects of the design phase. Strive to fully implement roles whose absence would have the greatest negative impact.

In regards to the exam environment, be fully aware of the subtle, or not so subtle, differences between the roles, and their respective responsibilities in each phase of the application design and development process. Understand the differences between roles. Understand when and where inherent differences will arise in the focus of the roles,

and the ramifications of failing to implement a given role, or the impact of assigning certain roles to the same individual. Pay careful attention to the differences between the roles of Product and Program Management. These can be difficult to distinguish.

In keeping the focus on roles, ensure that the chief participants in each phase of design (conceptual, logical, and physical) are able to fully perform the desired responsibilities. Most importantly, the conceptual phase can provide a hotbed for issues down the road. For this reason, complete fulfillment of the Program Management role is vital to ensuring that the foundation for the resulting application is strong and able to support future enhancements, scalability concerns, and efficient design.

—*Michael Lane Thomas, MCSE+I, MCSD, MCT, MCP+SB, MSS, A+*

With all this talk of components and systems, you might have guessed that Development plays a vital role in the logical design of a product. While Program Management still retains ownership over this part of Solutions Design, Development has the responsibility of deriving the business objects and services from the information provided in usage scenarios. In doing so, Development defines the objects and their related services, and ensures that there is sufficient detail. If the object and service definitions are incomplete or inconsistent, Testing, who is the other major player in logical design, catches it. Testing evaluates these definitions, ensures the logical design is valid, and also looks to see if the logical design as a whole is testable.

The other roles in the Team model aren't greatly involved during the logical design of the application. As shown in Table 11-5, Product Management looks at the services that evolve from the logical design to ensure that they accurately reflect the perceptions and requirements of the user. User Education looks at these same objects and services, to identify areas of the design that will require training, documentation, and other methods of user education. Finally, Logistics Management ensures that the services derived from the logical design can be applied to the available technologies and infrastructure.

Once the tasks associated with these roles have been completed, the results are passed forward to the physical design perspective of the Solutions Design

TABLE 11-5		
Team Roles and Responsibilities in the Logical Design Process	**Role**	**Logical Design Responsibilities**
	Product Management	Looks at the services derived in the logical design, to ensure they reflect user needs and views.
	Program Management	Has ownership of the logical design, and drives the logical design process. Also coordinates the efforts of the other team members.
	Development	Defines the objects and their related services, and ensures that there is sufficient detail.
	User Education	Analyzes the business objects and services to determine areas that will require training and materials for user education.
	Testing	Ensures that object and service definitions are complete and consistent, the logical design is valid, and that the logical design as a whole is testable.
	Logistics Management	Analyzes the services derived from the logical design to ensure whether they can be implemented into available technologies and infrastructure.

model. The abstractions of how the system will behave are transformed here to show how the system will actually be implemented. It's here that the physical constraints of technology are applied to the logical design, business objects and services are applied to components, and implementation and performance issues become paramount.

As with the other two design perspectives, Program Management has ownership of the physical design. In addition to driving the process and coordinating activities, Program Management keeps the lines of communication open among team members. If there are any issues dealing with whether the application design complies with the enterprise architecture, Program Management needs to ensure these issues are discussed and dealt with. Because the work performed on the logical design is applied to the physical design, Program Management also has the responsibility of ensuring that the integrity of the logical design is maintained.

Of the different roles in the Team model, Development bears most of the responsibility in physical design. This is because what goes into the physical design directly affects what coding will take place and how the application is built. By specifying how components will be packaged, and applying the logical design to the constraints of the physical environment, Development provides a majority of what goes into the physical design.

Testing also has a primary role in the physical design of a product. During this phase of the project, Testing develops the test procedures and criteria that will ensure the product works to specification. It also looks at the components that Development proposes to include in the finished product, and determines whether these components can actually be tested. If they are not testable, further work on the component will need to be done by Development. Along with Product Management, Testing looks at the physical design to ensure that the requirements still adhere to those in the usage scenarios.

In addition to the work performed by Testing, Program Management, and Development, the other members in the Team model perform their own activities, which either apply to the finished product or validate the physical design. This is shown in Table 11-6. Product Management looks at the physical design to determine whether it addresses the requirements and perceptions that were identified in usage scenarios, which were created in the conceptual design of the product. User Education takes advantage of the physical design perspective to plan the necessary training and user education materials that will support the product. Finally, Logistics Management plans the delivery, setup procedures, and other requirements for the product. These plans are passed onto the operation and support groups in the organization, and discussed so that the product will have a smooth rollout.

TABLE 11-6

Team Roles and Responsibilities in the Physical Design Process

Role	Physical Design Responsibilities
Product Management	Ensures that the physical design addresses the needs and views of usage scenarios.
Program Management	Has ownership of the logical design, and drives the physical design process. Ensures that the integrity of the logical design is maintained, and also coordinates the efforts of the other team members.
Development	Bears the greatest responsibility for the physical design of the product. Determines how components will be packaged, and how services will relate to the system.
User Education	Responsible for planning the training and other user education services that will support the product.
Testing	Plans test procedures for the product, and aids Product Management in ensuring that physical design still addresses the needs and views that were outlined in usage scenarios. Also works with Development to ensure that components are testable.
Logistics Management	Plans delivery, installation, and requirements necessary for the product, and discusses these plans with the operation and support groups in the organization.

Deriving the Physical Design

The physical design of your application is derived from the work done in the logical design. It's here that you determine how the logical design will develop based on the set of technologies you choose. While the logical design is technologically independent, the physical design applies the services, business objects, and logical database design to specific types of hardware and software.

As we saw in the previous section, each member of the team has a role in the physical design of the application, with Program Management, Development, and Testing taking on the primary responsibilities. The major activities performed during physical design include defining the interfaces to be used in the application, component packaging, and distribution. In performing these activities, the abstract business objects and services of the logical design are translated into physical components of the system.

Moving the logical design into a physical design is a step-by-step process that involves the following:

- Allocating services to components
- Deploying the components across a network
- Refining the packaging and deployment of components
- Specifying interfaces
- Validating the physical design

As we saw at the beginning of this chapter, a component encapsulates services that are accessed through its interface. Though each component works as a separate entity, and other programs can access its services, they are part of your application as a whole. Using the steps provided by the physical design process, you're able to achieve a stable and effective physical design for your application.

The first step in the physical design process is allocating services to components. The business objects from the logical design are translated into the components that will make up the application. The business objects are grouped by their related services. Depending on the service contained in the business object, it is grouped into user, business, or data service components. By separating the services in this manner, you determine what components will be created by the services they contain.

The next step is taking your components from the previous step, and determining how they'll be deployed across the network. This designates where components will be distributed on the network. If the application is for a single desktop, all components will reside on a single machine. If there is only one server on the network, components that provide services may reside on that server, while components to access the services will reside on each workstation. By determining the deployment of components across the network, each component is assigned to a specific node or machine on the network.

In determining the deployment of components on the network, there are a number of factors to consider. These include locality of reference, the interoperability of components, and data distribution issues that affect how components will work together, and where they will be placed. Support and reliability should also be considered, as you don't want components placed on unreliable servers or areas that will be difficult to access. Finally, you should also look at issues dealing with the security of your application, ownership, and the user interfaces when determining how components will be placed on the network. Each factor will influence how you decide to deploy components on the network. Such decisions will affect how well your application performs, and whether deployment will adhere to the needs of your users. These factors are discussed in the paragraphs that follow.

Of these different factors, *locality of reference* can have a big effect on how well your application performs. Despite being a rather cryptic phrase, locality of reference is a rather simple concept. It means putting a component in a location where it will be used, or near to where it will be used. For example, let's say you were creating an application for a large corporation, with offices in Tokyo and New York. The networks of these offices were connected by a WAN (Wide

Area Network) link between two servers. If users in New York were going to use specific components, you would put them on the New York server. The same goes for applications on a LAN (Local Area Network), where components are placed close to the users who use them. This decreases the amount of network use, and allows users to have faster access to services provided by the components.

Security is often an issue that must be addressed in application design, and it affects deployment. If your application depended on the security of a Windows NT server, you wouldn't want to deploy components to a Novell NetWare server. As such, security should be addressed when deciding where to put components on the network.

While the previous step is where preliminary decisions on component packaging and distribution are made, the next step refines these determinations of physical design. Performance and optimization are major issues of this step. Here you look at how the components are deployed, and determine whether they meet performance requirements. The refinement process also determines the size of each component (granularity), and how components should be assembled. It also looks at reusability issues, which affect whether other applications will be able to use the component.

The fourth step in the physical design process looks at the interfaces that allow interaction with the component. This can be a programmatic interface, which other components and your application will use, or a graphical user interface, which users can interact with. In creating these interfaces, components are able to consume the services supplied by other components.

The final step in the physical design process involves validating the work done in the previous steps. It's important that the services provided by components can be traced back to services in business objects. For every component in the physical design, you should be able to map its services to the services of business objects in the logical design. If you cannot do that with a component, then the physical design of that component is invalid, and you'll need to redesign it.

Evaluating Whether Access to a Database Should Be Encapsulated in an Object

Encapsulation is like a multivitamin capsule. Once you're satisfied with the contents of the capsule, you simply take one to access the vitamins inside. The same occurs when you encapsulate data access procedures or business logic in an object. You can create components that shield the user from the steps required to access data from specific data systems. Rather than a user needing to know how to view tables, manipulate data, stored procedures, and so forth in a SQL, Oracle, Paradox, or other system, they merely access the database through the component that's been created for them. They access the methods or properties they need in the component, and the component does the rest of the work for them.

Encapsulating access to a database is useful because the code used to access the database is kept separate from the actual application's code. The component exists as a separate entity, that is accessed through the properties and methods that are exposed to the calling code of the application. Code within the application accesses the functionality of the component. If the developer decides to change code within the component, the application on the workstation remains unaffected.

Encapsulating data access is particularly useful when dealing with legacy code. If you are creating a new application to access an old data system, you can encapsulate the procedures that access the old database. This saves users from having to know the commands for the older system, or needing to be retrained on how to use the archaic system.

When business rules change frequently in an organization, it's also wise to create components that contain business rules. You can control how data is accessed without having to rewrite the code of the actual application. Any procedures that control how data is accessed and manipulated, security functions for data access, and so forth are controlled through the component. This is accessed by code in the application that calls on the properties and methods of the component.

Designing the Properties, Methods, and Events of Components

Any component you create contains basic parts that make up the component, and determine its functionality. When you create COM classes to make up your COM component, you use properties, methods, and events to make up the characteristics of the class, which will subsequently become the characteristics of your component. *Properties* are used to read and set values for a specific attribute of the component. *Methods* define an interface for the component, and are used to invoke actions that the component can perform. This could include such things as adding items and printing. *Events* are the actions that are recognized by an object. Together they provide the functionality of the component, which the user or other components work with.

When designing the properties and methods of COM classes for your components, it's important to keep in mind that any developer who uses the component must know what properties and methods are provided. This means that class/type libraries should be used, so the developer can use the Object Browser to see a listing of properties, methods, and descriptions of each. Otherwise, or in addition to, you should provide documentation that outlines what properties and methods are provided, and what they are used for. In doing so, developers wishing to use the component can incorporate code into an application that calls on the features of your component.

Component Properties

A property is an attribute of your component. For example, the color of your display text is a property, and the Visible property of an object provided by your component determines whether it can be seen when the program runs. In designing the properties of your component, you need to decide on which properties you want the user or other components to access and possibly change.

A user can access the property of a component as they would the property of any other object. They're accessed through a public property procedure or a public variable that you've declared, and can include property values, property arrays, and read-only properties that are written in the code of your component. Any objects you provide to the user through your component should be implemented as a property procedure. This is because if you provided the object through a public variable, the value of the variable could be set to NULL. This could destroy the object, and cause runtime errors in your code. Properties should have a default value, which can be changed either programmatically or through an interface (such as a property sheet).

Component Methods

Methods are actions that an object can perform. Like the properties you design for your component, the methods of a component are invoked like the methods of any other object. Code is added to the application, which calls on the method of the component. The method then performs whatever action it has been programmed to perform.

A method is a Public Sub or Public Function procedure that's declared in the component, which is used to define your class. An example of this is the PrintForm method of a Form object in Visual Basic. When you use the PrintForm method in your programming code, the Form you specify will be printed. For example, let's say you had a Form named Form1 that you wanted to print. The following code would print it to the local printer:

```
Form1.PrintForm
```

In using this code, you'd be invoking the PrintForm method of the object Form1, and a depiction of the Form would be printed.

When you declare methods in your component, you should declare all of the arguments used as explicit data types. As we saw earlier in this chapter, certain data types are different sizes. Implicit data types, which don't have a data type attached to the argument, will by default be of the variant data type, which uses considerably more space than most other data types.

Arguments that take object references should have those references declared as a specific data type. This is done by declaring the type of data used in the argument, such as As MyObj rather than As Object or As Variant. This may not always be possible, but as a general rule you should try whenever you can. By declaring arguments as explicit data types, errors have a better chance of being caught by the compiler because of early binding. This will allow the error to be caught during compiling, rather than appearing as a runtime error when the user invokes the method.

Component Events

Events are actions that are recognized by an object. An example of an event is when a Form loads into memory (i.e., the Load event), or when a user clicks a button (i.e., the Click event). As you can see by this, some events are triggered by user interaction, while others are triggered by the application itself.

By default, any class you add to a Class module in a Visual Basic project will have two events associated with it: Initialize and Terminate. A Class module is a template for creating objects programmatically. The Initialize event occurs when an instance of a Class is created, and before any properties are set. It is used to initialize any data used by the Class, and can be used to load Forms used by the Class. Terminate occurs when the object variable is set to nothing or goes out of scope, and is used to save information, unload Forms, and any other tasks required to be done when the Class ends. Initialize is the first event that occurs between the two, and Terminate is the last.

Events can be added to any class in a component. All events are public, and can contain arguments like any other procedure. The difference between arguments in procedures and those in events are that events can't have named, optional, or ParamArray arguments. In addition, events can't return values. If you need a value returned, you should design functions, which return values, that can be used by the user or programmatic interface.

QUESTIONS AND ANSWERS

What is the purpose of a prototype?	Prototypes are used to validate the design of an application, and allow users and customers to actually see what the interface of your application will look like. In doing so, you will get better feedback on different aspects of the design early in the design stages.
Who has ownership of the design process?	Program Management has ownership of the conceptual, logical, and physical design.
Why would I want to enforce referential integrity in my database?	Referential integrity is used to ensure that for every row existing in a foreign key, there is a corresponding row in the primary key. It also keeps related data from being changed or deleted, because you need to delete the relationship between tables before you're able to delete the primary key.

CERTIFICATION SUMMARY

The Solutions Design model is comprised of conceptual, logical, and physical design perspectives. It also ties together the Application and Team models. The Application model breaks your application into distinct types of services, which consist of User Services, Business Services, and Data Services. As we saw in this chapter, using these models allows you to design component-based solutions that are integrated into a successful software product that meets the requirements of users.

Throughout the Solutions Design process, each team member has specific duties. While Program Management retains ownership throughout the conceptual, logical, and physical design perspectives, the responsibilities of other team members change. At no time is any member of the team left out of the design process.

Because the user interacts with your product through the user interface, there are specific design issues that must be considered when creating the interface. This includes such things as navigation and input validation, and establishing appropriate means of output. Should the user experience problems using your application, online user assistance is implemented into the user interface, to provide clarification on the difficulties they are experiencing.

Prototypes provide a way of generating feedback from customers, end users, and other interested parties. Evolutionary prototypes are built on, and used in the construction of the end product. Throwaway prototypes are discarded once they've been used to validate the design and generate feedback. In constructing either kind of prototype, it is important to follow user-interface standards, organizational rules, and other elements that are part of the end product's design.

Database design is a complex process that consists of identifying, documenting, and implementing the data requirements of the business. Normalization is part of good database design, and reduces data redundancy. Business rules and constraints can be used to enforce referential integrity, and control what data a user can enter. Denormalization pulls your database back from the rules of normalization, enabling it to work faster. Through the techniques used in this chapter, you can design an efficient database that meets the needs of the user.

Physical design takes the abstract business objects, services, and logical database design and applies them to the constraints of the physical environment. Here, technological constraints are applied to the logical design. The physical design consists of a process of allocating services to components, deploying components on a network, refinement, specifying interfaces, and validation of the physical design.

✓ TWO-MINUTE DRILL

❑ *Solutions Design* is a model that provides different perspectives on how to design a business solution, and is essential in designing component-based solutions.

❑ Solutions Design model is made up of three separate processes: conceptual design, logical design, and physical design.

❑ *Business objects* are abstract representations of real-world things or concepts (such as orders and customers).

❑ The requirements of an application fall into one of three tiers: User Services, Business Services, and Data Services.

❑ The user interface provides the end user with the ability to view and manipulate data, through units of application logic.

❑ The Data Services tier is also called the *data source tier*, and is responsible for defining, maintaining, and updating data.

❑ When one business object calls on services in another business object, this is called a *business object dependency*.

❑ Prototypes fall into two categories: throwaway and evolutionary.

❑ A *throwaway prototype* is created for the sole purpose of getting feedback from users, and validating the design of the user interface.

❑ An *evolutionary prototype* is incorporated into the building of the actual product.

❑ Data modeling is where you define the structure of your database, through a process of identifying the data and data requirements of the business, documenting this information, and implementing the requirements into your application's design.

❑ Normalization is a set of rules that the logical database design should satisfy.

❑ Primary keys identify rows that make up the table, while foreign keys are used in relationships to reference other tables.

❑ *Referential integrity* is a system of rules that can be applied to relationships through your DBMS.

❑ *One-to-many relationships* are the most common type of relationship used in databases.

❑ *Many-to-many relationships* can have each table matching multiple rows in one another.

❑ *One-to-one relationships* are the least-used type of relationship. This is because one row in a table can match only one row in another table.

❑ *Data validation* ensures that the values users type in are correct and accurate, by validating the data in one of several ways: data type validation, range checking, code checking, and complex validation.

❑ *Data type validation* looks at the type of data a user inputs, and determines if it is the correct type.

❑ *Range checking* is a type of validation that looks at the range of a particular data type.

❑ In a number of the applications your create, *code checking* may be used to determine whether certain actions are taken.

❑ In addition to the previously mentioned forms of data validation, which check the basic input of the user or lookup values, there may be times when more *complex validation* procedures are required.

❑ *Business rules*, also known as *business logic*, are the policies and procedures that dictate corporate behavior.

❑ *Constraints* are business requirements that enforce what a user can input into specific columns of your database.

Answers to Exercise 11-2

1. The first three fields have a common use, and thus require a related input validation. The user either enters the customer's ID number *or* their first and last name, then presses the OK button. This means

that the OK button should check to see that the first and last name fields have input and the ID number is empty, or vice versa. If both have input, the wrong account could be brought up, and an error would result.

2. None of the fields require input validation on the data type used in the field.

3. The last two fields, exam cost and total cost, shouldn't accept input. The data is entered in these fields by the application.

4. The exam number field requires input in a specific format. If users entered more than three letters of the customer's last name, or more than six digits after these letters, a warning should result. The wrong input could result in an error.

5. The coupons field can't accept more than two or less than zero coupons.

Answers to Exercise 11-3

1. ToolTips are the better choice for explaining the purpose of the navigation buttons. A ToolTip allows users to discover a button's function by resting their mouse pointer on the button.

2. A status bar could be used to provide brief instructions. When the user clicked on either the ID number field or either of the name fields, an instruction such as "Enter ID or Name, then click OK" could appear. A drawback to this type of assistance is that status bars are generally located on the bottom of the GUI, and so may be overlooked.

3. Help files can be used to provide detailed help. The Help menu should be placed rightmost on the menu bar. F1 could also invoke the Help file.

Answers to Exercise 11-4

1. Some users are connecting remotely, some users are visually impaired or blind, while others require hard copy that can be filed and soft copy to be archived.

2. HTML output could be used for both remote users, intranet archives, and blind/visually impaired users. Printer output will provide hard copies for filing. Audio files could be used, though they would take up more storage space than HTML.

3. Print preview and other print features, e-mail, browser functionality, and audio could be incorporated into the application.

Answers to Exercise 11-5

1. The menu system has inappropriate use of menus. The Help menu should always be rightmost. The File menu should always be leftmost. The Edit menu should be to the right of the File menu, with View beside that.

2. The Close menu item has the shortcut key CTRL-Z assigned to it. This is a common shortcut key that undoes the last action performed, and should be changed.

SELF TEST

The Self Test questions will help you measure your understanding of the material presented in this chapter. Read all the choices carefully, as there may be more than one correct answer.

1. Asimov Robotics has been having a problem with the application used in its sales division. This application is used to take orders from customers. A number of times, users of the application have been failing to enter shipping addresses, leaving the textbox for this purpose blank. While customers have been charged for their order, the shipping department hasn't been able to send out the order, since they have no way of knowing where it should be shipped. What is required for this application?

   A. Validation of the design

   B. Prototyping

   C. Input validation in the application used by sales

   D. Input validation in the application used by shipping

2. You create two tables, with each table having a one-to-many relationship to a third table. The primary key of this third table is comprised of foreign keys from each of the other two tables. What kind of relationship is this?

   A. Linked relationship

   B. Junction relationship

   C. Many-to-one relationship

   D. Many-to-many relationship

3. The military has contracted you to design a database. You assign a record number as the primary key for a table, which also contains a column that holds the serial numbers of enlisted personnel. No two people can have the same serial number, but you don't want to use this column as the primary key. What will you do?

   A. Set up a default constraint on the primary key column.

   B. Set up a unique constraint on the column for serial numbers.

   C. Set up a check constraint that matches the primary key to the serial number column.

   D. Set up a one-to-one relationship between the primary key and the serial number column in this single table.

4. An insurance company has contracted you to design a database. When insurance agents get information on new policyholders, they find that customers occasionally don't bring all of their information to the insurance office with them. As such, you can expect that certain fields won't be completed until a later time. How will you incorporate this issue into your design?

   A. Set up a default constraint on the primary key column.

B. Set up a default constraint on the columns that will be filled in later, and ensure that none of these fields are the primary key column.

C. Set up a check constraint that checks to see whether the field to be completed later isn't empty.

D. Set up a unique constraint on the columns that will be filled in later, and ensure that none of these fields are the primary key column

5. You are designing an application for an organization that frequently changes its business rules. You need to determine an effective method of keeping up with these changes in your application design. What is the best method of doing this?

A. Incorporate the business rules into the code of the actual application users will run on their workstations. When changes to business rules occur, change this code.

B. Incorporate the business rules into a COM component. When changes to business rules occur, change the code in the actual application run on user workstations.

C. Incorporate the business rules into a COM component. When changes to business rules occur, change the code in the component.

D. Don't incorporate any business rules into your design.

6. Which of the following is an example of data type validation?

A. A Y2K problem occurs in the application. The data type validation looks at the date, and corrects the error.

B. The user types his or her name into a String field. Data type validation would find this an error, and inform the user.

C. The user types his or her name in a numeric field. Data type validation looks at the type of data a user inputs, and determines if it is the correct type.

D. There is no type of validation for data types.

7. Which of the following design perspectives map requirements to abstract business objects and the services these objects need to provide?

A. Conceptual

B. Logical

C. Physical

D. Tautological

8. Which of the following define whether something or someone is a business object? (Choose all that apply.)

A. It is something (or someone) the system is required to know about.

B. It is something (or someone) the system isn't required to know about.

C. It is something (or someone) the system gets information from, or provides information to.

D. It is the system used to retrieve and provide information.

9. A user rests the pointer on a button on a toolbar. A small colored box appears containing information. What kind of user assistance is this?

    A. ToolTips

    B. StatusBox

    C. Status bar

    D. Help file

10. Which of the following should not be considered as a primary method of user assistance, but used as a secondary means?

    A. ToolTips

    B. Status bars

    C. Help files

    D. HTML Help files

11. You want to incorporate validation that checks if the value entered by a user is over the maximum value, or under the minimum value, of the data type for a field. What kind of validation will you use?

    A. Data checking

    B. Range checking

    C. Value checking

    D. Input checking

12. Purchasing has asked you to design a database application that will be used to catalog companies your organization buys from, their products, and the cost of each product. While purchasing buys from numerous companies, they don't buy the same product from multiple companies. You decide to create a Company table, listing the business information, and a Product table that lists each of the products to be purchased. What relationship will you apply to these two tables?

    A. One-to-one

    B. One-to-many

    C. Many-to-many

    D. No relationship needs to be specified

13. Which of the following design perspectives of the Solutions Design model identifies an application's requirements through specifications and usage scenarios?

    A. Conceptual

    B. Logical

    C. Physical

    D. Tautological

14. You want to enforce referential integrity between two tables in two separate databases. When you attempt to do so, you find that you cannot. Why?

    A. The related tables must belong to the same database.

    B. The primary key in each table must be identical.

    C. The foreign key in each table must be identical.

    D. Referential integrity has already been set.

15. Which of the following would be used to display the name of a control accessed through a button on a toolbar?

    A. ToolTips

B. Status bars

C. Help files

D. HTML Help files

16. You are determining data types appropriate for different forms of data that will go into your database. One of the data types you need to determine is for a field that confirms whether a customer has previously ordered. If they have, the answer will be true. If not, false. What is the most appropriate data type?

A. Numeric

B. String

C. Boolean

D. QA

17. You have created a user interface that has the following icons: a piece of paper representing the opening of a document, a floppy disk representing saving a file, and a fax machine representing fax services. What are these examples of?

A. Data model

B. Prototyping

C. Metaphors

D. Similes

18. You have decided to hold a meeting of end users, customers, and other interested parties to get feedback on your user interface design. You have decided to construct a display model of the user interface, which will be discarded later, to generate feedback. What have you decided to construct?

A. A data model

B. A throwaway prototype

C. A evolutionary prototype

D. A temporary user interface

19. In the physical design of a software product, which team member has ownership of the design process?

A. Product Management

B. Program Management

C. Development

D. Logistics Management

20. Which is considered the primary input device for applications running under Microsoft Windows operating systems?

A. Keyboard

B. Mouse

C. Pen

D. All of the above

A

Self Test
Answers

Chapter I Answers

1. Under MSF, how is *infrastructure* defined?

   A. The technology needed to support an enterprise computing environment

   B. The total set of resources needed to support an enterprise computing environment

   C. The standards needed to support an enterprise computing environment

   D. The public works that make up the city where resources are located
   B. Under the MSF definition, infrastructure is the total set of resources needed to support an enterprise computing environment.

2. Which of the following is made up of the four perspectives of business architecture, application architecture, information architecture, and technology architecture?

   A. Infrastructure model

   B. Process model

   C. Enterprise Architecture model

   D. Architectural model
   C. The Enterprise Architecture model consists of the four perspectives business architecture, application architecture, information architecture, and technology architecture.

3. Which model breaks an application into User Services, Business Services, and Data Services?

   A. Process model

   B. Application model

   C. Tiered model

   D. Enterprise Architecture model
   B. The Application model breaks an application into three tiers of services: User, Business, and Data Services.

4. Which role in the Team model is responsible for the smooth rollout of the product?

   A. User Education

   B. Development

   C. Deployment

   D. Logistics
   D. Logistics is responsible for the smooth rollout of a product.

5. Which phase of the Process model results in the Vision/Scope Approved milestone?

   A. Envisioning

   B. Stabilization

   C. Deployment

   D. Building
   A. The Envisioning phase of the Process model results in the Vision/Scope Approved milestone.

6. Which of the following represents the total cost based on industry averages?

   A. Baseline

   B. Benchmark

   C. Basemark

   D. Benchline
   B. The benchmark is the total cost based on averages in the industry.

7. Which model has users brought in during the design process so their needs can be anticipated by the project?

    A. Enterprise Architecture

    B. Solutions Design

    C. TCO

    D. Application
    B. The Solutions Design model anticipates user needs by bringing users into the project during the design process.

8. The Application model promotes the use of COM. Which of the following are built on the component object model? (Choose all that apply.)

    A. ActiveX controls

    B. OLE

    C. Solutions Design model

    D. System Management
    A, B. ActiveX controls and OLE are both built on the component object model.

9. The IT life cycle is comprised of three stages under MSF. What are these three stages? (Choose all that apply.)

    A. Plan

    B. Build

    C. Monitor

    D. Manage

    E. Stabilize
    A, B, D. The IT life cycle is comprised of three stages: plan, build, and manage.

10. Which model expands the logistics role to include three new areas in a team?

    A. Team

    B. Logistics

    C. Infrastructure

    D. TCO

    E. Enterprise Architecture
    C. The Infrastructure model expands the logistics to include three new areas in a team: System Management, Help Desk, and Communication.

11. The Process model breaks the development cycle into four phases. What are these phases?

    A. Envisioning, Planning, Developing, Stabilizing

    B. Envisioning, Planning, Building, Managing

    C. Vision/Scope, Planning, Developing, Stabilizing

    D. Envisioning, Planning, Deploying, Stabilizing
    A. The Process model breaks the development cycle into the following four phases: Envisioning, Planning, Developing, and Stabilizing.

12. The Solutions Design model is comprised of different perspectives that provide focus in designing applications. What are these perspectives? (Choose all that apply.)

    A. Conceptual

    B. Logical

    C. Illogical

D. Physical

E. Planning
A, B, D. The three perspectives used in the Solutions Design model are Conceptual, Logical, and Physical.

13. Which role in the Team model is responsible for making decisions that determine delivery of the right product at the right time?

A. Product Management

B. Program Management

C. Logistics

D. Development
B. Program Management is responsible for making decisions that determine delivery of the right product at the right time.

14. What models make up the Microsoft Solution Framework?

A. The Team, Planning, Application, System Management, Enterprise Architecture, Infrastructure, and TCO models

B. The Product Management, Project Management, Development, Design, Testing, User Education, and Logistics models

C. The Team, Process, Application, Solutions Design, Enterprise Architecture, Infrastructure, and TCO models

D. The Team, Process, Product Management, Project Management, Development, Design, Testing, User Education, and Logistics models
C. MSF is made up of the Team, Process, Application, Solutions Design, Enterprise Architecture, Infrastructure, and TCO models.

15. Which phase of the Process model results in the Scope Complete/First Use milestone?

A. Envisioning

B. Planning

C. Developing

D. Stabilizing
C. The Developing phase of the Process model results in the Scope Complete/First Use milestone.

16. Which phase of the Process model results in the Release milestone?

A. Envisioning

B. Planning

C. Developing

D. Stabilizing
D. The Stabilizing phase of the Process model results in the Release milestone.

17. Which service in the Application model is associated with the programmatic interface or user interface?

A. Data Services

B. Business Services

C. User Services

D. Application Services
C. User Services is associated with the user interface and/or programmatic interface.

18. Which of the following models promotes users becoming involved in the design process, so they can address key issues such as usability and user requirements?

    A. Application

    B. Team

    C. Solutions Design

    D. Process
       C. In the Solutions Design model, users become involved in the design process, addressing such key issues as usability and requirements.

19. In which perspective of the Solutions Design model are the structure and communication of elements in the solution laid out?

    A. Logical

    B. Conceptual

    C. Physical

    D. Planning
       A. In the logical perspective of the Solutions Design model, the structure and communication of elements in the solution are laid out.

20. The Enterprise Architecture model consists of four perspectives. Which perspective deals with standards and guidelines for laying out the software and hardware supporting an organization?

    A. Application

    B. Business

    C. Information

    D. Technology
       D. Technology architecture is the perspective that deals with standards and guidelines for laying out the software and hardware supporting an organization.

Chapter 2 Answers

1. What is the key goal of Product Management?

    A. Delivery within project constraints

    B. Delivery to product specifications

    C. Satisfied customers

    D. Smooth deployment and ongoing management
       C. The key goal of product management is satisfied customers. They get the customer's requirements, form and manage a business case, and administer to the expectations of the customer.

2. Which phase in the Process model results in the Scope Complete/First Use milestone?

    A. Envisioning phase

    B. Planning

    C. Developing phase

    D. Stabilization phase
       C. The Developing phase results in the Scope Complete/First Use milestone.

3. What milestone is associated with the creation of a vision statement or vision/scope document?

    A. Vision/Scope Approved

B. Project Plan Approved

C. Scope Complete/First Use

D. Release
A. The Vision/Scope Approved milestone creates a shared vision of a project, which is outlined in a vision statement or vision/scope document.

4. Which of the following is associated with User Services? (Choose all that apply.)

A. Creating a business plan

B. Programmatic interface

C. Graphical user interface

D. Enforcement of business rules
B, C. Programmatic interface and graphical user interface are associated with user services.

5. Which of the following are elements of a business case?

A. Analysis of the customer's business need

B. Proposed and alternative solutions

C. Quantitative and qualitative benefits

D. All of the above

E. None of the above
D. A business case consists of an analysis of the customer's business need, a proposed solution to the business need, alternative solutions that were considered but rejected (and why), and quantitative and qualitative benefits of the proposed solution.

6. Which service in the Application model provides Create, Read, Update, and Delete capabilities to an application?

A. User Services

B. Business Services

C. Middle-tier Services

D. Data Services
D. Data services provides Create, Read, Update, and Delete capabilities to an application.

7. Jennifer is a graphic artist who is working on a graphics-intensive application. To deal with this graphics-intensive process, the application she works with offloads some of the processing to a server's CPU. Which layer of the Application model has dealt with this situation?

A. User Services

B. Graphic Services

C. Middle-tier Services

D. Data Services
C. While offloading graphics-intensive processing isn't a business service, it is one of the services that maps to the middle tier. It doesn't fall into the category of being a user service or a data service, so it is considered a middle-tier service.

8. How is testing performed by the members in the Testing team role? (Choose all that apply.)

A. Randomly check all areas of a solution.

B. Schedules are used to determine when a product is tested.

C. Business cases are used to put testers in the role of the potential user, so they can randomly check areas like a real user.

D. Strategies and plans are used to fine defects, bugs, and errors.
B, D. Schedules are used by Testing to specify when an area of the product will be tested. Strategies and plans are used to find defects, bugs, and errors in a product.

9. The WidgetSoft project has a budget of $25,000, and is to be completed by September 8. The project experiences a few problems. Though it is completed on time, it is over budget by $5000. Which goal has not been met?

A. Delivery to product specifications

B. Smooth deployment and ongoing management

C. Delivery within project constraints

D. None of the above. Since it was completed on time, all goals were met.
C. Delivery within project constraints was not met, since the project went over budget.

10. Which of the following is true of versioned releases?

A. The current version of a program should meet the current requirements of the user.

B. The current version of a program should meet future requirements of the user.

C. The current version of a program should meet obsolete requirements.

D. The current version of a program should meet all conceivable requirements of the user.
A. The current version of a program should meet the current requirements of the user. Future requirements and additional features can be added to later versions.

11. Which team role corresponds to the key goal of enhancing user performance?

A. Development

B. Testing

C. Program Management

D. User Education
D. User Education has the key goal of enhancing user performance.

12. Which team role corresponds to the key goal of a smooth deployment and ongoing management?

A. Development

B. Program Management

C. Testing

D. Logistics
D. Logistics has the key goal of smooth deployment and ongoing management.

13. Your project team has set up a meeting to establish priorities for a project to deal with tradeoffs. What tool will you use to determine a strategy for dealing with tradeoffs?

A. Triangulated relationship

B. Business case

C. Shopping list

D. Tradeoff matrix
D. A tradeoff matrix is used to determine a strategy and establish priorities in a project when dealing with tradeoffs.

14. Your project team has just completed the Scope Complete/First Use milestone. What phase will come next in the development life cycle?

A. Planning

B. Envisioning

C. Developing

D. Stabilization
D. After the Scope Complete/First Use milestone, the development life cycle enters the Stabilization phase.

15. Project teams often depend on external groups. Which groups are members in the development role dependent on?

A. Customers

B. Senior management

C. Operations and support teams

D. None of the above

E. All of the above
D. Development has no external interdependency with other teams. By being internally focused, they aren't distracted from the role of building a product and can focus on their work without having to worry about outside interference.

16. Project teams often depend on external groups. Which project roles have an external group dependency with customers? (Choose all that apply.)

A. Product Management

B. Program Management

C. Testing

D. Logistics
A, B. Product management and program management both have an external group dependency with customers.

17. The project team has just handed responsibility of the product to operations and support teams, which is an indication of which milestone?

A. Vision/Scope Approved

B. Project Plan Approved

C. Release

D. Scope Complete/First Use
C. The Release milestone is where the project team hands over the product or service to operations and support.

18. How do the different layers of the Application model communicate with one another? (Choose the best answer.)

A. Service requests

B. ActiveX components

C. The Application model is a theoretical design. There is no need for actual communication.

D. The layers perform different activities, and have no need to communicate.
A. The layers of the Application model communicate through service requests.

19. Which of the following best defines a *business rule*?

    A. It is a policy that determines how team roles are assigned.

    B. It is a policy used to determine how a business task is performed.

    C. It is determined by the requirements of a customer, and used to specify the user interface.

    D. It is the criteria used in creating a business case.
    B. Business rules are policies used to determine how a business task is performed.

20. How should you increment a large project into multiple versioned releases?

    A. Ask what users want, then add all features requested at that time to the current release.

    B. Address the most important needs of the user, and add additional functionality to later releases.

    C. Add all possible features to a program, so that new ideas can be added later.

    D. See what the competition does first, then release a similar program.
    B. Large projects are incremented into versioned releases by addressing the most important needs of the user, and adding additional features to later releases.

21. Which of the following is not a phase in the Process model?

    A. Envisioning

    B. Planning

    C. Developing

    D. Release
    D. Release is the milestone that results from the Stabilization phase of the Process model.

22. Which of the following best describes vision?

    A. It is an optimistic view of a project's goals, where no consideration is given to the goals of the project.

    B. It is an unbridled view of a project's goals, with no consideration given to the constraints of a project.

    C. It defines the limitations of a product or service, and determining what can be done within the project's constraints. It is synonymous with scope.

    D. It is a view of project priorities, which establish where tradeoffs in a project will take place.
    B. Vision is an unbridled view of a project's goals, with no consideration given to the constraints of a project.

23. The Team model is made up of six roles and six goals. In your zeal to get a project started, one of the roles isn't assigned to anyone, leaving one of the six goals not represented by anyone. How will this affect the project?

    A. The Team model is designed for redundancy. It won't affect the project.

    B. It will result in extra work for other members, but the Process model deals with this contingency.

C. The project will fail.

D. It depends on which role hasn't been assigned, and what goal isn't achieved as to whether the project will succeed or fail.

C. If a team role or a single goal isn't assigned to someone, the project itself would fail. All six goals must be achieved for the project to succeed.

24. Delivery within project constraints is a key goal addressed by the Team model. Which role is associated with this goal?

A. Product Management

B. Program Management

C. Development

D. Logistics

B. The key goal associated with Program Management is delivery within project constraints.

25. Which phase in the Process model ends in the Project Plan Approved milestone?

A. Envisioning

B. Planning

C. Developing

D. Stabilization

B. The Planning phase ends with the Project Plan Approved milestone.

26. The Application model is a tiered model for solution development. From top to bottom layer, what are the tiers of this model?

A. Data Services, Business Services, User Services

B. User Services, middle-tier services, Data Services, Business Services

C. User Services, Business Services, Data Services

D. Business Services, middle-tier services, Data Services

C. The Application model is made up of three layered services. From top to bottom these are: User Services, Business Services (and other middle-tier services), and Data Services.

27. Each role in the Team model has different responsibilities. Which of the following is a responsibility of User Education? (Choose all that apply.)

A. Acting as advocate for the customer

B. Designing, creating, and testing materials to assist the user

C. Smooth deployment and support management

D. Acting as advocate for the end user

B, D. User education acts as an advocate of the end user. This is different from advocacy for the customer. While the customer pays for the product, the end user is the person who uses it. This role is responsible for designing, creating, and testing materials that assist the user. Online assistance, manuals, wizards, and training materials fall into the realm of user education.

28. You are working with a tradeoff matrix that has the Optimize column for Features (Scope) checked, indicating that a

maximum benefit strategy will be used. What does this mean?

A. As many features as possible will be shipped with the current version.

B. Features essential to the main functionality of the product will be shipped.

C. Features will be dropped from the current version.

D. It means your job is in jeopardy.
A. When the Optimize column for Features (Scope) is checked, a maximum benefit strategy is used, and it is accepted that as many features as possible will be shipped with the current version of the product.

29. What key goal in a project maps to the role of Testing?

A. Delivery to product specifications

B. Release after addressing all issues

C. Smooth deployment

D. Delivery within project constraints
B. Testing has the key goal of releasing a product or service after addressing all issues.

30. Which of the following is created in the Planning phase of the Process model? (Choose all that apply.)

A. Vision statement

B. Vision/scope document

C. Functional specification

D. Planning specification
C. The functional specification is

created during the Planning phase of the Process model.

31. Which of the following is a true statement?

A. Business rules change more frequently than business tasks.

B. Business tasks change at the same rate as business rules.

C. Business tasks change more frequently than business rules.

D. Business tasks change each time a business rule changes.
A. Business rules change more frequently than business tasks.

32. What are benefits of modular design in development? (Choose all that apply.)

A. It breaks a large project into subprojects.

B. It improves morale.

C. It allows different parts of a project to be developed parallel to one another.

D. It takes longer to complete a project.
A, B, C. Modular design allows a project to be broken into smaller subprojects. Since developers are able to see the progress of development and look forward to working on the next subproject, morale is improved. By having modules worked on by different developers, the parts of a project are developed parallel to one another, improving the speed of development.

33. You are using a tradeoff matrix, and notice that the Optimize column for the

Schedule row is checked. What does this indicate?

A. The ship date for the product is to be as soon as possible.

B. The product will not meet its previous ship date.

C. The product is to be shipped at a later date.

D. The product must keep its current ship date.
   A. When the Optimize column of the Schedule row is checked, an early-to-market strategy is used. This strategy specifies that the ship date for the product or service is to be as soon as possible.

34. Different roles of the Team model have dependencies on external groups. On which external group does User Education have a dependency?

A. Customer

B. Operations and support teams

C. End user

D. Senior management
   C. User Education has the role of enhancing the user's experience with a product or service. As such, its dependency is with the end user. This is not necessarily the same as the customer. While the customer pays for the product, it is the end user who actually uses it.

35. Which team role has the responsibility for creating the functional specification for a product?

A. Product Management

B. Program Management

C. Development

D. Logistics
   B. Program Management has the responsibility of creating the functional specification. This is done by taking the requirements outlined by Product Management, and specifying what will be created.

36. You are using a tradeoff matrix and notice that the Accept column of the Schedule row is checked. What does this indicate?

A. The ship date for the product is to be as soon as possible.

B. The product will not meet its previous ship date.

C. The product is to be shipped at an earlier date.

D. The product must keep its current ship date.
   B. When the Accept column is checked in the schedule row, a tradeoff is made with the ship date, and it is accepted that the product will not meet its previous due date for release.

37. You are working on a large project that's taking considerable time. This is affecting morale, and developers are getting depressed working on the project. What can you do to solve these problems?

A. Fire the developers and hire a subcontractor to finish the project.

B. Break the project into larger projects.

C. Break the project into smaller projects.

D. Scrap the project.
   C. Breaking a large project into smaller projects can decrease development time, as parts of the project can be developed parallel to one another. This improves morale, as developers can see progress in a project, and look forward to the next subproject.

38. A milestone occurs at the end of a phase in the Process model. What does a milestone indicate? (Choose all that apply.)

A. The project is complete.

B. One phase of the project is complete, and another is ready to begin.

C. The point in time where members synchronize their efforts.

D. A phase needs to be repeated.
   B, C. A milestone indicates the point where one phase of a project ends and another begins, and the point in time that members of a team should synchronize their efforts.

39. One of the team roles in the Team model is Development. What is the key goal associated with this role?

A. Delivery within project constraints

B. Delivery to product specifications

C. Release after addressing all issues

D. Enhanced user performance
   B. Delivery to product specifications

is the key goal associated with Development.

40. Which of the following is correct?

A. The Planning phase results in the Scope Complete/First Use milestone.

B. The Envisioning phase results in the Vision/Scope Approved milestone.

C. The Developing phase results in the Release milestone.

D. The Stabilization phase results in the Project Plan Approved milestone.
   B. The Envisioning phase results in the Vision/Scope Approved milestone.

Chapter 3 Answers

1. A risk has a risk probability of 100 percent. What does this mean?

A. The success of the project is ensured.

B. There is no risk, or chance of a problem occurring.

C. The risk has already become an actual problem.

D. The failure of the project is ensured.
   C. When a risk has a risk probability of 100 percent, it means that it has already become an actual problem.

2. Part of a project has been contracted out to a small software company. The developers at this firm were on strike for two weeks, causing work to fall behind by this amount of time. The owner of the firm tells you he's sorry, and that this strike has cost his software firm $5000 in

business. What is the risk impact to your project?

A. two weeks

B. $5000

C. There is no risk impact. This impacts the contractor, not you.

D. one week
   A. Since work from the contractor has fallen behind by two weeks, the risk impact is two weeks to your schedule.

3. What are the four key areas of risk action planning?

A. Research, acceptance, management, avoidance

B. Research, management, transfer, avoidance

C. Identify, assess, action, track, control

D. Assess, research, management, avoidance
   A. The four key areas of risk action planning are research, acceptance, management, and avoidance.

4. Which step in the risk management process results in the generation of a risk action form?

A. Identification

B. Risk analysis

C. Risk control

D. Risk tracking

E. None of the above
   E. A risk action form results from the work done in the risk action planning step of the risk management process.

5. Which step in the risk management process is the first time a Top 10 Risk List is generated?

A. Identification

B. Risk analysis

C. Risk control

D. Risk tracking

E. None of the above
   B. The Top 10 Risk List is generated in the risk analysis step of the risk management process. This is revised in later steps of the process.

6. Which of the following represents the amount of loss that would occur if a risk became an actual problem?

A. Risk category

B. Risk impact

C. Risk exposure

D. Risk identifier
   B. Risk impact represents the amount of loss that would occur if a risk became an actual problem.

7. Which of the following deals with risks before they result in loss, or become actual problems?

A. Reactive risk management

B. Proactive risk management

C. Preliminary risk management

D. All forms of risk management
   B. Proactive risk management deals with risks before they result in loss, or become actual problems.

8. Which of the following is best defined as the overall threat to a project?

   A. Risk

   B. Risk context

   C. Risk exposure

   D. Risk probability

   C. Risk exposure is the overall threat to a project. It is calculated by multiplying the size of loss by the probability of loss.

9. Which of the following must be included in a risk statement?

   A. The risk or risks that may be an issue to the project

   B. The source of a risk

   C. The expected consequence

   D. Risk control measures

   E. Crisis management issues

   A, B, C. Risk statements must include the risk source, associated risks, and the expected consequence of the risk. If any of these are missing, the risk statement is incomplete.

10. Which of the following best describes a risk?

    A. The certainty of loss

    B. The certainty that a problem will result

    C. The possibility of loss

    D. An object, person, or structure that causes the certainty of loss

    C. Risk is the possibility of loss.

11. You are using a risk assessment table, shown next. What is the risk exposure of the project?

Risk	Probability of Loss	Size of Loss (Weeks)	Risk Exposure (Weeks)
Redesign required due to inadequate design.	20 percent	5	

    A. 20 percent

    B. 5

    C. .04

    D. 4 percent

    E. 1

    E. The risk exposure is calculated by multiplying the two fields representing size of loss and probability of loss together. This means that the answer would by 1 (which is 5 × 20 percent, or 5 × .20).

12. Which of following is not a goal of risk management?

    A. Reduce the probability that the risk will actually occur.

    B. Keep the consequences associated with a risk constant.

    C. Reduce the extent or magnitude of loss that could result from the risk.

    D. Change the consequences associated with the risk.

    B. Keeping the consequences associated with a risk constant is not a goal of risk management. The goals of risk management are to reduce the probability that the risk will actually occur, reduce the extent or magnitude of loss that could result from the risk, and to change the consequences associated with the risk.

13. Which of the following specifies the focus area, risk factor category, and risk factor?

   A. Risk probability

   B. Risk source

   C. Risk context

   D. Risk consequence
      B. The risk source specifies the focus area, risk factor category, and risk factor.

14. Which of the following would contain a contingency plan to deal with a risk?

   A. Risk statement

   B. Risk action plan

   C. Top 10 Risk List

   D. Risk status report
      B. In addition to providing an initial plan of action, the risk action plan also includes a contingency plan to be used if the initial plan fails.

15. Delays in one area have a cascading effect on other areas. It results in tasks not being completed on time. Which of the following risk categories is this most directly linked to?

   A. Budget and cost

   B. Schedule

   C. Action planning

   D. Risk management
      B. Schedule is the risk category being affected most by this situation. Time is what's being affected, as delays in one area are eating into others.

16. Below is part of a table used in risk management. What is it an example of?

Risk	Probability of Loss	Size of Loss (Weeks)	Risk Exposure (Weeks)
Design is inadequate — needs reworking.	25 percent	8	2
Schedule is overly optimistic.	50 percent	2	1

   A. Risk assessment table

   B. Risk factor chart

   C. Top 10 Risk List

   D. Risk statement
      A. The table shown is an example of a risk assessment table.

17. Which of the following details the duties and actions to be performed in managing the risk?

   A. Due dates

   B. Personnel assignments

   C. Action items

   D. Risk sources
      C. Action items detail the duties and actions to be performed in managing the risk. Due dates are used to specify when the action item is to be completed

by, while personnel assignments show who is to perform the action item.

18. You are filling out a risk statement form and reach an area that asks for the risk consequence. What information will you enter in this area?

    A. A description of the loss that will occur, or results of the risk if it becomes an actual problem

    B. A description of the consequences expected if the suggested action plan succeeds

    C. A description of how managing this risk will affect the schedule of the project

    D. A description of the alternative action plan
    A. A risk consequence is a description of the consequences or loss that will occur if the risk becomes an actual problem

19. Which of the following best describes risk probability?

    A. It represents the likelihood that a loss will occur.

    B. It represents the certainty that a loss will occur.

    C. It represents that a loss has already occurred.

    D. It is calculated by multiplying risk exposure by risk impact.
    A. Risk probability represents the likelihood that a loss will occur.

20. When creating risk action plans, you have decided that no further action is necessary for a particular risk. What key area of risk action planning does this decision fall into?

    A. Research

    B. Acceptance

    C. Management

    D. Avoidance
    B. Acceptance is when you decide that no further action is necessary for a risk, and accept things as they stand.

Chapter 4 Answers

1. You have decided to use the Process model on a software development project. Which phase will your team start with in using this model?

    A. Envisioning

    B. Planning

    C. Developing

    D. Stabilizing
    A. The Envisioning phase is the first phase of the Process model.

2. Which of the following milestones are reached only after business constraints, which may adversely affect the project, are identified?

    A. Vision/Scope Approved milestone

    B. Project Plan Approved milestone

    C. Scope Complete/First Use milestone

    D. Release milestone
    A. In order to attain vision/scope

approval, the project team and the customer must reach agreement on several key points. One of these is identifying business constraints that may affect the project. Other key issues include agreeing on the overall vision for the project, which business requirements should be addressed first, setting a time frame for the project, risks that are associated with the project, and the required effort expected to complete the project.

3. During the Planning phase, which team role is responsible for ensuring that expectations are met in the product design?

   A. Project Management

   B. Development

   C. User Education

   D. Product Management
   D. During the Planning phase, Product Management collects and analyzes information that is germane to user expectations. It is responsible for ensuring that these expectations are met in the product design.

4. Which of the following milestones demands the signoff that the functional specification/design specification will meet the desired requirements?

   A. Vision/Scope Approved milestone

   B. Project Plan Approved milestone

   C. Scope Complete/First Use milestone

   D. Release milestone
   B. The Project Plan Approved milestone is considered to have been reached when the Program Management team signs off that the functional specification will meet the desired requirements, that there is sufficient accountability for each function, and that the schedules are realistic.

5. The project team has just achieved the Vision/Scope Approved milestone. What phase of the Process model will your team now use?

   A. Envisioning

   B. Planning

   C. Developing

   D. Stabilizing
   B. The Planning phase occurs after the Vision/Scope Approved milestone of the Envisioning phase has been achieved. It is the second phase of the Process model.

6. You are creating a project structure document to outline the structure of the project you're currently working on. What information will be included in this document? (Choose all that apply.)

   A. Project plans

   B. How the project will be managed and supported

   C. Administrative structure of the project team

   D. Other information that the project team may find useful, such as e-mail addresses and phone numbers

B, C, D. The project structure document includes such information as how the project will be managed and supported, the administrative structure of the project team, and other information that may be helpful to the project team.

7. You have reached the end of a project, and have decided to review the project to determine what went well, and which problems could have been avoided. Which deliverable is this?

    A. Master project plan

    B. Project plan

    C. Milestone review

    D. Golden master
    C. A milestone review is used to evaluate the project, and determine common problems and successes that occurred in the Process model.

8. You have reached a point in the project where no additional changes or additions will be made to the product. What deliverable does this represent?

    A. Master project plan

    B. Project plan

    C. Functional specification

    D. Frozen functional specification
    D. A frozen functional specification is when no additional changes or additions are made to the functional specification of the product.

9. You have reached a point in the project where no additional changes or additions will be made to the product. In what phase of the Process model does this occur?

    A. Envisioning

    B. Planning

    C. Developing

    D. Stabilizing
    C. During the Developing phase of the Process model, the functional specification is frozen, allowing no further changes or additions to be made to the product.

10. Which role of the Team model is responsible for the team achieving the Vision/Scope Approved milestone?

    A. Program Management

    B. Project Management

    C. Product Management

    D. Logistics
    C. Product Management has ownership of the Envisioning phase. It is the responsibility of this role to see that the team achieves the Vision/Scope Approved milestone.

11. The project has reached the point where the application has been designed, and development has begun. Which milestone is the project team now working to achieve?

    A. Developing

    B. Stabilizing

    C. Scope Complete/First Use

D. Release

C. When the project team reaches the point where the application has been designed, and development has begun, they are in the Developing phase of the project. During this phase, the project team is working to achieve the scope Complete/First Use milestone.

12. You are looking through the deliverables produced during the current phase of the project, and notice that the source code includes fixes to bugs that were found during testing by the Testing team. Which phase of the project are you currently in?

A. Scope Complete/First Use

B. Developing

C. Release

D. Stabilizing

D. During the Stabilizing phase, the source code includes fixes to bugs that were found during testing. While source code is also a deliverable of the Developing phase, the solution hasn't undergone testing by the Testing team and doesn't include these fixes. The other two choices provided in this question are milestones, not phases of the Process model.

13. The project team is working to achieve the Scope Complete/First Use milestone. Which of the following team roles has ownership of achieving this milestone? (Choose all that apply.)

A. Development

B. Product Management

C. Logistics

D. User Education

A, D. During the Developing phase, the team roles of Development and User Education have ownership.

14. The project team is working to achieve the Release milestone. Which of the following team roles has ownership of achieving this milestone? (Choose all that apply.)

A. Development

B. Logistics

C. Testing

D. User Education

B, C. During the Stabilizing phase, the team roles of Logistics and Testing have ownership.

15. Which of the following acts as a contract between the project team and customer? When approval is given on this deliverable, the project team is able to start development on the product.

A. Golden release

B. Frozen functional specification

C. Functional specification

D. Project plan

B. If the functional specification suits the needs and requirements of the user, the team is given the go-ahead by the customer to start development.

16. You have finished the product and are now ready to release the solution. What

will you use to create copies of the application to release to users?

A. Master release

B. Golden release

C. Zero-bug release

D. Deployment release
   B. The golden release is the finished copy of the product that will be used to make copies released to users.

17. You are creating a schedule for your team and decide to use bottom-up, task-level estimates. Who will provide the estimates required for performing individual tasks?

A. Project Management

B. Product Management

C. The person performing the task

D. The team leader of the person who performs the task
   C. Bottom-up, task-level estimating means that the person who does the work determines how long it will take.

Chapter 5 Answers

1. Complete this sentence: *Enterprise architecture* _____

   A. consists of people, process, and technology.

   B. is the intersection of people, process, and technology.

   C. consists of the Process model and Team model.

   D. means *technology infrastructure.*
      A. Enterprise architecture consists of people, process, and technology.

2. Which is an example of an enterprise architecture process?

   A. Managers

   B. TCP/IP

   C. Billing

   D. Microsoft Project
      C. Processes are neither the technology nor the people, but the procedures (such as billing) that people follow, often using technology.

3. Which is not a technology infrastructure category?

   A. Data transmission links

   B. Local area network architecture

   C. Protocols and transports

   D. TCP/IP
      D. All are elements of the infrastructure, but TCP/IP is an example, not a category.

4. The MSF Process model does not include

   A. Milestones

   B. Phases

   C. Teams

   D. Deliverables
      C. The MSF Team model (not the Process model) addresses team makeup.

5. Which milestone happens before the Planning phase?

   A. Vision/Scope Approved

B. Project Plan Approved

C. Scope Complete/First Use

D. Envisioning
A. The Envisioning phase ends with the Vision/Scope Approved milestone, and then the Planning phase begins.

6. Complete the following sentence: Vision addresses _____

A. the nature of the solution.

B. how the business will change with the new solution.

C. team makeup.

D. testing.
B. Vision addresses how the business will change with the new solution.

7. Which does not affect scope?

A. Resources

B. Schedules

C. Solution functionality

D. Planning
D. Scope puts real-world limits onto the vision, so it is beyond the Planning phase.

8. Which interim milestone occurs first?

A. Draft Vision/Scope

B. Final Vision/Scope

C. Team Formation Complete

D. Vision/Scope Approved
C. Before you can get consensus on your vision, you need to have the complete team together.

9. Which team has responsibility for articulating the vision?

A. Development

B. Program Management

C. Logistics Management

D. Product Management
D. Product Management must articulate vision to the team and to customers.

10. A SMART vision/scope document is

A. Specific, Measurable, Achievable, Results-based, and Time-oriented

B. Significant, Marketable, Achievable, Ready, and Testable

C. Sloppy, Marked, Amiable, Red, and Typed

D. Specific, Measurable, Action-oriented, low Risk, and Timely
A. Specific, Measurable, Achievable, Results-based, and Time-oriented.

11. The Conceptual Design Complete interim milestone is a part of which phase?

A. Envisioning

B. Planning

C. Developing

D. Deploying
B. Planning is the time when you put your conceptual design together.

12. Which is not an interim milestone of the Planning phase?

A. Conceptual Design Complete

B. Design Specification Complete

C. Master Project Plan Complete

D. Lab Testing Complete
    D. Lab testing occurs in the Developing phase.

13. The security plan is a part of which deliverable of the Planning phase?

    A. Conceptual design document

    B. Design specification

    C. Master project schedule

    D. Master project plan
        B. The design specification includes several parts, one of which is the security plan.

14. Complete the following sentence: The master project schedule _____

    A. evolves over time.

    B. stays set.

    C. is good for the Planning phase only.

    D. can by changed by development.
        A. The master project schedule cannot predict everything. As knowledge evolves, your team will reach consensus on how to change the schedule.

15. During planning, Development is responsible for _____

    A. user needs analysis.

    B. project plan.

    C. technology evaluation.

    D. design evaluation.
        C. Among other important tasks, the development team handles technology evaluation during the Planning phase.

16. Which test happens last in the Developing phase?

    A. Pilot

    B. Test lab

    C. Proof-of-concept

    D. Design test
        A. The test lab and proof-of-concept continue to operate, but the pilot is the last test before deployment.

17. Which does the Lab Testing Complete milestone mark?

    A. Real-world validation

    B. Technology validation

    C. Solution validation

    D. Software validation
        B. The test lab looks at the technologies involved in the solution.

18. Which is not a deliverable of the Developing phase?

    A. Pilot plan

    B. Training plan

    C. Rollout plan

    D. Project review
        D. Project review happens towards the end of the Deploying phase.

19. What does the business continuation plan do?

    A. Provides for transition to normal operations.

    B. Eliminates risk.

    C. Returns the company to an acceptable threshold of performance.

D. Returns the company to pre-failure.
C. The plan provides the first steps for disaster recovery during the project.

20. Which is not an interim milestone of the Deploying phase?

    A. Rollout Begins

    B. Training Complete

    C. Rollout Complete

    D. Program Review
    D. Stabilization Complete is the fourth interim milestone of the Deploying phase.

Chapter 6 Answers

1. Which milestone is owned by the User Education and Development roles in the Team model?

    A. Vision/Scope Approved

    B. Project Plan Approved

    C. Scope Complete/First Use

    D. Release
    C. User Education and Development have ownership of the Scope Complete/First Use milestone.

2. Which of the following is an internal interim milestone?

    A. Synchronization Points

    B. Management Review Meetings

    C. Post-Functional Specification Baseline Meetings

    D. Review and Validation of a Draft Functional Specification
    A. Synchronization Points are internal interim milestones. The project team uses them to coordinate efforts, and determine that the functional specification matches assumptions made by team members. Each of the other choices is externally visible, and thereby known to the organization.

3. Which role of the Team model adds buffer time to the schedule, and where in the schedule is buffer time added?

    A. Program Management adds buffer time to the end of the schedule.

    B. Product Management adds buffer time to each task in the schedule.

    C. Program Management adds buffer time to each task in the schedule.

    D. Development adds buffer time to the end of the schedule.
    A. Program Management adds buffer time to the end of the schedule.

4. What is the purpose of performing daily builds? (Choose all that apply.)

    A. Compiling files and components

    B. Linking files and components

    C. Exercising the system

    D. Ensuring that the application launches properly
    A, B, D. A daily build is used to ensure that files and components compile and link successfully, and that the

application launches properly without being hazardous to the system.

5. What are the four perspectives of the Enterprise Architecture model?

   A. Conceptual, application, information, and technology

   B. Conceptual, logical, physical, and technology

   C. Business, application, information, and technology

   D. Business, logical, information, and technology
   C. The four perspectives in the Enterprise Architecture model are business architecture, application architecture, information architecture, and technology architecture.

6. Which of the following best defines *modular design*?

   A. Modular design involves breaking a large project into modules that are designed to perform different and specific tasks and functions.

   B. Modular design is the design procedure for network applications that use modems.

   C. Modular design involves breaking large networking into modular networks that are designed to improve performance.

   D. There is no such thing as modular design.
   A. Modular design involves breaking a large project into manageable chunks

called modules. These modules are designed to perform different and specific tasks and functions.

7. Which other models does the Solutions Design model tie together to focus resources so they produce the most value? (Choose all that apply.)

   A. Process model

   B. Modular model

   C. Team model

   D. Application model
   A, C, D. The Solutions Design model ties together the Process, Team, and Application models to focus resources so they produce the most value.

8. What perspectives make up the Solutions Design model? (Choose all that apply.)

   A. Conceptual design

   B. Modular design

   C. Logical design

   D. Physical design
   A, C, D. The Solutions Design model is comprised of the conceptual, logical, and physical design perspectives.

9. You are designing a business solution, and have decided that at this point in the project, you will adopt a fixed-date mindset. The customer now comes to you and decides that she wants several new features added to the product. If these features aren't added, in addition to the other features already incorporated into the solution's design, then the productivity of users

will suffer. Which areas of the software development process can you trade off to implement these features?

A. Schedule

B. Resources

C. Features

D. Schedule and Resources

E. Resources and Features
B. Because all of the features must be included in the project, you can't trade off features. Since your team has adopted a fixed-date mindset, you can't trade off the schedule. As such, the only area where tradeoffs can be made are resources.

10. You have a project with a delivery schedule of six months. What should you consider implementing?

A. ActiveX components

B. Interim milestones

C. Major milestones

D. Interim delivery schedules
B. For delivery schedules that are over three months, you should consider using interim milestones. These break up a project and provide additional points at which the team can synchronize their efforts.

11. For which of the following milestones does Product Management hold responsibility?

A. Vision/Scope Approved

B. Project Plan Approved

C. Scope Complete/First Use

D. Release
A. Product Management holds responsibility for the Vision/Scope Approved milestone.

12. What kinds of interim milestones are there, and what is the difference between them?

A. There are no different kinds of interim milestones. They are only used for synchronization points for the team.

B. Internal interim milestones are announced to the organization, while external interim milestones have a beta release of the product available for public use.

C. Internal interim milestones are announced to the organization, while external interim milestones have a beta release of the product available for organizational use.

D. Internal interim milestones are known only to the project team, while external interim milestones are announced to the organization.
D. Internal interim milestones are known only to the project team, while external interim milestones are announced to the organization.

13. Which perspective defines the application portfolio of the enterprise?

A. Business

B. Application

C. Information

D. Technology
   B. The application architecture perspective defines the application portfolio of the enterprise.

14. Which of the following Enterprise Architecture perspectives correspond to the physical design perspective of Solutions Design?

    A. Business

    B. Application

    C. Information

    D. Technology
       D. The technology perspective of the Enterprise Architecture model corresponds to the physical design perspective of Solutions Design.

15. Which perspective of the Enterprise Architecture model corresponds to the Envisioning phase of the Process model?

    A. Business

    B. Application

    C. Information

    D. Technology
       A. The business architecture perspective corresponds to the Envisioning phase of the Process model. It is here that the business needs of the enterprise are acquired, and the vision statement, vision/scope document, and business cases are created.

16. In which of the following perspectives are the needs of the customer and user determined, and the idea of the solution is conceived?

    A. Technology

    B. Conceptual

    C. Logical

    D. Physical
       B. The conceptual design perspective is where the needs of the customer and user are determined, and the idea of the solution is conceived.

17. In which of the following perspectives are the structure and communication of elements making up your application laid out?

    A. Technology

    B. Conceptual

    C. Logical

    D. Physical
       C. In the logical design perspective, the structure and communication of elements making up your application are laid out.

18. Which perspective describes what the company needs to know to run the organization's business processes and operations, and how data and information are handled in an organization?

    A. Business

    B. Application

    C. Information

    D. Technology
       C. The information perspective describes what the company needs to

know to run the organization's business processes and operations, and how data and information are handled in an organization.

19. Which perspective provides standards and guidelines for laying out the software and hardware supporting an organization?

   A. Business

   B. Application

   C. Information

   D. Technology
   D. Technology Architecture provides standards and guidelines for laying out the software and hardware supporting an organization.

20. In which of the following perspectives are the constraints of technology applied to the logical design of the solution?

   A. Modular

   B. Conceptual

   C. Business

   D. Physical
   D. In physical design, the constraints of technology are applied to the logical design of the solution.

Chapter 7 Answers

1. What costs are included in a TCO assessment?

   A. Fixed and variable Costs

   B. Direct and indirect Costs

   C. Budgeted and unbudgeted Costs

   D. Discretionary and involuntary Costs
   B. Direct and indirect Costs. The direct costs are typically attributable to the implementation of IT in an organization. Indirect costs are still IT costs but may be hidden in the budgets of other departments.

2. What are the phase names of the TCO cycle?

   A. Plan, Do, Check

   B. Improve, Manage, Analyze

   C. Manage, Plan, Build

   D. Analyze, Develop, Test
   B. Improve, Manage, Analyze. Plan-Do-Check-Act is from Quality Assurance; Manage-Plan-Build is the Microsoft Solutions Framework IT life cycle; and Analyze-Develop-Test is the life cycle of applications development. This demonstrates one valid technique of arriving at a correct answer … eliminate all the wrong answers.

3. Which is not a goal of the TCO Manage phase?

   A. Monitor, track, and adjust affected projects.

   B. Establish an improvement cycle.

   C. Re-establish the baseline.

   D. Create what-if scenarios to simulate the costs and benefits of improvement projects.
   D. Create what-if scenarios to simulate the costs and benefits of improvement projects. This task is

part of the Improve phase of the TCO cycle.

4. What is not within the scope of TCO?

   A. Mainframe costs

   B. Peer support of end users

   C. Downtime

   D. Travel costs for computer consultants
   A. Mainframe costs. Microsoft intends to aid customers to get a handle on the costs of increasingly distributed components of IT.

5. Which of the following is not a benefit of screen prototyping?

   A. The users aid in the placement of text and input boxes to create a sense of ownership of the screens.

   B. The flow of the screens from task to task is based on the recommendations from the business community.

   C. The user documentation can be developed earlier in the development life cycle.

   D. The prototype may then be used as the application.
   D. The prototype may then be used as the application. Prototypes should never be used as the foundation of an application. Prototypes are rarely robust enough and, because they appear to be functioning applications, they may warp user expectations.

6. What is not included in the end-user TCO costs?

   A. The labor costs to restore an end user's workstation after they deleted the registry database.

   B. The labor costs for the end user to install a favorite spreadsheet application.

   C. The cost to upgrade an end user's favorite spreadsheet application.

   D. The labor costs for the end users to play a networked game of hearts during office hours.
   D. The labor costs for the end users to play a networked game of hearts during office hours. These may be costs to the organization, but they are not related to the implementation of IT.

7. During the Requirements Analysis phase, the idea is expressed that for any one order there may be multiple lines of ordered items. Which technique is best used to model this detail?

   A. Data Flow Diagramming

   B. Entity Relationship Diagramming

   C. Use cases

   D. Functional Decomposition
   B. Entity Relationship Diagramming. These are types of information or data entities. An order is the first entity and an order line item is the second entity. These two entities then contain fields and have a relationship to each other. All of these concepts are modeled on an Entity Relationship Diagram.

8. Which of the following organizational roles should be interviewed for the

Requirements Analysis phase in a new payroll application?

A. The employees who get paid

B. The payroll clerk

C. The CFO

D. All of the above

> **D. All of the above.** Each role is concerned with the business functions and may contribute significant, although different, viewpoints.

9. Which of the following is not a technique used in gathering requirements from the business community?

A. Initial data modeling

B. Review of the inventory of hardware in use

C. Questionnaires

D. Interviews

> **B. Review of the inventory of hardware in use.** In the Analysis phase, the technical hardware platform currently available is not considered in the business requirements.

10. Which of the following requirements might a warehouse manager state?

A. Need to know the cost of an item.

B. Need to track the physical location of an item.

C. Need to know the reorder quantity point of an item.

D. Need to know the vendor of an item.

> **B. Need to track the physical location of an item.** Although each organization implements business roles differently, a warehouse manager is concerned about item location and space consumed by that item. Definitions of roles are helpful in the Analysis phase.

11. Which of the following is not a step in the implementation of TCO?

A. Create a baseline set of data.

B. Recognize the issues that the analyzed data is highlighting.

C. Collect industry averages for analysis.

D. Measure progress toward resolving issues.

> **C. Collect industry averages for analysis.** Organizations such as the Gartner Group collect industrial averages. The organization doing a TCO assessment must then identify which industry average to use in their baseline.

12. Identify the statement that is not a business requirement.

A. Create an application to manage health improvement.

B. Allow the user to choose each food from a list of items.

C. Create a report of all food ingredients for a daily menu sorted by food type.

D. Allow the user to enter favorite recipes and calculate the nutritional breakdown

> **A. Create an application to manage health improvement.** This is too broad a statement. It must be broken into specific tasks to be a requirement.

This statement may be an objective of the business area application.

13. Select the business requirement from the following.

A. The application will run on NT 4 workstations.

B. The database for the application will be SQL Server.

C. Each food must have associated calories, fat, sodium, and cholesterol measures.

D. The application must have a web browser interface
C. Each food must have associated calories, fat, sodium, and cholesterol measures. The other choices are technical design constraints.

14. What role in the organization would state the following requirement: "Once a field has been entered and the return key pressed, the cursor must automatically position itself in the next field"?

A. The CFO

B. The CIO

C. The data entry clerks

D. The nutritional experts
C. The data entry clerks. This is a requirement stated by the individual responsible for daily work with the user interface screens.

15. Identify the tool not used in the Requirements phase of Applications Development.

A. Data Definition Language

B. Entity Relationship Diagram

C. Data Flow Diagram

D. Prototyping
A. Data Definition Language This defines the structure of the database and is a deliverable from the physical model of the database.

16. Identify the best reason to generate a requirements analysis document.

A. It can be used as an agreement contract between the technical team and the business community to manage scope creep.

B. It may be used for training new additions to the programming team.

C. A document can be mailed to geographically dispersed participants.

D. Laser printer paper make the best airplanes because it creases nicely
A. It can be used as an agreement contract between the technical team and the business community to manage scope creep. Although B and C are good answers, choice A is the best. Microsoft multiple-choice questions often ask for the "best answer."

17. Select the reason why the technical team does not create the business requirements.

A. The business users involved in the daily business activities know the business aspect better.

B. The requirements document would be filled with acronyms and technical terms if the IT team stated the requirements.

C. The document would be online rather than printed.

D. The technical team is not involved until after the Analysis phase

A. The business users involved in the daily business activities know the business aspect better. Although the business users specify the requirements, the technical analysts actually write the requirements. Realistically, the requirements document is a team effort, but the business user must understand it and sign off on it.

18. Select the analysis tool that aids in defining the workflow for the end user.

A. Data Flow Diagrams

B. Storyboarding

C. Entity Relationship Diagrams

D. Functional Hierarchies

B. Storyboarding. Although the Functional Hierarchy Diagram may suggest a navigational approach, storyboarding can clearly show the task-by-task flow of work.

19. The term *analysis paralysis* is best defined as:

A. What happens when the lead analyst does not agree with the statement of requirements by the business users.

B. A never-ending discussion of the minute details about how the application should function.

C. An iterative process of Prototype-Review-Modify.

D. The users cannot agree on the requirements.

B. A never-ending discussion of the minute details about how the application should function. Although the other choices may occur, paralysis is a direct result of wanting too much detail too early in the development cycle.

20. Which choice does not have potential to constrain a development project?

A. Financial Situation

B. Organization Politics

C. Training Needs

D. Vision statement for the business application

D. Vision statement for the business application. The vision should be all-encompassing. The scope then defines the boundaries, and the requirements must be defined within that scope.

Chapter 8 Answers

1. You are analyzing security requirements of the business, and want to establish the fault tolerance, based on what's available in the existing environment. You find that the organization's network uses NT servers. Which of the following levels of RAID will work with this type of network and provide fault tolerance? (Choose all that apply.)

A. RAID 0

B. RAID 1

C. RAID 3

D. RAID 5
B, D. Of the different levels of RAID, only levels 1 and 5 support fault tolerance. NT Server does support RAID levels 0, 1, and 5, but level 0 isn't fault tolerant.

2. Which of the following is the security context of an application?

A. The security attributes or rules that determine access to the solution and data

B. The effect security features in an application have on the existing security environment

C. The data and solution that are accessed

D. The security attributes that determine the security environment, and keep the existing security environment from being modified in any way
A. The security context of an application is the security attributes or rules that determine how a solution and data are accessed.

3. You are planning for effective maninntenance, and have decided to have data backed up at regular intervals to an external device. What method of data backup is this?

A. Replication

B. Mirroring

C. Dumping

D. Peeping
C. Dumping is when data is copied in a specific format to an external device.

4. You want to combine your maintenance plan with fault tolerance. Which of the following methods will provide this? (Choose all that apply.)

A. Replication

B. Mirroring

C. Dumping

D. Striping with parity
A, B. Replication and mirroring are both fault-tolerant, and have data copied to another location. Striping with parity is fault-tolerant, but data isn't copied to multiple locations.

5. After designing and developing an application that supports an average of 100 simultaneous users, the organization's users are now complaining that performance is bad at certain times of the day. When users log in to the solution in the morning and after lunch, or log off for lunch and at the day's end, the solution is incredibly slow. What is the most likely the reason for this?

A. During design, the peak requirements for the solution weren't acquired and applied to the design.

B. During development, the peak requirements for the solution weren't acquired and applied to the code.

C. The design of the solution took peak requirements into account, but not average acquirements.

D. The bandwidth is too high to deal with this number of users.
A. At certain periods, a higher number of users are accessing the solution to log on and log off. Though the average number of users was considered during design, the peak number of users wasn't. This has caused the system to become bogged down at certain times of operation.

6. There is a longer wait than desired in the time it takes for the database in your application to respond to requests. What is this called?

A. Response time

B. Legacy

C. Lactation

D. Latency
D. Latency is when there is a longer wait than necessary or than is desired in response times.

7. You have been hired to design a solution for a branch of the Canadian government, which is officially bilingual in English and French. All branches of this government require your application to support both languages. What must you implement into your design to accommodate this requirement?

A. Latency

B. Legacy

C. Localization

D. Parlezation
C. Localization adapts an application to support different languages and character sets, so that different areas and international markets are supported by the solution.

8. You are concerned about fault tolerance, and have decided to look into utilizing RAID. Which of the following can make your system less fault tolerant?

A. Disk striping without parity

B. Disk striping with parity

C. Mirroring

D. Disk duplexing
A. RAID 0 is disk striping without parity. This spreads data across several hard disks, but isn't fault-tolerant. If one hard disk fails, all of the data is lost. This means that RAID 0 actually makes your system less fault-tolerant. Rather than losing data on one hard disk when a fault occurs, you lose data on every disk in the striped set.

9. You are determining where backups of data will be stored to for a computer with a single, large hard disk. Which of the following devices could store backups, so that in the event your hard disk crashed, the backup data would remain safe? (Choose all that apply.)

A. Tape drive

B. CD-ROM

C. Local hard drive

D. Network hard drive

A, D. Tape drives or a network hard drive could be used for backups, and would keep the data safe in the event of a hard disk failure. Since the computer has a single hard disk, storing it to the local hard drive wouldn't keep the data that's been backed up safe. A CD-ROM is a "WORM" device—Write Once, Read Many—and is capable of only reading data. A writeable CD-ROM would be required to write the data, and would make a poor method of storage as each backup would require a new disk.

10. You are analyzing security requirements of the business, and want to establish the fault tolerance, based on what's available in the existing environment. You find that the NT servers on the network are set up to use disk mirroring. What will this provide in terms of fault tolerance?

A. Data will be spread across several disks, without error-correction information. If one disks fails, then data can be restored from the other disks in the set.

B. Data will be spread across several disks, with error correction. If one disks fails, then data can be restored from the other disks in the set.

C. Data will be copied to another partition on a separate hard disk.

D. Data will be copied to another partition on a separate hard disk, which also has a separate hard disk controller.

C. Mirroring is RAID Level 1. When this is used, an exact duplicate of data is copied from one partition to another (which should be on different hard disks).

11. Which of the following have a direct effect on quality control requirements? (Choose all that apply.)

A. RAID

B. Testing

C. Design

D. Error correction control

B, C. Design and testing are two primary components of quality control. Many problems can be avoided with good design, while testing allows defects to be found and fixed before the product is released.

12. Which of the following has a relation to quality control?

A. Schedule

B. Logistics

C. Process replacement

D. SQL Server testing

A. Quality control has an effect on schedule. When defects are found, they can increase the amount of time it takes before the product is ready for release. Projects that have too tight a schedule can lower the quality of the product.

13. Which of the following refers to the ability of an application to go beyond its original design, so that it has additional capabilities and greater functionality?

A. Availability

B. Extensibility

C. Scope

D. Scalability

B. Extensibility is the ability of an application to go beyond its original design. By incorporating extensibility into the design of your application, the solution is able to extend its capabilities, and provide additional functionality.

14. You need to determine the peak and average requirements of data being saved and retrieved from a database. On Tuesday, users of the previous database saved and retrieved a total of 20 GB of information. On Wednesday, they accessed 50 GB of data; on Thursday they accessed 60 GB; and on Friday they stored and retrieved 100 GB. What are the peak and average requirements for data access?

A. 57.5 GB average, and 100 GB peak

B. 50 GB average, and 100 GB peak

C. 100 GB average, and 57.5 GB peak

D. 60.5 GB average, and 100 GB peak

A. The peak requirement for data access is 100 GB per day, while the average is 57.5 GB (230 GB over 4 days, or 230 divided by 4).

15. You are analyzing security requirements of the business, and want to establish the fault tolerance, based on what's available in the existing environment. You find that the NT servers on the network are set up to use disk duplexing. What will this provide in terms of fault tolerance?

A. Data will be spread across several disks, without error-correction information. If one disks fails, then data can be restored from the other disks in the set.

B. Data will be spread across several disks, with error correction. If one disks fails, then data can be restored from the other disks in the set.

C. Data will be copied to another partition on a separate hard disk.

D. Data will be copied to another partition on a separate hard disk, which also has a separate hard disk controller.

D. When disk duplexing is used, an exact duplicate of data is copied from one partition to another on different hard disks. Each of these hard disks uses a separate hard disk controller.

16. Acme Tire and Spatula have hired you to design a solution. The customer, Mr. Acme, has admitted that he won't use the solution, but has some suggestions nonetheless. He states that most of the users of this web solution you're designing will be customers on the Internet. Sales will input information used in the solution, while accounting will make changes to any information that needs modification, such as tax rates. Which of the following will be your target audience?

A. The customer paying for the product (Acme)

B. The customer using the solution on the Internet

C. Accounting, who inputs tax and other data

D. Sales, who inputs data used in the solution

B. The customer who is using the solution on the Internet is the target audience. This is the primary user of the solution. This end user is thereby the entity that this solution will serve.

17. Backups are best associated with which of the following aspects of a solution?

A. Scalability

B. Availability

C. Maintenance

D. Extensibility

C. Backups are a maintenance issue.

18. Testing has found bugs in the software they've tested. They send it back to the developers to fix the problem. After modifying the code, the developers are satisfied. Where will the software go next to ensure quality control?

A. Logistics

B. It will be shipped to the customer

C. Testing

D. Program Management

C. After fixing defects found by Testing, Development sends the software back to Testing. Testing will then retest the software to determine if any additional problems have been introduced in the modified code.

19. You need to find a method of backing up data for a system that has no external storage devices, possesses a single hard disk, and has a network connection. Which of the following methods are available to you? (Choose all that apply.)

A. Dumping to a network drive

B. Replication

C. Dumping to an external device

D. Mirroring

A, B. Based on the information on this system, you are able to back up data or replicate it only to a network drive.

20. You are analyzing security requirements of the business and want to establish the fault tolerance, based on what's available in the existing environment. You find that the NT servers on the network are set up to use RAID Level 5. What will this provide in terms of fault tolerance?

A. Data will be spread across several disks, without error-correction information. If one disks fails, then data can be restored from the other disks in the set.

B. Data will be spread across several disks, with error correction. If one disks fails, then data can be restored from the other disks in the set.

C. Data will be copied to another partition on a separate hard disk.

D. Data will be copied to another partition on a separate hard disk, which also has a

separate hard disk controller
B. RAID Level 5 spreads data across several hard disks and includes error-correction information. If any one disk fails, the operating system can use the error-correcting information from other disks in the set to restore the information. Once you replace the failed drive, RAID 5 allows the information to be restored to the new disk.

Chapter 9 Answers

1. You are gathering information for the conceptual design of your application. In doing so, you identify the users who provided information, as well as their responsibilities and roles. What documentation you will put this into?

   A. User profile

   B. User scenario

   C. Usage scenario

   D. Vision statement
      A. A user profile identifies users who played a part in providing information, as well as their responsibilities and roles.

2. You are gathering information for the conceptual design of your application. In doing so, you document how the needs and perceptions of the system translate to actual tasks. You do this by writing down a step-by-step procedure of how business processes are executed. What kind of documentation is this?

   A. User profile

   B. User scenario

   C. Usage scenario

   D. Vision statement
      B. A usage scenario is documentation that depicts how the needs and perceptions of the system translate to actual tasks. This provides a step-by-step picture of how business processes are executed.

3. Which role of the Team model has ownership of the conceptual design, and is responsible for driving the conceptual design process?

   A. Product Management

   B. Program Management

   C. Development

   D. User Education
      B. Program Management has ownership of the conceptual design, and is responsible for driving the conceptual design process.

4. Which role of the Team model is responsible for gathering user input and validating usage scenarios?

   A. Product Management

   B. Program Management

   C. Development

   D. User Education
      A. Product Management is responsible for gathering user input and validating usage scenarios.

5. You are gathering information for the conceptual design of your application. You bring together team members, end users, and other interested parties to design the concept of your product. In the days that follow, you discuss business concerns that will affect the project. What information-gathering technique are you using?

A. User interviews

B. JAD sessions

C. JAG sessions

D. Shadowing
B. JAD (Joint Application Design) sessions bring team members, end users, and other interested parties together to design the concept of your product. No discussion on the functional design of the application takes place, but business concerns are addressed that affect the design of the project.

6. You are designing a database application for a user. The application will reside on the user's machine, but the user will connect to the database through a mapped network drive. What kind of solution is this?

A. Single-tier

B. Two-tier

C. Three-tier

D. *n*-tier
A. Since the user is connecting through a mapped network hard drive to the database, and everything else resides on the user's machine, this is a single-tier solution. Because the network drive is

mapped to the user's machine, the application acts as if it were a local hard drive.

7. A company has asked you to design a new database application, which will get data from a SQL server. The company currently has a solution in place. Applications on users' machines make requests directly to the SQL server, with no other servers being used in this process. The problem is that the network is slow because there are so many requests being made to the database server. The company insists that the database isn't to be broken into multiple databases in your design. What type of solution will you design?

A. Single-tier

B. Two-tier

C. *n*-tier

D. None. It is impossible to redesign the solution based on this criteria.
C. What is required here is an *n*-tier solution. Users can use an application on their machines to make requests from components you create. These components can reside on application servers between the user and the database server. As network traffic increases, more servers can be added between the user and the database server. This keeps the database intact, while improving the performance of the network.

8. The company for which you are designing an application asks if you can add browser

functionality to the application. When a user clicks on a toolbar button, or a menu item, this will bring up a Window that allows the user to browse the Internet. What technology will you incorporate into the application's design so users can have this functionality?

A.   Active pages

B.   EDI

C.   ActiveX controls

D.   POSIX
   C. Of the technologies listed, only ActiveX controls will provide the ability for your application to have Internet browsing capabilities.

9.   You are designing a business solution using the OSI model. This solution will access a database, and have built in e-mail capabilities. Which layer of the OSI model will the written solution directly access?

A.   Physical

B.   Application

C.   Internet

D.   Transit
   B. The Application layer is the layer that will be accessed by any network application you write. This is the layer that provides services that support such things as e-mail, database access, and file transfers. Also, except for the Physical layer, which corresponds to the media that will deliver the application's data, the Application layer is the only layer

listed as a choice that's in the OSI model.

10.   Your design includes COM components that can be reusable with other business solutions you create with development tools in Visual Studio 6. You need to select a development tool that supports COM. Which will you choose?

A.   Visual Basic 6

B.   Visual C++ 6

C.   Visual J++ 6

D.   All of the above
   D. All of the development tools in Visual Studio 6 support COM. This includes Visual Basic, Visual C++, and Visual J++.

11.   You have designed an application for your organization, but realize that with recent upgrades to the computers, the development team will need retraining. Your development team knows the Beginners All-Purpose Symbolic Instruction Code, and has experience creating text-based, console applications. For your application, they will need to create Windows applications and ActiveX documents. What will you have them retrained in?

A.   Visual C++, and then have them create ActiveX documents with the ActiveX Document Migration Wizard

B.   Visual Basic, and then have them create new ActiveX documents with the ActiveX Document Migration Wizard

C. Visual Basic, and then have them convert forms they create to ActiveX documents with the ActiveX Document Migration Wizard

D. Visual J++, and then have them convert forms they create to ActiveX documents with the ActiveX Document Migration Wizard

C. Since the developers already know BASIC (Beginners All-Purpose Symbolic Instruction Code), it would be easier and faster to have them retrained as Visual Basic programmers. They can then create applications using forms, and use the ActiveX Document Migration Wizard to convert the forms into ActiveX documents.

12. You have designed an application that will run in Windows. The computers that will use the application will have no network connection. Your development team consists of developers who specialize in Java programming. Which development tool should you use to develop the application you design?

A. Visual C++

B. Visual Java

C. Visual J++

D. None. Java is used only for Internet applications, and can't be used for Windows applications.

C. Visual J++ is used for Java programming, and can be used to create applications that run on the Windows platform.

13. You have designed a solution that will access data stored exclusively on a mainframe computer. When a request is sent to the mainframe, it will do all of the processing: retrieving the data, transmitting it back to the requesting computer, and displaying it on the terminal. What kind of solution is this?

A. Standalone

B. Centralized

C. Distributed

D. Client-server

B. A centralized solution takes requests from a terminal. It retrieves the data, with all processing taking place on the mainframe. It then transmits the data back to the requesting computer, and displays it on the terminal.

14. Splinky Sprockets has offices based in New York and London. New York is the main office, and 60% of the work is done there. Users at each of these locations need access to the same data, and both offices are connected with a WAN. What kind of solution will you design for this company, so that users have access to the same data, without having to wait long periods to connect to the database over the WAN?

A. Create a distributed solution with a database located on a server in New York. Have front-end applications on each of the users' computers to access this database.

B. Create a centralized solution. Have users connect to the database over the WAN line.

C. Create a distributed solution with a distributed database. Front-end applications will access the database residing on the server at their location, and the databases will be synchronized to replicate the data at certain intervals.

D. Create a collaborative solution, allowing data to be shared between each of the users. Users can interact with one another, and have their work follow a specified flow of information.
C. By creating a distributed solution with a distributed database, users can access the database on the server at their location through front-end applications. The back-end application resides on each of the servers at each location, and synchronizes the databases at specific intervals.

15. SuperDupe Comic Books has asked you to design an application for them. Their problem is that art drawn on computer for their comic books needs to go from the computer artist to the writer. Once the text has been added to the artwork, it then goes to the editor for approval, who sends it to copy editors and finally publishing. Any work generated by one user must be compatible with the work done by others. What kind of solution will you design? Choose the best answer.

A. Centralized solution, allowing all users to access the same data from a central location.

B. Standalone, allowing work to be printed or passed to other users on floppy disk.

C. Distributed solution, allowing all users to access the same data from a single server.

D. Collaborative solution, allowing data to be shared by users, and sent in a specified order from one user to another over the network.
D. Collaborative solutions allow groups of users to share data in a compatible format. They allow work to be sent from one user to another in a specified order.

16. Your local community has decided that the 911 emergency system currently in use is terribly out of date, and has hired you to design a new solution to store information taken by the operators of 911 calls. This information is critical, and needs to be able to complete committed transactions even in the event of a system failure. You need to determine what will be used to store this data. Which of the following will you choose?

A. Jet database created in Visual Basic 6

B. Visual FoxPro 6 database

C. Access 97 database

D. SQL Server database
D. SQL Server logs every transaction, so that in the event of a system failure, committed changes will be completed,

while uncommitted changes will rolled back automatically.

17. You are designing a database for a large insurance corporation. At any given time, up to 20,000 users will be accessing the database to store or retrieve information on policy holders. You need to determine what will be used to store this data. Which of the following will you choose?

    A. Jet database created in Visual Basic 6

    B. Visual FoxPro 6 database

    C. Access 97 database

    D. SQL Server database
    D. The only database that will support this kind of activity is SQL Server. All of the others should be used only for small numbers of users.

18. The network you're designing an application for consists of 100 users. The network has no connection to the Internet, and no corporate intranet currently in operation. Fifty of these users are low-level employees who don't have floppy drives. Twenty-five of these users are high-level employees who have both floppy drives and CD-ROM drives. You want to choose a method of deployment that will allow all of these users access to installation files. What method will you choose?

    A. Floppy-disk deployment

    B. CD-ROM deployment

    C. Put installation files on a web server, allowing users to access the installation files

    D. Put installation files on a network server, allowing users to access the installation files
    D. Not all users have floppy disks or CD-ROM drives, and no one has access to a web server as there is no intranet or Internet connections. The only method available to all users of your solution is network servers. By putting the installation files on a network server, and allowing users to access these files, this network-based deployment is the only solution that allows everyone access.

19. You have designed a database solution where users will access data from a server. A front-end application is designed as the GUI, allowing users to view and manipulate data. This front end sends requests to a back-end application residing on the server, which can handle requests from multiple users simultaneously. Processing is shared between the front- and back-end applications. What kind of solution have you designed?

    A. Standalone

    B. Centralized

    C. Distributed

    D. Static
    C. This kind of application is a distributed solution. Processing is shared

between the front-and back-end applications, with the back-end servicing requests from users using the front-end portion.

20. You are designing a distributed application for a company. Users will access data from a database server on the network. You need to design an application that will reside on each user's machine that will access data from the database server. No other servers will be used in your design. What type of solution will you design?

   A. Single-tier

   B. Two-tier

   C. Three-tier

   D. *n*-tier

   B. In designing this application, no servers (except for the database server) are to be used in the design. This means that three-tier or *n*-tier solutions won't be used, as no components will reside on servers between the user's workstation and the database server. Therefore you'll be designing a two-tier solution. The database server handles data management for multiple users, which users access through applications on their machines.

Chapter 10 Answers

1. Which statement best describes logical design?

   A. Logical design involves determining what attributes objects will have.

   B. Logical design is the process of identifying object behaviors.

   C. Logical design involves identifying objects and services from the conceptual design.

   D. Logical design is the physical implementation of conceptual design.
   C. Logical design involves identifying objects and services from the conceptual design. Logical design is the process of taking the user requirements from the conceptual design and mapping them to objects and services.

2. How is the logical design influenced by physical limitations?

   A. The logical model must be in accordance with available hardware.

   B. You must know what kind of hardware the components will run on before designing them.

   C. Available hardware capacity will determine the components' degree of granularity.

   D. Logical design is independent of physical limitations.
   D. Logical design is independent of physical limitations. You should not be concerned with the physical implementation at this point. This is purely an abstract model.

3. What is a benefit of logical design?

   A. It can facilitate later phases of design.

   B. It helps in planning hardware requirements.

C. It provides for good documentation.

D. It helps establish the database design.
   A. It can facilitate later phases of design. A good logical model will help later phases of development, such as in database design and when physically implementing the objects identified in the logical design.

4. Which attributes are present in a distributed application?

   A. Scalability, reliability, transaction management

   B. Scalability, reliability, efficiency

   C. Performance, scalability, transactions

   D. Efficiency, transactions, scalability
      B. Scalability, reliability, efficiency. A distributed application must exhibit efficiency in terms of performance. It must be reliable in terms of system availability, and it must be scalable to many users.

5. Why should objects provide as many services as possible?

   A. It simplifies development.

   B. Performance will be increased because there will be fewer components.

   C. They should contain attributes instead of services whenever possible.

   D. They shouldn't. They should be as self-contained as possible.
      D. They shouldn't. They should be as self-contained as possible. By keeping your objects self-contained, they will be more reusable and easier to maintain.

6. *Component granularity* refers to which of the following statements?

   A. The number of properties a component has

   B. The number of services a component provides

   C. The physical size of the component

   D. The number of input parameters a method call takes
      B. The number of services a component provides. The granularity of a component refers to the number of services or methods the component supports.

7. What is the easiest way to identify objects from the usage scenarios in conceptual design?

   A. Nouns are usually the best way to identify objects.

   B. Names are usually the best way to identify objects.

   C. Any phrase that contains a verb.

   D. This is what the prototype is for.
      A. Nouns are usually the best way to identify objects. The most common technique for identifying objects is to pick out the objects from the usage scenarios.

8. What is the difference between an object and a component?

   A. There is none.

   B. An object has services; a component has methods.

C. An object is instantiated from a class; a component is precompiled binary code.

D. An object has properties; a component doesn't.
C. An object is instantiated from a class; a component is precompiled binary code. An object is an instance of a class. A component is a precompiled executable, usually a .DLL file.

9. What is a usage scenario?

A. It's the same thing as user requirements.

B. The way in which the application uses the hardware.

C. It's the way in which users will interact with the system.

D. It describes the needs of the users.
C. It's the way in which users will interact with the system. Usage scenarios document the way in which users interact with their current system, or the expected interactions of a new system.

10. What characteristics must an object posses?

A. It must be something the system needs to know about. In addition, it must have behaviors and/or attributes.

B. It must have behaviors and/or attributes.

C. It must be able to store and retrieve data.

D. It must rely on other objects.
A. It must be something the system needs to know about. In addition, it must have behaviors and/or attributes. In order to qualify as an object, it must posses behaviors and attributes, and must be something the system needs to know about.

11. What are services?

A. They are the things the object knows.

B. They are how an object performs an activity.

C. Services determine how the data will be saved.

D. They are the actions an object performs.
D. They are the actions an object performs. Services are an object's behaviors. They are executed through the use of methods.

12. What are properties?

A. They are the things the object knows.

B. The rules that determine how a service is carried out.

C. Properties represent attributes.

D. They identify relationships between objects.
A. They are the things the object knows. Attributes, also known as properties, are the things an object knows.

13. What are the three types of relationships objects can have?

A. Ownership, Generalization, User

B. Ownership, Container, User

C. Ownership, Generalization, Subclass

D. Ownership, Subclass, Container
A. Ownership, Generalization, User. The three types of relationships are ownership (owns), generalization (is), and user (uses).

14. What is business logic?

    A. It determines where the components will reside.

    B. It determines how many services an object will have.

    C. It defines how an object will manipulate data.

    D. It defines how an object will retrieve data.
       C. It defines how an object will manipulate data. Business rules define the logic of how data is to be manipulated by your component.

15. Where should business rules be implemented?

    A. In the user services

    B. In the database using stored procedures and triggers

    C. In the Presentation layer

    D. In the middle tier
       D. In the middle tier. The bulk of business logic should be implemented in the middle tier or business layer whenever possible.

16. Which statement is true? (Choose all that apply.)

    A. An interface is a way of defining object properties.

    B. An interface should be immutable.

    C. An interface is just another term for service.

    D. An interface defines an object's services.
       B, D. An interface should be immutable. An interface is a contract between a client and a server and should therefore remain unchanged once implemented. An interface also defines the services the object contains.

17. What are the three service layers?

    A. User layer, Business layer, and Data layer

    B. User layer, Presentation layer, and Data layer

    C. Presentation layer, Data layer, and Data Services

    D. User layer, Business Services, Data layer
       A. User layer, Business layer, and Data layer. The three categories of services in a three-tier/three-service Application model are the User layer, Business layer, and Data layer.

18. Which phrase correctly identifies the User layer?

    A. The User layer contains user-related business logic.

    B. The User layer defines the data access strategy.

    C. The User layer defines the user interface.

    D. The User layer is the logical representation of the Presentation layer.
       C. The User layer defines the user interface. The User layer is the interface of the application.

19. Which best describes the Business layer?

    A. It acts as the liaison between the Data layer and the User layer.

B. It acts as the liaison between the User layer and the Presentation layer.

C. It acts as the liaison between the User layer and the business logic.

D. The Business layer is only in the Logical Design model. It is not physically implemented.

A. It acts as the liaison between the Data layer and the User layer. The services of the business objects in the Business layer act as a liaison between the User layer and the Data layer.

20. The Data layer consists of which of the following?

A. One database only

B. A variety of data sources

C. Any number of data sources, as long as they are all the same type

D. Any data source as defined by the application requirements

D. Any data source as defined by the application requirements. The data services may consist of a single data store, or a variety of them. The only limit is the technology and the application requirements.

21. What is the main benefit of the three-tier approach?

A. It uses more hardware.

B. It's easier to implement and deploy.

C. It's easier to maintain and adapts better to changing business needs.

D. There is none.

C. It's easier to maintain and adapts better to changing business needs. By separating the application into three logical tiers, it allows changes to be made to individual layers without affecting the other parts of the application.

22. What is a benefit of prototyping?

A. It allows developers a chance to test the usage scenarios.

B. It gives developers a chance to learn new development tools.

C. It lets users see an early cut of the application.

D. It allows users to express what they need the system to do.

A. It allows a chance to test the usage scenarios. The Prototype phase allows for the validation and refinement of the initial set of business objects developed from the usage scenarios.

23. What is the major source of risk in logical design?

A. Not finding enough objects for the nouns.

B. Finding more services than are needed.

C. The conceptual design and logical design don't reflect each other.

D. The conceptual design and logical design are too complex to model.

C. The conceptual design and logical design don't reflect each other. Perhaps the major source of risk is usage scenarios that aren't represented by objects and services, and vice versa.

When this happens, the conceptual design and logical design don't agree.

24. How can you avoid having to modify multiple components when a business rule changes?

    A. Implement all the rules in the User layer.

    B. Store them in the database as triggers.

    C. Use a two-tier approach instead.

    D. Encapsulate them into their separate objects by commonality.

    D. Encapsulate them into their separate objects by commonality. By abstracting common business rules into a common business object, you minimize the impact on your application when these rules change.

25. Which phrase indicates that the application is scalable?

    A. Adding more users causes a major performance hit.

    B. Adding more hardware seems to help slow performance.

    C. When only hardware capacity is increased, more users are able to use the application.

    D. More connections must be made available to handle more users.

    C. When only hardware capacity is increased, more users are able to use the application. An application is said to be *scalable* when the only change necessary to handle more users is to increase the capacity of the hardware.

Chapter 11 Answers

1. Asimov Robotics has been having a problem with the application used in its sales division. This application is used to take orders from customers. A number of times, users of the application have been failing to enter shipping addresses, leaving the text box for this purpose blank. While customers have been charged for their order, the shipping department hasn't been able to send out the order, since they have no way of knowing where it should be shipped. What is required for this application?

    A. Validation of the design

    B. Prototyping

    C. Input validation in the application used by sales

    D. Input validation in the application used by shipping

    C. Since users in the sales division have been leaving the shipping address field in the application blank, input validation in the application used by sales is required.

2. You create two tables, with each table having a one-to-many relationship to a third table. The primary key of this third table is comprised of foreign keys from each of the other two tables. What kind of relationship is this?

    A. Linked relationship

    B. Junction relationship

C. Many-to-one relationship

D. Many-to-many relationship
D. The relationship that has been set up by the one-to-many relationships between each of the two tables and the junction table is a many-to-many relationship.

3. The military has contracted you to design a database. You assign a record number as the primary key for a table, which also contains a column that holds the serial numbers of enlisted personnel. No two people can have the same serial number, but you don't want to use this column as the primary key. What will you do?

A. Set up a default constraint on the primary key column

B. Set up a unique constraint on the column for serial numbers

C. Set up a check constraint that matches the primary key to the serial number column

D. Set up a one-to-one relationship between the primary key and the serial number column in this single table
B. Unique constraints ensure that only unique values are entered into a column that isn't used as a primary key.

4. An insurance company has contracted you to design a database. When insurance agents get information on new policyholders, they find that customers occasionally don't bring all of their information to the insurance office with them. As such, you can expect that certain fields won't be completed until a later time. How will you incorporate this issue into your design?

A. Set up a default constraint on the primary key column

B. Set up a default constraint on the columns that will be filled in later, and ensure that none of these fields are the primary key column

C. Set up a check constraint that checks to see whether the field to be completed later isn't empty

D. Set up a unique constraint on the columns that will be filled in later, and ensure that none of these fields are the primary key column
B. Because the fields will be completed later, you should set up a default constraint on these columns. This could be a default entry of "To be filled in later" or a similar entry. You would need to ensure that none of these fields are the primary key column, as the primary key requires unique values, which the default constraint wouldn't provide.

5. You are designing an application for an organization that frequently changes its business rules. You need to determine an effective method of keeping up with these changes in your application design. What is the best method of doing this?

A. Incorporate the business rules into the code of the actual application users will run on their workstation. When changes to business rules occur, change this code.

B. Incorporate the business rules into a COM component. When changes to business rules occur, change the code in the actual application run on user workstations.

C. Incorporate the business rules into a COM component. When changes to business rules occur, change the code in the component.

D. Don't incorporate any business rules into your design.
   C. If business rules change frequently in an organization, you should incorporate business rules into a COM component. When changes to business rules occur, you change the code in the component. No changes then need to be made to the actual application's code.

6. Which of the following is an example of data type validation?

A. A Y2K problem occurs in the application. The data type validation looks at the date, and corrects the error.

B. The user types his or her name into a String field. Data type validation would find this an error, and inform the user.

C. The user types his or her name in a numeric field. Data type validation looks at the type of data a user inputs, and determines if it is the correct type.

D. There is no type of validation for data types.
   C. Data type validation looks at the

type of data a user inputs, and determines if it is the correct type.

7. Which of the following design perspectives maps requirements to abstract business objects and the services these objects need to provide?

A. Conceptual

B. Logical

C. Physical

D. Tautological
   B. Logical design maps the requirements identified in the conceptual design to abstract business objects and the services these objects need to provide.

8. Which of the following define whether something or someone is a business object? (Choose all that apply.)

A. It is something (or someone) the system is required to know about.

B. It is something (or someone) the system isn't required to know about.

C. It is something (or someone) the system gets information from, or provides information to.

D. It is the system used to retrieve and provide information.
   A, C. A business object is something (or someone) that the system is required to know about, and/or something (or someone) the system gets information from, or provides information to.

9. A user rests the pointer on a button on a toolbar. A small colored box appears

containing information. What kind of user assistance is this?

A. ToolTips

B. StatusBox

C. Status bar

D. Help file
   A. ToolTips are small, colored boxes containing information that appear when your mouse pointer rests on an object.

10. Which of the following should not be considered as a primary method of user assistance, but used as a secondary means?

A. ToolTips

B. Status bars

C. Help files

D. HTML Help files
   B. Status bars provide a secondary means of user assistance. Since they are often located a distance from controls in your user interface, users may ignore or not notice the information in the status bar. They should never be used as the primary means of user assistance.

11. You want to incorporate validation that checks if the value entered by a user is over the maximum value, or under the minimum value, of the data type for a field. What kind of validation will you use?

A. Data checking

B. Range checking

C. Value checking

D. Input checking
   B. Range checking is a type of validation that looks at the range of a particular data type.

12. Purchasing has asked you to design a database application that will be used to catalog companies your organization buys from, their products, and the cost of each product. While purchasing buys from numerous companies, they don't buy the same product from multiple companies. You decide to create a Company table, listing the business information, and a Product table that lists each of the products to be purchased. What relationship will you apply to these two tables?

A. One-to-one

B. One-to-many

C. Many-to-many

D. No relationship needs to be specified
   B. Purchasing doesn't buy the same product from multiple companies, but does buy products from each company. This means you'll need a one-to-many relationship between the two tables. In a one-to-many relationship, a row in one table can have many matching rows in a second table, but the second table can match only one row in the first table.

13. Which of the following design perspectives of the Solutions Design model identifies an application's requirements through specifications and usage scenarios?

A. Conceptual

B. Logical

C. Physical

D. Tautological

A. Conceptual design identifies an application's requirements through specifications and usage scenarios.

14. You want to enforce referential integrity between two tables in two separate databases. When you attempt to do so, you find that you cannot. Why?

A. The related tables must belong to the same database.

B. The primary key in each table must be identical.

C. The foreign key in each table must be identical.

D. Referential integrity has already been set.

A. To enforce referential integrity, the related tables must belong to the same database.

15. Which of the following would be used to display the name of a control accessed through a button on a toolbar?

A. ToolTips

B. Status bars

C. Help files

D. HTML Help files

A. ToolTips are commonly used to display the name of a control accessed through a button on a toolbar.

16. You are determining data types appropriate for different forms of data that will go into

your database. One of the data types you need to determine is for a field that confirms whether a customer has previously ordered. If they have, the answer will be true. If not, false. What is the most appropriate data type?

A. Numeric

B. String

C. Boolean

D. QA

C. The Boolean data type is used for true and false input.

17. You have created a user interface that has the following icons: a piece of paper representing the opening of a document, a floppy disk representing saving a file, and a fax machine representing fax services. What are these examples of?

A. Data model

B. Prototyping

C. Metaphors

D. Similes

C. These are examples of objects as metaphors. They allow the user to call on their existing knowledge of common items that represent features of the application.

18. You have decided to hold a meeting of end users, customers, and other interested parties to get feedback on your user-interface design. You have decided to construct a display model of the user interface, which

will be discarded later, to generate feedback. What have you decided to construct?

A. A data model

B. A throwaway prototype

C. An evolutionary prototype

D. A temporary user interface
   B. Throwaway prototypes are used to display how the user-interface design meets the needs of the user. After generating feedback on the design, such prototypes are discarded.

19. In the physical design of a software product, which team member has ownership of the design process?

A. Product Management

B. Program Management

C. Development

D. Logistics Management
   B. In each stage of design, conceptual, logical, and physical, Program Management has ownership of the design process.

20. Which is considered the primary input device for applications running under Microsoft Windows operating systems?

A. Keyboard

B. Mouse

C. Pen

D. All of the above
   B. The mouse is considered to be the primary input device for applications running under Windows.

B

About the CD

T his CD-ROM that accompanies this book contains a browser-based testing product, the *Personal Testing Center,* which is easy to install on any Windows 95/98/NT computer.

Installing the Personal Testing Center

Double clicking on the Setup.html file on the CD will cycle you through an introductory page on the *Test Yourself software.* On the second page, you will have to read and accept the license agreement. Once you have read the agreement, click on the Agree icon and you will be brought to the Personal Testing Center's main page.

On the main page, you will find links to the Personal Testing Center, to the electronic version of the book, and to other resources you may find helpful. Click on the first link to the Personal Testing Center and you will be brought to the Quick Start page. Here you can choose to run the Personal Testing Center from the CD or install it to your hard drive.

Installing the Personal Testing Center to your hard drive is an easy process. Click on the Install to Hard Drive icon and the procedure will start for you. An instructional box will appear, and walk you through the remainder of the installation. If installed to the hard drive, the Personal Testing Center program group will be created in the Start Programs folder.

Should you wish to run the software from the CD-ROM, the steps are the same as above until you reach the point where you would select the Install to Hard Drive icon. Here, select Run from CD icon and the exam will automatically begin.

To uninstall the program from your hard disk, use the add/remove programs feature in your Windows Control Panel. InstallShield will run the Uninstall program.

Choosing a Test Type

With the Personal Testing Center, you have three options in which to run the program: Live, Practice, and Review. Each test type will draw from a pool of over 220 potential questions. Your choice of test type will depend on whether you would like to simulate an actual MCSD exam, receive instant feedback on your answer choices, or review concepts using the testing simulator. Note that selecting the Full Screen icon on Internet Explorer's standard toolbar gives you the best display of the Personal Testing Center.

Live

The Live timed test type is meant to reflect the actual exam as closely as possible. You will have the option to skip questions and return to them later, move to the previous question, or end the exam. Once the timer has expired, you will automatically go to the scoring page to review your test results.

Managing Windows

The testing application runs inside an Internet Explorer 4.0 or 5.0 browser window. We recommend that you use the full-screen view to minimize the amount of text scrolling you need to do. However, the application will initiate a second iteration of the browser when you link to an Answer in Depth or a Review Graphic. If you are running in full-screen view, the second iteration of the browser will be covered by the first. You can toggle between the two windows with ALT-TAB, you can click your task bar to maximize the second window, or you can get out of full-screen mode and arrange the two windows so they are both visible on the screen at the same time. The application will not initiate more than two browser windows, so you aren't left with hundreds of open windows for each Answer in Depth or Review Graphic that you view.

Saving Scores as Cookies

Your exam score is stored as a browser cookie. If you've configured your browser to accept cookies, your score will be stored in a cookie named History. If you don't accept cookies, you cannot permanently save your scores. If you delete the History cookie, the scores will be deleted permanently.

Using the Browser Buttons

The test application runs inside the Internet Explorer browser. You should navigate from screen to screen by using the application's buttons, not the browser's buttons.

JavaScript Errors

If you encounter a JavaScript error, you should be able to proceed within the application. If you cannot, shut down your Internet Explorer browser session and re-launch the testing application.

Practice

When choosing the Practice exam type, you have the option of receiving instant feedback as to whether your selected answer is correct. The questions will be presented to you in numerical order, and you will see every question in the available question pool for each section you chose to be tested on.

As with the Live exam type, you have the option of continuing through the entire exam without seeing the correct answer for each question. The number of questions you answered correctly, along with the percentage of correct answers, will be displayed during the post-exam summary report. Once you have answered a question, click the Answer icon to display the correct answer.

You have the option of ending the Practice exam at any time, but your post-exam summary screen may reflect an incorrect percentage based on the number of questions you failed to answer. Questions that are skipped are counted as incorrect answers on the post-exam summary screen.

Review

During the Review exam type, you will be presented with questions similar to both the Live and Practice exam types. However, the Answer icon is not present, as every question will have the correct answer posted near the bottom of the screen. You have the option of answering the question without looking at the correct answer. In the Review exam type, you can also return to previous questions and skip to the next question, as well as end the exam by clicking the Stop icon.

The Review exam type is recommended when you have already completed the Live exam type once or twice, and would now like to determine which questions you answered correctly.

Questions with Answers

For the Practice and Review exam types, you will have the option of clicking a hyperlink titled Answers in Depth, which will present relevant study material aimed at exposing the logic behind the answer in a separate browser window. By having two browsers open (one for the test engine and one for the review information), you can quickly alternate between the two windows while keeping your place in the exam. You will find that additional windows are not generated as you follow hyperlinks throughout the test engine.

Scoring

The Personal Testing Center post-exam summary screen, called Benchmark Yourself, displays the results for each section you chose to be tested on, including a bar graph similar to the real exam, which displays the percentage of correct answers. You can compare your percentage to the actual passing percentage for each section. The percentage displayed on the post-exam summary screen is not the actual percentage required to pass the exam. You'll see the number of questions you answered correctly compared to the total number of questions you were tested on. If you choose to skip a question, it will be marked as incorrect. Ending the exam by clicking the End button with questions still unanswered lowers your percentage, as these questions will be marked as incorrect.

Clicking the End button and then the Home button allows you to choose another exam type, or test yourself on another section.

C

About the Web Site

Access Global Knowledge

A s you know by now, Global Knowledge is the largest independent IT training company in the world. Just by purchasing this book, you have also secured a free subscription to the Global Knowledge web site and its many resources. You can find it at **http://access.globalknowledge.com**.

You can log on directly at the Global Knowledge site, and you will be e-mailed a new, secure password immediately upon registering.

What You'll Find There...

The wealth of useful information at the Global Knowledge site falls into three categories:

Skills Gap Analysis

Global Knowledge offers several ways for you to analyze your networking skills and discover where they may be lacking. Using Global Knowledge's trademarked Competence Key Tool, you can do a skills gap analysis and get recommendations for where you may need to do some more studying. (Sorry, it just might not end with this book!)

Networking

You'll also gain valuable access to another asset: people. At the Access Global site, you'll find threaded discussions, as well as live discussions. Talk to other MCSD candidates, get advice from folks who have already taken the exams, and get access to instructors and MCTs.

Product Offerings

Of course, Global Knowledge also offers its products here, and you may find some valuable items for purchase—CBTs, books, or courses. Browse freely and see if there's something that could help you take that next step in career enhancement.

MICROSOFT CERTIFIED SOLUTION DEVELOPER

D

Programming
Conventions

A s with anything that's been around a while, there are conventions that apply to good programming. Conventions are a standardized way of doing things, and they often make things much easier in programming. They affect the structure and appearance of code, making it easier to read and maintain. There are naming conventions, coding conventions, and constant- and variable-naming conventions. Together they allow a programmer to look at the work of another, and help him or her in determining what is going on in code.

Coding Conventions

When you're programming, you should follow certain conventions in your code. This includes the placement of variables and the structure of the code itself. When you declare variables, you should always place them at the top of a procedure. You can place your variables anywhere before they are used, but you should always put them at the top. That way, any changes can easily be made after looking for the variables at the top of a procedure. You always know where to find them.

A good example of the usefulness of placing variables at the top of the code is an accountant declaring a variable to be a value that represents minimum wage. Minimum wage changes every few years. When it does, the accountant doesn't have to search through the code to change the variable; it is always at the top of the procedure. In such an example, the code might appear as follows:

```
Private Sub WrkWeek()
Dim curAnswer, curMinWage As Currency
Dim intHours As Integer
curMinWage = 6.85
Hours = 40
    curAnswer = curMinWage * intHours

    MsgBox curAnswer
End Sub
```

This example shows several things in addition to where to declare variables and assign values to them. First, it shows the importance of using meaningful names. By looking at intHours and curMinWage, you can automatically tell what they represent. While you could have used names like *x*, *y*, and *z* for variables, these names don't explain much about their purpose. This also applies to naming procedures. When you see a name like WrkWeek, you can determine that this probably has something to do with a work week.

This example also displays the use of spacing in your code. Visual Basic version 6 ignores white space (the spacing in your code where nothing appears). So indenting code and adding blank spaces to separate parts of code (by pressing ENTER) is ignored by VB. Though the compiler ignores the white space, its presence makes it considerably easier for programmers to read.

While a procedure or function should always deal with one task (such as calculating your paycheck or opening another form), you will always have parts of code that deal with different things. For example, declaring variables and code that deals with those variables are two different parts of code. You should leave a blank line between such items. If your code does different tasks, such as running a loop and displaying a message box, you should separate the code with blank lines. By doing this, your code becomes significantly easier to read.

You should also indent your code to show different tasks in your code. For example, using nested IF...THEN statements can be confusing if they are bunched together. If parts of the code are indented, it becomes easier to read. Compare the following example, and you can see the difference:

```
If x < y then                      If x < y then
If z>x then                            If z>x then
Msgbox "z is greater than y"               Msgbox "z is greater than y"
End if                                  End if
Msgbox "x is less than y"           Msgbox "x is less than y"
End if                              End if
```

When the lines of code are indented, you can easily see which END IF applies to which IF statement. You can also see what code applies to which IF...THEN statement. Indenting code organizes it so that you can read it much more easily.

If you have lines of code that are particularly long, stretching past the width of your code window, you should split the line of code across two or more lines. This is done with the line continuation character. This character is a space followed by an underscore; it makes your code easier to read, without affecting its performance. The following is an example of a single line of code, split across several lines with the line continuation character:

```
txtMyText.Text= "This is my line " _
& "that is split across several lines " _
& "of code."
```

While one statement should appear on each line of code, it should also be mentioned that you can put several lines of related code on the same line. This is done by using a colon (:) to indicate a separation between each statement. The following example shows how this is done:

```
Label1.Caption = "Hello World": Label1.BackColor = vbRed
```

This shows two related statements, separated by a colon. When VB reads this, it will recognize this as two different statements.

In addition to conventions that affect the appearance of your code, you should also use comments in your code. Comments can be placed in code by beginning your sentence with an apostrophe ('). Comments can be placed alone on a line, or at the end of a line of code. If you are placing the comment on a line by itself, you can also use the REM statement, which is short for remark. The REM statement is way of making comments that goes back to the early days of programming and is still used today. The following shows examples of comments in action:

```
REM This starts my program
Dim x As Integer 'This declares x as an integer
'The following line displays x
txtMyText.Text=x
```

In addition to showing how comments are used in code, this example shows how they should *not* be used. You should avoid commenting code that is obvious (stating that "This starts my program") and commenting on everything occurring in your code. Another bad example is explaining that a variable is being declared. Try to code with other programmers in mind.

Ask yourself, "Will this be obvious to another programmer?" If the answer is no, then comment it. In addition, keep in mind that, while a chunk of code makes sense to you now, it may not be so clear to you six months or a year from now. Commenting code avoids such problems.

on the job *A colleague of mine experienced a particularly funny example of bad commenting. He was working on some code written by a person who no longer worked for the company. While working on the code, he came across the comment "Don't touch this. It's important!" Since the code was being upgraded, he had to spend extra time determining if the code was still "important" or was now obsolete. Unfortunately, it was a particularly long and elaborate piece of code. I say this example is funny, because it happened to him, not me. It does illustrate the need to be straight to the point and explain things properly when writing comments.*

Object-Naming Conventions

Naming conventions allow you to look at an object and determine what it is. Rather than having to guess if MyLine is a label, text box, or who-knows-what, you should be able to look at an object's name and determine what it is. This is done by adding a prefix to the object's name to specify the type of object.

Table D-1 lists prefixes commonly used for controls in VB version 6. You should use these when naming objects in VB.

TABLE D-1			
Standard Prefixes for Object-Naming Conventions	**Control**	**Prefix**	**Example**
	3D Panel	pnl	pnlPanel
	ADO Data	ado	adoData
	Animated button	ani	aniEnter
	Check box	chk	chkBold
	Combo box, drop-down list box	cbo	cboListing
	Command button	cmd	cmdExit
	Common dialog	dlg	dlgOpen

Control	Prefix	Example
Communications	com	comModem
Control (used within procedures when the specific type is unknown)	ctr	ctrControl
Data	dat	datData
Data-bound combo box	dbcbo	dbcboOrders
Data-bound grid	dbgrd	dbgrdMyGrid
Data-bound listbox	dblst	dblstEmployee
Data combo	dbc	dbcLastName
Data grid	dgd	dgdBooks
Data list	dbl	dblCost
Data repeater	drp	drpDatRep
Date picker	dtp	dtpDatPic
Directory listbox	dir	dirDirect
Drive listbox	drv	drvSource
File listbox	fil	filFile
Flat scroll bar	fsb	fsbScroll
Form	frm	frmMain
Frame	fra	fraOptions
Gauge	gau	gauStatus
Graph	gra	graIncome
Grid	grd	grdOutcome
Hierarchical flexgrid	flex	flexPublisher
Horizontal scroll bar	hsb	hsbMove
Image	img	imgMyPic
Image combo	imgcbo	imgcboPicture
ImageList	ils	ilsMyImage
Label	lbl	lblFirstName
Lightweight check box	lwchk	lwchkMyBox

TABLE D-1

Standard Prefixes for
Object-Naming
Conventions *(continued)*

Control	Prefix	Example
Lightweight combo box	lwcbo	lwcboAuthor
Lightweight command button	lwcmd	lwcmdEnter
Lightweight frame	lwfra	lwfraSave
Lightweight horizontal scroll bar	lwhsb	lwhsbHorBar
Lightweight listbox	lwlst	lwlstPrice
Lightweight option button	lwopt	lwoptGross
Lightweight text box	lwtxt	lwoptFirst
Lightweight vertical scroll bar	lwvsb	lwvsbHigh
Line	lin	linMyLine
Listbox	lst	lstCustomer
ListView	lvw	lvwTitles
MAPI message	mpm	mpmMessage
MAPI session	mps	mpsSession
MCI	mci	mciVideo
Menu	mnu	mnuFile
Month view	mvw	mvwMonth
MS Chart	ch	chMyChart
MS Flex grid	msg	msgFlexGrid
MS Tab	mst	mstTab
OLE container	ole	oleFiesta
Option button	opt	optCanada
Picture box	pic	picMyPic
Picture clip	clp	clpPicClip
ProgressBar	prg	prgDataRate
Remote Data	rd	rdRemDat
RichTextBox	rtf	rtfDetails
Shape	shp	shpMyShape
Slider	sld	sldSlideBar

Control	Prefix	Example
Spin	spn	spnOutHere
StatusBar	sta	staMyStat
SysInfo	sys	sysMem
TabStrip	tab	tabTeStrip
Text box	txt	txtFirstName
Timer	tmr	tmrTest
Toolbar	tlb	tlbFunctions
Treeview	tre	treDirect
UpDown	upd	updDirection
Vertical scroll bar	vsb	vsbMyBar

TABLE D-1

Standard Prefixes for Object-Naming Conventions *(continued)*

Table D-2 shows the prefixes for Data Access Objects (DAO). You should use these prefixes when naming DAO objects.

DAO Object	Prefix	Example
Container	con	conMyCont
Database	db	dbCustomer
DBEngine	dbe	dbeVaroom
Document	doc	docMyDoc
Field	fld	fldFirstName
Group	grp	grpMarketing
Index	idx	idxGender
Parameter	prm	prmMyPara
QueryDef	qry	qryTopSales
Recordset	rec	recMyRec
Relation	rel	relFinance
TableDef	tbd	tbdPublishers
User	usr	usrMyUser
Workspace	wsp	wspMyWork

TABLE D-2

Prefixes for Data Access Objects

Variable-Naming Conventions

In addition to objects, you should also use naming conventions for variables. This will allow you to identify easily the data type of your variable, and avoid improperly matching data types. An example of such an error would be trying to multiply a Boolean data type called Answer by an integer named Amount. By using the prefixes of variable-naming conventions, you would rename these to intAmount and blnAnswer, and avoid such an error. Table D-3 lists the standard prefixes.

If you are using prefixes, I can't stress enough that you should give your variable a meaningful name. Renaming a variable called x to intx may follow the naming convention, but it hardly gives an accurate indication of what the variable is for. You should always try to name the variable something that indicates what it is being used for.

Using meaningful names is equally important when naming procedures, functions, and objects. You should try to determine what something is being used for, and name it accordingly. It is also wise to show the scope

TABLE D-3	Data Type	Prefix	Example
Variable-Naming Conventions	Boolean	bln	blnYesNo
	Byte	byt	bytOutaCrime
	Collection object	col	colComics
	Currency	cur	curMoola
	Date (Time)	dtm	dtmBDate
	Double	dbl	dblStarVal
	Error	err	errOopsy
	Integer	int	intAge
	Long	lng	lngDistance
	Object	obj	objMyAffection
	Single	sng	sngUnattached
	String	str	strName
	User-defined type	udt	udtCustomer
	Variant	vnt	vntMyVar

of a variable as being modular or global by prefixing it with the letters *m* or *g*, respectively.

While it may seem difficult to remember the methods and prefixes of conventions, they are well worth learning and using. In the long run, they will save you a substantial amount of time. You (and anyone who reads your code in the future) will certainly prefer taking a moment to look up a prefix rather than spending considerably more time searching through code to figure out the data type of a variable.

MICROSOFT CERTIFIED SOLUTION DEVELOPER

Glossary

accelerated keys (*See* **shortcut keys.**)

access keys Access keys allow the user to access a menu title, item, or object by pressing the ALT key with another key. Often confused with shortcut keys, but they are quite different.

accessibility Refers to the ability for everyone, despite any disabilities they may have, to be able to use your solution.

adjective calibration Method that uses a scale of verbs that describe the probability of a risk. (*See also* **risk.**)

administrators Users who have the highest level of security access to features in an application, and to the data that the solution uses.

application architecture Perspective in the Enterprise Architecture model that determines issues dealing with current applications and application models, and what changes may be necessary to these areas. (*See also* **Enterprise Architecture model.**)

Application model Addresses how applications are constructed to meet the needs of customers and users. This model promotes the use of COM (Component Object Model) components. These components are reusable and can be shared by other applications your team creates. The Application model breaks an application into a network of consumers and suppliers of services. (*See also* **consumer**, **supplier**, and **service.**)

attributes Also known as *properties*. The things your object knows. It's the data that's associated to the object. (*See also* **objects.**)

auditing Where activities performed by certain or all users are documented to a file, allowing a user (such as the administrator) to see what these users have done. The record showing the operations a user performed is called an *audit trail*.

availability   The ability of users to access and use the solution.

bandwidth   The network's capacity to carry information, measured in data transferred per unit of time, usually seconds.

Benchmark and Baseline phase   In the TCO model, the phase that calculates cost baselines, benchmarks, return on investments (ROIs), and validations. The benchmark is the total cost that's based on averages in the industry, while the baseline is the actual cost of the acquisition, management, and retirement of technology. (*See also* **TCO model.**)

betting scheme   Method of calculating risk probability that works as if you were betting money on particular risks; however, no money actually changes hands. (*See also* **risk.**)

BLOB (Binary Large Objects)   Includes such things as graphics, compiled code, tomes, and sound, which can cause serious performance issues.

bottom-up estimates   A chain-of-command principle, with those who are lower in a hierarchy reporting work estimates to those above them.

building   Where your product is moved from the paperwork of schematics to a physical form. Building takes information from the planning stage, and ensures that the business-driven application is created on budget and on schedule. One of the three stages in the Information Technology life cycle. (*See also* **planning** and **managing.**)

business architecture   Perspective in the Enterprise Architecture model that defines how the business works. It determines what the business does, its strengths, and its future. (*See also* **Enterprise Architecture model.**)

business case   A plan of action that's presented to senior management, and backs up a proposal for a project by providing facts and evidence about the project, and how it will be approached.

Business layer   Where all of the business logic and rules are contained. (*See also* **Data layer** and **User layer**.)

business object dependency   When one business object calls on services in another business object.

business objects   Abstract representations of real-world things or concepts (such as orders and customers).

business rules   Rules that define the logic of how data is manipulated by your components. These rules mirror the way the business domain you are modeling operates or does business.

Business Services   Also called *middle-tier services*. In a multi-tier application, Business Services enforces transactional integrity, business rules, and control sequencing. This layer also transforms the data acquired from Data Services into meaningful information that the user can use. (*See also* **multi-tier application**.)

calling conventions   The syntax to employ the service, the input parameters it accepts, and the output parameters the service will generate. (*See also* **interface contract** and **preconditions**.)

capacity   The volume or limit something can handle; can have a direct effect on the performance of your solution.

case analysis   The process of modeling how the user or users interact with the system.

Client   Role that performs most of the activities in a solution. These are the common users of an application, who often add and modify much of the data your solution will access.

Communications   Role in the Infrastructure model that is responsible for maintaining video, voice, and data communications in the project. (*See also* **Infrastructure model**.)

component granularity   The functionality that you design into your objects is referred to as component granularity. The more activities or services that your objects support, the coarser their granularity.

Component Object model (COM)   A standard that defines how objects can expose themselves, the life cycle of an object, and how object exposure works across networks and processes. COM components are reusable; you can invoke existing COM components from existing applications. Since COM is a platform-independent, distributed, object-oriented standard, it allows business applications and systems to be integrated with Internet technologies. When you create COM classes to make up your COM component, you use properties, methods, and events to make up the characteristics of the class, which will subsequently become the characteristics of your component.

Properties are used to read and set values for a specific attribute of the component. Methods define an interface for the component, and are used to invoke actions that the component can perform. This could include such things as adding items and printing. Events are the actions that are recognized by an object.

conceptual design   In the Solutions Design model, conceptual design is where the initial concept of the solution originates. It is here that the team develops an understanding of what the user needs from a solution. (*See also* **Solutions Design model**.)

connection pooling   Allows components to connect to data sources using a previously established connection. This dramatically reduces the overhead and wait time associated with connecting to a database.

constraints   Business requirements that enforce what a user can input into specific columns of your database.

consumer   A program or component that uses the services of another component.

daily build   Building the executable program by compiling it.

data buffering   Like a cache, where data is stored to improve the performance of various tasks being carried out.

data integrity   Business rules that can be used to ensure the integrity of your application's data.

Data layer   Responsible for maintaining, accessing, and updating data based on requests from the Business layer. (*See also* **User layer** and **Business layer.**)

Data Services   In a multi-tier application Data Services provides Create, Read, Update, and Delete services, along with such retrieval logic as order and joins. (*See also* **multi-tier application.**)

data validation   Ensures that the values users type in are correct and accurate.

database design   A complex process that consists of identifying, documenting, and implementing the data requirements of the business.

deliverable   A tangible result of the work performed.

Delphi method   Used to determine risk probability. (Also known as the *group consensus method.*) Each member provides an estimate on their own, along with the logic and reasons behind the estimate. Once this estimate and justification have been submitted, the members receive the estimates, along with the ratings, and re-evaluate their own submissions. After re-evaluating their work, each member submits revised estimates, and then discusses these estimates until they come to a consensus. (*See also* **risk.**)

denormalization   Allows you to selectively identify which tables and columns can break away from the normalization techniques you've used in your database. (*See also* **normalization.**)

Developing phase   Phase in the Process model where the functional specification and project plan are passed forward. Using this information as a baseline, the product or service begins to be built at this stage. The development team sets a number of interim delivery milestones, where the product goes through several cycles of testing, debugging, and fixing. (*See also* **Process model.**)

Development   Role in the Team model that is responsible for building or implementing a product or service that meets the requirements and needs of the customer. (*See also* **Team model.**)

direct costs   Predictable costs such as scheduled replenishments of supplies such as printer paper or diskettes.

dumping   When data is copied to an external device.

end users   The people who use the product on a day-to-day basis, and can tell you what specific needs the solution must address.

Enterprise Architecture model   A model that provides guidelines for planning, building, and managing technology infrastructures using four perspectives to help provide focus to key issues of a project: business architecture, application architecture, information architecture, and technology architecture. (*See also* **business architecture, application architecture, information architecture,** and **technology architecture.**)

Envisioning phase   Phase in the Process model where project requirements are defined. This phase keeps the team from spending effort on minor needs, or trying to make bad procedures or operations more efficient. (*See also* **Process model.**)

extensibility   The ability of an application to go beyond its original design.

external interim milestones   Are known outside of the development team, and are announced to the organization. (*See also* **internal interim milestones.**)

fault tolerance   The ability of a solution to function regardless of whether a fault occurred. In short, it is non-stop availability of a solution.

features   The requirements to be implemented into a product or service, and the quality and functionality of these items. One of the three elements of a project. (*See also* **schedule** and **resources.**)

flexible business solutions   Applications that are adaptable, easily modified, and have the feature of a consistent interface. Such applications allow users to perform more activities and perform more complex duties, without having to learn new applications.

foreign keys   Columns or combinations of columns with values that match the primary key of another table. The values of a foreign key are often unique and copy those of the primary key in the other table. Don't confuse foreign keys with primary keys. Primary keys identify rows that make up the table, while foreign keys are used in relationships to reference other tables. (*See also* **primary keys** and **relationships.**)

Forms   (*See* **normalization.**)

generalization/subclass relationship   One of the three types of relationships an object can have. In this type of relationship, an object is a specific type of another object. These are often identified when different objects have similar properties. (*See also* **ownership/container relationship** and **user/collaboration relationship**.)

Guest   Role that is generally given the lowest level of security. As its name implies, people who are simply visiting the application, and don't require a high level of access, have the role of Guest.

GUI (graphical user interface)   Visual display of an application for use by a human user. (*See also* **programmatic interface**.)

Help Desk   Role in the Infrastructure model that is responsible for providing assistance and ongoing support to the end user. (*See also* **Infrastructure model**.)

Hungarian Naming Convention   This has prefixes added to the names of controls and objects, which allow developers to recognize the purpose of those objects and controls. For example, cmd is the prefix for a command button, lbl for a label, and txt for a textbox.

Improvement phase   In the TCO model, the phase where ROI is calculated. Based on a strategy you create, this is calculated by simulating the impact of your recommendations on improvement and estimated cost savings. (*See also* **TCO model**.)

indirect costs   Includes costs not included in an IT budget. These costs are hidden in the expenses of the business departments of the organization.

information architecture   Perspective in the Enterprise Architecture model that describes how data and information are handled in a business so it can run effectively, and describes what the company needs to know to run the organization's business processes and operations. (*See also* **Enterprise Architecture model**.)

Infrastructure model   The total set of resources needed to support an enterprise computing environment. The resources included in this model are the following: technologies and standards, operational processes, and people and organizational resources. Team roles are expanded to include the following: Systems Management, Help Desk, and Communications. (*See also* **Systems Management**, **Help Desk**, and **Communications**.)

interface   The methods that the object exposes and are the gateways of communication between objects. They are what allow objects to communicate with one another and exchange data. Without these interfaces, objects would not know how to request or provide services to one another.

interface contract   A declaration of any preconditions for using the service, and the calling conventions. (*See also* **preconditions** and **calling conventions**.)

internal interim milestones   Are not known outside the development team because they are useful only for the team itself. (*See also* **external interim milestones**.)

locality of reference   Putting a component in a location where it will be used, or near to where it will be used.

logical design   In the Solutions Design model, logical design takes the information gathered from the conceptual design and applies it to technical know-how. While the requirements and needs of customers and users are outlined in the previous design perspective, it is here that the structure and communication of elements in the solution are established. Creating a logical design consists of mapping the business rules and user requirements identified to objects during conceptual design. These objects, which can most readily be identified from the user requirements as nouns, also provide services. These services in turn represent the rules and requirements of the business domain that you are modeling. (*See also* **Solutions Design model**.)

Logistics   Role in the Team model that is responsible for a smooth rollout of the product. Ensures that the installation and migration of a product to support and operations groups goes smoothly. (*See also* **Team model**.)

Management phase   In the TCO model, the phase where you measure what you actually achieved against what you hoped to achieve. The results of your work are compared to your objectives, which either validates or invalidates the strategy that was used. (*See also* **TCO model.**)

managing   Maintaining and improving the product. One of the three stages in the Information Technology life cycle. (*See also* **planning** and **building.**)

metaphors   A term or phrase that suggests a resemblance to something else. Can be used for objects in your application; for example, files holding data are stored in folders, which can be stored in cabinet files (like filing cabinets).

Microsoft Solution Framework (MSF)   A model based on the most successful practices available for making software projects succeed. Unlike some models that are purely theoretical, MSF is taken from the experiences of IT professionals.

milestone   A major turning point in the project that indicates progress. Not only marks the point where one phase of a project ends and another begins, it also indicates the point in time that members of a team should synchronize their efforts.

Minimum Cost strategy   This means that the allocation of resources should be kept to a minimum, so that costs don't go too high.

mirroring   This creates an exact duplicate of data, by copying data from one partition to another (which should be on different hard disks). If you use a separate hard disk controller for each hard disk in a mirror set, it is called *disk duplexing.*

modular design   Breaking a large project into smaller modules, or subprojects.

multiple versioned releases   Refers to the need to limit the scope of a current project and plan enhancements (new features) in future versions.

multithreading   When multiple threads of execution are used to process a task.

multi-tier application   The user interacts with the application through a user interface and/or programmatic interface, which is the User Services tier. The next tier controls sequencing, and enforces business rules and the transactional integrity of operations. The bottom tier is where data is stored, and where manipulations of data take place, such as Create, Delete, Read, and Update Services. (*See also* **User Services, Business Services,** and **Data Services.**)

NIH (Not Invented Here)   Idea that software products developed outside the organization should rarely be used.

normalization   A set of rules that the logical database design should satisfy. These rules are called *Forms,* and they ensure the proper design of your database. Forms include First Normal Form, where you determine that there are no duplicated groups or multi-value columns in the database; Second Normal Form, where you ensure that the non-key fields in your database depend on the entire primary key, and not just part of it; Third Normal Form, where you determine that non-key fields don't depend on other non-key fields; Fourth Normal Form, which requires that independent data entities are not stored in the same table when those entities have a many-to-many relationship with one another; Fifth Normal Form, which dictates that you should be able to reconstruct an original table from the tables created from breaking up the original table.

Not-to-Exceed strategy   Pressure to keep within the budget.

object pooling   Allows components to be recycled.

objects   The things from our requirements that we are modeling. They are often identified in the requirements as nouns. For example, if you scan through the requirements from the Conceptual Design phase, you may notice items being discussed such as a customer, an order, or an invoice. These things (nouns) are objects.

ownership/container relationship   One of the three types of relationships objects can have. Commonly referred to as a parent-child or one-to-many relationship. This is where one object owns or contains another type of object. (*See also* **generalization/subclass relationship** and **user/collaboration relationship**.)

performance   How well an application works under daily conditions.

perspective   In the Solutions Design model, a perspective is an outlook or viewpoint on something, which in this case is the design process of an application. (*See also* **Solutions Design model**.)

physical design   In the Solutions Design model, physical design is where requirements from the conceptual and logical perspectives are put into a tangible form. It is here that the constraints of technology are applied to the logical design of the solution. Physical design defines how the components of your solution, such as the user interface and physical database, work together. (*See also* **Solutions Design model**.)

planning   Creating strategies and evolving an enterprise architecture that will drive, or is adaptable to, changes in the business. One of the three stages in the Information Technology life cycle. (*See also* **building** and **managing**.)

Planning phase   Phase in the Process model where the customers and team members sit down and determine what will be delivered, and how it should be built. (*See also* **Process model**.)

preconditions   Conditions that must exist prior to using the service. For example, a database with certain tables may need to exist in order for the service to return the requested data. (*See also* **interface contract** and **calling conventions**.)

prefetching   When your solution anticipates additional data or data requests.

primary key   One column in the table that is used as an identifier. If more than one column is used as an identifier, it's called a *composite* or *compound primary key*. (*See also* **foreign keys** and **relationships**.)

proactive risk management   Deals with risks before they become problems that result in loss. (*See also* **reactive risk management**.)

process   Deals with how things will get done. Process deals with the methodologies of technology and management.

Process model   Clarifies what people are working toward, and the progress achieved from that work. Process focuses the team on issues relevant to different phases of the project, and allows members to see that they're on the right track with a project. (*See also* **Envisioning phase**, **Planning phase**, **Developing phase**, and **Stabilizing phase**.)

Product Management   Role in the Team model that is responsible for obtaining the customer's requirements of a product, and setting the vision for the product so everyone understands what it entails. (*See also* **Team model**.)

product specifications   Provide detailed descriptions for project requirements.

Program Management   Role in the Team model that is responsible for making decisions that determine delivery of the right product at the right time. (*See also* **Team model**.)

programmatic interface   Used by other applications to obtain information. (*See also* **GUI**.)

Project Plan Approved milestone   The Planning phase results in the Project Plan Approved milestone, providing the functional specification and schedule. The functional specification created here is the combined plans of members in each role of the MSF Team model, and details the requirements and commitments of the project. (*See also* **Planning phase.**)

Prototype phase   Allows you to validate and refine the initial set of business objects you developed from the usage scenarios and requirements list.

prototypes   Provide a way of generating feedback from customers, end users, and other interested parties. Evolutionary prototypes are built on, and used in the construction of the end product. Throwaway prototypes are discarded once they've been used to validate the design and generate feedback.

quality control   Determines the number of defects your product will have and have removed by release, thereby affecting the quality of the product.

RAID (Redundant Array of Inexpensive Disks)   A common method of fault tolerance. (*See also* **fault tolerance.**)

reactive risk management   Deals with risks after they've occurred. (*See also* **proactive risk management.**)

referential integrity   When referential integrity is set on a relationship, you ensure that for every row existing in a foreign key, there is a corresponding row in the primary key. (*See also* **relationships, foreign keys,** and **primary key.**)

relationships   Link two tables together, by having the primary key of one table referenced by the foreign key of another table. (*See also* **primary key** and **foreign keys.**)

Release milestone   The Stabilizing phase results in the Release milestone, where the product is shipped and put into service. (*See also* **Stabilizing phase.**)

replication   Allows all or part of a database to be copied to other machines on your network. Because each database is a replication of the other, users see a consistent copy of available data.

resources   Include such things as the people who work on the project, the technologies they work with, and the money available to use on a project. One of the three elements of a project. (*See also* **schedule** and **features.**)

response time   The difference in time between the end of a query or command to when the results of that query or command first begin to appear on the screen.

risk   The possibility of suffering some sort of loss. Inherent in any project, risk is an opportunity for success. Risk probability is the likelihood of events occurring, while risk impact is the amount of loss that could result.

risk assessment table   Documents the probability of loss and the size of loss associated with the risk. These two fields are multiplied to find the risk exposure.

risk factor chart   Used to organize and categorize risks, so it can be determined how critical certain risks are to a project.

risk impact   Measures the size of loss, or severity of adverse effects, if a risk results in becoming an actual problem. It is measured in currency for risks with a financial impact, time increments (e.g., days and weeks) for those with a time impact, or a subjective scale for other risks that don't fall into such obvious areas.

risk management   Process of identifying and dealing with areas of the project that can jeopardize success.

risk statement   Used to communicate the risks involved in a project, so that members can effectively manage them. Includes not only mentioning the symptoms of a risk, but what the results of a risk could be.

roaming users   Users who access your solution from more than one workstation, and thereby require having their preferences available from more than one computer.

robustness   How well components perform and handle unusual exceptions.

scalability   How well an application performs as the number of users increases.

schedule   A timetable with dates that define when parts of a project are due, and when the finished product or service is due to be completed. One of the three elements of a project. (*See also* **features** and **resources**.)

scope   The opposite of vision; reins in the features included in the vision, until it becomes something reasonable that the team can deliver. (*See also* **vision**.)

Scope Complete/First Use milestone   The Developing phase results in the Scope Complete/First Use milestone, where the product's functionality is assessed, and it is determined that rollout and support plans are in place before the product is delivered. (*See also* **Developing phase**.)

service   A unit of application logic, which is used to perform an operation, function, or some sort of transformation on an object.

service request   Communication among the three layers of the multi-tier application. (*See also* **User Services**, **Business Services**, and **Data Services**.)

shortcut keys   Allow users to quickly access features of your product. Rather than having to navigate to a menu title, access the menu, and then select a menu item, users can press a combination of keys on their keyboard to access the same command. Also called *accelerated keys*.

SMART vision/scope document   Specific, Measurable, Achievable, Results-based, and Time-oriented.

smoke tests   Building the program daily by compiling it, and then running a series of tests on it to ensure that it functions as it should. Used to detect major problems that go beyond seeing if the software launches properly.

Solutions Design model   Users become involved in the design process. By having them address key issues, such as usability and requirements, the team is able to determine that an application will be used and increase productivity. This model is comprised of different perspectives: conceptual, logical, and physical. (*See also* **perspective**, **conceptual design**, **logical design**, and **physical design**.)

Spiral model   Also called the *Rapid Application Development* (or *RAD*) *model*. It breaks a project into sub-projects, each of which deals with different risks in a project. Since each risk is addressed in the sub-projects, all risks in a project can be identified individually. MSF process model is partially based on the waterfall model. (*See also* **Waterfall model** and **Process model**.)

Stabilizing phase   Phase in the Process model with a primary focus on finding and fixing bugs that have appeared in the product. This phase occurs concurrently with code development, where the programming of the software product takes place. (*See also* **Process model**.)

stateless components   Do not maintain state between method calls.

supplier   Provides the requested service to this consumer.

Systems Management   Role in the Infrastructure model that is responsible for maintaining accountability for the systems and technology. This accountability is inclusive to the continued operation of this technology. (*See also* **Infrastructure model.**)

TCO (Total Cost of Ownership) model   Works on the basic premise that optimizing costs equals a better return on investment (ROI). In other words, by spending less, you have more money in your pocket. The TCO model approaches this objective by analyzing the cost areas in a business in a rational and proven method. TCO model uses an ongoing three-phase process: Benchmark and Baseline phase, Improvement phase, and Management phase. (*See also* **Benchmark and Baseline phase, Improvement phase,** and **Management phase.**)

Team model   Outlines well-defined roles for members of the team. Each role has its own mission, for which members in that role are responsible. (*See also* **product management, program management, development, testing, user education,** and **logistics.**)

technology architecture   Perspective in the Enterprise Architecture model that describes standards and guidelines for laying out the software and hardware supporting an organization. This perspective includes such things as operating systems, client/workstation tools, and hardware used by workstations and servers, printers, and modems. (*See also* **Enterprise Architecture model.**)

Testing   Role in the Team model that is responsible for making certain that a product works, and that issues such as bugs and errors are addressed before release. (*See also* **Team model.**)

Time and Materials strategy   Giving the team power to control risks and changes in a project by adjusting resources.

tradeoff   Where one element of a project is sacrificed so that another can fulfill the current needs.

tradeoff matrix   To establish priorities in a project when dealing with tradeoffs, a tradeoff matrix can be created to determine a strategy. This allows the team and customer to specify whether it is more important to stay on schedule or within budget, or to pass certain features off to future versions. A tradeoff matrix is simply a table that is used as a reference tool.

transaction   One or more separate actions that are grouped together, and executed as a single action.

user/collaboration relationship   One of the three types of relationships an object can have. This is where objects employ the services of other objects. They aren't a specific type of another object, nor are they owned by another object. They simply rely on some other object's specific functionality or service. (*See also* **container/ownership relationship** and **generalization/subclass relationship**.)

user communities   The parts of an organization that use IT services.

User Education   Role in the Team model that is responsible for enhancing the user's experience and performance with a product, by making the product easy to understand and use. (*See also* **Team model**.)

User layer   The interface of the application. (*See also* **Business layer** and **Data layer**.)

user requirements   The list of items that the application needs to be able to accomplish.

User Services   In a multi-tier application User Services is associated with the user interface and/or programmatic interface, provided by units of application logic. (*See also* **multi-tier application.**)

vision   The features and functionality you'd ideally like to see in a product. (*See also* **scope.**)

Vision/Scope Approved milestone   The Envisioning phase results in the Vision/Scope Approved milestone, where an agreement is made on what direction the project will take. Vision sets the ultimate goals of the project, while scope recognizes the limitations. (*See also* **Envisioning phase.**)

Waterfall model   Views the life cycle as a flow of steps. When one step ends, a milestone is reached. The milestone indicates that the step is assessed, and the next step begins in the development process. MSF Process model is partially based on the waterfall model. (*See also* **S**piral model and **P**rocess model.)

Year 2000 (Y2K) problem   The fact that most computer hardware and software has not been programmed to deal with the date change to the year 2000.

Zero-Defect milestone   Incremental internal release that passes testing without any defects, allowing developers work on the next set of features.

INDEX

O

P

Q

R

S

Custom Corporate Network Training

Train on Cutting Edge Technology
We can bring the best in skill-based training to your facility to create a real-world hands-on training experience. Global Knowledge has invested millions of dollars in network hardware and software to train our students on the same equipment they will work with on the job. Our relationships with vendors allow us to incorporate the latest equipment and platforms into your on-site labs.

Maximize Your Training Budget
Global Knowledge provides experienced instructors, comprehensive course materials, and all the networking equipment needed to deliver high quality training. You provide the students; we provide the knowledge.

Avoid Travel Expenses
On-site courses allow you to schedule technical training at your convenience, saving time, expense, and the opportunity cost of travel away from the workplace.

Discuss Confidential Topics
Private on-site training permits the open discussion of sensitive issues such as security, access, and network design. We can work with your existing network's proprietary files while demonstrating the latest technologies.

Customize Course Content
Global Knowledge can tailor your courses to include the technologies and the topics which have the greatest impact on your business. We can complement your internal training efforts or provide a total solution to your training needs.

Corporate Pass
The Corporate Pass Discount Program rewards our best network training customers with preferred pricing on public courses, discounts on multimedia training packages, and an array of career planning services.

Global Knowledge Training Lifecycle
Supporting the Dynamic and Specialized Training Requirements of Information Technology Professionals

- Define Profile
- Assess Skills
- Design Training
- Deliver Training
- Test Knowledge
- Update Profile
- Use New Skills

College Credit Recommendation Program
The American Council on Education's CREDIT program recommends 53 Global Knowledge courses for college credit. Now our network training can help you earn your college degree while you learn the technical skills needed for your job. When you attend an ACE-certified Global Knowledge course and pass the associated exam, you earn college credit recommendations for that course. Global Knowledge can establish a transcript record for you with ACE, which you can use to gain credit at a college or as a written record of your professional training that you can attach to your resume.

Registration Information

COURSE FEE: The fee covers course tuition, refreshments, and all course materials. Any parking expenses that may be incurred are not included. Payment or government training form must be received six business days prior to the course date. We will also accept Visa/ MasterCard and American Express. For non-U.S. credit card users, charges will be in U.S. funds and will be converted by your credit card company. Checks drawn on Canadian banks in Canadian funds are acceptable.

COURSE SCHEDULE: Registration is at 8:00 a.m. on the first day. The program begins at 8:30 a.m. and concludes at 4:30 p.m. each day.

CANCELLATION POLICY: Cancellation and full refund will be allowed if written cancellation is received in our office at least six business days prior to the course start date. Registrants who do not attend the course or do not cancel more than six business days in advance are responsible for the full registration fee; you may transfer to a later date provided the course fee has been paid in full. Substitutions may be made at any time. If Global Knowledge must cancel a course for any reason, liability is limited to the registration fee only.

GLOBAL KNOWLEDGE: Global Knowledge programs are developed and presented by industry professionals with "real-world" experience. Designed to help professionals meet today's interconnectivity and interoperability challenges, most of our programs feature hands-on labs that incorporate state-of-the-art communication components and equipment.

ON-SITE TEAM TRAINING: Bring Global Knowledge's powerful training programs to your company. At Global Knowledge, we will custom design courses to meet your specific network requirements. Call 1 (919) 461-8686 for more information.

YOUR GUARANTEE: Global Knowledge believes its courses offer the best possible training in this field. If during the first day you are not satisfied and wish to withdraw from the course, simply notify the instructor, return all course materials, and receive a 100% refund.

In the US:

CALL: 1 (888) 762-4442

FAX: 1 (919) 469-7070

VISIT OUR WEBSITE:

www.globalknowledge.com

MAIL CHECK AND THIS FORM TO:

Global Knowledge

Suite 200

114 Edinburgh South

P.O. Box 1187

Cary, NC 27512

In Canada:

CALL: 1 (800) 465-2226

FAX: 1 (613) 567-3899

VISIT OUR WEBSITE:

www.globalknowledge.com.ca

MAIL CHECK AND THIS FORM TO:

Global Knowledge

Suite 1601

393 University Ave.

Toronto, ON M5G 1E6

REGISTRATION INFORMATION:

Course title _____

Course location _____ Course date _____

Name/title _____ Company _____

Name/title _____ Company _____

Name/title _____ Company _____

Address _____ Telephone _____ Fax _____

City _____ State/Province _____ Zip/Postal Code _____

Credit card _____ Card # _____ Expiration date _____

Signature _____

Prepare for your Analyzing Requirements and Defining Solution Architectures Exam using the most effective Test-Prep CD-ROM available!

- Includes full version of MCSD Analyzing Requirements TEST YOURSELF Personal Testing Center.

- Reinforce your knowledge and improve your test-taking skills with challenging practice exams.

- Packed with powerful exam preparation tools, this CD-ROM will increase your chances of passing the exam.

ON THE CD YOU'LL FIND:

- Extensive, full-featured Web site that links all CD-ROM components together for fast access through your Web browser

- Complete electronic version of the study guide with fully hyperlinked table of contents

- MCSD Analyzing Requirements TEST YOURSELF Personal Testing Center with more than 220 questions offering a realistic exam experience. Features timed exams, expert answers, and detailed score reports by topic